Edward Meredith Cope

An Introduction to Aristotle's Rhetoric

Edward Meredith Cope

An Introduction to Aristotle's Rhetoric

ISBN/EAN: 9783337006846

Printed in Europe, USA, Canada, Australia, Japan

Cover: Foto ©Thomas Meinert / pixelio.de

More available books at **www.hansebooks.com**

AN INTRODUCTION

to

ARISTOTLE'S RHETORIC

WITH ANALYSIS NOTES AND APPENDICES

BY

E. M. COPE

SENIOR FELLOW AND TUTOR OF TRINITY COLLEGE, CAMBRIDGE.

> Un jour, disait Ibn-Rosohd (Averroes), Ibn-Tofaïl me fit appeler et me dit: "J'ai entendu aujourd'hui l'émir des croyants se plaindre de l'obscurité d'Aristote et de ses traducteurs: *Plût à Dieu*, disait il, *qu'il se rencontrât quelqu'un qui voulût commenter ces livres et en expliquer clairement le sens, pour les rendre accessibles aux hommes.*" Renan, Vie d'Averroès, p. 17.

London and Cambridge
MACMILLAN AND CO.
1867.

[Right of Translation reserved.]

VIRO EXIMIO

GEORGIO GROTE

HISTORICO PHILOSOPHO PRÆSTANTISSIMO

HOC OPUSCULUM

OBSERVANTIÆ ET HONORIS CAUSA

DEDICAVIT

EDVARDUS MEREDITH COPE

PREFACE.

THE following pages are introductory to an edition of the Greek text of Aristotle's Rhetoric, which has been long in course of preparation, and will appear as soon as it can be got ready. The general object which I have had in view in the present, and shall continue to pursue in the succeeding, volume, cannot be better stated than in the words of the Emir of the Faithful in the passage which I have selected for my motto; commenter ce livre et en expliquer clairement le sens, pour le rendre accessible aux hommes. In one word, it is, as far as I am capable of effecting it, to render Aristotle's Rhetoric thoroughly intelligible. It is a work worthy of all study, and one of the very best and completest, and I may add, one of the most original and characteristic, of this wonderful author's most original and multifarious writings. Explanation in its most comprehensive sense I take to be the first and foremost duty of the Editor of an ancient classic, to which all others are subsidiary and subordinate. Without seeking to underrate or depreciate the other services that may be rendered towards the elucidation of a deceased author, who wrote in a language long dead and forgotten by the world at large, and surviving only in the thoughts and affections of the few who have time or care to devote themselves to the study of it, and with a full acknowledgement of what we owe to those who have bestowed their special attention upon the critical, emendatory, palæographical, philological, or grammatical, departments of scholarship, I still cannot but think that the highest service that a scholar can render to literature and the unlearned is to bring, so as far as that may be possible, the great thoughts and great works of a bygone age, the representations of a state of feeling, of society, and of civilization, far removed from us and now hard to realise, within the range of modern apprehension and sympathy, and to make them at once intelligible and acceptable. This kind of light may be thrown upon ancient institutions and modes of thought best it is true by a searching and critical history, but in a lower degree and within narrower limits by a *good* explanatory commentary upon any important and characteristic work. The kind of illustration of which I am speaking will of course not be confined to a mere verbal or grammatical explanation of phrase and idiom, though that should certainly not be excluded. It should embrace not merely peculiarities of *expression* characteristic either of the author himself individually, or of his age and country, but also all that throws light upon the character, opinions, modes of thought, of himself and his age, and particularly upon the associations by which he was surrounded, the views and feelings prevailing in the society with which he mixed, which give their colour to his own thoughts, views and feelings, and upon which these often mainly depend : and this is more especially desirable in a commentary upon an *ancient* author, between whom and ourselves the difference in all these points is likely to be very wide. I write this with the fullest consciousness of the utter inadequacy of my own knowledge and abilities to realise this conception of an Editor's duty ; and indeed the deficiency of our actual knowledge of things and events, persons and circumstances, must often and in many points interpose an insuperable obstacle to any such realisation : still it may be well to keep it in view as a standard and an ideal to aim at, however far we may fall short in our efforts to attain it.

Judged by the standard of our modern notions of its value and importance, rhetoric might seem to be a subject rather below the dignity of a philo-

all others are subsidiary and subordinate. Without seeking to underrate or depreciate the other services that may be rendered towards the elucidation of a deceased author, who wrote in a language long dead and forgotten by the world at large, and surviving only in the thoughts and affections of the few who have time or care to devote themselves to the study of it, and with a full acknowledgement of what we owe to those who have bestowed their special attention upon the critical, emendatory, palæographical, philological, or grammatical, departments of scholarship, I still cannot but think that the highest service that a scholar can render to literature and the unlearned is to bring, so as far as that may be possible, the great thoughts and great works of a bygone age, the representations of a state of feeling, of society, and of civilization, far removed from us and now hard to realise, within the range of modern apprehension and sympathy, and to make them at once intelligible and acceptable. This kind of light may be thrown upon ancient institutions and modes of thought best it is true by a searching and critical history, but in a lower degree and within narrower limits by a *good* explanatory commentary upon any important and characteristic work. The kind of illustration of which I am speaking will of course not be confined to a mere verbal or grammatical explanation of phrase and idiom, though that should certainly not be excluded. It should embrace not merely peculiarities of *expression* characteristic either of the author himself individually, or of his age and country, but also all that throws light upon the character, opinions, modes of thought, of himself and his age, and particularly upon the associations by which he was surrounded, the views and feelings prevailing in the society with which he mixed, which give their colour to his own thoughts, views and feelings, and upon which these often mainly depend: and this is more especially desirable in a commentary upon an *ancient* author, between whom and ourselves the difference in all these points is likely to be very wide. I write this with the fullest consciousness of the utter inadequacy of my own knowledge and abilities to realise this conception of an Editor's duty; and indeed the deficiency of our actual knowledge of things and events, persons and circumstances, must often and in many points interpose an insuperable obstacle to any such realisation: still it may be well to keep it in view as a standard and an ideal to aim at, however far we may fall short in our efforts to attain it.

Judged by the standard of our modern notions of its value and importance, rhetoric might seem to be a subject rather below the dignity of a philosopher and unworthy of his express notice and study: but there were many peculiar circumstances in the social life of Athens during the latter part of the fifth century, and down to Aristotle's own time, which might well have the effect of attracting universal attention to this art. To say nothing of its natural and obvious value as a means of attaining distinction in public life, it had acquired a purely artificial and factitious importance by the ingenuity and accomplishments of its sophistical professors, who introduced it from Sicily, and established it in Greece proper; and especially at Athens, where it seems to have entirely superseded for a time the earlier system of education. During Aristotle's early residence at Athens, Isocrates and his rhetorical school were at the height of their reputation. The boundless assumption of this teacher and his lofty pretensions to 'philosophy' and general knowledge, contrasted with the actual reality of his literary and philosophical performances, as well as the real influence that he had acquired over his pupils and followers, seem to have moved the indignation of Aristotle to such a degree that he set up a rival rhetorical school to counteract it, and inaugurate a better system. This it was that gave him his first practical impulse to cultivate rhetoric as an art; and that he retained his liking for the study through life, is shown by the amount of attention that he continued to bestow upon it; for he not only seems to have occupied himself through a considerable part of his life in collecting the materials of the work that remains to us, but also of his lost writings, three at least appear to have been upon the subject of rhetoric. But he did for rhetoric what he has done for so many other branches of knowledge; he imparted to it an original character and a new direction, so that in his hands it became a system distinct and peculiar, with a new interest and value, which I believe I may say with truth no succeeding treatise on the subject has ever equalled. I may refer particularly in evidence of this novel character to the subtle and penetrating observations upon life character and manners in the first and second books which give a life and interest to the work such as no other art of rhetoric can pretend to. This and the logical element are perhaps the two most characteristic features of the Aristotelian system.

I have endeavoured in this Introduction to illustrate to the best of my power, as preparatory to the detailed explanation of the work itself, the general bearings and relations of this Art of Rhetoric in itself, as well as the special mode of treating it adopted by Aristotle in his peculiar system; I have collected and examined the available evidence upon one or two doubtful and obscure questions immediately connected with the subject, such as the date of the work itself, the Theodectea, and other works upon rhetoric, now unhappily lost, which Aristotle is believed to have composed; and have entered very fully, as the importance of the subject demanded, into the relations which rhetoric is made to bear in Aristotle's view to the kindred art of logic in its two varieties, demonstration or scientific method and dialectics. I have given a connected analysis or outline of the contents of the work itself; in some parts, where the obscurity of the text or the especial importance and difficulty of the immediate subject seemed to require it, in the form of a paraphrase; herein following the example of that excellent commentator Victorius: and with the view of relieving the commentary upon the text of certain notes which might have grown to a length too great for the space that could be there allotted to them, have thrown a few notices of matters that seemed to require longer and more detailed consideration into Appendices annexed to the first and third books. As a general appendix to the Introduction, and as offering a marked contrast to Aristotle's Rhetoric, and the best representative of the antagonistic system and method of his predecessors and the school of Isocrates, I have given a complete analysis of the rhetorical treatise known under the name of the Ῥητορικὴ πρὸς Ἀλέξανδρον, a work long attributed to

Aristotle and incorporated with his writings, but now by almost universal consent ascribed to Anaximenes. This latter question I have also examined, and have offered some arguments in favour of, at all events, a suspension of judgment upon a hypothesis certainly not yet beyond the reach of question, or even refutation. It has been my object also to show by this analysis what was the true character, and what the probable and natural result, of the teaching of the systems of rhetoric of this school, and the practice they inculcated; and how far therefore Plato was justified in the views that he held of their unscientific character and demoralizing influence.

And now, commending this little book to the students for whom chiefly it is intended, and with a hearty desire that it may help to throw a little light upon a great work in every way worthy of their study, but certainly requiring much elucidation; a work which, partly no doubt from the want of such aids, has been hitherto at least in this country somewhat unduly neglected by students and scholars, as well as Editors, who have been led away by the supposed superior attractions of the Ethics and Politics into other more flowery paths of Aristotelian literature; I will conclude this brief notice of the design and contents of this Introduction, and bring these prefatory remarks to a close.

TRINITY COLLEGE, *May* 31*st*, 1867.

ADDENDA.

p. 33. line 24 on the sentence ending "...may be obtained" add (note 2).
See on the same subject, and to the same effect, Bacon, de Augm. IV. 2. (Vol. I. p. 588. Ellis and Spedding. Ed.) or Advancement of Learning, Bk. II. (III. 371).

p. 127. Add to examples of $\sigma\tau o\iota\chi\epsilon\hat{\iota}o\nu$ in the sense of $\tau\delta\pi o s$, Rhet. ad Alex. c. 36 (37) 9. $\sigma\tau o\iota\chi\epsilon\hat{\iota}a$ κοινὰ κατὰ πάντων.

ERRATA.

p. 94. erase note 1.
p. 239. for CH. VI. read CH. XIV.

TABLE OF CONTENTS.

	PAGE
Aristotle's predecessors in the art of Rhetoric	1
appeals to the feelings	4
characteristics of Aristotle's Rhetoric	6
materials of rhetoric	8
rhetoric an art or a faculty?	14
Art, and its definitions	19
various views and definitions of rhetoric	27
date of Aristotle's Rhetoric	36
Aristotle's lost works on rhetoric, συναγωγὴ τεχνῶν, Γρύλλος, Θεοδέκτεια	49
demonstration or science; dialectics, rhetoric, in their mutual relations	67
syllogism, enthymeme, example	99
ἦθος, in rhetoric	108
πάθος, πάθη, in rhetoric	113
the three branches of rhetoric	118
τόποι, εἴδη, στοιχεῖα	124
Analysis of Aristotle's Rhetoric Bk. I. and Appendices	134—244
paraphrase of Bk. I. ch. 1.	134
paraphrase of Bk. I. ch. 2.	149
εἰκός, σημεῖον, τεκμήριον	160
paraphrase of Bk. I. ch. 3.	168
analysis of cc. 4—13	172
ἐπιείκεια, equity	190
analysis of cc. 14, 15. the ἄτεχνοι πίστεις	193
Appendices to Bk. I.	208
Append. A. to Bk. I. ch. 8. on the classifications of πολιτεῖαι in Aristotle, Plato, and Polybius	208
App. B. Bk. I. c. 9. ἔπαινος, ἐγκώμιον, μακαρισμός, εὐδαιμονισμός.	212
App. C. Bk. I. c. 10. the seven motives or sources of action	218
App. D. Bk. I. c. 11. on pleasure and its definitions	234
App. E. Bk. I. c. 14. ἄγραφοι, γεγραμμένοι νόμοι	239
Analysis of Aristotle's Rhetoric, Bk. II.	245—276

	PAGE
λύσις, ἔλεγχος, ἔνστασις	264—276
ᴬAnalysis and paraphrase of Aristotle's Rhetoric, Bk. III. and Appendices	277—400
General observations on style	279
ψυχρά, διπλᾶ ὀνόματα, γλῶτται, ἐπίθετα . .	286
purity, perspicuity, of style	293
propriety	297
rhythm in prose	303
the period, εἰρομένη and κατεστραμμένη λέξις . .	306
point and vivacity of style, τὰ ἀστεῖα, &c. . . .	316
Witticisms	319
Style in the three branches of rhetoric, the written style, the style of debate, declamatory, &c. . . .	323
τάξις, the divisions of the speech . . .	331
προοίμιον	337
topics of the same, διαβολή	344
διήγησις	348
πίστεις	355
ἐρώτησις, interrogation	362
ἐπίλογος, ἀνακεφαλαίωσις	366
Append. A. Bk. III. c. 2. ὀνόματα καὶ ῥήματα, early grammatical classifications	371
App. B. Bk. III. c. 2. Metaphor	374
App. C. Bk. III. ἁρμονία, ῥυθμός, μέτρον, μέλος, μέγεθος (τῆς φωνῆς): and especially on rhythm, in reference to III. 8. .	379
ῥυθμός, μέτρον, βάσις, ἄρσις, θέσις	387
App. D. Bk. III. c. 5. σύνδεσμος	392
App. E. Bk. III. cc. 15, 16, 17. ἀμφισβητήσεις, στάσεις, status, constitutiones causarum	397

Ῥητορικὴ πρὸς Ἀλέξανδρον.

Contrasted with Aristotle's Rhetoric, (and throughout) .	401
authorship	405
evidence of style	408
analysis of contents	415
moral character of the work	457

INTRODUCTION

TO

ARISTOTLE'S RHETORIC.

ARISTOTLE'S PREDECESSORS.

THE origin and growth of the art of Rhetoric have been traced from the earliest times, by Spengel in his Artium Scriptores, a work executed upon the model of, and intended to replace, Aristotle's lost treatise Συναγωγὴ τεχνῶν, a collection of the preceding 'Arts'[1]; very briefly by Westermann in his Geschichte der Griech. u. Röm. Beredtsamskrit. The same subject has been treated by myself in a series of papers published in the Journal of Classical and Sacred Philology, Nos. 5, 7 and 9[2]; and I need not here repeat what I have already said elsewhere.

Rhetoric, as an art—as a faculty or practice it is as old as human language and intellect—was born in Sicily, where its earliest professors Corax and Tisias practised and taught and quibbled: but it was soon transplanted by Gorgias and the wandering Sophists into Attica, where it grew and flourished in a congenial atmosphere and soil. In a state in which public speaking was an indispensable accomplishment

---

[1] The treatises on the art of rhetoric were so called par excellence, to mark the superiority of this over all other arts. Isocr. κ. τ. Σοφ. § 19. αἱ καλούμεναι τέχναι.

[2] I hope at some future time to republish these papers in a corrected and enlarged form, which may serve as a further introduction to the present work.

for a statesman or politician; and at Athens to be a politician was the rule rather than the exception; and in an unusually litigious society, where every citizen was obliged to plead his own cause in the law court, the value of such a powerful instrument of self-defence and personal aggrandisement was of course at once recognised[1], and the study became so popular that it completely supplanted, as the conservatives of Athens complained, the old-fashioned training by γυμναστική and μουσική, and supplied an education to the young men who were preparing for public life. The extant notices of the teaching of its professors and of the practices which they inculcated, as well as the contents of one remaining specimen of their writings, which I shall notice more particularly by and by[2], the substitution of plausible and sophistical reasoning for sound logic and scientific inquiry, the cultivation of quickness and dexterity and address at the expense of veracity and honesty and sincerity, their aim being 'persuasion' at any cost, to make the worse appear the better cause, to pass off falsehood for truth upon the hearers by a juggle of plausible arguments—all this would surely seem fully to justify the disapprobation and

[1] "When the only way of addressing the public was by orations, and when all political measures were debated in popular assemblies, the characters of Orator, Author, and Politician almost entirely coincided; he who would communicate his ideas to the world, or would gain political power, and carry his legislative schemes into effect, was necessarily a Speaker; since as Pericles is made to remark by Thucydides, 'one who forms a judgment on any point, but cannot explain himself clearly to the people, might as well have never thought at all upon the subject.'" Whately, Rhetoric, Introduction. The 'remark' which Whately has thus expanded, occurs in Thucydides II. 60. Pericles had just been laying claim to an equal capacity of judging what was right and expressing it in words, and adds, ὅ τε γὰρ γνοὺς καὶ μὴ σαφῶς διδάξας ἐν ἴσῳ καὶ εἰ μὴ ἐνεθυμήθη.

[2] In order not to break more than is necessary the thread of my story, I will reserve the evidences of the immoral tendency of the Sophistico-Rhetorical teaching derivable from their own writings for an Appendix: which will include an outline of the contents of the Rhetorica ad Alexandrum, now generally attributed to Anaximenes, at all events the only extant Τέχνη of this Sophistical school.

dislike of Plato and Aristotle, or indeed of any honest man and patriotic citizen, for this new system of education, without having recourse to the supposition of any unworthy prejudice entertained against them as rivals or charlatans, or an irresistible inclination to satire finding a convenient object in this particular class.

That these charges are not unfounded will appear, I think, from all the notices that remain to us of the systems and practice of this Sophistical School of Rhetoricians; and some acquaintance with the nature of their 'Arts,' the subjects they dwelt on and the precepts they delivered and the modes of arguing that they recommended will be of all the more importance, as it will illustrate by way of contrast, the novelty, the systematic completeness, the acute and varied observation of men and things which distinguishes Aristotle's 'Art of Rhetoric' from all others preceding and succeeding.

Aristotle himself in several passages of his work[1] gives us some account of the mode in which Rhetoric was treated by his predecessors in their system. He says that they had confined themselves almost exclusively to one branch of the subject the judicial namely or forensic, neglecting the higher and nobler department of deliberative, public, or Parliamentary speaking (the 'Ρητορικὴ πρὸς 'Αλέξανδρον, the only extant treatise belonging to the Sophistical School, is free at least from this defect); and that even in this they left un-

[1] Rhet. I. 1. 3, 4, 9, 10, 11. I. 2. 5. Compare III. 13. See also some remarks on the growth and progress of Rhetoric in de Soph. El. c. 34. 183. b. 25. et seq. He there refers, 183. b. 38, to the practice common amongst the rhetorical teachers of giving their pupils loci communes, select extracts of speeches, to learn by heart, as the dialecticians provided theirs with the most familiar and useful 'topics' of argument; implying apparently that some of these teachers did little else for them. This, he says, they called education. But in reality it was not the *art* of rhetoric that they taught them, but the products of the art: and a man might just as well profess to communicate an art for protecting the feet from injury, and then, instead of teaching the art of shoemaking, or providing the pupil with any means of making such things himself, present him with a great variety of ready-made shoes.

noticed the most important and the only scientific part of the subject, the theory of proof, and confined themselves to suggesting various arts and devices for working upon the emotions and affections of the audience, or describing the due arrangement of the contents and divisions of the speech, and such like comparatively trifling and insignificant matters, which are either positively vicious, or at any rate unscientific and 'beside the (real) question', ἔξω τοῦ πράγματος, extra artem—outside the limits of a genuine 'Art of Rhetoric'; of which the proper object is proof, and that alone. (III. 1. 5.) And all this is fully confirmed by Plato in the Phædrus, cc. 50, 51, 56 seq. and elsewhere.

Appeals to the Feelings.

It may be as well here by the way, though I shall have to return to it hereafter, to notice and explain an apparent contradiction between Aristotle's theory and practice in connexion with this subject of the defects of his predecessors: for it is quite certain that he *does* himself dwell in great detail upon the various modes of producing certain impressions on the minds of the audience, and exciting in them certain feelings, as of sympathy, compassion, indignation, resentment, kind feeling, and others, and that this occupies a considerable space in his work and is treated as a matter of great importance. The necessity of it is shown principally in the treatment of ἦθος, and πάθος; that is, in the mode of conveying a favourable impression to the audience of your own character and intentions, and in inspiring the listeners with such feelings and sentiments as are desirable for yourself and your own case, and adverse to the opponent. Now this may be done in two ways: scientifically, through the medium of the speech itself, which is indeed one of the modes of proof—of which there are three, πίστεις, ἦθος, and πάθος—and therefore forms part of the art of rhetoric in its strictest sense; and unscientifically, by the introduction of considerations ab extra or beside the real point, arguments ad hominem and ad captandum, such as *direct* appeals to the feelings, impassioned and exaggerated language (δείνωσις), or even, as was often done, the actual production of the widow and orphans or friends of a deceased person to excite compassion and blind the judges to the real merits of the case. This was indeed the constant practice in the Athenian law courts and public assemblies, and notoriously in the trial of the eight generals after the battle of Arginusae[1]. However there is always more room for the employment of arts of this kind in forensic than in public speaking (I. 1. 10): in the latter they are less serviceable, and therefore less used; and consequently this branch of Rhetoric is nobler and purer than the other, appeals to higher and more generous motives, and is more disinterested and liberal: in the practice of the Courts of law on the other hand there is more scope for trickery and chicanery (κακουργία), which indeed explains the preference of the Sophistical Rhetoricians for the forensic branch of the Art. But besides this scientific use of them, there is another reason for not excluding appeals to the feelings from the practice of rhetoric; they are justified to a certain extent, like the attention which must necessarily be paid to the composition and language, harmony and rhythm, of the speech (III. 1. 5), διὰ τὴν μοχθηρίαν τῶν ἀκροατῶν: the depraved judgment and taste of an ordinary audience *requires* this kind of 'flattery,' as Plato calls it, and the speaker is therefore *obliged* to give way; to relax the rigorous observance of the rules of his art, and to humour their perverted inclina-

---

[1] Nam et M'. Aquilium defendens Antonius, quum scissâ veste cicatrices, quas is pro patria pectore adverso suscepisset, ostendit, non orationis habuit fiduciam, sed oculis populi Romani vim attulit: quem illo ipso aspectu maxime motum in hoc, ut absolveret reum, creditum est. Quint. Inst. Orat. II. xv. 7. In § 8, the case of Servius Galba is quoted, and in § 9, the famous case of Phryne and the orator Hyperides. The story of Hyperides and Phryne is told by Athenaeus, XIII. 590. E. See also, Lycurg. c. Leocr. §§ 11—13.

tions. To some extent therefore the study and analysis of human motives passions and feelings belong to rhetoric, and are indeed an essential part of it: and the rules derived from it may be applied *through the speech* to excite certain emotions in the audience: this may however be carried a great deal too far: and the fault that Aristotle finds with the Arts of preceding Rhetoricians on this point is that they confined themselves to this indirect mode of proving their case, and neglected the more regular and scientific mode of proof by logical enthymeme. (I. 2. 5.)

CHARACTERISTICS OF ARISTOTLE'S RHETORIC.

From this explanatory digression we now return to the consideration of Aristotle's own Rhetoric, and the points of difference between his mode of treatment of the subject and that of his predecessors. That which gives its peculiar and distinctive character to his treatment of Rhetoric is, as he himself tells us, that he has established its connexion with Dialectics, the popular branch of Logic, of which it is a 'branch' or 'offshoot' or 'counterpart' or 'copy,' which enables him to give a *systematic* and scientific exposition of it as a special kind of reasoning and mode of proof: this had been totally overlooked by the preceding writers upon rhetoric, who as we have seen had confined themselves almost exclusively to matters outside of the Art, which do not properly belong to it. Subordinate to this however, and included in it, is another special characteristic which distinguishes his work from those that preceded and followed it, though he does not himself particularly notice it, the analysis namely of human character, motives, and feelings which gives it a great part of its value and interest. The adoption of this novel mode of treating the subject was in all probability due to the suggestions of Plato in the Phædrus, 271 C—272 B, 273 D, E, where it is pointed out, that as there is a great variety of 'souls,' i.e. minds and characters or dispositions, and a like variety of speeches, the latter, in order to produce the intended effect of 'persuasion,' must be duly adapted to the corresponding varieties of the former, and that for this purpose the study of human nature, characters and motives, is requisite[1]. But Plato, who was always more ready to project than carry out a scheme, contents himself with offering the suggestion: the execution of the plan was left to the great analyst and observer of Nature and human life; a task which he has fulfilled with his accustomed skill and sagacity. He is in fact the first, and we may add the last, who has treated Rhetoric comprehensively and systematically, in connexion and contrast with those branches of philosophy with which it stands in immediate relation.

With this general theory of rhetorical proof and its subor-

[1] This is all, I believe, that can fairly be inferred from Plato's language in the Phædrus; in proof of which I merely refer to the passages quoted, which speak for themselves. Spengel however, in a paper on Aristotle's Rhetoric published in the Transactions of the Bavarian Academy p. 28, comp. 8—11, thinks that Plato intended to mark the threefold division of rhetorical πίστεις, into πίστεις proper, ἦθος and πάθος, which Aristotle afterwards adopted from him and developed. I confess that I can see no trace of any such intention in the passages in question. The distinction of ἦθος and πάθη at any rate, as Aristotle understands it, is certainly not made out. What Plato *says* amounts to no more than I have expressed in the text. But in fact Plato acknowledges no *art* of rhetoric at all, and therefore would not have troubled himself about its divisions: and he expressly denies that Rhetoric, if a true art, can be confined to mere probabilities, τὰ εἰκότα, as its materials: ἔτυμος τέχνη ἄνευ τοῦ ἀληθείας ἧφθαι οὔτ' ἔστιν ὥστε μή ποθ' ὕστερον γένηται: whereas probability is the very basis and groundwork of Aristotle's system. Plato's object in this part of the Phædrus is to show that Rhetoric, if there be really such an art—περὶ πάντα τὰ λεγόμενα μία τις τέχνη, εἴπερ ἔστιν—must coincide with philosophy: that the true rhetorician must be also a dialectician (in his own, not Aristotle's, sense of the word), a complete philosopher, one who has a comprehensive and exact knowledge of all the relations of things. So far as he differs from the philosopher he is a quack and an impostor; so far as he coincides with him, his *art* is superseded. And essentially the same view of the art is taken in the Gorgias: a genuine τέχνη aims at truth; one which confines itself to mere probabilities, is no art at all, but a sham and an imposture.

dinate divisions, and the exemplification of its several εἴδη and τίποι, two-thirds of the entire work are occupied; it is not until the end of the second book and the commencement of the third that the contents of the latter of these, λέξις and τάξις, style and arrangement, including the divisions of the speech and their appropriate topics—the ordinary subjects of the preceding 'Arts'—are even named. Upon this circumstance, it may be mentioned in passing, has been founded an argument against the genuineness of this third book. I only mention it for the purpose of expressing my strong conviction of the utter groundlessness of any such suspicion. If the third book of the Art of Rhetoric did not proceed from the pen of Aristotle, all evidence of authorship derived from resemblance of style manner method and diction must be absolutely worthless[1].

THE MATERIALS OF RHETORIC.

Leaving for the present the important subject of the relation of Rhetoric, as a method or system of proof, to the Dialectical, and Demonstrative or Scientific Methods, to be reserved for subsequent consideration in more immediate connexion with the introductory chapters of the first book, we will now pass on to the examination of the rhetorical method in respect of its materials, the objects that it deals with.

Rhetoric, like Dialectics, may discuss anything: any problem that can be brought forward upon any subject

---

[1] Another argument against the genuineness of this book is derived from the entry in Diogenes' list of a work περὶ ῥητορικῆς α. β. which is *assumed* (1) to be correct (2) to designate our Rhetoric, and (3) to show that Aristotle's Rhetoric consisted of only two books. Brandis, in a paper on Aristotle's Rhetoric, in Schneidewin's Philologus, Vol. IV. No. 1., briefly argues the question of the genuineness of the book, and the probabilities of its earlier or later composition than that of the two preceding, and decides, like a man of sense, for the integrity of the work as we now have it.

whatsoever may be submitted to dialectical examination: and Rhetoric in like manner may deal with any topic that can be presented to it: it is περὶ ἅπαντος, περὶ τοῦ δοθέντος. Even science is not excluded from its domain[1]: only, if any question of special science has to be argued, as may sometimes happen in a court of justice, or any results or conclusions of science stated, the subject must be treated *popularly* and made intelligible to an unscientific audience: no long trains of demonstrative syllogisms can be admitted, no principles or axioms of any special science may be adduced or argued from: when dialectics or rhetoric deserts its *common* ground, and employs either the method or special principles (ἴδιαι ἀρχαί) of any particular science, it becomes something else; it quits its own province and trespasses upon an alien territory. It resembles dialectics also in being indifferent to the truth of its conclusions, so far as it is considered as an *art*, and the speaker as an *artist:* both of them argue indifferently on either side of a question, and may prove the affirmative or negative according as either of these happen to suit the reasoner's immediate purpose. This is one important point of difference between these two and science or demonstration: of this truth is the direct object, and the thinker is *not* indifferent to the conclusion.

Theoretically then Rhetoric is universal in its application: but practically it is limited for the most part to a particular class of phenomena, with which its two most important branches, the deliberative and the judicial, almost exclusively deal, namely human actions characters motives and feelings; and so it becomes closely connected with the study of Politics (including Ethics), which treats of moral social and political phenomena, of man as an individual and as a member of society. Hence it appears (Rhet. I. 2. 7) that Rhetoric may be considered as an offshoot, not only of Dialectics, but also of Politics: of the first, because the enthy-

---

[1] Compare Quint. Inst. I. 10, 34—49, on the study of Geometry.

meme, the rhetorical instrument of proof ($\pi\iota\sigma\tau\iota\varsigma$), is a kind of syllogism; and of the second, because the rhetorician has especially to take account of "characters and virtues and feelings and must know what each of them is in itself and its attributes or properties, and what is their origin and the modes of their excitement." Hence also rhetoric, "owing either to the ignorance or the quackery" of its preceding professors has "assumed the guise of Politics," and taken a place in general education to which it is by no means entitled. Now human actions characters and motives, as well as future events, and the facts and circumstances of daily life which are constantly brought into question, are by their very nature only contingent and probable; nothing can be *predicted* of them with certainty; they cannot be reduced to necessary laws, or form the subject of necessary conclusions: they are essentially 'probable,' $\epsilon\iota\kappa\delta\tau\alpha$, and only 'usual' $\dot{\omega}\varsigma\ \dot{\epsilon}\pi\dot{\iota}\ \tau\dot{o}\ \pi o\lambda\dot{v}$ (nothing can be pronounced of them *universally*), or $\dot{\epsilon}\nu\delta\epsilon\chi\delta\mu\epsilon\nu\alpha\ \ddot{\alpha}\lambda\lambda\omega\varsigma\ \ddot{\epsilon}\chi\epsilon\iota\nu$, 'contingent,' 'admitting of being in more than one way,' uncertain in the event: and hence rhetoric with few exceptions excludes the universal and necessary, and deals only with the probable; and this is the *essential* difference between it and the scientific or demonstrative processes. See Rhet. I. 2. 14. The matter of rhetoric, being such as is above described, consists in things that we deliberate about, $\pi\epsilon\rho\dot{\iota}\ \dot{\omega}\nu\ \beta o v\lambda\epsilon v\dot{o}\mu\epsilon\theta\alpha\ \kappa\alpha\dot{\iota}\ \tau\dot{\epsilon}\chi\nu\alpha\varsigma\ \mu\dot{\eta}\ \ddot{\epsilon}\chi o\mu\epsilon\nu$ Rhet. I. 2. 12; but no one deliberates about that which is unalterable or necessary, 'and can only be in *one* way,' $o\dot{v}\theta\epsilon\dot{\iota}\varsigma\ \delta\dot{\epsilon}\ \beta o v\lambda\epsilon\dot{v}\epsilon\tau\alpha\iota\ \pi\epsilon\rho\dot{\iota}\ \tau\hat{\omega}\nu\ \mu\dot{\eta}\ \dot{\epsilon}\nu\delta\epsilon\chi o\mu\dot{\epsilon}\nu\omega\nu\ \ddot{\alpha}\lambda\lambda\omega\varsigma\ \ddot{\epsilon}\chi\epsilon\iota\nu$, Eth. Nic. VI. 2. and so, as before, we conclude that we deliberate $\pi\epsilon\rho\dot{\iota}\ \tau\hat{\omega}\nu\ \phi\alpha\iota\nu o\mu\dot{\epsilon}\nu\omega\nu\ \dot{\epsilon}\nu\delta\dot{\epsilon}\chi\epsilon\sigma\theta\alpha\iota\ \dot{\alpha}\mu\phi o\tau\dot{\epsilon}\rho\omega\varsigma\ \ddot{\epsilon}\chi\epsilon\iota\nu$ Rhet. I. 2. 12 "for about things fixed and unalterable, past, present, or future, no one deliberates *under that supposition*, because there is nothing to be gained by doing so." Ib.[1] And con-

---

[1] Of the subjects which admit, and do not admit, of deliberation, there is an ingenious analysis in the Nicom. Ethics, III. 5. To the former of the two classes belong, things eternal and unchangeable, as the order of the uni-

sequently, rhetoric accepts *either* side of an alternative, and may conclude *either* of two opposites, τἀναντία συλλογίζεται. "Ars enim," says Antonius (Cic. de Orat. II. 7. 30) "earum rerum est quæ sciuntur: oratoris autem omnis actio opinionibus, non scientia, continetur. Nam et apud eos dicimus qui nesciunt, et ea dicimus quæ nescimus ipsi"—a different reason assigned for the same fact, that the sphere of the rhetorician is the contingent and variable and uncertain.

It follows of course from all this that rhetoric is not an exact science, which starts from peculiar axioms and principles of its own, and the conclusions of which are all universal and necessary: its processes must therefore be limited by the nature of its materials, the probable and contingent, and within that sphere it must rest. What is said of the study of Ethics, Eth. Nicom. I. 2, will apply equally to Rhetoric. "Such then is the aim of our science, which is a kind of Politics. The treatment of it must be considered sufficient if its distinctness and exactness be only in proportion to its subject matter (or materials) for nice elaborate finish (exactness in detail in carrying out the work) is not to be looked for in all subjects of inquiry alike, precisely as is the case with the productions of certain arts and manufactures [as bronze for example will not admit of so 'high a finish' as marble, or granite as alabaster]." Then, after speaking of the uncertainty and irregularity of men's motives and aims arising from their vacillating and erroneous notions of what

verse or the incommensurability of the diameter and side of the square; or even of things 'in motion' (liable to change) when the order of them is actually constant and invariable (ἀεὶ κατὰ ταὐτὰ γινομένων) whether that be a consequence of necessity or nature or proceed from any other cause, as the revolutions or risings and settings of sun and stars. Nor of things in which there is no constancy at all, as drought and rain; nor of things purely accidental. What we *do* deliberate about are things which are in our own power: everything which depends upon human volition and human action, and the sum of the whole is, that we deliberate about things which are not invariable, but usual, (things 'for the most part,' which generally conform to a rule) and of uncertain issue, and indefinite.

is καλόν, δίκαιον, ἀγαθόν, and the absence of fixed moral principles, he proceeds, "In dealing therefore with such materials and arguing from such (uncertain) premisses or principles, we must be content to exhibit the truth roughly (coarsely) and in mere outline[1]; and, as the materials and principles of our subject are mere general probabilities, to be satisfied with the like conclusions. And in the same way we are bound to acquiesce in the treatment of *any* (ἕκαστον) subject: for a cultivated intellect (the man of genuine sense, enlightment and power of judging, which is conferred by education and knowledge of the subject) is shown in looking for scientific exactness in any branch of knowledge only so far as the nature of the subject admits: for it seems to be much the same thing to be satisfied with plausible reasoning in a mathematician as to require exact demonstration from a rhetorician." Everything in rhetoric must be intelligible and popular: no long trains of syllogistic reasoning (comp. II. 21. 3) which ordinary people cannot follow: no rigorously exact definitions—this is specially mentioned in Rhet. I. 10. 19. δεῖ δὲ νομίζειν ἱκανοὺς εἶναι τοὺς ὅρους, ἐὰν ὦσι περὶ ἑκάστου μήτε ἀσαφεῖς μήτε ἀκριβεῖς—but only such as are popularly current and recognised: no appeals to the axioms or principles of the exact and special sciences, which require a special training and study, but only to those universal and general principles, which are common to all reasoning, and accepted and understood by all mankind alike[2].

[1] To exhibit the facts or phenomena in a mere rough sketch or outline; without *finishing* the picture by filling in all the details, παχυλῶς καὶ τύπῳ.
[2] To the same effect Hermogenes, τέχνη ῥητορ. περὶ τῶν στάσεων, sub init. ἔστι τοίνυν ἀμφισβήτησις λογικὴ ἐπὶ μέρους ἐκ τῶν παρ' ἑκάστοις κειμένων νόμων ἢ ἐθῶν περὶ τοῦ νομισθέντος δικαίου ἢ τοῦ καλοῦ ἢ τοῦ συμφέροντος ἢ καὶ πάντων ἅμα ἤ τινων. τὸ γὰρ ὡς ἀληθῶς τε καὶ καθόλου καλὸν ἢ συμφέρον ἢ τὰ τοιαῦτα ζητεῖν οὐ ῥητορικῆς. Cicero, Orat. XXXIII. 117. Erit igitur hæc facultas in eo, quem volumus esse eloquentem, ut definire rem possit neque id faciat tam presse et anguste quam in illis eruditissimis disputationibus fieri solet, sed quum explanatius tum etiam uberius et ad commune judicium popularemque intelligentiam accommodatius. de Orat. II. xxxviii. 159. Hæc enim nostra oratio multitudinis est auribus accommodanda, ad

With regard to the definitions in particular Aristotle's practice in this work is in strict conformity with his precept. Compare for example the elaborate and carefully constructed definition of virtue in the Nicomachean Ethics II. 6. init. which is a complete description of all the essential and characteristic points by which it is distinguished from other ἕξεις or 'states' intellectual and moral, with the extremely superficial and incomplete one given in Rhet. I. 9. 4: or the popular classification of the several forms of government in Rhet. I. 8, with the studied analysis and definitions of the same in Polit. III. 7—18 and IV. 1. and Eth. Nicom. VIII. 12. Another remarkable example is the definition of pleasure as a κίνησις in Rhet. I. 11. 1, which he himself argues against and condemns in Eth. Nic. X. 3.[1] Again in de Anim. I. 1. he points out the difference between the definitions of ὀργή which would be given by a natural philosopher and a dialectician: the one would say it is a ζέσις τοῦ περὶ καρδίαν αἵματος καὶ θερμοῦ, the other an ὄρεξις ἀντιλυπήσεως ἤ τι τοιοῦτον: the definition of this πάθος given in Rhet. II. 2. 1, making a very near approach to the latter. The one describes the feeling as it exhibits itself in the intercourse between man and man and is therefore suited for the purposes of rhetoric and dialectics, the other endeavours to penetrate into its true nature and to state what it *is* (τὴν οὐσίαν). Similarly the definition of the πάθη in general (λόγοι ἔνυλοι) which is found in the treatise de Anima (I. 1. 15.), and the few considerations that lead to it, are sufficient to show how different would have been the point of view and the consequent mode of treatment, had they been there analysed in detail, from that which is adopted as appropriate in the Rhetoric: in the former we should have had their nature and origin examined, and as far as possible accounted for, in

oblectandos animos, ad impellendos, ad ea probanda, quæ non aurificis statera sed populari quadam trutina examinantur.

[1] On the definition of pleasure. See also Eth. Eud. Z. 13. 1133. a. 14, 15., and Fritzsche's note.

connexion with the growth and development of the vital principle or soul pervading the entire animated world, and their essence expressed in a transcendental definition: in the latter they are described merely as they exhibit and express themselves outwardly, and with reference to the occasions and circumstances of their excitement, and the objects towards which they are directed[1]. τέκτων καὶ γεωμέτρης διαφερόντως ἐπιζητοῦσι τὴν ὀρθήν, ὁ μὲν γὰρ ἐφ' ὅσον χρησίμη πρὸς τὸ ἔργον, ὁ δὲ τί ἐστιν ἢ ποῖόν τι· θεατὴς γὰρ τἀληθοῦς. Eth. Nic. I. 9.

Rhetoric an Art or a Faculty?

So far we have been engaged upon a comparison of Aristotle's views of the nature and meaning of Rhetoric with those of his Sophistical predecessors, and a description of some of the leading peculiarities of his mode of treating the subject. We will now pass on to the consideration of his definition of Rhetoric, and the genus to which it belongs, whether science or art, faculty or practice; and compare it with other definitions, and other opinions that have been held upon the same subject.

Rhetoric is certainly not a science. We have already seen that when a rhetorician trespasses upon the field of science, or demonstration with its regular syllogisms and necessary and universal conclusions, he loses his proper character and becomes for the nonce a man of science; in this alien province he assumes an alien character.

According to the point of view from which it is regarded,

---

[1] See Brandis, tract on the Rhetoric in Schneid. Philol., u. s. p. 27. Brandis goes on to compare the two lists of πάθη, in respect of the selection and mode of treatment of them, which occur in the Nicom. Ethics II. 4. and the Rhetoric, II. 2—11, respectively: and afterwards proceeds to a more general comparison of the latter treatise with the Ethics and Politics in the points where they come into contact. On the definitions of Rhetoric, see Trendelenburg on de Anim. p. 177.

Rhetoric may be considered either as an art or a faculty. Quidam, says Quintilian, Inst. Orat. II. xv. 2., rhetoricen *vim tantum*, quidam *scientiam* sed non virtutem, quidam *usum*, quidam *artem* quidem, sed a scientia et virtute dijunctam, quidam etiam *pravitatem* quandam *artis*, id est κακοτεχνίαν nominaverunt. According to Cicero, de Orat. I. 21. 96. rhetoric is, vel studium vel artificium vel facultas. Compare de Invent. I. 1. 2. Looked at theoretically, absolutely in itself, and generally, ἁπλῶς, καθ' αὑτό, it is an art, laying down rules for practice and accompanied with illustrations in the shape of τόποι: so far as it manifests itself in its practical and relative aspect, and individually as exercised by its professors, πρός τι, καθ' ἕκαστον, it assumes the form of a δύναμις or individual faculty, which is exercised "in the consideration of the means of persuasion possible in any subject whatever," Rhet. I. 2. 1. Comp. § 7 and I. 4. 6. And so arts in their practical aspect are called δυνάμεις in Eth. Nic. I. 1. bis, again in X. 10, and Polit. III. 12. VIII. 1., where it is coupled with ἐπιστῆμαι, the same arts regarded from the theoretical point of view. It follows from this that Alexander Aphrod. can scarcely be right when he tells us near the beginning of his Commentary on the Topics that Dialectics and Rhetoric are called δυνάμεις because they are not bound to follow, or develope themselves in, one direction, but may conclude indifferently upon either side of any question proposed to them, ὁμοίως τὴν τῶν ἀντικειμένων δεῖξιν σκοπὸν ἔχουσι. Schol. ad Arist. p. 251. b. 39. Bekker. This is undoubtedly true of Dialectics and Rhetoric, but it is not true of Politics and the other arts to which the term is equally applied. To Politics and Ethics or the military art or medicine, it certainly is *not* a matter of indifference which side of a question they take; they aim at truth and reality, ἀλήθεια, and in so far partake of the nature of science. Indeed as Aristotle has expressly noticed this, Rhet. I. 1. 12. τῶν ἄλλων τεχνῶν οὐδεμία τἀναντία συλλογίζεται, it is all the more remarkable that Alexander should have overlooked it.

Alexander in his remark is referring to the antithesis of

δύναμις and ἐνέργεια. Of the former it is characteristic that it may be developed in opposite directions, that it is equally capable of producing contraries, whereas the developed actualised δύναμις, when it has become an ἐνέργεια, loses this capacity, and acquires one fixed direction from which it cannot depart. On the difference in this respect between physical and mental or moral δυνάμεις, and upon the entire subject, see Sir A. Grant, on Ethics, Essay IV[1].

But Art again is twofold; for either it may be regarded *subjectively*, as a ἕξις, or *state of mind*—and this is the view that is taken of it in the contrasted definitions of art and science, in Eth. Nicom. VI. 3 and 4. where it is divided into its two branches, πρακτική and ποιητική[2], according as it

---

[1] See further on this subject the note on the definition of rhetoric, in the introduction I. 2. 1.

[2] The author, probably Eudemus, seems in this passage, Eth. Nicom. VI. 4., to confine the term 'art' to rules and practice which end in production, that is, the fine arts and the useful or mechanical arts; which is in fact the modern definition of it. This I think cannot be really intended: it may however be meant to imply that art in its strictest sense, κατ' ἐξοχήν, is to be understood in this acceptation. It cannot be intended to exclude πρακτική, for Ethics, Politics, and Rhetoric, are all *practical*, and yet all are *arts*. Sciences they cannot be, for their materials and conclusions are alike only probable, contingent and variable, see the def. of ἐπιστήμη, Eth. Nic. VI. 3; and as they must be one or the other, and they are not sciences, it follows that they must needs be arts in one sense or other. It is true that all arts, even the mechanical, and those with them, have sometimes the term ἐπιστήμη applied to them, as in the Nicom. Eth. I. 1. above quoted; but this is only in the popular sense of the word, as applicable to any 'branch of knowledge:' and the distinction between ἐπιστήμη and τέχνη is very frequently disregarded, and the terms used as convertible both by Plato and Aristotle. See for example Plat. Phileb. 55. D—60, Polit. 304. B. αἱ περὶ χειροτεχνίας ἐπιστῆμαι, and Arist. Metaph. A. 1. passim. Sext. Emp. adv. Math. II. 6. notices this of Xenocrates. Sir W. Hamilton however, Lect. on Metaph. I. 118., looking merely at the definition of art in Eth. Nic. VI. 4., and without reference to other and conflicting passages, thinks that Aristotle (the definition is in all probability *not* Aristotle's) means to limit art to 'habit productive:' and goes on, in spite of Aristotle's own words, above quoted, to assign Rhetoric to this 'poetic' division of philosophy. And Brandis, Handb. &c. Aristoteles I. 147, 8., expresses a similar opinion, upon general considerations and without special reference to Aristotle. Nec potest ars non esse, says Quintilian, Inst. Orat. II. 17. 42., si ars est dialectice, quod fere constat;

ends in action or production; and in the latter acceptation is defined ἕξις¹ μετὰ λόγου ποιητική, "a conscious active state, a fixed intellectual habit and tendency, accompanied with reasoning or calculation, guided by general principles, working by rule, and not by mere instinct or experience, and tending to production"—or *objectively* as a system, or body of rules and principles, the general result of the preceding². In applying the term to Rhetoric Aristotle has usually the former, or subjective, acceptation in his mind—without however excluding the other signification—and by thus regarding the art from this point of view, practically and individually, as it is applied by the professor, brings it very nearly into coincidence with the other term, δύναμις, by which he designates it. It is, as we have already seen, and compare again Eth. Nicom. I. 1, a subordinate branch of πολιτική, the ἀρχιτεκτονική or master-craft, which prescribes to its subordinates their several provinces and functions, as the masterbuilder or architect to his workmen³. ὁρῶμεν δὲ καὶ τὰς

quum ab ea specie magis quam genere differat.

¹ Similarly, ἐμπειρία, τέχνη, ἐπιστήμη, are all ἕξεις, Anal. Post. II. 19. 100. 10, 11.

² This double use of τέχνη to express both a process and a result is common to it with many other kindred terms, as ἐπιστήμη, μέθοδος, πραγματεία, Plato's διαλεκτική, et sim. For example, μέθοδος, which usually denotes the scientific process, or pursuit of truth, is frequently employed to signify the special science or treatise which results from such a process. So in Polit. IV. 2. init. IV. 8. sub init. IV. 10. init. VI. 2. ἐν τῇ μεθόδῳ ('book,' discussion, or part of the treatise) τῇ πρὸ ταύτης, VII. 1, and 2. Metaph. M. 1. 1076. 9 ἐν τῇ μ. τῇ τῶν φυσικῶν περὶ τῆς ὕλης. and other passages from the Metaphysics and Topics cited by

Bonitz on Metaph. 983. 22. See also on πραγματεία Bonitz on Met. A. 6. 987. 30. and Waitz, on Anal. Post. II. 13. 96. b. 15., and (on μέθοδος) Comm. ad Anal. Post. I. 1. 71. a. 1. Similarly χυμός and ὀσμή in the de Anima and Parva Naturalia are used to denote the sense or process of sensation, and the object of sense; just as we ourselves employ the terms 'taste' and 'smell.' Comp. Trendel. on de Anima II. 9. 1. These are only a few examples of a common ambiguity. A great number of words in ·σις Gk. ·io Latin and ·ion Engl. such as sensation, perception, conception, discussion, terminations which denote some operation or process, have this double use.

³ So ἀρχιτεκτονικός is opposed to δημιουργοί, the inferior craftsmen and artisans, in Polit. III. 11. 11. (Oxf.) 1282. 3 (Bk.). In Phys. II. 2. 194. b. 3.

ἐντιμοτάτας τῶν δυνάμεων ὑπὸ ταύτην οὔσας, οἷον στρατηγικήν, οἰκονομικήν, ῥητορικήν. Eth. Nicom. I. 2. 6 (Oxf.) I. 1. (Bk.): and thus falls under the second head in the general division of science or philosophy, viz. πρακτικὴ ἐπιστήμη, φιλοσοφία, that department of knowledge whose end is practice or action[1]. So Quintilian, Instit. Orat. II. 18. 2. The passage is worth quoting, and seems to me to settle the question. It begins with a very clear and concise account of this threefold division of "arts," or philosophy, in general. Quum sint autem artium aliae positae in inspectione, id est cognitione et aestimatione, rerum, qualis est *astrologia*, sed ipso

the ἀρχιτεκτονικὴ τέχνη is said τὸ εἶδος γνωρίζειν, the inferior and subordinate arts only τὴν ὕλην.

[1] This division of philosophy and knowledge into θεωρητική, πρακτική, and ποιητική, defined severally by their τέλη or objects, truth, practice, and production, 'speculative' 'practical' and 'productive,' is set forth at length in Metaph. E. I. and assumed elsewhere as the only true and natural classification. See the reff. in Bonitz's note on 1025. b. 18. In this passage however the basis of the classification is a different one, viz. the origin or cause to which the objects upon which the speculation is exercised owe their existence. This gives rise to a twofold division of objects of knowledge, (1) things which are entirely independent of human action and human power, which are the objects of speculative philosophy, and (2) things whose origin does depend upon human will impulse and action, whether they terminate in the action or ἐνέργεια itself, as in Ethics, Politics, Rhetoric; or are carried on to an ἔργον, the production of something permanent and concrete, as in art proper. See the commencement of the Nicomachean Ethics. The other division, which appears incidentally in Top. I. 14. 105. a. 20, into Physics, Ethics, and Logic, which was afterwards generally adopted, and became eventually the recognised classification, (see Diog. Laert. I. 18. Sext. Emp. Pyrrh. Hyp. II. 13. adv. Matth. VII. 16. Seneca, Ep. 89. 8.) is not intended, as Waitz remarks in his note, for an exact and scientific division, but merely as one convenient for the use of dialecticians. This Aristotelian division of philosophy has been criticised and condemned, and the entire subject illustrated by Sir W. Hamilton, Lect. on Metaphysics, Vol. I. Lect. VII. His editor remarks (p. 114. not. a) that "the division of philosophy into Logic, Physics, and Ethics, probably originated with the Stoics," referring to Diogenes, and Pseudo-Plutarch. We have seen that at any rate it did not *originate* with them.

On πρᾶξις and ποίησις in the division of the sciences, see some remarks by Bernays "on the Dialogues of Aristotle," p. 58. seq.

rei cujus studium habet intellectu contenta, quæ θεωρητική vocatur: aliæ in agendo, quarum in hoc finis est, et ipso actu perficitur, nihilque post actum operis relinquit, quæ πρακτική dicitur, qualis est *saltatio:* aliæ in effectu, quæ operis quod oculis subjicitur consummatione finem accipiunt, quam ποιητικήν appellamus, qualis est *pictura:* fere judicandum est *rhetoricen* in actu consistere; hoc enim quod est officii sui perficit. And the chapter concludes § 5 Si tamen una ex tribus artibus (the three kinds above distinguished) habenda sit quia maxime ejus usus actu continetur, atque est in eo frequentissima, dicatur activa vel administrativa; nam et hoc ejusdem rei nomen est.

Rhetoric is a *practical* art.

From another passage of Quintilian, II. 17. 14, we learn that Aristotle himself argued against its being an art in his lost dialogue upon Rhetoric, the Gryllus. But, says Quintilian, this was only in accordance with his usual practice, quærendi gratiâ, to show what could be said on both sides of a question: sed idem et de arte rhetorica tres libros scripsit, et in eorum primo (I. 1. 1, 2.) non artem solum eam fatetur, sed ei particulam civilitatis (πολιτικῆς μόριον), sicut dialectices, assignat. This may help to account for his vacillation between τέχνη and δύναμις in the designation of rhetoric. See Bernays, die Dialoge des Arist. p. 63.

ART, AND ITS DEFINITIONS.

It may be well before we quit this subject of 'art' to enter a little more in detail into the views which were entertained upon it by the ancient philosophers, and some of its current definitions. We will begin with Aristotle, who in an interesting chapter at the opening of his Metaphysics gives an account of its nature and origin. The substance of this chapter is as follows. Knowledge varies in degree from the mere perception of phenomena to the knowledge of the highest and most universal causes: the order in the ascending scale is αἴσθησις, μνήμη, ἐμπειρία, τέχνη, ἐπιστήμη. Sensation of some kind is the distinctive mark of *animal* life: from sensation, in *some* animals, arises memory, and in proportion to the strength of this faculty is the force of intellect and the power of acquiring knowledge. In man, memory, by repetition of the same impression, gives rise to experience, ἐμπειρία, and from it proceed art, and ultimately science. Experience deals only with individuals, περὶ τὰ καθ' ἕκαστον, τῶν καθ' ἕκαστόν ἐστι γνῶσις, 981. 15.; but collecting its several memories of the same thing into one sum— the common properties being collected, the rest rejected. Bonitz.—it forms in some sort a general notion, yet never separated from these particulars, nor accurately defined. Art is a further process of generalisation from experience, "when from many mental impressions arising from experience a single universal conception is formed about their common properties," 981. 5. "For to have a conception that such and such a remedy is beneficial to Callias or Socrates when he has such and such a complaint is a case of experience: but to know that it is serviceable in all like cases (marked off from the rest, ἀφορισθεῖσι) determined under one kind is characteristic of art." Similarly in Rhet. II. 1. 11. we are told that art deals with classes (generalises), experience with individuals; but of these latter we can never attain complete knowledge because they are infinite: and the same example is used in illustration. The principle is then applied to Rhetoric and Dialectics. ἡ δὲ τέχνη τῶν καθόλου. Met. A. 1. 981. 16.

All real knowledge is the knowledge of causes; and it is this that constitutes the true superiority of art over experience—though in practice the skill derived from experience may often be more useful than the rules of art—"for empirics know the fact (the 'that,' τὸ ὅτι, that it is so) but not the why: but the others, artists and men of science, know the why, and therefore the cause." Hence it is that the master-craftsmen, ἀρχιτέκτονες, are more esteemed and held to be wiser than the handicraftsmen because they know the reason for all that they do; whereas the others work almost mechanically, by mere habit, like inanimate things. Another sign of knowledge is the power of teaching what we know, and therefore art is nearer to exact scientific knowledge than experience. And so also though the senses are the most authoritative organs of knowledge, yet as they know only particulars, not causes, nor universals, we do not attribute knowledge (in its strict and proper sense) to them. All this tends to show that *knowledge* is τῶν καθόλου and περὶ ἀρχάς or αἰτίας. Then follow some observations upon the order of the several arts and sciences in origin and dignity or value. The order of invention is inverse to that of dignity. The necessary and useful arts, πρὸς τἀναγκαῖα, πρὸς χρῆσιν, are first invented in the earlier and ruder stages of society: then come the ornamental and 'fine' arts, πρὸς ἡδονήν, πρὸς διαγωγήν, whose object is the adornment or embellishment of life and the gratification of a more refined taste: this is a mark of a more advanced stage of civilisation, when men have acquired wealth and leisure enough to allow them to devote themselves in some measure to the cultivation of their minds: and thirdly, there arrives a period when men have leisure enough to follow scientific pursuits and to seek truth and knowledge for their own sakes; and this is the age of theoretical science or philosophy. Hence it is that mathematics were originated by the Egyptian priests. By the same rule, that the value of knowledge is in proportion to the apprehension of cause, Metaphysics, ἡ πρώτη φιλοσοφία, which deals with first causes and ultimate principles, is the highest and most commanding, ἀρχικωτάτη, of all sciences, the apex and crown of the pyramid of knowledge.

The substance of the foregoing passage is repeated more concisely in the last Chapter of the Anal. Post. II. 19. 99. b. 34—100. 9.; and the resemblance is so close that the latter passage might be taken for a condensed epitome of the earlier part of the former. Art and science, as distinguished from ἐμπειρία, are found ἐν τῷ ἠρεμεῖν τὸ καθόλου ἐν τῇ ψυχῇ, τὸ ἓν παρὰ τὰ πολλά, ὃ ἂν ἐν ἅπασιν ἓν ἐνῇ ἐκείνοις τὸ αὐτό. (which may possibly be a reminiscence of Plato; the expression τὸ ἕν—τὸ αὐτό is at all events strictly Platonic). In this 'rest' of the universal in the mind—opposed to the κίνησις, the constant shifting and changing, of the particular and phenomenal in nature—the one universal notion gathered from the many individuals by abstraction of their common quality, art and science have their origin: these two being further distinguished by their aim and object, art being directed to, and employed upon production, περὶ γένεσιν, which, supported by the authority of Waitz, Comm. p. 431, si ad *agendum et faciendum* pertinet, I will interpret of 'practical' as well as strictly 'productive' ends; (see above, p. 16. n. 1. p. 18. n. 1.), science upon absolute truth and reality, περὶ τὸ ὄν.

The upshot of all this is, that ἐμπειρία is an *irrational* procedure; manifests itself in a merely mechanical mode of operation, working like a machine, and displaying a skill which results from nothing but habit and association, and is acquired by mere repetition; that it deals only with individual cases, and never rises to general conceptions or rules; or at least if it ever does form a general notion, this is never separated from the particular objects nor accurately defined; and as particulars are infinite and phenomena changeable they cannot in themselves convey any certain knowledge: art is a systematic rational, (μετὰ λόγου) procedure, or fixed intellectual character and tendency (Arist.), governed by *general* rules derived from experience, guided by general principles which are carried out in practice; its end and object is either action and practice, or the production of some concrete and permanent work. When it is said, as both Plato and Aristotle *do* say, that art implies a knowledge of causes, which as Aristotle tells us again and again is the characteristic of science or ἐπιστήμη properly understood, it is plain that the distinction between τέχνη and ἐπιστήμη is lost sight of, a confusion which, as I have already observed, is by no means uncommon with the ancient Greek philosophers. It is however this knowledge of causes which constitutes the certainty of an artist's knowledge, distinguishes him from the Empiric, and enables him to *predict* results; which in fact, says Plato in the Phædrus, would be the case with the Rhetorician if rhetoric could be made a true and genuine art[1]. This is the subjective aspect of art. Objectively it may be defined thus. An art is a body of general rules for practice, the application of which enables us to predict a given result.

This view of art and its distinction from empiricism which we derive from the above cited passages of Aristotle is in perfect agreement with Plato's opinions upon the same subject, as the following passage of the Gorgias, 501. A., will show. "What I said was, if I remember right, that cookery seems to me to be no art at all, but a mere empirical habit; medicine an art; meaning that the one, that is medicine, has inquired into the nature of that of which it treats and the *causes* of what it does, and can *give an account* of each of them: but the other enters upon the pursuit of the pleasure which is the object of all her care and attention quite unscientifically, without having bestowed any consideration upon either the nature or the cause of pleasure, and *proceeds in a manner absolutely irrational*, as one may say, without *the smallest calculation*, a mere knack and routine, simply *retaining the recollection of what usually happens*, by which you know in fact she provides all her pleasures." Again, 465. A. τέχνην οὐ καλῶ ὃ ἂν ᾖ ἄλογον πρᾶγμα: anything

---

[1] This power of looking forward to *future* results is likewise dwelt on by Plato as distinctive of the *artist*, the man of real knowledge and skill, in the Theætetus p. 178, and the fact of its existence alleged as a conclusive argument in favour of some objective standard of truth, against Protagoras' theory of the sole validity of the present subjective impression. See further on this matter in a paper on Mr Grote's Plato ('Theætetus', read before the Cambridge Phil. Soc. in May 1866, and since published, p. 27.

short of this is a mere ἐμπειρία, an acquired dexterity or knack.

And all this may be applied to determine what Aristotle's meaning is when he calls Rhetoric an art. In fact we may infer it from his own words at the commencement of the treatise, I. 1. 1, 2. where it is implied that Rhetoric may be made an art, because it can be systematised (ὁδοποιεῖν) and rules laid down to direct practice towards the attainment of a given end, namely to prove or seem to prove any point[1]; which agrees precisely with the views of the nature of art in general which we have already gathered from his other writings.

Another definition of art which became popular in later times—Quintilian says of it, Inst. Orat. II. 17. 41, that it was ab omnibus fere probatus—from its celebrity and some difficulties that attend the interpretation of it, deserves a few words of notice. It is attributed by Sextus Empiricus, Pyrrh. Hypot. III. 188 and 251, to the Stoics, and, so far at least as the word κατάληψις is concerned, is expressed in their technical phraseology. Sextus repeats it several times in the course of his works, sometimes in the naked form σύστημα ἐκ καταλήψεων, sometimes with the addition of συγγεγυμνασμένων, and in a passage adv. Math. B. πρὸς Ῥητορ. § 10, at full length, thus: πᾶσα τέχνη σύστημά ἐστιν ἐκ καταλήψεων συγγεγυμνασμένων καὶ ἐπὶ τέλος εὔχρηστον τῷ βίῳ λαμβανόντων τὴν ἀναφοράν. This, or something like it, is translated by Quintilian in the passage already cited, artem constare ex perceptionibus consentientibus et coexercitatis ad finem vitæ utilem. This however is at all events

---

[1] What he *says* is, that it may be systematised and a way paved towards the attainment of its objects, because it is certainly possible to discover the causes and the means of the success which rhetoricians meet with, whether they speak at random, without any care or training at all, or from an acquired habit. That is to say, that the modes in which their object is attained may be discovered, and reduced to general rules, which again may be applied to practice: and these are the various modes of proof, logical and ethical, which are the very body or soul of the art.

not a literal translation of the form of words used by Sextus, because Quintilian evidently construes συγγεγυμνασμένων as feminine with καταλήψεων, whereas in Sextus the former being connected with λαμβανόντων by καί is manifestly neuter: and the meaning of the words as given by Sextus must be, not that the apprehensions or conceptions *themselves* are drilled or exercised together (so as to act in common), but that this is the case with the things that they represent. But passing over this as of little importance, we will assume that the participle in the correct form of the definition belongs to καταλήψεων and is to be construed with it: and according to Quintilian, who translates σύστημα by consentientibus to express the uniformity of the impressions, the definition will mean, that art is a system of uniform conceptions drilled, i.e. brought to work, together to one common end; that end being something serviceable to human life and happiness[1]. By aid of this definition Sextus proceeds to demolish the claims of rhetoric to be considered an art at all, since he finds that its actual phenomena by no means agree with the terms of the other.

I have little doubt that this is the true meaning of the phrase, and we see that this interpretation has the authority of Quintilian in its favour. But Lucian, having occasion to employ the definition in his Parasite, c. 4, in applying it to test his παρασιτική, to see whether that is an art or not, goes on in the following chapter to compare the two in such a way as to furnish an explanatory commentary on the terms of the definition; and *he* evidently understands ἐγγεγυμνασμένων (as he writes it) of constant exercise or practice or application; so that according to him it means nothing more than "a set of consentient impressions exercised upon some end beneficial to human life."

Quintilian in the same passage, § 41, has given Cleanthes' (the Stoic, Zeno's pupil) definition of art, potestas via, id est

[1] The notion seems to be that of generalisation. A number of similar thoughts or impressions are gathered into a general rule of action.

ordine, efficiens, 'a faculty attaining its end by a systematic method,' which he says is equally applicable to Rhetoric with the preceding.

In Cicero de Oratore, I. 20. 92., Charmadas, the Academic, is made to give the following definition of art, quæ cognitis penitusque perspectis et in unum exitum spectantibus et nunquam fallentibus rebus continetur. This is the Platonic conception of a genuine art, and of course therefore cannot be applied to such a pursuit as Rhetoric which deals only with probabilities. Antonius notices this, c. 23. § 108, 9; admitting that by such a definition rhetoric is necessarily excluded from the sphere of art: but if we substitute a less rigorous one, a generalisation, viz., with a technical designation, a system of rules classified for application to practice, derived from the observation of clever and well informed men upon the usages and methods adopted by speakers in their ordinary practice[1]; he thinks that rhetoric may still retain the place that it has always held in popular estimation, as a member of the great family of Arts. Further on in the same work, c. 42. §§ 187, 8., a good summary account is given of the way in which art acts in combining and generalising and reducing to rule and system, and so making practically applicable, the scattered and desultory observations of phenomena already noted and existing in various departments of nature and human speculation, as grammar, music, geometry, astronomy, rhetoric; quæ rem dissolutam divulsamque conglutinaret et ratione quadam constringeret.

The entire subject of rhetoric as an art is ably discussed

---

[1] Quintilian II. 17. 5. styles this reducing rhetoric to mere 'observatio;' but it seems in fact to mean a great deal more: and I think that the interpretation I have given in the text to the words ab hominibus callidis ac peritis animadversa ac notata, verbis designata, *generibus illustrata*, partibus distributa, does not go beyond the import of them when fully developed, though that meaning is certainly rather vaguely and rhetorically expressed.

by Quintilian in an interesting and well reasoned chapter. Inst. Orat. II. 17, and the affirmative concluded against those who for various reasons, either that it is coeval with the existence of men in society and therefore antecedent to art, or that it has no peculiar subject matter and no definite end, which all genuine arts have, or that it contradicts itself by proving indifferently opposite conclusions, or others similar, denied its artistic character, and held it rather to be a natural gift or faculty developed and improved by habit and exercise.

Having dwelt so long upon the views and opinions of ancient authorities as to the nature of art and its relation to Rhetoric, we will pass over the Moderns with brief notice; referring merely for the discussion of these two questions, general and particular, to the Introduction to Campbell's Philosophy of Rhetoric; to Whately's Introduction to his Rhetoric; to the instructive chapter on the relation of art and science in Dr. Whewell's Philosophy of the Inductive Sciences, Bk. XI. ch. 8. (1st. Ed.); and the introduction to Lectures on Moral Philosophy 1839 and 1841 p. 40. by the same author: Dr. Whewell like Aristotle, points out the priority of art to science in the order of invention: also some observations on the various meanings of the term 'art,' in Sir G. C. Lewis' Method of Observ. in Politics. Vol. II. ch. XIX.

VARIOUS VIEWS AND DEFINITIONS OF RHETORIC.

We now proceed to give some account of the various definitions of rhetoric current amongst the ancient writers on the subject; which are all the more important, as by indicating the object and aim to which the art was supposed to be directed they throw some light indirectly upon the moral character of the art itself as thus understood, and of its professors whether schools or individuals. Quintilian in his second book, ch. XV, has given a very extensive list of definitions of the ancient rhetoricians from the earliest times down to his own, with critical remarks upon the defects and general bearings of them. He says he has selected only the most remarkable and those which have been most discussed; to go through them all was neither possible nor necessary for his purpose. This last observation may be applied to his own list, and I will follow his example by exercising a judicious selection out of his somewhat miscellaneous assortment of those that are most characteristic and due to the best known authors. A few comments and two or three corrections of careless misstatements are all that will be necessary in addition[1].

The views of the originators of the art, Corax, and Tisias, upon its nature and object may be gathered from Plato's description of the account Tisias gave of the rhetorician's functions, Phædr. 272. D, 273. A. and from a notice in Aristotle's Rhetoric. II. 24. 11. it appears that Corax' 'art' was completely occupied with the analysis and exemplification of the single 'topic' of τὸ εἰκός or the probable; of which Aristotle gives a specimen, and adds that the topic is neither more nor less than τὸν ἥττω λόγον κρείττω ποιεῖν, in other words, to subvert truth and justice. It will appear from this that, whether they actually adopted it as a definition or not, persuasion at any price, τὸ πείθειν without restriction or qualification, was their motto and their declared object; and 'the art or faculty of persuading' continued throughout to be the definition employed by the sophistical school of rhetoricians down to the time of Isocrates, and this it was that gave it its highly immoral character. This definition was at all events assumed by Gorgias the pupil of Tisias. He styled rhetoric πειθοῦς δημιουργός 'the artificer of persuasion,' as we learn from Plato's Gorgias, 453 A. 465 A. To the latter passage Quintilian alludes, Inst. Orat. II. 15. 18.

---

[1] I have treated the same subject of the ancient and some modern definitions of rhetoric in a paper published in the Journal of Classical and Sacred Philology, Vol. II. No. 5. p. 161—169, to which I will here venture to refer.

Gorgias apud Platonem persuadendi se artificem in judiciis et aliis cœtibus esse ait; de justis quoque et injustis tractare: and he again refers to Plato's Gorgias as the authority for the same statement in § 5. It is strange therefore that in the face of this he should attribute the origin of this definition and the view of the office and object of rhetoric which it implies, to Isocrates in § 4, as it seems impossible that he should have supposed Isocrates to be the elder of the two: and I can only account for the blunder on the supposition of its being a careless oversight, of which there are one or two other examples in this very chapter. Quintilian expresses some doubt of the genuineness of the τέχνη extant in his time which passed under the name of Isocrates, and contained this statement: but the statement itself is confirmed by Sext. Empir. adv. Math. B. πρὸς 'Ρητ. § 62. 'Ισοκράτης φησὶ μηδὲν ἄλλο ἐπιτηδεύειν τοὺς ῥήτορας ἢ ἐπιστήμην πειθοῦς. In the same passage, §§ 61, 62, Sextus attributes this opinion and definition of rhetoric to the followers or school of Plato and Xenocrates οἱ περὶ τὸν Πλ. καὶ Ξεν.,—whoever that may mean—to Ariston son of Critolaus, Hermagoras, and Athenæus, as well as Isocrates. These three are likewise mentioned by Quintilian, c. 15. §§ 14, 19, 23. and elsewhere, with the definition which they assigned to the art. These do not exactly correspond with those attributed to them by Sextus, although there is no absolute contradiction. Athenæus' *fallendi* ars, may be meant for an interpretation of the art of *persuasion*. To the list of writers on rhetoric who adopted this definition Quintilian adds the name of Cicero, who, pluribus locis scripsit (viz. de Orat. I. 31. 138. de Inv. I. 5. init. Acad. Post. I. 8. 32. In the last of these passages however the doctrine is not given as his own, but as held by the Academics and Peripatetics.) oratoris officium esse *dicere apposite ad persuadendum.* Quintilian justly condemns every definition of rhetoric which makes persuasion unqualified its object, on the ground that it includes too much, to pass over here the objections to it on moral grounds. Persuasion is not peculiar to rhetoric. Verum et pecunia persuadet, et gratia, et auctoritas dicentis, et dignitas, et postremo aspectus etiam ipse sine voce, quo vel recordatio meritorum cujusque, vel facies aliqua miserabilis, vel formæ pulcritudo, sententiam dictat. § 6. quoting illustrative cases, amongst them the famous one of Hyperides and Phryne (to which the *formæ pulcritudo* refers), and commending Gorgias and Theodectes for their addition of the qualifying 'dicendo' to the then current definition. §§ 7—10. But even this is insufficient; for it includes processes and influences which are not within the sphere of rhetoric; as those employed by meretrices, adulatores, corruptores. [This is going too far: so far as these 'persuade by speaking' they use rhetorical methods.] It is open also to another objection, that the genuine orator does not always *succeed* in persuading; whereas this form of the definition makes success essential to the art. Aristotle's modification of it, as we shall see by and by, removes this defect.

Plato's opinions upon rhetoric as it was understood and practised in his time have been already incidentally noticed. An art which he did not recognise as such he was not likely to take the trouble of seriously defining. He has it is true given a contemptuous description of it, which may pass for a definition, in the Gorgias, viz. that it is no true art at all, but a mere knack, or empirical habit, or routine, an ἐμπειρία or τριβή ('usus,' Quint. II. 15. 23) a process of 'flattery,' the object of which is to tickle the ears, to gratify and unfairly influence a popular and unintelligent audience: but Quintilian is so scandalised at the notion that an enlightened philosopher like Plato could have taken such a view of his favourite study, that he indignantly rejects this interpretation of Plato's opinions as a mistake arising merely from ignorance of what he has actually said. If those who have asserted this, he says, had not contented themselves with a few extracts unskilfully selected from the Gorgias, and had given themselves the trouble of referring to Plato's other volumes they never would have fallen into such an error. But he carefully abstains from quoting chapter and verse, and leaves his readers to find out for themselves in which of his other writings Plato has expressed a more favourable opinion of the art of rhetoric—at least in any sense in which it can be considered as rhetoric, or indeed an *art*, at all. Plato's real meaning, he continues, in the Gorgias and Phædrus is to show that the true rhetorician must also be a good man, or that the art of rhetoric cannot be complete without the knowledge of justice—which in fact, he adds, is his own opinion, §§ 24—29. This indeed we knew before; and we now see how an obstinate prepossession may lead an able and intelligent and clearsighted man utterly to misconstrue the opinions of another when they happen not to be in agreement with his own. I must also take the liberty to doubt whether Quintilian had either extensively read or carefully studied the works of an author whose views he can thus egregiously misinterpret: there is at all events little evidence of such acquaintance or study either here or elsewhere in his book.

But let us consider for a moment whether there are any such indications of a different opinion in Plato's other works, and particularly in his later writings in which, if any where, we might expect to find such a change. I confess I can find none: on the contrary what we do find as far as it goes seems to show that he maintained his unfavourable opinion, at all events of the prevailing study and practice of rhetoric, steadily to the end. In proof of his continued disapprobation of these, I will first notice—what seems to be conclusive on the point—the entire omission of it, the absence indeed of all allusion to it, in the course of study recommended for the philosophers and guardians of the model Republic. Surely if Plato when he wrote that work had recognised rhetoric as a useful and instructive art, he would not have denied his perfect governors all knowledge of that which he must in that case have considered so important an element in an education for public life. There is nothing very explicit in the Republic on this subject: what we do find there represents the old opinions as still strong in his mind. Compare for example II. 365 D, where Adimantus is made to say, in the true Platonic spirit, of the rhetorical instruction, εἰσί τε πειθοῦς διδάσκαλοι, σοφίαν δημηγορικήν τε καὶ δικανικὴν διδόντες, ἐξ ὧν τὰ μὲν πείσομεν, τὰ δὲ βιασόμεθα, ὡς πλεονεκτοῦντες δίκην μὴ διδόναι: or the contrasted pictures of the lives and characters and pursuits of the philosopher and politician, Rep. Bk. VI., and the corresponding ones in the Theætetus, in which the results of the education for public life consisting mainly in a rhetorical training are made to appear at a most manifest disadvantage; or again the θῶπας ἡδῦναι λόγους of the Theætetus, 175 E, which is very far from being descriptive of a scientific or even genuine artistic process. Look again to his latest work the Laws, where we find (XI. 937 D.) the reassertion in a summary way of all the old objections against the rhetorical education and practice. To what extent the use of rhetoric may be admitted into the art of government we learn from a passage of the Politicus, c. 42. 303 E seq. He here allows of a parænetic, hortative kind of discourses, homilies in fact, to be used under the direction of πολιτική, the royal or master art, whose office it is to prescribe to its subordinates (just like Aristotle's ἀρχιτεκτονική) to each its several function and limit, so that there may be no confusion or interference, but that each may act in its proper sphere, and all together form a harmonious and systematic whole. As it is to be applied to the mob, to keep them in order and persuade them to virtue, it must be of a purely popular character, διὰ μυθολογίας, moral instruction conveyed by way of fable and parable, not scientific or didactic, μὴ διὰ διδαχῆς. But surely this is something very different from an 'art of rhetoric.'

We now come to Aristotle, who, as we have already seen, modifies the sophistical definition in one important particular, in that he substitutes for the art or faculty of persuading, which assumes success to be essential, the faculty[1] (as I have pointed out, though in defining rhetoric he calls it merely a δύναμις, at the beginning of the treatise and incidentally everywhere else he *assumes* it to be a true art—see for instance I. 1. 12 and 14. even the name, ῥητορική, implies this) of observing or discovering in every case presented the possible means of persuasion, θεωρῆσαι περὶ ἕκαστον τὸ ἐνδεχόμενον πιθανόν. I. 2, 1, δύναμίς τις τοῦ πορίσαι λόγους. Ib. § 7. "a faculty of finding arguments." οὐ τὸ πεῖσαι ἔργον αὐτῆς, ἀλλὰ τὸ ἰδεῖν τὰ ὑπάρχοντα πιθανὰ περὶ ἕκαστον: because art depends in no respect upon the result, but only on the method employed: a patient may be treated secundum artem though he should die under the physician's hands; "for it is possible to treat artistically, by observing the proper rules and method, even those who are incapable of recovering their health": or as Napoleon was no less a general when he lost the battle of Waterloo. A similar modification is applied to the definition of χρηματιστική in Polit. I. 9. 10. Its office is not absolutely to make money, since rules most ably devised and applied *may* fail of their effect, but, τὸ δύνασθαι θεωρῆσαι πόθεν ἔσται πλῆθος χρημάτων, the ability to discover the sources and means from and by which wealth may be obtained. And again in another place, Topic. A. 3., οὔτε γὰρ ὁ ῥητορικὸς ἐκ παντὸς τρόπου πείσει, οὔθ᾽ ὁ ἰατρικὸς ὑγιάσει· ἀλλ᾽ ἐὰν τῶν ἐνδεχομένων μηδὲν παραλίπῃ, ἱκανῶς αὐτὸν ἔχειν τὴν ἐπιστήμην φήσομεν. Finally this consideration may serve as a further correction of that confusion of ἐπιστήμη and τέχνη which we just now noticed. Arts practical and productive are all exercised within the sphere of probability and the contingent, which is one of their distinguishing characters as contrasted with science. We cannot be *absolutely* certain either of the effect of a volition or action, or of the result of an artistic operation: art is *conversant* with causes and effects, but is not

---

[1] δύναμις, potestas, vis, Cic. and Quint.

master of them: exact science alone deals with the universal and the necessary. Quintilian criticises Aristotle's definition of rhetoric, II. 15. 13., in these terms : quidam recesserunt ab eventu, (give up the position that success is necessary to an artist) sicut Aristoteles, qui dicit: rhetorici est vis inveniendi omnia in oratione persuasibilia. Qui finis et illud vitium de quo supra diximus [persuadent enim dicendo, vel ducunt in id quod volunt, alii quoque, ut meretrices, adulatores, corruptores, § 11." Of the force of this I have already given my opinion: but the fact is that Aristotle's definition is really open to Quintilian's censure in this point, for it *does* leave out the qualifying 'in oratione' or 'in dicendo,' which Quintilian has wrongly introduced. He is indeed unusually careless in this chapter.] habet, et insuper quod nihil nisi inventionem complectitur, quæ sine elocutione non est oratio. That is to say, that it includes first too much, and then too little. The second objection is no doubt well founded: but we have already seen the reason of Aristotle's omission. In the first two books he takes no account of anything but the various modes of proof, which, as he justly says, do really constitute the essence of persuasion; the style, ornaments, arrangement, and delivery, though in themselves important enough, are by comparison mere accidents. The effect of this modification of the old definition is to withdraw the notion of the art in some degree from the exclusively practical application of it encouraged by the sophistical school, and to fix the attention rather upon its theory and method; in short it tends to a more scientific treatment of the subject.

Quintilian also cites another definition of rhetoric by Cicero, from the de Invent. I. 5, 6. which stands side by side with the one before mentioned, hanc oratoriam facultatem in eo genere ponemus, ut eam civilis scientiæ partem esse dicamus: corresponding herein with Aristotle who speaks of it, Rhet. I. 2. 7., as a παραφυές τι τῆς διαλεκτικῆς καὶ τῆς περὶ τὰ ἤθη πραγματείας ἣν δίκαιόν ἐστι προσαγορεύειν πολιτικήν, and in the passage so often already referred to of Eth. Nic. I. 1. as, together with οἰκονομική, and στρατηγική, one of the subordinate branches of πολιτική.

Theodorus, of Byzantium (§ 16.) described it as, vim (δύναμιν) inveniendi et eloquendi cum ornatu credibilia in omni oratione.

Anaximenes' treatise, if the ῥητορικὴ πρὸς Ἀλέξανδρον be really his, is distinguished by the absence of a definition of rhetoric: and that of Dionysius, which has a purely practical direction and consists in fact of little more than a collection of loci communes, choice extracts for study and imitation, is equally without one. I will omit the remaining definitions which are given in Quintilian's chapter, and are mere varieties and modifications of the others, and conclude with the author's own. This is brief and concise in expression, bene dicendi scientia §§ 34, 38, but very comprehensive in meaning, since it includes the possession of all virtues and accomplishments: nam et orationes omnes virtutes semel complectitur, et protinus mores etiam oratoris; quum bene dicere non possit nisi vir bonus.—an opinion which he had likewise expressed in the first section of this chapter. Cato the Censor took the same view as we learn from Seneca, Præf. ad Controv. I. p. 62. (quoted by Spalding) orator est, Marce fili, vir bonus, dicendi peritus.

Eloquence, that is rhetoric in practice, is defined by Campbell, Phil. of Rhet. init., "that art or talent (τέχνη or δύναμις) by which the discourse is adapted to its end." It is identical with Quintilian's definition, dicere secundum virtutem orationis, scientia bene dicendi. It exactly corresponds to Tully's idea of a perfect orator; optimus est orator qui dicendo animos audientium et docet et delectat et permovet. The *ends* of speaking are four: "every speech being intended to enlighten the understanding, to please the imagination, to move the passions, or to influence the will."

Whately in his Introduction has not given any exact definition of it: if the words "to prove is the proper office of the advocate" are to be interpreted as implying that rhetoric is 'the art of proving,' the definition is faulty, for it makes no distinction between rhetoric and logic.

I will conclude this part of my subject with the words of Bacon, who takes a very different view of the office and functions of Rhetoric from that of any of his Classical predecessors. "The duty and office of Rhetoric is to *apply Reason to Imagination* for the better moving of the will. For we see reason is disturbed in the administration thereof by three means; by Illaqueation or Sophism, which pertains to Logic; by Imagination or Impression, which pertains to Rhetoric; and by Passion or Affection, which pertains to Morality. And as in negotiation with others men are corrupt by cunning, by importunity, and by vehemency; so in this negotiation within ourselves men are undermined by Inconsequences, solicited and importuned by Impressions or Observations, and transported by Passions. Neither is the nature of man so unfortunately built, as that those powers and arts should have force to disturb reason, and not to establish and advance it: for the end of Logic is to teach a form of argument to secure reason, and not to entrap it; the end of Morality is to procure the affections to obey reason, and not to invade it; the end of Rhetoric is to fill the imagination to second reason, and not to oppress it: for these abuses of arts come in but *ex obliquo,* for caution." Adv. of Learning, Bk. II. Vol. III. p. 409 seq. de Augm. Scient. VI. 3. Vol. I. p. 671. Ellis and Spedding. Ed.

DATE OF ARISTOTLE'S RHETORIC.

So far we have been engaged upon the consideration of the general characteristics of the Aristotelian rhetoric, and have pointed out the peculiarities which distinguish his manner of treating the subject from that which was adopted by preceding and subsequent writers: we will now proceed to inquire whether we have any evidence which will enable us to fix the period of Aristotle's life at which this work was composed.

This question has been well discussed by Dr Max Schmidt in a little tract published at Halle in 1837, Commentatio de tempore quo ab Aristotele libri de arte rhetorica conscripti et editi sint; and by Brandis in the paper in Schneidewin's Philologus, Vol. IV. No. 1., über Aristoteles' rhetorik u. die griechischen ausleger derselben, already more than once referred to. These two writers have collected and weighed the evidence external and internal which is accessible to us upon the point, and to these, together with the aids incidentally derivable from the writings of Spengel, Stahr, and other Aristotelian expositors, I shall have recourse in the outline I am about to give of the leading facts and considerations which tend to throw any light upon the question[1]. As is usual in these cases the result is meagre and unsatisfactory: no certainty is attainable; and we have to content ourselves with sufficiently vague and indefinite conjectures as to the time and mode of the composition of the work.

It has been very justly observed that the internal evidence of the book itself, the constant references to events and persons connected with Athens, often unimportant or obscure, and if known at *Athens* probably known no where else, by showing that the work was addressed especially to an Attic audience, determine conclusively the *place* of composition as that city and no other. This will limit the possible date of composition to two periods, viz. the first and second residences of Aristotle at Athens, that is from B.C. 367 to 347, and again from B.C. 335 to 322. It seems equally

---

[1] Clinton, Fast. Hell. Vol. I. sub anno 334 B.C., referring to Rhet. II. 23. 6 and 24. 8, and to Dionysius Ep. ad Amm. who supposes ἡ περὶ Δημοσθένους δίκη to mean Demosthenes' 'case' for the Crown, an interpretation justly rejected by Victorius, Comment. p. 475, concludes that "we only know therefore that this treatise of Aristotle was [published] later than the year B.C. 338." We shall see that the limit of the period of publication may be brought down a year or two lower.

certain that the *final publication* of the work did not take place till the second residence of the author at Athens. The latest historical events alluded to in the Rhetoric are (1) II. 23. 6. an embassy to Thebes on the part of Philip, the Thessalians, and the rest of the allies, to induce the Thebans to grant Philip and his troops a passage through their territory into Attica, which occurred in 338 B.C. shortly before the battle of Chæronea—this is satisfactorily made out by Spengel in a tract published at Heidelberg, 1844. specimen Comment. in Arist. de arte rhet. L. II. c. 23. and Max Schmidt. op. cit. p. 16: and Dionysius commenting upon this passage says, Epist. ad Amm. c. 11. p. 740, Reiske, ὁ δὲ χρόνος οὗτος, ἐν ᾧ Φίλιππος ἠξίου Θηβαίους ἐπὶ τὴν Ἀττικὴν αὐτῷ δοῦναι δίοδον—and (2), II. 23. 18. the alliance which all the Greeks, with the exception of the Lacedæmonians, made with Alexander after the death of Philip in 336 B.C., here called κοινὴ εἰρήνη. This discovery is again due to Spengel, who proposes the explanation in *another* Specimen Comment. in Ar. libros de a. Rh., published this time at Munich, in 1839. Spengel adds, as a note in the margin, hoc quoque exemplum post illud tempus ab Aristotele Rhetoricam *elaboratam* esse docet. It seems to me that this is going too far: nothing can be fairly inferred from the reference except as to the date of *publication*. His general conclusion, stated in another and more recent paper upon Aristotle's Rhetoric, published in the transactions of the royal Bavarian Academy, Munich 1851, p. 42, is that the composition of the work may be assigned to somewhere about B.C. 330. The other reference in II. 24. 8. to 'Demosthenes' policy' which Demades said was the cause of all the mischief, is most likely also subsequent to the battle of Chæronea in 338, and would so far coincide with that of II. 23. 6; but *may* likewise possibly indicate some previous policy of Demosthenes, as that which he followed in promoting the Olynthian war; and is therefore not *quite* so trustworthy as the other.

As these are the latest events which are referred to in

the work, we may here pass over without special notice earlier references to persons and circumstances therein contained, of which Brandis has furnished a considerable list in his treatise p. 10, and proceed at once to the consideration of an argument derived from certain notices of Aristotle's pursuits in his earlier life, and the relations then subsisting between him and Isocrates, handed down to us from ancient authors. This, besides the light it throws upon the question now before us, has also an independent interest and importance of its own in its bearing upon Aristotle's pursuits and studies, and deserves on that account also a few minutes' attention.

Isocrates died in 338: any intercourse therefore that took place between them must have occurred during Aristotle's first residence at Athens, in the earlier period of his life. That there was at some time during this period an overt antagonism and rivalry between the rhetorician and the philosopher, and a mutual jealousy, which appears in the writings of the former (see Spengel in Trans. Bavar. Acad. Munich, 1851. p. 16, seq.[1]), but *not* in those of Aristotle, is placed beyond question, says Stahr, Aristotelia, I. 63. by the crowd of ancient witnesses who testify to it. These are Isocrates himself, who implies though he does not directly state it; Hermippus from whom Diogenes derived his information, Vit. Arist. a'. 2.; Dionysius, who quotes a sneer of Aristotle at the loads of Isocrates' forensic speeches which were hawked about by the booksellers, and adds that Aristotle wanted to 'befoul' him, ῥυπαίνειν, to bespatter him with calumny and abuse. de Isocr. jud. c. 18.; Diogenes, u.s. who quotes the verse of (Euripides'?) Philoctetes which Aristotle applied to his rival, αἰσχρὸν σιωπᾶν Ἰσοκράτην δ' ἐᾶν λέγειν,

---

[1] I confess that I cannot see the indications of this jealousy which Spengel finds in the *letter* to Alexander, the fifth of those ascribed to Isocrates, (of which he admits the genuineness) though it is barely possible that the allusions in it *may* be intended for Aristotle: in the other passages cited from his works this is plain enough.

with the substitution of 'Ἰσοκράτην for βαρβάρους as it stood in the original, and which Diogenes, apparently by a lapse of memory writes Ξενοκράτην, confounding times and persons; Athenæus, Deipn. II. 60. D.E, who tells us that one Cephisodorus or Cephisodotus, a pupil of Isocrates, was constrained to take up the cudgels in his master's defence, and to write four books κατὰ 'Αριστοτέλους, from which Stahr very fairly infers that Aristotle must have *written* something about Isocrates and his rhetoric to call forth all these *books;* Cicero, in various places, the most important of which is De Orat. III. 35. 141., which helps to fix the *time* of Aristotle's early rhetorical studies to the *later years* of his first residence at Athens, neque vero hoc fugit sapientissimum Philippum, qui hunc Alexandro filio doctorem accierit &c.; and lastly Quintilian who quotes the verse of the Philoctetes, and tells us in addition that Aristotle set up a rival school of rhetoric in *the old age* of Isocrates, his rhetorical lectures being given in the afternoon.

From all this it may naturally be inferred that this was the period at which Aristotle's attention was first directed to the study of rhetoric, and that the indignation which he felt at the undeserved popularity of Isocrates whom he looked upon as the perverter and corruptor of the genuine study of rhetoric, as one who by confining himself to the least important branch, the epideictic, and teaching his pupils merely to turn phrases and round periods instead of instructing them in the essentials of the art, exercised a malignant influence upon education in general—and this view was certainly well founded—that his indignation, I say, at all this induced him to set up a rival school in which rhetoric should be philosophically and systematically treated, for the use of which he *may* have drawn up a body of rules and precepts taking the form of an art of rhetoric. This is perhaps the ground of the opinion expressed, but with no reason assigned, by Niebuhr, Roman Hist. Vol. I. not. 39. that Aristotle's Rhetoric is one of those works of which the 'first sketch' belongs to the early period of the author's life, whilst it has continued to receive additions and corrections down to its close. This is in itself far from improbable, but is at the best a mere hypothesis: and I am at least equally inclined to agree with Brandis, op. cit. p. 8, 9., who after stating Niebuhr's opinion, and telling us that he was at first disposed to yield to his great authority, says that upon closer examination of the extant work he could see nothing which seems to point to an early period of composition, or to long and desultory elaboration; that on the contrary the regularity and uniformity with which the plan of it is carried through rather indicates a continuous and uninterrupted application: sie, (die Rhetorik), ist, as he says emphatically at the commencement of his dissertation, ein werk aus einem gusse[1].

But there are some other considerations connected with this question of the hostile relations of Aristotle to Isocrates which may assist us in deciding between the earlier and later residences at Athens as the probable period of composition of the Rhetoric. Victorius, as is well known, thinks he finds in Aristotle's extant work constant traces of this enmity in the shape of disparaging allusions and criticisms, which are directed against Isocrates, though he is never named in them. See for example his Commentary, pp. 507, 605. But this is in reality a complete delusion arising from a foregone conclusion on the part of the excellent commentator. Aristotle's notices of Isocrates are so far from being unfavourable that he draws a greater number of illustrations of excellences of style from him than from any other author; in a single chapter III. 10, as Spengel remarks, op. cit. p. 21., no less than ten are taken from the Πανηγυρικός, and so it is throughout. Of those which have been supposed to imply censure there is only one—the criticism upon the rule that the "narrative" must be "rapid", Rhet. III. 16. 4, which we

---

[1] I do not mean to deny that Aristotle wrote something upon Rhetoric at the earlier period of his quarrel with Isocrates—possibly the Theodectea—but only that it was the extant treatise.

know from Quintilian, IV. 2. 32., was to be found in Isocrates' τέχνη.—which is really liable to the charge: some of the other alleged satirical references have been examined by Schmidt and Brandis, ll. cc., and justly pronounced free from this imputation. There is absolutely no doubt upon the point; Spengel, Schmidt, and Brandis are all agreed about it; only the first of the three insinuates that as we have not Isocrates' art actually before us, and cannot therefore verify all the allusions that may be made to it, it may be dangerous to draw rash conclusions as to the non-existence of certain covert inuendos against it which may possibly lurk under general criticisms. However the absence of any evidence of ill feeling in the work itself, and the existence of it as an actual fact *at an earlier period* are perfectly reconcilable in themselves: and the former not only shows a humanity and courtesy and easy good temper on the part of Aristotle which it seems to me appears in all his Ethical writings at least, Ethics and Politics and Rhetoric, but may also incline us to adopt the later date for the composition of the Rhetoric, during his second residence in Athens. Nor is the early rivalry and opposition to Isocrates and his teaching in any way inconsistent with the almost universally favourable notices of him in the later work on Rhetoric, as Spengel has remarked. I have already observed that his antagonism was directed against his system of teaching and its mischievous results: to the merits of Isocrates' style, and the art on which it was founded, Aristotle never could have been insensible, and the care with which he had studied Isocrates' speeches is shown in the multitude of illustrations which he derives from them: and it is these and these alone that have attracted his approbation.

The fact is that although, as I am fully persuaded, Aristotle was a thoroughly kindly and good natured man, still it cannot be denied that a certain literary pugnacity [1]

---

[1] He says himself, arguing perhaps from himself, de Cœl. 294. b. 8. πᾶσι γὰρ ἡμῖν τοῦτο σύνηθες, μὴ πρὸς τὸ πρᾶγμα ποιεῖσθαι τὴν ζήτησιν, ἀλλὰ πρὸς τὸν τἀναντία λέγοντα.

and critical severity were characteristic of his habits of mind. He hardly ever mentions one of his philosophical predecessors except for the purpose of finding fault, and hence his supposed hostility to Plato, whose *doctrines* at any rate he certainly does lose no opportunity of attacking, though he seldom in return takes notice of any of his own very numerous obligations to his master. However, to suppose that the man who could write, or who could be supposed to have written, if they are not really Aristotle's, these two lines to Plato's memory,

Βωμὸν 'Αριστοτέλης ἐνιδρύσατο τόνδε Πλάτωνος,
ἀνδρός, ὃν οὐδ' αἰνεῖν τοῖσι κακοῖσι θέμις,[1]

and as a preliminary to one of the not least uncompromising of his attacks upon his writings—the criticism of the Laws to wit, in Polit. II. 6.—could speak of them in the terms that he there employs, could have been animated by a spirit of hatred or hostility or even jealousy towards his master, is to suppose that the beast preponderated over the angel in Aristotle's moral composition to a much greater extent than I can bring myself to believe. Indeed criticism and opposition being his ordinary rule of proceeding with his philosophical competitors, and compliment the rare exception, we shall be rather entitled to infer an exceptional esteem from the single compliment, than hatred or contempt or any other bad feeling from the frequent antagonism. When Bacon says that Aristotle corrupted Natural Philosophy with his Logic, Nov. Organ. I. 63., or that he tried to construct the world out of his Categories, there may perhaps be some foundation for the censure: but when he proceeds to talk of his pugnax et spinosa philosophia, Nov. Org. I. 89.; to compare him with the Turk that would "bear no brother near the throne," an image of jealousy and suspicion and rivalry of which he is so enamoured and thinks so extremely appropriate that he repeats it again and again, Nov. Org. I. 67.

---

[1] Quoted by Ammonius in his life of Aristotle.

de Augm. III. 4. (Vol. I. p. 563, Ellis and Spedding's Ed.) and elsewhere; or finally gives vent to the following piece of gratuitous spite, de Augm. III. 4. sub init.; Qua in re Aristotelis confidentiam proinde subit mirari, qui impetu quodam percitus contradictionis et bellum universæ antiquitati indicens, non solum nova artium vocabula pro libitu cudendi licentiam usurpavit, sed etiam priscam omnem sapientiam extinguere et delere annisus est—we merely presume that, blinded by a prejudice hastily taken up from a very incomplete acquaintance with Aristotle's writings, derived itself probably in a great measure at second hand from the schoolmen, and from his experience of the bad effects that had followed from the *abuse* of his method, showing themselves in the corruption of Natural Philosophy and the construction of worlds out of Categories, he took a very inadequate measure of the moral character as well as the acquirements of his greater prototype, and attributed to him most groundlessly feelings and motives which were at least as alien from Aristotle's temper as from his own[1]. The same hasty prepossession has been taken up in like manner by Montesquieu, whether derived from Bacon, or from his own independent judgment. He makes in the Esprit des Lois, XXIX. 19. the following, which I must be permitted to call, very foolish observation. Aristote voulait satisfaire tantôt sa jalousie contre Platon, tantôt sa passion pour Alexandre. There is only one more passage that I will bring forward on this subject, which however is neither unimportant nor uninteresting; and that, because I really think it settles the question as to the feeling which Aristotle entertained towards his master whilst controverting his doctrines. It is taken from Joannes Philoponus' reply to Proclus on the subject of the Eternity of the Universe, in which he tells us that Proclus in his defence of Plato's Timæus against Aristotle's objections, after enumerating, with citation of

[1] What shall we say for instance of Bacon's treatment of his contemporary Gilbert?

passages, the multiplied attacks of the latter upon the doctrine of ideas, to be found in the Ethics, the treatise on generation and decay, and the Metaphysics beginning middle and end, he concludes "and in his *dialogues* he most distinctly exclaims that he *can not* reconcile himself to this doctrine, though he feels that he shall expose himself to the suspicion of a quarrelsome (pugnacious) disposition by controverting it." καὶ ἐν τοῖς διαλόγοις σαφέστατα κεκραγώς, μὴ δύνασθαι τῷ δόγματι τούτῳ συμπαθεῖν, κἄν τις αὐτὸν οἴηται διὰ φιλονεικίαν ἀντιλέγειν. Quoted by Bernays, die Dialoge des Aristoteles, p. 48. by Heitz, Verlorene Schriften des Aristoteles, (Leipzig. 1865) p. 129, and by Rose, at full length, in his Arist. Pseudepigraphus, p. 718.: that is, Aristotle thought it *his duty* not to disguise his philosophical convictions even when they differed from those of his master, in spite of the imputation, false and unmerited (as plainly appears in the words), of hostility to Plato which he foresaw that it would bring upon him. The doctrines of a man's philosophy were in fact to the ancients what his religious convictions are amongst ourselves, and a philosopher might well regard it as a *duty* not to conceal them[1].

Another subject which may help to throw light (or obscurity) upon the period of Composition of the Rhetoric is the relation in which Aristotle stands to his great contemporary Demosthenes. It is a startling fact, equally so whether the Rhetoric was written during the first or second residence at Athens—for even upon the former supposition additions were constantly made down to at least 336. B.C.—that no sentence of Demosthenes' orations appears in it to illustrate any special beauty or peculiarity of rhetoric. *A* Demosthenes

---

[1] One more passage before closing this subject. Heitz. op. cit. p. 287. has these words—In dieser Weise werden die Briefe dazu benützt, um die Ungerechtigkeit des dem Aristoteles haüfig gemachten Vorwurfs der Undankbarkeit gegen Platon zu bekämpfen, quoting Vit. Marcel. p. 6. καὶ φαίνεται ἐν ταῖς ἐπιστολαῖς θαυμάζων Πλάτωνα, καὶ συνιστὰς τοῖς βασιλεῦσι τοὺς Πλάτωνι κατὰ γένος κοινωνοῦντας.

is indeed *mentioned* as the author of a lively comparison, Rhet. III. 4. 3., but it is probably not the orator who is meant. If indeed it *were* intended for the great orator, to mention him in such a way, to cite such an extremely unworthy and insignificant specimen of his powers and nothing else, would be almost as unaccountable as not to mention him at all[1]. According to Brandis, Handb. Aristoteles, I. 63. Demosthenes is named only once by Aristotle, and that is in Rhet. II. 24. 8, where a charge brought against his policy by Demades is cited as an example of the fallacy 'post hoc propter hoc', the interpretation of $\mu\epsilon\tau\dot{a}$ as if it were $\delta\iota\dot{a}$. Brandis remarks upon this that there is nevertheless no single trace of any enmity or ill will between them[2]. Schmidt on the other hand, u.s. p. 19, with much less reason and probability attributes this silence to political animosity. 'Aristoteles, Macedo, infestum animum etiam in hostem oppressum deponere non potuit,......Demosthenem per omnem vitam æqualem eodem aut supercilio despexit aut silentio pressit.' Credat Judæus.

Before leaving this subject we must not omit to notice the attempt made by Dionysius of Halicarnassus in his first

---

[1] Spengel says very coolly. Auffallend bleibt es, dass er für Staatsrede den Demosthenes ganz vernachlässigte, aus ihm ist kein einziges Beispiel angeführt; and that is all. Trans. Bav. Acad. u. s. p. 21. note.

[2] The name Demosthenes occurs three times in Aristotle's Rhetoric; Brandis of course supposes that only in one of these cases is the Orator intended. Of the two others, the one quoted in the text is supposed by Victorius and commentators in general to designate the Athenian general whom we find in Thucydides employed in the Peloponnesian war: of the other, II. 23. 3. ἡ περὶ Δημοσθένους δίκη καὶ τῶν ἀποκτεινάντων Νικάνορα, as we are absolutely ignorant of the persons and circumstances of the case, who Demosthenes was, who Nicanor, and what the δίκη, nothing whatever can be determined—see Buhle's note—It seems most probable that the Orator is *not* intended, though Dionysius, in spite of Greek and common sense, will have it that the reference is to the Speech for the Crown. Ep. ad Amm. I. c. 12. We learn further from the Scholiast on II. 23. 18. that the words καὶ τὸ μετέχειν τῆς κοινῆς εἰρήνης ποιεῖν τὸ προσταττόμενον are either a direct quotation, or the substance, of a passage in one of Demosthenes' speeches; but the author is not *named*.

Epistle to Ammæus to prove that Demosthenes owed nothing to the precepts and rules of Aristotle's Rhetoric, which was not *written*, *certainly* until Demosthenes' reputation as an orator was thoroughly established, that is the year 338 B.C. to which the historical allusion in II. 23. 6. refers, or the conclusion of the war, implied in II. 24. 8; and *probably* not until after the delivery of the Speech for the Crown, eight years later, to which he finds an allusion in II. 23. 3. (see above note 2. p. 10). The contents of the Epistle are of no great value or importance: it was easy enough for him to show from several historical references to contemporary events that the work was not *finished* till the year 338 B.C. at the earliest—he had not the sagacity to detect that which Spengel has discovered in II. 23. 18—and that it was not *published* before that date: but he says *written;* and this he has not shown; nor can it be gainsaid, though it be not demonstrated, that Aristotle in his earlier life had laid the foundations of his theory, and probably already sketched the outline of his system (I mean mentally, not in writing), based upon his master's suggestions in the Phædrus and perhaps upon oral communications from him, which was afterwards embodied in a work written at some uncertain period during his second residence in Athens and not completely finished or given to the world before at least the year 336 B.C. And with this not very satisfactory result of a long discussion, which is likewise the conclusion of Brandis, I will here leave this part of the subject.

To the examination of this question of the date of composition of the Rhetoric Brandis in the treatise so often referred to has appended an inquiry into the relation in which it stands to other works of the same author therein referred to expressly or by implication, in order so far to determine its comparative date.- In connexion with this he enters into a detailed and very instructive comparison of the Rhetoric with the Prior Analytics, the de Soph. Elench., the Ethics, Politics, and especially at great length with the Topics, for the particulars of which I must refer my readers to the work itself.

The conclusions with which we are more immediately concerned are as follows. There is at least one unmistakable reference to the Poetics, (Rhet. III. 2. 1404. b. 8. Poet. c. xxii.) which shows that this book was already written. Another reference, I. 2. 1356. b. 19, is made to the $\mu\epsilon\theta o\delta\iota\kappa\acute{a}$, a lost work upon some branch of Logic, 'probably occupying an intermediate place between analytics and dialectics.' The Topics of course were already completed; and the same may be said at least of the Prior Analytics, which are frequently referred to directly and indirectly. The case of the Posterior Analytics is not so clear. Brandis says p. 26 that as the immediate connexion of rhetoric is with dialectics rather than with analytics (scientific demonstration) we need not be surprised that there are no direct references to it in the Rhetoric, nor conclude on that account that this, or the tract de Interpretatione, had not been previously committed to writing. The *list* of Categories was certainly already prepared, Rhet. II. 7. 1385. b. 5: whether the *book* was written, is a different question which cannot be decided.

The three other subjects which may be expected to be brought into connexion with the treatment of Rhetoric, are Psychology, Ethics, and Politics;—and the books, consequently, de Animâ, the Nicomachean Ethics, and the Politics. Of the first of these there is no trace in the Rhetoric. The $\pi\acute{a}\theta\eta$ are treated quite independently of Physics and on purely rhetorical principles. The Ethics though not expressly named are never left out of sight: the principles appealed to are not different: only the popular mode of treatment which Rhetoric requires necessitates a different mode of handling and a different point of view, as we have before had occasion to observe. However as no distinct and decisive references are to be found in the one to the other, the comparative date of composition cannot be determined: all that can be positively pronounced is, that when the Rhetoric was written the author had the outlines of his Ethical system already definitely settled.

Lastly the Politics are actually mentioned by name, Rhet. I. 8. 7. and were therefore already in existence before the latter work was finally completed. No adverse inference can be drawn from the difference between the two classifications of forms of government severally adopted in Pol. III. 7 and Rhet. I. 8. In the former we have six, in the latter four or five, varieties of constitutions. This is easily explained. In the Rhetoric the distinction of the good and bad forms of popular government, of πολιτεία and δημοκρατία, peculiar to Aristotle, and included neither in the popular vocabulary nor in the schemes of preceding writers on Politics, is not recognised, because it would be unsuitable, perhaps unintelligible, to an audience of ἰδιῶται, who had no special knowledge of the subject: in the Politics on the other hand a scientific analysis requires the sixfold division.

ARISTOTLE'S LOST WORKS ON RHETORIC.

But next, was the art of Rhetoric now extant the *only* work upon this subject to which the capacious brain and amazing versatility of its author gave birth? By no means. Diogenes' list, v. i. 22 and 24., contains at least eight titles of works of which rhetoric must have been the subject; without counting one, περὶ συμβουλίας, which is included amongst them by Westermann Gesch. der Beredts. § 60. n. 4., and which, so far as a title is indicative of the nature of the contents of a work, might very well have treated of the deliberative or hortatory (τὸ συμβουλευτικόν) kind of rhetoric. The list of the 'Anonymus'[1], which as usual does not correspond with that of Diogenes[2], has nine titles of rhetorical works;

---

[1] An anonymous life of Aristotle, with a list of his works, first published by Menage in his notes on Diogenes Laertius v. 35, and reprinted by Buhle in his edition of Aristotle, Vol. I. p. 60. See Buhle's note.

[2] These lists are a great puzzle: they are absolutely irreconcilable, and nothing certain is known of them or of the sources from which they are derived, whether Hermippus or Andronicus or any or many others, and

but I cannot suppose that Aristotle wrote either eight or nine upon the subject. The lists *cannot* be correct, (see note) and one of the errors is probably that of exaggeration of the number of works. There are only three of these titles which we shall have to consider; two of them represent writings which we can with certainty from other authorities assign to Aristotle.

The Συναγωγὴ τεχνῶν in two books according to Diogenes, in one according to the 'Anonymus,' (this latter statement is confirmed by Cicero, de Orat. II. 38. 160) is one of these: it is authenticated, and its contents described by Cicero in three passages, de Inv. II. 2. 6. de Orat. II. 38. 160. Brut. 12. In the first and third of these he gives an account of its contents. It was a history of rhetoric from its earliest origin down to his own time, with an outline of the several systems of each of its professors, so that it would have served as a historical introduction to his own art, and doubtless accounts for his having contented himself in that work with the merest generalities in reference to his predecessors. We may also infer from this that it was an earlier composition than the extant Rhetoric. This is the work of which Spengel in his Artium Scriptores has attempted to supply the loss by a collection of the only too scanty notices left us by ancient rhetoricians and other authors, Greek and Latin, arranged in chronological order according to their contents, and forming a more or less connected sketch of the early history

the authority therefore of both or either of them we are utterly unable to determine, except where they are checked by the notices of other and more trustworthy writers. One thing however at least seems certain: that neither Aristotle nor any other human being could have written *all* the works that are assigned to him by either of the two lists. Fortunately in our case, they both agree in mentioning the three lost works which we shall have to consider. The author who has most recently treated this subject, is Heitz, in his Essay on the Lost Works of Aristotle, Leipzig, 1865. The book seems to be intended chiefly as an answer to the merciless and uncompromising scepticism of Valentine Rose in his two recent works, Aristoteles Pseudepigraphus, and de Arist. Libr. Ord. et Auctor.

and growth of Rhetoric from its origin to the time of Aristotle.

The subject which we are now engaged upon gives me occasion to point out that Cicero seems to have been acquainted with two works of Aristotle upon rhetoric, the συναγωγὴ τεχνῶν, and the now extant Art. This appears from the passage already referred to, de Orat. II. 38. 160. Aristotelem, cujus et illum legi librum in quo exposuit dicendi artes omnium superiorum, et illos in quibus ipse sua quædam de eadem arte dixit. In Orat. XIV. 46. we have as follows. Aristoteles adolescentes non ad philosophorum morem tenuiter disserendi, sed ad copiam rhetorum in utramque partem, ut ornatius et uberius dici possit, exercuit; idemque locos—sic enim appellat—quasi argumentorum notas tradidit, unde omnis in utramque partem traheretur oratio. The latter clause perfectly well describes, even though it be unintentionally, the method pursued in Aristotle's Rhetoric as we have it; the two first books are in reality a system of τόποι for the supply of arguments on both sides of any given question: the former clause (ad copiam rhetorum—exercuit) seems to me to describe a part of his method of teaching the adolescentes who frequented the school of rhetoric which he set up in opposition to Isocrates. He made them learn, as other rhetorical teachers before and after him, "Common places," select extracts from esteemed orations upon both sides of a question, which would be at once a model of style and a suggestion of argument. But whether or no this passage actually refers to our Rhetoric, or again § 94, where Aristotle is said to have included under metaphor both $μετωνυμία$ and $κατάχρησις$, [if it does, it is only by implication, for no such statement is directly made either here or in the Poetics, c. 21. on Metaphor], at all events § 114. is a most unmistakable reference to it, Atque etiam Aristoteles principio artis rhetoricæ dicit illam artem quasi ex altera parte respondere dialecticæ &c., and equally or still more so, §§ 192, 3, 4, 6, and 214. to Rhet. III. 8. 4, 5, 6. Now these two rhetorical works the Συναγωγὴ τεχνῶν, and the Art of Rhetoric are neither of them *dialogues;* the Gryllus *is*, which Cicero never mentions. And this brings me to the point which I had chiefly in view in making this digression, to show namely that Heitz's hypothesis, Verl. Schrift. Arist. p. 187, that Cicero's acquaintance with Aristotle's writings was confined exclusively to the dialogues, which indeed he expresses with considerable confidence[1] is totally devoid of foundation; and equally so the strange conclusion, p. 158. that Cicero bloss solche näher kannte die zu die verlorenen zählen. It appears on the contrary that it not only was not confined to the dialogues, but probably did not include all of them; for surely if Cicero had been acquainted with the Gryllus, imitator as he was of Aristotle's dialogues (Epist. ad Div. I. 9. 23. ad Attic. XIII. 19. 4), and himself the author of a dialogue upon Rhetoric, written too aristotelio more (l. c.), he could hardly have failed to mention it[2].

We now come to the second of the lost works on Rhetoric, the title of which is given in both lists, and their evidence supported by the authority of Quintilian. But Diogenes in this case authenticates his title by an actual reference to a notice in the work itself—if at least, as I myself believe, Bernays' conjecture (Dialoge des Ar. p. 62) is well grounded, that the statement in Diogenes, II. 55, φησὶ δ' Ἀριστοτέλης ὅτι ἐγκώμια καὶ ἐπιτάφιον Γρύλλου μύριοι ὅσοι συνέγραψαν, τὸ μέρος καὶ τῷ πατρὶ χαριζόμενοι, is derived from the dialogue itself, as seems most natural—and Quintilian also seems to have been acquainted with the work when he says, II. 17. 14, Aristoteles, ut solet, quaerendi gratia quaedam subtilitatis suae argumenta excogitavit in Gryllo, which certainly conveys the impression of personal knowledge: the statement is direct, and there is not even

---

[1] So haben wir allen Grund dieselben als die ihm ausschliesslich zu Gebote stehenden Quellen zu betrachten.

[2] On this mos aristotelius see Bernays, Dial. des Arist. p. 137. anm. 6. with Heitz's observation, Verl. Schrift. Ar. p. 150.

a shadow of intimation of information at second hand. The Gryllus who gave name to the dialogue was Xenophon's son who fell at the battle of Mantinea; whose untimely death, as we learn from Aristotle's dialogue, through Diogenes, attracted universal sympathy and commiseration, in part due to regard for his father. In giving the name of Gryllus to his dialogue, Aristotle seems to have been following a not uncommon custom of commemorating a departed friend, especially in the case of untimely death or melancholy accident, by a composition in his honour: and it is most probable therefore that it was composed shortly after the event. In another instance Aristotle has given the name of a deceased friend and pupil to a dialogue, Εὔδημος, ἢ περὶ ψυχῆς; and Theophrastus expressed his grief at the tragical end of Callisthenes in a dialogue which he named after him. Heitz, op. cit. 189, 9.

This authority for the existence of a dialogue on rhetoric by Aristotle called Gryllus, which indeed seems amply sufficient, is accepted without question by the sagacious Bernays, op. cit. p. 62, and the not over credulous Heitz, op. cit. p. 189, as well as by Spalding in his note on the passage of Quintilian. Only Rose hangs back and will not be persuaded. In his work de Arist. Libr. Ord. et auct. p. 31, he thus pronounces judgment on the question. Ita Hermippus in vita Theophrasti dixit de Gryllo Theophrasti (Diog. Laert. II. 55) eodem scilicet quem postea Andronicus (he means, as the compiler of the list in Diogenes; but this is a pure conjecture disallowed by Heitz) et Quintilianus Aristoteli tribuere mallent: and in the Pseudepigraphus, p. 76, he gives as his reason for assigning the Gryllus of Diogenes and Quintilian to Theophrastus rather than Aristotle, de Gryllo cur in vita Theophrasti potius quam Aristotelis Hermippus tractaverit, vix alia causa cogitari potest quam quod Theophrasti dialogum noverit judicaveritque eundem quem Aristotelis nomine vulgo inscriptum index Androniceus exhibebat &c. a most gratuitous conjecture founded upon an entire mistake. Let us see what Diogenes actually does say. One would think that Rose could not have read, or at least understood, the passage. He begins by giving an account of the death of young Gryllus at the battle of Mantinea; tells a story about his father Xenophon's behaviour upon the news of his death; and then continues—I will now give his own words—φησὶ δ' Ἀριστοτέλης ὅτι ἐγκώμια καὶ ἐπιτάφιον Γρύλλου μύριοι ὅσοι συνέγραψαν, τὸ μέρος τῷ πατρὶ χαριζόμενος. [in his Gryllus dialogue no doubt, in the descriptive 'scenery' of the introduction, as Bernays most reasonably supposes.] ἀλλὰ καὶ Ἕρμιππος ἐν τῷ περὶ Θεοφράστου καὶ Ἰσοκράτην φησὶ Γρύλλου ἐγκώμιον γεγραφέναι: and it is this last clause which is the sole basis and foundation of Rose's argument—if indeed it deserve to be so called. But why shouldn't Hermippus 'have written in his life of Theophrastus that Isocrates also wrote an eulogy upon Gryllus'? and what has this to do with Aristotle's dialogue? Rose seems to have overlooked the καὶ before Ἕρμιππος, and in some way which I cannot explain to have mixed up this last clause with the preceding. He first assumes as a fact, without a shadow of a foundation, that Theophrastus wrote a dialogue called Gryllus (de Gryllo Theophrasti in the first citation can mean nothing but this), which is certainly not stated by Diogenes, and I believe no where else— Diogenes says only that Hermippus in his life of Theophrastus tells us that Isocrates was one of the very numerous eulogists of Gryllus after his death—and then infers from the supposed mention of it in Hermippus' life of Theophrastus, first, that another of the same name by Aristotle could not have existed, and secondly, that Hermippus *must* have known that this assumed dialogue of Theophrastus was in fact the same as that which passed under the name of Aristotle in the list of Andronicus, that is, Diogenes. How Quintilian came to make the same mistake as Diogenes (in v. 22) he does not vouchsafe to explain. Heitz who believes neither in Rose's conclusion about the authorship of the Gryllus, nor in the derivation of Diogenes' catalogue of Aristotle's works from Andronicus, seems hardly sufficiently sensible of the deplorable lack of logic, the false assumptions and fallacious inferences, and the misinterpretation of the Greek text which distinguish this precious piece of criticism, when he says mildly, Der Nachweis den Rose gegen die Aechtheit des Gryllos...zu liefern gesucht hat, beruht auf zwei Voraussetzungen, von welchen weder die eine noch die andere hinreichende Sicherheit zu bieten scheinen. And at the end lets him and his reasoning off with an, ist ein um so weniger wahrscheinlicher Schluss. I am sorry to have been obliged to dwell so long upon this not very important matter: but when a writer undertakes to pronounce judgment ex cathedra and upon an extensive scale upon questions of interest, such as the genuineness or spuriousness of the works of a great and esteemed author, or the right or wrong ascription to him of any writing, and always with a strong bias towards the negative side, it is clearly worth while to examine whether or no these negative conclusions always rest upon a secure foundation before we abandon ourselves to his guidance and submit to the law that he so authoritatively lays down.

The next of the three lost works upon Rhetoric which may with some probability be ascribed to Aristotle is the so called Theodectea. As to the precise meaning of this term great difference of opinion has prevailed amongst the Aristotelian commentators and expositors; and since the question is very far indeed from being settled, I think it will be the best way to bring forward the evidence in detail, and examine each item separately, before we either state any opinions that have been entertained upon the subject, or attempt ourselves to arrive at any general conclusion.

We will begin with Aristotle himself. In the Rhetoric, III. 9. 9, we find, αἱ δὲ ἀρχαὶ τῶν περιόδων σχεδὸν ἐν τοῖς Θεοδεκτείοις ἐξηρίθμηνται. "The commencements of periods" as Victorius thinks, are not to be confined to the first words of them, but to be extended to the whole of the sentence:

and the phrase will therefore mean according to him, "the several modes of symmetrical construction of periods (that is by the use of ἀντίθεσις, παρίσωσις, παρομοίωσις, ὁμοιοτέλευτον) have been enumerated in the Theodectea." Now the first thing that strikes us here is that Aristotle must be referring to a work of his own: for his practice is, almost or altogether without exception, never to quote another's work *as an authority*, or as containing something necessary to the elucidation of the subject in hand, which he might himself have supplied, merely for the purpose of saving trouble. He refers to authors who have treated of the same matters as he is at the time engaged upon in order to criticise them, and to supply their defects, or to represent his own opinions and doctrines in favourable contrast. The references to Isocrates' speeches and others in the Rhetoric which we have previously noticed are of quite a different kind: they are *illustrations*, which Aristotle, departing from the usual practice of writers of arts of Rhetoric—exemplified in the ῥητορικὴ πρὸς 'Αλέξανδρον—preferred to draw from the known and accredited writings and speeches of others, rather than to make them for himself. I am for my own part so fully persuaded of this that I shall take it for granted that Aristotle in speaking here of the Theodectea means to refer to a work of his own. The *name* is probably analogous to that of the 'Nicomachean' Ethics, as Spalding on Quintilian II. 15. 10. and others[1] have thought, assigned by Aristotle to the treatise in compliment to his friend and pupil Theodectes the rhetorician and playwright; that is, that it was *named after* him, or bore his name: it cannot possibly mean *addressed to* him, as it has sometimes been interpreted. See Buhle, Aristotle, Introd. to Rhet. Vol. IV. pp. 4, 5. Sir A. Grant, Essays on Ethics, p. 14. The interpretation of the name given by Valerius Maximus, on which he founds a cock and bull story justly ridiculed by Spalding will be afterwards

---

[1] Compare Spengel, on the three Ethics ascribed to Aristotle, Trans. of Bav. Acad. 1841. p. 506.

mentioned in its chronological order. Meanwhile, I infer from the passage of the Rhetoric, that Aristotle in the earlier part of his career, probably whilst he was still carrying on his rhetorical school, composed a work upon this subject, mainly devoted to style and composition and arrangement, the contents "in extenso" of the third book of his extant Rhetoric, to which therefore the latter would naturally refer for fuller details; it would probably have treated at length of that artificial structure which was originated by Gorgias and consummated by Isocrates, with its manifold figures and devices; holding in all probability his own golden mean, and steering a middle course, like Cicero and all men of sense, and as he does himself in his Rhetoric, between the exaggerations and affectations of Gorgias and his school and the entire reprobation and exclusion of the use of them; and to this he gave the name of his friend Theodectes, himself a proficient in the art, and also the author of a treatise on it. Brandis, Handbuch &c. Aristoteles I. 100. seems to recognise the Θεοδέκτεια as a lost work of Aristotle.

And this we shall find to be in accordance with the next notice we have of the Theodectea in the spurious Epistle to Alexander prefixed to the 'Ρητ. πρὸς 'Αλέξανδρον, and written, as Spengel in his Commentary (and every one else[1]) admits, neither by Aristotle nor the author of the treatise that follows. We have no means of even approximating to the date of composition of this Epistle; all that we can say is, that when it was written Aristotle was known to have written a Theodectea, and that by some at least this was supposed to be the treatise which is known to us as the 'Ρητορικὴ πρὸς 'Αλέξανδρον. That this latter cannot possibly

---

[1] I mean of course every one who can distinguish between two totally different styles and contradictory statements and principles, and estimate the appropriateness of a composition to places persons and circumstances. It is however a melancholy fact that there have been men of learning within the present century who have not been able to discern that this letter could by no possibility have been the work of Aristotle. Such are Titze and Zell. See Stahr, Aristotelia, II. 209.

be the Theodectea mentioned by Aristotle himself in the Rhetoric, whether that be Aristotle's own work or any one else's, appears clearly from this, that in the Rhet. ad Alex. there is nothing whatever resembling in the remotest degree an "enumeration of the commencements of periods." It appears also from a reference in Cic. Orat. LVII. 194, where Theodectes together with Aristotle and Theophrastus are said to have agreed in their views about the use of the 'pæan' in rhetorical composition. There is not a word about the pæan in the Rhet. ad Alex. All that we can gather from it of any service to us in answer to the question what is the Theodectea, and who wrote it, is that the author of this letter believed, in common we may suppose with his contemporaries or some of them, that Aristotle *was* the author of *a* treatise that went under that name: and so far this is a confirmation of our interpretation of Aristotle's own words in the Rhetoric. Spengel in the note on this passage in his edition of Anaximenes, as he insists upon calling the author of this treatise, expresses a very decided opinion that the words have no intelligible meaning at all, and therefore that nothing whatever can be gathered from them. I am quite prepared to admit that the writer of the letters exhibits both ignorance and folly in a very high degree: but I think nevertheless that these particular words have a perfectly distinct meaning. They are, Περιτεύξῃ δὲ δυσὶ τούτοις βιβλίοις, ὧν τὸ μέν ἐστιν ἐμόν, [the author is writing in the person of Aristotle] ἐν ταῖς ὑπ' ἐμοῦ τέχναις Θεοδέκτῃ γραφείσαις, τὸ δὲ ἕτερον Κόρακος. "Herewith you will receive [literally, you will come across, light upon,] two volumes, of which one is my own, contained (or possibly 'consisting') in the art written (addressed) by me *to* Theodectes, [not *by* Theodectes, an error into which Spalding note on Quint. II. 15. 11. and others, Heitz for example, see Verl. Schr. Ar. p. 86., have fallen,] and the other a work of Corax." If ἐν ταῖς τ. is to be rendered "contained in" it is not very good Greek for "an extract from": if "consisting in", it of course means the whole treatise. And if this is the right interpretation, as I think it is, the passage will imply what I have already stated.

We now come to a piece of evidence which when rightly interpreted stands in opposition to the two preceding; at least upon the supposition that there can be only one Theodectea, and that, whatever that may mean, the 'art of Theodectes' must be the same with it. This consists in some verses of Antiphanes, a poet of the Middle Comedy, contemporary with Aristotle, preserved by Athenæus, IV. 134.B. which run as follows.

οὐχ ὁρᾶς ὀρχούμενον
ταῖς χερσὶ τὸν βάκηλον; οὐδ' αἰσχύνεται
ὁ τὸν Ἡράκλειτον πᾶσιν ἐξηγούμενος,
ὁ τὴν Θεοδέκτου μόνος ἀνευρηκὼς τέχνην,
ὁ τὰ κεφάλαια συγγράφων Εὐριπίδῃ.

It is a fragment of his Κᾶρες, see Meineke, Fragm. Comm. Græc. Vol. III. p. 59.

This description was applied by Max Schmidt, in the Essay already quoted, p. 11, to Aristotle, and it must be allowed that this interpretation of it is in itself tempting, and also at first sight commends itself favourably to the inquirer into the Theodectean mystery. The fourth line will then signify 'the only true discoverer (i.e. author) of the art of Theodectes': meaning that Aristotle laid claim to the authorship of the art of rhetoric which went under the name of Theodectes, viz. the Theodectea: and with the additional insinuation that the claim was without foundation. And this would bring the inference derivable from the present passage into harmony with the evidence of the two preceding, viz. that there was one work called the Theodectea, which was the work of Aristotle. But ἀμφοῖν φίλοιν ὄντοιν ὅσιον προτιμᾶν τὴν ἀλήθειαν, amicus Plato magis amica veritas; and truth compels us to admit that never was a theory more completely overthrown than this is by Trendelenburg in a communication made by him to Meineke and embodied by the latter in his note on the passage. Trendelenburg produces from Diogenes notices respecting the personal habits and studies of Heraclides Ponticus which correspond so exactly with the allusions of Antiphanes as to leave no reasonable doubt as to the person whom he intended to represent. We must consequently alter our interpretation of the verse in question to "the only man who ever made out, discovered the meaning of, Theodectes' art," which may be supposed to have been obscured by subtleties and ambiguities. Westermann in his Gesch. der Beredtsamkeit, § 68. n. 21, has a reference to a statement of Eudocia (the learned Empress who composed the 'Ιωνία or Violetum, a dictionary of history and mythology derived from the same sources as that of Suidas) that Theodectes ἔγραψε τέχνην ῥητορικὴν ἐν μέτρῳ. This was not unprecedented, for Evenus of Paros had done something of the same kind; Plat. Phædr. 267. A.; and if the statement be well founded, it would account for a good deal of the difficulty which according to Antiphanes attended the interpretation of Theodectes' art. I must add however that it seems to stand somewhat in contradiction to another extract from the Art of Theodectes, quoted by two anonymous writers on rhetoric, Walz. Rhet. Gr. VII. 33 and VI. 19. Spengel, Art. Script. p. 156. not., Rose, Arist. Pseudepigraphus, p. 141, ἔργον ῥήτορος, ὥς φησι Θεοδέκτης, προοιμιάσασθαι πρὸς εὔνοιαν, διηγήσασθαι πρὸς πίστιν, ἀγωνίσασθαι πρὸς ἀπόδειξιν, ἀνακεφαλαιώσασθαι πρὸς ἀνάμνησιν: which certainly does not look much like verse, but nevertheless goes far to establish the fact that Theodectes was the author of an art of Rhetoric.

Subtlety and ambiguity might in fact have been expected of him from the references to his works in prose and verse which we find chiefly in Aristotle, who very frequently quotes him in his Rhetoric, Poetics and Ethics. Hence we learn that he was a disciple of the Sophistical school of rhetoricians[1], and had adopted its artificial style and crooked

---

[1] Theodectes was a pupil of Isocrates, as well as Aristotle, and it was by the former that his character and literary habits were chiefly determined.

fallacious reasoning. See especially two of his τόποι in Ar. Rhet. II. 23 and 24. But what is more to our present purpose, we gather from this new interpretation of Antiphanes, writing as a contemporary of Theodectes himself, that he also was the author of an art of Rhetoric. And here we might stop in our investigation: for it seems by this time quite clear that there were *two* treatises on Rhetoric which both bore the name of Theodectes; one by Aristotle called the Theodectea, the other by Theodectes himself, called as usual ἡ Θεοδέκτου τέχνη. It does seem somewhat strange, though I believe it to be a fact, that this very simple and complete solution of the difficulty should not hitherto have occurred to any of the numerous scholars who have discussed the question[1]. The possibility of it however is so far recognised as to be sternly and uncompromisingly denied by Rose.

This is fully confirmed by Dionysius, de Isaeo Jud. c. 19. who in a chapter of which the object is to show that Isocrates was the most finished specimen *of his school* of rhetoricians, places Theodectes with several others amongst his imitators. Οὐδέ γε περὶ τῶν συμβιωσάντων Ἰσοκράτει, καὶ τὸν χαρακτῆρα τῆς ἑρμηνείας ἐκείνου ἐκμιμησαμένων οὐθενός, Θεοδέκτου λέγω, καὶ Θεοπόμπου, κ.τ.λ. which means as the Latin Interpr. renders it, neque de quoquam eorum qui Isocratis tempore vixerunt, et *characterem locutionis ejus exprimere conati sunt.* See also Epist. ad Amm. I. c. 2. where he speaks of the contemporaries of Isocrates and others as παραγγελμάτων τεχνικῶν συγγραφεῖς, καὶ ἀγωνισταὶ λόγων ῥητορικῶν, naming as instances Theodectes, and Philiscus, and Isaeus, and Hyperides and Lycurgus and Æschines. On this Rose, Pseud. Arist. p. 135, well remarks, argumenti (the contents of Theodectes' treatise) observatio, quo τεχνικὰ παραγγέλματα (mere precepts, hints to follow—one of these is censured by Aristotle, Rhet. III. 12. 6) in Isocrateorum fere modum auctor traderet, non artis ipsius naturam legesque explicaret cum Aristotele et Theophrasto. Add Athen. x. 451. E. Θεοδέκτην δὲ τὸν Φασηλίτην, φησὶν Ἕρμιππος ἐν τοῖς περὶ τῶν Ἰσοκράτους μαθητῶν, ἱκανώτατον γεγονέναι κ.τ.λ. See on Theodectes and his style, Müller, Hist. of Gk. Lit. c. XXVI. § 7.

[1] I must however make an exception in favour of Spalding, who does leave the question open whether there might not be two arts known by the name of Theodectes. Neque tamen si maxime τὰ Θεοδέκτεια sunt ipsius Aristotelis, protinus neges Theodecten quoque aliquid de arte oratoria composuisse... This had escaped me as I was writing the above. But no one has put this distinctly forward as an *explanation.*

The evidence of Cicero as to Theodectes and his writings counts for something. Besides the passage already quoted, Orat. LVII. 194, in which his Art of Rhetoric is plainly recognised by implication, we learn also from the Orator, LI. 172. that he attended the lectures of Aristotle, as supplementary, I conceive, to the instructions of Isocrates, from whom he manifestly derived his rhetorical style and practice. Cicero says, Ejus (i. e. of Aristotle) auditor Theodectes, in primis, ut Aristoteles saepe significat, politus scriptor atque artifex. This may probably have been intimated by Aristotle in his sketch of the early history of the art in the συναγωγὴ τεχνῶν: at all events there is nothing like it in the extant Rhetoric. And finally in c. LXIV. § 218, he is again named with Aristotle, Theophrastus, and Ephorus, as an authority for the use of the paean in rhetorical composition. From all which we may certainly conclude, that he wrote an Art of Rhetoric, and that Cicero was acquainted with it either at first or at second hand.

Next Quintilian, to whom I have already referred, in quoting Theodectes' definition of rhetoric, which was much the same as that of Gorgias, adds, sive ipsius id opus est, quod de rhetorice nomine ejus inscribitur, sive, ut creditum est, Aristotelis, Inst. Or. II. 15. 10. From this it seems that in Quintilian's time there was only one Art extant, or generally known, under this name: and Spalding (not. ad loc.) thinks that he has explained Quintilian's doubt on the subject (as I understand him, for his expressions are not quite clear) by his interpretation o' the name Θεοδέκτεια on the analogy of Νικομάχεια, which might mean either 'written by,' or simply 'bearing the name of,' Theodectes, and in the latter case written by Aristotle. There is nothing in this, as Spalding truly says, against the hypothesis of two works, one by each of these writers. This explanation is adopted by *Heitz. Op. cit.* p. 86. Subsequently Quintilian seems to have made up his mind that the Art belonged to Theodectes, *de cujus opere* supra dictum est. III. 1. 14.

We now come to Valerius Maximus, whose story about the Theodectea will not detain us long. The passage runs thus, VIII. 14. extern. 3. Aristoteles Theodecti discipulo oratoriæ artis libros quos ederet donaverat, molesteque ferens titulum eorum sic alii cessisse, proprio volumine quibusdam rebus insistens planius sibi de his in Theodectis libris dictum esse adjecit. The story which seems to admit of no rational explanation and to rest upon no foundation either of history or probability, was probably, as Spalding, note on Quint. II. 15. 10, conjectures, made up by Valerius himself or somebody else out of the reference in the Rhetoric III. 9. 9, to which the last words refer. It deserves no further notice.

In an anonymous author of an art of rhetoric, Rhet. Gr. Vol. I. p. 454, Ed. Speng., we find the words Ἀριστοτέλης δὲ ἐν ταῖς Θεοδεκτικαῖς τέχναις φησίν, ὅτι ὁ ἐπίλογος τὸ μὲν κεφάλαιον ἔχει προτρέψασθαι τοὺς ἀκούοντας; which also assigns the Theodectea to Aristotle, and confirms as far as it goes the description I ventured to give of the probable nature of its contents. Heitz in the work so often quoted does not refer to this passage. He supplies however another, from a 'semibarbarous' Scholiast upon the passage of the Rhetoric, ἐν τοῖς Θεοδεκτίοις] πρὸς τὸν Θεόδεκτον [sic] ἔγραφεν ὁ Ἀριστοτέλης ῥητορικήν, ἐν ᾗ ἀπηριθμήσατο τὰς τῶν περιόδων ἀρχάς, οἷαι ὀφείλουσιν εἶναι.

These are I believe all the notices of the Theodectea which ancient authorities have handed down to us; taken together they seem to me to show beyond reasonable dispute first, that Aristotle was the author of the Art called the Theodectea: and secondly, that there was besides this another Art by Theodectes himself, which also, according to the usual mode of designating them, bore his name. The latter I think *must* be admitted in deference to the statement of the *contemporary* writer Antiphanes.

Of the moderns who have treated of this subject I have already incidentally noticed several; and amongst them have referred to Max Schmidt's opinion upon the interpretation of the verse of Antiphanes (p. 23). This is taken from a complete essay upon this question of the Theodectea incorporated in his tract on the date of composition of Aristotle's Rhetoric pp. 3—13. His primary object is to determine the comparative dates of the Theodectea, presuming it to be Aristotle's, and the extant Rhetoric; but before that can be done a discussion of the several claims to the work of Aristotle and his pupil, and an examination of its nature and contents, is a necessary preliminary. He accordingly collects all the evidence from ancient authors who have touched upon the question, and from this shows first that the views of Aristotle and Theodectes differed widely upon the subject of rhetoric—this appears in two points; first the difference of the definition respectively given by the two authors, Theodectes (Quint. II. 15. 10) adhering substantially to the original definition of the sophistical school and his master Isocrates; Aristotle altering and improving it by 'recedens ab eventu': and secondly a precept which appeared in Theodectes' Art that the 'narrative' of a speech should be μεγαλοπρεπής and ἡδεῖα (Quint. IV. 2. 63.) is censured by Aristotle without naming the author, in Rhet. III. 12. 6.—but after all arrives at the conclusion that there was only one work called indifferently Θεοδέκτεια and ἡ Θεοδ. τέχνη, the joint production of Aristotle and his friend. And this is the way in which he reconciles the conflicting statements. Theodectes under Isocratean influences had composed an art of rhetoric which he submitted to the judgment of his preceptor, who *corrected* and enlarged it. [It would seem however from the preceding that Aristotle must have left *uncorrected* a good deal that he seriously disapproved of.] That afterwards in later life, Aristotle, when he came to write his own treatise on rhetoric, corrected (finally, I suppose) the errors of Theodectes, and, non admodum sollicitus cujusnam opus putaretur esse, in the third book quoted the joint, corrected and uncorrected, production as his own!

Of the more recent writers on this subject Heitz and Rose remain to be noticed. The former of the two is not very instructive on the matter: he seems to assume, though he does not expressly say so, that there was only one art that went by the name of Theodectes, and he arrives at no conclusion at all, referring to the passages, and then leaving them to tell their own story—in which they do not agree. He first cites the passage of the Rhetoric; then combats the sceptical views of Rose; next draws an inference as to the antiquity of the opinion that assigned the Theodectean Rhetoric to Aristotle from the title in Diogenes' list τέχνης τῆς Θεοδέκτου συναγωγή ā, and the reference in the letter to Alexander (which, as I remarked before, he mistranslates): then gives Valerius Maximus' story without comment; he thinks that the solution of the riddle of Valerius' story is to be sought in the verses of Antiphanes preserved by Athenæus, of which he says no more, except that Märcker's explanation of them is unsatisfactory. Lastly he borrows from Spalding without acknowledgment his explanation of the way in which the name Θεοδέκτεια came to be misinterpreted, and concludes with the citation of the 'Semibarbarous' Scholiast, which I have already given.

Rose's views on the question are stated in the imperious and magisterial style which seems habitual with him. Moreover he has changed his opinion; though the change of opinion has produced no corresponding change of tone, for the second is expressed in just as positive and peremptory language as the first, and has perhaps about an equal foundation in fact and reason. In the treatise de Arist. Libr. ord. et auct. p. 89. he was driven to the supposition that the Theodectea mentioned in Aristotle's Rhetoric, III. 9. 9, are to be understood of the frequent citations of Theodectes' dramas and declamations made in that work; 'a desperate attempt,' as Heitz truly says, 'to escape from a not very serious difficulty.' In his later work, the Arist. Pseudepigraphus, p. 135. seq., he bestows a much more careful con-

sideration upon the matter, and pronounces, it is hard to
see upon what grounds, that the clause in question which
contains the disputed word has been interpolated from the
margin, where a copyist had set down a gloss of some
commentator or grammarian, who was comparing [what he
supposed to be] the Theodectea of Aristotle[1]. If it *were*
Aristotle's, it could mean nothing else than he had supposed
it to mean in the other treatise, viz. the quotations from
his plays and prose writings; for Aristotle would never have
cited an 'art' of Theodectes under such a name, nor one
of his own, any more than he would have cited his Ethics
as τὰ Νικομάχεια. [I cannot see the force of the reasoning,
if indeed there be any, here. If the Ethics had been generally known by the name of Nicomachean, why should he
not have employed it to describe them? He had in fact
no occasion to do so because these were most probably the
only Ethics in existence during his lifetime, or at any
rate till his pupil Eudemus wrote the Eudemian. Then,
and not till then, it became necessary to distinguish them
by a specific name. But the case of the rhetorical works
was different. Upon this subject there were most probably
already two works of his own in existence, the συναγωγὴ
τεχνῶν, and the Gryllus, or περὶ ῥητορικῆς; and this at
least might easily have been confounded with the Theodectea, if that had been simply called ἡ ῥητορική or τὰ
ῥητορικά, as Rose seems to suppose necessary when it was
referred to by Aristotle himself; and at the time when he
was using the word he was actually writing another Rhetoric
with no special title at all. I ask, how could he avoid
giving the Theodectea a distinctive name?] However the

[1] I have given what I suppose to be the meaning of the original words which are merely qui compararet Theodectea Aristotelis. As I understand him to deny altogether the existence of such a work as a genuine 'Aristotle's Theodectea,' I can only presume that the meaning is intended as I have rendered it: or perhaps it may be, 'the Theodectea falsely ascribed to Aristotle.'

best way of meeting the difficulty is to suppose, as we have seen, that the clause is *not* Aristotle's, but inserted by some scribe from the margin: or if that is not sufficient, we are offered two alternatives in a note; we may suppose either the third book, or the entire Rhetoric to be spurious! Is not this mere trifling? As to an independent art of Theodectes, he denies the existence of this in toto. 'It is quite certain [no reason is given except that Aristotle who so frequently quotes his writings never mentions his Art] that there was no 'art' of Theodectes except that which is attributed (falsely?) to Aristotle, and wherever the doctrines of Theodectes are referred to it, is this PseudAristotelian work that is to be understood.' But enough of Rose, and his sceptical dogmatism.

THE RELATIONS OF DEMONSTRATION OR SCIENCE, DIALECTICS, AND RHETORIC.

Having, tant bien que mal, dispatched this preliminary matter, we can now proceed to examine the nature and peculiarities of the three kinds of proof or πίστεις which constitute the body and substance of the art of rhetoric, and the two logical instruments which it employs, corresponding in dialectics (and science) to syllogism and induction, viz. the enthymeme and example.

And first we will consider the relation in which Rhetoric stands to Dialectics on the one hand, and scientific demonstration on the other.

Dialectics and rhetoric are both of them supplementary to science and its method, which is confined to the universal and necessary. Dialectics on the other hand is the 'Logic of Probabilities', and, like its 'offshoot' Rhetoric, deals solely with the contingent and uncertain, τὸ ὡς ἐπὶ πολύ, and τὸ ἐνδεχόμενον ἄλλως ἔχειν. Dialectics, well expressed by the Latins as ars disserendi, the 'art of discussion', is more usually devoted to speculative inquiries: though theoretically its province is not confined to any special class of subjects, but includes and may deal with every proposition or problem that can be submitted to it, even those of science, *provided* they be not treated on peculiar scientific principles (ἀρχαὶ ἴδιαι), and the conclusion be left an open question. The arguments of these discussions ought to be reducible to regular syllogism, and are always carried on by question and answer between the questioner or assailant ὁ ἐπιχειρῶν, ὁ ἐρωτῶν, and the maintainer of the thesis or respondent ὁ ἀποκρινόμενος. Rhetoric again is confined to a particular class of probabilities and contingencies, such namely as we can deliberate about, things which depend upon ourselves, and are in our own power to do or to abstain from, τὰ ἐφ' ἡμῖν, to effect or to prevent, to thwart or promote; and as these are for the most part either human actions or things immediately depending on them, Rhetoric thus becomes associated with Politics, or Ethics, which takes account of men in society and as individuals, and analyses their motives, and feelings, and actions, their habits and tendencies, virtues and vices. Rhetoric, like Dialectics, takes either side of a question, and proves the affirmative or negative indifferently: and it *proves*, or tries to prove, its propositions—not merely examines or discusses them. And this it does in a *continuous discourse*.

The difference between Logic and Rhetoric has been represented by the ingenious comparison of the closed fist and the open hand: the reasonings of logic are 'close', the thoughts compressed, and the style condensed: in rhetoric the reasoning thoughts and language are expanded, discursive, diffuse. This illustration is ascribed by Cicero, de Fin. II. 6. 17, Orat. XXXII. 113, and by Sextus Empiricus, adv. Math. II. πρὸς ῾Ρητ. § 7, to Zeno the Stoic, and its application explained by both. However its author seems to have applied it differently on different occasions, for in another place, Acad. Pr. II. 47. 145, he tells us that Zeno described the different degrees or modes of apprehension of truth, visus, assensus, comprehensio, scientia, by the different degrees of compression of the hand. The passage is interesting and worth quoting. Et hoc quidem Zeno gestu conficiebat. Nam quum extensis digitis adversam manum ostenderat, *visum* inquiebat hujusmodi est. Deinde quum paullum digitos constrinxerat, *assensus* hujusmodi. Tum quum plane compresserat pugnumque fecerat, *comprehensionem* illam esse dicebat. Qua ex similitudine etiam nomen ei rei, quod ante non fuerat, κατάληψιν imposuit. Quum autem laevam manum admoverat, et illum pugnum arcte vehementerque compresserat, *scientiam* talem esse dicebat. To give the other side, I will transcribe from Sextus his explanation of the logical application, with which that of Cicero exactly corresponds. Ζήνων ὁ Κιττιεὺς ἐρωτηθεὶς ὅτῳ διαφέρει διαλεκτικὴ ῥητορικῆς, συστρέψας τὴν χεῖρα καὶ πάλιν ἐξαπλώσας ἔφη, τούτῳ, κατὰ μὲν τὴν συστροφὴν τὸ στρόγγυλον καὶ βραχὺ τῆς διαλεκτικῆς τάττων ἰδίωμα, διὰ δὲ τῆς ἐξαπλώσεως καὶ ἐκτάσεως τῶν δακτύλων τὸ πλατὺ τῆς ῥητορικῆς δυνάμεως αἰνιττόμενος. Cicero, Quod latius loquerentur rhetores, dialectici autem compressius. Both of them in their explanations seem unnecessarily to confine the illustration to difference of *style*. Not so Bacon, de Augm. Scient. Lib. VI. c. 3. [p. 673. Vol. I. Ellis and Spedding]. Porro non eo tantum differt Dialectica (which is not to be understood of the special Dialectic of Aristotle) a Rhetorica, quod, ut vulgo dicitur, altera instar pugni, altera instar palmae sit; altera scilicet presse, altera fuse *tractet;* verum multo magis quod Dialectica rationem in suis naturalibus, Rhetorica qualis in opinionibus vulgi sita est, consideret.

So far of the leading differences of Analytics, Dialectics, and Rhetoric in general. We will now consider them more closely and particularly. I have already to some extent gone over the ground which we are now about to enter upon a second time, and have sketched in outline what I am now going to fill up in detail. I hold with Plato, that in some things οὐδὲν οἷον τὸ πολλάκις ἀκούειν. In a subject of some difficulty and importance, repetition not only enables the expositor to illustrate and elucidate his explanations by representing the same facts in different language and from different points of view, but by familiarising the student with unaccustomed conceptions aids in an equal degree both the comprehension and the memory of one who is perhaps entering for the first time upon a new subject of inquiry. Without further preface or apology I proceed to fill up the outline by exhibiting in detail the points of difference between the three modes of reasoning or proof, by scientific demonstration, by the dialectical, and the rhetorical method.

The difference in the mode of treatment which must be applied to the same subject matter by a science[1] like Politics, and a popular and practical art such as Rhetoric, is very clearly stated in Rhet. I. 4. 4. "To look for an exact enumeration and a regular division into 'kinds' of the ordinary subjects of men's deliberations [he is speaking of the συμβουλευτικὸν γένος of rhetoric], and further to enter into every possible definition and distinction according to the scientific method, would be out of place on the present occasion, because this does not belong to an art like Rhetoric, but to one more intelligent and true [ἐμφρονεστέρας which looks into the nature and causes of things, and is therefore better informed, and capable of *instructing*, and again, ἀληθινῆς, which having truth for its sole object uses the regular

---

[1] πολιτική is here so called, § 7. I have before drawn attention to the frequent disregard of the technical distinction of τέχνη and ἐπιστήμη even by the Greek Philosophers. The author is here speaking loosely. At the beginning of the Nicomachean Ethics we are expressly told that the study of man, his motives and actions, does not admit of strictly scientific treatment, of demonstration, and the use of syllogism, precisely because in this practical department of Philosophy, there is nothing universal and necessary; human motives and actions, with which Politics are especially conversant, can *not* be reduced to rule and system, so that causes and effects can invariably be traced in them. However it can be treated more scientifically than Rhetoric; by comparison it may be regarded as a science; which is doubtless all that is meant here.

scientific method, πρὸς ἀλήθειαν οὐ πρὸς δόξαν]; and a great deal more has been already assigned to it [by the Sophistical Professors who confounded it with πολιτική itself. I. 2. 7.] than really belongs to its peculiar sphere of observation." And further, § 6, any dialectician or rhetorician who attempts to convert his faculty [δύναμις, rhetoric and dialectics being here regarded as the practice of *individual* professors, see above, p. 15. seq.], into a science, so far as he succeeds will be unconsciously and unintentionally obliterating the very nature of his pursuit, and in reconstructing it pass over into sciences which have for their provinces each its special and definite subject matter of *things*, and not mere *words*, which is all that really belongs to rhetoric and dialectics.

Now, to state summarily the characteristics of science, ἐπιστήμη, as distinguished from other methods of investigation. First, science has truth, and truth alone for its object; it is directed πρὸς ἀλήθειαν and is satisfied with nothing short of it. This is θεωρία, or θεωρητικὴ φιλοσοφία. Practical philosophy, including rhetoric (and dialectics?), must be content with mere δόξα, the sphere of the probable and contingent. Science is therefore not indifferent to the character of its *conclusions*, whether they be true or false; all these must be universal and necessary, because nothing else is real knowledge: nor can it like dialectics and rhetoric take *either* side of a disputed question (συλλογισμὸς ἀντιφάσεως). Its method is that of strict *demonstration*, ἀπόδειξις: and its instruments (1) the regular syllogism, which *deduces* the universal from axioms and first principles, which are themselves (the major premisses or universals of the syllogisms) obtained by (2) *induction from particulars*. All our knowledge, even that of the highest and ultimate truths axioms and first principles (ἀρχαί) of reasoning, must be derived from induction (δῆλον δὴ ὅτι ἡμῖν τὰ πρῶτα ἐπαγωγῇ γνωρίζειν ἀναγκαῖον, Anal. Post. II. 19. 100. b. 3.): these are themselves at once incapable, and independent of, demonstrative proof, neither can the knowledge (ἐπιστήμη) of them be so acquired,—because if proof of *every thing* were necessary for its acceptance it must go on ad infinitum: proof must ultimately depend upon something *accepted as truth*; it must rest ultimately on belief—and they are apprehended and verified by the highest faculty, the νοῦς or intuitive reason[1]. One peculiarity of science which distinguishes it alike from dialectics and rhetoric, is that which is brought into view in the passage of the Rhetoric with which I commenced this inquiry. It is that every science has first principles of its own, ἴδιαι, οἰκεῖαι ἀρχαί, which are peculiar to itself, and cannot be transferred to any other. These are distinguished from the κοιναὶ ἀρχαί, the ultimate and universal principles common to, and the necessary foundation of, every kind of reasoning—such are, *most probably*, the simplest and most elementary axioms of space and number, that the whole is greater than its part, that two and two make four, for if these and such as these were not to be depended upon it would seem that no process of reasoning in any subject could be long carried on; and *probably* also, I should suppose, for it is nowhere definitely stated, such principles as the Being of a God, substance, and suchlike ideas which belong to the category of τὸ ὄν, and fall under the province of Metaphysics; but *certainly*, because the first of these is constantly cited in illustration of them, the fundamental principles of Logic, the law of contradiction, of identity, of excluded middle, and of reason and consequent (see Sir W. Hamilton, Lect. on Logic. Vol. I. Lect. 5.)—and denote the peculiar and special axioms, postulates, and definitions, which each science is obliged to take for granted without demonstration, and cannot discuss with-

---

[1] Such appear to be the results of the reasonings of that very interesting and rather obscure chapter, the nineteenth and last of the Posterior Analytics. At first sight there might seem to be a contradiction, as if our knowledge of ultimate principles were obtained both from sensation and experience by way of Induction—the sensationalist theory—and also were antecedent and intuitive, as the Idealists hold. My solution (for there is a problem to be solved) in the text I am glad to find confirmed by Zeller, in his Philosophie der Griechen Vol. II. § 25. His judgment is summed up in a single sentence, p. 387, 1st ed.

out trespassing upon the province of a still higher and *common* science, viz. Metaphysics; ἡ πρώτη φιλοσοφία[1]. Dia-

---

[1] Anal. Post. I. 32. 88. b. 20. αἱ γὰρ ἀρχαὶ διτταί, ἐξ ὧν τε καὶ περὶ ὅ. αἱ μὲν οὖν ἐξ ὧν κοιναί, αἱ δὲ περὶ ὃ ἴδιαι, οἷον ἀριθμός, μέγεθος. Some of the ἴδιαι ἀρχαί, as the definitions of geometry and arithmetic, are given, Anal. Post. I. 10. 76. b. 3. See also, Anal. Post. I. 9. 76. a. 16. and I. 11. 77. a. 26. Met. Γ. 1. 1003. 26. The first philosophy investigates τὰς ἀρχὰς (*the* first principles, i. e. the κοινάς) καὶ τὰς ἀκροτάτας αἰτίας. And on the subject of πρώτη φιλ. as distinguished from the sciences. Met. Γ. 3. Joh. Philoponus in his commentary on Anal. Post. 88. a. 36, illustrates the κοιναὶ ἀρχαί by the principium contradictionis, and the axiom that things which are equal to the same thing are equal to one another: and Aristotle himself uses the same illustration (the princ. contrad.) at 88. b. 1. οἷον τὸ πᾶν φάναι ἢ ἀποφάναι, (*both* can't be done at once) and elsewhere. Aristotle's ἴδιαι or οἰκεῖαι ἀρχαί correspond closely with the 'Fundamental Ideas,' which in Dr. Whewell's Novum Organum Renovatum form the basis of his classification of the Sciences; but include besides special axioms and definitions. From Metaph. Γ. 3. 1005. b. 17 we learn that in Aristotle's view the highest, and surest, and most infallible, and most universal of all these κοιναὶ ἀρχαί is the principium contradictionis, that the same thing cannot be and not be, or cannot be predicated and not predicated of something else, at the same time, in the same place, and under the same circumstances: a proposition which it is utterly impossible to deny. Besides τὰ κοινά and κοιναὶ ἀρχαί, these ultimate principles are also designated by the names, ἀποδεικτικαὶ ἀρχαί (so Bonitz), κοινὰ ἀξιώματα, and ἀξιώματα par excellence. Bonitz on Metaph. B. 2. 996. b. 26. Waitz on Anal. Post. I. 2. 72. a. 17. They are ἀνυπόθετα, like Plato's highest idea, and ἄμεσα 'immediate,' indemonstrable, known "immediately" by intuition. Anal. Post. II. 19. 99. b. 21. and c. 9. 93. b. 22. Trend. El. Log. Ar. § 51. Compare also de Gen. Anim. II. 8. 12 and 13. where the οἰκεῖαι ἀρχαί are practically illustrated; § 9. λέγω δὲ λογικὴν (τὴν ἀπόδειξιν) διὰ τοῦτο, ὅτι ὅσῳ καθόλου μᾶλλον, πορρωτέρω τῶν οἰκείων ἐστὶν ἀρχῶν. In concluding this note, I will take the liberty of borrowing from Mr. Grote's Plato, I. 229. note, a quotation upon this subject from M. Jouffroy's Preface to Transl. of Reid. "Toute science particulière, qui, au lieu de prendre pour accordées les données *a priori* qu'elle implique, discute l'autorité de ces données—ajoute à son objet propre celui *de la logique*, (compare λέγω δὲ λογικὴν in the passage of de Gen. Anim. quoted above) confond une autre mission avec la sienne, et par cela même compromet la sienne: car nous verrons tout-a-l'heure, et l'histoire de la philosophie montre, quelles difficultés présentent ces problèmes qui sont l'objet propre de la logique; et nous demeurerons convaincus que, si les différentes sciences avaient eu la prétention de les éclaircir avant de passer outre, toutes peut-être en seraient encore à cette préface, et aucune n'aurait entamé sa véritable tâche."

lectics and Rhetoric have none of these οἰκεῖαι ἀρχαί. They deal with 'words' or discussion in general: and have to argue upon any problem or proposition that can be presented to them: Rhetoric however only theoretically; practically it is limited to subjects connected with Politics. Such then briefly stated are the province and materials, the method, and the instruments of science.

"The object proposed in the following study or treatise, says Aristotle at the beginning of his Topics, the analysis of the system of Dialectics, is to find a method (a scientific systematic procedure) by which we shall be able to draw logical conclusions (συλλογίζεσθαι) on any question proposed to us from probable materials (or premisses):" which will very well serve for a definition of the art of dialectics; and the syllogism by which it effects its proofs is further defined and contrasted with ἀπόδειξις or scientific demonstration, in these terms "That is demonstration, when the syllogism consists of (when its premisses and conclusions are) certain and primary principles, (ἐξ ἀληθῶν καὶ πρώτων. τὰ πρῶτα, here stand for the primary principles from which a science is deduced: its οἰκεῖαι ἀρχαί. Anal. Post. I. 2. 72. a. 5. ἐκ πρώτων δ' ἐστὶ τὸ ἐξ ἀρχῶν οἰκείων. Top. l. c. τὰ μὴ δι' ἑτέρων ἀλλὰ δι' αὑτῶν ἔχοντα τὴν πίστιν,) or of propositions immediately derived from such; whereas the dialectical syllogism is that which draws its conclusions from the sphere of the probable alone. The cardinal distinction therefore between science and dialectics, between the demonstrative and the dialectical syllogism, is that the former aims at and deals with exact knowledge and truth, or in other words, that the premisses and conclusions of its syllogisms are universal and necessary; dialectics, which also aims at proof and uses the same instrument of reasoning as scientific demonstration, derives all its propositions from probable and uncertain materials.

Dialectics again is the art of debating or discussing, ars disserendi, the art of maintaining a thesis and confuting an adversary. This is another of its essential characteristics, and a point of distinction between it and ἀπόδειξις; Top. Θ. 1. 155. b. 26. πᾶσα ἡ τοιαύτη πραγματεία πρὸς ἕτερόν ἐστιν. Comp. b 7 and 10. The object of the entire system of the Topics is to find arguments and to dispose them (τάττειν) in such a way as to carry your point, and reduce your adversary to silence. Hence at the beginning of Book Θ., where after having despatched the subject of the invention of arguments the author comes to treat of their arrangement, he observes, that the invention of topics is common to the philosopher and dialectician, the disposition of them and the conversion of them into questions is peculiar to the latter; because the entire treatment of dialectics has reference to some one else (πρὸς ἕτερόν ἐστι) that is, to an opponent; whereas the philosopher, a solitary investigator, so long as the propositions of his syllogisms are 'true and known,' gives himself no concern about the admission of them by a respondent, and therefore arranges his proofs with the sole object of making his demonstration as clear and cogent as possible; whilst the dialectician, who depends upon the concessions of his opponent, is obliged to use art in the construction and arrangement of his syllogisms, and to conceal the conclusion at which he would arrive, for fear the adversary should take the alarm prematurely, and refuse to admit some principle or proposition which is necessary to the proof of his position. So Soph. El. c. 2. 161, b. 1. διδασκαλικοὶ λόγοι (i. q. ἀποδεικτικοί) οἱ ἐκ τῶν οἰκείων ἀρχῶν ἑκάστου μαθήματος, καὶ οὐκ ἐκ τῶν τοῦ ἀποκρινομένου δοξῶν συλλογιζόμενοι.

Dialectics are universal in their application; not confined like ἀπόδειξις to certain definite subjects (οἰκεῖα, ὑποκείμενα): οὐδεμίας ἐπιστήμης ἀφωρισμένης, Rhet. I. 1. 1. οὐχ ἑνός τινος γένους ἀφωρισμένου...ἡ διαλεκτική. I. 1. 14. περὶ συλλογισμοῦ ὁμοίως ἅπαντος τῆς διαλεκτικῆς ἐστιν ἰδεῖν. I. 1. 11. οὐκ ἔστιν ὁ διαλεκτικὸς περὶ γένος τι ὡρισμένον[1], Soph. El.

---

[1] περὶ or ὑπὸ γένος τι ὡρισμένον. This belongs to the definition of science. All the special sciences are ὑπό τι γένος ὡρισμένον, as Zoology ὑπὸ

11. 172. a. 12. περὶ πάντων ἐστί, Ibid. 28. περὶ ἁπάντων διαλέγονται, Metaph. Γ. 2. 1004. b. 19. περὶ πᾶσαν ὕλην τῇ δυνάμει χρῆται. Alex. Aphrod. ad Topic. sub init.: and employed to a certain extent and at some time or other by every one. διὸ πάντες καὶ οἱ ἰδιῶται τρόπον τινὰ χρῶνται τῇ διαλεκτικῇ καὶ πειραστικῇ, πάντες γὰρ μέχρι τινὸς ἐγχείρουσιν ἀνακρίνειν τοὺς ἐπαγγελλομένους ... ἐλέγχουσιν οὖν ἅπαντες κ.τ.λ. Soph. El. 11. 172. a. 30—35. and the same is said of rhetoric, Rhet. I. 1. 1.

The materials which it employs in the construction of its προτάσεις, propositions or premisses, and προβλήματα problems, (questions or propositions expressed alternatively, Top. A. 4. 101. b. 20. 104. a. 5. and Waitz's note) are in every case τὰ ἔνδοξα, τὰ ὡς ἐπὶ τὸ πολύ, τὰ ἐνδεχόμενα ἄλλως ἔχειν, probable matter, contingent, uncertain, such as current popular opinions and maxims; truths it may be[1], but neither universal nor necessary; or, if they are so in themselves, as in the case of the universal axioms to which lies the ultimate appeal in all reasoning alike (τὰ κοινά), not assumed as such, but left to depend upon the concession of the adversary, who may deny them if he sees fit. Top. A. 1. 100. a. 20. 30. c. 10. 104. a. 8. seq. The reason of this is explained, Rhet. I. 1. 12. Hence it is repeatedly said that philosophy or science, or the demonstrative method is directed to truth, and has truth for its sole object, dialectics to opinion. πρὸς φιλοσοφίαν κατ' ἀλήθειαν περὶ αὐτῶν πραγματευτέον, διαλεκτικῶς δὲ πρὸς δόξαν. Top. A. 14. 105. b. 30. Θ. 13. 162. b. 32. Anal. Pr. I. 30. 46. a. 8. Rhet. I. 4. 4, 5, 6. These materials are described, Top. A. 1. 100. b. 21, as "the opinions

τὸ τῶν ζώων γένος, Botany ὑπὸ τὸ τῶν φυτῶν γ. Medicine ὑπὸ τὸ τοῦ ὑγιεινοῦ καὶ νοσώδους γ. 'opposites' in each genus—where there are such—being always under the same science. In other words, a science always embraces the whole extent of its genus.

[1] Alex. Aphrod. Comm. ad Topic. 100. b. 21. p. 12. διαφέρει δὲ τὸ ἔνδοξον τοῦ ἀληθοῦς οὐ τῷ ψευδὲς εἶναι, ἔστι γάρ τινα ἔνδοξα καὶ ἀληθῆ, ἀλλὰ τῇ ἐπικρίσει. Compare Rhet. I. 1. 11. where we are told that these popular opinions and maxims are oftener true than false, because οἱ ἄνθρωποι πεφύκασι πρὸς ἀλήθειαν ἱκανῶς καὶ τὰ πλείω τυγχάνουσι τῆς ἀληθείας.

of all the world, or of the great majority, or of Philosophers ('the learned,' 'Clerks' τοῖς σοφοῖς); and of these, either universally, or of the most part, or of the best known or of the highest reputation." Examples of both classes of propositions, those which are universally or generally received, and those which pass current only amongst philosophers and are not accepted by the vulgar, are numerous in the Topics. Instances of the former are the maxims, It is one's duty to do good to one's friends, and harm to one's enemies [this is the 'Classical' morality throughout]; the γνῶθι σεαυτόν, μηδὲν ἄγαν, καιρὸν γνῶθι, χαλεπὸν ἐσθλὸν ἔμμεναι, and other like popular adages and proverbial maxims of practical wisdom: to the latter belong such as these; opposites fall under the same science (as health and disease under that of medicine); all that is good is pleasant, or the reverse; the world is eternal; the paradoxes of Antisthenes ὅτι οὐκ ἔστιν ἀντιλέγειν, of Heraclitus ὅτι πάντα κινεῖται, of Melissus and Parmenides, ὅτι ἓν τὸ ὄν—all these are open to dispute; and moreover it is often difficult to draw the line of separation between the two classes, and to decide which is a popular and which is a philosophical dictum. However for the purposes of dialectics they are all alike regarded as 'probable.' It appears from these and other examples—as it is expressly stated, Top. A. 10. 104. a. 33,—that any proposition, however remote from vulgar apprehension, and however special in its character, even the axioms and conclusions of the special sciences, *may* be subjected to dialectical discussion, provided only it be treated as 'probable,' that is, the question be left open to debate, and not laid down as a necessary truth. However when scientific questions are dialectically handled, they are not to be treated scientifically, argued, that is, from the principles proper to the science to which they severally belong, for that would be to quit the province of dialectics and to trespass upon the domain of demonstration and science. See Soph. El. 2. 161. b. 1. (quoted p. 39). The scientific investigator starts with certain principles as axioms of his science which he cannot allow to be disputed: the dialectician may call anything in question: he may assume the affirmative or negative of any proposition at his pleasure: Anal. Post. I. 2. 72. a. 8, πρότασις δ' ἐστὶν ἀποφάνσεως τὸ ἕτερον μόριον, ἐν καθ' ἑνὸς διαλεκτικὴ μὲν ἡ ὁμοίως λαμβάνουσα ὁποτερονοῦν, ἀποδεικτικὴ δὲ ἡ ὡρισμένως θάτερον, ὅτι ἀληθές. ἀπόφανσις δ' ἀντιφάσεως (contradictio, opposite assertion, affirmative and negative) ὁποτερονοῦν μόριον. Comp. π. Ἑρμην. c. 11. 20. b. 23. θατέρου μορίου τῆς ἀντιφάσεως. Ib. v. 27. δεῖ γὰρ δεδόσθαι ἐκ τῆς ἐρωτήσεως ἑλέσθαι ὁπότερον βούλεται τῆς ἀντιφάσεως μόριον. Soph. El. 2. 165. b. 3. διαλεκτικοὶ (συλλογισμοὶ) οἱ ἐκ τῶν ἐνδόξων συλλογιστικοὶ ἀντιφάσεως. Dialectics therefore differ from demonstration in this as well as other points, that the man of science is not allowed to choose which side of an alternative he will take, ὁποτερονοῦν τῶν μορίων δοῦναι, Soph. El. 11. 172. a. 16.: whereas, in the passage Soph. El. 2. 161. b. 1., above referred to it is said that dialectics ἐκ τῶν τοῦ ἀποκρινομένου δοξῶν συλλογίζεσθαι—comp. Top. Θ. 1. 155. b. 7—16—the respondent takes whichever alternative of the 'problem' he pleases, and from that, or with that, the conclusion must be deduced. And as the premisses are merely probable, and truth is not strictly speaking the object of the debate, the conclusion arrived at, dialectically considered, is a matter of indifference, provided it be obtained by following exactly the syllogistic method: and as the affirmative or negative of any proposition may be taken for a premiss, so the conclusion may be affirmative or negative indifferently. That pleasure is or is not the good, that motion is or is not possible, that friends are or are not to be well treated, are conclusions equally valid in dialectics, though when they are looked at from the scientific point of view as principles of Ethics or Physics, one only of the alternatives in each case can be a true and sound conclusion. In dialectics the *form* is everything, the truth or falsehood of a position is a matter of indifference. Hence dialectics, and also Rhetoric, are said τἀναντία συλλογίζεσθαι "to deduce opposite conclusions"; the truth or falsehood of any given proposition may be proved alike by them. τῶν μὲν οὖν ἄλλων τεχνῶν οὐδεμία τἀναντία συλλογίζεται, ἡ δὲ διαλεκτικὴ καὶ ῥητορικὴ μόναι τοῦτο ποιοῦσιν· ὁμοίως γάρ εἰσιν ἀμφότεραι τῶν ἐναντίων. Rhet. I. 1. 12. Compare Top. I. 2. 101. a. 35, δυνάμενοι πρὸς ἀμφότερα διαπορῆσαι. Still the dialectician, even as a dialectician, may have a natural preference for the side of a problem which is generally held to be true, because a paradox is harder to maintain, and less likely to carry conviction. Rhet. u. s. ἀεὶ τἀληθῆ καὶ τὰ βελτίω τῇ φύσει εὐσυλλογιστότερα καὶ πιθανώτερα ὡς ἁπλῶς εἰπεῖν.

The uses of the dialectical method, that is of the technical exposition of the rules which regulate the practice of debate, the invention and analysis of propositions and arguments, and the various artifices that may be employed in maintaining one's own thesis and detecting the fallacy and refuting the objections of the opponent, are according to Aristotle Top. A. 2. three: a fourth is subsequently added, which is in fact virtually contained in the preceding. A systematic method and rules of art are useful 1. πρὸς γυμνασίαν, 'for exercise,' as an aid to the practice of disputation, δυνάμεως χάριν, to cultivate the faculty; a technical method will give us facility in seeing what is to be proved and how to prove it. This use of dialectics is illustrated by Top. Θ. 14. 164. a. 12. seq. 2. πρὸς τὰς ἐντεύξεις, in conducting arguments which necessarily arise in common conversation. In dealing with ordinary people who are incapable of following a scientific demonstration, and comprehending scientific definitions, we must have recourse to probable principles and to arguments upon probable grounds[1]: and this mode of

---

[1] The explanation in the text is that of Alexander Aphrod., and differs from that of Waitz, if I rightly understand his note on the passage. It is however fully confirmed by the parallel passage in Rhet. I. 1. 12. ἔτι δὲ πρὸς ἐνίους...πρὸς τοὺς πολλοὺς ἐντεύ- ξεως. where reference is made to this place of the Topics. Alexander interprets ἐντεύξεις, τὰς πρὸς τοὺς πολλοὺς συνουσίας. In this second use of dialectics we are on common ground with rhetoric.

arguing it is the business of dialectics to teach. When we know what the opinions of the vulgar are, says Aristotle, we shall be able to meet them upon their own grounds. 3. πρὸς τὰς κατὰ φιλοσοφίαν ἐπιστήμας. The use of the dialectical method, and the habit of arguing upon either alternative of a question, τὸ πρὸς ἀμφότερα διαπορῆσαι, will quicken our discernment of the truth or falsehood of scientific demonstrations and conclusions. Compare Top. Θ. 14. 163. b. 9, πρός τε γνῶσιν καὶ τὴν κατὰ φιλοσοφίαν φρόνησιν τὸ δύνασθαι συνορᾶν καὶ συνεωρακέναι τὰ ἀφ' ἑκατέρας συμβαίνοντα τῆς ὑποθέσεως οὐ μικρὸν ὄργανον· λοιπὸν γὰρ τούτων ὀρθῶς ἑλέσθαι θάτερον. "It is the office of the same faculty" as he says Rhet. I. 1. 11. "to discern the truth (the object of science) and that which resembles truth (i. e. τὸ ἔνδοξον)... and therefore sagacity as applied to popular and probable opinions belongs to the same mental constitution as that which is applied to the discovery of scientific truth." 4. πρὸς τὰ πρῶτα τῶν περὶ ἑκάστην ἐπιστήμην ἀρχῶν. Compare Anal. Post. I. 11. 77. a. 26—29. Aristotle had begun the chapter by saying that the uses of dialectics are three: he now adds a fourth, which, as Alexander and Waitz have both noticed, is already implied in the preceding. It means that as the first principles of any special science cannot be demonstrated by the science itself, ἐπειδὴ πρῶται αἱ ἀρχαὶ ἁπάντων εἰσί, as they are *to it* ἀνυπόθετοι, absolute and independent, and must be taken for granted without proof; (because demonstration must ultimately depend for its support upon something external to itself, otherwise it would be carried back ad infinitum and never stop; and this basis in every special science is provided by its specific ἀρχαί—see the beginning and the last chapter of the Analytica Posteriora—) these, if they are to be investigated at all, must be investigated through the medium of the all sifting all questioning method of dialectics, placed upon the lower level of probability, and thus undergo an examination in utramque partem. Similarly of the κοιναὶ ἀρχαί, Metaph. K. 5. 1062. a. 2. περὶ τῶν τοιούτων (τῶν ἀρχῶν, the principium contradictionis and the ultimate axioms of all reasoning) ἁπλῶς μὲν οὐκ ἔστιν ἀπόδειξις, πρὸς τόνδε δ᾽ ἔστιν. Ib. v. 30. ἀπόδειξις μὲν οὖν οὐδεμία τούτων ἐστὶν ἁπλῶς, πρὸς μέντοι τὸν ταῦτα τιθέμενον ἀπόδειξις. Cum specie quadam veritatis, διαλεκτικῶς, probari possunt ei qui nobiscum disputat. Waitz. Comm. ad Topic. p. 436. Brandis, Handb. Arist. I. 144. has these words. Die Dialektik bahnt *untersuchend* den weg zu den principien der begriffsbestimmungen, die weisheit oder wissenschaft in strengerem sinne des worts erkennt sie, see also not. 48[1]. See on this same subject, Poste, Introd. to Transl. of Post. Anal. pp. 21 and 32. The view taken by him of this relation of dialectics to science is not unlike that of Zeller. A good description of the dialectical practice as recommended

---

[1] Zeller, Phil. der Gr. II. 384, 5. (1st Ed.), puts the following interpretation on this fourth use of dialectics. The axioms and principles on which the special sciences are based are indemonstrable by that science, and can only be arrived at by induction. But from the infinity of particulars no induction (i. e. the inductio per enumerationem simplicem, as it was understood by Aristotle) can be complete, and the axioms therefore are always more or less liable to uncertainty. To rectify this in some degree and confirm their validity we may have recourse to the common opinions and general probabilities of the case. These when examined and sifted and classified will furnish a sort of induction, after a dialectical investigation, which consists in setting them one against another taking alternately either side of each question. It is on this principle, says Zeller, that Aristotle himself proceeds in his scientific writings. Before he enters upon the dogmatic statement of the principles on which he himself bases the science, he goes through a series of ἀπορίαι, examining the preceding views on their various sides, and thus bringing them into collision with one another. These dialectical discussions furnish tests of the results of the preceding inductions, which can thus be brought under one point of view and harmonised, and so become the preparation and foundation of the dogmatic development. I am not sure that Zeller is not going a little beyond Aristotle in his interpretation of this passage. I doubt if the question of induction entered into his meaning at all. I should rather suppose that all that he means to say is this, that whereas these fundamental principles of the sciences are incapable of demonstration, dialectics may at any rate be made useful, by discussing and trying them, and submitting them to 'cross examination', and showing what is to be said pro and con, in establishing for them a high degree of probability, which is all that dialectics can do.

and exemplified by Plato, is to be found in Grote's Plato, c. VI. Vol. I. p. 229. and elsewhere.

These three uses of dialectics are very well and briefly described by Brandis, in his treatise über Aristoteles' rhetorik, p. 12, and I will therefore quote his own words. Die Topik soll, Nach, Arist. Top. I. 2., auf dreierlei gerichtet sein, auf (geistige) Übung (πρὸς γυμνασίαν), auf anweisung zur debatte (πρὸς τὰς ἐντεύξεις), auf Vorbereitung für die philosophischen wissenschaften (πρὸς τὰς κατὰ φιλοσοφίαν ἐπιστήμας), d. h. für die wissenschaften im eigentlichen sinne des worts. *Den zweiten zweck hat sie mit der rhetorik gemein;* diese soll anweisen durch gemeinhin angenommenes (διὰ τῶν κοινῶν) in der rede zu überzeugen (ποιεῖσθαι τὰς πίστεις καὶ τοὺς λόγους).

The distinction between philosophy, which employs the demonstrative or scientific method and dialectics with its spurious branch sophistic, is further illustrated by a passage of the Metaphysics, Γ. 2. 1004. b. 17. After describing the field embraced by the speculations of the 'philosopher' and pointing out that his inquiries are directed to τὸ ὂν ᾗ ὄν, that is, being and its essential properties (πάθη καθ' αὑτά, ἴδια), regarded in themselves and apart from the accidents connected with, or properties remotely deducible from them, the author proceeds; σημεῖον δέ. οἱ γὰρ διαλεκτικοὶ ταὐτὸν ὑποδύονται σχῆμα τῷ φιλοσόφῳ· ἡ γὰρ σοφιστικὴ φαινομένη μόνον σοφία ἐστί, καὶ οἱ διαλεκτικοὶ διαλέγονται περὶ ἁπάντων, κοινὸν δὲ πᾶσι τὸ ὄν ἐστιν· διαλέγονται δὲ περὶ τούτων δῆλον ὅτι διὰ τὸ τῆς φιλοσοφίας εἶναι αὐτὰ οἰκεῖα. περὶ μὲν γὰρ τὸ αὐτὸ γένος στρέφεται ἡ σοφιστικὴ καὶ ἡ διαλεκτικὴ τῇ φιλοσοφίᾳ, ἀλλὰ διαφέρει τῆς μὲν τῷ τρόπῳ τῆς δυνάμεως, τῆς δὲ τοῦ βίου τῇ προαιρέσει. ἔστι δὲ ἡ διαλεκτικὴ πειραστικὴ περὶ ὧν ἡ φιλοσοφία γνωριστική, ἡ δὲ σοφιστικὴ φαινομένη, οὖσα δ'οὔ. One proof that the domain of philosophy embraces the entire range of things existing is derived from a comparison between it and dialectics and sophistic. Since these two "covertly assume the disguise of philosophy," the objects of the three must be coextensive. For sophistic is nothing but sham philosophy, and every question may be discussed by the dialectician, whilst being is common to all three. So that they all "revolve about," (versantur circa[1]) turn upon, are occupied with, the same class of subjects: only dialectic differs from philosophy in the mode in which the faculty is exercised, and sophistic in the purpose of the life (of the Professor), in the moral end and intention[2]. For dialectic is tentative where philosophy aims at exact knowledge, and sophistic is a sham and not a real philosophy. Philosophy and dialectics may discuss the same questions: and each of them has the $\delta \acute{v} \nu a \mu \iota s$, the faculty or latent power, of dealing with them in the same way: but this $\delta \acute{v} \nu a \mu \iota s$ is developed in different directions, and in the actuality, $\grave{\epsilon} \nu \epsilon \rho \gamma \epsilon \acute{\iota} a$ (the complete development and exercise), they differ in the mode of exercising it: for whilst philosophy proceeds from true and certain principles to necessary conclusions, and investigates the very truth of things, dialectics, whose sphere is popular and current opinion, aiming not at truth but at the refutation of an adversary, in the process of sifting propositions and arguments, tries (experiments upon) and tests the truth, and thus accidentally helps to illustrate it. Philosophia a veris profecta principiis ipsam cognoscit veritatem, dialectica verum tentat modo et experitur, et profecta a vulgi opinionibus viam quasi parat philosophiæ. Bonitz ad h. l. Dialectica ab iis proficiscens quæ in communi hominum opinione versantur ($\tau \grave{a}$ $\check{\epsilon} \nu \delta o \xi a$) in utramque partem disputat et difficultates ita quasi exagitat ut verum indagetur et ad artium principia patefiat accessus. Trendel. El. Log. Arist. Not. ad § 33. p. 103. $\pi \epsilon \iota \rho a \sigma \tau \iota \kappa \acute{\eta}$[3] according to this explana-

[1] Quint. II. 15. 15. Quidam enim circa res omnes, quidam circa civiles modo versari rhetoricen putaverunt.

[2] Comp. Rhet. I. 1. 14. ὁ γὰρ σοφιστικὸs...κατὰ τὴν δύναμιν.

[3] Waitz translates πειραστική quæ propositum habet ut tentet adversarium note on 172. a. 21, a sense which seems to be suitable to the word when it is applied to *a special branch of dialectics*, as it is in p. 165. b. 4—6, where see Waitz's note: because in this application of it the characteristic, from which the name is derived, is that it

tion is nearly equivalent to ἐξεταστική in Top. A. 2. 101. b. 3.: πειραστική and πειραστικός are so frequently applied in the Topics to dialectics and the dialectician, as to be almost convertible with them, for instance, Soph. El. ii. 172. a. 36. 171. b. 9. πεῖραν λαβεῖν 172. a. 23. 183. b. 2. διαλεκτική and πειραστική are however in the treatise de Soph. El. sometimes distinguished as separate branches of the general art of debate. See Soph. El. c. 2. and c. 8. 169. b. 25. 171. b. 4. 172. a. 30. 183. b. 4.

The foregoing remarks will serve also to explain another passage of the Metaphysics, to be compared with that already cited; Bk. K. 3. 1061. b. 7. ἥ γε μὴν διαλεκτικὴ καὶ ἡ σοφιστικὴ τῶν συμβεβηκότων μέν εἰσι τοῖς οὖσιν, οὐχ ᾗ δ' ὄντα, οὐδὲ περὶ τὸ ὂν αὐτὸ καθ' ὅσον ὄν ἐστιν.

In further illustration of this distinction of philosophy and dialectics I will quote one more passage from the Soph. El. c. 11. 172. a. 11—36. because it is very explicit, and describes this in detail. "The dialectician," we are there told, "does not deal with any special or definite class of subjects, οὐκ ἔστι περὶ γένος τι ὡρισμένον, nor is his function to demonstrate anything (δεικτικός i. e. ἀποδεικτικός), nor does he belong to the family of the 'universalists'¹ (men of science,

argues from the opinions *of the opponent.* πειρᾶσθαι and ἀποπειρᾶσθαι frequently denote "to put to the proof," "to try an adversary's strength," as Plat. Theæt. 154. D. ἐκ περιουσίας ἀλλήλων ἀποπειρώμενοι. 157. C. &c. But when it is applied to dialectics in general, the other meaning seems to be the true one; as may be inferred from πειραστικὴ περὶ ὧν ἡ φ. γνωριστική. in Metaph. l. c. On πειραστική, see further in Poste, Introd. to Transl. of Post. Anal. p. 21. seq. A different distinction is given by Waitz on Soph. El. c. 2. between διαλεκτικοί and πειραστικοί illi quidem (colligunt) ex iis quæ omnibus probari solent, hi vero

ex iis quæ probantur adversario. But dialectics as commonly understood (when *not* expressly distinguished from πειραστική) always includes this latter characteristic.

¹ οὐδὲ τοιοῦτος οἷος ὁ καθόλου. ὁ καθόλου is an elliptical phrase, which may be supplied, either by understanding the simple ὤν, and then it will be parallel to Plato's οἱ ῥέοντες, οἱ ἱστάντες, in the Theætetus, used to designate the maintainers of the views of universal motion and universal rest, the Heracliteans and Eleatics, by a sort of personification of the doctrine itself, and in this case ὁ καθόλου 'the universal' stands for one who deals ex-

whose propositions and conclusions are 'universals'):" all these being characteristic of the scientific demonstrator. "For neither can *everything* be included under one genus," the <u>dialectician disputes about *everything*, and therefore cannot be a man of science,</u> "nor if it were, is it possible for all existing things to be reduced under the same first principles." Every science is subordinate to and based upon certain special first principles: if the dialectician were a 'man of science,' that is, the professor of any special science, the entire field of things existing, which all fall within his province, must be referrible to or deducible from, the same special first principles: but this is impossible. "Consequently no demonstrative art (τέχνη) is interrogative," presents an alternative, and argues from the answer of the opponent; propositiones ex quibus demonstrationem conficit, num sibi concedantur ab adversario non quaerit, sed ponit. Waitz. "for it cannot assume (δοῦναι 'to offer;' but since the 'offering' of a thesis to another for his acceptance presupposes that the offerer accepts or assumes its truth, so δοῦναι here is equivalent to 'assume') either branch of an alternative indifferently (like dialectics), because <u>a syllogism</u> (that is, such a syllogism as science requires to prove its propositions) <u>cannot be constructed from both</u> (affirmative *or*

clusively with the universal: or clse, and perhaps more naturally, ἀποδεικνύων or συλλογιζόμενος may be understood, and the meaning will be substantially the same, 'one whose demonstrations or conclusions are always universal.' This is in fact one of the distinguishing characteristics of science. All sciences, and all arts so far as their theory and rules are concerned, operate in the sphere of the universal; τέχνη and ἐπιστήμη are τοῦ καθόλου, ἐμπειρία τοῦ καθ' ἕκαστον. Metaph. A. I. 981. a. 16. and c. 2. See Bonitz. Comment. p. 49. And this sufficiently distinguishes the man of science from the dialectician, who at any rate does not *confine himself* to the discussion of universal problems. Waitz however is not satisfied with this, and referring to Anal. Post. I. 4. 73. b. 26., understands it thus, qui ex iis solis colligit quae cum ipsa rei natura necessario conjuncta sunt. The ellipse he does not explain.

Compare Rhet. I. 2. 9. τὸ δὲ τινῶν ὄντων...ἢ καθόλου, ἢ ὡς ἐπὶ τὸ πολύ, ἐκεῖ μὲν συλλογισμὸς ἐνταῦθα δὲ ἐνθύμημα καλεῖται.

negative). But dialectic is interrogative. Had it attempted demonstration—though I don't say *all* its propositions—at any rate its primary highest axioms and special principles, it never could have converted into questions," (proved by way of interrogation in the dialectic manner. If dialectics affected a scientific method, it must have conformed to the laws of science; and it would have had some special principles, οἰκεῖαι ἀρχαί, from which to deduce its propositions. But the dialectical method is *essentially* interrogatory; if it abandons that method it ceases to be dialectical; and so leaves all its propositions and principles at the mercy of the opponent. And this shows at once that it cannot be scientific: were it so, it would have special principles, axioms and definitions, of its own, and these could not be left dependent upon the judgment or will of another, for that would deprive the supposed science of its only basis and foundation[1].) "For if the other party refused to concede them, it would have no materials left to furnish a reply to his objection. Dialectic is also Pirastic"—here is another difference between dialectics and science—"for neither is Pirastic a science like geometry, but a faculty that may be possessed even by one who is ignorant of science. For it is possible for a man who is ignorant of the subject in question to examine another who is equally ignorant, provided his propositions be not derived from assumed scientific knowledge, or from the special and peculiar principles of the science, but merely from

---

[1] οὐκ ἐρωτᾷ ἀλλὰ λαμβάνει (assumes) ὁ ἀποδεικνύων. Alex. Aphrod. Comment. ad Top. 172. a. 18. Compare Anal. Post. I. 11. 77. a. 31. ἡ δὲ διαλεκτικὴ οὐκ ἔστιν οὕτως ὡρισμένων τινῶν. οὐ γὰρ ἂν ἠρώτα. ἀποδεικνύντα γὰρ οὐκ ἔστιν ἐρωτᾶν διὰ τὸ τῶν ἀντικειμένων ὄντων μὴ δείκνυσθαι τὸ αὐτό. In demonstration, where only one solution of a given problem can be true, and that necessarily follows from the given principles, where the same conclusion will not follow (μὴ δείκνυσθαι τὸ αὐτό) from the assumption of either alternative, the affirmative or negative, of a given principle or proposition (τῶν ἀντικειμένων ὄντων)—the first principles of the science cannot be left open to question, nor can the assumption of them be allowed, as in dialectics, to depend upon the concession of an opponent.

their ordinary consequences; (ἐκ τῶν ἑπομένων, a knowledge of things gained by mere experience and routine, Waitz.) which are such that a man may very well be acquainted with them without a knowledge of the art (sic) itself, but of which the ignorance is absolutely incompatible with any knowledge of the art at all. Consequently it is plain that πειραστική is not a science of any definite branch of knowledge: whence it follows that it is universal in its application; (and thus in some sense may be applied to the sciences themselves) because all arts and sciences employ certain universal axioms, besides the special axioms &c. peculiar to each (καὶ κοινοῖς τισίν). Accordingly everybody, even those who make no profession of science (οἱ ἰδιῶται), make use after a fashion of dialectics and πειραστική: for every one to a certain extent undertakes to examine (ἀνακρίνειν) the pretensions of Professors (of any art or science. This is πειραστική when distinguished, as a subordinate branch, from διαλεκτική.) And these (which everybody appeals to) are the universal principles (τὰ κοινά). For *these* they know equally well themselves" (as the men of science)—they have an unconscious and undeveloped knowledge of them: they know them after a fashion and can apply them, though not perhaps with perfect exactness—"though their expression of them may be very defective in precision[1]. And so every one practises this art of testing and confutation; for they employ unsystematically and unscientifically a practice of which dialectics is the scientific and systematic method, and every one who tries or tests arguments by the syllogistic art is a dialectician." Compare with these last remarks Rhet. I 1. 1. where precisely the same thing is said of rhetoric.

Now let us, although all this has been stated or implied already, repeat by way of summary the principal points of

---

[1] κἂν δοκῶσι λίαν ἔξω λέγειν. The meaning of this is not quite certain. I have adopted Mr. Poste's translation. ἔξω λέγειν may also, I think, mean, to deviate from the rules by which the application of these axioms should be regulated.

agreement and disagreement between science and dialectics, and then illustrate these by an example.

Both of them alike follow a rigorous method: alike they employ syllogism and induction, the latter in collecting their principles and major premisses, the former in deducing their conclusions; the highest and most universal principles of reasoning, τὰ κοινά, which lie beyond and are antecedent to the special principles of the several sciences, are common to both alike.

But whilst science from universal and necessary principles, some of them always special and peculiar to each science, the latter of which it assumes a priori and will not suffer to be called in question or submit to the caprice of an opponent, deduces universal and necessary conclusions, and all the materials that it employs are impressed with the same character of universality and necessity, which alone constitute exact knowledge and truth, the sole object and aim of science; whence it is said to be περὶ τὸ ὄν—dialectic on the other hand is περὶ τὸ συμβεβηκός, its sphere is the probable, its principles current popular opinions: it is universal in its application, and may deal even with the principles and propositions of science, only in that case they are not to be treated as necessary, but regarded like all the rest as only probable and open to question; it is indifferent to truth, and aims only at proving its point, and thereby refuting an adversary, whose existence is always assumed in every dialectical discussion, even when it is carried on in a man's own brain and in his own study; it therefore regards every thing as an open question, takes either side of an alternative indifferently, concludes as readily the negative as the affirmative (τἀναντία συλλογίζεται); it depends absolutely for its arguments upon the concessions of the opponent, real or imaginary: to it the form or method is everything, the truth of the conclusion nothing, except so far as it follows legitimately from the exact observance of the rules of the syllogism, which is its instrument.

The Mathematician, for instance, starting from the principles of his science and following a rigorous method necessarily concludes in one way; he *cannot* prove that two straight lines may enclose a space, or that the three angles of a triangle are *not* equal to two right angles; not that he has any personal interest in proving that the three angles of a triangle are equal to two right angles: in this respect it is a matter of perfect indifference to him whether they are equal or unequal; but only one of them can be true, and he is constrained by his principles and his method to arrive at one single conclusion and at no other. The dialectician following *his* method is equally indifferent to the conclusion to which his arguments lead him: as a philosopher he may have his own private opinion upon the eternity of the universe or the possibility of motion; as a moralist he may hold that the opinion that the good is nothing but pleasure, or virtue mere knowledge, is false; but as a dialectician following his rules of art he argues upon either side of these questions and concludes either way with equal facility. It might seem at first sight that the truth of the conclusion is *not* a matter of indifference to the dialectician any more than to the man of science; but this misapprehension arises from not distinguishing between the debater and the man. The questions which usually come under discussion, questions of morals or politics, physical problems, philosophical theories, are such as very often involve important practical interests, the solution of which may materially affect the well being of the individual and of society. If a man maintain false views upon such questions he may be a bad philosopher, and if he seek to disseminate them knowing them to be false, he may be a bad man; but if he force an opponent to assent to his thesis, and refute the opposing theory by arguments without a flaw, he is a good dialectician. Against those who object to the cultivation of dialectics and rhetoric upon the ground of the mischief which may arise from the misuse of it, Aristotle replies Rhet. I. 1, that they are like all powerful and therefore dangerous weapons, which when *misapplied may do infinite harm* : but this is no valid objection to the *use* of them for lawful and beneficial purposes, and therefore to the acquisition of skill in the employment of them by practice and study : that these, like all other arts, should be cultivated for the use and not for the abuse of them ; in order to know what the method of reasoning is, and how to employ it to refute what is false and injurious, and maintain and defend what is true and salutary.

The dialectical method as described by Aristotle in the terms which have been cited from his works may be readily illustrated from the arguments which form the staple of most of the Platonic dialogues or (not quite so well) from Bp. Berkeley's philosophical dialogues. We have for example a Sophist first laying down some antisocial or immoral doctrine ; he is encountered by Socrates, a debate ensues and issue is speedily joined. Socrates undertakes to refute the position and sustains the part of ὁ ἐρωτῶν, ὁ ἐλέγχων, ὁ ἐξετάζων, ὁ ἐπιχειρῶν, the questioner or assailant, the Sophist being the respondent, or maintainer of the thesis, ὁ ἀποκρινόμενος, ὁ ὑπέχων τὸν λόγον. The principles maintained and the positions assumed are all probable and open to question, the appeal being in all cases made either to current maxims and opinions or to those ultimate principles which are common to and the foundation of all reasoning. The respondent takes either side ὁποτερονοῦν μόριον of the alternatives offered by the assailant and the latter is obliged to argue from the admissions of his opponent ἐκ τῶν τοῦ ἀποκρινομένου δοξῶν συλλογίζεσθαι ; the conclusion which is finally elicited from the concessions of the adversary may be the affirmative or negative of the position originally laid down, συλλογίζεται τἀναντία, this being to the dialectician a matter of indifference so long as the forms of argument are duly observed, though to the philosopher or the man it may be of vital importance.

Of this general art of debating Rhetoric is a special

branch. Aristotle commences his treatise on Rhetoric with the remark that it is the counterpart of Dialectics. The full import of the term (ἀντίστροφος) there employed, implying exact correspondence in detail, will be explained in the note on that passage. There are however so many points of difference between them in respect of form and substance, (dialectics for example necessarily implies an argument by question and answer—from which indeed it takes its name— and an opponent whose concessions furnish the data on which the adversary founds his argument; rhetoric is expressed in continuous speeches addressed to a special audience, political or judicial, and in consequence derives its materials almost exclusively from politics in the larger sense, since it almost invariably turns upon political social and moral questions; nor again has the mode of argumentation the same formal character in the latter that it has in the former art; to which many minor points of difference might be added) that the word cannot, or at least ought not to, be applied here in its strict signification, but probably denotes no more than a general correspondence or analogy. Of the four terms employed by Aristotle to express the connexion of Rhetoric with Dialectics, ἀντίστροφος, ὁμοίωμα, μόριον, παραφυές Rhet. I. 1. 1. I. 2. 7. the two last seem best to describe the relation in which they stand to one another. Dialectics is the mother science of probable reasoning which handles every question; and rhetoric, which argues practical questions of politics and Ethics, (one member of her family, with a strong family likeness,) a subordinate "branch" or "department", an "offshoot" or "scion".

Still although its sphere is thus practically limited, theoretically considered it embraces as wide a range of subjects as dialectics. περὶ οὐδενὸς ὡρισμένου οὐδετέρα αὐτῶν ἐστὶν ἐπιστήμη Rhet. I. 2. 7 comp. I. 2. 1. I. 1. 14 περὶ τοῦ δοθέντος ὡς εἰπεῖν. I. 2. 1[1]: both of them are mere arts or

---

[1] Alexander Aphrod. on Top. 100. a. 19 has the following remark. προσ- κείμενον τὸ περὶ παντός (the addition of περὶ π. to the description of δια-

faculties of supplying arguments, Rhet. I. 2. 7. Its office is not properly speaking to persuade, though it was usually so defined in the rhetorical schools and treatises, as that of dialectics is not to convince or refute: but as the conditions of the latter art are satisfied and its end attained when arguments are found and a method pursued which are capable of refuting an opponent and reducing him to silence, so in like manner the end of rhetoric does not require the actual persuasion of an audience, which is often rendered impossible by causes altogether independent of the rhetorician, as prejudice or stupidity, but its function is "to ascertain the possible means of persuasion on a given subject." τὸ ἰδεῖν τὰ ὑπάρχοντα πιθανὰ περὶ ἕκαστον. Rhet. I. 1. 14; the *artistic* process consisting in the mode of treatment, and not including the result; as is likewise the case with medicine and all other practical arts.

The probable and the contingent are the province and the materials of both alike; of dialectics, *everything* that can be brought under this denomination: of rhetoric, human actions and motives and characters, and in general everything that we deliberate about, and which is in our own power[1]. Like dialectics again it does not affect demonstration (ἀπόδειξις). When ἀπόδειξις or συλλογισμός is applied to rhetorical arguments as it sometimes is, it is not used in the technical sense of scientific demonstration, but stands

λεκτικὴ) χωρίζει πως τῆς ῥητορικῆς τὴν διαλεκτικήν. οὐ γὰρ ὁμοίως περὶ παντὸς προβλήματος ἡ ῥητορικὴ συλλογιστική. ὕλη γὰρ μᾶλλον τῷ ῥήτορι τὰ ἠθικά τε καὶ πολιτικὰ προβλήματα, ἃ δι' ἐνδόξων πειρᾶται καὶ αὐτὴ ἀποδεικνύναι. This is quite true; but Alexander forgets that in the Rhetoric (l. c.) Aristotle had said the reverse: else he would have told us that this universality of application is merely theoretical; an orator *may* speak or argue upon any subject whatever; but practically he seldom *does* speak upon any but political and moral questions. I have here left the ἐπιδεικτικὸν γένος altogether out of the account, because it is entirely subordinate to the other two: though even in this kind of rhetoric, as we may gather from Isocrates' extant orations, the subject of these declamations was generally taken from Politics or History.

[1] On the objects of deliberation see Eth. Nic. III. 5.

for 'proof' and 'reasoning' in general—nor does it pretend to *teach* anything (διδασκαλική) I. 2. 1. I. 1. 12 διδασκαλίας γάρ ἐστιν ὁ κατὰ τὴν ἐπιστήμην λόγος...ἀλλ' ἀνάγκη διὰ τῶν κοινῶν ποιεῖσθαι τὰς πίστεις. *instruction* is conveyed by science and its *peculiar* principles and method; rhetoric argues with the universally accepted principles and current opinions of mankind. Again, I. 2. 21, of the τόποι of which the materials of rhetoric consist, the one kind, the κοινοὶ τόποι, loci communissimi, as the topic of degree τοῦ μᾶλλον καὶ ἧττον, will convey no instruction on any definite subject, being equally applicable to all; and the other, τὰ ἴδια or εἴδη, topics derived from special subjects or sciences, as physics, ethics, politics, in proportion to the knowledge and exactness with which the rhetorician or dialectician selects his premisses from them, he will insensibly be carried beyond the boundaries of his own art into an alien and special science: for any 'principle' that he lights upon (that is, any of the ἴδιαι or οἰκεῖαι ἀρχαί of the sciences) will belong not to dialectics or rhetoric but to that science whose principles he has thus adopted.

Though the rhetorician is not strictly and formally dependent like the dialectician upon the concessions of an adversary, yet he is so in some sense upon his audience; for in ordinary cases he can only assume such principles and sentiments in conducting his argument as he knows will be acceptable to them, or which they are prepared to admit; for which purpose he has to study their characters. See for example the topics in Rhet. I. 9. and the popular sentiments there appealed to.

The art of rhetoric too, like that of dialectics, teaches how to argue on both sides of a question indifferently, τἀναντία συλλογίζεται, τἀναντία δεῖ δύνασθαι πείθειν, Rhet. I. 1. 12.. This follows as a consequence from the nature of the materials with which it has to deal. None of these are universal and necessary; and a case which is merely probable, always leaves the alternative open to proof. Such questions have necessarily two sides; and therefore the art of rhetoric teaches how to maintain the affirmative or negative as the occasion may chance to require. Not that the orator need argue both sides of the same question, or be indifferent to the side which he does take, as Aristotle adds; but that he may be acquainted with the method, and prepared to meet the fallacies of an ignorant or dishonest reasoner. That an art may be abused is no proof of its inutility or immorality: everything may be misused, and most especially the choicest and best gifts and accomplishments and the most useful and necessary arts, health, strength, wealth, abilities, medicine, military skill and science.

I have already entered at some length, in speaking of the characteristic peculiarities of Aristotle's treatise on Rhetoric, into the differences in the mode of treatment of any subject required by the rigorous exactness of scientific inquiry and demonstration on the one hand, and the popular method of 'persuasion' employed by Rhetoric on the other: and I have exemplified this difference especially in the treatment of definitions, illustrating it by a comparison of some of the most striking of these as they appear in the scientific or quasi scientific treatises of the Politics, Ethics, de Animâ, and in the Rhetoric[1]. For the further illustration of this difference I will refer my readers to Brandis' article on Aristotle's Rhetoric in Schneidewin's Philologus, Vol. IV. No. 1., which I have already several times had occasion to mention. He has entered into a very elaborate comparison of the Rhetoric with all the other works of Aristotle with which it in any way comes in contact, first and foremost and in the fullest detail with the Topics—which thus furnishes a contrast of the *dialectical* and rhetorical manner of dealing with the same topics of argument—and also the Analytics, the de Animâ, the Nicomachean Ethics, and the Politics. It is so concisely expressed that any epitome or abbreviation would do it injustice, and it is far too long to admit of being

[1] This occurs in the earlier part of the Introduction, not here printed.

quoted here entire. I must confine myself to a very general description of its contents, and to one or two of the parallel cases by way of illustration, to which I will add one or two of my own.

From the comparative survey of the Topics and the Rhetoric it appears that the choice and comprehension of the topics illustrated are determined by the nature and limits of the arts to which they severally belong. Dialectics of course which discusses every thing treats the subject much more comprehensively, and introduces many divisions and distinctions which are omitted in the corresponding analyses of the Rhetoric. The practical limitation of the application of the rules of rhetoric to human actions and characters excludes a great number of the general topics of dialectics, and of their subordinate divisions, as useless for the purposes of the other art. Thus in the analysis of the fallacious enthymemes in Rhet. II. 24,—corresponding to the de Soph. El., the treatise on logical fallacies appended to the topics,—of the first general division of these fallacies, those namely which arise from the misuse of language, παρὰ τὴν λέξιν, out of the five or six different kinds which are distinguished in the Topics, only two appear in the Rhetoric (the fallacies arising from ambiguous, homonymous, words, and from deceptive combinations and separations): of the seven kinds of the other division[1], fallacies ἔξω τῆς λέξεως, such as originate in causes beyond the range of language—he will not allow the distinction of πρὸς τοὔνομα and πρὸς διάνοιαν, as if thought could be independent of language—recognised in the Topics, only four are to be found in the Rhetoric. But this is not all; besides the omissions, there are in both cases additions of topics suitable only to rhetoric; to the first of the two divisions are added the three first topics of § 2, and δείνωσις, 'exaggeration' (for the purpose of exciting the emotions and passions)

---

[1] This is an instance of the logical division by 'dichotomy'; the two classes being fallacies of language and not-language. Its value may be measured by this example.

§ 4., a topic especially appropriate to this art and absolutely excluded from the art of debating: in the second, the fallacy ἐκ σημείων, § 5., which is noticed in the Soph. El. c. 5. 167. b. 8. but with the remark that it belongs to rhetoric, and that of § 10., are over and above the kinds *expressly distinguished* in the dialectical treatise.

This will serve as a specimen of the different mode of treatment required by dialectics and rhetoric in the selection of topics. Passing on to the Analytics we find in the explanation and definition of the instruments and materials of rhetoric, as σημεῖον, τεκμήριον, παράδειγμα, a technical logical analysis and detail, which is omitted as unsuitable in the rhetorical treatise, and replaced by descriptions much more popular and practical; as may be seen by a comparison of the treatment severally bestowed upon them at the end of the second book of the Prior Analytics and in the second chapter of the Introduction to the Rhetoric.

Of the three remaining works which might afford us the means of comparing scientific with rhetorical treatment, in the de Anima the doctrine of the πάθη or 'affections,' the discussion of which in detail would have brought the two works into contact, is omitted, and the subject dismissed with some very general reflexions and a transcendental definition near the opening of the book. Had it been thoroughly gone into, the treatment of the subject would most certainly have differed widely from that which is adopted in the Rhetoric, where they are considered merely in respect of their external manifestation, of the sort of persons against whom they are directed, and the motives and means by which they may be excited or allayed: and consequently those only are selected for discussion which are most easily brought under the influence of the speaker.

In the Ethics and Politics as compared with the Rhetoric we have already drawn attention to the definition of virtue in the former, and the classification of forms of government in the latter, as very striking illustrations of the scientific mode of dealing with those subjects in contrast with the popular method of the Rhetoric. These of course are not omitted in Brandis' list. We may further compare the two lists of special virtues in the Ethics and Rhetoric—most of these are common to both systems; and Brandis finds in the latter work hints and indications of the Ethical distinction of moral and intellectual virtues, and of the famous doctrine of the mean[1]. The list in the Rhetoric has all the moral virtues of the Ethics with the exception of the nameless mean between φιλοτιμία and ἀφιλοτιμία: the minor and social virtues which mark the well bred gentleman are omitted. The principle of selection is stated I. 9. 6. and is characteristic of rhetoric. It is, that the highest virtues are those which are most useful to society (τοῖς ἄλλοις). At the end of the list are added the two intellectual virtues of the 6th book of the Nicom. Ethics, φρόνησις and σοφία, practical, and philosophical or speculative (θεωρητική) wisdom. One singular mark of the unscientific character of this work, which has escaped the observation of Brandis, is that πραότης which in this list and equally in that of the Ethics is a *virtue*, that is a ἕξις, figures in Rhet. II. 3. as one of the πάθη.

One more illustration of the distinction between dialectical or rhetorical and scientific treatment, and one more passage descriptive of the manner in which rhetoric deals with its materials, shall bring this subject to a close. In the Topics and the Rhetoric alike the author's object is to show by an analysis of the different sources or heads from which arguments may be derived, where they may be looked for—this is in fact the meaning of τόπος, the "place," locus or regio,

---

[1] I think that Brandis here ascribes a little too much Ethical philosophy to the Rhetoric. Of the two passages which he adduces in support of this view, one, I. 6. 21. καὶ οὗ μή ἐστιν ὑπερβολή, τοῦτο ἀγαθόν, has certainly nothing to do with the doctrine of the mean: and in the other, I. 9. 29. 'excess' is no doubt spoken of in contrast with virtue, but neither the 'defect,' nor the 'mean,' is mentioned. Καὶ τοὺς ἐν ταῖς ὑπερβολαῖς ὡς ἐν ταῖς ἀρεταῖς ὄντας certainly does not *require* the doctrine of the mean to make it intelligible.

where they haunt, and are to be found when wanted: the notion is that of a game-preserve, or a district in which a particular product or commodity, such as minerals for example, abounds, or an armoury or magazine where a store of weapons or other things is kept for use; or generally, '*the place*' for anything—and how they are to be applied. To take the instance referred to by Waitz, Comm. on Anal. Post. p. 297, the treatment of definition. In the Analytics the nature and construction of a true definition are investigated; in the Topics, VI. 4. seq., we are taught simply what kind of definitions may be successfully assailed. In the Analytics, (Anal. Post. I. 26.) and Topics (VIII. 2) it is shown that a direct or categorical demonstration is to be preferred to a reductio ad impossibile or absurdum : but in the former the proof of this is drawn from the fact that the direct demonstration is derived from principles or premisses anterior to, and therefore higher and better than, those from which the other is deduced, and more nearly related to the subject of the demonstration; the direct process is shorter, easier, and more convincing; in the Topics the reason given is that this is less easily combated and refuted.

In the fourth Chapter of the first book of the Rhetoric he opens the examination of the first and most important of the three branches of the art, the δημηγορικόν or συμβουλευτικὸν γένος, with some introductory observations upon the extent to which the analysis of this department of his subject should be carried in conformity with the requirements of a practical art. After pointing out the necessary limitations of the area from which the topics suitable to public speaking are to be drawn, he proceeds to say that an exact enumeration and precise division by kinds of the subjects which usually fall under discussion, and an attempt to define them accurately in the way which would be required by the scientific method of procedure, κατ' ἀλήθειαν, would be altogether out of place on an occasion like the present; and then goes on, in a passage already quoted, to tell us what rhetoric is, and how it and its mother dialectics are distinguished by the universality of their application from the sciences which have each its own special field of study and observation; at the same time very decidedly intimating that in a popular and practical art like Rhetoric we are to expect nothing but a popular and practical mode of treatment.

SYLLOGISM. ENTHYMEME. EXAMPLE.

The subject that offers itself next for our consideration is the logical instruments which rhetoric employs in its popular and probable reasonings, the most important of its three πίστεις, or modes of persuasion; the other two being the ἤθη and πάθη. These are, as was to be expected, merely varieties of the two sole instruments of all reasoning, συλλογισμός and ἐπαγωγή, the deductive and inductive method of proof.

We must first however premise that besides these three kinds of logical, and quasi logical or indirect and moral proofs, which belong essentially to the art or system, there is another and totally distinct kind of proof which is unscientific, extraneous to, and independent of, the art and its practice. But though they are strictly speaking outside of the art and its system, they may still be treated systematically, and as in the other cases the employment of these also may be guided and governed by certain general rules: and such rules are laid down in Bk. I. ch. 15. where the treatment of them is described. These are the ἄτεχνοι πίστεις of the judicial branch, to which they all belong; evidence, the question (βάσανος), laws, documents or contracts, and oaths. They differ from the other kind, the ἔντεχνοι πίστεις, in this, that whereas these are of our own making and originate in ourselves, and are supplied by the instrumentality of the speech itself, the others are extraneous to ourselves, already in existence independently of ourselves and our own exertions, προϋπῆρχεν, ready for use when wanted. This distinction is very clearly put in the Rhet. ad Alex. c. 8. § 2. εἰσὶ δὲ δύο τρόποι τῶν πίστεων. γίνονται γὰρ αἱ μὲν ἐξ αὐτῶν τῶν λόγων καὶ τῶν πράξεων καὶ τῶν ἀνθρώπων, αἱ δ' ἐπίθετοι (adventitious) τοῖς λεγομένοις καὶ τοῖς πραττομένοις· (τὰ μὲν γὰρ εἰκότα καὶ παραδείγματα καὶ τεκμήρια καὶ ἐνθυμήματα καὶ γνῶμαι καὶ τὰ σημεῖα καὶ οἱ ἔλεγχοι πίστεις ἐξ αὐτῶν τῶν λόγων καὶ τῶν ἀνθρώπων καὶ τῶν πραγμάτων εἰσίν, ἐπίθετοι δὲ μαρτυρίαι ὅρκοι βάσανοι. The one therefore must be invented—hence the 'inventio' of Cicero and the Latin Rhetoricians—the others lie ready to hand and have only to be advantageously employed. Rhet. I. 2. 2.

And we can now proceed at once to the consideration of the two great instruments of all proof and reasoning alike, scientific or demonstrative and probable, syllogism and induction, or, in their rhetorical form, enthymeme and example.

All knowledge and instruction are acquired and conveyed by one or other of these two processes, syllogism, and induction; all belief rests upon principles so derived: the one is a demonstration (ἀπόδειξις) from universals, the other from particulars: universals (whether they *exist* independently or not, which is not here determined) can only be *known* to us by induction. Anal. Post. I. 18. δῆλον δὴ ὅτι ἡμῖν τὰ πρῶτα ἐπαγωγῇ γνωρίζειν ἀναγκαῖον. Ib. II. 19. 100. b. 3. At the commencement of the same treatise we are told that every method of teaching and learning rests alike upon preexisting knowledge: this is not only the case with Mathematical science and every other art (as he calls them), but the syllogism and induction of the dialectician are equally dependent upon previous knowledge (axioms and first principles), which the one (syllogism) takes for granted upon authority (ὡς παρὰ ξυνιέντων), whilst the other (induction) proves the universal from the knowledge which he has acquired of particulars from the clear evidence of sense. The 'persuasion' of the orator is produced by exactly the same processes; for his enthymeme is a form of syllogism, and his example of induction. To the same effect, in the Anal. Pr. II. 23. 68. b. 9. ὅτι δ' οὐ μόνον οἱ διαλεκτικοὶ καὶ ἀποδεικτικοὶ συλλογισμοὶ διὰ τῶν προειρημένων γίνονται σχημάτων (the 'figures' of the syllogism: it must be remembered that Aristotle reduces induction to a syllogistic process), ἀλλὰ καὶ οἱ ῥητορικοὶ καὶ ἁπλῶς ἡτισοῦν πίστις καὶ καθ' ὁποιανοῦν μέθοδον, νῦν ἂν εἴη λεκτέον. ἅπαντα γὰρ πιστεύομεν ἢ διὰ συλλογισμοῦ ἢ ἐξ ἐπαγωγῆς. Lastly, Eth. Nicom. VI. 3. ἐκ προγιγνωσκομένων δὲ πᾶσα διδασκαλία, ὥσπερ καὶ ἐν τοῖς ἀναλυτικοῖς λέγομεν· ἡ μὲν γὰρ δι' ἐπαγωγῆς, ἡ δὲ συλλογισμῷ. ἡ μὲν δὴ ἐπαγωγὴ ἀρχή ἐστι καὶ τοῦ καθόλου, ὁ δὲ συλλογισμὸς ἐκ τῶν καθόλου. εἰσὶν ἄρα ἀρχαὶ ἐξ ὧν ὁ συλλογισμός, ὧν οὐκ ἔστι συλλογισμός· ἐπαγωγὴ ἄρα[1]. Anal. Post. I. 18. 31—40. II. 19. 100. b. 2.

The enthymeme in Rhetoric occupies the place of the

[1] I have quoted this last clause partly on account of the bearing that it has on the question of the authorship of this 6th book of the Nicomachean Ethics. This is not the place to enter at length upon such an inquiry: I will only observe that there seems to be here a decided indication of non-Aristotelian authorship. I have in an earlier part of this introduction endeavoured to determine from the Posterior Analytics, where the question was most likely to be scientifically discussed, and the author's deliberate opinion stated, what Aristotle's views were upon the ultimate source and origin of our knowledge, and although from a careful consideration of the chapter in which these views are most explicitly stated, (Anal. Post. II. 19.) and from the unmistakable language of 100. b. 3., we were obliged to conclude that Aristotle held that all knowledge is ultimately derived from observation by induction, yet at the same time he seems to admit the necessity of some faculty, which is the νοῦς, to verify and authenticate by its intuitive intelligence the ultimate axioms on which all reasoning is founded, so that we may be enabled to depend absolutely upon their authority. But in this 6th book of the Nic. Eth. the writer seems to me to go beyond Aristotle, by asserting without qualification or modification 'that whereas there are principles of reasoning from which the syllogism (deductive reasoning) is derived, and these cannot be deduced by syllogism, there remains nothing but induction upon which they can rest.' Here induction is all in all, and the intuitive reason is nothing: the only organ of truth which is implied in this view is sensation, from which in the order of experience, memory, comparison, abstraction, generalization, the universal, we arrive at the ultimate and highest principle, beyond which we cannot rise.

syllogism in demonstration and dialectics; it is in fact the 'rhetorical demonstration,' ἔστι δ' ἀπόδειξις ῥητορικὴ ἐνθύμημα. Rhet. I. 1. 11. συλλογισμός τις, 'a kind of syllogism,' II. 22. 2. that is, not that it is a form of demonstration proper, but that it stands to the probable proofs of rhetoric in the same relation that demonstration does to science, as its principal instrument of proofs. The most explicit account of it is given in Rhet. I. 2. 9. After describing the syllogism[1] as "a conclusion from certain given premisses (of which the truth must be previously ascertained) that something else, and different from them (ἕτερον—this is denied by Mill and the opponents of Formal Logic, but we are here only concerned with Aristotle—) by reason of them (διὰ ταῦτα) and besides them (παρὰ ταῦτα), because they are what they are (τῷ ταῦτα εἶναι)," Aristotle continues " (a conclusion) either universal or (for the most part, ὡς ἐπὶ τὸ πολύ) general and probable, is called in the former case a syllogism, in the latter an enthymeme." So that it appears from this, as from Anal. Pr. II. 27, that the only *essential* difference between the two is that the one leads to a necessary and universal, the other only to a probable conclusion.

The definition of the rhetorical enthymeme given in the Anal. Pr. II. 27. is, omitting the interpolation ἀτελής, " a syllogism from probable propositions or signs:" (compare Rhet. I. 2. 14.) to which is added in Rhet. I. 2. 13. "and consisting of few propositions or premisses, and often of less than those of which the primary (or normal) syllogism is composed." The first of these is, as it is bound to be in a scientific treatise, the definition which expresses the essence of the enthymeme, that is, the genus, syllogism, and the differentia which distinguishes it from other kinds of syllogism. The distinctive difference is this, that its premisses and conclusions are never more than probable and contingent, which follows from the nature of its materials, human

---

[1] Compare Top. Λ. 1. 100. a. 25. ἔστι δὴ συλλογισμὸς λόγος ἐν ᾧ τεθέν- των τινῶν ἕτερόν τι τῶν κειμένων ἐξ ἀνάγκης συμβαίνει διὰ τῶν κειμένων.

actions, characters, motives, emotions. The addition to the definition in the Rhetoric, which has been usually regarded by Logicians as characteristic and essential, is not so in fact as Sir W. Hamilton has shown at length (Lect. on Logic, XX. Vol. I. p. 386. seq.); for a syllogism founded upon εἰκότα and σημεῖα, and expressed at full length with all its terms premisses and conclusion complete, would be just as much an enthymeme as the incomplete one, which wants one or other of these, in common use, the curtum enthymema of Juvenal[1]. Still the suppression of one or other of the premisses or of the conclusion is so invariably attendant upon its ordinary use, that it may at least be regarded as what Aristotle would have called a συμβεβηκὸς καθ᾽ αὑτό, "an inseparable accident" of the enthymeme; and as such Aristotle himself speaks of it, in the passage of the Rhetoric

---

[1] The view of the distinctive characteristic of rhetoric given in the text was adopted mainly in deference to the decided opinion expressed by Sir W. Hamilton. I am now however convinced that he is wrong, and return to the opinion which I had myself previously formed upon the question. If the only difference between the rhetorical enthymeme and the syllogism lay in the probability of the one and the certainty of the other, it would leave no distinction remaining between the dialectical syllogism and the rhetorical enthymeme: besides which the position is not true of the dialectical syllogism, whose materials and conclusions are all probable and nothing more. Plainly the difference between the two latter is one of *form*. The syllogism is complete in all its parts; the enthymeme incomplete; one of the premisses or the conclusion is *invariably* wanting. If further proof were needed, it would be found in this, that the relation of the example to induction is precisely similar. The example is an incomplete induction: a general inference derived from a *single instance*, instead of being collected from an exhaustive assemblage of similar instances. Again the argument, that a syllogism from probabilities expressed at full length would be just as much an enthymeme as the incomplete one, rests upon an utterly unfounded assumption, which assumes the theory to be proved, and presents us with another of those petitiones principii for which Sir W. Hamilton has lately become so famous (see Mill's Examination). *If*, as I affirm, and as Aristotle seems to imply also from insisting so much upon it in his Rhetoric, the characteristic distinction between enthymeme and dialectical syllogism *does* reside in the incompleteness of the former, the complete syllogism is *not* the same as the incomplete enthymeme.

above cited and the continuation of it. The examples that he gives here and in III. 17. 17. have, the one the major, the other the minor, premiss omitted: the two supplied by Trendelenburg from Seneca's Medea 934 (occidant; non sunt mei. Pereant? mei sunt. or dialectically, Non sunt mei; ergo occidant. Sunt mei; ergo non pereant.) both want the major premiss: see another example in Quintilian, v. 14. 26.: and similarly the illustrations of the enthymeme given by Sir W. Hamilton, Lect. on Logic, I. p. 392, and in Thomson's Laws of Thought § 120 p. 247, are all marked by this same characteristic, as it is in fact and in practice, though not theoretically, and therefore not included in the definition. Sir W. Hamilton likewise illustrates the enthymeme without conclusion. See also on this same subject Trendelenburg El. Log. Arist. § 38. p. 110. and on the divisions, use, and application of the enthymeme Rhet. II. 22.

In the Rhet. ad Alex. cc. 8 and 11, the enthymeme instead of one of the two kinds of rhetorical proof allied to logic, is considered (as by Isocrates and the orators in general, Spengel, not. ad loc. c. X.) as a peculiar species of $\pi i \sigma \tau \iota \varsigma$, one amongst many special $\tau \acute{o} \pi o \iota$ or classes of arguments, sententia cui qualiscunque $\dot{\epsilon} \nu a \nu \tau \acute{\iota} \omega \sigma \iota \varsigma$ est (Spengel, l. c.). "a proof drawn from any kind of opposition." $o \dot{\upsilon} \mu \acute{o} \nu o \nu \tau \grave{a} \tau \hat{\wp} \lambda \acute{o} \gamma \wp$ $\kappa a \grave{\iota} \tau \hat{\eta} \pi \rho \acute{a} \xi \epsilon \iota \dot{\epsilon} \nu a \nu \tau \iota o \acute{\upsilon} \mu \epsilon \nu a, \dot{a} \lambda \lambda \grave{a} \kappa a \grave{\iota} \tau o \hat{\iota} \varsigma \ \ddot{a} \lambda \lambda o \iota \varsigma \ \ddot{a} \pi a \sigma \iota \nu$. c. 11.[1] (Mansel, note on Hamilton, Logic, I. p. 390): the other $\pi \acute{\iota} \sigma \tau \epsilon \iota \varsigma$ being, $\epsilon \mathord{i} \kappa \acute{o} \tau a, \pi a \rho a \delta \epsilon \acute{\iota} \gamma \mu a \tau a, \tau \epsilon \kappa \mu \acute{\eta} \rho \iota a, \gamma \nu \hat{\omega} \mu a \iota, \sigma \eta \mu \epsilon \hat{\iota} a,$ $\ddot{\epsilon} \lambda \epsilon \gamma \chi o \iota$. Cicero, Topic. XIII. 55, admitting that the term enthymeme is properly applicable to every kind of sententia, "thought" or "saying, dictum," says that nevertheless as a rhetorical term it is confined to one particular kind of argument, ex contrariis conclusa, quæ ex contrariis conficiatur: this kind especially being designated 'enthymeme' par excellence, as the most acute smart and striking, just as

---

[1] This difference in the meaning affixed to 'Enthymeme' is of course, as Spengel has also remarked, one of the many proofs of diversity of authorship of Aristotle's Rhetoric, and the 'Ρητορικὴ πρὸς 'Αλέξανδρον.

Homer is called by the Greeks "*the* poet;" and he illustrates it by these examples,

> Hunc metuere? alterum in metu non ponere?
> Eam quam nihil accusas damnas; bene quam meritam esse autumas,
> Dicis male mereri?
> Id quod scis prodest nihil; id quod nescis obest.

"A reasoning from contraries or contradictories" Hamilton, l. c. This coincides with the meaning given to it by the author of the Rhet. ad Alex.; and also with one of the three, or four, assigned to it by Quintilian, v. 10. 1, viz. (1) omnia mente concepta, a thought in general (so Dionysius Halicarn., quoted by Hamilton, but by no means peculiar to that author) (2) sententia cum ratione (Aristotle's application of the term) (3) argumenti conclusio vel ex consequentibus vel ex repugnantibus: and these, omitting the first, are explained and illustrated, v. 14. 1., and again § 24. In v. 14. 1 the argumentum ex consequentibus appears to be identified with the sententia cum ratione of v. 10. 1; for the former is there called propositio conjunctaque ei protinus probatio, and again, ratio et propositio, and imperfectus syllogismus: and to this description the illustration from Cicero pro Ligario exactly corresponds. In VIII. 5. 9, the following description seems to be borrowed from Cicero's Topics. Enthymema quoque est omne quod mente concipimus: proprie tamen dicitur quæ est sententia ex contrariis; propterea quod eminere inter ceteras videtur ut Homerus *poeta*, *urbs* Roma.

As the enthymeme is an imperfect syllogism, so is the example an imperfect induction: the former omits either premiss or the conclusion; the latter instead of collecting its universal from all the known and accessible instances, contents itself with one or two, from which the universal is *inferred*.

The description of παράδειγμα 'example' as a logical argument is given in Anal. Pr. II. 24, and is in perfect accordance with the account given of it in Rhet. I. 2. It concludes not inductively from "the part to the whole," from the particular to the universal, nor deductively from "the whole to the part," from the universal to the particular, but from particular to particular, ὡς μέρος πρὸς μέρος. To take Aristotle's own instance. You wish to know whether a war between the Athenians and Thebans is an evil. You take an analogous case, ὑπὸ τὸ αὐτὸ καθόλου, in which the result is *known*, as the war between the Thebans and Phocians (D), which you know to have issued in the destruction of the latter, and therefore was certainly an evil. From this last known case you *infer* the general principle that all wars between neighbours are evils, and you can now construct your syllogism. A. evil. B. war between neighbours. C. a war between the Athenians and Thebans.

All wars between neighbours B. are evil A.
The war between the Ath. and Theb. C. is a war between neighbours B.
Therefore the war between the Ath. and Theb. will be an evil.

And the proof is from particular D. to particular C. through the universal assumed or supposed to be collected from D. (ληπτέον)[1]. It is also necessary for this kind of proof that the relation between the middle and the third term should be known. Aristotle had stated at the commencement of the chapter that an example is a case, ὅταν τῷ μέσῳ τὸ ἄκρον ὑπάρχον δειχθῇ διὰ τοῦ ὁμοίου τῷ τρίτῳ. "when it is shown by means of a term analogous to the third term that the extreme (major) is predicable of the middle." The conclusion of the general rule or principle from a single instance is of course a case of imperfect induction, just as the enthymeme is an imperfect syllogism: and the process of proof in the example is up and down,

---

[1] Compare Rhet. II. 25. 8. on παραδείγματα, Τὰ δὲ δι' ἐπαγωγῆς διὰ τοῦ ὁμοίου, ἢ ἑνὸς ἢ πλειόνων, ὅταν λαβὼν τὸ καθόλου εἶτα συλλογίσηται τὰ κατὰ μέρος διὰ παραδείγματος.

ascendendo and descendendo, from the known instance to the general rule and thence downwards to the particular conclusion required, and thus ὡς μέρος πρὸς μέρος. It is in fact an argument from analogy assuming the validity of a regular induction, and therefore no perfect demonstration but a mere probability. Waitz has this note on the passage, Vol. I. p. 533. Jam non demonstrat quod proposuit 68. b. 38. et quod exemplo demonstrari dicit 69. a. 11, predicari majorem terminum de medio; sed majorem minori tribuendum esse probat. Quod cur fecerit apparet ex iis quæ dicit vs. 19 de discrimine inductionis et exempli: nam per inductionem nihil probatur de termino minore; per exemplum de minore, quippe quem medius complectatur, comprobatur quod de medio valet. I have shown by the analysis of the process that *both these* are proved or assumed to be so. See likewise on the same subject Trendelenburg, Elem. Log. Arist. § 38. p. 111. also Thomson, Laws of Thought § 120. p. 249. "In the example the proof is not of one particular judgment by another, but of a particular by means of a universal for which another particular is the sign." and Sir W. Hamilton, Lect. on Logic. Appendix. Vol. II. p. 360.

Of the use and application and the several kinds of enthymemes an account is given in Rhet. II. 22.; the next chapter (23.) contains an enumeration of the principal τόποι, 'heads,' 'types,' of enthymemes, which may be employed either for direct categorical proof, or conversely and negatively in the way of refutation of the same argument: rhetoric being double edged and capable of being employed to prove ὁποτερονοῦν τῶν μορίων, either side of a question.

Of the two logical instruments that belong to rhetoric, ἐνθύμημα and παράδειγμα, the former is the more useful to the rhetorician, and more frequently employed: it is in fact the very body or substance of proof, σῶμα τῆς πίστεως, Rhet. I. 1. 3.; all the other modes of argument as well as style, arrangement, and delivery, being regarded for the nonce as non-essentials, accidents, or mere ornamental appendages, with neither strength nor weight, like the dress and external appliances as compared with the body itself[1]. Again in the same chapter, § 11., it is called κυριώτατον τῶν πίστεων the most valid and authoritative or convincing of rhetorical arguments, or means of persuasion. So the syllogism in dialectics is βιαστικώτερον, more cogent, and πρὸς τοὺς ἀντιλογικοὺς ἐνεργέστερον, though induction is πιθανώτερον, σαφέστερον, and κατὰ τὴν αἴσθησιν γνωριμώτερον, Top. A. 12. 105. a. 16.: and similarly in Rhet. I. 2. 10, πιθανοὶ μὲν οὖν οὐχ ἧττον οἱ λόγοι οἱ διὰ τῶν παραδειγμάτων, θορυβοῦνται δὲ μᾶλλον οἱ ἐνθυμηματικοί. In apparent contradiction to this is the assertion in Probl. XVIII. 3. that an audience is better pleased with examples, because an example is particular, and therefore 'nearer' and 'better known' to us, more within the compass of our ordinary knowledge and experience, just as it is described in the Topics, l. c.; whereas the enthymeme is an ἀπόδειξις ἐκ τῶν καθόλου ἃ ἧττον ἴσμεν ἢ τὰ μέρη[2].

ἨΘΟΣ.

So far of the strictly logical πίστεις, and their instruments[3]. Two other kinds of proof remain to be considered. The term ἦθος or ἤθη in Rhetoric, when applied in its ordinary sense, is employed to denote one of the three kinds of

---

[1] This contrast is more usually conveyed by opposing the soul, the source of life and activity, to the inert matter of the body. So in the Schol. ad Hermog. Prolegom. we find, οἱ παλαιοὶ ὥσπερ τι ζῷον τὸν λόγον ὑπέθεντο ἐκ σώματός τε συνεστηκότα καὶ ψυχῆς· ψυχὴν μὲν καλοῦντες τὰ ἐνθυμήματα καὶ τὴν δύναμιν τὴν διὰ τῶν κεφαλαίων συνισταμένην· σῶμα δὲ τὴν φράσιν καὶ τὸ ἔξωθεν κάλλος, ὃ ποιεῖν εἰώθασιν αἱ ἰδέαι.

[2] If I might venture to suggest a solution of this difficulty, it would be that different kinds of arguments may be suited to the taste of different kinds of audiences.

[3] The further consideration of the logical affinities of rhetoric, the analysis of fallacious syllogisms in II. 24, and of λύσις with its ἔλεγχος and ἐνστάσεις c. 25. I will postpone for the present, and take them in the order in which Aristotle himself has placed them as an appendix to the theory of πίστεις at the end of the second book.

arguments or modes of persuading into which all rhetorical proofs are divided, namely (1) πίστεις *direct* logical proofs which appeal to the reason, and *indirect* moral proofs of two kinds, those namely (2) which appeal to the moral sense and (3) to the feelings[1]. Of these two the former is the ἦθος ἐν τῷ λέγοντι or τοῦ λέγοντος, Rhet. I. 2. 3, 4., which consists in conveying to the audience a favourable impression of *your own* character (auctoritas, Quint. III. 8. 12), in making them believe *by the speech itself* that you are an honest man and incapable of misrepresenting the facts of the case, intelligent enough thoroughly to understand them, and well disposed to your hearers and their interests. In this way you express *your own character* in the speech; it is the ἦθος τοῦ λέγοντος that is herein represented. The third, the πάθη (affectus, Quint. u. s.), is employed for the purpose τοῦ τὸν ἀκροατὴν διαθεῖναί πως, of inspiring *the audience* with certain feelings, of putting them in a state of mind, favourable to yourself and adverse to your opponent. These three kinds of proof are all effected secundum artem by means of the speech itself, and are thereby distinguished from the ἄτεχνοι or unscientific, which are not invented by the speaker, but lie ready to hand requiring only to be employed to advantage. Now this kind of ἦθος is most important, nay essential, to the success of the speech: for the opinion of any audience as to the credibility of a speaker depends mainly upon the view they take of his intentions and character intellectual and moral; his ability to form a judgment, his integrity and truthfulness and his disposition towards themselves; to one they will listen with attention respect and favour; another, if they

---

[1] Rhet. I. 2. 3—5. Cicero, de Orat. II. 27. 115, 6. Ita omnis ratio dicendi tribus ad persuadendum rebus est nixa: ut probemus vera esse quæ defendimus; ut conciliemus nobis eos qui audiunt (ἦθος); ut animos eorum ad quemcunque causa postulabit motum vocemus (πάθος). Ad probandum autem duplex est oratori subjecta materies; una earum rerum quæ non excogitantur ab oratore, sed in re positæ ratione tractantur: . . . . . altera est, quæ tota in disputatione et argumentatione oratoris collocata est. On the same subject, Quintilian V. I. I. and the following.

look upon him as of the opposite character, they will regard with dislike and impatience and an inclination to disbelief and criticism. See also Rhet. I. 9. 1. and compare Rhet. I. 2. 3, 4 with the description of ἦθος in Bk. II. c. 1.

But besides this there are two other kinds of ἦθος that may be expressed in the speech, which must be distinguished from the preceding. To the first of these belong the ἤθη τῶν πολιτειῶν, in Rhet. I. 8. 6., and the characters enumerated and analysed in the series of chapters Bk. II. 12—17 inclusive. The object of the preceding was, as we have seen, to exhibit *the speaker's own character* in and by the speech so as to produce a favourable impression of his intelligence virtue and good intentions upon the audience, and in repeating the enumeration of the three kinds of proof in I. 2. 7. Aristotle speaks of the second as ἤθη καὶ τὰς ἀρετάς, meaning by 'the virtues' these same qualities, φρόνησις ἀρετή εὔνοια, and nothing else. But this second kind, the characters of constitutions or forms of government, and of the different periods of life, youth, manhood, old age, and the different orders and degrees of society, the rich, the well-born, the powerful, and so forth, are to be studied for the purpose of accommodating our language to the tone and sentiments prevailing under certain forms of government, and characteristic of or peculiar to certain ages and conditions of life, and thereby conciliating the audience when it happens to be composed of members of one or other of these classes. Thus democratic sentiments should be avoided before an audience which is known to hold aristocratic or monarchical views on the subject of government, and vice versa. The young and the old are actuated by different motives and differ in their principles and opinions: appeals to their understanding and feelings must be made in accordance with their known sentiments and habits of thought: and so on for the rest. That this is the true interpretation of this class of ἤθη as Aristotle meant it appears from Rhet. II. 13. 16. after the analysis of the characters of youth and age, in which he himself indicates its mode of application. τῶν μὲν οὖν νέων καὶ τῶν πρεσβυτέρων τὰ ἤθη τοιαῦτα· ὥστ' ἐπεὶ ἀποδέχονται πάντες τοὺς τῷ σφετέρῳ ἤθει λεγομένους λόγους καὶ τοὺς ὁμοίους, οὐκ ἄδηλον πῶς χρώμενοι τοῖς λόγοις τοιοῦτοι φανοῦνται καὶ αὐτοὶ καὶ οἱ λόγοι. Meaning—for the *expression* is incorrect, the reasoning from πρότασις to ἀπόδοσις being a non sequitur[1]—that as all men readily accept, like to hear, words and sentiments in accordance with their own character and resembling themselves, i.e. those that they themselves are in the habit of using, we may act upon this, for it is now clear enough how we must proceed in the endeavour to assume ourselves and impart to our speeches any of the characters above described[2]. Therefore although it is true that this latter species *may be* regarded merely as a variety of the former, yet it is certain that they are not identical; for though the latter in a sense may be referred to the ἦθος ἐν τῷ λέγοντι, yet it differs from the preceding both in the object aimed at and the kind of character that has to be assumed: unless indeed it be supposed that the assumption of the tone and sentiments of the different ages orders and degrees of our audiences, being designed to conciliate them, are all modes of showing our εὔνοια to them: but I cannot believe this to have been Aristotle's intention. The object of these chapters II. 12—17, and their connexion with the general scheme of proof which characterises Aristotle's rhetoric, is very clearly and concisely expressed by Brandis (in Schneidewin's Philologus, u. s. p. 5).

---

[1] Unless indeed we suppose that ἐπεὶ ἀποδέχονται πάντες is merely equivalent to ἀποδεχομένων πάντων, and that οὐκ ἄδηλον κ.τ.λ. is not intended to be a *consequence* of the protasis.

[2] It might almost seem as if Cicero had this very distinction in his mind when he wrote the following passage of the Orator, c. XXI. § 71. at all events it is in exact correspondence with our interpretation of Aristotle. Est autem quid deceat oratori videndum, non in sententiis solum sed etiam in verbis. Non enim omnis fortuna, non omnis honos, non omnis auctoritas, non omnis ætas, nec vero locus aut tempus *aut auditor omnis* eodem aut verborum genere tractandus est aut sententiarum, semperque in omni parte orationis, ut vitæ, quid deceat est considerandum: quod et in re de qua agitur positum est et in personis, et eorum qui dicunt, et *eorum qui audiunt*. (ἦθος ἐν τοῖς ἀκροωμένοις).

I have dwelt so long on this distinction, which is obvious enough in itself and plainly enough marked by Aristotle, because Spengel, to whose learning and acuteness all students of this author are so deeply indebted, has as it seems to me strangely confounded the two; and, overlooking the treatment of the ἤθη proper in II. 1., speaks of it as contained in the Chapters from 12 to 17 inclusive which form an appendix to the πάθη. See Spengel's paper in the Transactions of the Bav. Acad. 1851, über die Rhetorik des Aristoteles, pp. 30—32. But not only does this supposition disregard the marked difference between the two kinds of ἤθη, it also breaks through the order of treatment of the several branches of his subject which Aristotle seems to have proposed to himself; and as Spengel makes a great point of this proposed order in discussing the state of the text in reference to the order in which these very same modes of proof are placed by Aristotle, it does seem most especially incumbent upon him not to violate it himself. But this he does. He tells us that Aristotle in his introduction and elsewhere places these proofs in the order, πίστεις, i. e. εἴδη and τόποι, πάθη, ἤθη; transposing the two last in accordance with his view that Bk. II. cc. 12—17 contain the treatment of the ἤθη proper: but *Aristotle's* order as may be seen by reference to the passages, see particularly I. 2. 7., is πίστεις, ἤθη, πάθη, throughout. Compare II. 1, 2, 3, 4, and I. 9. 1. τὸ ἦθος, ἥπερ ἦν δευτέρα πίστις, which seem decisive on the point. And this also appears to be the natural order of treatment.

The third variety of ἦθος (different again from the preceding) which may be introduced into the speech belongs to *style*, and accordingly appears only in Bk. III. It is a kind of painting or ornament, but aids the proof in some slight degree by imparting to the speech an air of truthfulness and fidelity. It occurs usually and is most appropriate in the second division of the speech, διήγησις or narrative; and it is accordingly treated briefly under this head in Rhet. III. 16. 8, 9. When we have occasion to pourtray or describe any person, we ought to be acquainted not only with the special characteristics of the individual, but also with the generic marks which distinguish the class to which he belongs; whereby the narrative will gain in liveliness, our portrait or description in faithfulness, and our accuracy in these minutiæ will convey a favourable impression to the audience of our trustworthiness in general. This will be best illustrated by the author's own words, Rhet. III. 7. 6. Καὶ ἠθικὴ δὲ αὕτη ἡ ἐκ τῶν σημείων δεῖξις, ὅτι ἀκολουθεῖ ἡ ἁρμόττουσα ἑκάστῳ γένει καὶ ἕξει. λέγω δὲ γένος μὲν καθ' ἡλικίαν, οἶον παῖς ἢ ἀνὴρ ἢ γέρων, καὶ γυνὴ ἢ ἀνὴρ καὶ Λάκων ἢ Θετταλός, ἕξεις δὲ καθ' ἃς ποιός τις τῷ βίῳ· οὐ γὰρ καθ' ἅπασαν ἕξιν οἱ βίοι ποιοί τινες. That is, in representing or pourtraying any person whom we may want to notice or describe, we must take care to keep distinct the characteristics of age, sex, nationality, and moral character: and we should be sufficiently well acquainted with all these to be able duly to paint them with our words so as to give life and accuracy to the portraits that we draw. ἠθικὰ τὰ ἑπόμενα ἑκάστῳ ἤθει, οἷον ὅτι ἅμα λέγων ἐβάδιζεν· δηλοῖ γὰρ θρασύτητα καὶ ἀγροικίαν ἤθους. III. 16. 9. And this is the third method by which the speech may be made to express *character*. These are the dramatic ἤθη, character-drawing, which belongs equally to poetry and painting, and in tragedy is second in importance only to the μῦθος or plot. This was one of the excellences of Sophocles, who was said to be δεινὸς ἠθοποιεῖν. See Poetics, c. VI.; and on the 'characters' of tragedy, and their four requisites, moral goodness, propriety, resemblance (to the original), and consistency or keeping, Poet. c. XV.

ΠΑΘΟΣ.

As a sequel to the examination of the ἤθη, and preliminary to the consideration of the following chapters of the second book, 2—17, we will now give some account of the πάθη or moral affections as Aristotle understands them.

And first of πάθος in general. Πάσχειν, "to suffer something," is used to express the 'being in any state or condition, the having any feeling or *affection* whatsoever.' This most general sense is found in the ordinary language, as Arist. Pac. 696, of Sophocles, εὐδαιμονεῖ, πάσχει δὲ θαυμαστόν. he's affected in an extraordinary way, "he's in a wonderful state." Eur. Hippol. 340 ὦ παῖ, τί πάσχεις; "child, what ails thee?" What is thy mental condition? Arist. Rhet. II. 16. 1. πάσχοντές τι (affected in some way) ὑπὸ τῆς κτήσεως τοῦ πλούτου. Ib. § 2. εἰκότως τοῦτο πάσχουσιν "this feeling is natural to them." Hence πάθος, ὅ τι ἄν τις (or τι) πάσχῃ is an 'affection,' and hence 'quality' or 'property,' or even 'phenomenon' of any kind; and in this general sense it is applied not merely to men and their feelings and states bodily and mental, but to every variety of objects real or conceivable. It is sometimes any 'accident,' anything that can happen to, or belong to, any one or any thing, as in Plato, Parmen. 136. B. ὡς ὄντος καὶ οὐκ ὄντος καὶ ὁτιοῦν ἄλλο πάθος πάσχοντος, or anything that can be predicated of another, as even the finite and the infinite, Ibid. 158. E. At the opening of the seventh book of the Republic it stands for the imaginary state or condition of the denizens of the cave, ἀπείκασον τοιούτῳ πάθει τὴν ἡμετέραν φύσιν παιδείας τε πέρι καὶ ἀπαιδευσίας· ἰδὲ γάρ κ.τ.λ. and in c. 3. of the same book p. 518. B. it denotes 'all that has happened to a man,' or 'his soul,' τὴν μὲν εὐδαιμονίσειεν ἂν τοῦ πάθους τε καὶ βίου. 'properties' in Phileb. 17. D. ἐν ταῖς κινήσεσι τοῦ σώματος ἕτερα τοιαῦτα ἐνόντα πάθη.

We come now to Aristotle; who employs it like Plato to denote 'properties' or 'qualities' in general. So, according to the Pythagoreans, Metaph. A. 5. 985. b. 29. δικαιοσύνη is a πάθος, or property, of numbers, and two lines further on, "they perceived in numbers the properties and proportions (πάθη καὶ λόγους) of harmonies." 986. a. 5. τὰ τοῦ οὐρανοῦ πάθη καὶ μέρη. Ib. 17. τὸν ἀριθμὸν νομίζοντες ἀρχὴν εἶναι καὶ ὡς ὕλην τοῖς οὖσι καὶ ὡς πάθη καὶ ἕξεις. See also Γ. 2. 1004. b. 10. These πάθη Bonitz, on 985. b. 23., explains as πάθη καθ' αὑτά, ἴδια, οἰκεῖα, or συμβεβηκότα καθ' αὑτά, not inherent in the essence or definition, but 'inseparable accidents,' definitæ qualitates.

In Metaph. Δ. 21, this general signification of πάθος is narrowed to that of 'changeable qualities,' ποιότης καθ' ἣν ἀλλοιοῦσθαι ἐνδέχεται, as black and white, sweet and bitter, heavy and light, i. e. 'sensible' or 'secondary' qualities (Compare c. 24, 1020. b. 9.), and to the 'changes' themselves: and hence (he continues) the term πάθος in its ordinary acceptation of 'suffering' is applied par excellence to a special variety of these changes, viz. to injurious change, or change for the worse, and especially 'painful injuries,' and amongst these again, especially to 'the most serious calamities and pains,' 'sufferings and disasters,' τὰ μεγέθη τῶν ξυμφορῶν καὶ λυπῶν[1].

Thirdly, as applied to the mind and moral nature, πάθος is any natural *affection;* anything, feeling, sensation, thought, to which our minds (in the widest sense, ψυχαί) are naturally liable—quidquid animo accidit, Trendel. de Anim. p. 205—as a 'sensation' or 'impression on the senses', Categ. c. 8. p. 9. a. 28. seq.; and even νοεῖν 'thinking' is included, de Anim. I. 1. 11., on the supposition that it is not independent of φαντασία, and therefore connected with the bodily organs.

In this general application the πάθη are defined, de Anim. I. 1. 15. λόγοι ἔνυλοι or (as may be gathered from the context) εἴδη ἐν ὕλῃ τὸ εἶναι ἔχοντα καὶ οὐ χωριστά, "forms that have their essence or being in matter, and are inseparable from it." These "psychical phenomena," Grant, Essays

---

[1] If Aristotle will excuse me for differing from him, this is *not* the way in which πάθος acquires that meaning. 'Suffering' or 'being affected, in any way' is the primary and original sense of the word, and all the rest are derivative.

on Arist. Ethics, p. 236, act in and through the bodily organs, they are inseparable from the body and from material conditions—Compare the entire argument, de Anim. I. 1. 11—19. These are 'modes of consciousness,' 'properties' or 'phenomena' of ψυχή, in all its forms and phases, animal, mental, moral.

But we must now make a further distinction, and separate the moral from the sensible and intellectual πάθη; and we may call this subordinate variety 'the feelings, or affections, or sensibilities or emotions of our moral nature'; adding to the preceding definition οἷς ἕπεται ἡδονὴ καὶ λύπη as the distinctive *difference*. See Eth. Nicom. II. 4 (Bekk.) II. 5. 2. (Oxf.). Rhet. II. 1. 8.

We now turn to the psychical analysis in the two passages just referred to. The πάθη therein described are regarded as the fundamental elements or groundwork of our moral constitution: they lie dormant in the soul or mind until they are called into play by some exciting cause which stimulates them to active exercise, ἐνέργεια, and so actualises them. In the chapter of the Ethics they are merely enumerated, not defined. Besides the πάθη we have δυνάμεις and ἕξεις as constituent elements of our moral nature, and "it is *assumed* that every mode of the mind must be one of three things, either a feeling, a faculty, or a state." Grant, note on Eth. Nic. II. 5. 1. The πάθη are *passive* phenomena of our constitution: to call them into action we require δυνάμεις or faculties, καθ' ἃς παθητικοὶ (capable of feeling) τούτων λεγόμεθα, οἷον καθ' ἃς δυνατοὶ ὀργισθῆναι ἢ λυπηθῆναι ἢ ἐλεῆσαι. "Capacities of feeling those emotions when excited." And the ἕξεις, "the developed, acquired, settled, states, the fixed and determined habits", are *in a moral sense* virtues and vices according as these feelings and sensibilities have taken a right or a wrong direction, and have grown into confirmed states or habits, conformable to or deviating from the moral standard (the mean as determined by φρόνησις or ὁ φρόνιμος) under the influence of habit and education. [The reasons for not using the term "passions" to express these πάθη here or in any psychological analysis, are given by D. Stewart, Outlines of Mor. Phil. § 158., and Whewell, Elem. of Mor. § 64.]

Before quitting this subject I will quote some observations of Brandis (op. cit. p. 27) upon a comparison of the two lists of the πάθη given respectively in Eth. Nicom. II. 4. and in the second book of the Rhetoric. We need not be surprised, says Brandis, that the lists do not exactly correspond. Anger; love and hatred; fear and its opposite (or opposites), fearlessness, daring, rashness; mercy or compassion; envy; emulation, appear in both enumerations; but in the Ethics gratitude and a disposition to kindness and benevolence (χάρις), as well as modesty and its opposite shamelessness, are omitted; and also νέμεσις, righteous indignation at unmerited success or prosperity—but this last, together with αἰδώς, is added at the end to the list of *virtues* in the analysis of Eth. II. 7., where they are introduced (not as virtues, but as πάθη) because they conform to the law of the mean. Brandis has omitted to notice this, as well as the curious fact that πραότης which is a virtue or ἕξις in the Ethics is entered amongst the πάθη, as the opposite to ὀργή, in Bk. II. of the Rhetoric—but all this only tends to show the great vacillation and inconsistency of Aristotle's views on the psychological department of Ethics, which Sir A. Grant points out in his Essays on the Ethics. The place of these omitted πάθη is supplied in the Ethical enumeration by the insertion of ἐπιθυμία, χαρά, and πόθος. The second of these, joy, is left out in the Rhetoric, as Brandis thinks, because it is an emotion not easily excited by rhetoric, or at any rate that element of it in which it is distinguished from pleasure, which required a separate treatment in another place. πόθος is only a variety of ἐπιθυμία: and the omission of these from the list of πάθη in the Rhetoric, whilst it is included in that of the Ethics, is due again to Aristotle's indistinct conception of the true nature of these πάθη, so that his opinions on the subject are determined by the particular object which at the time he happens to have in view. Hence in the Ethics, where his object is merely to distinguish the faculties and affections from the ἕξεις or permanent states, in order to show that virtue is to be included amongst the last, he might very well introduce 'desire' and 'longing' amongst the πάθη; whilst in the Rhetoric he excluded them from it, and connected his examination of them with the treatment of pleasure and pain in I. 11—which is in fact a more suitable place for them, seeing that it is pleasure and pain that give occasion to their manifestation.

THE THREE BRANCHES OF RHETORIC.

Leaving for the present the εἰκότα, σημεῖα, the probable materials of enthymemes, and τεκμήρια, constant, inseparable signs, the only, and those rare, cases in which a necessary conclusion can be drawn by rhetoric, till we come upon the exposition of them in the place assigned to them by Aristotle himself in his Introduction I. 2. 14—18[1], we will now proceed to describe the three kinds of rhetoric, with their several characters, objects, and materials, and the topics general and special which are either common to all of them, τόποι, κοινοὶ τόποι, or peculiar and appropriated to each, εἴδη.

Rhetoric has three branches, a division which is determined by the characters of the several kinds of audiences which the orator has to address, and by the end, τέλος, which he has consequently to keep in view in each case[2]. Every

---

[1] See below, p. 159. seq.

[2] Arist. Rhet. I. 3. 1. Cic. de Invent. I. 5. 7. de Orat. I. 31. 141. Quint. III. 3, 14. 4, 1. Aristotle appears to have been the first who made this division, and distinguished the Epideictic or declamatory, demonstrativum genus, from the deliberative and the forensic branches. This may be *inferred* from Cic. de Inv. I. 5. 7. and Quintilian II. 21. 23. III. 7. 1. It is directly stated, III. 4. 1. Theon, Progymn. ap. Spengel, Rhet. Gr. II. 61. τῆς γὰρ ὑποθέσεως εἴδη τρία, ἐγκωμιαστικόν, ὅπερ ἐκάλουν ἐπιδεικτικὸν οἱ περὶ Ἀριστοτέλην, δικανικόν,

rational action, and every artistic procedure, looks to an end, and by that end is determined.

The first and noblest, though hitherto neglected, branch is the συμβουλευτικὸν γένος, so called because its principal object and materials is deliberation, and hence in Latin it is deliberativum genus: again, because it is principally employed in addressing public assemblies it receives the name of δημηγορία (Rhet. III. 16. 11. III. 17. 5.) or τὸ δημηγορικὸν γένος, τὰ δημηγορικά (Rhet. I. 1. 10. alib.), and sometimes from the Latin Rhetoricians, as Cicero and Quintilian, of concio, or genus concionale. (Quint. III. 4. 1 in III. 8. 14, 15. He thinks that this is too narrow a view to take of this branch, nam et consultantium et consiliorum *plurima* sunt genera): and lastly from its office of προτροπή and ἀποτροπή, suadendi et dissuadendi, it is sometimes called προτρεπτικόν and suasoria oratio. (Quint. III. 8. 6.)[1] The counsellor's function, ἔργον, is to exhort or recommend and dissuade, συμβουλῆς τὸ μὲν προτροπὴ τὸ δὲ ἀποτροπή; his end, τέλος, object or aim, τὸ συμφέρον καὶ βλαβερόν, the expedient or advantageous and injurious or pernicious, Political Expediency: (all the objects of deliberation are in the category of quality, says Quintilian, VII. 4. 2., facienda ac non facienda: appetenda vitanda: quæ in suasorias quidem maxime cadunt, sed in controversiis quoque sunt frequentia: hac sola differentia, quod illic de futuris, hic de factis agitur. conf. Rhet. I. 6. 1. On the τέλη Cic. de Inv. II. 4. 12 and 51 and 156. Topic. XXIV. 91. The Auct. ad Herenn. III. 2. 3. reduces the three τέλη to one, utilitas, subdivided into tutum et honestum[2]). With respect to these τέλη in general it may be

συμβουλευτικόν. On the division of the 'Ρητ. πρὸς Ἀλέξ., double or triple, see Spengel in his note on the (so called) art of Anaximenes, p. 99. and 228. Also Art. Script. p. 182.

[1] It is probable that a general's speech to his soldiers comes under this head: it is at any rate of a hortatory kind. Aristotle never mentions it.

[2] The Rhet. ad Alex. makes the τέλη of deliberative rhetoric six in number: τὸν προτρέποντα χρὴ δεικνύειν that the objects of his recommendation are just, legal, expedient, fair and noble (καλά), pleasant, and easy of

observed that the author does not mean absolutely to confine any one of them to a special branch, and Cicero in the passages of the de Invent. above quoted includes the honestum with the utile as the object of the genus deliberativum; they all συμπαραλαμβάνουσι τὰ ἄλλα, take in the rest as adjuncts and subordinate considerations, the special τέλος being *characteristic*, and the most prominent object of the genus. The *time* of the public speaker is the future. Demosthenes adds τὸ παρόν 'the present fact' to τὸ μέλλον as the object of the σύμβουλος, τὸ δὲ μέλλον ἢ τὸ παρὸν τὴν τοῦ συμβούλου τάξιν ἀπαιτεῖ. de Cor. p. 292 § 192. and, by implication, de Pace, at the opening. And this 'present time' is likewise slipt in, contrary to the theory, by Aristotle himself, I. 6. 1. προτρέποντα ὡς ἐσομένων ἢ ὑπαρχόντων; and again, I. 8. 7. Deliberative rhetoric, as we have seen, derives one of its names, τὸ δημηγορικόν, from the circumstance of its being usually addressed to public assemblies and on subjects of national interest. Theoretically speaking however this need not be so, though practically it is for the most part thus limited. For in the first place advice may be given privately, which is just as much προτροπή and ἀποτροπή as the other. Rhet. I. 3. 3. II. 18. 1.: and secondly, in some cases the distinction between the συμβουλευτικόν and the ἐπιδεικτικὸν γένος almost vanishes, as in Isocrates' Panegyric and Panathenaic speeches, each of which was addressed to a national assembly, and the former designed to recommend a national policy, union against the Persians. The end of these is *ostensibly* τὸ συμφέρον, political expediency, and the time referred to, the future. But the real object of the speaker is the display of his own powers of composition, and so *immediate* or present, and therefore these are properly referred to the head of declamatory or epideictic speeches, made for ostentation's sake and to gain applause.

This branch of oratory must plainly derive its materials,

attainment: and ὁ ἀποτρέπων must show that the course from which he dissuades is the opposite of all these.

And the ends of the epideictic kind are the same. c. 2. § 4. c. 4. § 1.

εἴδη or προτάσεις, chiefly from Politics in its narrower or special sense.

The second branch of Rhetoric is addressed to one or more judges, and is called τὸ δικανικόν or δικαστικόν, judicial or forensic speaking, judiciale or forense genus, practice in the law courts and before judicial tribunals. It comprises accusation and defence as its parts, κατηγορία and ἀπολογία: its τέλος is τὸ δίκαιον καὶ ἄδικον; justice in accusation, injustice, or rather the removal of it, in defence. (This seems the only way of explaining the *double* end: though it is plain that justice in either case is the real object—no one avowedly aims at injustice—and the other is added in all probability merely to make the end of this parallel to the other two): and its time is the past; (comp. Quint. VII. 2. 3) for accusation and defence must always turn upon acts already committed. This is the kind of rhetoric which occupied according to Aristotle nearly the whole attention, and the entire arts or τέχναι, of his predecessors; because, Rhet. I. 1. 10, this kind of practice admits of more sophistry and chicanery than the deliberative—ἧττόν ἐστι κακοῦργον ἡ δημηγορία.

The forensic kind of rhetoric plainly requires the study of some parts of Ethics, as the theory of Justice; and Jurisprudence, which belongs to Politics.

The third branch is inferior to the two preceding in extent, importance and interest. It is the ἐπιδεικτικὸν γένος, demonstrativum genus, the demonstrative, showy, ostentatious, declamatory kind: so called because speeches of this sort are composed for 'show' or 'exhibition', ἐπίδειξις, and their object is to display the orator's powers, and to amuse an audience (Quint. VIII. 3. 11.)—who are therefore θεωροί rather than κρίται, like spectators at a theatre, or a contest for a prize, Rhet. II. 18. 1. I. 3. 2—rather than any serious interest or real issue at stake[1]. This is sometimes called πανήγυρις or

---

[1] From this arises a twofold division of rhetoric into πραγματικόν, where there *is* some real interest at stake, or ἀγωνιστικόν, where there is a

τὸ πανηγυρικόν (as by Dionysius, Ars Rhet. VIII. 4. Nicol. Soph. Progymn. ap. Spengel, Rhet. Gr. III. 477. Syrian. ad Hermog. ap. Speng. ad Rhet. ad Alex. p. 99. and Art. Scr. p. 184.) because these ἐπιδείξεις were often delivered at the πανηγύρεις, the general assemblies at Olympia and the other national games. It also sometimes goes by the name of ἐγκωμιαστικόν or laudatory. To this class belong funeral orations[1], πανηγυρικοὶ λόγοι, speeches for the πανηγύρεις, and panegyrics in the modern sense (of which Isocrates' ἐγκώμιον Ἑλένης is an instance); and in general, literary compositions in rhetorical or periodic style which have no practical purpose in view—whence it is said of them, Rhet. III. 12. 5. ἡ μὲν οὖν ἐπιδεικτικὴ λέξις γραφικωτάτη· τὸ γὰρ ἔργον αὐτῆς ἀνάγνωσις—they are meant rather to be read. Quintilian thus characterises this branch of rhetoric. Ubi emolumentum non in utilitate aliqua, sed in sola laude consistit. Inst. Orat. III. 8. 7. Tota est ostentationis. Ib. § 63. Well known examples are the speeches in Plato's Phædrus and Symposium; most of Isocrates' speeches, and such like. Cicero, Orat. II. 37. (Compare XIII. 42.) comprises under the head of ἐπιδείξεις, laudationes scriptiones historiæ et tales suasiones qualem fecit Isocrates Panegyricum. Sometimes these laudationes assumed the aspect of a burlesque, and we read of Polycrates, who had a reputation for the composition of these ἔπαινοι, writing one in praise of mice (Rhet. II. 24. 6.), another in commendation of pots, χύτραι, and a third of counters, ψῆφοι (mentioned by Menander the Rhetorician): an encomium upon salt, ἅλες, is noticed by Plato, Symp. 177 B, and Menander περὶ ἐπιδ., without the author's name; and the same is again referred to, together with another upon humble bees, βομβυλιοί, by Isocrates, Helen. § 12.[2] A pane-

struggle or effort, which implies something substantial at issue; and ἐπιδεικτικόν, where the end is mere display. Syrianus ad Hermog. ap. Spengel, Art. Script. p. 184.

[1] On Plato's Menexenus, and funeral orations in general, see Grote's Plato, Vol. III. ch. 31.

[2] This distinction of serious and burlesque ἐπιδείξεις is noted by Ari-

gyric upon the lyre by Lycophron the Sophist is mentioned by Alexander Aphrod. in his Commentary on Soph. El. 174. b. 30. There were also ἐγκώμια παράδοξα, as that of Alcidamas upon death. He wrote another in praise of poverty, and a third περὶ Πρωτέως τοῦ κυνός. Menander. περὶ ἐπιδεικτικῶν. ap. Speng. Rhet. Gr. III. 346.

Of this branch ἔπαινος and ψόγος are the constituent parts; its τέλος, τὸ καλὸν καὶ αἰσχρόν, honour and dishonour, the noble and the base, fair and foul, right and wrong: and its time, the present.

Here again some acquaintance with Ethics, which determines what is καλὸν and what αἰσχρόν, is necessarily required.

And thus it appears that in all the three branches alike the materials which the orator handles, his εἴδη or special topics, must be almost entirely derived from Politics, the science which treats of man in his social condition, ἡ περὶ τἀνθρώπινα φιλοσοφία, Eth. Nic. X. 10. sub fin., "the study of human conditions and of the relation of man to man in society," and therefore includes Ethics, which analyses human nature in the individual, investigates his functions, ἔργον, and his character, ἦθος, and habits, his end and aim, τέλος, and thence prescribes his rule of conduct. So that not only do the two kinds of moral (or immoral) proof, the assumption of a virtuous character, and appeals to the feelings, require some knowledge of Ethics, but we now see that no reasoning in any of the three branches of rhetoric can be carried on without it; and we are entitled to conclude, ὥστε συμβαίνει τὴν ῥητορικὴν οἷον παραφυές τι τῆς διαλεκτικῆς εἶναι καὶ τῆς περὶ τὰ ἤθη πραγματείας, ἣν δίκαιόν ἐστι προσαγορεύειν πολιτικήν. Rhet. I. 2. 7. And of these two, dialectics gives the *form*, Politics supplies the *matter*.

stotle, Rhet. I. 9. 2. ἐπεὶ δὲ συμβαίνει καὶ χωρὶς σπουδῆς καὶ μετὰ σπουδῆς ἐπαινεῖν πολλάκις οὐ μόνον ἄνθρωπον ἢ θεὸν ἀλλὰ καὶ ἄψυχα καὶ τῶν ἄλλων ζῴων τὸ τυχὸν κ.τ.λ.

ΤΟΠΟΙ, ΕΙΔΗ, ΣΤΟΙΧΕΙΑ.

And this brings us to the consideration of the form which these materials assume in a system of rhetoric, when they appear as τόποι or κοινοὶ τόποι and εἴδη, general and specific topics.

The object and use of τόποι in general is to aid the memory. Top. Θ. 14. 163. b. 24. Cicero, Top. § 2, speaks of Aristotle's Topics as, disciplina inveniendorum argumentorum. See also de Orat. II. 86. 354. and 358, and on the use of τόποι, Rhet. II. 22. 10.

But first of the meaning of the term τόπος, locus, or topic.

This is very clearly stated by Cicero and Quintilian. The former in his Topics, II. 7., gives the following explanation: ut igitur earum rerum quæ absconditæ sunt demonstrato et notato loco facilis inventio est; sic quum pervestigare argumentum aliquod volumus, locos nosse debemus: sic enim appellatæ ab Aristotele sunt hæ quasi sedes e quibus argumenta promuntur. Itaque licet definire locum esse argumenti sedem. In de Orat. II. 34. 147. the τόποι are compared to the haunts of game; atque hoc totum est sive artis sive animadversionis sive consuetudinis nosse regiones intra quas venere et pervestiges quod quæras. Ubi eum locum omnem cogitatione sæpseris, si modo usu rerum percallueris, nihil te effugiet, atque omne quod erit in re occurret atque incidet; and again, § 174, to veins or mines, where metals may be looked for; ut enim si aurum cui, quod esset multifariam defossum, commonstrare vellem, satis esse deberet si signa et notas ostenderem locorum, quibus cognitis ipse sibi foderet, et id quod vellet parvulo labore, nullo errore, inveniret: sic has ego argumentorum notas quærenti demonstravi ubi sint: reliqua cura et cogitatione eruuntur: and in de Fin. IV. 4. 10. they are further compared to stores or thesauri which may be had recourse to on occasion for a supply of arguments; e quibus locis quasi thesauris argumenta depromerentur. Quintilian, V. 10. 20—22 is particularly distinct in his explanation, which is exactly to the same purport as Cicero's, and perhaps borrowed from him. Locos appello...sedes argumentorum quibus latent (lurk, like wild beasts; where *game* is to be looked for), ex quibus sunt petenda. Next they are compared with the haunts or regions where animals of any particular kind may be found when wanted. Nam ut in terra non omni generantur omnia, nec avem aut feram reperias ubi quæque nasci aut morari soleat ignarus; et piscium quoque genera alia planis gaudent, alia saxosis, regionibus etiam litoribusque discreta sunt, nec helopem nostro mari aut scarum ducas; ita non omne argumentum undique venit, ideoque non passim quærendum est. Multus alioqui error, et exhausto labore quod non ratione scrutabimur non poterimus invenire nisi casu. At si scierimus ubi quodque nascatur, quum ad locum ventum erit facile quod in eo est pervidebimus. Lastly Aristotle himself, Rhet. II. 26. 1. describes τόπος as a head or genus under which many enthymemes or rhetorical arguments fall or are collected; τόπος, εἰς ὃ πολλὰ ἐνθυμήματα ἐμπίπτει[1].

A τόπος therefore is a 'place' or 'region,' *the* place where you may look for something you want with the certainty of finding it, or a store which may be drawn upon to meet an occasional requirement: and in its application to rhetoric means a 'head' (capita, Cic. de Orat. II. 34. 146) or 'genus' or general conception, which includes under it a large stock of special arguments of the same kind. The advantage of referring special arguments to these general heads, is that you know where to find them when wanted, like game in their haunts, or metal in a metalliferous district or in a vein,

---

[1] Theon, in his Progymn. c. 7. περὶ τόπου, (Spengel. Rhet. Gr. II. 106.) gives a different version of the metaphor. According to him 'place,' means 'head quarters' or 'the place from which you sally out to attack an enemy,' and equivalent to ἀφορμή: and τόπος has accordingly been defined by some, ἀφορμὴν ἐπιχειρημάτων. But this explanation is neither so natural, nor so applicable to the circumstances of the case as that of Cicero and Quintilian.

or any plant or animal in the particular habitat or region to which it belongs; or like goods in a store, or arms and ammunition in a magazine or arsenal: *the* place where they may all be found. A passage of Cicero, de Orat. II. 30. 130. may be quoted in further explanation of the term itself and the use of topics. As in writing, we ought to have the letters that we require to use ready at hand, and not to be obliged to hunt about for them whenever we want them; so when a case is to be argued we should have a stock of arguments all ready classified, arranged in 'places' where we can make sure of finding them, and ticketed and labelled as it were in their repository, or like bottles in the bins of a cellar, so that they offer themselves to us at once as soon as they are required. And to precisely the same effect, XXXIV. § 146.

But we have next to notice a distinction between different kinds of τόποι, which as far as Rhetoric is concerned is peculiar to Aristotle's system. Τόποι as a general term is subdivided into εἴδη special or specific, and τόποι proper, or κοινοὶ τόποι universal topics: and τόπος is frequently used in *both* these senses. The εἴδη or ἴδια, the specific topics, are as he expressly tells us Rhet. I. 2. 21, so called because they are species or kinds subordinate to and forming part of the several sciences, chiefly Ethics and Politics, which come in contact with rhetoric and furnish it with its propositions, προτάσεις, and enthymemes. As distinguished from these, the τόποι or κοινοὶ τόποι are those general topics of argument which are universally applicable to all sciences, the εἴδη being confined each to its own; since no ethical enthymemes can be applied to physical subjects and vice versa: but the topics of degree, τοῦ μᾶλλον καὶ ἧττον, of amplification and depreciation, τοῦ αὔξειν καὶ μειοῦν, of past and future, of possible and impossible, which are *the* topics, τόποι, or κοινοὶ τόποι 'universal' topics, are alike applicable to all the materials of the several sciences from which the εἴδη are derived, and are thus 'common' to all. Aristotle's language is so very distinct on this point in the passage quoted that it cannot be mistaken. λέγω γὰρ διαλεκτικούς τε καὶ ῥητορικοὺς συλλογισμοὺς εἶναι περὶ ὧν τοὺς τόπους (the κοινοὶ τόποι of degree, probability and improbability and the rest, as appears immediately afterwards from the *example* given οἷον ὁ τοῦ μᾶλλον καὶ ἧττον τόπος) λέγομεν· οὗτοι δ' εἰσὶν οἱ κοινῇ περὶ δικαίων (Ethical) καὶ φυσικῶν (Physical) καὶ περὶ πολιτικῶν (Political) καὶ περὶ πολλῶν διαφερόντων εἴδει (i. e. *special* sciences) οἷον ὁ τοῦ μᾶλλον καὶ ἧττον τόπος. I. 2. 20, and again, § 22. λέγω δὲ εἴδη μὲν τὰς καθ' ἕκαστον γένος (of sciences, Ethics, Politics, Physics, &c.) ἰδίας προτάσεις, τόπους δὲ τοὺς κοινοὺς ὁμοίως πάντων (i. e. the κοινοὶ τόποι and the τόποι ἐνθυμημάτων of cc. II. 23. and 24.). Nevertheless Schrader, on II. 20. 1., and Spengel, in Trans. of Bav. Acad. p. 38, where this is distinctly *implied*, conceive the name εἴδη to be applied to the former because they are species of each of the three *genera of rhetoric*, the κοινοὶ τόποι being universally applicable to all three. It is perfectly true that Aristotle does so *treat* the ethical or political εἴδη, as subordinate to the three divisions or branches of rhetoric, and it is equally true that the κοινοὶ τόποι are common alike to all three, and that they *might* therefore have been so called for the reason assigned: but the language of the second chapter above referred to leaves no doubt that *Aristotle* gives them the name of εἴδη because they are species subordinate to the several sciences, from which they are borrowed, as genera, and not because they happen to be treated under the heads of the three branches of rhetoric.

Another term by which they are frequently designated is στοχεῖα, as in Rhet. I. 2. 22. ult. I. 6. 1. II. 26. 1. II. 22. 12. στοιχεῖον for τόπος is found likewise in the Topics. Δ. 1. 121. b. 11. c. 6. 128. a. 22. Z. 5. 143. a. 13. c. 14. 151. b. 18. and Cicero has, Top. IV. 25. locis...tanquam elementis quibusdam. The reason why they are so called appears from the Chapter on στοιχεῖον, Metaph. Z. 3. στοιχεῖον is an 'ultimate element', something either altogether indivisible, or divisible only into *similar parts*. The term may be variously applied, as in a language to its ultimate divisions, or letters; in bodies, to their elements, indivisible component parts, or atoms; in geometry to points, στιγμαί, the ultimate elements of space; in reasoning or proof, to the simplest and normal form of syllogism, the first figure: and in the Anal. Post. I. 23. 84. b. 22. it stands for ἄμεσοι προτάσεις, propositions 'immediately' or intuitively apprehended, 'without the intervention of the middle term', when subject and predicate are seen simultaneously by the νοῦς or intuitive reason.

A τόπος therefore, the genus or head of a multitude of *similar* and individual τόποι of the same kind, may be called a στοιχεῖον or 'element' of enthymematic reasoning, because it is only further divisible into *similar* parts, and thus corresponds with the definition of the latter. And this will enable us to enter fully into Aristotle's meaning when he says, Rhet. II. 26. 1. τὸ γὰρ αὐτὸ λέγω στοιχεῖον καὶ τόπον· ἔστι γὰρ στοιχεῖον καὶ τόπος, εἰς ὃ πολλὰ ἐνθυμήματα (many enthymemes *of the same kind*) ἐμπίπτει, and in II. 22. 12. στοιχεῖον δὲ λέγω καὶ τόπον ἐνθυμήματος τὸ αὐτό. And these are the heads of families of similar enthymemes which are enumerated and exemplified in II. c. 23.[1]

There are accordingly three kinds of τόποι; (1) the εἴδη, the special materials, or specific premisses, derived mainly from Politics and Ethics; these may also be designated by the general name, as they are in Rhet. II. 22. 16, τόποι τῶν εἰδῶν. Most enthymemes are derived from the εἴδη, I. 2. 22. and the latter are expressly distinguished from the τόποι ἐνθυμημάτων. III. 1. 1. ἔστι γὰρ τὰ μὲν εἴδη τῶν ἐνθυμημάτων, τὰ δὲ τόποι[2]. (2) The second kind is the κοινοὶ τόποι, or τόποι alone, for the general name is applied alike to all. These are so called, because, as we have seen, they

---

[1] Waitz in his note on στοιχεῖον, Comment. ad Organ. 84. b. 21. omits to explain the application of the term to 'topics': nor does Bonitz. ad Metaph. 1014. b. 3—6. supply the deficiency.

[2] On εἴδη, and τόποι in general, see Poste, Introd. to Transl. of Anal. Post. p. 24.

can be applied to all the materials of Rhetoric, and to its three branches alike. They are four in number, Rhet. II. 18. 3—5. and c. 19. possible and impossible, δυνατὸν καὶ ἀδύνατον; fact past and future, τὸ γεγονὸς καὶ τὸ μέλλον; degree, τὸ μᾶλλον καὶ ἧττον; and amplification and depreciation, τὸ αὔξειν καὶ μειοῦν. These are 'common', to the εἴδη the materials of Rhetoric and to its three branches; κοινὰ γὰρ ταῦτα πάντων τῶν λόγων, Rhet. I. 12. 2. περὶ τῶν κοινῶν, II. 18. 2. They are analysed and exemplified in II. c. 19. and from them of course are to be distinguished the κοιναὶ πίστεις of the succeeding chapter, which are the two universal instruments of proof, enthymeme and example. These general τόποι can be applied to the εἴδη, and also employed as τόποι ἐνθυμημάτων—see II. 23. 4, 5—or as τόποι of fallacious enthymemes, as δείνωσις in II. 24. 4. The distinction between the εἴδη and κοινοὶ τόποι is very clearly stated in Rhet. I. 3. The former are the special materials of the orator's enthymemes, and may be classified under the heads of the three branches of rhetoric; although the name is really given to them because they are *species*, or specific topics, of the γένος or science to which they severally belong. They are the topics to which the three τέλη of the several branches of rhetoric, τὸ συμφέρον καὶ βλαβερόν, or in other words, τὸ ἀγαθὸν καὶ κακόν, τὸ δίκαιον καὶ ἄδικον, τὸ καλὸν καὶ αἰσχρόν, give rise. The κοινοὶ τόποι, four in number, which are enumerated and determined in § 8, are common to all these, and in so far *universally* applicable to the εἴδη *and* to the three divisions of rhetoric. (3) Thirdly we have the τόποι ἐνθυμημάτων and φαινομένων ἐνθυμημάτων which are to be distinguished from the two preceding; heads of families of similar arguments out of which enthymemes may be constructed. Some of these are 'common topics', in the sense of their being applicable to all the three branches of rhetoric; others are confined to the dicastic branch. All of them may be used either way, argued either on the affirmative or negative side, II. 23. 1. Rhetoric τἀναντία συλλογίζεται.

The communes loci of Cicero and Quintilian and the Latin Rhetoricians seem to be more comprehensive, and capable of a more extensive application than those of Aristotle's three divisions. They are thus defined by Cicero, Orat. 36. § 136. qui communes appellati sunt eo quod videntur multarum iidem esse causarum, sed proprii singularum esse debebunt; de Orat. III. 27. 106. quia de universâ re tractari solent: and are illustrated by examples in various places, Cic. de Orat. III. 27. 106, 7. de Invent. II. 16. 50. Auct. ad Herenn. II. 3, 5. 9, 13. 10, 14. 15, 22. 16, 24. 17, 26. 30, 48, 9. Quint. v. 12. 15, 6. From these examples it seems that any subject or topic of a general character, that is capable of being variously applied and constantly introduced on any appropriate occasion, is a locus communis; any common current maxim, or alternative proposition, such as rumoribus credi oportere et non oportere, suspicionibus credi oportere et non oportere, testibus credi oportere et non oportere et similia de Invent. l. c.: compare the passages of the Auct. ad Heren. Again invidia, avaritia, testes inimici, potentes amici, (Quintil.) may furnish loci communes; or they may be constructed de virtute, de officio, de æquo et bono, de dignitate, utilitate, honore, ignominia, and on other moral topics. Cic. de Or. III. 27. 107. u. s. To the same effect Hermogenes, Progymn. c. 6. ap. Spengel. Rhet. Gr. vol. II. p. 9. κοινὸς τόπος λέγεται, διότι ἁμόττει περὶ παντὸς μὲν ἱεροσύλου (for example), ὑπὲρ παντὸς δὲ ἀριστέως. This use of communes loci is also exemplified in the orations or "School Exercises" (Müller. H. G. L. c. XXXIII. § 2.) of Antiphon. See for example de Cæd. Herod. § 87, and § 14, compared with περὶ τοῦ χορευτ. § 3 and § 2. where the same τόπος is repeated in nearly the same words, and applied to two similar cases. These loci communes were sometimes illustrated by examples of the mode of treating them rhetorically by the teachers of the rhetorical schools, such as Protagoras, Gorgias and Antiphon himself, and given to the pupils as models of argument or of style to be committed to memory. Such loci communes are referred to by Aristotle in a passage, de Soph. El. c. 34. 183. b. 36. seq. previously quoted, p. 3. not., but not under that name; λόγους γὰρ οἱ μὲν ῥητορικοὺς οἱ δὲ ἐρωτητικοὺς (dialectical) ἐδίδοσαν ἐκμανθάνειν, εἰς οὓς πλειστάκις ἐμπίπτειν ᾠήθησαν ἑκάτεροι τοὺς ἀλλήλων λόγους....οὐ γὰρ τέχνην ἀλλὰ τὰ ἀπὸ τῆς τέχνης διδόντες παιδεύειν ὑπελάμβανον κ. τ. λ. and this practice continued in use in the Roman schools. Bacon likewise in de Augm. Scient. Lib. v. c. 3. speaks of the collection of an apparatus for rhetorical purposes, which he says may be of two kinds, either a store of subjects of arguments and common places, quam vocamus Topicam (these are more like Aristotle's τόποι), or a stock of ready-made arguments and speeches upon the most common subjects of controversy, which he calls Promptuaria; and these last correspond to the loci communes of the Latin Rhetoricians. Protagoras is said by Cicero to have been the first composer of communes loci in his sense; Brut. c. 12. Protagoras scripsit rerum illustrium disputationes, quæ nunc appellantur communes loci.

Upon the various divisions already described; the modes of proof or persuasion, πίστεις[1], ἤθη, and πάθος; the εἴδη and τόποι; the three genera or branches of rhetoric; are founded the plan and method of treatment of the work in its two first books. Another and more fundamental division which has been already incidentally mentioned, p. 7, is that which distinguishes the two first books from the third, and is not even noticed until we come to the end of the second and the beginning of the third book. The two first are occupied with an account of the instruments and modes and materials or topics of rhetorical proof, which is the

---

[1] The term πίστεις applied to rhetorical proofs, because they are *not* demonstrative or scientific, ἀποδεικτικαί, but only probable, or modes of persuading, is no invention of Aristotle. It appears in the Rhet. ad Alexand. cc. 7, 8, and elsewhere; in Isocrates, ἀντίδ. § 256, 278, 280.; and in Plato; only in the last of the three, not as distinctive of, and specially applicable to, *rhetorical* proof.

essential part or 'body' of the art: the rest being comparatively of no importance, a mere appendage or external ornament, like dress or jewels to the person. This is why the contents of the third book on style, arrangement, and delivery, λέξις, τάξις, and ὑπόκρισις, are left so long unnoticed: it is because they are unworthy to occupy the attention until all the more important and material subjects of the art have been thoroughly analysed and examined and exhibited in detail. The three parts of rhetoric are distinguished by Cicero, Orat. § 43., in one of those succinct and expressive phrases which preeminently distinguish the Latin language; quid dicat, quo quidque loco, quomodo.

In Aristotle's own introduction in the three first chapters, to which after the dispatch of so much preliminary matter we have at length arrived, the province of the art is marked out, its limits determined, its instruments, materials and principal divisions are in general terms defined analysed and explained. The obscurity of this part of the work is so great, especially to those who are as yet unacquainted with the technicalities of Aristotle's Logic and the intricacies of his style, that I have here as in the third book for a similar reason, that is, on account of the extreme brevity and compression and elliptical character of the composition, had recourse to a running commentary or paraphrase with occasional translation, in order to supply a clue of connexion which may guide the inexperienced reader through what I may call without exaggeration the tangled wilderness of Aristotle's ordinary writing. That Aristotle could and did write well we know from Cicero's frequent and glowing eulogiums on the beauties of his lost dialogues: that he could also write excessively ill and obscurely, that he could omit to express at least two thirds of his meaning and leave it to be supplied by the reader's ingenuity, that he could involve himself in a maze of endless subtlety and confusion in the discussion of some transcendental problem Physical or Metaphysical, 'and find no end in wandering mazes lost', that he could often repeat himself, or again confuse his readers by the absence of all indication as to whether he is speaking in his own person, or quoting or even refuting the doctrines of another, and that his trains of reasoning in general have sometimes a rambling, discursive, and unconnected character—all this is but too well known to the readers of his Physics, of his de Animâ, of his Metaphysics, and indeed of nearly all his extant writings, in the very best of which these unpleasant peculiarities will occasionally appear. There are many parts of the Rhetoric, especially the third book, which have to me all the appearance of notes of lectures, jotted down in a commonplace book, to be filled up expanded and illustrated when they were orally delivered to his class; and though I by no means assert that this is true of the entire work, still it may be a good reason for dealing with such parts in the manner that I propose; and I am in this also following the example of Victorius' excellent Commentary.

ARISTOTLE'S RHETORIC.

BOOK I. CHAP. I.

THE art or faculty of rhetoric as it is variously called, the one term describing it as a theory or system, the other regarding it from the practical side, as a faculty or practice in finding arguments, δύναμις τοῦ πορίσαι λόγους, I. 2, 7., is the counterpart, ἀντίστροφος[1], or as it is afterwards more correctly expressed (the differences between it and rhetoric being too considerable to admit of its being properly designated as an exact counterpart, implying that the two arts resemble one another as closely as στροφή and ἀντιστροφή in a regular lyrical ode) a copy, ὁμοίωμα, offshoot, branch, παραφυές, or subordinate part, μόριον, of dialectics, both of them being employed upon subjects common after a fashion (τρόπον τινά, i. e. in a certain sense, up to a certain point; it is not *absolutely* true, because there *are* differences in this respect between man and man, some using them much more than others) to all men alike, and neither of them confined like other arts and sciences to one particular definite class of objects and inquiries. Medicine, for example, deals with one particular genus or department of things, τὸ ὑγιεινὸν καὶ νοσερόν, geometry with the properties of magnitude, τὰ τοῦ μεγέθους πάθη, or of space, arithmetic with numbers: botany is περὶ φυτῶν, zoology περὶ ζῴων, and the like: whereas rhetoric and dialectics have no one special subject of their own, but exercise themselves indifferently upon any question that is set before them, περὶ τοῦ δοθέντος, I. 2. 1[2]. In consequence of this universality of application every one at some time or

---

[1] See the note on ἀντίστροφος, I. I. I.   [2] See above, p. 75.

other has occasion to make use of them; for every one is constantly liable to get engaged in a discussion [indeed at Athens, where dialectical disputation was so fashionable, and more especially while Socrates was alive and prowling about the streets and public places seeking whom he might confute, the difficulty must rather have been to keep out of it] in which he must sustain the part of assailant, critic, or maintainer of a thesis, of questioner or respondent in a dialectural debate[1], or to be driven to the use of rhetoric in accusation or defence. Most people it is true do this either altogether at random without any regular system rule or method at all, or else they acquire a practical skill, still independent of system, an ἐμπειρία or knack falling short of genuine 'art', which is due to the familiarity or habituation (συνήθεια) which arises out of the exercise of the acquired habit (ἕξις). But the very possibility of these two modes of procedure, and the undoubted success with which they are often carried on, show plainly by their frequent recurrence that causes and effects must be traceable in the processes, and therefore that they may be systematised (ὁδοποιεῖν), and a body of rules drawn up by which they will be converted into arts, and success *ensured* so far as the rules of art can ensure it. [It is the knowledge of *causes* by which art is distinguished from mere ἐμπειρία. See on 'art', ante, pp. 19—23]. It appears therefore that rhetoric may be treated as an art systematically, if not scientifically[2]. (See especially, c. 4.

---

[1] ἐξετάζειν to sift, crossexamine here represents the assailant or questioner in the dialectical combat, ὁ ἐπιχειρῶν, ὁ ἐλέγχων, ὁ ἐπιχειρῶν, and ὁ ἐξετάζων himself; the opponent is the maintainer of the thesis, ὁ ὑπέχων τὸν λόγον, ὁ ἀποκρινόμενος, the respondent. See the description, above, p. 90.

[2] The complete definition of art, as it is understood both by Plato and Aristotle, is, a systematic and *rational* procedure, governed by general rules derived from experience, but distinguished from mere ἐμπειρία, practical skill or routine, which is irrational (Plat. Gorg. 465. A.) growing merely out of habit and practice, by the apprehension of *cause* (Plat. Gorg. 501. A. Arist. Met. A. 1. and elsewhere), and the recognition of *general* principles. Art deals with universals and not particulars. Rhet. I. 2. 11. Met. A. 1.

§§ 4—6.) As it is, the compilers of the so-called 'arts' have supplied us with a very small portion of what really constitutes an *art of rhetoric*, and that is proof—not scientific demonstration, but the kind of proof that rhetoric admits[1]— the legitimate and most effective instrument of 'persuasion', the reputed *end* of the art; which can most readily be reduced to rules of art, and admits of the nearest approach to scientific treatment. Of enthymeme, the form of syllogism which rhetoric employs in drawing its conclusions, which is in fact "the body", the solid substantial matter of proof,— to which all other kinds of indirect proof, such as the influence of character, or appeals to the feelings, interests, passions of judge or audience, are subsidiary and subordinate, standing to the other in the relation of mere adjuncts or external appendages ($\pi\rho\sigma\theta\hat{\eta}\kappa\alpha\iota$), like dress or ornaments to the person—their works are absolutely silent; whilst they confine themselves to the treatment of such non essentials as some of those above described, which are properly speaking no part of rhetoric at all, are 'beside the subject', $\xi\xi\omega\ \tau o\hat{v}$ $\pi\rho\acute{a}\gamma\mu\alpha\tau os$, and mere appeals ad captandum to the judges. And therefore, if all trials were conducted as they even now are in some cities, and particularly in the best governed, the pleaders who strictly adhered to the rules laid down in these systems of rhetoric would have nothing whatever to say: in some places they actually put in practice what is universally

---

[1] Viz. $\pi\iota\sigma\tau\epsilon\iota s$. Rhetorical proofs are so called, first because $\tau\grave{o}\ \pi\epsilon\acute{\iota}\theta\epsilon\iota\nu$ being assigned as the object of the art, $\pi\acute{\iota}\sigma\tau\iota s$, belief, is the proper and natural result; and secondly because the sphere of rhetoric being probability, and none of its premisses or conclusions with very few exceptions necessary, scientific demonstration, $\dot{a}\pi\acute{o}\delta\epsilon\iota\xi\iota s$, is excluded, and belief is the highest degree of certainty to which the orator can attain. The use of the term $\pi\acute{\iota}\sigma\tau\epsilon\iota s$ as applied to rhetorical proofs, because they *are* popular and not demonstrative or necessary, is no invention of Aristotle. It occurs frequently in the Rhet. ad Alex. see cc. 7, 8, &c. and in Isocrates in the same application, $\dot{a}\nu\tau\iota\delta$. §§ 256, 278, 280, &c. Plato uses the word frequently, but never, I think, in this strictly technical sense, though the meaning is often implied. Of the nature and import of 'persuasion,' an *excellent* account is given by Mr Bain, Senses and Intellect, Bk. II. Ch. 2. § 40. part of this is unintentionally repeated from the note, p. 131.

approved in theory, and allow no 'travelling out of the record', no arguments or persuasive arts which have not a direct and immediate bearing upon the case before the court. This is the practice in the Court of the Areopagus, and it is certainly right: to appeal to a judge's passions and feelings, to attempt to excite in him anger, jealousy, compassion, is to warp him ($\delta\iota\alpha\sigma\tau\rho\acute{\epsilon}\phi\epsilon\iota\nu$), and prevent him from exercising a *right* (straight and even) and sound judgment; and is just like wilfully making the rule crooked which you are about to apply to test something which you want to make straight. Besides this, it is plain that the parties in an action strictly speaking have nothing to do but to prove their point; whether the fact is so or not, whether the thing alleged has or has not been done; whether it is 'great or small', important or trifling, 'just or unjust',—except in cases where these points have been already determined by the legislator —is for the judge to decide, who wants no instruction from the parties before him on such matters as these. § 6.

We may observe here that laws enacted on sound principles should as far as may be determine everything themselves, and leave as little as possible to the decision of the judge: first, because it is easier to find one or a few with sufficient wisdom and capacity for legislation and judicial decision than a large number similarly endowed; and secondly, because legislation arises from long previous consideration, allows plenty of time to deliberate upon the operation and effect of a proposed enactment, its adaptation to the wants and character of the people for whom it is intended, and its harmony with the rest of the system, and so forth; whereas the decisions of a judge or an assembly are given on the spur of the moment, without much time for reflexion, and are therefore always liable to error, the one in point of justice, the other in regard of the true interests of the state[1]. But the most important consideration of all

[1] αἱ δὲ κρίσεις ἐξ ὑπογυίου, ὥστε χαλεπὸν ἀποδιδόναι τὸ δίκαιον καὶ τὸ συμφέρον καλῶς τοὺς κρίνοντας. κρίνειν, as Victorius notes, is here used with

in favour of this view, is that the legislator's decisions are not partial or particular, but universal, and also directed to the future: he lays down general rules with reference to future acts and events, in which he himself has no immediate interest; but when we come to ($ἤδη$) the judge and assembly-man, *they* have to decide upon things present, in which they are, or may be, directly concerned, and definite, special cases, in which their interests and affections may be engaged—whereas 'universals' are of an abstract nature, and interest nobody—and so from this conjunction of their personal feelings and private interests with the case before them, their judgment, or power of decision, is obscured or clouded ($ἐπισκοτεῖν$), and they are unable to discern the truth. Questions of fact, however, past present and future, are a necessary exception to the application of this principle: these cannot be foreseen by the legislator, and it is therefore impossible for him to provide for them by any general regulations; they must necessarily be left to be decided as the occasion arises by the ordinary judges[1]. § 8.

a double reference to judicial decision and legislative deliberation; in both cases there is a *judgment* or *decision*: $τὸ δίκαιον$ being the object of the former, $τὸ συμφέρον$ of the latter. This is confirmed by the introduction of $ἐκκλησιαστής$ in the next sentence. Compare § 10, also I. 3. 2, and II. 18. 1. where it is shown how the decision of the $κριτής$ may be extended to all the three kinds of rhetoric. In the epideictic branch his *judgment* becomes *criticism*, and he is a *critic*.

[1] On this same question of the necessary insufficiency of *general laws* in their application to *particular cases*, see Polit. III. 11. sub fin. To supply these deficiencies, $περὶ ὅσων ἐξαδυνατοῦσιν οἱ νόμοι λέγειν ἀκριβῶς$ $διὰ τὸ μὴ ῥᾴδιον εἶναι καθόλου δηλῶσαι περὶ πάντων$, one of the 'rulers,' $τὸν ἄρχοντα$, or states officer must be called in. The rule or theory is that a state should be governed by general laws as far as they can possibly be made to reach; but as they cannot provide for all cases that may arise, a great deal must of necessity be left to the discretion of individuals, and the intervention of some temporary and occasional authority is therefore required. The nature of this authority must be determined by the circumstances of the case. In Politics and affairs of state it is the $ἐκκλησία$ or general assembly that is called in to pass *particular measures*, $ψηφίσματα$, on any special occasion, to provide for special emergencies — this is the

From what has been said it is plain that writers upon rhetoric, in defining the contents of the several divisions of the speech, the prooemium, narrative and the rest (Rhet. III. cc. 13—19.), are dwelling upon points which are beside the real subject which is before them; for these contents consist of nothing but precepts and directions for putting the judge into some particular state of mind and feeling, to excite in him, that is, such emotions as are favourable to their own cause and adverse to that of the opposite party: the true method of scientific proof, or rather artistic persuasion, which makes the really accomplished and successful rhetorical rea-

definition of ψήφισμα as opposed to the νόμος or general law: ὅτι περὶ ἐνίων ἀδύνατον θέσθαι νόμον, ὥστε ψηφίσματος δεῖ, Eth. Nic. v. 14—in legal proceedings it is of course the judge, one or many, the κριτής or δικαστής, that has to interpret the written law, apply it to particular cases, and if need be modify its severity. This is in fact the province of ἐπιείκεια, Eth. N. v. 14., which is a merciful and indulgent consideration or tendency, especially applied in the mitigation of the rigour of the written statute—ἐπιείκεια is consequently defined, ἐπανόρθωμα νομίμου δικαίου, a correction, rectification, of strict legal justice. Under certain circumstances (circonstances atténuantes) the rigour of the law must not be enforced. αἴτιον δ' ὅτι ὁ μὲν νόμος καθόλου πᾶς, περὶ ἐνίων δ' οὐχ οἷόν τε ὀρθῶς εἰπεῖν καθόλου.

On this point Plato, though he holds theoretically that the *true* politician, one who has a perfect and scientific knowledge of the *art* of government, ought to be absolute, for the public benefit, not for his own, Polit. 296. D. seq., like a physician or pilot, 297. D. sq.—at 298. E. the ab-

surdity of the democratic theory and practice is held up to ridicule—yet allows that, when this perfection of scientific government is not to be attained, the authority of the laws should be paramount. This is ὁ δεύτερος πλοῦς, the second best course. 300. A. B. Though the irregularities and inconsistencies, ἀνομοιότητες, of human beings and their actions are such that no absolute general principles or rules can be constantly applied to them, 294. B, and hence one would prefer, were it possible to find such an one, a perfect human statesman as governor and legislator who can adapt himself to these ever varying circumstances; yet in consequence of the infinity of the special cases that arise, and the impossibility of settling them all singly and in detail, πῶς γὰρ ἄν τις ἱκανὸς γένοιτ' ἄν ποτε, ὥστε διὰ βίου ἀεὶ παρακαθήμενος ἑκάστῳ δι' ἀκριβείας προστάττειν τὸ προσῆκον;—time strength and patience would alike fail the judge in such an office—although no one would *willingly* limit his powers and control his judgment by laying down absolute and general rules of action, this must nevertheless be done. 295. A. B.

soner (ἐνθυμηματικός), they do not even attempt to explain. § 9.

[It has been already observed (ante, p. 4), and need here be only briefly repeated, that it may seem that Aristotle in these remarks is arguing against himself, and cutting the ground from under his own feet; for his system by no means excludes appeals to the feelings, and τὸ τὸν ἀκροατὴν διαθεῖναί πως (c. 2. § 3.) is one of the three modes of proof which are effected by means of the speech itself, and therefore fall under the province of the art. But he is to be understood as speaking only comparatively, whilst he is pointing out the defects in the existing 'arts' and their mode of dealing with rhetoric. They occupied themselves almost exclusively with these matters, which strictly according to the theory of the art are really ἔξω τοῦ πράγματος. For if judges and popular assemblies were what they ought to be, all such appeals to feelings and interests would be as unnecessary as they are irregular, and proof alone, logical proof, of the question under consideration would be all that is required: but unfortunately they are not, and therefore διὰ μοχθηρίαν τῶν ἀκροατῶν (III. 1. 5. compare I. 1. 10. and I. 2. 5.), in consequence of the defects of the audience, we must accommodate ourselves to circumstances; and since the introduction of such topics is usually necessary to the success of the pleader and orator, they must consequently enter into a complete system of rhetoric, which is to be a guide to practice: only they are to be kept subordinate, and scientifically (methodically) treated, both of which conditions the preceding writers on rhetoric failed to fulfil: they are not the immediate or proper subject, and ought not to be made the 'body' of the speech, or of the rhetorical treatise.]

And this is in fact the reason why they have totally neglected the deliberative, hortative, or public kind of speaking, and devoted themselves exclusively to the forensic or judicial branch; although both of these form parts of the same system, and the same mode of treatment is equally applicable to both; and although the former is nobler and larger and more liberal (or 'statesmanlike,' or 'more worthy of a citizen,' vid. not. ad loc.)—being employed upon the settlement of questions in which important state interests are involved—than the other in which private interests are principally concerned, and the petty disputes that arise out of the ordinary every day dealings between man and man (τὰ συναλλάγματα): it is because the practice of the law courts allows more room for the introduction of this extraneous matter, and for the use of trickery and chicanery (ἧττόν ἐστι κακοῦργον ἡ δημηγορία δικολογίας) than that of the public assembly, which is κοινότερον, that is, in which the interests and issues which are taken into consideration are wider and more general, and encourage a more frank and candid and liberal tone and habit of mind than the special and private interests, and the often paltry and trifling matters which supply the topics of the pleader[1]. Such tricks and devices, dishonest alike and unscientific, as the sophistical rhetoricians recommend in their treatises and have recourse to in their practice, are in fact less available in the public assembly, because there the audience are deciding upon their own affairs (περὶ οἰκείων) in which they necessarily feel a deep interest: accordingly all that they want is *proof* that the course proposed is for their advantage, and every thing beyond and beside this is likely to be disapproved and rejected as unnecessary and out of place: whereas in a court of law, the judges—and especially a large miscellaneous body of dicasts like that of which the Athenian courts were composed—have usually no direct interest in the questions that are brought before them, and may be regarded as indifferent to the issue: it is therefore considered neces-

---

[1] κοινότερον is rendered by Victorius quod a multitudine quoque et imperitis tractatur, more popular, more within the reach of the vulgar apprehension: but I think that the meaning that I have given to it in the text is at least equally derivable from the Greek, and far more suitable to the context and general sentiment of the passage.

sary to conciliate them (bring them over, ἀναλαβεῖν), and awaken in them a factitious interest in favour of the parties by appeals to their passions and feelings: the absence of any real interest renders them especially liable to be led away by these; they are diverted from the consideration of the merits of the case by the artificial excitement thus raised; they yield to the influence, lend themselves to the more plausible speaker, give sentence in his favour, and the case is *decided*, but not *judged* (διδόασι τοῖς ἀμφισβητοῦσιν, ἀλλ' οὐ κρίνουσιν). And all this accounts for the exclusive attention which this school of sophistical rhetoricians has bestowed upon the forensic branch of their art, because it is here that the artifices and sophistry which are distinctive of their school can be but brought into play. To prevent these evil consequences in the administration of justice, the law, as has been already observed, in some cases actually prohibits the employment of any such indirect means of unduly influencing the judges: in the assembly, the members who have to decide are sufficiently interested in the result to guard against it themselves. § 10.

Now it is plain that the scientific treatment of rhetoric, that is, the reduction of it to general rules of art, must occupy itself mainly, if not exclusively, with proof. This proof, since rhetoric is confined within the sphere of the probable, and does not admit of strict scientific demonstration (ἀπόδειξις), leads to no more certain result than πίστις, belief, a mode of conviction produced by the persuasion (τῷ πείθειν) of the speaker. Still it is a *kind* of demonstration (ἀπόδειξίς τις), because we entertain the strongest persuasion or conviction of any thing which we suppose to have been demonstrated. [This seems to be somewhat of a non sequitur. The *inference* would be rather the other way; that ἀπόδειξις is a kind of πίστις: which is in any case the truer statement, seeing that belief is much more *general* than demonstration.] The form assumed by this rhetorical demonstration is that of the enthymeme: and this is in fact, speaking *generally*, (ἁπλῶς)—because it is possible that an 'example', or even one of the 'unscientific proofs' (ἄτεχνοι πίστεις) may be more telling on any particular occasion— the most powerful and convincing of all the modes of persuasion employed by rhetoricians. Now this enthymeme is a variety of the syllogism; and the province of dialectics —and therefore of rhetoric, its branch offshoot or copy— embraces the consideration of every kind of syllogism alike[1], demonstrative, dialectical, sophistical, rhetorical. And it is clear from all this that a thorough acquaintance with the materials of syllogism, the propositions or premisses of which they are constructed, and the modes of their construction, with the addition of a knowledge of the special subjects of enthymemes, things contingent, viz. or of uncertain issue, and probable, especially things which we deliberate about, as human actions and their consequences; and the differences between them and 'logical' (meaning here 'demonstrative' Vict. or rather complete and regular, not incomplete like enthymemes) syllogisms, is the readiest way to supply a

[1] ὅτι δὲ οὐ μόνον οἱ διαλεκτικοὶ καὶ ἀποδεικτικοὶ συλλογισμοὶ διὰ τῶν προειρημένων γίγνονται σχημάτων, ἀλλὰ καὶ οἱ ῥητορικοί, καὶ ἁπλῶς ἡτισοῦν πίστις, καὶ ἡ καθ' ὁποιανοῦν μέθοδον, νῦν ἂν εἴη λεκτέον. Anal. Pr. II. 23. 68. b. 9.

How far, and in what sense, dialectics may be applied to the investigations of science and its syllogisms, has been already explained, ante, pp. 80, 81, and note; and the general connexion of dialectics and rhetoric, p. 91. seq.

In the text is added after διαλεκτικῆς, ἢ αὑτῆς ὅλης ἢ μέρους τινός. Mr Poste in his Introd. to Transl. of Anal. Post. p. 18. n. 2. says of this, "general logic seems to be called a part of dialectics." And Victorius takes a similar view of the meaning.

He thinks that μέρος refers to the two books of the Prior Analytics which treat of the construction and varieties of the syllogism in general, equally applicable to all kinds; as above described: 'dialectics' is therefore here to be understood as comprehending the entire theory of reasoning or logic in all its branches. I cannot agree with this, and think it much more probable that by "a part or branch of dialectics" Aristotle means the treatise on Fallacies, de Soph. Elench., appended to the Topics or *treatise on dialectics*, just as the treatment of rhetorical fallacies, or fallacious enthymemes, is appended to the analysis of the τόποι ἐνθυμημάτων in Rhet. II. 24. μέρος αὐτῆς therefore is introduced for the purpose of including the fallacious branch of the art.

student with enthymemes, and so to qualify him for the successful practice of rhetoric. For although demonstrative science, of which syllogism is the appropriate instrument, has exact truth for its sole object, whereas Dialectics and Rhetoric deal only with the contingent and probable, yet since it belongs to the same faculty to discern truth and that which resembles it, and men in general have a natural aptitude for discerning truth, and mostly *do* arrive at it when it is their aim; so, sagacity in discerning and dealing with probabilities implies the same sort of mental dispositions as those which lead to truth, and the same kind of intellectual operations and processes will cultivate these dispositions towards both: and the study of the syllogistic method which belongs to demonstration and tends to the establishment of the verum, will be equally serviceable to the dialectician and rhetorician, whose syllogisms begin and end in nothing but the verisimile. § 11.

Now although the unscientific treatment of the subject, and the exclusive leaning towards the lower branch of the art, together with the sophistry and chicanery promoted and encouraged by this, which we have noted in the writings and practice of preceding Rhetoricians, have not unnaturally brought reproach upon the Art and the employment of it in general, yet Rhetoric nevertheless when rightly applied has its proper use and value: for we must not argue from the abuse to the use of any art. Rhetoric has four uses. For, first, it is corrective: it may be employed to prevent the triumph of fraud and wrong when the scale of justice might otherwise incline to their side: for truth and justice have *a natural superiority* over falsehood and wrong which the use of rhetoric enables them to assert against perversion and imposture; and therefore whenever wrong decisions are given and truth and justice defeated, it must needs be the fault of the parties themselves[1] who have neglected this

---

[1] The explanation in the text, which was first suggested to me by Mr Munro, makes αὐτῶν reflexive, for αὑτῶν. This use of the pronoun is so

invaluable instrument for the exposure of fraud and sophistry and for the setting forth of their case in its true and proper light. That falsehood and wrong should thus be allowed to prevail by the mere indolence or ignorance or carelessness of those who might avail themselves of it is reprehensible and deserving of censure : rhetoric *corrects* this ; it is therefore 'corrective' of this social defect.

Secondly it is 'instructive', that is, to certain classes of people, and to a certain extent, within the limits of probability. With a great many people, in fact all popular audiences, a popular method of proof, avoiding the technicalities of exact demonstrative science, is necessary in trying to convince them; which we are obliged to endeavour to do, whether we have to persuade them that such and such a course of policy is expedient, or that such and such a settlement of a legal question is fair and right. 'Instruction' $διδασκαλία$ (comp. de Soph. El. c. 2. quoted above, p. 75.) in its strict and proper sense, by the scientific or exact demonstrative or regular syllogistic method, even if we had the exactest scientific knowledge of our subject, would be thrown away upon ordinary hearers, and we must meet such upon their own ground, by reference to popular and current opinions, and the universal and universally accepted axioms and principles of reasoning ($τὰ\ κοινά$): this has been already stated in the Topics (A. 2. see above, p. 79.) of the mode of meeting ordinary·people in argument ($ἔντευξις$). Rhetoric therefore in this limited sense is 'instructive'.

Thirdly, Rhetoric is 'precautionary and suggestive': the study of it tends to put us on our guard against the sophistries and fallacies of others. It is characteristic of dialectics

common as hardly to need illustration; but it is illustrated by Waitz on Anal. Pr. 55. a. 14. Victorius' interpretation of $αὐτῶν$ by $τῶν\ ἐναντίων$, "the opposites" of truth and justice, viz. falsehood and wrong, cannot be right. The conclusion, $ὥστε$, would in this case have no meaning; for how can it be said that in cases of unjust decisions the defeat of truth and right by their opposites is a *consequence* of the natural superiority of the former?

and of this art, that they both undertake to prove opposites, to argue on either side of a question, for the affirmative or the negative indifferently. But we may have the faculty without exercising it directly in actual practice—for we have no right to persuade people of what is false or wrong—but it may be kept in reserve and made available for detecting fallacies in others: and we may habituate ourselves to the examination of either side of any given question so that in any particular case in which we are concerned we may know how it really stands ($\pi\hat{\omega}\varsigma\ \check{\epsilon}\chi\epsilon\iota$), the actual state of the case, on which side the truth and right actually lie [so Schrader. Victorius "to see how the thing is actually done—how to do it if necessary." The other is doubtless right]; or if the adverse party employs unfair arguments, that we may be able on our side to meet and refute them. Now this office of 'concluding opposites' is amongst all arts peculiar to dialectics and rhetoric. To those two alone, abstractedly considered, the truth of the conclusions they draw is a matter of indifference: so long as they are correctly drawn according to the rules which the arts prescribe, the theory and end of the arts are satisfied. Not that there is absolutely *no* difference however between the two sides of a question or two opposite conclusions, even in reference to the arts themselves and the application of them, and independently of all other considerations: for what is true and right, better and more advantageous, is always, so to speak, easier to prove, and more convincing when proved than its opposite, which is a *paradox*. Rhetoric is 'precautionary' or 'preventive', and 'suggestive'.

The fourth use of rhetoric is for 'defence'. The arguments in favour of rhetoric on this ground are derived from the analogy of the use of the bodily faculties and instruments: it is accounted disgraceful to be unable to defend oneself with one's hands, or the body in general: much more shameful must it be to be unable to use speech in self-defence, and all the more in proportion as it is more characteristic of man (Polit. I. 2¹) than the use of the members of his body. Rhetoric is 'defensive'.

Lastly if the great amount of mischief that may be caused by the unfair use of this 'faculty of words' be objected to the cultivation and practice of it, such an argument from the abuse to the use may be applied alike to the condemnation and discouragement of everything that is good and useful, except virtue, and is more conclusive against each in exact proportion to its excellence and utility, as strength, health, wealth, military skill; for just in proportion to the amount of service that each of them may be made to render to their possessor and to society at large by the right and proper use of them, is the amount of damage which the unfair and unjust employment of them may produce: they are all dangerous or mischievous if misused, but no one thinks that they are on that account not to be desired and pursued and cultivated. §§ 12, 13.

It has thus been made plain that rhetoric is not confined to any one special and definite class of subjects, but is universally applicable, like dialectics, and that it is valuable and beneficial when used aright: it is clear likewise that its object and special function is not 'to persuade', absolutely and without qualification—this is, τὸ ὁρίζεσθαι οὐ τὸ πρᾶγμα, ἀλλὰ τὸ πρᾶγμα εὖ ἔχον ἢ τετελεσμένον, Top. Z. 12. 149. b. 24.: this makes the result or success (eventus, Quint.) necessary to the definition of an art—as the current definition erroneously assumes, but to discover and put in prac-

---

[1] ὁ δὲ λόγος ἐπὶ τῷ δηλοῦν ἐστὶ τὸ συμφέρον καὶ τὸ βλαβερόν, ὥστε καὶ τὸ δίκαιον καὶ τὸ ἄδικον· τοῦτο γὰρ πρὸς τἆλλα ζῷα τοῖς ἀνθρώποις ἴδιον, τὸ μόνον ἀγαθοῦ καὶ κακοῦ καὶ δικαίου καὶ ἀδίκου καὶ τῶν ἄλλων αἴσθησιν ἔχειν. Speech, as contrasted with mere *voice*, φωνή, which is given to man for the purpose of *expressing moral distinctions*, is therefore the faculty by which he is distinguished from the rest of the animals. Hoc enim, says Cicero, de Orat. I. 6. 32., uno praestamus vel maxime feris, quod colloquimur inter nos et quod exprimere dicendo sensa possumus.

On speech as distinctive of humanity, see Whewell Elem. of Morality § 430. Max Müller, Lect. on the Science of Language, Lect. IX. 1st series. J. S. Mill, System of Logic, Bk. IV. Ch. iii.

tice the available means of persuasion on any subject: the successful result is not necessary to the notion of art: that consists in employing the proper method. It is so in all arts. The function of medicine, for instance, is not strictly speaking to restore a patient to health, but to promote or forward his cure so far as circumstances permit: for it is quite possible to treat secundum artem even those who are necessarily debarred from the enjoyment of health[1].

It appears also that there is a spurious fallacious branch of rhetoric[2], corresponding to the theory of fallacies, the de Sophisticis Elenchis, in dialectics, included in either case as a subdivision under the general art: for the difference between sound and genuine, and sophistical reasoning, lies not in the faculty or art itself, nor in the method followed, but in the moral purpose, προαίρεσις, of the reasoner; the faculty is the same in both: only in the one case—in rhetoric —the sophistical reasoner passes under the one general name of ῥήτωρ or Rhetorician, in the other there is a distinction of names as well as of objects, and the one is called a Dialectician the other a Sophist[3].

Having thus determined what rhetoric is, or ought to be, that it is an art, and when properly used an honest and useful art, we must next proceed to examine its 'method', the

---

[1] Top. A. c. 3. ἕξομεν δὲ τελέως τὴν μέθοδον, ὅταν ὁμοίως ἔχωμεν ὥσπερ ἐπὶ ῥητορικῆς καὶ ἰατρικῆς καὶ τῶν τοιούτων δυνάμεων. τοῦτο δ'ἐστὶ τὸ ἐκ τῶν ἐνδεχομένων ποιεῖν ἃ προαιρούμεθα. οὔτε γὰρ ὁ ῥητορικὸς ἐκ παντὸς τρόπου πείσει, οὔθ' ὁ ἰατρικὸς ὑγιάσει· ἀλλ' ἐὰν τῶν ἐνδεχομένων μηδὲν παραλίπῃ, ἱκανῶς αὐτὸν ἔχειν τὴν ἐπιστήμην φήσομεν. Comp. Z. 12. u. s. de Anim. III. 9. 8. Metaph. A. 1. Eth. Nic. III. 5. βουλευόμεθα δὲ οὐ περὶ τῶν τελῶν, ἀλλὰ περὶ τῶν πρὸς τὰ τέλη. οὔτε γὰρ ἰατρὸς βουλεύεται εἰ ὑγιάσει, οὔτε ῥήτωρ εἰ πείσει, οὔτε πολιτικὸς εἰ εὐνομίαν ποιήσει......ἀλλὰ θέμενοι τέλος τι, πῶς καὶ διὰ τίνων ἔσται σκοποῦσι. See also above, p. 33.

[2] This is treated in Rhet. II. 24.

[3] More briefly thus: there is a sophistry in rhetoric as well as in dialectics, and the definition of both turns upon the same distinction; that is, it resides not in the faculty, but in the moral purpose: only in the one case the Sophist passes under the general name of rhetorician; in the other we distinguish name as well as thing.

instruments and processes which it employs in arriving at its conclusions, the rules and means or sources or materials (πῶς τε καὶ ἐκ τίνων, the latter especially referring to the προτάσεις, premisses or propositions, from which as materials the enthymemes are constructed and the conclusion deduced) by which the proposed object, the persuasion of the hearers, may be attained. And we commence the inquiry with the definition of our subject. § 14.

BOOK I. CHAP. II.

Rhetoric may be defined, not as heretofore the 'art of persuading', because as we have already seen the result is not necessarily included in the meaning of the term 'art', but 'the faculty of discerning or finding in any question presented to it that which is adapted to produce persuasion, or the possible means of persuasion': the 'art' of rhetoric being here regarded in its practical application by the individual orator[1]. This is peculiar to rhetoric: every other art (except

[1] Quintilian's criticism of Aristotle's definition, that it includes too much and too little, has been already commented on, p. 34. To the same effect he adds, II. 15. 16, omnia subjecisse oratori videtur Aristoteles, quum dixit, vim esse dicendi, quid in quaque re possit esse persuasibile. On the same ground, of including too much, the definition of Aristotle is criticised by the Scholiast on Apthonius, quoted in Gaisford's Animadv. ad Arist. Rhet. p. 30. The author says that the universal, περὶ ἕκαστον, requires the limitation πολιτικόν, to mark the proper sphere of rhetorical study and practice; (this, though absent from the definition, is amply supplied by Aristotle in the body of the work:) and further that the πιθανὸς λόγος (this gives the sense, not the exact words of the definition) must be limited by the addition of διεξοδικός 'narrative,' to distinguish it from the 'interrogative' dialectics; with which it is confounded by the omission of this and the preceding differentia; for dialectics alone, Top. A. init., is in reality περὶ παντός. However, as we have seen Rhetoric *is theoretically* of universal application, though *in practice* the field of operations is confined to Politics in its widest sense, to man in society, and his actions, motives, feelings, and character. The Scholiast accordingly approves of the definition of Dionysius of Halicarnassus, who describes it as a δύναμις τεχνικὴ πιθα-

dialectics, as should have been added) has a special 'subject', ὑποκείμενον, the materials which supply its premisses or propositions, as medicine deals exclusively with what is wholesome and unwholesome, geometry with the properties of magnitudes, arithmetic with numbers, and so on: whereas it is the province of rhetoric to discover that which conduces to persuasion in any subject whatsoever: and therefore we say that the art has no special determinate class of things to which its rules and processes are applied. § 1.

Of rhetorical proofs there are two kinds, scientific and unscientific. By the unscientific are meant, all such as are 'preexistent,' προυπῆρχεν, independent of ourselves and our own efforts and actions; as witnesses, torture, documentary evidence, such as contracts, and so forth; by scientific, those that may be conducted and established by the processes and rules of the art, and by our own agency: the one kind is ready to hand, and has only to be properly *employed*, the other must be *invented;* [hence the Latin term Inventio.][1]

Of the proofs which are furnished through the instrumentality of the speech itself, and therefore scientifically or systematically, there are three kinds, one residing in the character of the speaker, the second in the feelings and emotions produced in the audience, and the third, which is proof in its proper sense, logical, direct proof, in the speech itself, by proving or seeming to prove; the last words ex-

νοῦ λόγου ἐν πράγματι πολιτικῷ τέλος ἔχουσα τὸ εὖ εἰπεῖν; and this certainly is a very complete definition. It does not appear in his extant τέχνη, which is occupied with quite other matters.

Of Alexander's explanation of the term δύναμις as applied to Rhetoric I have already spoken above pp. 15, 16. I will here add as a supplement a passage of Eustratius on Eth. Nic. x. 9. 18. (quoted by Zell) which takes the same view, δυνάμεις ἐκάλουν οἱ παλαιοὶ τὰς ἐπιχειρούσας εἰς τἀναντία,

οἷον ῥητορικὴν διαλεκτικήν, ἐπιστήμας δὲ τὰς μὴ τοιαύτας, οἷον ἀριθμητικὴν γεωμετρικὴν φυσικήν. Let me further add to the argument against this explanation of the application of the term δύναμις to rhetoric previously given, that Aristotle's own language is in contradiction of it. In Rhet. I. 2. 7, Dialectics and Rhetoric are said to be δυνάμεις—*not* τοῦ τἀναντία συλλογίζεσθαι, but—τοῦ πορίσαι λόγους.

[1] On the ἄτεχνοι πίστεις, see I. 15.

pressing the sophistical branch which is a necessary appendage to rhetoric as to dialectics. Persuasion is conveyed by the character of the speaker when the speech is so expressed as to prepossess the audience in favour of the orator's credibility: which is effected by leading them, always through the speech, to ascribe to him three virtues or good dispositions of mind, φρόνησις the intellectual virtue of practical wisdom, which contrives means to an end (Eth. Nic. VI.), and enables him to judge what is right and expedient, ἀρετή moral virtue, or integrity of character, which will prevent him from trying to deceive them, and thirdly εὔνοια, good intentions, to themselves, their party, or their cause (Rhet. II. 1). We put faith more readily and in a higher degree in persons whose character we approve as a general rule; but more especially in doubtful or 'probable' cases, where opinions differ, and no exact certainty is attainable: and here our confidence is entire. This however must be effected through the speech, and not be left to depend upon any previous impression of the speaker's character: and herein it differs from Cicero and Quintilian's auctoritas. It is so far from being true, as some writers on the art assert, [who these are we do not know: not Isocrates, nor the author of the Rhet. ad Alex. for both of them assert the contrary. Isocr. Antid. §§ 276—280. Rhet. ad Al. c. 39. 2.] that the influence of character contributes nothing to the speaker's power of persuasion, that it might almost be said that this is the most effective (κυριωτάτην) of all kinds of proof[1]. Rhetorical proof or persuasion is conveyed through

---

[1] See Plut. Vit. Phocion. 744. A. (quoted by Gaisford). ἐπεὶ καὶ ῥῆμα καὶ νεῦμα μόνον ἀνδρὸς ἀγαθοῦ μυρίοις ἐνθυμήμασι καὶ περιόδοις ἀντίρροπον ἔχει πίστιν.
Of the influence of auctoritas, or the authority of character in general, see Quintilian Inst. Or. IV. 1. 6—12. As a particular exemplification of it I will quote two famous examples, the one historical, the other fictitious. The first is what Quintilian, V. 12. 9, where the story is very briefly told, truly calls nobilis Scauri defensio. Q. Varius Sucronensis ait Æmilium Scaurum rempublicam P. R. prodidisse; Æmilius Scaurus negat. And that is the defence. It is to be re-

the hearers when by the speech any emotion is excited in them; for very different decisions are given under the influence of joy and grief, of love and hatred: and it is to this branch of the art alone, to these 'appeals to the feelings' that the preceding and present professors of it have hitherto directed their studies and their efforts. This subject shall be examined in detail when we come to the treatment of the πάθη, the 'affections' or emotions. (Bk. II. cc. 2—11.) Thirdly *the speech itself* is the organ of proof when we have shown directly the truth, or apparent truth, of anything by the arguments or materials and means of persuasion that the subject supplies. §§ 2—6.

Such being the nature of these three modes of rhetorical proof, it is plain that the employment of them requires the study of character, of the virtues, and of the affections or emotions—of the last the nature (τί ἐστι) and qualities (ποῖόν τι) and the sources or materials (ἐκ τίνων) and modes (πῶς) of their excitement—and the power of deriving arguments from these: and hence it appears that Rhetoric is an offshoot or scion, as we may call it, not only of dialectics, but also of Ethical science, which may fairly be called Politics or Practical Philosophy. And this explains the reason why its

marked that Quintilian here omits the prenomen; which I should hardly conceive it possible for a *Roman* under the circumstances to have actually done. The same story is told at greater length, but not improved, by Asconius in his Comment. on Cic. pro Scauro, of which a few fragments remain quoted by Orelli, Onomast. Tull. II. 19. Asconius omits the gentile name, Æmilius; I should suppose with equal improbability. Lastly Valerius Maximus Lib. III. by diluting it so as to deprive it of all its emphatic brevity, destroys at once its point force and interest.

The only other exemplification of the influence of *auctoritas* which I will refer to is Virgil's noble simile in the first book of the Æneid,

Ac veluti magno in populo cum sæpe
    coorta est
Seditio, sævitque animis ignobile vulgus,
Jamque faces et saxa volant, furor arma ministrat—
Tum pietate gravem et meritis si forte virum quem
Conspexere, silent, arrectisque auribus adstant;
Ille regit dictis animos et pectora mulcet.

Professors assume the mask or disguise, ὑποδύονται ὑπὸ τὸ σχῆμα, of Politics and Political philosophers, whether it be from ignorance, or from quackery, ἀλαζονεία, or any other human infirmity: for it is in fact nothing but a branch or copy of Dialectics, as we said at the beginning of this book: ['We' did in reality say something more; for we called it ἀντίστροφος, an exact parallel or counterpart; but we now see that the connexion between the two is better represented by a different name, and so we correct ourselves.] since neither of them has for its subject of investigation the nature or constitution, πῶς ἔχει, of any special class of things, but both are mere "faculties of supplying arguments."

So much on the faculty and province of these two arts, and their mutual relation; we now proceed to the *instruments* of proofs. § 7.

Of direct logical proof, or apparent proof, there are here, as in dialectics, only two modes, one the inductive, the other the syllogistic or the seeming syllogistic, method: for in Rhetoric the example is a kind of induction, and the enthymeme a kind of syllogism: the enthymeme may be called a rhetorical syllogism, the example a rhetorical induction. In rhetoric the only instruments of proof are enthymeme and example: so that if it be true of reasoning in general that it must all be carried on and by every one (ἢ ὁντινοῦν) either by way of syllogism or induction—as it is clearly stated in the Analytics, (An. Pr. II. 23. 68. b. 13, An. Post. init., also I. 18. 81. a. 40, II. 19. 100. b. 2.)—one or other of the one (enthymeme or example) must needs be the same with one or other of the other (syllogism or induction). [All proof by reasoning is thrown into the form, either of syllogism or example: the only modes of rhetorical proof are enthymeme and example: therefore, enthymeme must be a variety of syllogism and example of induction.] The difference between enthymeme and example may be plainly inferred from the Topics, where the syllogistic and inductive processes have been previously explained; it may be *inferred* I say from what is there said[1], that to derive a general conclusion or rule from an observed similarity in a number of particular cases is in Dialectics induction, in Rhetoric example; whereas the (deductive) conclusion that from certain assumed premisses something *else* (*different* from them) follows besides them, *by reason* of their being what they are (and nothing else), either universally (as in demonstrative science) or generally (as in dialectics and rhetoric), is in the one case called syllogism and in the other enthymeme. And it is plain that rhetoric enjoys both these advantages (syllogism and induction)—(ἀγαθόν here, as in II. 20. 7., stands for 'something that is good and useful')—for what has been said (of dialectics) in the Methodica (a lost work on some branch of Logic, of which beyond the reference and the simple mention of it by

---

[1] The passages in the Topics to which I suppose the references to be made, give exactly the same account of syllogism and substantially of induction as we have here in the Rhetoric; and from these descriptions, now that we know that enthymeme is a kind of syllogism and example a kind of induction, we may readily *infer* the difference between the two. Aristotle does not say, as has been generally supposed, that this difference has been *stated* in the Topics, but only that it can be *inferred* from the statements there made; and by making ἐκεῖ γὰρ π. σ. κ. ἐπ. εἰρ. πρότερον an explanatory parenthesis, and then connecting ὅτι τὸ μὲν κ.τ.λ. with the preceding words, we obtain the meaning that I have rendered in the text. The parallel passages in the Topics, are A. I. 100. a. 25, for the syllogism, ἔστι δὴ συλλογισμὸς λόγος ἐν ᾧ τεθέντων τινῶν ἕτερόν τι τῶν κειμένων ἐξ ἀνάγκης συμβαίνει διὰ τῶν κειμένων, and nearly the same words repeated, de Soph. El. c. 1. 165. a. 1., which present a sufficiently close resemblance to the definition in the Rhetoric: and for the induction, Top. A. c. 12. 105. a. 13. ἐπαγωγὴ ἡ ἀπὸ τῶν καθ' ἕκαστον ἐπὶ τὰ καθόλου ἔφοδος.

Spengel in Trans. Bav. Acad. p. 43. Brandis, über Arist. rhet. p. 13. Heitz, Verlor. schrift. de Arist. p. 82, 3, and Sauppe there quoted; and before these Victorius and Muretus; all suppose that Aristotle is directly quoting as from the Topics the *difference between* Enthymeme and example: and as this is not to be found in that work, they have recourse to various expedients of transposition of clauses and omission of them as interpolated—which Heitz, who would leave out all the words from ἐκ τῶν τοπικῶν to ὁμοίως ἔχει, carries to the greatest length—all of which I will ask my readers who are desirous of seeing their proposed alterations to look for in their own writings: for the difficulty which they take so much trouble to overcome vanishes, as it seems to me, before the explanation here given.

Diog. Laert. v. 29. nothing whatsoever is known) is equally applicable here—for there are two kinds of speeches in rhetoric, in one of which enthymemes predominate, in the other examples, and in like manner two kinds of speakers similarly distinguished. Of these two, though that which (proceeds by) chiefly employs examples is just as effective in the way of persuasion as the other, yet the enthymematic kind of speech is more popular and applauded[1]. The cause and origin of them (so Vict.), and the mode of their employment we will describe hereafter (II. 20—24.); let us now determine more explicitly what they are. §§ 8—10.

First of all τὸ πιθανόν is a relative notion; that which is persuasive must be persuasive to some one; persuasion must have an object: secondly, persuasion acts either directly and immediately, like an intuition or sense, when the statement seems convincing and credible at once and by itself, or by its own virtue, without the aid of reasoning; or else by the intermediate process of a proof derived from considerations, arguments, or premisses similar to those just described, such, namely, as carry immediate conviction; and thirdly no art looks to the individual or particular as its object and aim, as medicine to Socrates or Callias—it does not investigate what is wholesome or unwholesome to *him* individually—but always to classes or universals, [this is one of the characteristics of 'art' as distinguished from ἐμπειρία, Metaph. A. I.] to one of such and such a constitution, or to several of the same sort—particulars being infinite and not to be comprehended in our knowledge—accordingly [of the *three* προτάσεις the ἀπόδοσις follows from the third *only*] rhetoric will not consider what is probable only to this or

[1] Of these two great instruments of reasoning it is further said, Rhet. I. 9. 40, that the example is more suitable to the deliberative branch of rhetoric, because we decide upon what is future by reference to past examples: the enthymeme to the forensic branch, because the past admits more of proving and assigning causes by reason of the obscurity that attends the investigation of it. To the same effect, III. 17. 5. The same is said of the use of πίστεις in forensic rhetoric in Rhet. ad Alex. c. 7. § 2.

that *individual*, Socrates or Hippias, but that which is probable to members of a given class, τοῖς τοιούτοις, men of such and such a sort or kind, of a given character and qualities, like dialectics. Both of them, though they may theoretically be applied to argue any possible question or problem, yet practically both are limited; for both of them alike derive their problems and theses not from any question taken at random and without consideration, ἐξ ὧν ἔτυχεν, senseless or immoral it may be, nor from the views and opinions of all persons alike, for fools, madmen, idiots have *some* fancies, φαίνεται γὰρ ἄττα καὶ τοῖς παραληροῦσιν; but dialectics from subjects which really require discussion, to see on which side of a disputed question the truth really lies, and rhetoric from the subjects of ordinary deliberation[1]. The province and function of the latter lie in the things that we are accustomed to deliberate about, things probable merely and contingent, where we have no 'arts' ready made to furnish us with general rules for their decision; and it addresses itself to a popular audience, to hearers who are unable to take in at a glance (συνορᾶν), to take a simultaneous or *comprehensive* view of, the several steps of a protracted argument, or to carry in their minds a long chain of reasoning. That is to say, from the character of the audience who are usually unaccustomed to long trains of close and connected reasoning, the mode of argumentation, as well as the materials, the opinions maxims and principles appealed to, must be all alike *popular*. Now we deliberate about things contingent and probable, which appear, (are supposed,) to admit the possibility of opposite conclusions views and

---

[1] Top. A. 10., 104. a. 4. οὐ γὰρ πᾶσαν πρότασιν οὐδὲ πᾶν πρόβλημα διαλεκτικὸν θετέον· οὐδεὶς γὰρ ἂν προτείνειε νοῦν ἔχων τὸ μηδενὶ δοκοῦν, οὐδὲ προβάλοι τὸ πᾶσι φανερὸν ἢ τοῖς πλείστοις· τὰ μὲν γὰρ οὐκ ἔχει ἀπορίαν, τὰ δ' οὐδεὶς ἂν θείη. On the proper subjects of discussion, see Eth. Eud. I. 3, where the principles laid down are precisely similar to those of the Topics and Rhetoric. Eudemus is applying them to determine the proper subject of Ethics. τοῖς παραφρονοῦσιν is there represented § 1., by τοῖς παιδαρίοις, καὶ τοῖς κάμνουσι καὶ παραφρονοῦσι.

results; in respect *either* of the truth or falsehood, the right or wrong of them, as opinions; or their probable issue, as events, or future courses of action to be recommended or discouraged, in so far as they are good or evil, expedient or prejudicial, where the event is unknown or the exact truth cannot be ascertained: for no one ever deliberates about things which offer no alternative, which can only exist or issue in one way, things necessary, τὰ μὴ ἐνδεχόμενα ἄλλως ἔχειν,—at least on that supposition; for of course such matters *may* be argued in ignorance that they are fixed and unalterable, and we have no power to determine them, [see on the proper objects of βούλευσις, Eth. Nic. III. 5]—because there is nothing to be gained by it. §§ 11, 12.

It is possible to reason and to draw conclusions, either by a connected chain of demonstration from propositions and premisses, the truth of which has been previously demonstrated by syllogism, or from such as have not yet been regularly and scientifically concluded, but require syllogistic demonstration because they are *not* probable : now both of these must be unfit for the use of the rhetorician, who has but a popular and unscientific audience to address ; the first must plainly be difficult to follow from its length, the judge (the hearer in all the three branches may be called 'a judge', see above p. 137, n. 1.) being presumed to be a 'simple' person, ἁπλοῦς; the second will make no impression on the minds of the audience, will not be readily accepted and credible to them, because they are not gathered from admitted facts or probable acknowledged principles, but on the contrary require proof; and from this it necessarily follows that the materials of both enthymeme and example must be things which may usually, for the most part, be other than they are, liable to change, contingent and variable; the example as a kind of induction, the enthymeme as a syllogism. The enthymene is deduced from few premisses (is a syllogism whose major premiss is so evident that it needs little or no previous proof. Schrader.), and often (*always*,

I believe; else what remains to distinguish it from the dialectical syllogism?) consists of fewer propositions (including the conclusion) than the primary or normal syllogism (the syllogism of the first figure : or, the typical, normal, original syllogism of which all the rest are only varieties) : because if any of these is already well known—and the propositions of the rhetorician *are* well known, being popular and current maxims and opinions, and generally accepted rules and principles, which he uses for the major premisses of his arguments—there is no occasion to state it at all; the listener will supply it for himself. Suppose for example, we wish to show (as in an epideictic or panegyrical speech) that Dorieus[1] has been victor in a contest for which a crown is the prize; we need only say that he has won an Olympic victory; the major premiss, that all Olympic contests have a crown for the prize may be omitted, because it is universally known. The *syllogism* at full length is,

    All Olympic contests (and therefore victories) have a crown for the prize;
    Dorieus won an Olympic victory;
    Ergo, Dorieus had a crown for his prize.

The *enthymeme* omits the well-known major, and merely argues that,

    Dorieus won an Olympic victory;
    and therefore, had a crown for his prize. § 13.

The materials or propositions of which enthymemes are constructed are only in very rare cases 'necessary': the objects of our decisions and investigations are almost always variable, admitting of opposite issues : for the object of deli-

---

[1] Dorieus is here selected as one of the most famous of Olympic victors. His second victory furnishes Thucydides with a date for the 89th Olympiad, B.C. 428. ἦν δὲ 'Ολυμπιὰς ᾗ Δωριεὺς 'Ρόδιος τὸ δεύτερον ἐνίκα. His two other Olympic victories were won in the preceding and following Olympiads, B.C. 432 and 424. Pausanias VI. 7. 1. παγκρατίῳ νικήσας ὀλυμπιάσιν ἐφεξῆς τρίσιν. Besides these he likewise gained eight victories at the Isthmian, and seven at the Nemean games. Ibid. § 2.

beration and inquiry (which supply the materials of rhetoric) is human action; and since no action, possibly with this or that exception, ὡς ἔπος εἰπεῖν, (in consequence of the freedom of the will) is subject to necessary laws, all of them must be contingent and undetermined. Again, the premises and principles from which we deduce our conclusions must be derived from others of the same kind, neither universal nor necessary, but only possible, ἐνδεχόμενα, and *generally* true: whereas science draws necessary conclusions from necessary premisses—which has been already explained in the Analytics[1]. And from all this it plainly follows, that the materials which go to the construction of enthymemes, though they *may* be necessary, yet are for the most part, with few and rare exceptions, only probable, and generally, not universally, true; whether they are referred to present facts as opinions, or to future events as contingencies. These materials are εἰκότα and σημεῖα: and as the enthymemes *are* derived from them, it follows that these two must be identical with the same materials as previously divided into necessary and probable each to each; the necessary portion of the σημεῖα, the τεκμήρια, being the ἀναγκαῖα of the other division, the remaining σημεῖα and εἰκότα coinciding with the second[2]. § 14.

[1] Anal. Pr. 1. 8. where three degrees of certainty are distinguished, ὑπάρχειν, ἐξ ἀνάγκης ὑπάρχειν, ἐνδέχεσθαι ὑπάρχειν. Comp. c. 13. 32. b. 4. where the same three are differently expressed, the necessary; and two kinds of possibility; the usual τὸ ὡς ἐπὶ τὸ πολύ, the next degree; and the indefinite, where the chances are even whether the things be so or not, to which belongs the family of accidents, τὸ ἀπὸ τύχης.

[2] This seems the only possible interpretation of ἀνάγκη τούτων ἑκάτερον ἑκατέρῳ ταὐτὸ εἶναι. It cannot mean that εἰκότα and σημεῖα are the same one with the other, which is not only a false statement, but a most faulty expression. Even if the interpretation in the text be the true one—and I see no other—the expression is very incorrect; taken literally it is not true: the σημεῖα as a whole, are not identical with the ἀναγκαῖα. A seeming, but unreal, interpretation φαινομένη ἐξήγησις, of the passage, is to understand by τούτων ἑκάτερον ἑκατέρῳ ταὐτὸ 'each of the two things' last mentioned, the εἰκότα and σημεῖα; the meaning being supposed to be 'that either of these is the same as the other,' in so far as each of them

ΕΙΚΟΣ, ΣΗΜΕΙΟΝ, ΤΕΚΜΗΡΙΟΝ.

As preliminary to the account, which follows in the chapter on which we are engaged, of the materials of the rhetorician's enthymemes, the εἰκότα, σημεῖα, and τεκμήρια, we will first transcribe from the Organon, Anal. Pr. II. 27, the logical description of them there given, and not repeated in the Rhetoric.

Εἰκός and σημεῖον are not the same thing: εἰκός is a probable proposition or premiss; what is known to be or not to be, or to turn out or not to turn out (γίγνεσθαι, follow, as a resulting *event*, or physical *growth*, or general *consequence*), *usually* in such and such a way; any thing that follows a general, not universal, rule, is said to be 'probable;' as hatred follows envy, or love attends the objects of affection, for the most part, not invariably[1].

is only ὡς ἐπὶ τὸ πολύ. But to say nothing of the objections to this, already noticed, it is plain that with this interpretation the consequence asserted in the text does not follow: for how can the resemblance to one another of εἰκότα and σημεῖα in respect of their being no more than probable follow from the fact that enthymemes are constructed out of them, when we had been told just before that some of the materials of the enthymemes are *necessary* τεκμήρια? And besides all this the statement of the *identity* of εἰκός and σημεῖον would be contradicted by the negation of the same in Anal. Pr. II. 27. (in the passage which follows in the text.)

[1] A very different account of εἰκός is given in the Rhet. ad Alex. c. 8. § 3. and the unscientific and immoral character of the mode of treatment and motives suggested, which characterised the 'Arts' of the sophistical school of rhetoricians, is made very

clearly to appear. The 'probable' is that which, when it is stated, at once suggests to the hearers similar examples which they have already present in their minds. As when a man says that he wishes his country to be great, or prosperity to his friends and misfortune to his enemies, every one supposes this to be probable, because he is conscious of the existence of similar feelings in himself. There are accordingly three kinds of probability available for the rhetorician, arising from the three different sources of interest supplied by our nature. The first has reference to the πάθη or feelings of the audience; their present mood of mind; contempt or terror, pleasure or pain, or any other emotion by which they happen to be influenced. These the speaker must ascertain, and to these he must appeal, and humour them by his speech, συμπαραλαμβάνειν τοῖς λόγοις. Secondly, their habits and associations must be studied in the same way, and the

A sign affects to be, would be if it could, βούλεται εἶναι, (and herein it is distinguished from the probable proposition, which *is already* probable) a demonstrative proposition, necessary or probable (the τεκμήριον necessary, the σημεῖον proper probable): for anything that accompanies an existing thing or fact, or precedes or follows anything that happens or comes into being, is a sign either of its existence or of its having happened[1]. Now an enthymeme is a kind of syllogism whose materials are εἰκότα and σημεῖα; and of the latter there are three kinds corresponding to the place of the middle term in the three syllogistic figures. If the sign is the invariable accompaniment of the fact to which it bears witness, it is a τεκμήριον, a certain or necessary sign, and this can be thrown into a syllogism of the first figure, with an irrefutable conclusion. Let A be conception (κύειν), B milk (the middle term), C a woman. Here the sign is invariable; the milk is the invariable accompaniment of conception. We can therefore say,

All B is A.
C is B.
∴ C is A.

and in this case the sign, milk, which is here the middle

---

speech accommodated to them. And thirdly, their interests or profit (κέρδος) must be in like manner appealed ‑to, "for we are often led by this to do violence to our nature and our character." § 7. Every thing when represented in any of these three ways will appear probable.

[1] The sign is well enough defined by the author of the Rhet. ad Alex. c. 13. § 1. σημεῖον δ' ἐστὶν ἄλλο ἄλλου, οὐ τὸ τυχὸν τοῦ τυχόντος οὐδ' ἅπαν παντός, ἀλλὰ τό γ' εἰθισμένον γίνεσθαι πρὸ τοῦ πράγματος ἢ ἅμα τῷ πράγματι ἢ μετὰ τὸ πρᾶγμα. His τεκμήριον is altogether different from Aristotle's,

c. 10. Cicero de Inv. I. 29. 46, gives the following account of 'the probable.' Probabile autem est id, quod fere solet fieri, aut quod in opinione positum est, aut quod habet in se ad hæc quandam similitudinem, sive id falsum est sive verum. In eo genere quod fere solet fieri, probabile hujusmodi est: si mater est, diligit filium: si avarus est, negligit jusjurandum. In eo autem quod in opinione positum est, hujusmodi sunt probabilia: impiis apud inferos pœnas esse paratos; eos qui philosophiæ dent operam non arbitrari deos esse.

term, is a certain and infallible indication of the fact of conception.

The same example of a τεκμήριον is given in the Rhetoric. Philoponus ad Arist. de Anim. I. fol. 7. b. illustrates it by smoke and fire; and the changes of the moon (τὸ οὕτω φωτίζεσθαι, that she is lighted as she is) are a certain sign of her spherical form.

Another kind of sign, which may give rise to a syllogism in the third figure, is never more than probable, and is always susceptible of refutation. Suppose we say that it is a sign that all wise men are good, because Pittacus is wise and good. The syllogism takes this form—

Pittacus is good
Pittacus is wise
All wise men are good,

but this conclusion is never safe from refutation (ὁ διὰ τοῦ ἐσχάτου, the third figure, λύσιμος) because we have no right to draw a <u>universal conclusion from</u> two particular premisses: in the third figure we can have only a particular conclusion.

The following sign gives rise to a syllogism in the *second* figure. Here the middle term is the predicate of both premisses, as in the third it is the subject. We say, paleness is a sign of conception. As before let A be pale, B conception, C a woman. The (assumed) syllogism runs thus. Conception is pale (implies paleness).

This woman is pale,
∴ this woman has conceived.
B is A.
C is A.
∴ C is B.

"but no correct syllogism can be constructed with the terms of this kind: for it does not follow, because a woman that conceives is pale, and this woman is pale, that she must necessarily be pregnant." The syllogism is in fact faulty: A and B in the major premiss are not convertible. It does not follow that because all pregnant women are pale all pale women are pregnant, and therefore C's paleness is no certain proof of her prégnancy. In the second figure the conclusion must always be *negative*. It appears from all this that there is only one kind of sign that is a τεκμήριον; when it is invariable, and universally true, and can therefore be expressed in a syllogism of the first figure. It is to be observed that the distinctive name τεκμήριον does not occur in the Analytics, though the *thing* itself is defined and illustrated by the first of the three examples. One would infer from this that the specific name was an afterthought, and the distinction not completely made out until the Rhetoric was written. The distinction is of course *implied* in the addition of ἀναγκαία to ἔνδοξος πρότασις in 70. a. 7. in the definition of σημεῖον.

It is again remarked, Rhet. II. 24. 5. that the sign, i.e. the σημεῖον proper, as distinguished from the τεκμήριον, cannot be embodied in a conclusive syllogism. Examples of fallacious conclusions from signs are given de Soph. El. c. 5. 167. b. 8. and in Rhet. II. 24, §§ 5. and 7.

Such is the logical exposition of the σημεῖον and τεκμήριον; in the Rhetoric we shall find the description of them much more popular.

Ch. 2. § 15. That which is 'probable,' εἰκός, usually happens; 'the probable' therefore is 'that which usually happens;' but this, the ordinary definition, is not absolutely true, οὐχ ἁπλῶς; it requires some qualification. *Necessary* things may be also said 'usually to happen,' they are habitual and something more. There are two limitations necessary; first that the probable consists of things which *may* be other than they are (which *cannot* be said of things necessary); and secondly that it stands towards the conclusion to be proved, πρὸς ἐκεῖνο πρὸς ὃ εἰκός, towards that to which its (general) probability is directed, i.e. the *particular* probable case which has to be proved, in the relation of universal to particular. Whereas in the case of signs, one kind of them stands in the relation of particular to universal—as when a

11—2

man argues that such and such a particular case or instance is the sign of the prevalence of a general rule including *all* such cases; as in the second example given above, when it is inferred from the particular case of Pittacus, or Socrates. § 18, that all wise men are good—the other has the relation of universal to particular, and is illustrated in § 18. as when we infer from an *assumed* general rule that all hard or quick breathing is a sign of fever, to a particular case of quick respiration which is supposed to indicate a fever. Of these two kinds, the necessary sign is called τεκμήριον: the other, which is not necessary, has no special name to distinguish it from its congener, but goes by the general name of the entire family, σημεῖον. By 'necessary signs' are meant, those that can be made into a demonstrative syllogism, and therefore this kind of sign is a τεκμήριον. This may be gathered from the opinion of the speakers themselves who employ them, and from the derivation of the word. For the one suppose themselves to have made use of a τεκμήριον whenever they think their assertion cannot be refuted, as it is then proved and concluded, πεπερασμένον; and this very word πεπερασμένον by the side of τεκμήριον reminds us that in the old language τέκμαρ (or τέκμωρ, as Homer writes it) and πέρας meant the same thing: so that τεκμήριον is a 'conclusive sign or proof.' σημεῖον, λυτὸν, ἀσυλλόγιστον, II. 25. 12. τεκμήριον, ἄλυτον, συλλελογισμένον. Ib. § 14. Of signs that stand to the conclusion in the relation of particular to universal, there are two kinds: the first may be thus illustrated: Socrates is wise and just, therefore all wise men are just. A sign of this kind can always be refuted, even though the particular proposition be true, because it cannot be converted into a regular demonstrative syllogism. The other kind, included under the general name σημεῖον, is in fact a τεκμήριον, and if the proposition stated be true, is incontrovertible: this arises from the fact that in these cases the connexion between the sign and the thing concluded is uniform, and therefore, as far as we know, necessary: as when the inference is drawn from the milk in a woman's breasts to the birth of a child; or from the existence of fever to disease in general. This is the only kind of sign which, if the alleged fact be true, is incapable of refutation. Of the sign that stands to the conclusion in the relation of universal to particular the following may be taken as an example: it is a sign that a man has a fever when he breathes hard: this assumes that all that breathe hard have a fever and therefore A has a fever. But though the fact be true that a man does breathe hard when he has a fever, yet here the connexion between hard breathing and fever is not a necessary connexion, it is not invariably true that hard breathing implies fever; the terms are not 'convertible,' fever and hard breathing are not coextensive: and therefore 'a sign' of this kind is always capable of refutation. The nature and differences of 'the probable,' of 'sign;' and of 'necessary inference' which have been briefly stated here, have been more explicitly determined in the Analytics (An. Pr. II. 27.), together with the reasons why some of them can be expressed in regular valid syllogisms, whilst others can not. §§ 15—18.

It has been already stated that example is a kind of induction, and the sources or materials of its propositions described (§§ 9—13). The example stands neither in the relation of part to whole (as in induction, by which the universal is gathered from the particular and individual), nor in that of whole to part (as in the opposite process of deduction or syllogism, which concludes from the universal to the particular), nor as whole to whole (the conclusion from universal to universal, likewise effected by syllogism), but in the relation of particular to particular, of like to like; when the example, and the analogous fact that is to be inferred from it, are both under (i.e. species of) the same genus, but the one is better known than the other. For instance if we wish to prove that Dionysius' motive in asking for a body-guard was that he had a design upon the tyranny, because Peisistratus had already asked for one with the same intention, and Theagenes at Megara: in fact from all the cases that we *do* know we may draw the same inference as to Dionysius' motive, with which we are not yet acquainted: and all these 'examples' or cases are under the same general rule or principle (the same genus or universal), that when a man has a design upon the tyranny he demands a body-guard. The universal rule thus arrived at is thus made the major premiss of a syllogism and from it we may now *deduce* the conclusion required in the particular case of Dionysius. [see above, pp. 106, 7.] § 19.

The nature of the propositions of which enthymemes are constructed, those proofs which are taken for demonstrative but really conclude nothing but what is probable, has been already explained. But the most important distinction of enthymemes, which is to be found also in the syllogistic system of dialectics, has been almost entirely overlooked: it is that there is a double division of them; one sort (is in accordance with, ἐστὶ κατά) specially belongs to rhetoric, as also to dialectics, whilst the others are proper to other arts and faculties, either in actual existence or not yet established: and thence the distinction more readily escapes the notice of speakers, [omit τοὺς ἀκροατάς, which is contrary to the sense, with Spengel.] who in proportion to the 'appropriateness' of the method[1] that they adopt, that is, to the degree of precision and exact scientific detail which they introduce into the handling of their subject, in the same degree overstep or transgress (μεταβαίνουσιν) the proper limits of their art. The meaning of this will be more clearly conveyed if it be expressed more at length, in greater detail. § 20.

Dialectical and rhetorical syllogisms and enthymemes (which is included in 'syllogisms', here to be understood

---

[1] On the 'appropriate method,' see Poste, Introd. to Transl. of Post. Anal. p. 20, and notes. Gaisford follows Muretus' emendation μᾶλλον... ἢ κατὰ τρόπον, and explains κ. τρ. by δεόντως. See his note (in Animadv. ad Arist. Rhet.) p. 56. Also Schrader on the same place, p. 55, 6.

as a general term for any kind of deductive reasoning) have for their special and peculiar province what are called οἱ τόποι[1], par excellence; the loci communissimi namely, which may be applied alike to the propositions of a variety of sciences different in kind, Physics, Ethics, Politics. Such a 'topic' is that of "the more or less" or 'degree'; for it will be just as easy to construct a syllogism or enthymeme out of this on an ethical, as on a physical subject or any other of the like; and yet all these (sciences) differ in kind. Distinct from and subordinate to these are the special topics (ἴδια or εἴδη) that belong to, or may be derived from, each kind of science or subject severally; each science or subject of investigation having premisses or propositions of this kind peculiar to itself: as there are propositions in Physics from which no ethical syllogism or enthymeme can be constructed; and again Ethical propositions which will furnish no conclusions in Physical science. The former, the common or universal Topics, will convey no instruction in any special branch of science or inquiry, because they have no 'subject' ὑποκείμενον, no particular class of objects to the study and illustration of which they are especially devoted; in employing the others, the εἴδη, the orator, in proportion to the care he has taken and the judgment he has shown in the selection of his propositions, and to the degree of 'appropriateness' in the propositions selected, will find that he has in the same proportion quitted his own particular province, and has trespassed on the domain of an art different from dialectics and rhetoric: for if he light upon first principles (that is, the ἴδιαι ἀρχαί, the axioms and definitions of the special sciences, he no longer retains the character of a dialectician or rhetorician but assumes that of a student or professor of any science whose principles he has adopted. However most enthymemes are derived from these εἴδη, special and peculiar; few comparatively form the common or universal. Here

[1] More literally, "the objects or materials of dialectical and rhetorical syllogisms are the same as what we call *the* topics."

therefore, as in dialectics, we must make a distinction between the εἴδη and the τόποι, out of which enthymemes may be constructed. By the former are meant the peculiar propositions included under any given class of things (classed as objects of study and science); by the τόποι classes of arguments common to every one of these alike[1]. Let us speak first of the former: but first of all we have to determine ('to find') the number of the 'kinds' of Rhetoric; in order that, when we have done so, we may discover in each case separately, what are their elements or τόποι, and their special propositions. §§ 21. 22.

BOOK I. CHAP. III.

The kinds or branches of Rhetoric are three, determined by the kinds of audience to whom speeches are addressed: for, the speech being made up of three parts, the speaker, the subject of the speech, and the persons addressed, the 'end' has reference to the last; and as everything is defined by its end or object (ὁρίζεται ἕκαστον τῷ τέλει, Eth. Nic. III. 10.), it is this which determines the divisions of rhetoric. The listener must be either a spectator, θεωρός, (a listener for mere amusement like a spectator at the games or in a theatre) or a judge; and a judge either of the past or of the future. But all three may be regarded as judges (comp. II. 18. 1). The member of the Assembly may be taken as an instance (οἷον ἐκκλησιαστής, meaning that though he is only one of a number of judges of the future, yet he is so in a peculiar sense, par excellence, and far the most important

---

[1] We learn from this passage what the term 'species' εἴδη has relation to as its genus. These special topics are species of the genera of the sciences which fall under rhetorical treatment. They are also *treated* as species under the three genera or branches of rhetoric, though it is not from this relation that the *name* is borrowed. They are *not* species of the τόποι or loci communissimi: with these they have no connexion, except that the τόποι can be *applied* to any of them if required.

representative of the class) of a judge of the future; the dicast or juror in a court of law is a judge of the past; the 'spectator' may be regarded as a 'judge' of the faculty or skill shown (δυνάμεως), and his 'judgment' or decision is shown in 'criticising'; he is in fact a 'critic'. There are therefore necessarily three kinds of rhetorical speeches, the deliberative or public kind of speaking, the judicial, and the panegyrical, or declamatory (epideictic or show speeches). The advice which is given by the deliberative, hortative, or political speaker consists of two parts or elements, exhortation, encouragement, and dissuasion; for those that offer advice to their friends privately always do one or the other. Forensic speaking is exercised in either accusation or defence; one or the other of which is necessarily the office of both parties in a legal process. To the epideictic or declamatory orator belong praise and blame, encomium and censure. The 'times' which are the spheres of operation of these three are for the counsellor or deliberative speaker the future (present time being also sometimes included, see I. 6. 1, 8. 7.)—for his advice is always (so to speak) directed to some future object whether in exhorting or dissuading; for the judge in the law court the past—for accusation and defence have always reference to something already done—; to the declamatory speaker the present time is most properly assigned; for though he often refers to the past in the way of reminiscence, and to the future in the way of anticipation, yet it is to the present character and condition of the object of his declamation that he really and substantially directs his approbation or censure: [so that even in a funeral oration the orator's 'time' may still be considered as the present.]. Each of the three has a distinct end and object in view: the counsellor's arguments are directed to what is expedient or injurious—Political Expediency is the usual subject of the public speaker—when he exhorts or encourages to a course of action, he advises it because it is 'better', more to the interest of his audience; or if he dissuades, it is because the course of policy from which he wishes to divert them is 'worse', or disadvantageous, inexpedient for them: every other consideration, just and unjust, fair and foul, right and wrong, when taken into their argument is subordinate and subsidiary, only with reference to, or to promote, this his principal end.

[As Aristotle has failed to illustrate this very important distinction, it will be well to say a few words in explanation of it. No orator, unless in very rare and special cases, can absolutely confine himself to expediency as the *sole* motive of action, because if this is directly and nakedly stated the minds of any ordinary audience are revolted and alienated thereby: seldom indeed does it happen that any speaker dares, like the Athenian envoys in their dialogue with the Melians (Thuc. Bk. v.), to assert that it is the duty of a state to consult its own interests at the expense of all the obligations of justice and mercy. Still this is his main point, the predominating principle to which he appeals, and the doctrine of expediency is therefore characteristic of this genus. Justice and honour are taken in, when they are appealed to, as adjuncts, συμπαραλαμβάνει § 5., and occupy a quite subordinate position. Though subordinate, such considerations are nevertheless, except in such extreme cases as the one already cited, always taken into account: and even Cleon in his cold-blooded and cruel argument for the extermination of the Mitylencans finds himself obliged to throw a specious veil of justice over his unscrupulous policy, ἐν δὲ ξυνελὼν λέγω, πειθόμενοι μὲν ἐμοὶ τά τε δίκαια ἐς Μυτιληναίους καὶ τὰ ξύμφορα ἅμα ποιήσετε. Thuc. III. 40.]

The parties in a legal case have for their object the just and unjust; every thing else that they introduce is subsidiary and relative to this. Those that commend or censure, in epideictic oratory, have the fair and foul, honour and disgrace, right and wrong, for their end; and all the rest they likewise refer to these. As a sign that the thing specified in each case *is* the real object that each kind of speaker has in view, we may refer to the fact that in many cases the speaker could hardly contend for any thing else beyond his own special object, that so and so is either expedient or just or noble: as for instance a man on his trial often would not care to contend that the act with which he is charged either was not done at all, or did no harm; but that it was unjust or a crime he never could be brought to allow; if he did, there would be no need of a trial at all. In the same way counsellors, though they are ready to abandon every other consideration, will never admit either that what they are recommending is inexpedient, or what they are dissuading profitable; as to the *injustice* of reducing their unoffending neighbours to slavery, *that* they pay no attention to at all (they utterly disregard). And so in like manner, in praising and blaming, the speakers never consider whether the acts of the object of their panegyric or censure were beneficial or injurious; nay they often assign it to their hero's praise that he neglected his own interest in the pursuit of some noble and great action, as when Achilles went to the rescue of his friend Patroclus though he knew that he must die for it, when he might have lived had he refrained: to *him* life was indeed precious, but such a death was more glorious. § 1—6.

From what has been said it is plain that these three, the expedient, the just, the fair and noble, are the subjects from which the rhetorician must chiefly and primarily gather his premisses and propositions, because these are the materials of the probabilities, signs, and necessary inferences, which constitute the rhetorician's premisses: the entire syllogism is constructed of propositions (including the conclusion as a πρότασις? or, ἐκ 'derived from', meaning that the conclusion or result of the reasoning is deduced from the two premisses?), and the enthymeme is a kind of syllogism composed of the premisses or propositions before mentioned. These are the ἴδιαι προτάσεις, τὰ ἴδια, or εἴδη, borrowed from Ethics and Politics. Secondly, since all rhetoric is conversant with human action, and all actions, past and future, must be possible, none impossible; and nothing that has not happened or will not happen can ever have been done, or is capable of ever being done at any future time, the rhetorician in all the three branches of the art must necessarily be supplied with premisses in the general topics of the 'possible and impossible', and of 'fact past and future. These are topics common to all the three branches of rhetoric, as are likewise those of 'magnitude', excellence, importance, absolute and comparative—the latter of the two the topic of 'degree', τὸ μᾶλλον καὶ ἧττον, the former amplification and depreciation, τὸ αὔξειν καὶ μειοῦν—which can be applied alike to good and bad, just and unjust, fair and foul, either absolutely in themselves, or relatively to one another, and therefore are κοινοί, common to persuasion and dissuasion in deliberative rhetoric, to accusation and defence in judicial, and to commendation and censure in epideictic. These are the topics, special and common, in which the rhetorician must necessarily be furnished with a stock of propositions to draw upon for use. We have next to analyse individually the subjects or contents of each of the three branches of the art, first of the deliberative which offers advice, secondly of the epideictic, and thirdly of the forensic variety. §§ 7—9.

BOOK I. CHAP. IV.

We have first to discover what *are* the good and bad things which the counsellor and deliberative orator gives his advice about: since they do not *all* come within his sphere, but only those that are possible, that may be brought to pass or not (things contingent); nothing which must of necessity be, now or hereafter, or which cannot possibly exist or be made to exist, can be the subject of advice or exhortation. But even possible things, that may or not be, are not all included in the counsellor's province; for there are some natural and accidental gifts and advantages, as personal beauty, health, strength, or the gifts of fortune, as wealth acquired by finding a treasure, or any other piece of good luck, which are desirable no doubt, but not being within our own control are not fit subjects for advice. But it is plain that advice is confined to those things that we deliberate about; and these are all such as may be referred to ourselves as authors and agents, or 'of which the origin of generation (i. e. of bringing about, or effecting) is in our own power'. For in deliberating or advising we always carry back our inquiries until we have arrived at this point; until we have ascertained, namely, whether what we are consulting about be in our power to do or not. §§ 1—3.

Now to go through an exact and complete enumeration and division into kinds of all the objects of men's ordinary business and deliberations, and further to attempt to define them with the degree of precision which would be required by the exact scientific method, would be altogether out of place in a work like the present, because inquiries of this nature do not belong to a popular art like rhetoric, but to a more 'intelligent' and 'exact' method (ἐμφρονεστέρας καὶ μᾶλλον ἀληθινῆς, one which works more with its eyes open, can see deeper into the nature of things, deduce *certain* and *necessary*, and not like rhetoric mere probable conclusions, and is in general more instructive, philosophical, or scientific[1]), and a great deal more has been already assigned to it than really belongs to its own proper objects of inquiry. For, as has been before observed, rhetoric is a combination of the logical branch of science (ἀναλυτικῆς, meaning of course dialectics, which is here improperly included in Analytics, the doctrine of the *demonstrative* syllogism: ἀναλυτική being here put for Logic in general[2]), and the

---

[1] Comp. I. I. 12. διδασκαλίας γάρ ἐστιν ὁ κατὰ τὴν ἐπιστήμην λόγος. I. 2. 21. κἀκεῖνα (the κοινοὶ τόποι) οὐ ποιήσει περὶ οὐδὲν γένος ἔμφρονα. Metaph. Λ. 1004. b. 25. ἔστι δὲ ἡ διαλεκτικὴ πειραστικὴ περὶ ὧν ἡ φιλοσοφία γνωριστική. de Soph. El. c. 2.

[2] Poste, Introd. to Tr. of Anal. p. 19.

Ethical branch of Politics, and corresponds to dialectics together with its sophistical appendage, the art of fallacious reasoning. "But the further we recede in the treatment of dialectics or rhetoric from the conception of them as mere practical faculties (δυνάμεις, τοῦ πορίσαι λόγους I. 2. 7) and attempt to construct or establish them as sciences, in that same proportion shall we be unconsciously effacing their true nature, by transgressing, in our attempt to *re*construct or *re*constitute them (ἐπισκευάζειν, to *re*model or *re*fashion, *alter* the form), their proper limits, and trespassing upon the province of sciences of certain definite subject-matters[1]." The proper business of the two arts is merely to find topics of argument and apply to them a correct logical method; except so far as the materials of rhetoric are derived from Ethics and Politics, they have no special subject-matter like the sciences; of which Arithmetic has its numbers, Geometry its 'properties of magnitude', Anatomy the structure of animal bodies, Botany its plants, Zoology its living sentient animals.

Still, so far as an analysis of some of these topics (i.e. the Ethical and Political materials) is useful for the purposes of the rhetorician, we will now proceed to enter upon it: carefully abstaining from any encroachment upon the domain of the Political Philosopher, and leaving something still remaining (ἔτι) for his inquiries. §§ 4—6.

We shall now quit this detailed paraphrase, and state the contents of the following chapters merely by way of summary and in outline, so as to trace the connexion and sequence of the treatment of the several parts of the system; until we come to the third book, in which the extreme brevity and elliptical obscurity of the style will render it desirable to resume the method of a running commentary.

The remainder of the first book is accordingly occupied

---

[1] "If you try to convert Dialectic from a method of discussion into a method of cognition, you will insensibly eliminate its true nature and character." Grote, Plato, Vol. I. p. 234 note z.

with the analysis of the εἴδη, derived from Political and Ethical materials, and arranged under the heads of the three branches of rhetoric, the deliberative, the epideictic, and the forensic; the order in which they are actually treated. The 15th chapter is an appendix on the ἄτεχνοι πίστεις. These are to furnish the materials of the *logical* πίστεις. The ethical or indirect πίστεις are derived from two sources, the ἦθος and the πάθη, which, together with some supplementary ἤθη of a peculiar kind, are treated in the first seventeen chapters of the second book, the ἦθος being very summarily dealt with in the first chapter; for the analysis of its topics we are referred *back* to the chapter on the virtues, I. 9, for the treatment of ἀρετή and φρόνησις; and *forwards* to the following analysis of the πάθη for the topics of εὔνοια and φιλία. In the 18th chapter of Bk. II. the subject of the logical πίστεις is resumed; the κοινοὶ τόποι are exemplified in c. 19, the κοιναὶ πίστεις discussed and illustrated in c. 20, 21, 22; and from c. 23 to the end of the book we have a selection of τόποι described which may furnish the rhetorician with classes of serviceable enthymemes; then a similar selection and illustration of fallacious enthymemes; and finally the various modes of refutation and solution of arguments and objections appropriate to rhetoric. The third book is occupied with the treatment of style, delivery, and the divisions of the speech, a part of the work which is mentioned now for the first time in the concluding words of the second.

Ch. 4. § 7. Aristotle begins the analysis of the various εἴδη by borrowing from Politics the principal questions and subjects with which the deliberative or <u>public speaker</u> will have to deal. These resolve themselves into five, which are the chief matters of national interest; viz. finance or revenue, (πόροι), war and peace, the defence of the country, exports and imports, or trade, and legislation. The public speaker must be in some sense a statesman, so far at least as to have a popular knowledge of these and similar objects of national concern. The analysis will furnish him with materials for his enthymemes; and some of the items of the information which he must possess are given in detail under general heads or εἴδη.

There is a very remarkable discrepancy between the two lists of the subjects of ordinary deliberation in a legislative assembly which we find here and in the Politics, IV. 4. In the latter we have in addition to some of the Topics of the Rhetoric, συμμαχία καὶ διάλυσις, concluding and breaking off alliances; decisions in legal cases involving the penalties of death; banishment and confiscation, περὶ θανάτου καὶ φυγῆς καὶ δημεύσεως; the control of the accounts of officers of state, περὶ τῶν εὐθυνῶν; whilst those of commerce (exports and imports), the defence of the country, and finance, which appear in the Rhetoric, are omitted. Neither of them is, or is intended to be complete and exhaustive; and why the divergence should be so unusually wide it is not easy to guess. Certainly the popular character of rhetoric, and the comparatively scientific treatment of Politics, will not here account for it.

Ch. 5. Again, happiness is the end of all human action individual and collective, the end therefore with reference to which men choose and avoid: accordingly to this all exhortation and dissuasion must ultimately be directed. Hence the analysis of happiness and its parts. Here we are introduced into the province of Ethics, but we have no comparative views, no disquisitions, no ἀπορίαι, above all no scientific definition, such as we find in the Ethical treatise. The definitions of, or rather opinions about, happiness in § 3., are all of the most popular kind; they express several of the current and prevailing notions as to the nature and meaning of the term; such as are generally known, or if not, likely from their probability to be generally accepted. Virtue, though an essential element of happiness, comes more properly under the ἐπιδεικτικὸν γένος of which τὸ καλόν, honestum, is the τέλος; it is therefore reserved to be treated under that head, in c. 9.

Ch. 6. The end of συμβουλή is τὸ συμφέρον, 'the interest' of the individual or the nation, especially political expediency. But all that is συμφέρον is ἀγαθόν; and hence 'good' is the subject of the analysis of the sixth chapter. In § 3. there is a series of definitions of good of precisely the same character as those of happiness in the chapter preceding. This as well as the other is introduced by the characteristic ἔστω, let it be assumed that any of these definitions is sufficient; it is not required that they should be exact, so long as they are accepted and intelligible. In the first three sections the *general principles* are laid down, in the remainder of the chapter these are applied and illustrated.

Ch. 7. This seventh chapter contains the application of the κοινὸς τόπος of 'degree,' τὸ μᾶλλον καὶ ἧττον, to the subject of the last, viz. good. It is introduced with the remark, that as we often have to choose between two good things, it is not enough to know what is good absolutely, but we must also be able to decide between two different goods, and to judge of them comparatively and relatively: we want to know what is more and less good in general and in particular cases, and hence the application of the topic of degree to the εἴδη of the last chapter.

Some of the sections of this chapter are obscure from the extreme brevity of expression and confusion of style: it will be well to explain them here, in order to avoid encumbering the text with long notes on the several passages.

DEFINITIONS OF GOOD REPEATED FROM CH. 6, AND OF GREATER AND LESS GOOD.

Good, § 3, is that which is desirable for its own sake and not for any thing else : or it may be called, the universal aim, or object of desire: or it might be defined what every thing, or if not every thing, at any rate every thing that is possessed of, or could acquire, reason and practical wisdom would choose (even the lower animals, or inanimate objects if they could get them; compare c. 6 § 2.) and all that tends to produce or to preserve such things; and every thing of which this is the accompaniment;—here he breaks off, and introduces a parenthesis suggested by the first two definitions; but that which is the object of all actions and aspirations is the 'end', and it is to this end that every thing else is directed; and good in the highest sense, in and for itself, is that which is 'thus affected', presents these characteristics or phenomena (ταῦτα such as we have described), or stands in this relation to, itself; that is, is the end in itself—such is good: and since the property of the greater is to exceed the less, and the less is contained in the greater, it necessarily follows that the larger number of good things is 'a greater good' than a single one or a smaller number; provided the one good or the smaller number, as the case may be, is reckoned into the account of the larger number in question. That is to say, for instance, virtue, health, wealth, strength, personal beauty are superior to virtue alone: but this *one* must be admitted into the class with the rest; for it may be that virtue alone outweighs all the rest put together. If virtue be not 'enumerated with them' the proposition need not be true. This is Schrader's explanation of συναριθμουμένου, and is doubtless the true one. A different one is given by Sir A. Grant in his note on Eth. N. I. 7. 8.

ἐπεί...ἀνάγκη are grammatically protasis and apodosis; but the latter is not a consequence of the former, nor in *necessary* connexion with it. The protasis merely states a fact, enumerates some different notions, and some particular varieties of 'good' in a general sense. The ἀνάγκη does not in any way depend upon this, for what has the meaning and definition of good to do with the superiority of the larger number to one or fewer? The 'necessity' is argued from this, that the larger number contains the smaller and the smaller is contained in it, omne *majus* continet in se minus. τὸ δ' οὗ ἕνεκα—πεπονθός, is as already observed a parenthesis suggested by the preceding. This is a not very uncommon instance of Aristotelean carelessness in writing.

The topic of 'consequence', § 5, τὸ ἑπόμενον, appears in the Topics, Γ. 2. 117. 5. where it is treated more briefly than it is here, and only two cases included under it τὸ ἕπεσθαι πρότερον καὶ ὕστερον. The notion of 'consequence', τὸ ἕπεσθαι, is extended *technically* to attendants, concomitants, connexions of various kinds; thus we have a prior or antecedent, as well as a posterior or subsequent 'consequent'. The same word, as well as its synonym ἀκολουθεῖν, is often used elsewhere in the same extended signification.

These 'consequents' have been already mentioned I. 6. 3., where only two of them, the contemporaneous, simultaneous, or coincident, ἅμα; and the consequent proper, the succeeding, ὕστερον. To these are now added the prior or antecedent, which is implied in ἐφεξῆς, ('succession' may be interpreted of what precedes, as well as of what succeeds, any thing else) and the ἑπόμενον δυνάμει 'the potential or virtual consequent or concomitant', that which is *implied in* the other. And further in the Topics B. 8. 113. b. 15. seq. we find a fifth, 'reciprocal consequents', ἡ κατὰ τὴν ἀντίφασιν ἀκολούθησις, otherwise ἀντικατηγορουμένως, where two terms or propositions are 'convertible', ἀντιστρέφει.

The application of the topic to the three examples given is as follows. When B follows A, but not reciprocally, then A is greater, superior to, more important, of higher value than B. Thus life always follows or accompanies health; without life health is impossible; or, health implies life. Consequently since life is necessary to health, but health is not necessary to life—the 'consequence' is not reciprocal—health in this point of view may be considered superior to life. This is a case of 'simultaneous' (ἅμα) 'consequence' or connexion. So of knowledge and learning: learning necessarily implies knowledge, as following, subsequent to, it, ὕστερον: but the converse is not true; knowledge, (immediate knowledge for instance, as the perceptions of the senses and the intuitive apprehension of the νοῦς) does not necessarily imply learning. *In this sense* therefore—it *is* a paradox, *only* true in this sense—learning may be considered superior to knowledge because it implies it, but not *reciprocally*. This I think is a fair interpretation of this second example, which is thus brought into conformity with the other two, as an *illustration* of the general topic of μᾶλλον καὶ ἧττον. Schrader however regards it not as an exemplification of the rule of superiority, but as a mere *example* of the second kind of consequents. His reason is, nec tamen de omnibus consequentium generibus propositionem ipsam vult intellectam, sed de iis tantum quæ reciproce non consequuntur. Discere autem et scire utique reciprocantur: ut enim vere dixero, *didicit, ergo scit;* ita contra pariter verum est, *scit, ergo didicit.* But I have already shown that there is a sense in which they are *not* reciprocal, that learning is *not* always the accompaniment of, or implied by, knowledge: and so Schrader's objection falls to the ground. The third example is also a case of non-reciprocity; where the consequent resides perpetually or virtually δυνάμει, ἐνυπάρχει ἡ χρῆσις, in the antecedent; as cheating is implied, virtually contained (ἐνυπάρχει), in sacrilege; by the rule, omne majus continet in se minus. Schrader observes truly enough on the whole of this Topic, that it belongs rather to dialectics than to rhetoric.

If we wish to determine, § 6, the comparative superiority of two things A and B, we may do so by referring them both to a third thing C: if the excess of A above C, is greater than that of B, A will be greater than B. Thus if A be 12, B 9, and C 6, 12, which exceeds 6 by a greater number than that by which it (6) is exceeded by 9, will be greater than 9. Or as Schrader suggests, if the Dictator has more power compared with the Prætor than the Consul, the Dictator is greater than the Consul. A comparison of this sort must always be made between things of the same kind; otherwise there can be no common standard to which to refer them. We cannot for example compare health and wealth in this way. But it seems that it never can have any practical value or really facilitate the determination of the comparative value of two given things. To take the case of motion, suggested by Victorius; if we have to decide upon the relative speed of two horses we shall gain nothing by referring them both to the speed of a third: they are all referred ultimately to the same standard, the amount of space traversed in a given unit of time; this is the real measure, and the introduction of the third horse rather interferes with than helps the calculation. The principle of the Topic is undeniably true, but as it seems to me useless to the Rhetorician.

Ch. 8. The orator must not only be acquainted with the manners, customs, institutions, resources, deficiencies, and all that the true interest of the state requires, but he must also be conversant with the various forms of existing governments; because political expediency is his end and object, and this expediency or state interest has immediate reference to the form of government, consists in fact in things which tend to maintain it in its integrity[1], and it is by an appeal to their interest that people are most readily persuaded. Besides this, it is the governing body whose 'declarations' or decisions give the law to the people, and the governing body varies in every different form of constitution; and therefore the public speaker must be acquainted with the nature of the governing body, and its several varieties under the various forms of government. §§ 12. Accordingly a very brief description is given of the existing constitutions under four heads, democracy, oligarchy, aristocracy, and monarchy.

The treatment of this subject in the present chapter, as compared with Polit. III. 7—18. and IV. and Eth. Nic. VIII. 12., in which it is likewise handled, affords an excellent illustration of the difference between the methods appropriate to a scientific and a popular treatise such as Rhetoric. The divisions and definitions of forms of government as they are

---

[1] The constitution is the state's life. Pol. IV. 11. sub init. ἡ γὰρ πολιτεία βίος τίς ἐστι πόλεως.

here described are merely such as were popularly current and recognised by the popular language; compare Polit. IV. 7. init.; and because they were so recognised would serve best for a popular and general audience: whereas in the Ethics the division is totally different and much more exact; and in the Politics the different constitutions are all carefully studied and analysed in detail, definitions discussed, and a scientific division—the same essentially as that which is proposed in the Ethics—established[1]. Or again compare the requirements of the practical statesman or deliberative orator as they are described here in the Rhetoric with the objects of inquiry laid down and enumerated in the Politics, at the opening of Book IV, and again at the conclusion of the second chapter, as falling within the province of the scientific statesman or Political Philosopher.

The study of the various forms of government is likewise necessary to the deliberative orator for the purpose of giving an 'Ethical' character to his speech, (see above p. 110) by the introduction of what may be called in general terms a political character or tone. A certain tone and certain sentiments and language are peculiar to the members of each state according to the nature of the constitution under which they live. The citizen of a democratic republic has views and sentiments and associations and a set of terms in conformity with these, and will not listen with patience to expressions or suggestions which are *not* in conformity with them; he will disapprove of oligarchical or monarchical sentiments, and be pleased with such expressions as fall in with his own notions and experience and habits of thinking. The orator must accommodate his language to these associations, and use democratic language to the members of a democracy, oligarchical to an oligarchical audience, and so

---

[1] I will reserve for an Appendix at the end of this book an account of these two classifications, to one of which Aristotle himself refers us, § 7, and compare them with those of Plato, which we find in his Politicus and Republic. See Appendix A. to Bk. I.

on for the rest: τὸ μὲν γὰρ ἑκάστης ἦθος πιθανώτατον ἀνάγκη πρὸς ἑκάστην εἶναι. § 6.

With the eighth chapter the analysis of the deliberative branch of rhetoric is brought to an end. It concludes with a brief summary of the contents of the preceding chapters, 4—8, and the remark that the mode of treatment of these topics has been in accordance with the requirements of the present occasion; that is to say, popular, in conformity with the 'probable' and popular nature of the materials of the subject. The author refers his readers to the Politics for a fuller and more exact discussion of the matters handled in the last chapter. διηκρίβωται γὰρ ἐν τοῖς πολιτικοῖς περὶ τούτων.

Ch. 9. The second branch of rhetoric, the ἐπιδεικτικὸν γένος, here taken out of its usual order—it is usually put last as the least important of the three—is dispatched in a single chapter. Its contents are the objects of praise and censure, ἔπαινος and ψόγος being the ends and the constituent parts of the declamatory species. From these therefore all its topics must be derived; and we consequently have to analyse ἀρετή and κακία, τὸ καλόν and τὸ αἰσχρόν, and in general all that merits and generally receives praise and blame.

The definitions of virtue and the virtues at the commencement of this chapter illustrate, like that of happiness in c. 5. § 3. and of good in c. 6. § 2., and the Classification of Constitutions in the preceding, the popular method of treatment required by Rhetoric. It is worth while to compare the definition of virtue as it is presented here with the celebrated one of the Nicomachean Ethics, II. 6. "Virtue" it is here said § 4, " as is generally supposed (ὡς δοκεῖ), is a faculty capable of supplying or producing and preserving good things; or a faculty capable of conferring many great services or benefits, in fact of doing any thing in every thing." This last part of the definition, which is, as Victorius tells us, a proverbial phrase, implies an universal ability or capacity, exercised with a good object in view—that is, if we are to repeat εὐεργετική with πάντων, and not rather to understand the more general ποιητική as implied in it, which I rather prefer, as expressing universal ability or excellence in any thing, without any qualification. This includes all 'excellence' of every kind, physical, mental, and moral. Now contrast this with the Ethical definition. "Virtue is a fixed, permanent, conscious, developed, acquired state (all this is implied in ἕξις) of mind or character, manifesting itself in a deliberate moral purpose (προαιρετική), residing in a mean state, *relative* to ourselves (no absolute standard of morality), the mean being determined by reasoning or calculation (λόγῳ), not however by the individual, subjective, calculation, but by the *general, objective*, standard, of practical wisdom, or the (concrete) man of practical wisdom (ὡς ἂν ὁ φρόνιμος ὁρίσειεν)."

The difference between the definitions of the individual virtues in the two treatises is not so glaring. The lists of virtues given here and in the Ethics, II. 7., are substantially identical. In the Rhetoric the nameless mean between φιλοτιμία and ἀφιλοτιμία is omitted, doubtless because it *is* nameless, and would therefore not be recognised by a popular audience: and for the same reason the three social and conversational virtues (περὶ λόγων καὶ κοινωνίας), ἀλήθεια, a frank, straightforward plainness and simplicity in language and demeanour, (the mean between bragging and swaggering, ἀλαζονεία, and mock-humility, εἰρωνεία); εὐτραπελία, or well-bred pleasantry; and φιλία, friendliness of manner, are excluded; being invented by Aristotle himself, and *not* commonly accepted as virtues; and with them, the so-called virtues consisting in a mean state of two emotions or feelings, πάθη, viz. αἰδώς modesty, and νέμεσις righteous indignation[1]. The *two* intellectual virtues, (Eth. Nic. VI.) σοφία speculative wisdom, or philosophy, and φρόνησις practical wisdom, the special virtue of the statesman (a practical philosopher) are

---

[1] On moral indignation, see Whewell, Elem. of Morality, § 56.

introduced; and justice, which in the Ethics is reserved for subsequent and separate treatment. The chapter is mainly occupied with the analysis into their εἴδη of ἀρετή and κακία, καλόν and αἰσχρόν. Besides the episode on ἔπαινος and ἐγκώμιον in §§ 33, 34 which I reserve for the appendix to this book[1], we have one more general observation, which deserves to be quoted here, in § 40. that, namely, of all the κοινὰ εἴδη —meaning τόποι, with which are here included the two universal instruments of reasoning—that of αὔξησις 'amplification', is most appropriate to this epideictic branch of rhetoric; the example, παράδειγμα, to the deliberative, because we decide upon the future by a divination or presentiment derived from the past; and the enthymeme to the forensic, because past facts most readily admit of being proved by reason of their uncertainty.

Ch. 10. In this chapter we pass to the judicial or forensic kind of rhetoric, of which the parts are accusation and defence, and the end justice and injustice (explained as before). Hence an analysis of the latter, and the study of the feelings and impulses, the characters and objects, of wrong doers, are necessary for the forensic pleader: and this falls naturally under three heads; 1st the objects and causes and motives which lead men to commit wrong; 2nd the characters of the wrong doers; and 3rd the characters and conditions that render men liable to wrong. Injustice or wrong doing assumes the forms of different vices according to the kind of defect which predominates permanently or at the moment, and inclines the vicious man to go wrong in that particular direction, and also according to the circumstances of the case and the particular temptation offered. Thus ἀδικία may be manifested in illiberality in affairs of money, of licentiousness in bodily pleasures, of cowardice in danger, and so on for the rest. These subjects either have been already treated in the analysis of the virtues in c. 9, or are re-

---

[1] On ἔπαινος, ἐγκώμιον, μακαρισμός and εὐδαιμονισμός, §§ 33, 34, see Appendix B. to Bk. I.

served for future treatment in the 2nd book with the πάθη. So that we proceed at once to the consideration, as aforesaid, of the motives and objects of wrong doing, of the characters of wrong doers, and of those who are most exposed to ill treatment and wrong. § 5. And first we must determine the motives or causes of wrong doing, what are the objects and aims which men propose to themselves either to pursue or avoid when they commit injustice: it is plainly the accuser's business to see how many and what sort of these universal motives are applicable to the defendant; the latter must discover how many and which of them he is not liable to be suspected of, and are *not* applicable to his case. The treatment of this subject occupies the remainder of this chapter and c. 11. The two remaining topics are analysed in c. 12. The sources or causes of all action, and therefore of justice and injustice are seven; three external and beyond our control, accident, nature (natural disposition or tendency), and external force or compulsion: and four of which the cause and origin lie within ourselves, which subjects them to our control; habit, reasoning or calculation, passion, that is, anger and resentment, and desire. § 8. A detailed examination of these—which they well deserve—would, if introduced here, occupy too much space, and divert attention from our present object, which is to supply a connected *general* account of Aristotle's system of rhetoric, and a guiding thread through its details. I have therefore treated them separately in an Appendix to this first book (Appendix C), where they are examined, and illustrated (or obscured—this especially in the case of τύχη—) by a comparison with the treatment which they receive in other passages of the author's works.

Ch. 11. It is found from the analysis of the last of these, desire, as a spring of action, that pleasure as well as genuine good is the object of our desires, and therefore a proper subject for rhetorical inquiry. Good, in the shape of τὸ συμφέρον, a man's *real* interest, has been already analysed, c. 6: and we may now therefore proceed at once to the consideration of pleasure. This is accordingly done; and after a repeated warning, § 19, that we are to look for no scientific exactness in our definitions, but only that they shall be clear and intelligible, there follows in c. 11, the promised analysis of pleasure, with which the chapter is entirely occupied. I will deal with this subject as I have done with the sources of action in the preceding chapter, and for the same reason; and a similar examination of pleasure, and comparison with Aristotle's views of it as expressed elsewhere, will be found in Appendix D at the end of this book.

Ch. 12. is devoted to the analysis of the two remaining heads of the treatment of ἀδικία, viz. the characters and dispositions, which (1) dispose, and (2) expose, men to wrong. πῶς ἔχοντες καὶ τίνας ἀδικοῦσι. § 1.

Ch. 13. In this chapter we have an analysis and classification of actions, right and wrong, just and unjust, for the use of the forensic orator, or pleader in a court of law. These have a double division in reference to laws and persons; each of which again admits of two subdivisions. *Laws* are either (1) special, whether written or unwritten, or (2) universal and natural: and *offences* or wrongs, (and their opposites, right and just acts) may be committed against (or beneficial to) either (1) individuals, as adultery or assault, or (2) the state or community, τὸ κοινόν, as desertion; and similarly the opposites. §§ 1—4. The distinction here taken is the same as that upon which the distinction of civil and criminal procedure is made to rest in the Attic law. The grievance complained of, which has to be adjusted or punished, is an injury either to a private individual (πρὸς ἕνα καὶ ὡρισμένον, § 3), or to society at large: the former is the object of a civil action, ἀγὼν ἴδιος, δίκη ἰδία, or δίκη in its special sense; the latter of a criminal prosecution ἀγὼν δημόσιος, δίκη (in its general sense) δημοσία, γραφή: here the state is aggrieved, and therefore ὁ βουλόμενος, any duly qualified citizen, may prefer an indictment. But the latter is again subdivided into the cases, in which (1) the offence against the individual is immediate, and against the state mediate, and that (2) wherein the state is immediately offended, and the individual mediately. In the former of these two cases the process would be properly denominated ἰδία γραφή, a criminal prosecution or indictment (such is the case of Demosthenes against Midias); in the latter δημοσία γραφή, a state prosecution, or impeachment; though in fact these terms are seldom found in actual use. See Meier u. Schömann, Attische Process, Bk. III. § 2.

We have next, § 5, a definition of τὸ ἀδικεῖσθαι 'wrong received', which is, 'to suffer intentional injustice'; in accordance with the statement already made, c. 10, § 3, that injustice, to be such, must always be intentional. The deliberate intention is thus necessary to constitute an act of real 'injustice', and forms the characteristic mark of ἀδικεῖν and ἀδίκημα, by which it is distinguished from ἀτύχημα a mere accident, and ἀμάρτημα a mistake; though by either of these the same amount of *positive injury* may be inflicted; vice and crime being always characterised by the προαίρεσις, § 10. The voluntary intention is determined by knowledge; that is, by the *particular* knowledge of the circumstances of the case—as of the nature and instruments of any particular act in question, such as the foil which has lost its button and so become a *dangerous* weapon, or the gun that was loaded when it was thought to have been discharged. In such a case the *particular* ignorance is admitted in excuse of the act, which does not now amount to a crime; though death may equally ensue from a mistake or an accident, and the *injury* be as great as it could be if it were inflicted with malice prepense. But *general* ignorance, of moral distinctions or right and wrong, cannot similarly be pleaded in extenuation or justification of a crime committed: here the agent is responsible for the knowledge of them, as well as for the formation of his own habits and character: herein in fact lies the distinction between virtue and vice. See further in Eth. Nic. III. 2 (Bekk.). Hence we have, § 7, the following distinction of various classes of ἐγκλήματα, charges, complaints, actions, prosecutions. They have reference either to one individual, or to the community at large; a wrong may be committed (1) in ignorance, ἁμάρτημα, or (2) unintentionally, by mere accident, ἀτύχημα, or (3) with full knowledge and intention; and in the latter case either with deliberate immoral evil purpose, προελομένου, or (4) intentionally and with knowledge, but in a fit of uncontrollable passion, διὰ πάθος, i. e. θυμὸν or ὀργήν. This same subject is also discussed in Eth. Nic. v. 10. (Bekk.), where four degrees of wrong or criminality are distinguished, which correspond precisely with those already given from the Rhetoric[1]. ἄκοντος is the accidental case, ἀτύχημα; ἀγνοοῦντος the error or mistake, ἁμάρτημα; and of the two cases where the act is ἐκ προαιρέσεως, the one is an ἀδίκημα, intentional but not deliberate, as a wrong committed in an overpowering fit of passion, μὴ προβουλεύσας; the last only is the real genuine ἀδικία, showing as it does the malus animus, the engrained evil habit, the ἕξις, the confirmed state of *vice*, or the malice prepense, πρόνοια, of the ἄδικος properly so called. The threefold division, with which I commenced this paragraph, is the more usual one, and I think simpler and better. It is found in the Rhet. ad Alex. c. 5. § 9, 10. And to this Aristotle himself returns later on in this Chapter, § 16. Compare also, Magn. Mor. I. 34. §§ 26, 7, 8[2].

Next, in §§ 9—11, we have a little disquisition upon the definition of crime and the distinctions of crimes, which in a subsequent treatise on rhetoric would have come under the head of the στάσις ὁρική, one of the variously classified στά-

---

[1] This precise correspondence especially in a case where, as with this fourfold division, the view is certainly not the usual one, might furnish an argument in favour of attributing the fifth book of the Nicom. Ethics to Aristotle rather than Eudemus. But I refrain from entering on this thorny subject.

[2] Themistius, Orat. I. p. 15. c. (quoted by Gaisford) giving an account of this classification, absurdly enough describes ἁμάρτημα as πάθους κίνησις σφοδροτέρα, ἐπιθυμίας τινὸς ἢ ὀργῆς ἄφνω προεξαλλομένης, οὐ συνενδούσης ὁλοκλήρου τῆς ψυχῆς τῷ κινήματι; thereby identifying ἁμάρτημα with the third of Aristotle's four classes, acts διὰ θυμόν or πάθος, omitting the true ἁμάρτημα altogether. Gaisford takes no notice of the blunder.

σεις, status, or legal issues[1]. It is here called the ἐπίγραμμα, the inscription or designation of the offence, which determines the mode of trying the case, and the court before which it should be brought for trial. The same blow, for example, may be interpreted as an act of ὕβρις and render the culprit liable to a γραφή or public prosecution; or as a simple αἰκία or assault, in which case the penalty or amends may be settled by a δίκη or private action between the parties; and similarly the same act may be construed either as sacrilege ἱεροσυλία, or as mere theft κλοπή; and so on. This status is called in Latin nomen or finitio, by Cicero and Quintilian. The 'status' in general are termed ἀμφισβητήσεις, in Rhet. III. 16. 6 and 17. 1; it was not till later that they received the technical name of στάσεις. Aristotle seems here to include another of the στάσεις with the ὁρική, which is usually distinguished from it; namely ποιότης or qualitas: and in fact the two are not always very clearly distinguishable. As we shall be called upon in pleading our causes to apply the proper names to the charges which we bring, and to distinguish the several 'qualities' of offences, it is necessary to be so far acquainted with these definitions and distinctions of crimes, as to know what is the legal interpretation of theft, murder, adultery, ὕβρις, "in order that, whether we wish to prove that such and such an act comes under such and such a legal designation, or the contrary, we may be able to construe it fairly and aright." § 10.

The remainder of the Chapter is occupied with the question of the difference between τὸ δίκαιον and ἐπιείκεια or equity, together with the distinctions of νόμος γεγραμμένος and νόμοι ἄγραφοι, which are connected with the former. The latter of the two subjects shall be reserved for separate treatment in the Appendix to this book (Appendix E); the former, equity, shall be considered here.

Equity, we are told, § 13, "is a kind of justice, but

[1] On the στάσεις or status and their divisions see note on Rhet. III. 15. in this Introduction.

beyond the written law," τὸ παρὰ τὸν γεγραμμένον νόμον δίκαιον. This omission of the legislature is partly intentional, partly unintentional; the latter, when something that should have been inserted and defined is overlooked; the former, when it is necessary to lay down a general rule, and this rule has exceptions which cannot be foreseen and determined; and also by reason of the infinite variety of possible cases that may arise, no two of which are exactly alike. Whence the universal rules of law require constant modification and adaptation to circumstances, and this is equity, 'the mitigation of the austerity' (Sopater ap. Stob. in Gaisford's Not. Var.) or the relaxation of the exact rigour of the written law, and a leaning to the side of mercy, indulgence, liberality. So τὸ ἐπιεικές is defined in Eth. Nic. v. 10., ἐπανόρθωμα νόμου ᾗ ἐλλείπει διὰ τὸ καθόλου, "a rectification of the (written) law, to supply deficiencies consequent upon its universality." And in the same chapter we find the following; "when it is necessary to speak generally, and impossible to do so with rigorous exactness, the law takes the general case, lays down the general rule; being well aware of the error committed, but right nevertheless. For the error is not in the law nor in the legislator, but in the nature of the case or circumstances." No law for instance can enter into all details, and provide for all exceptional cases in determining penalties in exact proportion to the size or material of a weapon with which a wound has been inflicted. It lays down a general rule; a wound inflicted by an iron weapon, or by iron in general, renders the offender liable to such and such a penalty. But this must not be so rigorously interpreted as to bring under its operation the case of a man who happens to be wearing an iron ring upon the hand with which he strikes a blow: because here he is only following a usual custom, and the nature and character of the instrument that inflicts the wound in no respect aggravates the crime. But the law cannot foresee and provide for all this infinite variety of special cases; and here therefore equity steps in to mitigate and modify its rigorous application, § 14. Quintilian, Inst. Orat. VII. 6. 8, quotes an exactly similar case. Qui nocte cum ferro deprehensus fuerit, alligetur. Cum anulo ferreo inventum magistratus alligavit. The law had enacted that any one found abroad at night "with iron in his hand[1]", meaning of course 'armed with a steel weapon', was liable to be taken up and put in prison. The magistrate acting upon the general rule apprehended a man who wore an iron ring: 'equity' would have required that an exception should be made in this case.

Equity therefore in its widest sense is 'merciful *consideration*'. It takes into account, and makes allowance for ἀτυχήματα and ἀμαρτήματα, (see above on § 5.) accidents and mistakes, distinguishing them from real injustice or crime, ἀδικία, ἀδίκημα, which is wrong done with deliberate evil intent, § 16. And all leanings to the side of mercy, compassion for and sympathy with human infirmities, is of the nature of equity. In the three following sections, down to the end of the chapter, this quality of ἐπιείκεια is further illustrated by the enumeration of several τόποι, or collections of cases in which it shows itself. As, for instance, in looking to the lawgiver rather than the law in interpreting the latter; (this is explained by Eth. Nic. v. 14. 1137. b. 20. ὃ κἂν ὁ νομοθέτης αὐτὸς οὕτως ἂν εἴποι ἐκεῖ παρών, καὶ εἰ ᾔδει ἐνομοθέτησεν ἄν), and to the meaning rather than the words of the law itself; and to the intention rather than the action in estimating the degree of criminality; and to the whole rather than to a part of any transaction; and to the past or general character rather than the present temper of an offender: to remember benefits rather than injuries, and benefits received rather than those conferred; to put up with wrong; to prefer an amicable, to a violent or legal, settlement of a dispute; or if it cannot be decided in this way, to prefer arbitration, where

---

[1] Our language here does not admit of the same degree of ambiguity as the Latin. For first ferro may mean both 'in' and 'on' 'his hand': and secondly the same word will stand for the 'iron' of the ring, and the 'steel' of the sword or dagger.

equity is the rule, to a law court where the judge usually decides by the letter of the law: all characteristic of a considerate, candid, fair, merciful, forgiving, temper, and spirit and disposition; and expressing a character far more amiable than any of the so-called virtues—which are in reality so many characters—of the Nicomachean Ethics.

Ch. 14. In this chapter the common topic of degree, τὸ μᾶλλον καὶ ἧττον, is applied to injustice, as it was before to τὸ ἀγαθόν in c. 7.

Ch. 15, the last of the book, is occupied with the examination and analysis of the ἄτεχνοι πίστεις, already briefly referred to in I. 2. 2. These, according to Aristotle, are five in number; laws, evidence of various kinds, μάρτυρες, the question βάσανος, contracts or documents (tabulæ, Quint.), and oaths. The contents of this chapter furnish a very striking illustration of that characteristic of rhetoric (and dialectics) which has been previously noticed. viz. that it τἀναντία συλλογίζεται; I. 1. 12. and elsewhere. Every argument or topic of this chapter can be retorted against the opponent; the affirmative or negative of every proposition stated is alike susceptible of proof. §§ 1. 2.

And first of the use to be made of *laws* in the pleadings of the law courts and discussions of the general assembly. If this written law happen to be against us the following τόποι, classes of arguments, will be serviceable. First of all we may appeal to the unwritten, universal laws [see c. 13. 3. 2. and Append. E. to Bk. I:], and to the *equitable* construction of the written ones, in opposition to the strict letter of the law, as furnishing the grounds of a fairer decision: or we may say that the juror's oath, that he will decide according 'to the best of his judgment', shows by the latitude it allows him that he was not intended always to follow the precise words of the written law: or that equity and the universal law never vary because they are 'according to nature', whilst written laws are liable to constant change; and quote Sophocles' Antigone[1] in

[1] Antig. 450. seq.

confirmation of our view: similarly we may argue that real justice is 'true', that is, certain and infallible, and salutary to man and society, whereas the justice of the written law is a mere apparent or sham justice, which is liable to numerous errors and can *not* satisfy the wants of society and lay down a rule sufficient to meet all cases that may arise. Summum jus is often summa injuria; and hence it is said that the written law "does not do the proper work of the law", does not fulfil its proper function, which is to do justice equally to all. Cic. de Leg. I. 15. And further we may say, that the judge is like a tester of coin, and it is his very office to distinguish between spurious and genuine justice. Again, that it is the sign of a better man to appeal to, practise, and abide by, the unwritten rather than the written law [because the latter enforces obedience by inflicting penalties of which *fear* therefore is the motive, and a base one; whereas the obedience to unwritten law is spontaneous; it is a proof of a nobler and better nature, a more generous spirit, a more confirmed habit of virtue, to do right spontaneously, without the expectation of reward or dread of penalty. See Rhet. I. 7. §§ 12 and 16. Oderunt peccare boni virtutis amore; Oderunt peccare mali formidine pœnæ.]: or again, if the written law that is opposed to us be also in opposition to any other popular law in good repute, or be self-contradictory, or clash with another law of the same code; of the latter case (Victor.) an instance is when, as sometimes happens, one law enacts that all contracts be valid, whilst another interdicts the entering into any engagement contrary to the law. Again we must examine the law to see if its terms are ambiguous, so as to be able to twist it either way to our purpose, and decide according to which of the two constructions[1]

---

[1] In this passage ἀγωγή is the ductus legis, as we say ductus litterarum. Via et ratio ducendi legem in hanc vel illam partem. H. Stephens. ap. Gaisf. that is, the *turn* given to it, the *construction* put upon it, τὸ δίκαιον is τὸ ἀκριβοδίκαιον the letter of the law; τὸ σύμφερον here represents the equitable or liberal interpretation which forms part of the notion of equity—supr. c. 13.

the rule of strict justice or of expediency—as either happens to suit us—can be applied to the interpretation of it; and then treat, or use, it accordingly. Lastly we may urge that circumstances have altered since the enactment of the law, and therefore that it no longer applies. §§ 3—10.

If on the other hand the written law favours our side of the question, we must interpret the oath that the dicasts take to decide "according to the best of their judgment," not as implying the right to give any decision beyond the letter of the law, or to modify its application in any way, but that it is administered merely to save them from the guilt of perjury in case they happen to mistake the meaning of the law. Secondly, in maintaining the superiority of the written law when it tells in our favour, and the consequent expediency of abiding by its decision, we may use the following argument. It may be laid down as a general principle "that no one chooses abstract or absolute good, but that which is good to himself", that viz. which is adapted to his particular wants and circumstances. (And this is probably a reference to Rhet. I. 7. 35. where it is affirmed that the particular good by the individual is superior to good in general or absolute good.) Hence we infer (this is Schrader's explanation) that the actual written laws of a given state being deliberately adapted to the persons and circumstances of the members of that state, and to the security of its government, are to be preferred to those which upon abstract and general considerations might be regarded as the absolute best: they are therefore to be carefully maintained and none of their enactments disregarded or infringed. [This is a genuine specimen of a rhetorical enthymeme. The major premiss is expressed in the general rule or principle laid down, the minor and conclusion being both omitted.] Again we may argue that not to use the laws or law is as bad as having none at all: as they are enacted so must they be applied. Or we may derive a rule from the other arts and apply it to legislation. In every art the artist is the supreme authority.

No patient should try to be 'wiser than his physician'; nor should the judgment of any ἰδιώτης be preferred to that of the accomplished artist, the man of skill in his profession. The mischief caused by any error that the physician or professional person, in this case the lawgiver, may commit, is outweighed by the danger of weakening the authority of the ruling power: the habit of disobedience is a worse evil than any mistake that the legislator can make. Or lastly, that to seek to be wiser than the laws is the very thing that is forbidden by all laws that are approved. §§ 11, 12.

Next of evidence. On this subject we have first to distinguish the kinds of evidence; and we find that there is a twofold division of witnesses and authorities, first into old and new, ancient and modern or contemporary, and again into those that share the risk and those that do not, but are outside (ἔξω) or beyond the reach of all danger. 'Ancient Witnesses'[1] are poets, whose verses are sometimes quoted as evidence and authorities for the past, as prophets and diviners are for the future: proverbs likewise are used as confirmatory evidence in support of a general precept or advice offered. To this class of modern, recent, contemporary witnesses or authorities, belong all living men of weight and reputation (γνώριμοι), who have already pronounced sentence or given a decision upon any question that happens to be under discussion, as Eubulus quoted a saying of Plato as an authority in his speech against Chares. To the class of contemporary witnesses belong likewise all those who share the risk of a trial in which they are giving evidence, in so far as they are liable to penalties not merely if they are found guilty, but even if they are suspected, [δόξωσι, so Victor.] of perjury: whereas the ancient witnesses, being long dead and gone, are of course exempt from all chance of danger or punishment. This latter class of witnesses who actually appear in court and run the risk of being punished for false

---

[1] Compare Cic. Top. xx. 78. oratores, philosophos, poetas, historicos, ex quorum et dictis et scriptis sæpe auctoritas petitur ad faciendam fidem.

evidence can only testify to facts: whether such and such a thing has been done (γέγονε) or not, whether so and so is true (ἔστι) or not: in the decision of questions relating to the *quality* of an act, as whether it is just or unjust, expedient or inexpedient (the introduction of these latter words shows that evidence given in the general assembly, in favour for example of any scheme of policy, as well as the courts of law is here taken into account), they can have no voice: this indeed is not the office of the witness, but of the judge. [Also by the hypothesis, they are only ordinary every day people, and not jurists or philosophers; who can state facts, but cannot set up for authorities as to the nature and quality of actions.] Of the three classes of witnesses already enumerated, the ancients, the living authorities, and those that appear in court to give evidence, the first are by far the most trustworthy, because they are absolutely out of the reach of corruption; their judgments have received the sanction of time and stood the test of examination, and as authorities are absolutely unexceptionable. The second class are also very trustworthy, but in a less degree. These are they that pronounce their decisions from a distance (ἄπωθεν), not on the spot like the witnesses actually present in court; that is to say, have pronounced it some time before the similar question, actually under discussion, had arisen. §§ 13—16.

Arguments on the subject (i. e. the value) of evidence are of the following kind. If you have no witnesses to produce yourself, you may argue that the decision should rest upon the probabilities of the case; and that this in fact is the meaning of deciding—as the juror's oath runs—'according to the best of one's judgment;' or you may say that probabilities cannot be bribed to impose upon one, witnesses may; and that they can never be found guilty of perjury. [This topic is excellently illustrated by a passage of Cicero pro Cælio c. 9. quoted by Victorius]. If you *have* witnesses and your adversary has *not*, you can urge that probabilities are not responsible, not amenable to justice, or subject to penalty, and that the evidence of witnesses would never have been required at all in a case, if mere arguments had been sufficient for the investigation of it. Witnesses may be called either in our own defence or against the antagonist; and they give evidence either to facts or character; so that plainly no one ever need be at a loss for serviceable evidence: for if we cannot produce evidence of fact, either in agreement with our own case or opposed to that of our adversary, at all events as a pis aller we can always find witnesses prepared to give testimony as to character, either to our own virtues and respectability, or to the worthlessness of our opposite. So far of witnesses in general. If we have any particular point to prove about a witness, as that he is friendly, or hostile, or indifferent, or of good or bad character, or intermediate, neither the one nor the other, we must derive our proofs from the same sources and materials from which we take our ordinary rhetorical arguments, or enthymemes. These are the εἴδη, here called by the general name of τόποι, the materials of enthymemes. Thus, if we want to show that a witness is friendly or the reverse we must have recourse to the analysis of the πάθη of φιλία and ἔχθρα and μῖσος, where we shall find the indications and manifestations of these affections described, (Rhet. II. 4.), which we must then apply to our argument: or if we desire to make him appear respectable or infamous, we refer to the characteristics of virtue and vice described under the τόποι, or rather εἴδη, of ἀρετή and κακία in I. 9. §§ 17—19.

On the subject of contracts, bonds, or agreements of any kind expressed in writing, (documents, tabulæ, Cicero and Quintilian), the speech may be made use of either for magnifying or destroying their credit with the judges; our course of procedure being determined by the consideration whether we or our adversaries have such documents to produce. Their credit will be in exact proportion to the respectability of their subscribers ("those who have put their names upon them") and custodians; the latter because the integrity of those who have had them in their keeping is a proof that they have not been tampered with. And hence it appears that these may be dealt with in precisely the same way for the purpose of establishing or destroying their credit as we have already described in the case of witnesses. When there is no question about the *existence* of the contract, if it be on our side (οἰκείας), all that we have to do is to "magnify" it, or uphold its credit. One way of effecting this is to call it a "law;" because a contract may really be considered as a private or special and partial law: and it is not the contract that gives validity to the law, but the law to a *legal* contract. In fact, speaking generally, the law itself may be regarded as a contract[1], and therefore to violate its conditions (ἀπιστεῖν, disobey it) or to attempt to upset it, is the same thing as abolishing or cancelling a law. And besides this, most of the ordinary dealings of men with one another (συναλλάγματα), as buying and selling, letting and hiring, in fact all voluntary transactions, are matters of contract; so that if contracts be invalidated, all customary intercourse of men with one another is as good as abolished. All the other arguments appropriate to this subject lie so entirely upon the surface, that they may be passed over here as obvious. If our opponent have the documents upon his side, first, we may argue from the analogous case of an adverse *law;* viz. that it would be strange indeed if we were compelled to abide by a defective or unjust contract, whilst we hold that illframed and

---

[1] The law a contract, νόμος συνθήκη. This is positive law, lex scripta, not the κοινός, ἄγραφος νόμος, which is *natural* and *moral* law. These positive obligations, variously determined in different communities, have been taken by these societies upon themselves, and the members have agreed together, as it were, have entered into a sort of (implied) contract with one another to conform to them. This remark is not intended to give any countenance to the sophistical doctrine, maintained by Thrasymachus and Callicles and Hobbes, that *all law* is a mere convention of society, and has no absolute basis or principles. See Whewell, El. of Mor. §§ 96 and 816 on the 'social contract,' and a *similar* observation in Arist. Pol. I. 6. init. compare III. 9. 8. καὶ ὁ νόμος συνθήκη, καὶ ἐγγυητὴς ἀλλήλοις τῶν δικαίων.

injurious *laws* are not to be obeyed. Or, secondly, that it is for the judge, and not the contract, to decide the question at issue; no mere written agreement ought to weigh against general considerations of justice. And, as supplementary to and enforcing this latter argument, we may proceed to say that justice cannot be changed or perverted, have its nature altered, by fraud or force, because it is natural (φύσει οὐ νόμῳ); whereas contracts are altered by fraud, under false impressions and pretences, and under compulsion. Besides this, we may examine the contract to see if it is opposed to any law, written or universal; and of the former to those of our own or of foreign countries; and next, to any other contracts antecedent or subsequent; and then argue, either that the later one is valid, and therefore the earlier, which contradicts it, must be invalid, or else the earlier is right (sound, valid, legal), and the later a fraud; whichever happens to suit our case. Also we may take *expediency* into account, and try to show that the fulfilment of this contract in question would be contrary to the interest of the judges: and a number of other topics of the same kind, too obvious to require enumeration. §§ 20—25.

Torture, the question, furnishes a kind of evidence, which is *supposed* to be especially trustworthy, because it is given under compulsion, the truth being as it were *forced from* the party under examination. On this subject likewise there is no difficulty in discovering what may be said on either side. If we have evidence of this kind to bring forward in support of our own case (οἰκεῖαι), we must of course exalt the authority of it, and argue that this is the only kind of evidence which can be absolutely relied on[1]: if it is against us and on the side of the opponent, it may be quashed or discredited (διαλύοι ἄν τις) by putting forward what is actually true about torture in general: namely, that men under the stress of torture are just as likely to say what is

[1] Some arguments in favour of the use of torture are to be found in Rhet. ad Alex. c. 17. § 1.

false as what is true; whether by a resolute persistence in the refusal to reveal the truth, or from a readiness to accuse others falsely in expectation of (in order to obtain) a speedier release. (Rhet. ad Al. 17. 2.) The speaker should also be able to refer to known precedents with which the judges are acquainted, of constancy and resolution of men under torture, of a steady refusal to reveal the truth and betray their accomplices, and such like. ["It may be urged further that evidence under torture cannot be true, or to be depended on, because there are some men who are fat witted (insensible) and thick-skinned and resolute enough to endure any amount of torture without flinching"—the remainder of the sentence as it stands seems to have no meaning, "whereas those of an opposite temper, the cowardly and cautious or timid, are confident enough before they come in sight of what they have to endure, or before they have actually witnessed the sufferings of the others (αὐτῶν, viz. τῶν παχυφ. καὶ λιθοδ. καὶ δυνατῶν), so that torture is in no way to be relied upon[1]—" For even if we suppose that something has been lost after καταθαρροῦσιν, to this effect, "although cowards &c. are confident enough before they are put to the question, yet when actually in the hands of the executioner they are sure to flinch and lose all courage, and so their evidence becomes worthless," which seems the most natural solution of the difficulty, still the position itself, that cowards are

[1] The above sentence δεῖ δὲ λέγειν— πιστὸν ἐν βασάνοις, though preserved in the text of the best MS. (Aᶜ. Gaisf.), is un-Aristotelian in its language (the word καταθαρρεῖν in particular has no authority earlier than Polybius) wanting in the old Latin version, and already implied in what precedes. It is therefore properly rejected by Victorius, Bekker and Spengel, as either a gloss, or, as Spengel thinks, an extract from some other rhetorical treatise introduced by the Transcribers. Aristotle in the foregoing remarks upon torture, even if the last clause be omitted as spurious, shows his animus in a very unusual way. The argument adduced in favour of the use of it rests upon a mere assertion unsupported by facts. The convincing arguments are all on the other side. It plainly appears that his opinion as to the use of torture in extracting evidence is that it is cruel, unnecessary, and futile.

courageous enough until they come within the actual sight of danger, is so questionable, and the observation itself so irrelevant and superfluous, that we are driven to the conclusion that the corruption is more deeply seated and irremediable.] § 26.

Oaths admit of a fourfold division. The oath may be tendered and accepted, or neither, or the one without the other, i.e. either tendered and not accepted, or accepted and not tendered[1]. And this fourfold division may be further extended by the addition of cases in which an oath has already been taken by either of the two parties. The arguments for not tendering the oath are such as these: that men are easily induced to perjure themselves; and further, that if the other party take the oath tendered, the prospect of gain will overrule any scruple of conscience which he might have had about forswearing himself, he will take the oath and keep the money (οὐκ ἀποδίδωσιν, not make restitution); whereas *you* are so confident in the goodness of your cause, that you think the judges are sure to condemn him *unless* he takes an oath and perjures himself; and therefore from both these considerations it is better not to offer it (so Victor.): and thirdly, because it is better to leave the decision of the case to the honour of the judges whom one *does* trust, than to that of the other party whom one does not, (lit. this risk that one runs before the dicasts, by leaving the decision to their honour and good faith, is to be preferred to deciding it by the oath of the opponent; because the one can be trusted, the other cannot). If you refuse it, it is because taking an oath from

---

[1] ὅρκον διδόναι is to offer an oath to another, when you call upon your adversary to swear to the truth of his statements. λαμβάνειν to accept it thus offered, and make oath yourself. Quintilian's offerre jusjurandum, v. 6. 1. is 'to offer *to take* the oath': Aristotle's διδόναι is with him 'deferre,' and λαμβάνειν, recipere. In Demosthenes and the Orators the usage of the terms is the same as Aristotle's; except that sometimes δέχεσθαι is substituted for λαμβάνειν. And so Æschylus, Eumen. 429. ἀλλ' ὅρκον οὐ δέξαιτ' ἄν, οὐ δοῦναι θέλει. On the derivation, original signification, and early usage of ὅρκος see Buttmann's Lexilogus, sub voce.

mercenary motives, "bartering it against money," is a scandal and an infamy, unworthy of a man of honour. Or you may argue thus; "Had I been a rogue I should have swallowed it at once; for it's better to be a knave for something than for nothing: that is, Had I been a knave without scruple or remorse I should certainly have taken the oath; for I should have gained something by it, and if one *is* to be a knave, it is better to derive some benefit from one's knavery: now had I taken it I should have gained my cause at once and the property at stake; by not taking it, I leave the issue to the decision of the court, and run the risk of losing it: and therefore the refusal to take it (τὸ μή) proceeds from a virtuous motive, and not from the fear of perjuring myself; it is not because I should forswear myself if I did take it that I now refuse. And Xenophanes' verse may be quoted in point (ἁρμόττει), that it is "no fair challenge from a Godless (unscrupulous, ready to swear anything) to a God-fearing man" (who has some scruples and belief in divine retribution), but it is like the case of a strong man challenging a weak one to fight, where all the advantage is on the side of the former. If you accept it, you may say that you have confidence in yourself and your own integrity, but not in the other, whose character and principles you do not know; you don't want *him* to swear. And you may reverse Xenophanes' dictum, and say that the fair way is for the Godless man to tender the oath, and the religious man to take it; and it would be monstrous for you, the interested party, (who are of course the εὐσεβής,) to refuse to take it, when the judges, whom the adversary requires to adjudicate for him in this very matter, and yet have no interest in it, are themselves sworn. If on the other hand you offer it, you must say that it is a mark of piety to entrust the decision to the Gods, to place the matter in their hands, and that your antagonist ought to require no one to judge the case but himself; and so you hand it over to him to decide. And again that it is absurd for him to refuse to take the oath, whilst he obliges the judges to take one in order to decide *in his own affairs*. The preceding four are all simple cases of accepting and rejecting an oath: but these again may be combined in pairs, as in the cases where (1) the one party is willing to accept the oath but not to tender it, or (2) to tender it but not to accept it, or (3) when he is willing to accept and tender it, or (4) when he will do neither. Now as these arise from combinations of the simple cases, so clearly the arguments applicable to them may be gathered from the combination of those that have been already suggested for the others. Lastly, if you yourself happen to have already made a deposition on oath with which your present deposition conflicts, you may argue that this is no perjury: for all perjury is injustice, and all injustice is voluntary: but in your case the former deposition was extorted either by force or fraud; now all such acts are *involuntary*, and therefore there was no 'injustice' or criminality in the matter. And here it should be argued (the conclusion drawn by argument) that perjury consists in the intention of the mind, not in the expression of the mouth; it is the intention and not the words that make the lie: now in your case there was no fraudulent intention because you were either deluded and acting under a mistake, or under compulsion and so far not responsible for the act, and therefore you cannot be guilty of perjury[1]. If on the other hand it is the adverse party who has made these inconsistent depositions, you are then to exclaim that one who abides not by what he has sworn subverts everything, all that is most sacred and precious amongst man. To take an instance; why are judges *sworn* to administer the laws faithfully, unless it be because men confide in the sanctity of an oath, and its binding power in enforcing an obligation? he who would subvert this, is destroying the very foundations of society. And, appealing to the judges, "you we require to observe in judging this

---

[1] This is Hippolytus' argument, in the famous ἡ γλῶσσ' ὀμώμοχ' ἡ δὲ φρὴν ἀνώμοτος.

case, the oath you have sworn and they (the adverse party) don't observe it themselves!" [or with ἐμμενοῦμεν. "and *we* (people in general, but especially the other side) can't observe it ourselves!" or with ἐμμενοῦμεν; "and are we not to observe it ourselves?"]; or any other arguments that may suggest themselves for the purpose of adding to the solemnity, importance, credit of an oath. §§ 27—33.

Such are the ἄτεχνοι πίστεις of which the orator and pleader have to avail themselves. This distinction of ἄτεχνοι and ἔντεχνοι πίστεις is due to Aristotle (Quint. Inst. Orat. v. 1. 1.), and derived from the following considerations. Arguments in support of a case may be supplied either from facts independent and external, which we don't make for ourselves; but find ready to our hand, and have to use to the best advantage; to confirm and magnify or depreciate and discredit (αὔξειν καὶ μειοῦν), according to the circumstances of the case, as they happen to be favourable to ourselves or the adversary. These are extra artem or ἄτεχνοι. The others, which alone deserve the name of purely scientific arguments, are those which arise out of and are suggested by the case itself, follow a scientific method, the rules of the Art of Rhetoric (διὰ τῆς μεθόδου); which we invent and apply from the resources of our own knowledge and ingenuity, "by ourselves and our own agency" (δι' ἡμῶν.) Arist. Rhet. I. 2. 2. Ad probandum autem duplex est oratori subjecta materies: una rerum earum quæ non excogitantur ab oratore, sed in re positæ ratione tractantur: ut tabulæ, testimonia, pacta, conventa, quæstiones, leges, senatus consulta, res judicatæ, decreta, responsa, reliqua, si quæ sunt quæ non ab oratore pariuntur, sed ad oratorem a causa atque a reis deferuntur; altera est quæ tota in disputatione et in argumentatione oratoris collocata est. Cic. de Orat. II. 27. 116. Ac prima quidem illa partitio ab Aristotele tradita consensum fere omnium meruit, alias esse probationes quas extra dicendi rationem acciperet orator, alias quas ex causa traheret ipse et quodam modo gigneret. Ideoque illas ἀτέχνους, id est inartificiales; has ἐντέχνους, id est artificiales, vocaverunt. Quintil. u. s. The same distinction is recognised by Dionysius de Lys. Jud. c. 19.

Cicero's list of these 'inartificial proofs' has been already quoted from the de Oratore. It omits Aristotle's 'oaths,' and adds several other subdivisions which may all be readily referred to the heads of νόμος or μαρτύρια. On the same subjects, Orat. Part. cc. 14, 34, Topic. c. 19, Auct. ad Heren. cc. VI. VII.

Quintilian's runs thus. Præjudicia, rumores, tormenta, tabulæ, jusjurandum, testes. To the last are added, v. 7. 35, quæ *divina* testimonia vocantur, ex responsis, oraculis, ominibus. The list almost coincides with Aristotle's; for the νόμοι of the latter may very well be included under Quintilian's præjudicia, which are previous decisions, and 'precedents' of all kinds: or on the other hand the præjudicia may be reckoned with the ancient and modern or contemporary 'authorities' in the Aristotelian class of 'witnesses.' Quintilian's 'public opinion,' fama atque rumores, publicum testimonium, v. 3., to which appeal may be made or not according as it is favourable or the reverse, is an addition of his own; though even this might easily be identified with a portion of the 'universal unwritten law' included by Aristotle with the νόμοι. Comp. Auct. ad Heren. c. 8. § 12.

Lastly the author of the Rhetorica ad Alexandrum in treating the subject distinguishes four kinds of ἄτεχνοι πίστεις, though without using this technical term; which may be taken as an indication—it scarcely amounts to a proof—that this work was written at all events before Aristotle's was published, since from that time forward this distinction seems to have been recognised by all writers on Rhetoric. The first of these is c. 15. § 6. ἡ δόξα τοῦ λέγοντος, novum argumentum cæteris rhetoribus ignotum (Spengel ad loc.). "To state your own opinion about the facts under discussion," is, as the context implies, to state your own view of the case and its bearings; not of course to dictate the decision to the judges, but to exhibit it in a favourable aspect; and in doing this you must make it appear that you have a full knowledge of the case and its details, the facts and the law, and that it is your interest to state the exact truth; on the other hand it must be shown that the adversary has no knowledge or experience in the matter, and that consequently *his* opinion, if he offers one, is worthless. The three others are evidence, torture, and oaths.

In concluding this part of our subject we will notice the definitions of these three, evidence, torture, and oaths, with which the author of the Rhet. ad Alex. prefaces his account of them; more especially as Aristotle has left them undefined. μαρτυρία is defined ὁμολογία συνειδότος ἑκοντός (Spengel. corr. for ἑκοντί) a statement of the facts of a case in agreement with our own (this only includes *favourable* evidence), by one who was a party to the transaction or privy to it, (so far Demosthenes, c. Aristocr. p. 640, § 63. μαρτυρία συνειδότος), and voluntary: the latter characteristic distinguishes it from βάσανος which is ὁμολογία παρὰ συνειδότος ἄκοντος, the evidence being extorted by compulsion. In fact Aristotle tells us, Rhet. I. 15. 26, though he distinguishes the two, that the βάσανος is but a subordinate species of μαρτυρία. ὅρκος is μετὰ θείας παραλήψεως φάσις ἀναπόδεικτος, "an unproved assertion under the divine sanction or authority, or with an appeal to God," and with the implied notion of punishment consequent upon perjury[1].

[1] παράληψις is properly 'adoption' as παραλαμβάνειν is 'to adopt,' as a wife, or son, or partner, or ally; to bring forward witnesses, in Demosth. c. Euerg. et Mnes. p. 1159. 27. and c. Phorm. 904. so that παράληψις is the adoption or bringing forward of the Gods as authorities or witnesses of the truth of your assertion, to give their sanction to your credibility; whilst at the same time you imply that you expect punishment if you swear falsely.

END OF BOOK I.

APPENDIX A. TO BOOK I. CH. VIII.

In Polit. III. 7., Aristotle, besides the *normal*[1] state, ἡ ἀρίστη πολιτεία, distinguishes six kinds of constitutions, which are afterwards subdivided each into several varieties. The ἀρίστη πολιτεία, or true ἀριστοκρατία, which may be either the government of one, μοναρχία, βασιλεία, or of several, according to the proportion of virtue moral and political in either, though its conditions and institutions should none of them be impossible (like those of Plato's Ideal Republic); yet under the ordinary conditions of humanity it is practically unattainable, and must remain a mere visionary scheme or theory, the object of our wishes, κατ' εὐχήν, rather than of our expectations. The six others are divided into three normal, ὀρθαί, and three abnormal, degenerate or corrupt forms, παρεκβάσεις, "deviations" from the true standard "to the worse" (παρά). They are monarchy, aristocracy, πολιτεία, democracy, oligarchy, tyranny. The two first in their highest and completest forms may be included theoretically in the ἀρίστη πολιτεία: but there are also lower forms of them, which in a classification may be referred like the πολιτεία to the normal class, but are practically treated, as they actually exist, with the other. (IV. 8). Monarchies in actual existence are classified and described, III. 14—17. The πολιτεία,

---

[1] I prefer this term to that of 'ideal' to characterise Aristotle's typical constitution, in order to mark a slight distinction between the two conceptions of the 'perfect state' as they appear respectively in Plato and Aristotle. Plato's state is purely ideal: he himself admits finally after some hesitation that it can never be realised in practice; and writes his Laws subsequently to correct it, and reduce it to a more practicable shape. Aristotle's admits in a somewhat higher degree of the possibility of realisation; though he too constantly implies, by the expression κατ' εὐχήν which he applies to it, that under human conditions the actual establishment of it here on earth is far from likely.

the normal form of the democracy, the government of the middle classes, (and therefore by the law of the mean the best practicable constitution), has no special name of its own, but is designated by that which is common to all constitutions. It is a mixture of oligarchical and democratical institutions, and in it the middle class, οἱ μέσοι, which is likewise the hoplite class, the heavy-armed infantry, οἱ τὰ ὅπλα ἔχοντες, οἱ ὁπλιτεύοντες, IV. 13,—the wealthy order forming the cavalry, the poorer sort having either light arms or none at all—has the supreme power. The distinction of the normal and abnormal governments is founded upon the τέλος of each, which always determines the definition—ὁρίζεται ἕκαστον τῷ τέλει, Eth. Nic. III. 10. 6: and this is τὸ συμφέρον. Hence all the forms of government which are directed to the interest of the governed are normal and right; all that have the private interest of the governor or governing class alone in view are severally deviations from the true standard of that form of constitution which each of them proposes to itself as its aim. To this latter class belong all the existing democracies, oligarchies, and tyrannies. The names by which they are known are derived from the governing body in each; but do not correspond to the true definitions of them, (III. 8. IV. 4. init. and 8.) which are determined not by the mere number of the governors but by the object and aim or theory of each particular constitution, ἐλευθερία and ἰσότης of democracy, πλοῦτος and εὐγένεια of oligarchy, and ἀρετή or παιδεία of aristocracy. This is perhaps directed against Plato, who adopts this view both in the Republic and Politicus.

The scheme laid down in Eth. Nic. VIII. 12. substantially coincides with this; the difference being chiefly in name. There are six forms, no mention being made of the perfect state, which pass one into another, the better into the worse in each pair, by natural degeneration; monarchy into tyranny —this *does* differ from the view taken in Pol. IV. 12. and V., where democracy in its extreme and lowest form, and oligarchy, are both said to degenerate into tyranny—aristocracy into oligarchy, and πολιτεία 'republic or polity,' into democracy. To the πολιτεία, which he *here* says is the name by which it is generally known, he gives the name of τιμοκρατική, adopted from Plato, Rep. VIII., but applied in a very different sense. It is a constitution, as it is described in the Politics, in which the majority have a share in the government, with a property qualification for admission into the governing class, all within these limits being equal. His scale of merit in these six agrees with the gradation of rank assigned to them in Pol. IV. 2. Monarchy is the best; because if it really mean anything, a monarch or sole ruler, worthy of the name, must be such in consideration of an immense superiority in virtue; and tyranny is the worst, on the principle that corruptio optimi fit pessima. Aristocracy comes next; then πολιτεία; then democracy, oligarchy, and tyranny. He is however not very consistent in his expressions on this point; for from different points of view each of the three normal forms seems in its turn the best. In Pol. III. 15. he gives the preference to aristocracy, because it is better to have several men of great merit, if they can be found, at the head of affairs, than one: and in III. 10, in arguing the question which of all possible governors, or classes of governors, is best entitled theoretically to the supreme power, he decides for the majority; because practically, though each individual of them may have only a small portion of virtue and intelligence, yet the collective sum of the whole must needs outweigh that of any single person or small number; and this is extended even to their judgment upon works of art.

This classification is derived in substance from Plato's Politicus; as he himself admits, Pol. IV. 2, where by τὶς ἀπεφήνατο Plato is intended. In that dialogue we have seven varieties of constitutions, viz. the ideal state, the only really ὀρθὴ πολιτεία, 302 C., and six others; called five, 291 D, but really capable of division, 302 D, and so divided by Aristotle, into six: three κοσμίαι or ἔννομοι (Aristotle's ὀρθαί), in which the governors use their powers well and observe the laws—πρὸς τὸ κοινὸν συμφέρον ἄρχουσιν, Aristotle, Pol. III. 7.— and three παράνομοι or ἀκόλαστοι (the παρεκβάσεις) vicious and licentious governments, in which they act for their own private interest, and disregard the laws and the welfare of their subjects. These form three pairs, monarchy and tyranny, aristocracy and oligarchy, and the two kinds of democracy, which are distinguished in fact, though not in name. Of these, in his opinion, monarchy is the best, and its corruption tyranny the worst: and the government of the people, or the many, being from its inherent feebleness incapable of anything great, bad or good, is the worst of the better forms, and the best of the worse, 302. E. seq. Similarly Aristotle, Eth. Nic. VIII. 12., calls a democracy the least bad of the three corrupt or vicious forms.

In the Republic there are nominally five, but in reality six, forms of government recognised. We have, as with Aristotle, monarchy as well as aristocracy included in the ideal or perfect constitution (VII. 540. D, IX. 576. D, 580. B. compared with 587. D); an ἀριστοκρατία, or government of the best, may be either of one or several. It cannot be of all, no commonwealth or republic in any shape; because no πλῆθος can ever acquire the requisite qualifications [note here the difference of view of master and pupil], the true and perfect science of government (Polit. 297. B); and, as one is much more likely to attain to this than several, the ideal state will most naturally be a monarchy, like the internal constitution of man under the sway of one supreme reason. 300 E. Next comes τιμοκρατία, or military government, with institutions like those of Sparta and Crete, all directed to war rather than peace, Rep. VIII. 547. E; in this τὸ θυμοειδές, the spirited, angry, zealous, active, energetic, emulous element of the human constitution predominates, and gives its character to the polity. Fourth is oligarchy. Fifth democracy, for the two forms of which he has only one name, Polit. 292. A: and sixth despotism. These pass from one into another by corruption and degeneration in regular order, the order in which they have been enumerated, until they arrive at the conclusion of the series, where the whole comes to an end. But, as Aristotle very pertinently asks (Pol. v. 12. ult.), why should they stop here? and how, if not, can the model state be produced out of the very worst of the whole number? The order of succession is well criticised on several grounds drawn from observation of real life and existing facts by Aristotle in the same Chapter.

Lastly Polybius, Hist. VI. cc. 3, 4., likewise recognises six forms of πολιτεῖαι, three normal and regular, βασιλεία, ἀριστοκρατία, δημοκρατία, and three which arise severally out of the depravation and corruption of each of the three preceding, tyranny from constitutional monarchy, oligarchy from aristocracy, and ochlocracy (ὀχλοκρατία, this is, I believe, the earliest use of this word) from democracy. The natural primary and original form of government, arising out of no art, system, or compact, is μοναρχία, the government of one: so that Polybius unconsciously adopts the patriarchal theory of the origin of government, which deduces it from the natural supremacy of the head of the family.

APPENDIX B. TO BOOK I. CH. IX.

Ch. 9. In §§ 33, 34, occurs a brief episode on ἔπαινος, and a distinction is drawn between this and ἐγκώμιον, μακαρισμός, and εὐδαιμονισμός. Since ἔπαινος and ψόγος are the constituent elements and the main business of the ἐπιδεικτικὸν γένος of rhetoric, it is important to know precisely what 'praise' is and how it is distinguished from other nearly allied and analogous conceptions. "Praise" we are told means, "words setting forth magnitude of virtue"; we must therefore (in using this branch of Rhetoric) show that men's *actions* are virtuous; ἐγκώμιον 'panegyric' is properly applied to facts, things done, results of action, ἔργα; all surrounding, concomitant circumstances, are added in the way of proof, (to help to convince, not as the proper object of the ἐγκώμιον), such as birth and education; because from these we draw an inference as to the character of the subject of the panegyric, arguing that fortes creantur fortibus, that virtue is hereditary, and that one who is educated in such and such a way will turn out so and so. And this is why we panegyrise men for *having done* this or that, (acts accomplished). These completed acts are signs of the moral state from which they proceeded (which is the real object of praise, as showing the προαίρεσις, in which virtue resides); for we should praise one who had not actually performed them if we believed him to have the disposition to do so." This somewhat confused statement seems to imply that ἔπαινος has always a moral character, is specially and properly applied to distinguish virtue, and therefore referred 'to moral actions' πράξεις, in which virtue is exhibited. ἔπαινος and ψόγος are in fact the moral approbation and disapprobation by which we naturally mark our sense of the distinction between virtue and vice. Butler, Diss. II. Of the Nature of Virtue. Whewell, Elem. of Morality, § 56. See Eth. N. I. 12. ὁ μὲν γὰρ ἔπαινος τῆς ἀρετῆς· πρακτικοὶ γὰρ τῶν καλῶν ἀπὸ ταύτης. I. 13. ult. τῶν ἕξεων τὰς ἐπαινετὰς ἀρετὰς καλοῦμεν. II. 4. κατὰ δὲ τὰς ἀρετὰς καὶ τὰς κακίας ἐπαινούμεθα ἢ ψεγόμεθα. II. 4. bis. And this is why we do not praise the Gods; because they are beyond the sphere of human virtue (X. 8), and therefore not fit objects of 'praise' being in fact above it, like happiness, and all that is best and greatest. Ibid. Similarly at the end of Bk. I. in distinguishing the intellectual from the moral virtues, he says that though σοφία is not a moral virtue, yet it is a virtue. ἐπαινοῦμεν δὲ καὶ τὸν σοφόν, we show that it is a virtue by *praising it*. τῶν δὲ ἕξεων δὲ τὰς ἐπαινετὰς ἀρετὰς λέγομεν. That praise and blame are the ordinary tests of virtue and vice is constantly repeated throughout all the Ethical works ascribed (two of them erroneously) to Aristotle. See Eth. Eud. II. 1. 1219. b. 9. οἱ ἔπαινοι τῆς ἀρετῆς διὰ τὰ ἔργα. Ibid. 1220. 4. ἀρετῆς δὲ εἴδη δύο, ἡ μὲν ἠθική, ἡ δὲ διανοητική. ἐπαινοῦμεν γὰρ οὐ μόνον τοὺς δικαίους κ.τ.λ. Ib. VII. 15. 1248. b. 19. seq. where it is shown that good which exhibits itself in moral action (πράξεις) is the proper object of ἔπαινος. Compare Magn. Mor. I. 2. 1183. b. 26. τὰ δ' ἐπαινετὰ οἷον ἀρεταί· ἀπὸ γὰρ τῶν κατ' αὐτὰς πράξεων ὁ ἔπαινος γίγνεται. and again, I. 35. 1197. 16. ἔστι δὲ ἡ φρόνησις ἀρετή...ἐπαινετοὶ γάρ εἰσιν οἱ φρόνιμοι, ὁ δ' ἔπαινος ἀρετῆς. I. 9. 1187. 19. ἔτι δὲ μαρτυροῦσιν οἵ τ' ἔπαινοι καὶ οἱ ψόγοι γινόμενοι· ἐπὶ γὰρ τῇ ἀρετῇ ἔπαινος. Cic. de Fin. IV. 18. Aristoteles, Xenocrates, tota illa familia, non dabit; quippe qui valetudinem, viris, divitias, gloriam, multa alia bona esse dicant, laudabilia non dicant. Archytas, ap. Stob. I. 13. γίνεται δὲ ὁ μὲν ἔπαινος ἐπ' ἀρετᾷ. And this view has been generally adopted by the succeeding Greek Rhetoricians.

ἐγκώμιον is said to be applied properly to ἔργα. This appears also in Eth. N. I. 12. u. s. τὰ δ' ἐγκώμια τῶν ἔργων, ὁμοίως καὶ τῶν σωματικῶν (not therefore exclusively a moral distinction) καὶ τῶν ψυχικῶν; upon which Zell, ἐγκώμιον pertinet ad res bene vel splendide gestas; and again Eth. Eud. II. 1. u. s. καὶ τὰ ἐγκώμια τῶν ἔργων; and a little farther on, διὸ ἕτερον εὐδαιμονισμὸς καὶ ἔπαινος καὶ ἐγκώμιον· τὸ μὲν γὰρ ἐγκώμιον λόγος τοῦ καθ' ἕκαστον ἔργου, ὁ δ' ἔπαινος τοιοῦτον εἶναι καθόλου (again marking the moral character of the object of 'praise'), ὁ δ' εὐδαιμονισμὸς τέλος. ἐγκώμιον therefore according to Aristotle is properly applied to facts, deeds done, achievements accomplished; not to actions in operation πράξεις, which have a more exclusively moral character[1]. [See Eth. N. II. 1. on the formation of a

---

[1] This is Brandis' view of the distinction between the two words. He says in his excellent little tract, über Aristoteles' Rhetorik, in Schneidewin's Philologus, IV. 1. p. 30. "Auch dass das lób oder das löbliche sich auf die handlungen beziehe, das enkomium auf die werke...". My own interpretation was quite independent, adopted before I had become acquainted with Brandis' work.

virtuous character.] All the other ordinary objects of panegyric, as birth, wealth, accomplishments, strength, and such like 'concomitants,' are introduced for the purpose of confirming and strengthening the conviction in the minds of the audience that the deeds alleged are rightly attributed to the object of the panegyric; because such talents and advantages natural and acquired imply a capacity for the performance of them: but the deeds themselves are the real matter of the encomium; nam genus et proavos et *quæ non fecimus ipsi Vix ea nostra voco*. It is only what a man has done himself that can really make him illustrious; διὸ, says Aristotle, ἐγκωμιάζομεν πράξαντας; it is only *after* the deeds have been performed that we panegyrise their authors. At the same time these deeds have so far a moral character that they are indications[1] of the moral habit of the performer of them. The *moral* ἕξις we praise in any case, even if it does not exhibit itself in any actual reality, as long as we believe the individual in question to be τοιοῦτος 'of that character', possessing the virtue potentially (i.e. ready for use if required), and capable and inclined (by acquired habit) to exercise it. So that to sum up, ἔπαινος is praise, the expression of moral approbation and therefore is referred principally to motives and character: the object of ἐγκώμιον is facts, acts realised; the virtue is included by implication, but is here secondary and nonessential: the τὰ κύκλῳ being admitted by way of support and confirmation.

This is only one of several distinctions that have been drawn between ἔπαινος and ἐγκώμιον, nor indeed is the term ἔπαινος confined, except in Ethical writings, to this its moral acceptation. In the ordinary language it is used in the most general sense of praise, however derived and however be-

---

[1] σημεῖα, only *signs*, not necessary consequences: for a great victory might possibly be won by accident, without either skill or courage on the part of the commander, or an act of splendid munificence performed from a merely selfish motive; and yet these ἔργα might be made the subjects of ἐγκώμιον; whence the need of proof from the concomitants.

stowed. Nor is the distinction between the two terms generally observed: Aristotle confounds them himself in the very next sentence. § 35. Alexander the Rhetorician quoted by Gaisford in his collection of Not. Var. p. 127[1], informs us that some made no distinction between the two words in question, (one of these may be the author of the 'Ρητορικὴ πρὸς 'Αλέξανδρον), and then proceeds to enumerate four. 1. That ἔπαινος is confined to the eulogy of a single virtue, ἐγκώμιον goes into detail and may include any number of them; it may also be extended to all natural, acquired, and accidental gifts, accomplishments, endowments, advantages, as γένος, παιδεία, τροφή, πρᾶξις, ἀπόγονοι, εὐκλεὴς θάνατος. 2. that the difference between them consists in the mere length and amount; ἔπαινος being simple and concise, ἐγκώμιον long and elaborate, carried into detail, as in the preceding definition. 3. That ἔπαινος is ἀληθής; properly denotes true, genuine, sincere praise, to which the judgment gives its assent; which is due to virtue alone; ἐγκώμιον, is πιθανόν; the set show speech for festivals and holidays is only πιθανόν, does not aim at truth, but only at plausibility; does not carry with it the assent of the judgment, or sincerity on the part of the speaker, who is only trying to make an impression on his audience: as for instance when Polycrates composed his panegyrics upon pots and pebbles, he had no real admiration of them, but was only exercising his ingenuity in the invention of plausible arguments. This distinction though taken from a different point of view falls in very well with that of Aristotle. It makes the object of ἔπαινος to be virtue, as the only thing really worthy of approbation; and regards the other as fallacious and liable to, or even careless of, error, which as we have seen according to Aristotle's view it might very well be. Alexander considers this the best of the

---

[1] Gaisford calls him Menander. The passage is printed in Walz and Spengel's collection of Greek Rhetoricians as the work of Alexander, an extract from his 'Ρητορικαὶ ἀφορμαί 'rhetorical magazine.' Did Gaisford misread the word Alexander?

four definitions which he quotes. 4. The fourth may be intended for Aristotle's own distinction such as I have described it, but if so, the latter half is strangely disguised. It gives Aristotle's own words for the definition of ἔπαινος, λόγος ἐμφανίζων μέγεθος ἀρετῆς, and for that of ἐγκώμιον, λόγος ἐμφανίζων πράξεις καλάς. The distinction between πρᾶξις and ἔργον I have already pointed out. 'The details' which enter into some of the above definitions are probably included also in that of Aristotle in the words τὰ κύκλῳ.

The same subject is touched upon by the author of the Ῥητ. πρὸς Ἀλέξ. c. 36 init. He does not distinguish the two words; in fact after saying that ἔπαινος properly belongs to virtue he yet § 4 continues, τὰ τῆς ἀρετῆς δικαίως ἐγκωμιάζεται; adding τοὺς γὰρ ἰσχυροὺς καὶ τοὺς καλοὺς καὶ τοὺς εὐγενεῖς καὶ τοὺς πλουσίους (Aristotle's 'concomitants') οὐκ ἐπαινεῖν ἀλλὰ μακαρίζειν προσήκει. Μακαρίζειν is applied to what according to Aristotle should be expressed by ἐγκωμιάζειν, and the latter is substituted for ἐπαινεῖν.

Definitions and distinctions of the same are also found in other and later writers on rhetoric, as Aphthonius, προγυμνάσμ. (Rhet. Græc. II. 35. Ed. Spengel) and Hermogenes προγυμν. (Rhet. Gr. II. 11.); both of these coincide with the second of Alexander. See also Nicolaus Sophistes, προγυμνάσματα. in Rhet. Græc. III. 478. who gives the same explanation as Alexand No. 1.

The following is Vater's explanation. πρᾶξις est actio, quatenus agitur, ἔργον res gesta, facinus perpetratum. πράξεως igitur consensus cum præceptis virtutis demonstrandus est, et hæc est *laus*. In laudatione (ἐγκωμίῳ) vero res gestæ enumerantur et describuntur, et orator laudatione fungens operam non in eo ponit ut ostendat hanc partem propositi huic virtuti, illi illam convenire: hoc sumit, et amplificando magnitudinem rei exprimit.

μακαρισμός and εὐδαιμονισμός are identical; and superior (μεῖζον καὶ βέλτιον) to the two others, which they include, as happiness itself includes virtue. We learn from the parallel passage in Eth. N. I. 12. that these terms are applicable to all that is highest and best and most perfect, as the Gods, heroes and god-like men, and happiness.

APPENDIX C. TO BOOK I. CH. X.

This classification of causes of action is arrived at as follows. All our actions either originate in ourselves, or have their origin external to and independent of us; either they are under our own control or not. Of the latter there are two cases, accident and necessity; and necessity again may be subdivided into two, nature, and external force constraint or compulsion. So that actions over which we have no control fall under three heads, accidental, natural, and compulsory. Again of the other class of actions which originate in ourselves, ὧν αὐτοὶ αἴτιοι, and of which therefore we have the control, some are due to an acquired habit, some to our natural impulses, either rational or irrational, of which the rational impulse is the calculating or reasoning faculty λογισμός, which always has good for its aim and object; the irrational are two, anger or passion, and desire, the object of which is pleasure real or apparent. Hence we have seven causes or sources of action, accident, nature (natural bent, disposition, tendency, 'propension,' as Butler calls it) external force or compulsion, habit, reasoning or calculation, passion, i.e. anger, resentment, and desire. §§ 7, 8. In §§ 12—18. we have the following definitions of them: and in § 19. we are again reminded that in definitions for rhetorical purposes we are not to look for ἀκρίβεια, exact, mathematical, scientific accuracy, which is here out of place; all that is required being distinctness and freedom from obscurity, μὴ ἀσαφεῖς εἶναι, so that they may be readily apprehended. Comp. I. 5. 15. οὐδὲν ἡ ἀκριβολογία χρήσιμος ἡ περὶ τούτων εἰς τὰ νῦν, and elsewhere.

τύχη is defined by negatives, § 12. Actions are ascribed

to it, of which the cause is indefinite, such as are not directed to any particular object or end (ἕνεκά του), and occur arbitrarily, neither always, nor generally, nor according to any regular prescribed law or fixed order. (τεταγμένως)[1]. [Grant. Ess. on Ethics. p. 221. illustrated by Phys. II. 5. 4.] This plainly appears, he says, from the general definition of τύχη. The definition in question is found in the Physics II. 5. 197. a. 5.[2] αἰτία κατὰ συμβεβηκὸς ἐν τοῖς κατὰ προαίρεσιν τῶν ἕνεκά του, that is "an accidental cause, operating within the sphere of things that have an end in view, and within that again, in the sphere of the voluntary, and of actions with a purpose." In c. 6. 197. b. 1, he adds, ἡ μὲν γὰρ τύχη καὶ τὸ ἀπὸ τύχης ἐστὶν ὅσοις καὶ τὸ εὐτυχῆσαι ἂν ὑπάρξειεν καὶ ὅλως πρᾶξις· διὸ καὶ ἀνάγκη περὶ τὰ πρακτὰ εἶναι τὴν τύχην. By τὰ ἕνεκά του, "things with a purpose," are meant, in general, ὅσα τε ἀπὸ διανοίας ἂν πραχθείη καὶ ὅσα ἀπὸ φύσεως[3]: and τὰ τοιαῦτα ὅταν κατὰ συμβεβηκὸς γένηται, ἀπὸ τύχης φαμὲν εἶναι. Compare Anal. Post. II. 11. 95, 2—9, where τὰ ἀπὸ διανοίας are said to be either ἕνεκά του, or ἀπὸ τύχης, but not both together; and the chapter ends with the emphatic statement ἀπὸ τύχης δ' οὐδὲν ἕνεκά του γίνεται. Ib. b. 21. ὅσα ἀπὸ διανοίας are actions or their results, as οἰκία, ἀνδρίας, ὑγίεια, σωτηρία, (Anal. Post. II. 11. 95. 4, 5), which are originated and suggested within ourselves, the produce as it were of our own intellect (in what sense actions can be said to proceed from the intellect see in de Anim. III. 10. 3.); ὅσα ἀπὸ φύσεως, are things which grow and are developed by a natural law to a certain end, but are

---

[1] It is hard to say whether αἰτία, or ὅσα (i. e. the actions), should be repeated as the nominative to γίγνεται; that is whether we are to understand that the cause operates, or the actions are produced in these ways. Perhaps the word γίγνεται is more appropriate to the actions than to the cause, and the passage should be so understood.

[2] The contents of this chapter are epitomized in Metaph. K. 8—on which see Bonitz. Comm. ad Metaph. p. 22—where the same definition of τύχη is given.

[3] All nature is ἕνεκά του: there is design and purpose in all natural operations. Phys. II. 8. 199. a. 13—8.

incapable of 'action:' and for the same reason inanimate things, beasts, and children are incapable of it, because they have no will, no 'moral purpose,' by which πρᾶξις moral action is determined. (It is plain however that προαίρεσις in the definition is employed in its widest sense, 'will' or 'purpose' in general, and not confined to 'moral' actions. This appears from the whole tenour of the discussion, and more particularly from the illustration—to be presently quoted—for there surely is no *moral* purpose implied in going to recover payment of a debt.) Of these however τὰ ἀπὸ φύσεως are afterwards withdrawn from the sphere of τύχη and assigned to that of ταὐτόματον—which includes τύχη, c. 6. 197. a. 36, though it is distinguished from it, 197. b. 18—22.— and τὰ ἀπὸ τύχης limited to actions with a purpose, ὅσα ἀπὸ ταὐτομάτου γίνεται τῶν προαιρετῶν τοῖς ἔχουσι προαίρεσιν[1]. The apparent contradiction between the definition in the Physics and Metaphysics ll. cc. ἐν τοῖς κατὰ προαίρεσιν τῶν ἕνεκά του, and of the Rhetoric where it is said ἔστι δ' ἀπὸ τύχης...(ὅσα) μὴ ἕνεκά του γίγνεται; with which compare Post. An. II. 11. 95, 8. ἀπὸ τύχης δ' οὐδὲν ἕνεκά του γίγνεται; may be thus reconciled. Actions and events that result from chance cannot in reality proceed from a purpose, the nature and meaning of chance, which is accidental, excludes the supposition. When it is said that they "lie within the sphere of that portion of acts ἕνεκά του, which are done with a purpose," they are spoken of as belonging to this class only as acts that would have been done with a purpose *if* they had not been accidental, if the actor had had previous knowledge of the circumstances of the case. This appears from the example by which τὰ ἀπὸ τύχης and τὰ ἀπὸ ταὐτομάτου

---

[1] Jam τύχη, ubi accurate distinguitur a ταὐτομάτῳ, eo in genere habet locum, quod a voluntate et consilio suspensum est. Bonitz ad Metaph. K. 8. 1065. a. 30.

On Chance and Spontaneity, according to the Aristotelian conception, as accidental causes, irregular agencies in which, unlike true causes, the observation of the past affords no ground for the prediction of the future, see Grote's Plato. c. 37. III. 497.

are illustrated, 196. b. 33. "as, to take an instance, the lender would have come (to a certain place) to get back his money, (for repayment of his loan) had he known (that he should find his debtor there): he *did* come not for this purpose, but he *happened* to come and do this for the purpose of recovering his money: and this, though he was not in the habit of visiting the place, nor of necessity: the end (τὸ οὗ ἕνεκα), the recovery of the money, is not (in this case) one of those things that has its cause in itself (τὰ ἀπὸ φύσεως), but one that proceeds from moral purpose and (so) from the intellect: and *then* it is said to proceed from 'chance'." Which appears to be rather a confused way of expressing this; that τὰ ἀπὸ τύχης belong to that class of actions in which intention or purpose is usually shown, which might have been done with a certain end in view; only in these accidental cases it is excluded by ignorance or some other cause: as in the case cited, the creditor might have gone, and would have done so for the purpose of getting back his money, if he had known that he should meet his debtor there: he did *not* know it; the meeting, and therefore the recovery of the loan, was accidental.

The αἰτία ἀόριστος in the definition of the Rhetoric is explained by Phys. II. 5. 196. b. 28. τὸ μὲν οὖν καθ' αὑτὸ αἴτιον ὡρισμένον, τὸ δὲ κατὰ συμβεβηκὸς ἀόριστον· ἄπειρα γὰρ ἂν τῷ ἑνὶ συμβαίη: and Metaph. K. 8. 1065. a. 25. τὸ δ' οὐκ ἀναγκαῖον ἀλλ' ἀόριστον, λέγω δὲ τὸ κατὰ συμβεβηκός· τοῦ τοιούτου δ' ἄτακτα καὶ ἄπειρα τὰ αἴτια. It is added, Phys. 197. a. 8. ἀόριστα μὲν οὖν τὰ αἴτια ἀνάγκη εἶναι, ἀφ' ὧν ἂν γένοιτο τὰ ἀπὸ τύχης. Ὅθεν καὶ ἡ τύχη τοῦ ἀορίστου εἶναι δοκεῖ καὶ ἄδηλος ἀνθρώπῳ, καὶ ἔστιν ὡς οὐδὲν ἀπὸ τύχης δόξειεν ἂν γίγνεσθαι, and this is repeated in the Metaphysics, 1065. a. 32. See also Phys. 197. a. 18—21. καὶ τὸ φάναι εἶναί τι παράλογον τὴν τύχην ὀρθῶς· ὁ γὰρ λόγος ἢ τῶν ἀεὶ ὄντων ἢ τῶν ὡς ἐπὶ τὸ πολύ, ἡ δὲ τύχη ἐν τοῖς γιγνομένοις παρὰ ταῦτα· ὥστ' ἐπειδὴ ἀόριστα, τὰ τοιαῦτα, καὶ ἡ τύχη ἀόριστος.

With the words (ὅσα) γίγνεται μήτε ἀεὶ μήτε ὡς ἐπὶ τὸ πολὺ μήτε τεταγμένως, §12, compare Phys. II. 5. init. ἐπειδὴ ὁρῶμεν τὰ μὲν ἀεὶ ὡσαύτως γινόμενα τὰ δὲ ὡς ἐπὶ τὸ πολύ, φανερὸν ὅτι οὐδετέρου τούτων αἰτία ἡ τύχη λέγεται οὐδὲ τὸ ἀπὸ τύχης, οὔτε τοῦ ἐξ ἀνάγκης καὶ ἀεὶ οὔτε τοῦ ὡς ἐπὶ τὸ πολύ : and again (in the illustration) 197. a. 3, "had the creditor gone with the *purpose* (of getting his debt paid) or *with that intent;* or had he been in the *constant* habit of going, ἢ ἀεὶ φοιτῶν, or had it been his usual habit to exact payment of his debts, ἢ ὡς ἐπὶ τὸ πολὺ κομιζόμενος, the result would not have been accidental, *chance* would not have been the cause of it, οὐκ ἀπὸ τύχης. Compare also, Eth. Eudem. VII. 14. 6, ἀλλὰ μὴν ἥ γε φύσις αἰτία ἢ τοῦ ἀεὶ ὡσαύτως ἢ τοῦ ὡς ἐπὶ τὸ πολύ, ἡ δὲ τύχη τοὐναντίον.

Yet after all, though for a moment, and in deference to popular opinion and popular language, Phys. II. 5. 196. b. 14. πάντες φασί, II. 4. 196. a. 11—17, Aristotle, following in this respect his usual practice, for with him an established current prevailing opinion is always a strong argument in favour of the truth of any view, allows to chance the *name* of cause, yet he subsequently virtually retracts the admission, and by defining this as an 'accidental' kind of cause (Phys. II. 5. passim.) deprives it of all valid title to that name. For this in fact contradicts the very notion of cause, to which constancy and uniformity of operation are absolutely essential. It is, as he himself says in the same chapter, just as much a cause of an action or event, and no more, than whiteness or musical skill is the cause of a house, when the architect happens accidentally to be possessed of either of these two qualities. 196. b. 26. 197. a. 14. 'Chance' is in fact nothing more than a name employed to cover our ignorance of the true cause of a thing. See also Anal. Post. I. 30., in which he excludes τύχη from the domain of scientific investigation and demonstrative proof, on the ground that it comes under the head neither of τἀναγκαῖα, nor of τὰ ὡς ἐπὶ τὸ πολύ; and all syllogisms alike must draw conclusions of one or the other kind.

The various statements of Aristotle on this subject of chance as a cause are very contradictory and confusing. Besides the contradiction, real or apparent, already pointed out, in Rhet. I. 5. 17, he tells us in speaking of εὐτυχία, which is ὧν ἡ τύχη ἀγαθῶν αἰτία, that this chance may in some cases be the cause of things which are ordinarily due to art or nature; as health, which is a work of art, and personal beauty or tall stature, which are *natural* gifts, may also be accidental; which is directly opposed to the statements of the Physics II. 6. 197. a. 36, already quoted. In fact Aristotle writes upon this subject like one who had formed no definite opinion upon it, nor attempted to reconcile the difficulties it involves. Further on in the same section we are told that chance is the cause of all unexpected blessings, i.e. such as are beyond calculation παρὰ λόγον, and deviate from the ordinary rule. These he illustrates by four examples, of which the first again belongs to τὰ ἀπὸ φύσεως.

On the same subject see further Eudemus, in his Ethics VII. 14, where he is discussing the nature and meaning of εὐτυχία; and Spengel's commentary, in his paper 'on the Ethical writings ascribed to Aristotle,' published in the transactions of the Bavarian Academy, pp. 544—548. Eudemus is more than half inclined to come to the conclusion just stated, that τύχη as an αἰτία is a mere delusion and a name given by us to express an *unknown* cause; and eventually he resolves εὐτυχία 'good fortune' into two kinds, the one φύσει, proceeding from nature as its source, the other θεία, from the divine favour, thus excluding τύχη altogether as its source or origin, though the name is derived from it.

On chance as a cause or supposed agent see Bentley, Boyle Lectures, Lect. V.; Butler, Analogy, II. 4. 3; the references in Grote's Plato, Vol. I. 76. note k. and Stewart there quoted, on the Epicurean theory; and in the same work Vol. II. p. 184. note f.

In his note on Anal. Post. I. 30. 87. b. 19, Waitz has written out the passages bearing on this subject from the Physics and Metaphysics. On the relation of chance to Nature in Aristotle's philosophy, see the excellent remarks of Grant in Essays on Ethics, p. 221.

The next definition is that of φύσις as a cause of action, § 13. "Things are said to be 'by nature' when the cause is in themselves and regular (acts uniformly), when the operation is always, or almost always, in the same way. The exceptions—when the course of nature is not absolutely uniform—need not be scientifically gone into to ascertain whether these aberrations from the ordinary rule are due to nature itself in some sense, or to any other cause. It would rather seem that chance is the cause of these latter." See Grant, Essays on Ethics p. 220. seq.

The definition of Nature given in the Physics, II. 1. 192. b. 13. seq., is as follows—τὰ φύσει ὄντα πάντα φαίνεται ἔχοντα ἐν ἑαυτοῖς ἀρχὴν κινήσεως καὶ στάσεως, τὰ μὲν κατὰ τόπον, τὰ δὲ κατ' αὔξησιν καὶ φθίσιν, τὰ δὲ κατ' ἀλλοίωσιν· and, as is subsequently added, καθ' αὑτὸ μὴ κατὰ συμβεβηκός. Examples are, all animals and their parts, plants, and the elements, earth air fire and water. All works of art are excluded; because these except by accident, so far as the material, earth or stone for instance, is concerned, have no principle or origin of motion or change in them, but this is communicated from without. The difference between καθ' αὑτό and κατὰ συμβεβηκός is thus illustrated, 192. b. 23. Health when produced by medical treatment is artificial, the product of art, not natural; and yet the physician may be said to be the origin of his own health, or to have its origin in himself. But this is only due to the *accident* of his being a physician; it is not the health that grows of itself, naturally. Philoponus observes upon this that Aristotle has not here given us a definition of Nature itself but of its activity or operation, (ἐνέργεια): for to say that Nature is the origin of motion or rest is not to tell us what Nature is, but what it does. He therefore thus supplies the omission. "Nature is a life or power pervading bodies, which forms and moulds them and regulates their motions; the origin of motion and rest is that which exists primarily in them, in itself and not accidentally:" the last words being taken from Aristotle. The last clause of the definition of the Rhetoric τὰ γὰρ παρὰ φύσιν—δέξειε δ' ἂν καὶ ἡ τύχη αἰτία εἶναι τῶν τοιούτων, stand in direct contradiction to Phys. II. 6. 197. b. 32. seq. μάλιστα δ'ἐστὶ χωριζόμενον τὸ ἀπὸ τύχης ἐν τοῖς φύσει γινομένοις· ὅταν γὰρ γένηταί τι παρὰ φύσιν, τότε οὐκ ἀπὸ τύχης ἀλλὰ μᾶλλον ἀπὸ ταὐτομάτου, γεγονέναι φαμέν. ἔστι δὲ καὶ τοῦτο ἕτερον· τοῦ μὲν γὰρ ἔξω τὸ αἴτιον, τοῦ δ' ἐντός[1].

On τὰ παρὰ φύσιν τέρατα, monstra, in animals, see further de Gen. Anim. IV. 3. ult. c. 4 init. c. 3. 767. b. 13. τὸ δὲ τέρας οὐκ ἀναγκαῖον πρὸς τὴν ἕνεκά του καὶ τὴν τοῦ τέλους αἰτίαν, ἀλλὰ κατὰ συμβεβηκὸς ἀναγκαῖον, ἐπεὶ τήν γ' ἀρχὴν ἐντεῦθεν δεῖ λαβεῖν. and Probl. X. 61.

Βίᾳ, 'by external force or compulsion,' § 14, is applied to actions 'which are performed indeed by the actors themselves and their own instrumentality, but contrary to their desires and calculations.' Here again the definition is at variance with what is elsewhere stated on the same subject. In the Nicom. Ethics, III. 1. sub init. we find, δοκεῖ δὲ ἀκούσια εἶναι τὰ βίᾳ ἢ δι' ἄγνοιαν γινόμενα. βίαιον δὲ οὗ ἡ ἀρχὴ ἔξωθεν, τοιαύτη οὖσα ἐν ᾗ μηδὲν συμβάλλεται ὁ πράττων ἢ ὁ πάσχων, οἷον εἰ πνεῦμα κομίσαι ποι ἢ ἄνθρωποι κύριοι ὄντες: which is in direct contradiction of the γίγνεται δι' αὐτῶν τῶν πραττόντων of the preceding. In Metaphys. Δ. 5. 1015. a. 26, the definition makes a nearer approach to that of the Rhetoric. τὸ βίαιον or βία is a species of the genus ἀνάγκη, τοῦτο δ' ἐστὶ τὸ παρὰ τὴν ὁρμὴν καὶ τὴν προαίρεσιν ἐμποδίζον καὶ κωλυτικόν. τὸ γὰρ βίαιον ἀναγκαῖον λέγεται...καὶ ἡ βία ἀνάγκη

---
[1] See Grant on φύσις, note on Eth. N. II. 1. 3.

τις...καὶ δοκεῖ ἡ ἀνάγκη ἀμετάπειστόν τι εἶναι, ὀρθῶς· ἐναντίον γὰρ τῇ κατὰ τὴν προαίρεσιν κινήσει καὶ κατὰ τὸν λογισμόν. Compare Anal. Post. II. 11. 94. b. 37. ἡ δ' ἀνάγκη διττή· ἡ μὲν γὰρ κατὰ φύσιν καὶ τὴν ὁρμήν, ἡ δὲ βίᾳ ἡ παρὰ τὴν ὁρμήν, ὥσπερ λίθος ἐξ ἀνάγκης καὶ ἄνω καὶ κάτω φέρεται, ἀλλ' οὐ διὰ τὴν αὐτὴν ἀνάγκην. παρὰ φύσιν ἡ βία. Rhet. I. 11. 3.

Ἔθει, ὅσα διὰ τὸ πολλάκις πεποιηκέναι ποιοῦσιν. "what we continue to do because we have often done the same before." § 15. This is I believe the only precise and explicit statement which Aristotle has given us about the meaning of the term, and is far enough from being a complete definition of it, even the genus being omitted.

ἔθος, like many other words, such as τέχνη, ἐπιστήμη, μέθοδος, πραγματεία, the Platonic διαλεκτική, is used in two different senses, to express a process, and a result, the formation of a habit, habituation, and the habit itself, acquired, developed, confirmed. (See above, p. 17. note 2.) The formation of a habit is the result of a law of association, arising from constant repetition: a certain course of action regularly follows certain antecedent circumstances: the two thus become inseparably connected in our practice as antecedent and consequent; under similar circumstances we always act in the same way. The connexion thus becomes permanent, and finally, inseparable when the habit is formed; which then becomes a law of our nature. The test of habit is that it makes what was originally irksome or painful, natural, easy, and pleasant; so that it ends by becoming a 'second nature' to us, φύσις ἤδη τὸ ἔθος, περὶ μνήμης καὶ ἀναμν. c. 2. 452. a. 27. τὸ εἰθισμένον ὥσπερ πεφυκὸς ἤδη γίγνεται. Rhet. I. 11. 3. And similarly frequent repetition gives rise to a law of suggestion and association; as a thing which we have often had in our minds is most readily suggested to us when we wish to recal it to our recollection; and so again τὸ πολλάκις φύσιν ποιεῖ. Ibid. ἔθος *as a process* is distinguished from ἕξις the established habit, which in fact is produced by it.

Eth. N. II. 1. 1, 3. (Grant, Essays on Ethics, p. 190.); as a *result* it must needs be identical with it. What was before said to be distinctive of ἔθος, that the test of it lies in the pleasure found in the acts resulting from it. Rhet. I. 11. 3, 4. οὕτω δὲ τὸ ἔθος ποιεῖ ἡδύ, is likewise distinctive of the ἕξις. Eth. N. II. 3. 1. On the formation of habits, and the Law of Contiguity which it exemplifies, see Prof. Bain's masterly treatise on the Senses and Intellect, p. 315 and the following: and on the four Laws of Association in general. The Moral Habits are analysed and discussed in the Vol. on the Emotions and Will, p. 500. seq. It is distinguished from φύσις a *natural* inclination or tendency; for in the latter this is fixed and unalterable, and acts only in one direction, but ἔθος may follow either of the two opposites; and therefore it cannot *properly* be applied to any natural operation, or φύσις, because in these no change can be effected by any amount of practice. The operation of nature is constant and invariable, that of habit has not this necessary uniformity, it follows only a *general* law, and may be altered. ἡ φύσις τοῦ ἀεὶ, τὸ δὲ ἔθος τοῦ πολλάκις. Rhet. I. 11. 3. Also, (Grant Eth. N. II. 1. 3. not. 3. I.) "φύσις is opposed to habit as the original tendency to that which is superinduced. VII. 10. 4. ῥᾷον ἔθος μετακινῆσαι φύσεως."

It is distinguished on the other hand, from μάθησις and τέχνη: from the first, Metaph. Θ. 5. 1047. b. 32, as a *mechanical* process (compare Grant's note on Eth. N. II. 1. 1. "a mechanical theory is here given both of the intellect and the moral character [ἡ δ' ἠθικὴ ἐξ ἔθους περιγίγνεται] as if the one could be *acquired* by teaching the other by a course of habits"), as αὐλεῖν the power of *blowing* the flute comes by repetition, mechanically; whereas μάθησις is an intelligent process by which the arts are acquired: from τέχνη, Metaph. A. I. 981. b. 5. for the same reason as the last, and because it leads only to ἐμπειρία practised skill, and makes men πρακτικούς merely, not σοφούς; art implying knowledge, especially the knowledge of causes. ἐμπειρία works by rule of thumb, the handicraftsman has merely acquired by practice the constant repetition of the process, the power of executing the work in which he is skilled, τοὺς χειροτέχνας (ποιεῖν) δι' ἔθος. Met. u. s.; the artist works by rules which he understands, and with a knowledge of causes and means and ends.

Habit, ἔθος, seems, says Grant, Essays, u. s., to be assumed by Aristotle, "as an acknowledged law of human nature". Δύναμις by the law or process of ἔθος is developed ultimately into ἕξις, an acquired and confirmed state; not intellectual, which comes from διδασκαλία; and the sum total of these constitutes the ἦθος or character; the name itself being derived from ἔθος, the process by which it is generated. Eth. N. II. 1. 1. and Magn. Mor. I. 6. 1186. a. 2. ἠθικὴ καλεῖται διὰ τὸ ἐθίζεσθαι. Plato, Legg. VII. 792. E. κυριώτατον γὰρ οὖν ἐμφύεται πᾶσι τότε τὸ πᾶν ἦθος διὰ ἔθος. A physical operation or process *may* be called an ἔθος; a 'habit' may be said to work in things physical, as fire rises and stones fall; but there is this marked difference between the physical and moral habit, that in the former the tendency is fixed and can only operate in one direction, "a stone could never acquire the habit of rising by being thrown ten thousand times into the air, nor fire of falling", Eth. N. II. 1. 2, but in the other it may take either of the two opposite directions and be developed either into a virtue or a vice.

Habit is the first of the four causes to which actions are due that originate in ourselves, τὰ δι' αὐτούς. The second is λογισμός, 'reasoning or calculation'. This mode of action is described as follows. "Actions are performed from rational motives or calculation which from the several kinds of goods above detailed[1] (cc. 6. 7), are thought to be advantageous,

---

[1] ἐκ τῶν εἰρημένων ἀγαθῶν. Victorius understands this as though the preposition ἐκ were superfluous, 'of, belonging to that class.' As far as the grammar is concerned this is perfectly admissible; but as it is the actions in pursuit of good, and not the good things themselves, that are here in question, the interpretation in the text is to be preferred.

(that is to say, in which the conception of the advantage of the action is derived from the kind of good, which we have analysed in detail, that it is supposed to aim at) either as ends or as means to an end, provided these advantages are the motives of the actions: because it *is* possible to do things that are advantageous, yet not for that reason, but for the pleasure that attends them; as is the case with the licentious, who are devoid of self-control." § 16. This is in agreement with the Aristotelian doctrine that the object of motion is always itself unmoved: but it is *not* in agreement with another principle laid down in de Anim. III. 10, on προαίρεσις, that the ὄρεξις or impulsive element of it is the *sole* origin of motive, with which the calculating part of it, the διάνοια or λογισμός has nothing whatsoever to do.

λογισμός is the reasoning or calculating faculty, 'the practical and discursive reason'. In the Nicomachean Ethics VI. 2. init. the rational soul, τὸ λόγον ἔχον, is divided into τὸ ἐπιστημονικόν and τὸ λογιστικόν; the former being the intuitive reason, ᾧ θεωροῦμεν τὰ τοιαῦτα τῶν ὄντων ὅσων αἱ ἀρχαὶ μὴ ἐνδέχονται ἄλλως ἔχειν, by which we discern necessary truth; and the other the discursive, reasoning faculty by which we apprehend the contingent and variable. ᾧ (θεωροῦμεν) τὰ ἐνδεχόμενα (ἄλλως ἔχειν). τὸ λογίζεσθαι is here the same as τὸ βουλεύεσθαι; and we never deliberate about necessary truths which cannot be other than they are; but usually λογίζεσθαι denotes 'reasoning' of all kinds. Grant observes in his note on Eth. N. VI. 1. 6 that elsewhere λογιστικόν rather expresses 'rational' in general, quoting passages from the de Animâ in which it occurs in this sense. Add Plato, Rep. IV. 4. 39. D, where τὸ λογιστικόν stands for the entire rational part of the soul. In Magn. Mor. I. 1. 1182. a. 18, 20. it is identified with τὸ διανοητικόν. 'the intellect'. In Anal. Post. II. 19. 7. we are told that it is like δόξα, liable to error, capable of being misled by a false show of truth, whilst ἐπιστήμη and νοῦς are unerring in their perception of truth, and can apprehend nothing else.

This faculty or element of the rational soul, the practical reason, is that of which φρόνησις, practical wisdom, which guides men in deliberation and the choice between right and wrong, is the special virtue; as σοφία, speculative wisdom or philosophy, is that of the ἐπιστημονικόν, the intuitive or scientific faculties, or part of the mind[1].

The calculating and practical faculty then is that by which we estimate, and are directed to, possible advantages, to be aimed at either as ends or means: and of these advantages the nature and the measure and the value may be gathered ἐκ τῶν εἰρημένων ἀγαθῶν, from the list of things good, and their degrees or comparative values, given in chapters 6 and 7. At the same time it is to be remarked that the performance of things useful and expedient does not always proceed from calculation or reasoning: such things may be due to accident, the motive and intention which prompt them being of a different kind, as pleasure.

In § 7 the λογισμός is said to be a λογιστικὴ ὄρεξις 'a calculating or reasoning impulse';—this serves in some degree to correct the contradiction above noticed—otherwise a βούλησις[2] or ἀγαθοῦ ὄρεξις; οὐδεὶς γὰρ βούλεται ἀλλ' ἢ ὅταν οἰηθῇ εἶναι ἀγαθόν. It is however the ὄρεξις guided by the reasoning powers that gives the impulse to motion and action; the intellect by itself can move nothing; διάνοια δ' αὐτὴ οὐθὲν κινεῖ. ἀλλ' ἡ ἕνεκά του (i.e. with the addition of ὄρεξις; see Grant's note) Eth. N. VI. 2. 5. and de Anim. III. 9. 7. οὐθὲν γὰρ μὴ ὀρεγόμενον ἢ φεῦγον κινεῖται ἀλλ' ἢ βίᾳ. and again: ch. 10. 2, 3. ἄμφω ἄρα ταῦτα κινητικὰ κατὰ τόπον, νοῦς καὶ ὄρεξις. νοῦς δὲ ἕνεκά του λογιζόμενος καὶ ὁ πρακτικός. ...ὥστε εὐλόγως δύο ταῦτα φαίνεται τὰ κινοῦντα, ὄρεξις καὶ διάνοια πρακτική· τὸ ὀρεκτὸν γὰρ κινεῖ, κ α ὶ δ ι ὰ

---

[1] Bonitz on Met A. I. 980. b. 28. gives the following definition of λογισμός 'eam rationem per quam, quid sit verum quid falsum, quid sit faciendum quid non, deliberamus, causasque in utramque partem perpendimus.'

[2] ἔν τε τῷ λογιστικῷ ἡ βούλησις γίνεται· καὶ ἐν τῷ ἀλόγῳ ἡ ἐπιθυμία καὶ ὁ θυμός. de Anim. III. 9. 5.

τοῦτο ἡ διάνοια, ὅτι ἀρχὴ αὐτῆς ἐστὶ τὸ ὀρεκτόν. So Cicero, de Off. I. 36. ult. cogitatio in vero exquirendo maxime versatur; appetitus impellit ad agendum. And this agrees with the conclusions of modern philosophers—see for example J. S. Mill, on Auguste Comte and Positivism. p. 101. and the same in Dissertations and Discussions, p. 121.

The two remaining causes of action are θυμός or ὀργή, and ἐπιθυμία. §§ 17, 18.

In the classification of these three last causes of human action, λογισμός, θυμός, and ἐπιθυμία, Aristotle is following the triple division of the human soul, the intellectual and moral part of man, as it is laid down in Plato's Republic: but with considerable modification. λογισμός the discursive *reasoning* faculty is only *part* of the intellectual portion of the soul, the higher and nobler speculative or intuitive reason being omitted, because it never does prompt to action. Again the θυμός, as merely equivalent to ὀργή, leaves out a great deal which is contained in the Platonic θυμοειδές; which includes spirit, zeal, enthusiasm, the vigorous, active, emulous elements of human character, besides mere anger, and just resentment or indignation. ἐπιθυμία as well as θυμός or ὀργή are both πάθη, according to the Aristotelian classification. Eth. N. II. 4.

In his more scientific works, as the Ethics and Politics, Aristotle usually adopts and argues from this Platonic division of the soul. He also accepts the other Platonic (so the Epitomizer in Magn. Mor. I. 1.) division into the rational and irrational elements, as in Eth. N. I. 13. Polit. VII. 14; only with the modification, that the 'irrational' element, the θυμός and ἐπιθυμία, may be considered rational in a sense, because they are capable of understanding the dictates of the reason, of listening to and obeying it. And this is also the basis of his division of virtues into intellectual, διανοητικαί, and moral, ἠθικαί. Nevertheless in de Anim. III. 9. 3, compare I. 5, 6., both of these are criticised together, and shown to be unsound and untenable. If we are 'to divide the soul into parts' at all, the division must be carried to a much greater length; indeed it seems that it might be carried to infinity.

θυμός and ὀργή, § 17, passion and anger, resentment of injury, real or supposed, are the causes of action of which punishment or vengeance is the object, τὰ τιμωρητικά. So in the chapter on ὀργή, II. 2. 1. it is defined, ὄρεξις μετὰ λύπης τιμωρίας κ.τ.λ. τιμωρία and κόλασις are two different kinds of punishment; punishment takes the form of vengeance, when it is inflicted by the offended person for his own sake and with a view merely to his own satisfaction; in the other case, when it is employed for the offender's sake to turn him from his evil ways, it is punishment proper, correction or chastisement. Plato, Gorg. 525. B. C., distinguishes two cases of τιμωρία or punishment in general; either for the correction and improvement of the offender ἢ βελτίονι γίγνεσθαι καὶ ὀνίνασθαι; or for example's sake, to deter others from the like offences; ἢ παραδείγματι τοῖς ἄλλοις γίγνεσθαι, ἵν' ἄλλοι ὁρῶντες πάσχοντα ἃ ἂν πάσχῃ φοβούμενοι βελτίους γίγνωνται. Compare Clem. Alex. Strom. VII. p. 895, quoted by Gaisford. Θεὸς δὲ οὐ τιμωρεῖται· ἔστι γὰρ ἡ τιμωρία κακοῦ ἀνταπόδοσις· κολάζει μέντοι πρὸς τὸ χρήσιμον καὶ κοινῇ καὶ ἰδίᾳ τοῖς κολαζομένοις.

There is however a different interpretation of τιμωρία which might be applied here, derived from a different division of punishments. This division is referred to by Aulus Gellius, N. A. VI. 14, quoted by Gaisford, and is to this effect. 'One kind is that which is called νουθεσία, κόλασις, or παραίνεσις, when the punishment is applied for the sake of castigation and improvement, &c.: the second is that which is called τιμωρία, and is employed for the maintenance of the dignity and authority of the person offended, lest it should suffer if no notice were taken of the offence; and from this the name itself is supposed to be derived, 'a conservatione honoris'. The third kind is the second of Plato's division, viz. when the punishment is inflicted for an example to others. It is possible, though I think not probable, that Aristotle may have had this signification in view in the distinction of κόλασις and τιμωρία.

For the further consideration of ὀργή we are referred to the treatise on the πάθη in Bk. II. c. 2.

ἐπιθυμία[1], the remaining incentive to action, § 18, is reckoned as one of the πάθη in Eth. N. II. 4, though it is omitted in the treatment of them in Rhet. II. 2—11. It is here said of it 'that it gives rise to all actions which have the appearance of being agreeable', (φαίνονται because the pleasure aimed at is often more apparent than real): and again in c. 11. § 5, it is called τοῦ ἡδέος ὄρεξις, 'an impulse towards what is agreeable.' ἐπιθυμία, desire, therefore is that πάθος or natural affection that excites us to pursue what is pleasant, or supposed to be so. ᾧ δ' αἴσθησις ὑπάρχει, τούτῳ ἡδονή τε καὶ λύπη καὶ τὸ ἡδὺ καὶ τὸ λυπηρόν, οἷς δὲ ταῦτα καὶ ἡ ἐπιθυμία· τοῦ γὰρ ἡδέος ὄρεξις αὕτη. de Anim. II. 3. 414. b. 4. and see further on ἐπιθυμία in ch. 11. § 5.

Continuing this subject the author tells us that the objects of voluntary action are good and pleasure, real and apparent; reckoning amongst these the real and apparent relief from real and apparent evil and pain, and the exchange of a less real or apparent evil and pain for a greater. It thus appears that good and pleasure are both necessary objects of rhetorical inquiry, and as the first has been already described and analysed (c. 6), we pass on in the next chapter to the subject of pleasure, after being warned, as before, that we are not to expect scientific definitions in a practical and popular art like rhetoric, but only such as may be readily apprehended by an unlearned audience; a precept which, as we have already seen and shall see throughout, is abundantly exemplified in this work.

---

[1] On the origin of desire, Plat. Phil. 36. A. B. Grote, Plato II. 569.

APPENDIX D. TO BOOK I. CH. XI.

Ch. 11. The eleventh Chapter therefore commences with a definition of pleasure. "Let us assume that pleasure is a kind of motion (an active state) of the soul (or of life, the vital powers) and a settling[1] (relapse), sudden (all at once) and sensible, into our proper nature; and pain the contrary."

This description of pleasure seems to be borrowed from Plato, of whose views on this subject gathered from his statements in the Philebus, Gorgias, Republic, and Timæus, I have given some account in my Introduction to the Translation of the Gorgias, p. liii. "Pleasure, especially sensual pleasure, the gratification of a bodily appetite, and some, but not all, mental pleasures, consist in the relief of a want, the filling up of a gap, the supply of the deficiency, of a certain part of the body, or of the entire bodily constitution, and a restoration of the whole system to the normal harmony of its condition." In the Philebus 31 D. "pain is represented as the λύσις τῆς ἁρμονίας of the bodily frame, and pleasure as the restoration of this balance or harmony, in the filling up of the void produced by this dissolution." See further, p. 32. B. 42. C. D[2]. The same view is found in Timæus 64. D. (where the word ἄθροον occurs, which seems to have been thence transferred by Aristotle to his definition in the Rhetoric); and in the Republic IX. 583. B—586. C. see particularly 584. C. and 585.

[1] See Grote, on Philebus, in his Plato, II. 566. sq. with the word κατάστασις here may be compared φύσεως καθεστηκυίας in Eth. Eud. VI. 13. 1153. a. 3., which is receptive of the higher pleasures of θεωρία; distinguished from τῆς καθισταμένης or ἀναπληρουμένης the process by which the pleasures of sense (in the Platonic doctrine) make themselves felt.

[2] So Lucretius, de Rer. Nat. II. 963.
Præterea quoniam dolor est ubi materiai
Corpora vi quadam per viscera viva, per artus,
Sollicitata suis trepidant in sedibus intus,
Inque locum quando remigrant, fit blanda voluptas.

A. Comp. Magn. Mor. II. 7. 1206. b. 20. It is therefore according to Plato a κίνησις or γένεσις. Phileb. 53. c. 54. E. a doctrine supposed to be that of Aristippus and his followers, and referred to in Eth. N. x. 3. Eth. Eud. VI. 12. Magn. Mor. II. 7. (Stallb. note on Phil. 53. c.) and so far adopted by Plato. A similar view was held by Kant. See the passage of his Anthropology, quoted by Dr. Badham, in Append. to Phileb. p. 102; and on this, Grant, Ess. on Ethics, p. 198.

It is to be observed that the definition commences with ὑποκείσθω ἡμῖν, 'let us assume'. Compare ἔστω introducing a definition, I. 5. 3. and 6. 2. This is to show that we are not to take this for an exact scientific description: it is a mere hypothesis, which will answer the purpose of the rhetorician well enough, and satisfy a popular audience, though when we come to examine it more closely we find that it is untenable. It is in fact in other passages of his writings both virtually and actually contradicted: but from the rhetorical point of view it is sufficient, because accepted. Aristotle's opinions upon the subject of pleasure appear to have undergone a change, which is shown in the discrepancy between the view taken in the Physics III. 8. 247 and 7. seq. and the conclusions arrived at in the treatise on pleasure in the tenth book of the Nicomachean Ethics; this later theory being completed and carried out by Eudemus in the sixth book of his Ethics (Eth. N. bk. VII.) chapter 13.

In the passage of the Physics he says. "All moral virtue has reference to bodily pleasures and pains, which consist either in the act, or the memory, or anticipation of them. Now those that are felt in the act are all sensible, reside in sensation (κατὰ τὴν αἴσθησίν εἰσιν), and therefore are put in motion by some sensible object; those which belong to memory and anticipation arise from these: for the pleasure arises either from recollection of our former feelings, or from anticipation of the future. It follows therefore that all pleasure of this kind must be produced by the objects of sense¹.'' In the following sentences he speaks of pleasures and pains as ἀλλοιώσεις τοῦ αἰσθητικοῦ. The words 'pleasures of this kind' might lead one to suppose that the description here given is confined to bodily pleasure or pleasure of sense; the intellectual pleasures as of taste and contemplation being designedly left altogether out of the account: yet it would seem rather that the theory is intended to include pleasures of all kinds, divided into two classes, the bodily pleasures of sense, and the intellectual pleasures of anticipation and retrospection, all of them alike being ultimately traceable to sensation: the pure pleasures of taste, as of eye and ear, being supposed to reside in the sensations of those organs; and those of θεωρία, speculation or philosophical contemplation being here unnoticed and unthought of.

A similar view seems to be implied in the curious definition of pleasure and pain given in the de Anim. III. 7. 431. a. 10. "Sensation (pure and simple)" we are there told "is mere speaking (that is, the mere utterance of detached words without the combination which gives the meaning; or 'words' as distinguished from 'propositions' which assert or deny something), or thinking: but when this is accompanied by pleasure or pain, then, as it were affirming or denying, the soul pursues or avoids. [i.e. it then does what may be compared to pronouncing a positive judgment that the one viz. is good and to be sought the other evil and to be avoided, which it *expresses* in action by pursuing the one and shunning the other.²] Pleasure and pain are therefore states of activity (consciousness, Grant) in relation to what is good and bad as such, operating by the discriminating faculty of the senses, τῇ αἰσθητικῇ μεσότητι³. This when it is ac-

¹ Comp. Rhet. I. 11. 6, 7.
² Eth. N. VI. 2. ἔστι δ' ὅπερ ἐν διανοίᾳ κατάφασις καὶ ἀπόφασις τοῦτ' ἐν ὀρέξει δίωξις καὶ φυγή. This comes from Plato, Sophist. 263. E. seq. comp. Theæt. 189. E. 190. A. Phileb. 38. D.

³ τῇ αἰσθητικῇ μεσότητι. The meaning of μεσότης as applied to sensation is explained in a preceding passage of Bk. II. c. 11. sub fin. sensation is there said to be μεσότης τῆς ἐν τοῖς αἰσθητοῖς ἐναντιώσεως, 'a mean state, a sort of balance or harmony, between

tually realised in action, κατ' ἐνέργειαν, becomes pursuit on the one hand or avoidance on the other." Compare II. 3. 414. b. 4. ᾧ δ' αἴσθησις ὑπάρχει, τούτῳ ἡδονή τε καὶ λύπη καὶ τὸ ἡδὺ καὶ τὸ λυπηρόν. And we have a similar sense of right and wrong, τοῦτο γὰρ πρὸς τἆλλα ζῷα τοῖς ἀνθρώποις ἴδιον, τὸ μόνον ἀγαθοῦ καὶ κακοῦ καὶ δικαίου καὶ ἀδίκου καὶ τῶν ἄλλων αἴσθησιν ἔχειν, Pol. I. 2. 12. Pleasure therefore according to this view, is an active realised operation of sense, which has a discriminating power to distinguish good and evil, and when actually developed and in active exercise impels us to seek and to shun. It is therefore both an αἴσθησις and a κίνησις. ἐπεὶ δ' ἐστὶ τὸ ἥδεσθαι ἐν τῷ αἰσθάνεσθαί τινος πάθους. Rhet. I. 11. 6.

This is controverted in Eth. N. X. 3 and 4. We are there informed that pleasure is not a motion, nor in time, nor divisible into parts, but entire and instantaneous in its operation like sight: and the third chapter closes very emphatically with the words, ἐκ τούτων δὲ δῆλον καὶ ὅτι οὐ καλῶς λέγουσι κίνησιν ἢ γένεσιν εἶναι τὴν ἡδονήν. οὐ γὰρ πάντων ταῦτα λέγεται, ἀλλὰ τῶν μεριστῶν καὶ μὴ ὅλων· οὐδὲ γὰρ ὁράσεώς ἐστι γένεσις οὐδὲ στιγμῆς οὐδὲ μονάδος, οὐδὲ τούτων οὐθὲν κίνησις ἢ γένεσις· οὐδὲ δὴ ἡδονῆς· ὅλον γάρ τι. c. 3. ult. Comp. Magn. Mor. II. 7. 1204. b. 5. ἔστι γὰρ πρῶτον μὲν οὐ πᾶσα ἡδονὴ γένεσις. κ.τ.λ. and Eth. Eud.

---

the two opposite extremes of each class of objects of sensation which are subject to the several senses, as sight between the opposite colours, black and white, or the visible and invisible; touch between hot and cold, or the palpable and impalpable; and so on. It is neither of them ἐνεργείᾳ, but both δυνάμει. The sense lying between these extremes and capable of apprehending both or inclining in either direction, has as a mean the power of judging or distinguishing, κρίνειν, the objects of sense, τὸ γὰρ μέσον κριτικόν. Similarly the αἴσθησις lying between the good and the bad may form its judgment between them and take the direction of either. When it verges towards the good, the feeling becomes one of pleasure, when towards what is bad, painful. When this sensation or feeling is developed and realised in activity, κατ' ἐνέργειαν, it becomes pursuit or avoidance δίωξις or φυγή.

VI. 15. 1154. b. 27, ἡδονὴ μᾶλλον ἐν ἠρεμίᾳ ἐστὶν ἢ ἐν κινήσει.

Further pleasure is not a sense x. 5. 7. though it is conveyed by and accompanies the action of the senses, κατὰ πᾶσαν γὰρ αἴσθησίν ἐστιν ἡδονή, ὁμοίως δὲ καὶ διάνοιαν καὶ θεωρίαν. 4. 5—here for the first time intellectual and speculative pleasures are mentioned—and again, καθ' ἑκάστην δ' αἴσθησιν ὅτι γίνεται ἡδονὴ δῆλον· φαμὲν γὰρ ὁράματα καὶ ἀκούσματα εἶναι ἡδέα. 4, 7. Neither is it as yet an ἐνέργεια or a ἕξις. It is said, (1) εἶναι ἐν τῇ ἐνεργείᾳ 4, 8. (2) ἕπεσθαι τῇ ἐνεργείᾳ § 9. 5, 11. Compare 5, 6. καθ' ἑκάστην ἐνέργειαν οἰκεία ἡδονή ἐστιν. (3) τελειοῦν τὴν ἐνέργειαν 4. 6, 8, 11. only not as a ἕξις ἐνυπάρχουσα (growing to perfection within it) but ὡς ἐπιγιγνόμενόν τι τέλος, "a superadded perfection", (Grant.) as something distinct from and without it. § 8. And so, "though they are so nearly allied, and the pleasure is so inseparable from the ἐνέργεια, that it is even doubtful whether they are not identical." c. 5, 6.; yet still they must be distinguished, ὥσπερ οὖν αἱ ἐνέργειαι ἕτεραι καὶ αἱ ἡδοναί 5, 7.[1] Pleasure is the necessary concomitant of every healthy ἐνέργεια. This doctrine is carried a step further by Eudemus in whose ethical scheme pleasure has now become an ἐνέργεια. His definition is, Eth. Eud. VI. 13 (Eth. N. VII. 13.) 1153. a. 14 ἐνέργεια τῆς κατὰ φύσιν ἕξεως ἀνεμπόδιστος· 'the unimpeded activity of the natural state' ἐνέργεια implying, the realisation of the latent faculty and its active exercise, that pleasure is an end in itself, and the consciousness of it[2]. According to this definition pleasure in

---

[1] "This definition then is equally applicable to the highest functions of the mind, as well as to the bodily organs. Even in the case of pleasure felt upon the supplying of a want, the Aristotelian doctrine with regard to that pleasure was, that it was not identical with the supply, but contemporaneously; that it resulted from the play and action of vital powers not in a state of depression, while the depressed organs were receiving sustenance." Grant, Essays on Ethics, p. 199.

[2] See Grote, Plato II. 503. note 9. and Bain, on the Emotions and Will,

its highest form of speculative philosophical pleasure, is identical with the highest happiness. In Metaph. Λ. 7. 1072. b. 14. sq. ἡ ἐνέργεια is represented as the pleasure of the Supreme Being; and because this is the nature of pleasure, all states of activity, waking, sensation, thinking give the highest pleasure; and to one of these all other pleasures, as those of anticipation and recollection, are due.

See further on this subject Grant, Essays on Ethics IV. 'on ἐνέργεια' p. 194 seq. and again 'on the doctrine of the mean' p. 206. On the passage of the Metaphysics above quoted Bonitz has the following note. Propterea (διὰ τοῦτο, quia ἡ ἐνέργειά ἐστιν ἡδονή) nobis hominibus voluptatem afferunt animae nostrae, et ejus quidem vel θρεπτικῆς vel αἰσθητικῆς vel νοητικῆς, actiones quales sunt ἐγρήγορσις, αἴσθησις, νόησις: quodsi qua alia praeterea voluptatem nobis afferunt, veluti spes vel recordatio, causa ex eo est repetenda, quod ad unam ex illis actionibus referuntur, διὰ ταῦτα i.e. διὰ ἐγρήγορσιν ἢ αἴσθησιν ἢ νόησιν. Brandis. Handb. Arist. II. 132. and not. 276. p. 131. n. 273. and Fritzsche's notes on Eud. Eth. VI. 13. particularly that on 1153. a. 14, 15.

The remainder of the chapter is occupied with a *catalogue raisonné* of things pleasant.

APPENDIX E. TO BOOK I. CH. VI.

The laws which Aristotle here designates as unwritten are only one branch of those which are usually understood by that term. The ἄγραφοι νόμοι, ἄγραπτα νόμιμα, which

there quoted. Mr Grote, who attributes the Eudemian Ethics to Aristotle, seems to make no distinction between the two theories, of which *the former* (that of Aristotle) must be according to his view the truer. It appears in fact to be more reasonable to consider pleasure the necessary accompaniment of an ἐνέργεια itself. Eudemus in going beyond his master has fallen into error.

he here calls κοινοί, are the great fundamental conceptions and duties of morality, derived and having their sanction from heaven, antecedent and superior to all the conventional enactments of human societies, and common alike to all mankind. On this 'Natural Law' to which all 'positive laws' should conform, 'the law of man's nature', see Whewell Elem. of Mor. § 380. who quotes this passage of the Rhetoric. These are "the sure and unwritten institutions of the Gods" which cannot be contravened by any human enactments, to which Antigone appeals when ordered by Creon to violate her duty to her slaughtered brother by leaving his body unburied, "for not to day and yesterday, but from everlasting these have lived, and none knows what time they came to light[1]", Antig. 450. seq.; the 'sublime laws' νόμοι ὑψίποδες, οὐρανίαν δι' αἰθέρα τεκνωθέντες, ὧν Ὄλυμπος πατὴρ μόνος, οὐδέ νιν θνατὰ φύσις ἀνέρων ἔτικτεν, οὐδὲ μήποτε λάθα κατακοιμάσῃ, of divine origin, eternal, soaring in a higher sphere far above all the changes and chances of human institutions, and beyond the reach of human interference; Œd. R. 865. In Xenophon's Memorabilia IV. 4. Socrates, in maintaining the theory of absolute and universal moral principles against the views of Hippias, who would reduce all morality to a mere convention, appeals to these ἄγραφοι νόμοι, which are universal, 'the same in every land' and of divine, not human, origin; and some of them are enumerated; as the worship of God, duty to parents, gratitude, the requital of benefits, which are universally established in men's opinions as right rules of conduct, though by no means universally observed. Two of these are ranked by

---

[1] So in Eurip. Suppl. 19.
εἴργουσι δ' οἱ κρατοῦντες (sc. μὴ θάψαι νεκρούς), οὐδ' ἀναίρεσιν
δοῦναι θέλουσιν, νόμιμ' ἀτίζοντες θεῶν.
and in the same play 526,
θάψαι δικαιῶ, τὸν Πανελλήνων νόμον σώζων.

and 537,
δοκεῖς κακουργεῖν Ἄργος οὐ θάπτων νεκρούς;
ἥκιστα. πάσης Ἑλλάδος κοινὸν τόδε,
εἰ τοὺς θανόντας νοσφίσας ὧν χρῆν λαχεῖν
ἀτάφους τις ἕξει.

Euripides, Antiop. Fr. 38., amongst the three fundamental duties of man.

τρεῖς εἰσιν ἀρεταί, τὰς χρεών σ' ἀσκεῖν, τέκνον,
θεούς τε τιμᾶν, τούς τε φύσαντας γονεῖς,
νόμους τε κοινοὺς Ἑλλάδος, καὶ ταῦτα δρῶν
κάλλιστον ἕξεις στέφανον εὐκλείας ἀεί.

The same distinction is taken, and the same moral precepts selected, by the author of the Ῥητ. πρὸς Ἀλέξανδρον. c. 2. § 6, 7. 'Justice' he says, is τὸ τῶν ἁπάντων ἢ τὸ τῶν πλείστων ἔθος ἄγραφον, defining right and wrong. τοῦτο δ' ἐστὶ τὸ γονέας τιμᾶν καὶ φίλους εὖ ποιεῖν καὶ τοῖς εὐεργέταις χάριν ἀποδιδόναι; for the performance of these and such like duties is not enforced upon men by written laws, but derives an immediate sanction from a law unwritten and universal, ἀλλ' εὐθὺς ἀγράφῳ καὶ κοινῷ νόμῳ νομίζεται. In Demosth. c. Aristocr. p. 639. the κοινὸς νόμος is the 'right of self-defence.' It is likewise recognised by Plato, Rep. VIII. 563. D.; and equally by the Latin writers, as Cicero, de Legg. I. 6. II. 4. and de Rep. III. 22. ap. Lactant. Inst. VI. 8., a very emphatic passage, translated in Whewell, Elem. of Moral. § 361. Add Archytas and Hierocles in Stobæus pp. 267. and 230. quoted by Gaisford in Notis variorum. Quintil. XII. 2. 3. leges quæ natura sunt omnibus datæ, quæque propriæ populis et gentibus constitutæ. And Aristotle himself, in a former passage of the Rhetoric, I. 10. 3. νόμος δ' ἐστὶν ὁ μὲν ἴδιος ὁ δὲ κοινός. λέγω δὲ ἴδιον μὲν καθ' ὃν γεγραμμένον πολιτεύονται, κοινὸν δὲ ὅσα ἄγραφα παρὰ πᾶσιν ὁμολογεῖσθαι δοκεῖ. and Eth. Nic. VIII. 13. 5.

In the Eudemian Ethics IV. 10. 1134. b. 18. seq. [Nic. Eth. V. 7. 1. Oxf. Ed.] what is here called κοινὸς νόμος receives the name of τὸ φυσικὸν δίκαιον; the written law is 'conventional' τὸ νομικόν; and the distinction between this natural justice or law, and the positive or written or conventional law, the ἴδιος νόμος of the Rhetoric (because it varies in different states), is very strongly brought out, and the latter exemplified. τοῦ δὲ πολιτικοῦ δικαίου (as opposed to τὸ οἰκονομικὸν δίκαιον) τὸ μὲν φυσικόν ἐστι τὸ δὲ νομικόν, φυσικὸν μὲν τὸ πανταχοῦ τὴν αὐτὴν ἔχον δύναμιν, καὶ οὐ τῷ δοκεῖν ἢ μή, νομικὸν δὲ ὁ ἐξ ἀρχῆς μὲν οὐθὲν διαφέρει οὕτως ἢ ἄλλως, ὅταν δὲ θῶνται διαφέρει, οἷον τὸ μνᾶς λυτροῦσθαι, ἢ τὸ αἶγα θύειν ἀλλὰ μὴ δύο πρόβατα. ἔτι ὅσα ἐπὶ τῶν καθ' ἕκαστα νομοθετοῦσιν, οἷον τὸ θύειν Βρασίδᾳ, καὶ τὰ ψηφισματώδη. Compare Rhet. I. 13. 2. κοινὸν δὲ τὸν κατὰ φύσιν· ἐστὶ γάρ, ὃ μαντεύονται πάντες, φύσει κοινὸν δίκαιον καὶ ἄδικον, κἂν μηδεμία κοινωνία πρὸς ἀλλήλους ᾖ μηδὲ συνθήκη. natural law, not a social contract, nor conventional; and 15. 6. ὁ κοινὸς κατὰ φύσιν. "Natural justice is law because it is right, conventional justice is right because it is law." Grant on Eth. N. v. 7. 1.

Such is the usual mode of distinguishing the ἄγραφοι and γεγραμμένοι νόμοι. But in the passage before us the unwritten law in a special sense, a branch of the former, and included in it, is introduced as a subdivision of the ἴδιος or local, special, law, and in § 12. the two kinds are thus described. "Right and wrong under the one consists in an excess of virtue (i.e. above the *legal* standard) or vice, in actions to which praise and disgrace or censure (moral approbation and disapprobation), and dishonour and honours and rewards are attached; as to be grateful and make due return to a benefactor, to be ready to assist one's friends and so forth (using the same examples as in the passages previously quoted): in the other the ἄγραφα νόμιμα mean equity, the correction of the deficiencies of the special and written law. For equity is a form of justice, but not included in the written law." On ἐπιείκεια see Eth. Eud. IV. (Eth. N. v.) c. 14. The law can only lay down general rules, but these often require modification in special cases. It is here that equity comes in to supply these necessary deficiencies, and it is usually exercised in mitigation of the strict rigour, the letter, of the law, τὸ ἀκριβοδίκαιον; and therefore becomes a law of mercy or clemency. It is ἐπανόρθωμα νομίμου δικαίου. ᾗ παραλείπει ὁ νομοθέτης καὶ ἥμαρτεν ἁπλῶς εἰπών, ἐπανορθοῦν τὸ ἐλλειφθέν, ὃ κἂν ὁ νομοθέτης αὐτὸς οὕτως ἂν εἴποι ἐκεῖ παρών, καὶ εἰ ᾔδει ἐνομοθέτησεν ἄν. Here therefore this second, subordinate kind of ἄγραφος νόμος is said to mean equity, the modification or mitigation of the rigour of the law, the supplementum juris or legis scriptæ, or *particular* decision adapted to the special occasion where the written *general* laws fail to meet the case, and in this corresponding to the ψήφισμα. And in c. 15. 6. τὸ ἐπιεικές is substituted for ἄγραφος νόμος in this second sense. See the whole passage §§ 3—6, from which it appears that this is the κοινὸς νόμος in a particular application. This same distinction is taken between the written and unwritten laws of a particular state in the Politics, VI. 5. sub init. τιθεμένους δὲ τοιούτους νόμους καὶ τοὺς ἀγράφους καὶ τοὺς γεγραμμένους οἳ περιλήψονται μάλιστα τὰ σώζοντα τὰς πολιτείας. At first sight the word τιθεμένους seems somewhat strangely applied to *unwritten* laws, but it is plain from this very application that the notion which is here uppermost in the mind of the writer is not that of equity—though this may be included—but rather the feelings on the subject of right and wrong, the notions habits and practices prevailing in any given society. These may be modified and cultivated, and so 'instituted' in a sense by education and other influences which the legislator has at his command. These identical ἄγραφα νόμιμα are interpreted by Plato in a parallel passage conveying the same distinction, Legg. VII. 793. D., ἔθη καὶ ἐπιτηδεύματα. The ἄγραφα νόμιμα in this sense form the necessary basis and supports, οἷον τεκτόνων ἐν οἰκοδομήμασιν ἐρείσματα, of the written laws, and they consist in these habits and practices, feelings and notions; so that the laws, written and unwritten, of any state may be resolved into νόμους, ἔθη, and ἐπιτηδεύματα. Legg. VII. 793. A—D. On this Stallbaum says, intelliguntur quæ more et consuetudine recepta sunt, non legibus publicis sancita. And he collects several passages in his note, (Legg. III. 680. A. ἀλλ' ἔθεσι καὶ τοῖς λεγομένοις πατρίοις νόμοις ἑπόμενοι ζῶσιν. VIII. 841. B. Politic. 295 A. &c. Dem. de Cor. p. 317. οὐ μόνον ἐν τοῖς νομίμοις (sc. τοῖς γεγραμμένοις νόμοις), ἀλλὰ καὶ ἡ φύσις αὐτὴ τοῖς ἀγράφοις νόμοις καὶ τοῖς ἀνθρωπίνοις ἤθεσι διώρικεν. and elsewhere. Thucyd. II. 37. μάλιστα (τῶν νόμων) ὅσοι τε ἐπ' ὠφελίᾳ τῶν ἀδικουμένων κεῖνται, καὶ ὅσοι ἄγραφοι ὄντες αἰσχύνην ὁμολογουμένην φέρουσιν. Arist. Pol. III. 11. 6. ἔτι κυριώτεροι καὶ περὶ κυριωτέρων τῶν κατὰ γράμματα νόμων οἱ περὶ τὰ ἔθη ἐστίν,) to show that ἔθη are often spoken of either as distinguished from (written) laws, or as forming an unwritten branch of law itself. Add to these Hierocles in Stobæus, l. c. ἔθος ἄγραφός τις εἶναι βούλεται[1] νόμος, and we shall have enough reason for concluding that this is what we are to understand principally by the νόμοι ἄγραφοι in the Politics, and probably here also, together with the equity expressly mentioned.

[1] βούλεται, would like to be, tries to be, would be if it could.

ARISTOTLE'S RHETORIC.

BOOK II.

AFTER the general introduction and the analysis of the εἴδη of Politics and Ethics and of the three branches of rhetoric, and the supplementary treatise on the ἄτεχνοι πίστεις, we might next expect the κοιναὶ τόποι and the enthymemes to follow; both because this seems to be the natural order, and also because in the second chapter of Book I., where our author is describing and explaining the divisions of his subject, he arranges them in the following order, πίστεις i. e. εἴδη, τόποι, ἤθη, πάθη. If this was his original intention he has abandoned it, supposing that the work as we have it is complete and undislocated,—and there is no sufficient evidence to the contrary—for instead of the promised arrangement of subjects, we find first the εἴδη, I. 4—15, then the ἦθος, II. 1., then the πάθη, II. 2—11, next, some supplementary ἤθη, II. 12—17, and finally the κοινοὶ τόποι, II. 19, and the τόποι ἐνθυμημάτων, genuine and spurious or fallacious, II. 23, 24.

Ch. 1. In the present chapter, after a brief recapitulation of the contents of the preceding book, § 1., and an argument on the importance of the indirect proof conveyed by the character of the speaker and the appeals to the sentiments and feelings of the audience; the first of which is more valuable and carries greater weight in deliberative, and the latter in forensic, rhetoric; and the reasons for the latter § 2, 3, 4; he proceeds in §§ 5—7 to point out the three requisites in the exhibition of the speaker's character *by the speech* for making a favourable impression on the audience, and giving him 'authority' with them. These are φρόνησις, ἀρετή, and εὔνοια; the first, to enable him to judge of the expediency of the policy he recommends, or the inexpediency of that from which he would dissuade the people; virtue, to lend weight and dignity to his words to obviate all suspicions of passion, prejudice, self-interest or any evil motive; and friendly intentions to, or regard for the interests of, the assembly he is addressing, §§ 5, 6. We are then referred for the analysis of the three, from which the means of assuming the appearance of these qualities may be ascertained, and the topics necessary for this purpose, backwards to the chapter on the virtues I. 9. (see I. 9. 1.) for φρόνησις and ἀρετή, and forwards to the πάθη, c. 4, for εὔνοια or φιλία[1]. §§ 7. 8. See further on the subject the account of the three kinds of ἦθος, above p. 108—13. and the illustrations of auctoritas given [p. 151. not. 1].

In §§ 8, 9, two general observations are given, introductory to the special treatment of the πάθη in the following chapters; first that the πάθη, of which he is here speaking, are the *moral* affections, which are therefore accompanied by pleasure and pain, such as anger, fear, compassion; and secondly, that in the analysis of them three things in each are to be regarded; the nature of them, what each affection is, and how each person is disposed that feels them; πῶς διακείμενοι ὀργίλοι (for instance) εἰσί; the ordinary objects

---

[1] Whately, in his Rhetoric ch. 2., observes that these three, good sense, good principle and good-will, are precisely the three qualities to which Pericles lays claim in his defence of himself before the Athenian assembly, Thuc. II. 60. I have already referred to this passage, p. 2. n. 1., for another purpose. Whately's comparison is not quite correct. In Aristotle the three qualities represent (1) *intellectual,* and (2) *moral*, virtue, φρόνησις or practical wisdom for discerning the means to an end (see Eth. Nic. VI.), the special virtue of a statesman, and ἀρετή moral virtue, for the reason before assigned. ἢ φρόνιμοι μὲν καὶ ἐπιεικεῖς II. 1. 6.; and (3) good-will and a friendly feeling and intentions towards the audience and their country and state institutions. In Thucydides they are four; judgment and decision to enable a man to see what is right and enforce it, the ability of the statesman or governor, and the (intellectual) virtue of the mind; secondly the power of expression, eloquence, the virtue of the tongue; thirdly patriotism, the virtue of the feelings; and fourthly, what might *possibly* be included in the preceding, probity and independence, freedom from all taint of corruption. It will be seen by this comparative statement, that the two lists, though there certainly is some resemblance between them, cannot be brought into exact coincidence.

of them, τίσιν εἰώθασιν ὀργίζεσθαι (carrying on the same *example*); and the ordinary occasions and circumstances ἐπὶ ποίοις, of their manifestation. If we are ignorant of any one of these, we shall find ourselves unable in case of need to excite the required emotion. Accordingly the detailed treatment of the several πάθη in the next chapters, 2—11, follows this rule and division[1].

Ch. 2—17. After the summary treatment of the ἤθη Aristotle next proceeds to the analysis of the moral πάθη, for the purpose of supplying the rhetorician with topics for his appeals to the feelings of his audience. On the πάθη in general I have already said something, above p. 113. foll.; and Brandis also, in his treatise on the Rhetoric, in Schneidewin's Philologus, pp. 26, 7, has some general observations upon them, and a comparison of the two lists in Eth. Nic. II. 4 and here; but as there is nothing in them that requires special notice, I may in this case likewise refer the reader to the tract itself. The list of the πάθη here given contains anger, and its opposite, meekness, gentleness, or calmness, mildness, and composure of temper, πραότης; love and hatred, or liking and disliking (φιλεῖν, like the French aimer, combining the stronger and the weaker feeling); fear and boldness or confidence; compassion; envy; emulation; which appear also in the list of the Ethics; shame and shamelessness reckless disregard of the opinion of others; gratitude or grace and favour, both included in χάρις; and righteous indignation, are found only in the Rhetoric. Instead of these last we

---

[1] For a genuine and really scientific explanation and analysis of the πάθη I refer my readers to Mr Bain's work on the Emotions and Will. Of those that enter into Aristotle's list, anger, resentment, righteous indignation, terror and confidence or courage, love and hatred, are included in Mr Bain's. But the classification and the mode of treatment are totally different. Founded upon observation and the actual study of human nature, Mr Bain's analysis need fear no comparison with the comparatively tentative, inaccurate, and incomplete psychology of Aristotle here or elsewhere in his writings, which I take to be the weakest point of that mighty Analyst and subtle observer.

have in the Ethics desire, joy, and longing, πόθος. And these are all analysed and examined from the three points of πάθη view described at the end of the last chapter, viz. their nature, their objects, and their occasions, or exciting causes and conditions. In treating them Aristotle confines himself strictly to his immediate subject: there are no general observations which might supply as before a link of connexion between the several parts of the entire subject, nor are there any episodes, as in some of the preceding chapters, which require a separate discussion. We may consequently omit any further notice of them here, and reserve the detailed explanation of them for the notes on the text.

The analysis or εἴδη of the πάθη carries us down to the end of chapter 11. From ch. 12. to 17 we have by way of appendix to the preceding dissertation an examination of certain ἤθη, which have been already described, and distinguished from the other ἦθος, above p. 110. These ἤθη are, as we have already seen, the *characters* that belong to certain ages and conditions of life, as youth, the prime of life, and old age; birth, wealth, and power: and the treatment of them is properly appended to that of the πάθη, τὰ δὲ ἤθη ποῖοί τινες κατὰ τὰ πάθη, because they are liable to vary in the audience under the above conditions and circumstances. For example, an assembly in which young men preponderate requires a different style and tone, and different topics in appealing to its feelings and passions, to one which is composed mainly of old men; rich men are not moved in the same way, by the same kind of appeals, as the poor; and so on for the rest. In every case the speaker must fall in with the prevailing tone of feeling and humour of his audience, and this in accordance with the time of life and condition of the whole of them, or the majority, if there be one[1].

---

[1] The import of these ' characters,' as of the ἤθη τῶν πολιτειῶν in I. 8. 6., and the use to which they are to be applied, may be thus expressed in other words. Certain ages and conditions of men are marked by different

II. 18. The 18th chapter forms a break in the subject, and landing place, whence the author looks back over the progress that he has made in his work, and forwards to what still remains to be accomplished. It is therefore of importance as marking out the divisions of the subject.

It will be well perhaps to enter here a little more fully into the consideration of the contents of this chapter, and to give a connected account of it in the way of paraphrase. The difficulty in the interpretation of it consists in this, that the conclusion ὥστε—ποιητέον does not follow from the protasis or antecedent ἐπεὶ δ' ἡ τῶν πιθανῶν—εἴρηται πρότερον. Now it is possible that Aristotle, careless as he so frequently is in connecting his sentences, may not have meant ὥστε to be the consequent to ἐπεί at all: but having originally intended to construct his sentence so that ἐπεί should have something correlative to it, omitted that, and varied his construction, leaving ἐπεί pendent with nothing to correspond to it: and that ὥστε may have merely the vague meaning 'and so, after all this, the next thing is', marking a mere continuation and not a direct consequence. There is a similar piece of carelessness in II. 13. 16. and in I. 7. 3. where it is noticed in the Commentary[1]. Spengel (Trans. Bav. Acad. p. 35) supposes that

and peculiar characteristics. A speaker is always liable to be confronted with an audience in which one or other of these classes forms the preponderating element. In order to make a favourable impression upon them, he must necessarily adapt his tone and language to the sentiments and habits of thought prevailing amongst them, and the feelings and motives by which they are usually influenced. And for this purpose he must study their characters, and make himself acquainted with their ordinary motives and feelings and opinions. And the following analysis will supply him with topics for this purpose. That this (in spite of Spengel) is the true interpretation of these ἤθη, and their use in Rhetoric, and that they are therefore to be distinguished from the ἤθη properly so called of Bk. II. ch. I., of which the *object*—to prove by the speech that you are *yourself* of a certain character, and that character exhibited in three particular virtues, quite distinct from the elements of the ἤθη here— and (therefore) the *materials* are alike different, any one may convince himself by simply referring to II. 13. 16., in which the object and use of them are explained.

[1] See also Zell on Eth. Nic. VII. 14. p. 324, and Spengel on the Rhetoric

the sentences ἐπεὶ δ' ἢ—βουλεύονται are a mere expansion of the passage II. 1. 2. Ἐπεὶ δὲ—κατασκευάζειν; and accordingly in his recent recension (in his edition of the Rhetores Græci) rejects the entire passage as an interpolation: a proceeding, as it seems to me, unjustifiable and unnecessary. However, if we retain the text as it stands, and there really seems to be no sufficient reason for altering it, the false connexion of ἐπεί and ὥστε, and of the sentences which they introduce—unless upon the above supposition—remain unaccounted for.

The disorder may be rectified and the whole passage naturally and rationally explained by merely supposing that a sentence has been lost before ὥστε, and that the connexion of the whole was somewhat as follows. It will be observed that in the passage II. 1. 2., to which Spengel refers this, the fact that every kind of speech is addressed to a judge of *some kind* is assigned as *a reason* for treating the ἤθη and πάθη as a part of Rhetoric. "Since all rhetorical speeches are addressed to a judge, which is obviously true in the two first kinds, and substantially, though not strictly, absolutely, ἁπλῶς, in the declamatory or epideictic—for there the spectators may be regarded in this light—[I have therefore entered at length into the analysis of the ἤθη and πάθη because the assumption of a certain character by the speaker himself with a view to conciliate these same judges, and the production of certain emotions in the judges or audience, are just as necessary as the proofs proper. Now the ἤθη I have treated under such and such heads (see II. 1. 5. sq.)] and have also discussed the πολιτειῶν ἤθη in my chapters on deliberative rhetoric (I. 8., in fact), and so (ὥστε) this part of my

in Trans. of Bav. Acad. 1851. p. 34 on this careless introduction of ὥστε following ἐπεί after a parenthesis.

Muretus, who is followed by Vater, considers λοιπὸν ἡμῖν διελθεῖν to be the apodosis to the ἐπεί at the beginning of the Chapter. But to this Spengel reasonably objects, that there is a second ἐπεὶ δέ, the introduction of which between the first ἐπεί and the apodosis is quite contrary to the Aristotelian usage.

subject is finished and determined, and we may now proceed to what further remains to be considered."

I will now give a connected paraphrase of the principal contents of this chapter. All rhetorical speeches and arguments, of which persuasion is the object ($\pi\iota\theta\alpha\nu\hat{\omega}\nu$), are addressed to a judge of some sort; because if Rhetoric is the art of persuasion, there must be in every use of it somebody to persuade; and looks to a judgment or decision: when we know and have decided any thing there is no further need of argument. This judge may be either one or several: for whether you are actually pleading a cause in a court of law, or recommending or opposing a measure in the assembly, or conversing, or giving advice, or carrying on a dialectical argument with a single person in private, still whenever you try to *persuade*, you constitute the person addressed, real or imaginary, (the latter, when you are arguing with yourself perchance against an assumed principle or theory, $\pi\rho\grave{o}\varsigma\ \acute{v}\pi\acute{o}\theta\epsilon\sigma\iota\nu$, the opposing theory standing in this case in the place of the opponent or judge who has to be convinced) the judge of your arguments, to him they are directed, and with him rests the decision. It is the same with Epideictic speaking, when there is no real interest at stake, no $\acute{a}\gamma\acute{\omega}\nu$, but the speech is a mere amusement or made to display the author's abilities: the 'spectator' in this case fills the place of the 'critic' or judge; he decides, what is alone here in question, the merits of the composition. However in the strict and absolute sense of the term it is only in public and forensic speaking that there is a true judge. The supplement which I have given in the preceding paragraph I need not here repeat; and this brings us to the end of § 1. Returning to the text § 2 we have next a recapitulation of the subjects already treated, and an indication of what is to follow down to the end of c. 23. First are mentioned the $\pi\acute{\iota}\sigma\tau\epsilon\iota\varsigma$ proper, or direct proofs, which have been analysed as $\epsilon\check{\iota}\delta\eta$ under the three heads of deliberative, forensic, and declamatory rhetoric, and made to supply 'popular principles' $\delta\acute{o}\xi\alpha\iota$, and 'premisses' προτάσεις, for the construction of rhetorical arguments (Enthymemes): secondly, the ἤθη and πάθη, both included under the one head of ἠθικὸς λόγος, which as both appeal to and are descriptive of the moral sense and the moral elements of the human constitution, and derive their materials alike from Ethics, is properly held to comprehend them both.

And now that these have been dispatched, we have next to consider the κοινοὶ τόποι, and the enthymemes, which together with 'example' (the Rhetorical induction), the analysis of the fallacious enthymeme, and the modes of meeting and refuting it, will carry us through the subject of rhetorical proof in all its branches, and at the same time to the end of the second book. The κοινά or κοινοὶ τόποι here mentioned are the 'common' or 'universal' classes of arguments which may be applied alike to all εἴδη, as of Politics, Ethics, Physics, and also to each of the three branches of Rhetoric[1]; and are thus distinguished from the εἴδη, which furnish 'appropriate' topics derived from the sciences which feed rhetoric, and are *specially* applicable to each of the three, and treated, as we have seen, *severally* under each. It remains therefore "in pursuance of our original design," "in fulfilment of our original proposal," ὅπως ἀποδῶμεν τὴν ἐξ ἀρχῆς πρόθεσιν, § 5, to review first these universal τόποι or classes of arguments. The κοινοὶ τόποι are four in number, §§ 3, 4. c. 19. 27.; for although it is possible to make them five by separating τὸ δυνατόν and τὸ ἀδύνατον, or six by counting τὸ αὔξειν καὶ μειοῦν or μέγεθος καὶ μικρότης, and τὸ μᾶλλον καὶ ἧττον or τὸ μεῖζον καὶ ἔλαττον, separately as two topics, and the author's language on the point does seem to vary: yet we may infer from the treatment of them in

---

[1] The κοινὰ πᾶσι τοῖς εἴδεσιν and the things which κοινὰς ἔχει πᾶσι τοῖς εἴδεσι τὰς χρήσεις, of the Rhet. ad Alex. c. 7. §§ 1, 3., though analogous to Aristotle's κοινά in respect of their universality and applicability to all three kinds of Rhetoric, yet differ from them in the particular things which they denote. They include such generally applicable notions as justice, expediency, pleasure, and characteristics of style, propriety, perspicuity, brevity, moderation, and so forth.

four divisions in c. 19, and from the expressions above quoted, (to which may be added a note in 19. 26, where μέγεθος and μικρότης and μείζον and ἔλαττον are summed up under *one* head in the phrase ὅλως μεγάλων καὶ μικρῶν,) that he does in fact regard them as four, neither more nor less. Though these common topics, as their name implies, may be all applied to each of the three branches of rhetoric, yet it will be found in practice that the topic of amplification and depreciation or detraction is most appropriate to the epideictic kind, (comp. I. 9. 40. and Rhet. ad Alex. c. 7. 2,) the topic of fact past, to the dicastic, and of future to the hortatory or public speaker, § 5. In I. 12. 2, δυνατόν and ἀδύνατον are said to be κοινὰ πάντων τῶν λόγων. In the passage just referred to, I. 9. 40, these κοινοὶ τόποι are oddly and incorrectly enough styled κοινὰ εἴδη, which seems like a contradiction in terms; the εἴδη being distinguished from the τόποι, when each is used in its proper sense, by the very circumstance that the εἴδη are special, and the τόποι common or universal.

Ch. 19. The nineteenth chapter contains the analysis of these four κοινοὶ τόποι into their subordinate topics, and points out the modes of their application. They are as we have seen, the possible and impossible, fact past, fact future, and magnitude *and* degree. The last of them, τὸ αὔξειν καὶ μειοῦν, we are again told at the end of c. 26, includes the topic of 'greater and less' or degree. For the analysis and handling of it we are referred again to the συμβουλευτικά, I. 7, and 8, on 'good' general and particular, and 'goods' comparative. The application of the topic of degree to injustice in c. 14., is not expressly alluded to. Good he says, § 26, includes the τέλη of all three branches of rhetoric, τὸ συμφέρον, τὸ δίκαιον, and τὸ καλόν; and therefore the analysis of good is equally applicable to each of them, and will furnish in each topics for magnifying or depreciating; consequently there is no necessity for dwelling any longer on this topic here.

Ch. 20. We next come to the two κοιναὶ πίστεις, the universal instruments of all rhetorical reasoning, the enthymeme and example. These are 'universal' even when compared with the κοινοὶ τόποι of the last chapter, and still more with the εἴδη preceding, being applicable to all of them alike. Both of these as contrasted with enthymeme and example may be called ἴδια, a term which is applied to them in § 1. ἔπειπερ εἴρηται περὶ τῶν ἰδίων. The γνώμη which is a part of enthymeme—a species of enthymeme, either the major premiss or the conclusion being alone expressed, and constituting the γνώμη; the two premisses, or the minor and conclusion, being in either case left to be understood—is not to be distinguished from it, and the κοιναὶ πίστεις are only two. It seems from the treatment which γνώμη receives in the Rhet. ad Alex. c. 12., that it had been actually distinguished from the enthymeme, and treated separately as a different kind of argument. Hence the necessity of the observation here, § 1, and the explanation, just quoted, in c. 21. 2.

The 'example', as a logical argument, has been already described, p. 105—7. In the present chapter the example, παράδειγμα, is first divided into its several kinds, and then the mode of its application exemplified.

There are two kinds of examples, real or historical, and fictitious: and the latter are again divided into two (1) παραβολή, (similitudo, Quint. v. 11. 1; collatio, Cicero, according to Quint. v. 11. 23) "comparison, illustration," general analogies borrowed from real life, of which Aristotle instances τὰ Σωκρατικά, the analogies which Socrates drew from political and social life in proof or support of some political or moral rule which he wished to establish (analogy applied inductively), of which a pertinent example is given § 4: and (2) λόγοι, either (a) "fictions, tales, fables, (erzählungen), analogous cases derived from works of fiction, as poetry, (Quint. v. 11. 17.) tragedies for example, or the Homeric poems—compare Cicero. Top. XX. 78. oratores, philosophos, poetas, historicos, ex quorum et dictis et scriptis sæpe auctoritas petitur ad faciendam fidem. Hermogenes, Progymn. περὶ μύθου, ult. φαίνονται δὲ καὶ οἱ ῥήτορες αὐτῷ (τῷ μύθῳ) χρησάμενοι ἀντὶ παραδείγματος.—or (β) "fables" proper, like those of Æsop and Stesichorus quoted by Aristotle, or Menenius Agrippa's apologue of the belly and the members, referred to by Quintilian, v. 11. 19.[1] Quintilian adds a third

[1] λόγοι. When λόγος and μῦθος are distinguished, λόγος is a 'tale,' real or fictitious; μῦθος is 'a fable,' and more especially one of Æsop's. The definition of a fable is given by Eustathius ad Od. ξ. 508., Il. Λ. p. 855. αἶνος (the older word to express it) λόγος μυθικὸς ἐκφερόμενος ἀπὸ ἀλόγων ζῴων ἢ φυτῶν πρὸς ἀνθρώπων παραίνεσιν. Comp. Hermogenes, περὶ μύθου, Progymn. 1. Spengel Rhet. Gr. II. 1. It is a fictitious story with a moral or didactic purpose (τὸν μῦθον πρῶτον ἀξιοῦσι προσάγειν τοῖς νέοις, ὅτι τὰς ψυχὰς αὐτῶν πρὸς τὸ βέλτιον ῥυθμίζειν δύναται...πάντως δὲ χρήσιμον πρός τι τῶν ἐν τῷ βίῳ. Hermog. u. s.) derived from irrational animals or plants; the characteristic feature being, that it invests irrational or inanimate objects with the language, sentiments, and actions of the human race. These fables, says Quintilian, v. 11. 19., were generally known under the name of Æsop, though he was not the real originator of them; nam videtur earum primus auctor Hesiodus. They had been collected, and passed under his name. The earliest on record is Jotham's fable of the Bramble and the Trees, in the Book of Judges, ix. 8. Two or three other examples from the Old Testament are cited by Dr R. Williams, Hebrew Prophets, p. 249, note. The αἶνος in Odys. ξ. 469–506, is of a different kind; being merely a fictitious narrative *with a purpose*. The next in point of antiquity, likewise called αἶνος, is the fable of the Hawk and the Nightingale, in Hesiod. Op. et D. 200. Then come in the order of time, Archilochus' αἶνοι, Fragmm. 80, 82, Bergk. The Fox and the Eagle; and the Ape and the Fox [Reynard has always played a leading part in these compositions.] see Mure, H. G. L. III. 170. Αἴνον Græci vocant, et Αἰσωπείους ut dixi λόγους et Λιβυκούς, nostrorum quidam, non sano recepto in usum nomine, apologationem. Quint. l. c. § 20. Compare Theon, Progymn. c. 3. Speng. Rhet. Gr. II. 72. Hermogenes. u. s. The name of 'Libyan' is likewise applied to them by Æschylus in a fragment of the Myrmidons, Dind. Fragm. 123, ὡς δ' ἐστὶ μύθων τῶν Λιβυστικῶν λόγος. The fable here quoted by Æschylus, and cited from the Libyan collection, is the famous one of the Eagle slain by an arrow for which his own wing had supplied the feather; it is alluded to by Aristophanes, Av. 808.; and applied by Waller

That eagle's fate and mine are one,
Who in the dart that made him die
Espied a feather of his own
With which he wont to soar so high.

and by Byron on the death of Kirke White in English Bards and Scotch Reviewers.

Another collection of these fables seems to have been known under the name of 'Sybaritic:' Arist. Vesp. 1259, ἢ λόγον ἔλεξας αὐτὸς ἀστεῖόν τινα Αἰσωπικὸν γελοῖον ἢ Συβαριτικόν. Three or four examples of these are given at the end of the play. They were usually called by the collective name

species, παροιμίαι "proverbs," quod est velut fabella brevior, citing Cicero's non nostrum onus; bos clitellas. Some proverbs are γνῶμαι. Rhet. II. 21. 12. Such 'proverbial' fables are to be found in the Proverbs of Solomon. See Prov. vi. 6. xxx. 24—28. Cicero, de Invent. I. 19. 27. treats of some of these forms of 'example,' and classes them under the general head of (ornamental) narrative. His 'historia' corresponds with Aristotle's first kind: fictitious narratives, and invented cases of analogy, λόγοι, he calls argumentum, "ficta res, quæ tamen fieri potuit;" and the μῦθος or 'fable proper,' the second species of λόγοι, is with him fabula. Angues ingentes alites, juncti jugo, is the example given.

With regard to the use and application of these παραδείγματα in their various forms, we are told that the 'fictitious examples,' λόγοι, are more used in public speaking, because it is easier to invent them than to find actual precedents or facts, πράγματα, in history; one well versed in literature (φιλοσοφία) will always be able to supply them: nevertheless the real analogous facts, if they can be found, are far more serviceable in the way of proof of the expediency, for example, of some particular course of policy in question, because for the most part future events do under similar circumstances really correspond with the past. If you have no enthymemes, no regular logical arguments, which are always more telling because *they* carry the actual proof, you must use your examples as proofs; if you have, as evidence or authorities, *after* the enthymemes as an 'epilogue': because when they are put first they look like the particulars of an induction, which is seldom appropriate to the rhetorician; whereas if

of Αἰσώπειοι. Hermog. u. s. ὀνομάζονται δὲ ἀπὸ τῶν εὑρόντων οἱ μὲν Κύπριοι, οἱ δὲ Λιβυκοί, οἱ δὲ Συβαριτικοί, πάντες δὲ κοινῶς Αἰσώπειοι λέγονται, διότι τοῖς μύθοις Αἴσωπος ἐχρήσατο πρὸς τὰς συνουσίας. See also π. ἰδεῶν. β'. II. II. 240. See Philolog. Mus. I.ᵢp. 280. Bentley on Æsop's Fables (Dissertation appended to the Phalaris); and on the Fable, Müller. H. G. L. c. xi. § 14.

With this signification of αἶνος, compare αἰνεῖν in its older sense 'to tell, or mention,' in Æsch. Suppl. 175. Agam. 98, 1458. Choeph. 546, 1002.

they are subjoined to the enthymemes they more resemble the additional evidence of witnesses, and witnesses always carry weight. If you put them first, you will require a great number (for your induction), if last, even one is sufficient; for a *single* witness that can be relied on is always of service. §§ 7—9[1].

Ch. 21. The following chapter is on γνῶμαι, which are as we have seen a kind of enthymeme, but with only the major premiss or the conclusion expressed—all the rest in either case being left to be inferred.

A γνώμη is according to Aristotle a *general moral* sentiment[2], § 2. Now most enthymemes being derived from ethical materials, and conveying a maxim, or a precept, or a rule of action, either the major premiss or the conclusion of an enthymeme, whenever it conveys some general principle, is a γνώμη; and if we add the reason of this general maxim in the shape of a premiss we have a regular enthymeme. The conversion of a γνώμη into an enthymeme is illustrated in Rhet. III. 17. 17. Sunt item sententiæ, says the Auctor ad Heren. IV. 17. 24., quæ dupliciter efferuntur, sine ratione et cum ratione—and he then proceeds to illustrate them: the former, sine ratione, is the γνώμη proper, when no reason is given, but only the general sentiment enunciated; the latter is a genuine enthymeme, one premiss and a conclusion. See the whole chapter on Sententiæ. In complete accordance with this is the description of the second of Quintilian's three kinds of enthymeme, sententia cum ratione. Inst. Orat. V. 10. 1. Compare on γνῶμαι or sententiæ in general Quint. Inst. Or. VIII. 5. Aphthonius, προγυμν. (ap. Spengel, Rhet. Græc. II. 25) defines, classifies, and exemplifies them. Hermogenes Progymn. (Ibid. II. 7.) defines γνώμη in nearly the same terms as Aristotle, omitting however the *morality*. He also, like Aphthonius, classifies and illustrates them, chiefly

---

[1] On the subject of παράδειγμα and its validity as an argument, see further, Introd. p. 105. foll.

[2] γνωμολογία δὲ ὡς, δεινὸν ἡ πονηρία. Schol. on Plat. Phædr. 267. c.

from Homer and the Tragic poets, and using nearly the same examples as Aphthonius. The treatment of the γνώμη by the author of the Rhet. ad Alex. differs in some points from that of Aristotle; in one particular there is a very unusual accordance. His definition is, c. 12., "a summary statement of your *private* judgment upon things in general", a general maxim founded upon individual opinion. There are two kinds of γνῶμαι, he continues, one when the maxim is generally popular and accepted; the other when it is contrary to received opinions and takes you by surprise; in the latter case only is it necessary to add a reason for it; in the former when it is neither unknown nor discredited the reason may be dispensed with. The maxim should be appropriate to the occasion; if it be not, it will have an awkward appearance (σκαιόν, gauche) and will look as if it were 'hanging on' (ἀπηρτημένον), a mere appendage, without proper connexion. The rest of the chapter is occupied with illustrations of different sorts of γνῶμαι. To return to Aristotle. In accordance with—most probably not borrowed from—the division of γνῶμαι in the Rhet. ad Alex. he divides them into four kinds, § 7. First, they are either accompanied or not with an ἐπίλογος, an addition or appendage, afterwards called αἰτία and ἀπόδειξις; by Cicero and Quintilian, ratio. (See p. 105). Secondly, these maxims or general sentiments require this reason or (partial) demonstration when they are either contested, or such as you don't expect and have never heard before, new and strange, or contrary to your own previous opinions. Otherwise, when they are generally accepted and approved (ἔνδοξα, Rhet. ad Alex.) they want none. Hence we obtain our fourfold division. The two first are distinguished by requiring and having *no* additional reason; (1) Those that are already familiar and approved, requiring no additional reason: and (2), those that are intelligible and acceptable per se and at first sight. Of those that have this explanatory appendage one class (3) is a part of an enthymeme—it is in fact a complete enthymeme (see above, p. 102, foll.), and part of a *syllogism*—and a second (4) is of an enthymematic character, but not strictly speaking a part of an enthymeme. In this last kind the reason or ground is conveyed in the γνώμη itself: as when we say ἀθάνατον ὀργὴν μὴ φύλασσε θνητὸς ὤν, the first four words constitute the maxim or precept, the two last give the reason. And this kind is the most effective and popular. [because it is condensed, and therefore vivid and striking.] Of the two classes that require the ἐπίλογος, the first, the surprising and unlooked for maxims, may either have the appendage put first, and then the γνώμη used as a conclusion; or else the latter may be made to precede, and the reason or explanation added subsequently. The second class, which consists of those which are not paradoxical, but only not readily intelligible, since there is no prejudice against them to be overcome, but they merely require explanation, should have this explanation made as terse and concise (στρογγυλώτατα) as possible, § 7. In such cases laconic apophthegms and enigmatical sayings are appropriate as appendages. The use of maxims and general sentiments is proper to old age, unbecoming at any earlier period of life, like story-telling; and they require experience and knowledge of the circumstances in those that employ them: when any one attempts to introduce them without the requisite knowledge they become coarse and foolish: as appears in the practice of rustics, who are great coiners of maxims, and by no means averse to exhibit their skill in this particular, §§ 8. 9. An illicit or unfounded generalisation is most appropriate in loud indignant complaint or the exaggeration of passion (σχετλιασμῷ καὶ δεινώσει), ['Varium et mutabile semper foemina', 'Frailty thy name is woman', οὐδὲν γειτονίας χαλεπώτερον, § 15. are examples.] and this may be introduced either at the commencement or after the 'demonstration', that is, the assigning of the reason, § 10. Maxims that are popular and in every one's mouth may be employed if they happen to be in point; for from their being so well known and often repeated they are as it were universally admitted and approved, § 11. Some *proverbs* may be used as γνῶμαι, § 12. Maxims that have become public property and proverbial, like γνῶθι σεαυτόν, μηδὲν ἄγαν, may be controverted, either in order to heighten the passion or pathos; or, if the maxim be of questionable truth or morality, to represent your own character in a more favourable light. In doing this you should contrive by the expression itself, or the statement of the γνώμη, to make clear your own moral predilections; or if not you must add the reason of your disapproval of the maxim in question, §§ 13, 14. These γνῶμαι are an immense help to the speech, partly owing to the ignorance and want of taste of the audience, who are pleased to hear any sentiment, which they entertain partially, stated in general terms—as, if a man had a bad neighbour or worthless children, he would like to hear any one say οὐδὲν γειτονίας χαλεπώτερον or, nothing can be more absurd than the procreation of children. So that you must guess what the sentiments of your audience may happen to be, and then accommodate your generalisations to them, § 15. Another still more signal service that γνῶμαι render to a speech is that they give it a moral character. All speeches have this moral character in which a moral purpose is plainly indicated. Now all γνῶμαι have their effect, because they always contain a declaration (ἀποφαίνεσθαι), carry with them a judgment, upon the objects of moral choice or preference or purpose, and therefore if their morality be sound, they impart a *good* moral character to the speech, § 16.

Ch. 22. The twenty-second chapter commences with some observations upon the use of enthymemes in general: it points out certain considerations which must be taken account of, or rules to be observed in the employment of them. The arguments must be as brief as possible; no long chains of reasoning and concatenated syllogisms, (like the propositions of Euclid), οὔτε πόρρωθεν δεῖ συνάγειν, § 3.—Comp. I.

2. 12, 13—which an unlearned assembly unused to a connected chain of ratiocination would find difficult to follow; and as simple and precise as possible, οὔτε πάντα δεῖ λαμβάνοντας συνάγειν; where οὐ πάντα means as few as possible, not to prove what is already plain, to introduce nothing that has not an immediate bearing on the question, or overload the proof by putting in all the steps of an argument where any of them are obvious. Comp. § 10. Again, we must avoid the error into which men of science and philosophers are apt to fall in addressing a popular audience, that namely of always endeavouring to draw *universal* conclusions, and always stating universal principles (οἱ μὲν γὰρ τὰ κοινὰ καὶ καθόλου λέγουσιν), which with the uneducated usually make less impression than arguments derived from particulars, things with which they are familiar, and which strike their senses, and are of daily experience, ἃ ἴσασι καὶ τὰ ἐγγύς. [This is otherwise expressed by the often recurring phrase τὰ ἡμῖν γνωριμώτερα]. We are therefore not to argue from any opinions whatsoever—things 'necessary' and 'universal' come under the general head of 'opinions'—nor from any notions and maxims hastily taken up and uncertified—οὐκ ἐξ ὧν ἔτυχεν, φαίνεται γὰρ ἄττα καὶ τοῖς παραληροῦσιν, I. 2. 11—but we are to select certain definite and special maxims, current opinions, and probabilities in general, which are certified and accredited by 'judges' properly qualified, τοῖς κρίνουσιν, or by those whose judgment the audience are ready to accept, οὓς ἀποδέχονται. Another error in the use of enthymemes akin to the preceding, the misuse of 'universals', is to aim at 'necessary' conclusions from necessary premisses; whereas we have already seen that the ordinary materials and conclusions of rhetoric are and can be nothing more than probable and contingent. § 3.

The author next dwells particularly upon the importance of a thorough and detailed acquaintance with the subjects or materials from which these arguments are to be derived. Hence the advantage of the τόποι or εἴδη, the classification under definite heads of all the circumstances that are required to be known about any thing that Rhetoric has to deal with, for the purpose of rightly applying it to the proof direct or indirect of any given case. Such are the qualities or properties of good and bad, just and unjust, enumerated in the first book; the delineation of the affections or emotions, which we have to impart to the judges or audience, in the second; and the characteristics of the three qualities ability, virtue, and goodwill, which we have to assume ourselves; as well as the characters of the different forms of government, and of certain ages conditions and degrees of men, the knowledge of which will, enable us to adapt our time and language to the feelings and sympathies of our audiences, according to the form of government under which they live or the age, rank, station, of any of them. Further, these items of knowledge must be definite and precise, not vague and indefinite: and in selecting our topics for argument or illustration we must employ not only as many as possible for the sake of widening the basis of our argument, but carefully choose such as are most closely connected with the matter in hand, ἐγγύτατα τοῦ πράγματος, or nearly related to it, οἰκειότατα, the most appropriate and characteristic, and the least general, ἧττον κοινά. §§ 4—12.

Next of the two kinds of enthymemes, δεικτικά, demonstrative, used in *direct* proof, and the establishment of a proposition, affirmative or negative : and ἐλεγκτικά refutative, which refute, or conclude the negative *of the opponent's* argument[1]. Of the former he says that the process is, τὸ ἐξ ὁμολογουμένων συνάγειν, which can mean nothing else than,

---

[1] ἔλεγχος δὲ συλλογισμὸς ἀντιφάσεως τοῦ συμπεράσματος, de Soph. El. I. 165. a. 2. redarguit, qui colligit quod repugnat ei quod *ab adversario* coactum est. Waitz. Comp. 168. a. 35—37. See also Anal. Pr. II. 20. 66. b. 10. ὥστ' εἰ τὸ κείμενον εἴη ἐναντίον τῷ συμπεράσματι ἀνάγκη γίνεσθαι ἔλεγχον·

ὁ γὰρ ἔλεγχος ἀντιφάσεως συλλογισμός. Rhet. III. 9. 8. ἔλεγχος συναγωγὴ τῶν ἀντικειμένων. Trendel. El. Log. § 40. Thomson's Laws of Thought, p. 271. τῶν ἐνθυμημάτων τὰ ἐλεγκτικὰ μᾶλλον εὐδοκιμεῖ τῶν δεικτικῶν, and the reason of this, Rhet. III. 17. 13.

as the Interpreters explain it, to draw conclusions from admitted principles, i. e. the probable universal rules and maxims generally and popularly recognised, which are the materials of our 'major premisses'': of the latter, that it consists in τὸ τὰ ἀνομολογούμενα συνάγειν, which from the nature of the ἔλεγχος, and a comparison of II. 23. 23, and 30. διὰ τὸ συναγωγὴν ἐναντίων εἶναι τὸ ἐλεγκτικὸν ἐνθύμημα must mean to draw conclusions at variance with the opponent's conclusions or positions, "*unacknowledged by him.*" [This is one way of understanding it, though the word ἀνομολογούμενα is used in a more restricted sense than its parallel and contradictory, ὁμολογούμενα².] §§ 14. 15. To these two kinds a third is added in § 17, the φαινόμενον ἐνθύμημα, opposed to τὰ ἴντα 'realities', the semblance of an enthymeme, the sham fallacious sophistical argument. See c. 24.

The chapter concludes with another summary review of the contents of the work past and to come. The εἴδη, Political and Moral, which form the materials of the πίστεις, have been collected and reduced to heads (τόποι), and the various characters, affections, and states (i. e. virtues or any confirmed settled habits,) of humanity, so far as is necessary for the purposes of the rhetorician, enumerated and analysed. We have next to collect and classify some specimens of heads of rhetorical arguments in general (as oppposed to the

---

[1] Top. VIII. 6. 160. a. 14. Ὅσοι δ' ἐξ ἀδοξοτέρων τοῦ συμπεράσματος ἐπιχειροῦσι συλλογίζεσθαι, δῆλον ὡς οὐ καλῶς συλλογίζονται.

[2] ἀνομολογούμενα, may perhaps be translated as above. The word is used instead of ἀντικείμενα or ἐναντία for the sake of the antithesis. Otherwise, and more naturally, it may mean "not agreeing, harmonising with," "inconsistent," and so, 'opposed to.' ὁμολογεῖν and ὁμολογεῖσθαι are used to express agreement. See Rhet. L 15. 18. II.

23. 23. Anal. Pr. I. 34. 48. a. 21. ἀνομολογούμενα τοῖς προειρημένοις. de Gen. et Corr. II. 4. 11. Hist. Anim. III. 2. 1. de Gen. Anim. I. 21. 4. III. 10. 25. This sense in the *middle* voice is rare; Liddell and Scott, in their Lexicon (Ed. II), give *one* reference to Xenophon, Mem. I. 2. 57, ὡμολογεῖτο, 'assented;' but no instance of the participle. Plato has an example, Phædr. 265. D. and see Buttmann, Auctarium ad Gorg. Heind. § 108. p. 495. A.

special εἴδη), equally applicable to all the three branches of rhetoric (καθόλου περὶ ἁπάντων), marking the distinction between the refutative and the demonstrative kinds—this is the subject of c. 23.—and then we will pass on to the consideration of the "apparent", sham, unreal, fallacious enthymeme (c. 24), a chapter in rhetoric corresponding in dialectics to the treatise περὶ Σοφιστικῶν ἐλέγχων appended to the Topics; after which we shall proceed to consider the modes of answering an adversary and refuting his arguments (λύσις); either by counter syllogism or enthymeme, a regular ἔλεγχος in detail; or by ἔνστασις, an instantia or 'objection', directed against one of his premisses, c. 25. And with this, after a brief appendix upon αὔξειν and μειοῦν, and an observation upon a certain difference of classification of demonstrative and refutative arguments in dialectics and rhetoric in c. 26, the treatment of 'proofs' the means of rhetorical persuasion, πίστεις is concluded, and with it the second book.

Ch. 23. Of the two kinds of enthymeme described in the last chapter Aristotle now proceeds in this twenty-third to give specimens and illustrations. It is in fact an analysis and classification or reduction to their several heads, τόποι, of the most serviceable enthymemes or rhetorical arguments, applicable to deliberation and accusation and defence, to Parliamentary or public speaking, and the practice of the Courts of Law, and in one instance, § 14, to the laudatory and vituperative, the epideictic branch of rhetoric. The intention seems to have been, as I have stated it, to illustrate both kinds of enthymemes, the demonstrative ἀποδεικτικά, and refutative ἐλεγκτικά; but as a matter of fact Aristotle has almost confined himself to the former; as indeed seems to be implied by the opening words, § 1. ἔστι δὲ εἷς μὲν τόπος τῶν δεικτικῶν ἐκ τῶν ἐναντίων. Of course demonstrative arguments can be employed equally well on the other side for the purposes of refutation, which follows from the nature of the ἔλεγχος, the same in *form* as the demonstrative syllogism, and differing from it only in this, that it draws the opposite conclusion: ὁ γὰρ ἔλεγχος ἀντιφάσεως συλλογισμός. Anal. Pr. II. 20. p. 66. b. 10. de Soph. Elench. 1. p. 165. a. 2. ἔλεγχος δὲ συλλογισμὸς μετ' ἀντιφάσεως τοῦ συμπεράσματος. Rhet. II. 25. 2. τὸ μὲν οὖν ἀντισυλλογίζεσθαι (the ἔλεγχος) δῆλον ὅτι ἐκ τῶν αὐτῶν τόπων (as have been already enumerated under the head of δεικτικά or ἀποδεικτικά) ἐνδέχεται ποιεῖν. This is especially the case with the topic of εἰκός, which can always be retorted upon an adversary; compare the τόπος of c. 24. § 11.; and Agathon's τάχ' ἄν τις εἰκὸς αὐτὸ τοῦτ' εἶναι λέγοι Βροτοῖσι πολλὰ τυγχάνειν οὐκ εἰκότα; and the amusing story of the logical encounter between Corax and Tisias told in the Prolegomena to Hermogenes (see Journal of Classical and Sacred Philology. No. 7. Vol. III. p. 44), and also by Aulus Gellius of Protagoras and his pupil Euathlus. And in fact in 23. 2. after the apparent limitation of the τόποι of the chapter to the demonstrative kind of enthymemes, he immediately adds in the same sentence, ἀναιροῦντα μὲν εἰ μὴ ὑπάρχει, κατασκευάζοντα δὲ εἰ ὑπάρχει "in the way of upsetting or refutation if you have none of this kind of argument in your favour; or if you have, as a confirmatory argument" (lit. in the way of establishing or proving your case). Compare c. 24. § 3. and c. 26. 3. οὐδὲ τὰ λυτικὰ ἐνθυμήματα εἶδός τι ἐστὶν ἄλλο τῶν κατασκευαστικῶν κ.τ.λ. There is however one τόπος, § 23, which is expressly called ἐλεγτικός; and the succeeding one, § 24, also falls under this head. However the treatment of the ἐλεγκτικὸς συλλογισμός in general properly comes under the analysis of λύσις in c. 25.

These topics are then illustrated in detail, §§ 1—29; and the chapter concludes with two remarks upon enthymemes in general, § 30.

The refutative or destructive enthymeme is always more popular, gains more credit and applause, than the constructive or demonstrative, because the former is the 'conclusion of opposites in little,' ἐν μικρῷ, in a small compass, because the syllogisms are not drawn out in extenso; and two things are always made clearer, and are better understood when they are placed side by side so as to admit of immediate comparison; whereby they throw light upon one another. The same observation is repeated in nearly the same words, III. 17. 13.

But of all syllogisms (or enthymemes) those are most applauded of which the result is foreseen by the audience from the very beginning: not because they are superficial, for in fact the hearers (think they are rather deep, and) are pleased with their own ingenuity in thus anticipating the conclusion of the argument; and those which are clear and consecutive enough to allow them just to keep pace ($\tau o \sigma o \hat{\upsilon} \tau o \nu$ $\hat{\upsilon} \sigma \tau \epsilon \rho \acute{\iota} \zeta o\upsilon \sigma \iota \nu$ $\ddot{\omega} \sigma \tau \epsilon$) with the steps of the argument as they are successively delivered.

Ch. 24. As an appendix to the preceding treatment of the regular constructive and refutative enthymemes, and corresponding to the treatise $\pi \epsilon \rho \grave{\iota}$ $\sigma o \phi \iota \sigma \tau \iota \kappa \hat{\omega} \nu$ $\grave{\epsilon} \lambda \acute{\epsilon} \gamma \chi \omega \nu$, on Logical Fallacies, added as a ninth book to the Topics, the analysis of the normal dialectical syllogism, we have next a chapter on fallacious *rhetorical* arguments, or apparent, not real, enthymemes. These are classified like the former under their respective $\tau \acute{o} \pi o \iota$ or heads. The objection on moral grounds which may be alleged against the introduction of an analysis like this; an art of cheating which might furnish the sophist and dishonest reasoner with a stock of arguments to be applied to purposes of fraud and deception; has been already anticipated in I. 1. 12., where the author is speaking of a different kind of abuse of rhetoric. We ought to be acquainted with these artifices, not in order to put them in practice ourselves, but that we may not be ignorant of their nature and use, and so may be enabled to detect and expose any unfair arguments employed by another: just as the legislator or politician who has to establish and maintain a constitution must study the measures and enactments not only conservative, but also destructive, of the institutions appropriate to the form of government which he has in view; in order to avoid the latter, and to guard against their evil consequences. Polit. VI. 5. init. The exposition is likewise required to complete the system.

Of these fallacious enthymemes ten τόποι are explained and illustrated. The last includes one of the modes of misusing the topic of τὸ εἰκός, (τὸ μὴ εἰκὸς εἰκός, κακουργότατον τῶν ἐπιχειρημάτων, Dion. Hal. Ep. ad Amm. I. c. 8.); namely the illicit substitution of absolute for particular, or relative probability. This, says he, is τὸ τὸν ἥττω λόγον κρείττω ποιεῖν, the making the worse prevail over the better cause, which was Protagoras' profession, the art which he undertook to teach to his pupils. The indignation which this excited, he continues, was fully justified; for it is false, an apparent not a real argumentation, a sham and a fraud; it follows no artistic method, but is *mere* rhetoric and quibbling, § 11.

Ch. 25. Of λύσις. The following chapter treats of the modes of refuting an adversary's position and arguments, premisses and conclusions. The general term that expresses this is λύειν, λύσις, διαλύειν, and syllogisms are said to be λυτοί or ἄλυτοι, capable or incapable of refutation, and arguments λυτικοί.[1]

---

[1] Similarly λύειν λόγους, as Plato Gorg. 509. A. Ar. Rhet. I. 1. 12. III. 2. 13. λύειν ἀπορίαν, διαβολάς, Rhet. ad Alex. 37. 12, 13, 29. in the sense of "to explain, resolve, refute." The metaphor from which this application of the word is borrowed is explained by Aristotle himself, Metaph. B. 1. ἡ γὰρ ὕστερον εὐπορία λύσις τῶν πρότερον ἀπορουμένων ἐστί· λύειν δ' οὐκ ἔστιν ἀγνοοῦντας τὸν δεσμόν. Eur. Hippol. 668, 771. κάθαμμα λύειν. Compare also Poet. XVIII., where λύσις is opposed to δέσις, πλέκειν, and πλοκή. The original meaning therefore is "to untie a knot;" either 'to resolve' as a difficulty, or 'to undo' what an opponent, for example, has done, and so, 'to refute' a conclusion or argument. It is found likewise in much the same sense in the common language, 'to do away with,' 'get rid of,' and sometimes 'to break or violate.' The metaphor however in these cases seems to be a different one, to "resolve a thing" viz. into its elements, or "break up" a system or organized whole, and so bring to an end. Hence we have λύειν νείκεα (Homer), φόβον, ἔχθραν, πόλεμον, διαφοράν, φιλίαν, σπονδάς, διαθήκας (to cancel a will), προφάσεις, τέχνας (Æschines), νόμους. Similarly in Latin we have solvere, diluere, solutio (Cicero), dissolutio

Syllogisms and enthymemes are of two kinds, constructive, of which the object is to establish something positive, and destructive, where the object is to upset or subvert an opposing proposition or conclusion by proving the negative. This is refutatio or reprehensio (Cic. de Inv. I. 42. 78.) in the later systems. The ordinary technical names of these two processes are συλλογισμὸς δεικτικός and ἐλεγκτικός, σ. κατασκευάζειν (to construct) and ἀνασκευάζειν or ἀναιρεῖν 'to upset or refute,' see for example, II. 2. 27; 24. 4. Hence ἐνθυμήματα κατασκευαστικά, II. 26. 3. Quintilian has confirmare and destruere, II. 4. 18. λύσις therefore may be defined ἀπόδειξις or πίστις (in rhetoric) ἀνασκευαστική. It has two kinds; τὸ ἀντισυλλογίζεσθαι, which is the ἔλεγχος, to prove the opposite, or subvert an opponent's conclusion, by a regular counter-syllogism, or in rhetoric, enthymeme[1]; and ἔνστασις, instantia, an instance contrary, or objection[2]. ἔνστασις is thus defined in c. 26. § 4, τὸ εἰπεῖν δόξαν τινὰ ἐξ ἧς ἔσται δῆλον ὅτι οὐ συλλελόγισται ἢ ὅτι ψεῦδός τι εἴληφεν. The one therefore is general, the other special. The former proves the contrary of the adversary's position as a whole; the latter singles out a particular point, premiss or flaw in the reasoning, which vitiates the conclusion. There is no difference in form between the λυτικά and κατασκευαστικὰ

(Auct. ad Heren. I. 3. 4.); solvere argumentum, solvitur quæstio (Quintilian V. 5. 2. III. 7. 3.), objecta diluere Ib. IV. 2. 26. causæ faciles ad diluendum Ib. §§ 27, 8., diluere argumentationem Cic. de Inv. I. 52. 99, vim et acrimoniam, Ib. II. 48. 143. et passim. Solvitur ambulando, of the argument against the possibility of motion: and so we say, 'to solve a problem or riddle' and 'the solution of a difficulty.' Other terms expressive of 'refutation' are ἀναιρεῖν and ἀνασκευάζειν, applied to the destructive syllogism, and opposed to κατασκευάζειν said of the constructive ἀνασκευή and κατασκευή are defined by Hermogenes, Progymn. in Speng. Rhet. Gr. II. 8.

[1] On the ἔλεγχος see further on c. 22.

[2] The word ἔνστασις first acquires its technical logical denotation in Aristotle. We find however ἐνέστηκε expressing an obstacle or objection in Plato's Phædo, 77. D. and ἐνστῆναι in a similar sense in Isocr. Phil. § 39. The primary meaning which gives rise to this secondary sense is 'to stand in the way' as an obstacle or impediment.

ἐνθυμήματα, and therefore no necessity for analysing them separately: the τόποι are the same for both, 26. 3. III. 17. 14. τὰ δὲ πρὸς τὸν ἀντίδικον οὐχ ἕτερόν τι εἶδος, ἀλλὰ τῶν πίστεων ἔστι τὰ μὲν λῦσαι ἐνστάσει τὰ δὲ συλλογισμῷ. Compare Cicero, de Inv. I. 42. 78, hæc fonte—infirmari.

Of the logical character and mode of application of the ἔνστασις, the second kind of λύσις, no general account is given in the Rhetoric: this is supplied in the Analytica Priora, II. 26. p. 69. a. 37. seq., where the following description of it is given. The ἔνστασις, instantia, instance, special objection, is distinguished from the ἔλεγχος in this, that whereas the latter takes the form of a counter syllogism in detail, with a *conclusion* opposite to that which it undertakes to refute, the ἔνστασις is directed against one of the *premisses* of the adverse syllogism; it is a counter proposition or assertion, πρότασις προτάσει ἐναντία, or instance to the contrary: if the objection be valid and capable of proof the opposing syllogism is disproved. It differs from the proposition or premiss, i.e. the universal premiss, in this that it can be either universal or particular; contradictory either of the universal proposition as a whole, or of a part or item of it. This latter, the particular objection, is the only one that is exemplified by Aristotle, and is in fact the form which the ἔνστασις or 'instance' usually assumes [and from which the meaning of the word *instance* in its modern acceptation is derived[1]]. The conclusion is drawn either in the first or the third of the syllogistic figures: in the first when the ἔνστασις is universal, and opposed to the universal major of the syllogism to be refuted, as for example when we oppose to the general assertion that the science of two opposites is universally the same, the counter universal assertion that none

---

[1] The literal meaning of ἔνστασις, which stands for ἐνστημα, the process or position for the object in that position, seems to be 'something that stands in the way,' as an obstacle or impediment, thwarting and running counter to a contrary proposition; and hence an 'objection,' quod objicitur, which indeed very nearly represents precisely the same notion.

is so: or in the third when we take a single 'instance' as an 'objection' to the general principle, that of the two opposites the known and the unknown the science or knowledge cannot be the same. In this second case it is only proved that the rule is not universally true, that it admits of exceptions; but in both cases alike the counter syllogism is overthrown. Of this third figure Thomson, Laws of Thought, p. 173, note, says, "Useful for bringing in examples, and for *proving an exception to some universal statement.* Thus if it were stated that all intellectual culture improved the heart and conduct, it would be natural to say in this Figure, Mr. A. does not act as he ought, yet Mr. A. is a person of cultivated mind, therefore one person at least of cultivated mind does not act as he ought." And in like manner in the example of Aristotle the syllogism will be,

> Things known and unknown cannot fall under the same science,
> But Things known and unknown are opposites,
> Therefore (in one instance at least) opposites do *not* fall under the same science,
> Or, the principle that all opposites fall under the same science is *not* universally true[1].

Q.E.D.

Of ἐνστάσεις there are four varieties, derived (1) from the opposing enthymeme itself, or (2) from an analogical case, or (3) something opposite, or (4) from a previous decision. In the first, suppose the enthymeme concluded that all love is good and respectable; we may interpose an objection in two ways, either (α) universally, that every kind of want or deficiency (of which love is one) is bad, or (β) partially,

---

[1] On ἔνστασις and λύσις, besides the Chapter of the Anal. Pr. above referred to, see Thomson, Laws of Thought, § 127. The division there adopted does not coincide with that of Aristotle, with whom λύσις is the genus, and ἔλεγχος and ἔνστασις the two subordinate species. See also Trendelenburg. Elem. Log. Arist. § 41. Also compare Rhet. II. 16. 4. and Cic. de Orat. II. 53.

by a particular 'instance,' that the proverb Καύνιος ἔρως, the particular case of the incestuous passion of Byblis for her brother Caunus, shows that at all events there is *one* exception. The third kind, from opposites, which is taken before the second, is thus illustrated. The enthymeme or conclusion which you wish to refute is, "that the good man does good to all his friends," or in other words, that doing services to one's friends is a conclusive and universal proof of goodness. No, says the opponent, taking the opposite to this, the bad man does not always do his friends harm: a *bad man* may do good to his friends: benefits conferred on friends are no necessary proof of virtue. The second class of objections, derived from like cases, is illustrated by the following example. The enthymeme is to prove that ill treatment always produces hatred or that hatred is always a proof of ill-treatment. The reply is, that if this were so, the opposite, kind treatment would always produce love: but this is not the case: those who are well treated don't *always* love their benefactors: and therefore hatred is *not* a necessary proof of ill treatment. The fourth kind of ἔνστασις is borrowed from a 'previous decision of men well known and famous;' as the enthymeme, that allowance should be made for a drunken man when he commits a crime, because he does it in ignorance, may be met by the authority of Pittacus, who enacted a heavier penalty for a crime committed in a state of intoxication. With this last variety of ἔνστασις compare the topic of κρίσις in c. 23. 12., and the topic of μάρτυρες in I. 15. 15.

Now as the enthymemes and the conclusions of the rhetorician are never more than probable, except in the single instance of the τεκμήριον or necessary sign, being all derived from probable materials, εἰκός, παράδειγμα, σημεῖον; and as they are consequently none of them without exception or necessary, but being probable can be nothing more than contingent and variable, it is plain that they must be in every case open to exception and objection, and can always be refuted *in this sense*, that it can always be shown that they are neither necessary nor invariable. But this mode of refutation is in reality unfair and fallacious: what the objection has properly to prove is that the *probable* enthymeme is *improbable*, not that the conclusion is not universal and necessary, which is the mode of refutation appropriate to *demonstrative* reasoning[1], "and therefore also" § 8, "it is always possible to take an unfair advantage, more easily however in defence than in accusation, by means of this paralogism: for since it is by probabilities that the accuser always endeavours to prove his case, but refutation by showing the improbability and by showing the non-necessity are two different things, and that which is only probable (only 'for the most part,' only generally true) is always liable to exception—for if it were not it would not be mere probability, but constant and necessary—this being so, I say that the judge is led to suppose, if the refutation be made in this way (by showing that the opposing argument is not *necessary*), either that the accuser's case is not probable, or else that it is not for *him* to decide, misled by the fallacy above described: for he is not required to decide by necessary demonstration alone, but also by the probabilities of the case: and that in fact is the meaning of 'deciding according to the best of his judgment.' It is not enough therefore for the defendant to prove by way of refuting the accusation that he necessarily was not guilty of the offence with which he is charged: he must also show that it was not probable" —meeting his adversary upon his own ground.

In other words: as the orator's conclusions are never, ὡς ἔπος εἰπεῖν, i.e. with the exception of the one case of the τεκμήριον, more than probable, they are always liable to an

---

[1] In § 8 Spengel has included the words δι' ἐπαγωγῆς in brackets, probably as an explanatory gloss on δι' ὁμοίου; and Victorius long ago expressed his suspicion that the words had been importunè inculcata. It seems to me that the words may be very well retained, in the sense of 'by an inductive process,' a process, that is, of imperfect, not complete, induction, which is in fact the definition of an Example. See on the Example and its logical description, ante, p. 105. foll.

objection: and here the defendant, or in general any one who has to *answer* an argument, has, and constantly takes, an unfair advantage: ἀεὶ ἔστι πλεονεκτεῖν ἀπολογούμενον. He imposes upon the judges or audience by showing that the preceding speaker's conclusions are not *necessarily* true; which can always be done, because that which is only 'for the most part,' only *generally* true, τὸ ὡς ἐπὶ τὸ πολύ, must from its very nature admit of exceptions. The judge however, to take a particular case, is often deluded by the paralogism, when the defendant has shown merely that so and so has not necessarily happened or is not necessarily true, when he ought to have shown that it was not probable. The judge confounds the two and thinks that the defendant has really made out his case; and as the accuser has not shown that the offence was necessarily committed, lets the other off. He supposes either that the probability of the case has not been made out, or else that the whole thing is so uncertain that at all events it is not *his* business to decide it. But this is a mistake, and shows an ignorance of his actual duties, and of the meaning of the oath that he takes on entering his court: for that oath, 'that he will decide according to the best of his judgment[1],' means precisely this, that he will accept probabilities, the contingent, and the uncertain, and make the best of them; and will not always require absolute and necessary truths, facts, and arguments, as the grounds of his decision.

This refutation of a probable argument by one of superior probability will be effected by producing an objection of a higher degree of probability than the argument or premiss that it is meant to refute. The degree of probability of a fact or event is estimated by the number of analogous facts or events that can be quoted in support of it; if these paral-

---

[1] Τὸ γνώμῃ τῇ ἀρίστῃ κρίνειν, comp. I. 15. 5., is usually expressed by γν. τῇ δικαιοτάτῃ κρ., and was part of the dicast's oath. Compare Demost. c. Bœot. de Nom. 1006. 27. ἀλλὰ μὴν ὧν γ' ἂν μὴ ὦσι νόμοι γνώμῃ τῇ δικαιοτάτῃ δικάσειν ὀμωμόκατε. c. Aristocr. 652. 25. adv. Lept. Arist. Pol. III. 16.

lel cases are numerous, the fact or event in question is probable: and therefore the probability of an ἔνστασις will be increased in proportion as the circle of similar facts and events which it represents widens, and their number increases. This increase of probability, μᾶλλον τὸ ὡς ἐπὶ τὸ πολύ, says A., may be effected in two particulars, the time and the circumstances of the case. To take an instance—suppose you are charged with a crime for which your adversary makes out a probable case; to this you oppose an objection which gives a contrary but, as you argue, a more probable view of it: this increase of probability may consist either in the different time assigned, or in different circumstances of the case: if you can make out that there is more analogy in the ordinary course of events for your account of the case in respect of the time and circumstances of it, your account is more probable than that of the accuser, and your argument prevails. This use of 'the time,' is illustrated by the examples given in II. 23. 6., 'the topic of time.' [This seems to me to be the only way of bringing the two particulars in which the increase of probability of the ἔνστασις may be effected into conformity with the preceding description of the mode in which it is to be done, ἐνδέχεται τοιαύτην εἶναι: which is, to make it μᾶλλον ὡς ἐπὶ τὸ πολύ, "more general, more in accordance with the usual course of events, or in accordance with a greater number of cases of a similar kind." Victorius understands the words ἢ χρόνῳ ἢ τοῖς πράγμασιν, a tempore, cum crebro; a rebus, cum plurima ita fiunt, which can mean no more than from the frequency of similar cases, *and* from the frequency of similar cases. And not only does this interpretation do away with the distinction between the two modes, but also it would seem that τῷ χρόνῳ can hardly signify 'crebro,' which would rather be expressed by τῷ πόσῳ or τῷ ἀριθμῷ. Portus, quoted by Gaisf. in Not. Var., explains them thus; to take account of (1) times and (2) circumstances: τῷ χρόνῳ ut supra de Helena, Quicquid pater liberis concedit, id liberis facere licet; at non semper, sed dum ejus in potestate sunt.

τοῖς πράγμασιν, ut, Decet filium persequi injurias patris; sed in alienis personis, non in matre: et jure potius quam vi. But I cannot see how either of these could be said to *increase the probability of an objection*, which is what the context requires.] §§ 8—11.

'Signs', and enthymemes founded upon signs, are always liable to refutation, even though they be real and genuine, as was observed at the beginning of this work (I. 2. 18.); because no argument from a sign can ever be put in the form of a regular demonstrative syllogism—it wants the universal major—which is shown in the Analytics. (Anal. Pr. II. 27).

The mode of refuting examples is the same as that which is employed against probabilities. ·If we have a contrary instance to produce which does not conform to the rule laid down by our opponent, the refutation must be directed against the *necessity* of the opponent's proposition; and similarly if we have several analogous instances to the contrary, or the *same thing* occurring *several times:* but if the number and frequency of the similar cases, the superiority of probability, be on the side of the opponent, we are reduced to contend, either that the example cited on the other side is not a case in point, does not prove the general rule, or that the thing can't be done in the same way (οὐχ ὁμοίως Vict.), or that there is some difference or other between the case which the opponent desires to establish and that which he takes for his example. §§ 12, 13.

Enthymemes arising from τεκμήρια are the only rhetorical arguments that are incapable of refutation. The σημεῖα can always be refuted because they cannot be thrown into the form of a regular syllogism: but the τεκμήρια can; and therefore they are not refutable on *this* ground at least. This is plain from the Analytics (II. 27. Compare Rhet. I. 2. §§ 16, 17, 18). In this case it only remains to us to show that the τεκμήριον is imaginary, has no real existence, or is no real τεκμήριον. If both can be proved, that it does exist, is real, and is a τεκμήριον, *then* indeed it is absolutely irrefutable. For when once a thing is demonstrated its truth becomes clear and indisputable. § 14.

Ch. 26. This short chapter is added as an appendix to the preceding analyses, and contains two statements, probably meant to correct certain erroneous opinions or classifications of one or more preceding writers upon Rhetoric. The opinions controverted are not found at all events in the Rhet. ad Alex.

First of αὔξειν and μειοῦν, amplification and depreciation[1]. We have been already told in c. 18. that this is one of the κοινοὶ τόποι, loci communissimi, applicable ἀπάντων τῶν λόγων, to every kind of speech, and to every εἶδος or special topic, in all the three branches of rhetoric. It is therefore not a mere τόπος ἐνθυμήματος. Αὔξειν and μειοῦν are of much wider application than a τόπος ἐνθυμήματος. They are in fact ἐνθυμήματα themselves; specially applicable to one particular class of subjects, the great and small, and employed, chiefly in the epideictic branch (comp. I. 9. 40.), in showing that things are or are not important or distinguished or valuable; just as there are classes of arguments, including many τόποι, to prove that things are good or bad, just or unjust, and the like.

Secondly, § 3., there is no difference in kind between demonstrative or constructive and refutative or destructive enthymemes in rhetoric. In the latter, you either *demonstrate* by a counter-syllogism (ἀντισυλλογιζόμενος) that your adversary's conclusion is false; or you meet and overthrow his argument by an ἔνστασις; which is no syllogism or enthymeme at all, and therefore does not constitute a different *kind of enthymeme.*

---

[1] The Latin equivalents of these terms are, exaggerare, augere, tollere, amplificare on the one hand, extenuare, abjicere, minuere, on the other. Quint. VIII. 3. 40. Cic. de Orat. III. 26. 104, 5. Orat. §§ 125. 127. The Rhet. ad Alex. has ταπεινοῦν and ταπείνωσις in the place of μειοῦν and μείωσις. c. 18, 2. et passim.

BOOK III.

Ch. 1. So far we have been occupied with the materials of rhetoric; the different kinds of arguments suitable to each of its three branches have been distinguished and set forth in detail, together with the sources from which they are derived: the sources of proof being three, either direct, by actual demonstration, or indirect[1] by the assumption of a certain character by the speaker himself, or by stirring up certain emotions in the audience; and of the first of these the several species have been analysed, παραδείγματα, γνῶμαι, ἐνθυμήματα, &c., and the modes of answering them, λύσεις, pointed out. § 1, and II. 26. 5. This concludes the treatment of inventio: there remain λέξις, elocutio, including ὑπόκρισις pronuntiatio and actio, and τάξις dispositio, on which Aristotle now enters[2]. And first of λέξις, or 'style', which is here made to include 'delivery'. 'For it is not enough to know what to say, we must also know how to say it:' and this necessity arises from a defect of the art of rhetoric on the one hand, and of the audience on the other: for if rhetoric were a science like geometry (§ 6), nothing but perspicuity would be required; and if the audience were what they ought to be and attended only to the proofs adduced, all graces of style, as all appeals to the passions, (I. 1. 3—10) would be out of place: all that the orator in such a case should aim at, would be a colourless medium, to speak so as to give neither pleasure nor offence. (§ 5) Aristotle begins his treatise on style with a few remarks upon the second and subordinate division of it, viz. ὑπόκρισις or delivery. This subject, with the exception of a few notices by Thrasymachus

---

[1] Comp. I. 1. 4. οὐ περὶ τοῦ πράγματός ἐστιν, ἀλλὰ πρὸς τὸν δικαστήν.

[2] These, together with the appeals to the feelings, which entered into the treatment of the parts of the speech, were the subjects on which Aristotle's predecessors had mainly dwelt, τὰ ἔξω τοῦ πράγματος τεχνολογοῦσιν I. 1. 9. Cic. Orat. § 43, reduces the partes rhetoricæ to three, as Aristotle; quid dicat, quo quidque loco, quomodo.

in his ἔλεοι, had been as yet unattempted (§ 3 and 5) by writers upon rhetoric; and it is in fact more independent of art, more the gift of nature, than the other branches of λέξις (§ 7); and also might seem beneath the dignity of serious philosophical inquiry, φορτικόν, § 5. The management of the face, mouth, arms, and body, which are included by the Latin Rhetoricians, Cicero and Quintilian, under the head of actio, are unnoticed by Aristotle, and only the regulation of the voice, as regards volume, pitch or accent, and time or measure, which vary according to the emotion that is to be represented, is touched upon. § 4. ὑπόκρισις is therefore confined by Aristotle to 'declamation', and is classed with that of tragic actors and rhapsodists, § 3. Passing on to the consideration of style in its ordinary acceptation of 'the choice and arrangement of words and the composition of these in sentences', he proceeds to say, that mere style, as distinguished from thought and matter on the one hand, and from delivery, declamation and action, pronuntiatio, on the other—as it is found for example in speeches which are intended to be read[1], and not delivered in a court of law or public assembly, οἱ γραφόμενοι λόγοι, such as those of Isocrates who is probably here referred to—deserves to be cultivated on its own account[2] as a means of securing the prizes (ἆθλα), of applause and public favour. § 7. But the treatment of style must be limited by the subject before us. It is true that the cultivation of style originated with the poets, because their business is imitation; and words and the voice itself are the chief instruments of such imitation; and also that the earlier rhetoricians of the school of Gorgias, finding from the example of some poets that a reputation might be gained by mere sound without sense, copied them, and adopted a style approaching to poetry in its language and artificial combinations: but this is vicious: and that it is so, we may

---

[1] ἡ ἐπιδεικτικὴ λέξις γραφικωτάτη III. 12. 5. Quint. III. 8. 63.

[2] That is, independently of its *indirect* effect upon proof; διαφέρει γάρ τι πρὸς τὸ δηλῶσαι ὡδὶ ἢ ὡδὶ λέγειν. § 6.

learn from the example of the poets themselves: for the tragedians have by this time abandoned their peculiar language and measure, and employ a diction and a metre conforming as nearly as possible to the ordinary language of common life[1]. It is plain therefore that we are not required here to enter into the niceties of poetical language and composition—*That* is properly reserved for the Poetics. §§ 8—10.

GENERAL OBSERVATIONS ON STYLE.

The chapters on λέξις, on the virtues of style, are from 2—12 inclusive. This part of the subject is implicitly divided into two[2] parts; the treatment of single words, cc. 2—4, and the combination of them in sentences; to the end that the style be pure, grammatically correct, lucid, ornate or dignified, harmonious or rhythmical, lively, pointed and impressive, and adapted to the subject in hand. cc. 5—12. Some writers on Rhetoric refer the ἀρεταὶ λέξεως, the various excellences of style, to four heads; and these are all found in Aristotle, though the division is not accurately made, nor the order regularly followed. These four are purity, perspicuity, ornament, and propriety[3]. This division, already current,

---

[1] This was especially the case with writers like Aristotle's contemporary and pupil Theodectes, who was both rhetorician and dramatic author; and the writers of the middle and new Comedy.

[2] These two divisions are not kept very carefully distinct; see for example, c. 5 § 3, 4.

[3] On Purity, see Campbell Phil. of Rhet. Bk. II. c. 3. init. It implies three things, that the words be English: that the construction and arrangement of them be conformable to the English idiom: and that the words and phrases be used in that sense which custom has affixed to them. The opposite errors, are barbarism, solœcism, and impropriety. Quint. deprehendat quæ barbara, quæ impropria, quæ contra legem loquendi composita. Treated by this author as a branch of grammar. I. 5. VIII. I. (but not exclusively.) Aristotle's definition of solœcism seems to be the same, from the examples of it in Top. IX. 173. b. 17 seq. It is =βαρβαρίζειν, Ib. 165. b. 20. Purity is the foundation of style, solum quidem, et quasi fundamentum oratoris vides locutionem emendatam et Latinam, Cic. de Clar. Or. LXXIV. 258.: what this implies

(Cic. de Or. I. 32. 144.,) is adopted by Cicero de Oratore, III. cc. 10—55. See § 37. Purity, Latine loqui, is treated in §§ 38—47. Compare Orat. XXIII. 79. Perspicuity, sermo dilucidus, plane dicere, in §§ 48—50. Ornament, ornate dicere, the ornaments, figures, and numbers or rhythm, of speech, in §§ 52—207. And Propriety, aptum, quid maxime deceat in oratione §§ 208—212. The same division is followed by Quintilian I. 5. 1. and VIII. cc. 1. 2. 3. seq. to the end of IX.; except that he does not place the last under a distinct head, but includes it under ornatus. Propriety must regulate the choice of ornament in making a speech attractive, as it does that of topics in confirming an argument. It is in the use of this last that the true virtue of rhetoric consists: to speak with purity and perspicuity, is rather to avoid faults than to attain excellence, VIII. 3. 1.; and in this therefore propriety may be most signally shown. These four qualities of style are implicitly recognised by Aristotle in the two first sections of this chapter, purity being first perhaps implied in σαφήνεια, and afterwards expressly stated in c. 5. § 1, 'Ελληνίζειν: and in that chapter purity and perspicuity are discussed in conjunction. Propriety is directly mentioned and afterwards enlarged upon in cc. 7. and 12.: and the ornamental character, at least in the choice of words, expressed by the terms μὴ ταπεινὴν ἀλλὰ κεκοσμημένην, τὸ ἐξαλλάξαι, σεμνοτέραν, and ξένην τὴν διάλεκτον: compare τὸ ξενικόν in § 6, and Poet. XXII. 3. σεμνὴ δὲ καὶ......παρὰ τὸ κύριον. The examination and criticism of the different kinds of ornaments of style occupy the remaining chapters, with the ex-

see in de Orat. III. 11. 40, 41. Comp. I. 5. 1. ἀρχὴ τῆς λέξεως τὸ 'Ελληνίζειν. (Puritas) Latine atque emendate loqui. Quint. VIII. 1. 2. to avoid barbarisms, to observe the rules of grammar, &c. (Perspicuitas) propria verba, rectus ordo, non in longum dilata conclusio; nihil neque desit, neque superfluat. Id. VIII. 2. 22. What this includes is summed up by Cic. de Orat. III. 13. 49. Lastly, Orat. XXIII. 79. Sermo purus erit et Latinus; dilucide planeque dicetur; quid deceat (propriety) circumspicietur; unum aberit, quod quartum numerat Theophrastus in orationis laudibus, ornatum illud, suave et affluens.

ception of 5 and 7, from 2 to 11 inclusive; c. 12 belongs to the head of propriety.

Campbell in his Phil. of Rhet. Bk. II. ch. 5. says. "Besides purity, which is a quality entirely grammatical, the five simple and original qualities of style, considered as an object of the understanding, the imagination, the passions, and the ear, are, perspicuity, vivacity, elegance, animation, and music." The four last would be included by the Latin Rhetoricians under ornatus. "By vivacity" he says Ibid. p. 3. "resemblance is attained; by elegance dignity of manner." Propriety is omitted apparently as inseparable from all the six qualities, and not independently attainable—as it certainly may appear in them all. Perhaps for this reason the triple division is more philosophically exact.

According to the auctor ad Heren. IV. 12 the virtues and graces of style may be classed under three heads. 1. Elegantia, which includes purity and perspicuity; quæ facit ut unumquodque pure et aperte dici videatur: distribuitur in latinitatem et explanationem. See the rest of § 17. in which Latinitas, and the vices of style which it avoids, solœcismus and barbarismus (all this being a part of grammar) and explanatio, quæ reddit apertam et dilucidam orationem, are defined. 2. compositio, quæ facit omnes partes orationis æquabiliter perpolitas; regulates the composition, construction, collocation, of words and sentences so as to avoid all harshness and inelegance (to the ear) arising from a vicious arrangement of words, as hiatus, alliteration, repetition of the same word, of the same termination, hyperbaton, and clauses too long to be conveniently pronounced in a breath. 3. dignitas, quæ reddit ornatam orationem, varietate distinguens. In this classification the contents of (2) may otherwise be distributed over perspicuity and ornament; the excellences implied in the avoidance of the two last of the six faults named being reducible to the head of perspicuity, and the four others falling under that of ornament.

Hermogenes, π. ἰδεῶν τομ. α΄ c. 1. (vol. II. pp. 268, 274, Spengel.) adopts a sevenfold division. σαφήνεια, μέγεθος, κάλλος, γοργότης, ἦθος, ἀλήθεια, δεινότης. Most of these are again subdivided. Purity is altogether omitted: σαφήνεια includes perspicuity, and the rest may be referred to the third of Quintilian's divisions.

Diogenes Laert. Zenon. VII. 59. ἀρεταὶ δὲ λόγου εἰσὶ πέντε, Ἑλληνισμὸς, σαφήνεια, συντομία, πρέπον, κατασκευή. In this list, which agrees with that of Cicero with the addition of συντομία, conciseness, this latter quality is defined, λέξις αὐτὰ τὰ ἀναγκαῖα περιέχουσα πρὸς δήλωσιν τοῦ πράγματος: πρέπον, λέξις οἰκεία τῷ πράγματι: and κατασκευή (apparatus, furniture, ornament), λέξις ἐκπεφυγυῖα τὸν ἰδιωτισμόν (common, everyday language); and therefore corresponds precisely with Aristotle's ξενικόν, and ξένη λέξις.

The observations upon style in the Rhet. ad Alex. are contained in cc. 23—29. They are slight, scanty, and fragmentary. They include precepts and remarks upon the kinds of words, the composition of words, rules for attaining perspicuity of style, amongst which are some elementary grammatical notices c. 26, and explanation and illustration of the rhetorical figures ἀντίθεσις, παρίσωσις, παρομοίωσις, invented by Gorgias, and the prominent characteristic of his compositions and those of his followers of the 'Sicilian' school. From these Isocrates derived them, to whose school the author of this treatise plainly belongs.

Ch. 2. The first virtue of style, says Aristotle, is perspicuity, σαφῆ εἶναι: for as the office of language is to express our meaning, if this be obscure it fails to do so, and does not fulfil its proper function. Next, it must be neither too low mean creeping degraded, nor stilted pompous extravagant, but appropriate to the subject. Of the various kinds of words, into which ὀνόματα and ῥήματα[1] (nouns, adjectives, and verbs, Poet. XX. 8, 9) may be divided, viz. κύρια[2], γλῶτ-

---

[1] ὀνόματα and ῥήματα, see Appendix A. to Bk. III.

[2] κύριον (ὄνομα) is the 'proper' word, by which any object is designated, and commonly employed to express it. It is therefore opposed to all the other kinds of words; to all figurative, foreign, archaic, or in any way 'uncommon'. It is therefore distinguished from γλῶτται and the rest, not only

ται, μεταφοραί, κόσμοι, πεποιημένα, ἐπεκτεταμένα, ὑφῃρημένα, ἐξηλλαγμένα· (common, foreign, metaphorical, ornamental, [embellishments, ornamental *epithets* I think, which are otherwise omitted], invented, extended, contracted, altered. Twining.) Poet. c. XXI, the first sort only conduce to perspicuity; all the rest may be employed to add dignity grace and ornament to language, and divest it of its mean everyday commonplace character. To alter or vary language, ἐξαλλάξαι, in this way invests it with a higher dignity; for we feel towards language just as we feel towards men; 'familiarity breeds contempt' for the words we are constantly

here, but also in the enumeration of Poet. c. XXI., where the two are thus defined; λέγω δὲ κύριον μὲν ᾧ χρῶνται ἕκαστοι, γλῶτταν δὲ ᾧ ἕτεροι. On the different varieties of nomina propria, see Quintilian, VIII. 2. 1—11. Τὸ κύριον is opposed ξένον or ξενικόν, any term that is not 'proper' and 'usual', any foreign or strange word, that strikes one as singular and unusual. Diodorus Siculus, XII. 53. applies the phrase τὸ ξενίζον τῆς λέξεως to the affected exaggerated style of Gorgias and its 'foreign' ornaments. See Whately Rhet. ch. III. § 1. Words, as regards their use in writing or style, are in the Poetics, XXI. 4, somewhat arbitrarily divided into seven classes; the κύρια, and six kinds of ξένα or extra-ordinary. Of the logical or grammatical division adopted by Aristotle I have spoken in the Appendix A. to this book. I will add some other divisions of the Latin Rhetoricians, Cicero and Quintilian. The passages will illustrate some of Aristotle's technicalities.

First, Cicero, de Orat. III. 37. 149. Ergo utemur verbis aut iis quæ propria (κύρια) sunt, et certa quasi vocabula rerum, pæne una nata cum rebus ipsis; aut iis quæ transferuntur (μεταφορά, verba *tralata*,) et quasi alieno in loco collocantur; aut iis quæ novamus, et facimus ipsi. Here there are only three classes; words 'proper', metaphors, and a third novel, which we *make* ourselves (Aristotle's πεποιημέναι); and probably also meant to include those which we *introduce* ourselves, the γλῶτται and ἐξηλλαγμένα. Again, de Or. III. 38. 152, tria sunt igitur in verbo simplice quæ orator adferat ad illustrandum atque exornandam orationem [here the κύρια are omitted, and only the ornamental words classified.]; aut inusitatum verbum (γλῶτταν), aut novatum (πεποιημένον), aut translatum (μεταφοράν). Orat. XXIV. 80. propria et usitata; aliena; videlicet, translatum, factam aliunde ut mutuo, aut factum ab ipso, aut novum et priscum et inusitatum. Verba singula, may be divided, according to Quintilian, I. 5. 3, into, nostra aut peregrina; aut simplicia aut composita; aut propria aut translata; aut usitata aut ficta. And in VIII. 3. 24. he gives three divisions, propria, ficta, translata.

meeting in everyday intercourse, whilst 'strangers' assume a higher importance and interest and dignity in our eyes. Hence we are to aim at a 'strange' i.e. unusual, not familiar, novel, out of the common way, diction, ξένην ποιεῖν τὴν διά- λεκτον; people *admire* strangers whom they don't see every day, and "admiration" (τὸ θαυμαστόν, 'the marvellous', anything that excites our curiosity,) is agreeable. But this source of interest is to be used much more sparingly in prose than in poetry; because in the latter the subject and the characters being further removed from everyday life can be more appropriately clothed in corresponding language. However even in poetry, a fortiori in prose[1], the language must be accommodated to the subject, and raised or lowered in accordance with it. But this being the case (διό), admitting as we must the necessity of this from the attention that ornament necessarily attracts, we must be particularly careful to avoid all appearance of art and elaborate study in the choice and composition of language, because this always arouses the suspicions of an audience, and the manifest artifice makes them apprehend deceit[2]. Of this natural style

---

[1] ἐν τούτοις in prose. Vict. In this case καί signifies 'also', and nothing more; 'in prose as in poetry'. But I think the sense is better and more in accordance with the general argument of the passage, if we understand τούτοις of the preceding viz. poetry; and then καί is 'even', and the argument a fortiori. Poetry from the elevation of its subject admits of a good deal of exaggeration in language, but even in poetry the language must be adapted to the subject.—et tragicus plerumque dolet sermone pedestri—the use of fine language by a slave or a child, or on a mean and trifling subject is ridiculous: "but even here (in what we were just speaking of, poetry) there is a propriety which consists in a lowering or elevation of the tone according to circumstances: and if this be true *even* of poetry where a more lofty tone is allowed, what must be the case with rhetoric and its prose?"

[2] ὑπέδειξε. The ὑπό may either signify 'underneath,' as a guide or rule to follow; the metaphor taken from the tracing of lines *underneath* by a writing master for the pupil to follow or write *over;* see Protag. 326. D. ὑπογράψαντες τῇ γραφίδι, and κατὰ τὴν ὑφήγησιν τῶν γραμμῶν, which explains the metaphor. There is a large family of compounds with ὑπό in this sense, of which ὑφηγεῖσθαι is the one that most frequently occurs: the enumeration of them I must reserve for a more appropriate place. ὑποδεικνύναι

in which art has concealed art Euripides gave the earliest specimens[1]; some of his best effects are produced not by the employment of forced metaphors and bombastic stilted phraseology, γλῶτται, διπλᾶ ὀνόματα, and such like, but by careful selection of words out of the common language of the

itself is used by Herodotus, I. 189, and Xenophon, Œcon. XI. 18, in this sense. Otherwise, the ὑπό may express the *under* tone; the primary notion, which is extended to convey the idea of faintness, softness, feebleness, and hence a low or slight degree of anything. In this case ὑπέδειξε will mean, as I have rendered it, 'gave us a glimpse, or hint, or specimen':. and so Isocr. Paneg. § 93, ὑπεφαίνετο. Thuc. I. 77. 5.

[1] In illustrating the 'concealment of art' by Euripides' writings, Aristotle is of course referring to the poet's ordinary and better style, which was celebrated for its easy simplicity and terse neatness, τὸ στρόγγυλον, Arist. Σκην. Καταλ. Fragm. 397. Dind. [See Thirlwall, Hist. of Greece, c. XXXII. Vol. IV. p. 262. Ed. 1. and Müller, Hist. Gr. Lit. XXV. 7.]; for there are occasional affectations and singularities especially in the later plays, which Aristophanes has criticised and parodied in the Frogs. Archimelus, the author of the Epigram on the difficulty of imitating Euripides, Anthol. II. 64. seems to have more than agreed with Aristotle as to the amount of art employed by the poet in disguising the pains and labour that the construction of his sentences had cost him: he says of his style,

λείη μὲν γὰρ ἰδεῖν καὶ ἐπίκροτος (smooth as a beaten road)· εἰ δέ τις αὐτὴν

εἰσβαίνει, χαλεποῦ τρηχυτέρη σκόλοπος.

Of the care which the orators bestowed on disguising their art, on effacing as much as possible all marks of study and premeditation from their speeches, there are some curious examples in Isocrates' περὶ ἀντιδ. §§ 140, 159, 310, 320. Though this speech, as the author tells us himself at the beginning of it, was not only a written composition, but never even intended for any thing but to be read, yet, in order to give the appearance of reality to the defence of his character and studies, supposed to be delivered in a court of law in answer to a charge brought by one Lysimachus—of which the main bulk of the entire work consists—he introduces passages, such as those already referred to, of which the only meaning and intention is to suggest the notion of an extemporaneous harangue. It afterwards became a recognised convention in the orator's *practice*, and was introduced even in speeches actually delivered in the assemblies and law courts: it seems to have been thought that without the use of such artifices the impression of vraisemblance or reality would not be produced. Even Demosthenes and Cicero condescended to have recourse to them; the former in the speech against Meidias, written but never delivered; the latter, under the same circumstances, in his second Philippic.

day, which are combined so as to produce a pleasing and poetical character. § 5.

Of the several kinds of words, already mentioned, most, as foreign and archaic, double or compound and 'invented' (manufactured by the author for the occasion) words are to be rarely and sparingly employed in prose, for the reason before mentioned (i.e. that they make prose stilted and unnatural, being most frequently above the dignity of the subject)—the only kinds suitable to prose are the common, familiar (or appropriate, proper) terms and metaphors—the proof of this being that these and these alone occur in common conversation. If the orator confines himself to these, his style may be novel and ornamental, yet without forcing itself unduly upon the attention, and perspicuous. And these are the excellences of style. Of two other kinds of terms homonyms and synonyms, (see the Categ. init.) the former are of service to the sophist in passing off his fallacies, the latter (such as πορεύεσθαι and βαδίζειν) to the poet.

The rest of this Chapter is occupied with directions for the invention and use of metaphors, the most striking and important and generally useful ornament of speech. This subject may be more conveniently reserved for an Appendix. See Appendix B to Bk. III.

Ch. 3. From the virtues or excellences, we pass on in this chapter to the defects, of style. Faults of taste, τὰ ψυχρά, ψυχρότης, are exhibited in the use of compound words; of words archaic and foreign, or so obscure from their rarity as to require interpretation; of epithets, or ornamental and descriptive additions; and last but not least, of metaphors. These are all illustrated in detail, chiefly from the vicious compositions of Gorgias and his follower Alcidamas. The subject of metaphor is separately treated in Appendix B, at the end of this book: of the three remaining we will now say something.

On ψυχρόν in general, see Demetrius, π. ἑρμην. §§ 114—127. Vol. III. pp. 287—290 (Rhet. Gr. Spengel.). According to him it is the vice akin to, that is, the abuse or excess of μεγαλοπρέπεια; and is defined by Theophrastus, τὸ ὑπέρβαλλον τὴν οἰκείαν ἀπαγγελίαν; an inflated, stilted, bombastic, turgid phraseology, "which goes beyond the proper style of narrative." In Xenophon also, Symp. VI. 7, the term is applied to an expression a little too lofty for common conversation, for which Socrates apologises. In § 119, Demetrius compares it to ἀλαζονεία; καὶ καθόλου ὁποῖόν τί ἐστιν ἡ ἀλαζονεία, τοιοῦτον καὶ ἡ ψυχρότης· ὅ τε γὰρ ἀλαζὼν τὰ μὴ προσόντα αὐτῷ αὐχεῖ ὅμως ὡς προσόντα, ὅ τε μικροῖς πράγμασι περιβάλλων ὄγκον, καὶ αὐτὸς ἐν μικροῖς ἀλαζονευομένῳ ἔοικε. In § 116, Aristotle's fourfold division of ψυχρά is quoted from this chapter. In Latin ψυχρότης is represented by frigidum et insulsum. (Cicero and Quintilian). The origin of the metaphor appears in Quintilian, II. 4. 29; fastidium movere velut frigidi et repositi cibi; words and phrases that have lost all their savour, and become cold and insipid, "flat, stale, and unprofitable". And likewise in Demosthenes, c. Mid. p. 551, 13. ἑῶλα καὶ ψυχρά 'stale and cold'; of crimes that by this time have lost all their interest; and opposed to πρόσφατος, 'fresh'. A specimen of inflated phraseology, arising from the misuse of verba nova, prisca, duriter aliunde translata (harsh metaphors), graviora quam res postulat, is given by the Auct. ad Heren. IV. 10. 15.

διπλᾶ ὀνόματα, supr. c. 2. 5; Poet. XXI. 1, 2, where they are defined. They are compound words, [ἁπλᾶ is not confined to words of one syllable, Gräfenhan ad loc.] which may have either one member significant and the other not, or both significant. All the examples given in this chapter, probably with the exception of κατενορκήσαντας—a preposition being a σύνδεσμος is a φωνὴ ἄσημος, Poet. XX. 6.—are of the latter sort. The former means a compound word of which one of the elements has no *independent* signification, such as prepositions; if adverbs are ὀνόματα (See Append. A to Bk. III. not. 1.) words compounded with them must belong to the second class. Most of the examples quoted being compounded with adjectives fall also under the second class. By Quintilian, VIII. 3. 43, they are called *duplicia verba*, a phrase borrowed from Cicero, Orat. Part. c. 6, where the form is *duplicata*. On the frequent employment of these in dithyramb, see Philoxenus ap. Athen. XIV. 642. B.; and the note on Rhet. III. 2. 3. χρησιμωτάτη ἡ διπλῆ λέξις τοῖς διθυραμβοποιοῖς.

γλῶτται are, according to the definition Poet. XXI. 6. *foreign* words[1], in a particular sense; such as σίγυνον, a Cyprian term for a kind of dart; Plut. de Aud. Poet. c. 5. Also words 'obsolete' and 'archaic,' Dion. de comp. verb. c. 3. p. 15. (Reiske), where they are distinguished from ξένα: Galen. Interpr. gloss. Hippocr. (ap. Gräfenhan ad Poet. l.c.), ὅσα τοίνυν τῶν ὀνομάτων ἐν μὲν τοῖς πάλαι ἦν συνήθη, νυνὶ δὲ οὐκέτι ἐστί, τὰ μὲν τοιαῦτα γλώσσας καλοῦσι. Eustath. ap. eund. interprets it, ἀπεξενωμένην διάλεκτον: of this the two words put into the mouth of Gorgias, (Plato, Gorg. 450. B,) κύρωσις and χειρούργημα, are examples: the Scholiast remarks upon them, χ. καὶ κ. οὐκ εἴρηται· αἱ δὲ λέξεις Γοργίου ἐγχώριοι· Λεοντῖνος γὰρ ἦν. On voces inusitatæ, Cic. de Orat. III. XXXVIII. 153. Quintilian, I. 1. 35, interpretationem linguæ secretioris, quas Græci γλώσσας vocant. Ib. I. 8. 15, glossemata, id est voces minus usitatas. Putting all this together, it appears that the term γλῶτται includes all words that are so unusual, obscure, and little known, either from their being seldom employed, or because they have become obsolete, or belong to a foreign language or dialect, as to require a 'glossary', or explanation[2]. All the examples in

---

[1] This special application of the word γλῶττα may help to throw light upon the disputed question as to the meaning of γλώσσαις or γλώσσῃ λαλεῖν in Acts ii. 4. and the first Epistle to the Corinthians. There seems to be little doubt that it must mean in both, 'speaking in a foreign language, or foreign languages'. See Alford on Acts ii. 4. and Ep. I. to the Corinth. xiii. 1.

[2] αἱ μὲν οὖν γλῶτται ἄγνωτες. Rhet. III. 10. 2. Another reason for avoiding the employment of obsolete and little used words is given by Quintilian, VIII. 2. 12. It is that from their obscurity they carry with them the appearance of pedantry and affecta-

this chapter are of obsolete words, found only in the earlier poets. On verba inusitata as an element of ψυχρότης, compare Cæsar's maxim, in Aul. Gell. I. 10; quod a Gaio Cæsare in primo de analogia libro scriptum est, habe semper in memoria et in pectore, ut tanquam scopulum sic fugias inauditum atque insolens verbum. Gräfenhan, Gesch. der Philol. I. 187. in treating of this subject, points out how particular attention was directed to these γλῶτται by the teachers who instructed children in Homer. These drew up lists of obsolete words occurring in his text, with explanations (hence 'glosses', 'glossary') for the use of their pupils. Being contradistinguished from ὀνόματα κύρια, Poet. XXI., words belonging to the dialect in use at the time, they include also 'provincialisms', dialectical varieties (such as the word cited in illustration by Aristotle in the text,) and *may* thus be distinguished from 'barbarisms', or terms of a *foreign* language, ξενικά, ἐθνικὰ ὀνόματα. See also Ernesti, Lex. Techn. Græc. s.v.

ἐπίθετα from the examples here given (there are two more c. 2. § 14.) are not confined to what we now understand by 'epithets', single adjectives; but include any ornamental or descriptive addition to an ὄνομα κύριον. Quintilian describes them, VIII. 3. 43, as ad nomen adjuncta (from Cicero, Orat. Part. c. 6.), comp. VIII. 6. 29, where Tydides, Pelides, are epitheta. In VIII. 6. 40. they are called apposita: a nonnullis 'sequens' dicitur. Comp. Ib. § 43, where ille qui Nu-

tion. Obscuritas fit etiam verbis ab usu remotis; ut si commentarios quis pontificum, et vetustissima fœdera, et exoletos scrutatus auctores, id ipsum petat ex his quæ inde contraxerit, quod non intelliguntur. Hinc enim aliqui formam eruditionis affectant, ut quædam soli scire videantur. He proceeds to include technical terms of art, and dialectical and local peculiarities of phraseology. The use of archaisms is illustrated by Persius in a well known passage, Sat. I. 77.

Sunt quos Pacuvius et verrucosa moretur
Antiopa, ærumnis cor luctificabile fulta.

Well translated by Gifford,

Where in quaint tropes Antiopa is seen
To—prop her dolorifick heart with teen.

mantiam et Carthaginem evertit, is an 'epithet' of Scipio. See Ernesti, Lex. Techn. Græc. s.v.

Ch. 4. From the consideration of metaphors in c. 2., and their abuse c. 3., we proceed to that of the simile, εἰκών, which is a kind of metaphor with the addition of the particle of comparison; comp. III. 10. 3. A simile is in fact an expanded metaphor; as a metaphor is a contracted simile Cic. de Oratore III. 39. 157.; or a resemblance expressed in a single word. Quint. VIII. 6. 8, 9. In totum autem metaphora brevior est similitudo; eoque distat quod illa *comparatur* rei quam volumus exprimere, hæc *pro ipsa re* dicitur. Comparatio est cum dico fecisse quid hominem, ut leonem; translatio cum dico de homine, leo est. In consequence of this distinction, metaphor, translatio, is treated by the Auct. ad Heren. IV. 34. 45, under verborum exornatio; similitudo, simile, IV. 45. 59, under sententiarum exornatio. εἰκών, μεταφορὰ πλεονάζουσα. Demetr. π. ἑρμ. III. 284. (Speng. Rhet. Gr.) Similes therefore are to be derived from the same sources, and are subject to the same rules as metaphors, § 2; but they belong rather to poetry than prose, and even in the latter are to be used sparingly. Ib. The two may easily be converted the one into the other as occasion requires. A metaphor which has been approved can be converted into a simile, and similes which have gained a reputation and become favourites can be employed as metaphors, with the explanation or details omitted, (λόγου δεόμεναι): a simile is a metaphor 'writ large' with the details filled in; this is λόγος. § 3.

The concluding observation upon the use of metaphor, § 4, ἀεὶ δὲ δεῖ—φιάλην Ἄρεος, requires some special notice. Aristotle here says that "the proportional metaphor"—the last of the four kinds of metaphor, Poet. XXI. 7.—"must always correspond reciprocally (backwards and forwards,) from one to the other, and in words under the same genus." If you can with propriety call a goblet 'Dionysus' shield' (it stands to Dionysus 'in the same proportion' as the shield to

Ares, i.e. it is his characteristic appendage, and therefore the shield and the goblet both 'fall under the same genus', and are ὁμογενῆ, this *genus* being 'the characteristic appendage of a deity'; and so the two can be 'reciprocally transferred') then you can invert the application reciprocally, and call the shield Ares' goblet. This illustration of the 'proportional metaphor', is given again at full length as an exemplification of this kind of metaphor in Poet. XXI. 12, and also more briefly in Rhet. III. 11. 11. It certainly seems from the terms in which Aristotle refers to it that he approved of the metaphor. Tyrwhitt observes, in his note on the passage of the Poetics p. 175. (ed. 3. 1806.) that it was not received by all with equal favour. We learn from Athenæus, X. 433. D. that the author of it was Timotheus the famous dithyrambic poet of the 5th and 4th centuries B.C., and the great innovator in the dithyrambic style. Antiphanes, the contemporary poet of the middle comedy, had made a satirical allusion to the metaphor in a passage which Tyrwhitt has thus restored from the text of Athenæus, where the words are given in a corrupt and mutilated form.

—ᾔτει δ' ἥρως θ' ὅπλον·
φιάλην Ἄρεως κατὰ Τιμόθεον·
ξυστόν τε βέλος.

The metaphor became celebrated, and was imitated by later writers; see Casaubon, Comm. ad Athen. p. 728.

Another example of the proportional metaphor is given by Aristotle in Poet. XXI. 13. "what old age is to life that is evening to the day", and therefore evening and old age are ὑπὸ τὸ αὐτὸ γένος or ὁμογενῆ: the genus being, a waning or declining state, close, or latter end. Therefore they can be reciprocally transferred: we may call either old age the evening of life as Empedocles did, δυσμὰς βίου (and Æschylus, Agam. 1123. βίου δύντος αὐγαῖς, and Plato, Legg. VI. 867. ἡμεῖς δὲ ἐν δυσμαῖς τοῦ βίου), or the evening the old age of the day.

Demetrius περὶ ἑρμῆν. § 79, (Rhet. Gr. III. 280. Speng.) has a remark upon these passages of the Rhetoric and Poetics, which he evidently refers to though without naming them, to qualify the *too general* principle here laid down. The reciprocity is not uniform: οὐ πᾶσαι μέντοι ἀνταποδίδονται, ὥσπερ αἱ προειρημέναι, (from the 'resemblance,' for instance, of the general, pilot, and charioteer; that is, that they all fall under the same class or genus of 'guiders' or 'directors,' so that the one may be substituted for the other; we may call the commander 'pilot of the city', or the pilot 'ruler of the ship'.) ἐπεὶ τὴν ὑπώρειαν μὲν τῆς Ἴδης πόδα ἐξῆν εἰπεῖν τὸν ποιητήν, (Homer, Il. Υ. 59., πόδες πολυπίδακος Ἴδης. Β. 824. ὑπαὶ πόδα νείατον Ἴδης. He also speaks frequently of the 'knees', κνημοί, of Ida.) τὸν δὲ τοῦ ἀνθρώπου πόδα οὐκέτι ὑπώρειαν εἰπεῖν. Schrader, not. ad loc., gives another instance of non-reciprocity in this kind of metaphor: Sparta may be called one of the eyes of Greece, but an animal's eye cannot be called a Sparta.

The chapter concludes with the words, ὁ μὲν οὖν λόγος συντίθεται ἐκ τούτων. This observation which may easily be passed over, is significant, and marks a division of the subject. Hitherto we have been occupied with single words as ornaments of speech, which constitute the component elements of discourse. We now proceed to consider the requirements of style mainly in reference to construction, composition, arrangement of words in sentences, and their connexion; under the heads of (grammatical) purity, c. 5; dignity, c. 6; propriety, c. 7; rhythmical harmony, c. 8; the construction of periods, c. 9; liveliness, point and vigour, c. 10; vivacity of style, including witticisms, in continuation of the same subject, c. 11; and propriety in relation to different styles respectively suitable to the three genera of Rhetoric, c. 12.

Ch. 5. Accordingly, we next enter upon the second division of the subject λέξις, the combination namely of words in sentences, and the connexion of the latter in harmonious periods. And first of the origin or foundation, ἀρχή,—the first thing to be considered, the basis of all ornamental construction and expression, which are *subsequent*,—of all style, τὸ Ἑλληνίζειν, Ἑλληνισμός, Purity; pure emendateque loqui, Vict.; the opposite being σολοικίζειν. § 7. What is implied in Purity has been already pointed out (note on Purity, p. 279.). Aristotle distributes its contents under five heads: (1) the use of connecting particles and the proper connexion of sentences or clauses[1]: (2) the direct expression of our meaning by the simple and appropriate terms; the avoidance of pompous or vague periphrases, sua cujusque rei appellatio, Quint. VIII. 2. 1. proprietas. See the examples given in the two following sections, and compare VIII. 6. 59—61, on periphrasis, or circumlocutio; and Cicero, de Div. II. 64, quoted by Schrader: (3) the avoiding of ambiguous words and phrases—illustrated by Quintilian, VIII. 2. 6. Demetr. π. ἑρμ. §§ 196—202. on perspicuity—unless your object be to mystify or mislead; to disguise a lack of meaning, for instance, or as is the case with oracles, and the practice of diviners and soothsayers, whose intention is to conceal their meaning. These two last rules belong more properly to 'perspicuity'; and the former of them is referred to that head by Quintilian in the passage cited. The author of the Rhet. ad Alex. c. 26. 1. combines these two precepts in one brief rule, πρῶτον μὲν οὖν ὀνομάζω τοῖς οἰκείοις ὀνόμασιν ὅ τι ἂν λέγῃς, διαφεύγων τὸ ἀμφίβολον. (4) the due observance of the genders of nouns, as they were distinguished by Protagoras[2]; and (5) of (grammatical) num-

---

[1] On σύνδεσμος, see Appendix C, at the end of this book.

[2] ὡς Πρωταγόρας τὰ γένη τῶν ὀνομάτων διῄρει, ἄρρενα καὶ θήλεα καὶ σκεύη. This is commonly supposed to be the grammatical classification still in use, of masculine, feminine and neuter. I have endeavoured to show in the Cambridge Phil. Journal, No. VII. Vol. III. p. 48—50, that this is a mistake; the examination of a passage of the de Soph. El. c. 14. is made to lead to the conclusion, that the true interpretation of Protagoras' division is, that it is a classification founded not upon a grammatical, but upon a *real*, or natural, basis; and that ἄρρην, θῆλυς, σκεῦος, mean, not masculine, feminine, and neuter, but male, female, and inanimate. Ἄρρενα and θήλεα would therefore be confined to the designation of masculine and feminine *proper* names, and to words denoting distinctions of *sex* in men and animals,

ber. § 6. This classification, which is very imperfect, and seems to include two distinct and dissimilar things under one general head, is reducible to two heads, grammatical correctness or observance of the laws of language, and especially your own language, and perspicuity.

Again, a composition must be such as to be easily read, or, which is much the same, delivered—compare Quintilian, VIII. 2. 17—; and herein a due regard to punctuation is required: inattention to this is one of the causes of the extreme obscurity of Heraclitus' writings. Compare also Demetrius, π. ἑρμ. § 192. τὸ δὲ ἀσύνδετον καὶ διαλελυμένον ὅλον ἀσαφὲς πᾶν· ἄδηλος γὰρ ἡ ἑκάστου κώλου ἀρχὴ διὰ τὴν λύσιν, ὥσπερ τὰ 'Ηρακλείτου· καὶ γὰρ ταῦτα σκοτεινὰ ποιεῖ τὸ πλεῖστον ἡ λύσις. and Theon, Progymn. π. διηγήματος. § 187. (II. 82. Rhet. Gr. Spengel.) also Quintilian, VII. 9. 7., who exemplifies it[1]. This precept again belongs to Perspicuity.

Further, the 'solecism' is to be avoided of coupling a word with two others which can only with propriety be applied to

or to any conceptions, as God, to which sex could be attributed. σκεύη would include the names of all other objects, natural and artificial, real and abstract. This last class would comprise many words which *grammatically* are masculine and feminine, that is, which have the masculine or feminine article; ἃ κλῆσιν ἔχει ἄρρενος ἢ θήλεος. de Soph. El. l. c. This view is confirmed by the use of the term σκεῦος itself; which may stand very well to represent inanimate objects—see Plato, Soph. 219. A. Gorg. 506. D.—but not for grammatical neuters, οὐδέτερα; for a large proportion of names of σκεύη are masculine or feminine: ἀσκός, κλίνη, μάχαιρα, φιάλη, κερκίς, κάρδοπος κ.τ.λ. Aristotle's μεταξὺ ὀνόματα, Poet. XXI. de Soph. El. l.c.—see 173 b. 32 —appear to have the same signification. Alexander's commentary on the latter is entirely in favour of this view. Gräfenhan, Gesch. der Phil. § 25, Vol. I. p. 116, who mistakes the point, takes no notice of this.—It is of course not meant that Protagoras first distinguished male and female, but only that he first introduced the distinction into the analysis of language.

[1] No reader of Aristotle, who has suffered from his inattention to this very same essential of perspicuous writing, can fail to be amused with the naïveté and happy unconsciousness which he here shows in laying down a rule for others which he is constantly violating himself; and to such an extent, as to be a source of much obscurity in his writings; and in criticising others for a fault of which he is perpetually guilty: it is indeed a grave case of Satan rebuking sin.

one of them; as when ἰδεῖν is connected in construction with ψόφον as well as χρῶμα, instead of αἰσθάνεσθαι, which is common to both[1].

The last precept, which belongs likewise to perspicuity, is to avoid μεταξυλογία, i.e. the introduction of a number of details in the middle of a sentence, to the interruption of the construction, and the confusion and annoyance (Theon) of the hearers. [I refer here to Theon's Progymnasmata, in Speng. Rhet. Gr. Vol. II. p. 82, 3.] Quintilian calls this interjectio, VIII. 2. 15. He says it is a frequent fault of historians and orators, ut medio sermone aliquem inseruit sensum. It is in fact 'Parenthesis'[2].

Ch. 6. Treats of ὄγκος, "swelling," grand, majestic style, point or dignity of style, amplitudo, grandis oratio, Vict.[3].

---

[1] This form of violation of propriety, or of the laws of logic, or of syntax, which resides in the use of an inappropriate combination, is common enough in the Tragic poets; of whom Æschylus is the chief offender in this respect. What shall we say to ἐν' οὔτε φωνήν...ὄψει, Prom. Vinct. 22. or to κτύπον δέδορκα, Theb. 103 and elsewhere? Sophocles is nearly as bad with his δοῦπον κλύω in the Ajax, and ἀχὼ τηλεφανής. Philoct. 189. Other examples might be cited from Euripides and various prose authors—but, ecce iterum Crispinus, here we catch Aristotle again in flagrant delict, breaking his own rule; of which εὐόφθαλμον ἀκοῦσαι, Polit. II. 8., is a violation not to be surpassed in enormity. When it occurs in authors of credit it is called by the grammarians, not a blunder, but a figure: and this with the kindred σύλληψις, is illustrated at great length from Tacitus, by Bötticher in his Lexicon Taciteum, Proleg. pp. 87—90. I will only add two examples of this carelessness—for that is what it really is—from the elaborate and immaculate Isocrates, and that too from his most celebrated work, the Πανηγυρικός. See § 26, a glaring instance; and a still worse, § 80, καὶ σωτῆρες ἀλλὰ μὴ λυμεῶνες ἀποκαλεῖσθαι.

[2] It is the abuse and not the use of Parenthesis which is here in reality censured. As I myself have made great use of the figure throughout this Introduction, I feel bound to say on its behalf, that the use of it is very important and valuable, when you have a brief observation to make, too short for a note, and closely connected with the immediate subject; which it illustrates though it may not be essential, or, in a commentary, included in the text. It should therefore for the most part be employed in *explanation*, or *suggestion* of something arising immediately out of the subject.

[3] The word is frequently applied to style by the later writers on Rhetoric, to designate sometimes a beauty,

It presents a very near resemblance to σεμνότης; σεμνόν like ὀγκωδές is almost characteristic of epic poetry. This is called by the Auct. ad Heren. IV. 13. dignitas; and is described, quæ reddit *ornatam* orationem varietate distinguens: hæc in verborum et in sententiarum exornationem dividitur. This amplitude or dignity may be communicated to our style by the observation of the following rules. 1. To substitute the definition or description of a thing for the naked or direct and 'proper' term, ὄνομα κύριον: but if brevity be our object the reverse:—both of these are found in the Rhet. ad Alex. 23. 3—5., and perhaps come from Isocrates—or again if there be anything ugly, foul, indecent, disagreeable, or unbecoming in what we wish to express, if these qualities are inherent in the λόγος, i.e. in the conception or description, in the object described, or the associations suggested, we are to employ the direct designation; if in the term itself, the description. 2. To use metaphors and ornamental additions or 'epithets'; only not so frequently as to give a poetical character to our composition. 3. To use the plural for the singular, as the poets often do. 4. In combining adjectives or pronouns with substantives to write the phrase at full length, repeating the article; not to connect both together with one, non copulare vincireque uno articulo duos casus, sed utrique suum assignare. Vict. Conciseness requires the contrary method. 5. To add the copula, and avoid asyndeton. In concise writing omit the copula yet without asyndeton; πορευθεὶς διελέχθην, not πορευθεὶς καὶ διαλεχθείς, nor πορευθεὶς διαλεχθείς. 6. To employ for the purpose of amplification the device adopted by Antimachus[1], the poet of Claros, ἐξ ὧν μὴ ἔχει λέγειν; who in describing the Bœotian hill Teumessus, introduces first all the beauties and advantages which it does *not* possess: this process may be carried ad infinitum. This topic may be applied either to good or bad qualities, as the

sometimes a deformity, see Ern. Lex. Techn. Hermog. π. ἰδεῶν. II. 286 bis. and 341. Demetr. III. 287. 30 &c.

[1] On Antimachus see Schrader and Buhle's notes, Düntzer, Epic. Fragm. p. 99.

occasion requires. Similar to this is the use by the poets of privative epithets, which express the absence of some quality; as ἄχορδον or ἄλυρον applied to μέλος, of the trumpet[1]: and as some of them (Æschylus especially) qualify an over daring metaphor by the addition of one of these as Ζηνὸς ἀκραγεῖς κύνες, ἄναυδος ἄγγελος (of the dust). Compare Demetr. π. ἑρμ. III. 282 ἔνιοι δὲ καὶ ἀσφαλίζονται τὰς μεταφορὰς ἐπιθέτοις ἐπιφερομένοις, ὅταν αὐτοῖς κινδυνώδεις δοκῶσιν, ὡς ὁ Θέογνις παρατίθεται τὸ φόρμιγγα ἄχορδον ἐπὶ τοῦ τῷ τόξῳ βάλλοντος. κ.τ.λ. These words of Theognis are cited Rhet. III. 11. 11.

Ch. 7. Propriety in style, the subject of this chapter, is manifested mainly in two particulars, ἦθος and πάθος, both of them common to the Poet and Rhetorician, but less prominent and obtrusive in the works of the latter. They are therefore treated in the Poetics as well as here, but in them more elaborately and in greater detail, in proportion to the superior importance which they assume in Poetry. The ἤθη, so far as they belong to style, I have separated from the other two classes, and distinguished them as the 'dramatic' kind in a former part of this Introduction pp. 112, 13. In these the propriety is shown by representing each class and disposition, γένος καὶ ἕξιν, § 6, in its proper 'character'; that is, by assigning to each certain marks or signs, σημεῖα, which are usually characteristic of them in *language*, sentiments, and opinions: "for the man of education and refinement would neither use the same words, nor in the same

---

[1] This is an instance of 'a proportional' metaphor: ἐν ταῖς μεταφοραῖς ταῖς ἀναλόγον. The proportion is according to Vict. Trumpet : sound of trumpet (auonymous) :: lyre : μέλος (the proper name for the sound of the lyre). If therefore you substitute the second for the fourth, or the fourth for the second, you have a proportional metaphor. But to qualify the harshness of this substitution, from the want of similarity between the two sounds, the epithet ἄλυρον is added. Examples of the latter are extremely common in the Tragic poets. Æsch. P. V. 822. Ζηνὸς ἀκρ. κύνες 899. ἀρδις ἄπυρος. Διὸς πτηνὸς κύων. κῶμον ἀναυλότατον. Phœn. 818. θίασον ἀβάκχευτον. Orest. 319. μηνυτῆρος ἀφθέγκτου. Eumen. 245. ἀπτέροις πωτήμασιν, ib. 250.

way (ὡσαύτως, meaning probably both in pronunciation and association), as the clown or boor;" nor do men at different periods of life, in boyhood, manhood, and old age, nor the two sexes, nor the natives of different countries, Lacedæmonian and Thessalian, either speak or think alike. In the πάθη propriety manifests itself in the due adaptation of your language to the emotion that you intend to express in your 'appeals to the feelings' of the audience. Anger has one language and one set of words and a particular tone, compassion another, admiration and approbation a third, contempt one totally different, and so on for the rest. But in all these cases alike 'propriety' requires the observation of one rule, that the art be disguised; you must not by exaggerated or inflated language or by an undue lowering of the tone, allow your audience to discover that you are acting a part and trying to mislead them. When you have produced the impression that you are yourself under the influence of high passion or excitement, or when you have already excited your hearers to a state of passion or enthusiasm, you may then raise the tone of your expression to a high pitch, and use long and poetical words: men commonly use such language themselves when violently excited, and they construe your exaggerations as 'signs' of the real existence of the emotions which you are endeavouring to express.

So much for the general subject of the chapter; we will now proceed to consider some of the details.

Of Propriety, τὸ πρέπον, decorum. Cic. Orat. XXI. 70. aptum. Quint. I. 5. 1. apta oratio XI. 3. 30. quid aptum sit, hoc est quid maxime deceat in oratione. Cic. de Or. III. 55. 210. ad id quodcunque agetur apte congruenterque dicere Ib. III. 10. 37[1].

---

[1] In Poet. XXIV. 23. Ar. observes that elaboration of style should be reserved for the ἀργὰ μέρη of a composition; all brilliancy of *expression* interferes with the effect of passages in which the interest depends upon 'the thought' and character, διάνοια, and ἦθος. πάθος is omitted designedly; see Rhet. III. 7. 11.

This quality of style consists in a due proportion, ἀνάλογον, or accommodation of language to subject, as lofty to lofty, low to low; and also (which is in reality a subordinate part of the other) in the due representation by language of, or accommodation of language to, the character and emotions which the speech is intended to express. Cic. de Or. l.c. § 211.

What this 'proportion' implies, or what is implied by παθητικὴ λέξις, is explained in § 2[1]. This adaptation of language to the expression of emotion conveys an appearance of *reality to the* speech, comp. c. 16. § 10., even though it be purely artificial and uncalled for by the circumstances of the case, and so imposes upon the hearers; who because men really feel what the speech so graphically pourtrays under the alleged circumstances, argue from the truth of the delineation to the truth of the fact[2]: and besides this people always sympathise with the expression of feeling, whether real or assumed. And so the orators understanding what an effect the delineation of passion has upon the minds of an audience often try to overwhelm and confound them

---

[1] On ἦθος and πάθος in style, and what they mean, Cic. Orat. 37. § 128. affectus, including both, impart the entire spirit and soul to a speech, Quint. VI. 2. 7. 8. On the whole subject of ἤθη and πάθη, and their use in Rhetoric, see above p. 108. and foll. On the dramatic ἦθος comp. Poet. c. VI. 24. It is always indicative of the character or quality of the προαίρεσις. Rhet. II. 21. 16. III. 16. See also Poet. XV. 4. δεύτερον δὲ τὰ ἁρμόττοντα, κ.τ.λ. defined and illustrated by Alexander, π. σχημάτων, περὶ ἠθοποιΐας, 15. Rhet. Gr. (Spengel) III. 21. There is a full description and explanation of it in Rhet. III. 16. 8.

[2] The fallacy consists in assuming that because a given consequent follows a given antecedent, the consequent necessarily implies the antecedent, which is false, Poet. XXIV. 18. οἴονται γὰρ ἄνθρωποι κ.τ.λ. In the case before us the emotions represented do no doubt arise from the facts stated: but it does not follow that they may not arise from something else. The fallacy consists in the conversion, or assumption of the reciprocity, of antecedent and consequent. The language used *is* the ordinary sign of emotion, which *does* usually arise in men as a consequence of such facts as those alleged: the antecedent is then falsely inferred 'reciprocally' from the ordinary, but not universal or necessary, consequent.

with the noise they make, in assuming a tone of rage, terror, indignation, scorn and so on, [Vict. understands θορυβοῦντες in a transitive sense, 'tumultu in animis eorum excitato': this makes it almost synonymous with καταπλήττειν.] §§ 3— 5. Style may be made 'ethical', (this is connected with the preceding, Vict.) to represent character, morata oratio, by using language conformable to that of the class or disposition or character, that you wish to represent. Every class as boy, adult, old man, the different ages, sexes, countries are each characterized by a language of their own, and the same is true of moral and intellectual ἕξεις, virtue and vice; the brave and the timid, the wise man and the fool, the temperate and the licentious, the cultivated man and the boor, all use a different language and a different tone. However it is not the fact that all ἕξεις that give a definite character to life can be distinctly represented in speech. Physical and some intellectual 'states' must be excepted. §§ 3—7. The following remark πάσχουσι δέ τι...§ 7, is merely suggested by the preceding, and is added, in accordance with a not unfrequent practice of the author, as a parenthetical note, and so has no very close connexion with the general subject of the Chapter. It is in some sense, τρόπον τινά, an appeal to the feelings, in this way. It describes a trick for making an impression upon the hearers, πάσχ. τι οἱ ἀκροαταί, to which the λογογράφοι, those who write speeches in their closets for the use of others, (Victorius thinks that Isocrates, whose speeches are full of this artifice, is especially aimed at) have recourse to them usque ad nauseam, to a nauseous excess, κατακόρως. This is to appeal to the supposed universal belief or feeling upon some point which the author wishes to enforce upon his audience. The unsuspecting listener falls into the trap: takes for granted that mankind in general really do think and feel as the orator assumes, and not liking to stand alone in his views or sentiments accepts the speaker's assertion. § 7. The word κατακόρως, the nauseous excess into which some fall in the use of the preceding device, according to Victorius, suggests the following observation, which applies alike to all the previous rules of propriety[1], ἁπάντων τῶν εἰδῶν ἐστιν: that we must have regard, namely, to fitness of time and place in the use of every τόπος and every ornament of style. § 8. For every exaggeration or daring innovation, as in the use of language, every bold flight of imagination, every excess, as in dwelling unusually upon any point (this connects it with the preceding), the remedy or corrective (of the bad impression which may possibly be made on the audience) is to acknowledge it as a fault by anticipation; to apologise beforehand for the assumed error or extravagance. Quintilian's description, VIII. 3. 37, where he refers to this passage, reading προεπιπλήσσειν, is a complete commentary and illustration of this artifice. The sense of the words δοκεῖ γὰρ ἀληθὲς εἶναι...§ 9, is exactly rendered by Quintilian, 'in quo non falli judicium nostrum solicitudine ipsa manifestum est.' The hearer takes it to be all true and sound and right, ἀληθές, because he sees that it is deliberate; that it is not said at random, but has been carefully considered. § 9. The greatest care and pains are always requisite to give the speech a natural and unstudied character: the rule 'ars est celare artem' is of the utmost importance in effecting the end and object of a speech, persuasion or conviction. This applies equally to proportion, as an element of propriety. It has been laid down that a certain proportion of style, tone, and manner, to the subject is always to be observed: but this if carried too far will defeat its own object: the study will appear; and the suspicions of the hearer will be aroused. For instance, there is a proportion in the tone of voice and manner of delivery, the expression of the features and the action, to the words delivered: these however should not be employed all at once; if the words have a harsh sound, (σκληρὰ ὀνόματα are exemplified by Hermog. π. ἰδεῶν α'. 11.

[1] So Victor.; but perhaps it is still more general, and means, "is of universal applicability."

300 and 359. Rhet. Gr. Speng.) the voice and the features and all the rest should not be made to assume a harsh expression, or else the study becomes apparent (I suppose he means that it will appear affected and overdone): whereas if one or two of them are made to correspond, and the rest not, the same effect is produced, whilst the artifice escapes notice. This however is not to be understood to mean that we are to rush into the opposite extreme[1] (Schrader)—dum vitant stulti vitia in contraria currunt—and pronounce for instance harsh words in a soft voice, or vice versa, (or perhaps better as Vict., to use soft and mild language in describing harsh things and the reverse; in total violation of the precept of τὸ ἀνάλογον given in § 2); for this destroys the vraisemblance, the plausibility of the speech: and most of all if the language of passion be not accompanied with appropriate tone and gestures; for in that case no one would believe that the emotion is really felt: or if affecting or exasperating circumstances be described in cold and measured language, no effect at all by comparison will be produced. § 10. The use of compound words, of ἐπίθετα, of strange unusual or foreign words, is most suitable to the language of passion: a man in a passion may use language which would be affected and intolerable in one free from that emotion; or again such words may be employed when the orator has 'gained possession of', overmastered, his audience, and worked them up to enthusiasm; such is the language of inspiration; and being themselves in a state akin to this, they accept and approve of the terms appropriate to such a condition. This is also the reason why this style is suitable to poetry; for poetry is inspired. These words, uncommon and exaggerated, may likewise be em-

---

[1] If this is the right interpretation of the paragraph,—it is that of Vict. and Schrader, and I see no other—οὖν must be wrong. We want a restrictive or adversative particle, μέντοι, or something similar; not a continuative or inferential one. Can the οὖν and δέ after ἐάν in the two clauses have changed places?

ployed ironically: as Gorgias did. Arist. Pol. III. 1. 9. (see Schneider); and Plato in the Phædrus. 338. D. (bis).

Ch. 8. On Rhythm. Prose Composition should be neither metrical nor altogether devoid of measure or rhythm: when applied to practice and the affairs of common life a complete metrical structure makes a composition unnatural, and the manifest artificiality totally deprives it of all truth and reality, of all power of moving the feelings and producing conviction[1]. At the same time it diverts the attention of the hearers, who instead of attending to your statements or arguments are waiting for the recurring cadence of your rhythm; just as the children in the market place have got so accustomed to the invariable reply to the herald's proclamation, 'whom does the freed man choose for his patron or attorney?' that they chime in by anticipation with the usual burden of the song, 'Cleon'. The audience of the orator who speaks in metre are ready, like the children, to anticipate the close of the sentence § 1. On the contrary that which is altogether destitute of rhythm is like the formless infinite, which only takes shape and substance by the imposition of the definite form[2]; ($\pi\acute{\epsilon}\rho as$, the Pythagorean doctrine in Plato Phileb. 23. c. et seq. from whom this is borrowed.) but this form is rhythm, not metre: all that is indefi-

---

[1] See Longinus c. 4f. ap. Vict. Cic. de Orat. III. 57. 216. Orat. 62. 209.

[2] The $\mathring{a}\pi\epsilon\iota\rho o\nu$ is only $\delta\upsilon\nu\acute{a}\mu\epsilon\iota$ not $\acute{\epsilon}\nu\epsilon\rho\gamma\epsilon\acute{\iota}\varrho$ as Ar. expresses it. See Metaph. Θ. 6. 1048. b. 9. infiniti ea est potentia quæ nec progrediatur nec possit unquam progredi ad actum. Bonitz. $\mathring{a}\pi\acute{\epsilon}\rho a\nu\tau o\nu$, $\pi\epsilon\pi\epsilon\rho\acute{a}\nu\theta a\iota$, $\pi\epsilon\rho a\acute{\iota}\nu\epsilon\tau a\iota$ Vict. Mag. und Schrader all translate, terminari, finiri. But rhythm which is itself indefinite, see Quint. IX. 4. 50. and Böckh. de Metr. Pind. c. 3, cannot introduce a limitation in this sense, of bringing to a conclusion: this is the property of metre as distinguished from rhythm, Quint. l. c. If this translation be adopted, $\pi\epsilon\rho a\acute{\iota}\nu\epsilon\tau a\iota$ $\mathring{a}\rho\iota\theta\mu\hat{\varrho}$ $\pi\hat{a}\nu$, must mean that everything finite can be numbered, or everything that can be numbered is finite: but this seems not to agree with what immediately follows in the next clause. The translation in the text seems to me to make much better sense.

On the use of these rhythms in prose, Cic. Orat. 64.; who qualifies the exclusive preference of Aristotle for the Pæon.

nite, being beyond the grasp of our knowledge, is unpleasing: τῶν ἀπείρων πῶς ἐνδέχεται λαβεῖν ἐπιστήμην; Metaph. B. 4. 999. a. 27. It is number that imparts this definiteness to every thing (number represents law according to the Pythagorean conception); and the 'number' of composition is rhythm; of which metres are so many sections. § 2. Prose therefore must have rhythm, but not metre, which would convert it into a poem. This rhythm however is only to be carried to a certain point, and not to be carried systematically through the structure of the composition; the βάσεις must not be continuous. § 3. (This is explained by Hermogenes, Demetrius, and Cicero, quoted in Append. C.) Of rhythms there are three kinds; the heroic, iambic, and pæonic. (See further on this subject Append. C.) Of these the heroic is too solemn and dignified for prose, too remote from the language of common conversation (reading οὐ λεκτικός[1]) and wanting in harmony [this is referred by Gaisf. to Demetrius' specimen of spondaic rhythm. But on the one hand, the spondaic is the least common of the three varieties of heroic rhythm, dactylic, anapæstic, and spondaic, and therefore would be the least likely to be selected as the representative of the

[1] The reading οὐ λεκτικός, which suggests itself at once from a passage of Demetrius, π. ἑρμ. § 42. ὁ μὲν ἡρῷος σεμνὸς καὶ οὐ λογικός, and adopted by Victorius, is at first sight a most plausible emendation of Aristotle's text; but then ἁρμονίας δεόμενος, applied to the heroic measure, seems neither true in itself, nor in accordance with what is said of it elsewhere, as by Dionysius de Comp. Verb. quoted in the text. Gaisford's interpretation, who understands it of the 'spondaic' rhythm of Demetrius, limits most unnaturally and improbably the signification of ἡρῷος. Nor is the explanation, that when the heroic measure is said to be 'wanting in harmony', all that is meant is that its particular kind of harmony is not suited to prose, a more natural or probable interpretation of *those words*. We must have recourse to a parallel passage of the Poetics, IV. 19, for an emendation, adopted by Spalding, on Quint. IX. 4. 76., Bekker. and Spengel, καὶ λεκτικῆς ἁρμονίας δεόμενος. In the Poetics the passage runs, ἐξάμετρα δὲ ὀλιγάκις (people use in ordinary conversation) καὶ ἐκβαίνοντες τῆς λεκτικῆς ἁρμονίας: which corresponds so precisely with what Aristotle is *made to say* by the alteration in the Rhetoric, that there can be little doubt of its being the true reading. The emendation was originally proposed by Vinc. Madius and accepted by Tyrwhitt, ad loc.

entire class; and again, of this same rhythm, Dionysius, de Comp. verb. c. 18. p. 109, Reiske, says the very opposite: Δακτυλικὸς πάνυ ἐστὶ σεμνὸς καὶ εἰς κάλλος ἁρμονίας ἀξιολογώτατος]; the iambic on the other hand has the opposite defect; it is too colloquial and familiar, and below the dignity of the higher prose style[1]—Aristotle is still speaking of this measure as it appears in *prose:* no one would say that the iambic *verses* of Æschylus or Sophocles are wanting in dignity—and this appears from the fact that the Greek language even in common conversation falls naturally into the iambic measure. comp. Poet. IV. 19. The trochaic measure again is too lively light and tripping, (Poet. IV. 18.) and more suitable to the licentious buffoonery of the old Comedy[2]: this appears in the tetrameter as it was originally employed. These two constitute only one rhythm. There remains therefore the third, the Pæonic rhythm, which has been used by all Rhetoricians from the time of Thrasymachus[3], though none of them has defined it. It is closely connected with the two preceding rhythms, or ratios, λόγοι—lying in fact between the two, (Cic. Orat. 57. 191)—$1:1, \frac{3}{2}:1, 2:1$. The heroic and iambic are to be rejected for the reasons given above, and also because they are too 'metrical', too suggestive of the cadence of regular verse; the pæon, which does not alone constitute a metre or verse[4] (see Herm. El. Metr. p. 121), is free from this defect, and so obtrudes itself less upon the ear. Of the Pæons only one is employed, and that at the beginning of the sentence (so Vict.)[5], whereas

[1] Cic. Orat. LVII. 192.

[2] In comparing the trochaic tetrameter to the κόρδαξ or comic dance, Aristotle means to say that it wants steadiness, sobriety, and dignity. See the description of it by Donaldson in Dict. Antiq. p. 277. and Müller, H. Gr. L. XXVIII. 7. dignitatem non habet. Cic. Orat. LVII. 193. On the κόρδαξ see further Interpp. ad Arist. Nub. 540. Casaubon ad Theophr. Char. 6. περὶ ἀπονοίας. Harpocrat. s. v. κορδακισμός. Demosth. Olynth. II. p. 23, 13.

[3] Quint. IX. 4. 87. says he invented it.

[4] Pæon minime est aptus ad versum. Cic. Orat. 57. 194.

[5] Vater's suggestion that τελευτῶντες has dropt out before καὶ ἀρχόμενοι had occurred to me independently. Perhaps however καὶ alone may

of the two kinds[1], opposed to one another, ‿‿– and –‿‿, the former is adapted to the beginning, the latter to the end: for a short syllable at the end carries with it an appearance of incompleteness, and as it were mutilates the rhythm: the period should be broken off at a long syllable, and the end *marked*, not however by the copyist, as by a full stop or marginal note, marking the beginning or end of a sentence, παραγραφή[2], but by the rhythm coming to an abrupt and decided close.

Ch. 9. The Period[3].

So far of the harmonious flow of the sentence in respect of the distribution of the quantities of the syllables of which it is composed: the next thing that we have to consider is the structure of the sentence itself, in respect of the arrangement of its words and subordinate clauses. In this view there are two kinds of style[4], called severally εἰρομένη[5],

be so interpreted; "at the beginning as well" (as at the end).

[1] So Cic. de Or. III. 47. 183. Quint. IX. 4. 96.

[2] διὰ τὸν γραφέα, παραγραφήν, see Vict. note and Cicero quoted by him; and Ernesti, Lex. Techn. s.v. παραγραφή.

[3] On the Period, besides the authors hereafter to be quoted, see Dissen, Introd. essay to Dem. de Cor. p. XXIV.; p. XXXIV. on Arist. Rhet. III. 9. 4.; and on ἀντικειμένη λέξις, p. XL. seq.

[4] Dionysius, de adm. vi dic. in Demosth. init., distinguishes three varieties of style. First, that which is represented by Thucydides, the αὐστηρὰ λέξις or ἁρμονία, described at length by Dionysius, de Comp. Verb. c. 22. This is a rough, harsh, uncouth, awkward style, without neatness, smoothness, or careful construction, like a wall built of rough unhewn stones, thrown together without fitting or adaptation; and is characterised by exaggeration and affectation in ornament and construction. The second is the λιτὴ καὶ ἀφελὴς λέξις, the smooth, simple, easy style of Lysias and Thrasymachus. And the third lies between these, as a *mean*, μέση λέξις; it is the periodic style of Isocrates. See further on this subject in a paper 'on the Sophistical Rhetoric', in Camb. Journal of Philology, No. IX. Vol. III. p. 268. seq.

[5] The εἰρομένη λέξις, or 'jointed style' (Mure) is called by Demetrius (π. ἑρμ. περὶ περιόδων. § 12) διηρημένη, 'di*s*jointed', and a little farther on, διαλελυμένη, and διερριμένη, all implying the same want of connexion and coherence and systematic arrangement. Aquila, § 18, quoted by Gaisford, Not. Var., characterises this style by the terms, soluta, perpetua; as though it ran on for ever, having no natural termination. In Auct. ad Heren. IV. 11. 16, this loose kind of

and κατεστραμμένη, or ἡ ἐν περιόδοις λέξις. The first is the style of Herodotus and the earlier λογογράφοι, Cadmus, Acusilaus, Scylax, Hecatæus, Diogenes of Miletus, Charon, Hellanicus &c. (see Mure, Hist. of Gk. Lit. Bk. IV. cc. ii. iii.) In it the sentences and clauses are strung together, εἰρόμενοι, hang one from another, like the links of a chain, or the joints of a reed, or onions on a rope, with no other connexion than that which is supplied by the σύνδεσμοι, or connecting particles. This is compared by Aristotle to the ἀναβολαί or preludes of dithyrambs, in which the rambling, flighty, incoherent character of the modernised dithyramb[1] chiefly showed

composition, without any internal principle of cohesion, is called, dissolutum genus orationis, quod est sine nervis et articulis, ut hoc modo appellem fluctuans, eo quod fluctuat huc et illuc, nec potest confirmare neque viriliter expedire se. This is illustrated by an example: and the style opposed to it, the periodic, thus characterised: diffluit enim totus (sermo dissolutus) neque quidquam *comprehendens perfectis verbis amplectitur*. Isocrates περὶ ἀντιδ. § 184 has συνείρειν of 'concatenation'; and Demetrius applies the term συνείρεσθαι to the 'stringing together' of periods.

[1] ἀναβολαί. Arist. Pac. 827—831. Av. 1385. seq. where Cinesias is made to describe the present flighty and aerial state of his art. Pind. Pyth. I. 7. προοιμίων ἀμβολαί. Arist. Probl. XIX. 15. The Schol. on Aristoph. l.c. (referring to Homer, Od. a. 155.) explains it, as usual, τὰς ἀρχὰς τῶν ᾀσμάτων. Twining on Poet. note 17. p. 180, has this remark, "ἀναβολαί... meaning, I think, evidently, the long, irregular, *protracted*, Odes of the more modern dithyrambic poets; such as those of which he speaks in the Problem. For the word ἀναβολή here,

does not, I believe, signify exordium, procemium, as usually understood, but was probably the name by which these ᾠδαὶ μακραὶ καὶ πολυειδεῖς were distinguished, and opposed to the old and simple Dithyrambic *in stanzas*." I can see no reason for understanding the word here in this novel and unnatural sense: it is plain that the reason for singling out the commencement or prelude, and distinguishing it from the rest of the ode, in these passages in which the characteristics of the altered dithyramb are brought into notice, is that the ἀναβολή was *the* part of the ode in which these characteristics were most prominently displayed. Müller, Hist. Gr. Lit. c. XXX. § 3. seems to regard these ἀναβολαί as simply musical, without words.

The antistrophic dithyramb of Arion, Stesichorus, and afterwards of Pindar, was first relaxed in its structure, rhythm and musical accompaniment by Lasus of Hermione (flor. circ. B.C. 522.), by innovations which impaired its set, formal, systematic or antistrophic character. This relaxation was carried still farther by the 'Attic Dithyrambists' (i.e. of the Attic style or period, not native Athenians), Mela-

itself; whilst the regular dithyrambic chorus in its earlier antistrophic form, as used by Arion, Stesichorus, Pindar, is likened to the regular, organized, system of the periodic construction. The εἰρομένη λέξις, says Twining, on Poet. n. 17. p. 180, "has no other unity than that which copulatives give it, nor any other *measure* (i. e. rhythm) than the completion of the *sense*, and the necessity of taking breath[1]." As the type and exemplar of this style Herodotus is selected by Aristotle, Hecatæus of Miletus by Demetrius, π. ἑρμ. § 12. It is there described as ἡ εἰς κῶλα λελυμένη οὐ μάλα ἀλλήλοις συνηρτημένα. τὰ πλεῖστα τοῦ Ἡροδότου are also included.

The opposite to this is the periodic called by Aristotle κατεστραμμένη; a term adopted by Demetr. l. c., who refers

nippides of Melos [the *popular* judgment of this writer is given by Xenoph. Memor. I. 4. 3. and specimens of his style are to be found in Bode, Gesch. d. Hell. Dichtk. Vol. II. Pt. 2. p. 295. seq.]. Ion of Chios, Philoxenus, Cinesias, and Timotheus, at the end of the 5th and during the first half of the 4th century B.C. It seems from Aristoph. Pac. and Av. ll. cc. that the compositions of both Ion of Chios (Pac. 835) and Cinesias were distinguished by this rambling, incoherent, extravagant, character, and daring flights; Cinesias appears not only in Aristophanes' Birds, but also in Plato's Gorgias, 501. E, as a poet who wrote merely to give his hearers pleasure, without any regard to their instruction: and in the Nubes 333. the word ᾀσματοκάμπται is coined to designate the rhythmical and musical *variations* and twists and tricks and quavers of this new fangled poetry and music. Its authors and composers are fed by the Clouds, whom they celebrate in return. Philoxenus is parodied in the Plutus, 290. (Müller.) On this subject in general see Bode, Gesch. d. Hell. Dichtk. Vol. II. Pt. II. p. 111. seq. and 290. seq. and Müller's excellent account of these changes Hist. Gk. Lit. c. XXX. Aristotle, in Probl. XIX. 15., states the fact of these innovations, and accounts for them by the increasing fondness for imitation or mimicry, wherein he coincides with other writers. To this was due the dropping of the Chorus in Tragedy, and the recitation of the Dithyramb by single performers, because these alterations both lend themselves to imitation. He cites the parallel case of the abandonment of antistrophic construction in the tragic Monodes, or τὰ ἀπὸ σκηνῆς. The fragments of the Dithyrambs are to be found in Bergk's collection. Poet. Lyric. Gr. pp. 837—868.

[1] So Cicero, de Orat. III. 44. 175. 'ille rudis (orator) incondite fundit quantum potest, et id quod dicit spiritu non arte determinate.' Opposed to this is the εὐανάπνευστος λέξις of § 5.

directly to Aristotle. In a period the members are integral parts of one whole, having a relation to it and to one another The characteristic of the period, and that which distinguishes it from the εἰρομένη λέξις, is the organization of the sentence; the internal construction which adapts the several parts to one another so as to form a perfect whole[1] which has a beginning and end in itself, independently. (Arist.)[2]. This is expressed by κατεστραμμένη, 'compact, condensed, concentrated[3]', and implied in the definition of the period given by Demetr. u.s. σύστημα ἐκ κώλων κ.τ.λ.; and likewise in the description given of it by Dionysius, de Lys. Jud. 6, ἡ συστρέφουσα τὰ νοήματα καὶ στρογγύλως ἐκφέρουσα. The character ascribed to this construction of sentences by the term περίοδος is that of a definite self-containing completeness[4]: a 'circuit' is complete in itself, like a circle; when a man makes a circuit he comes round again to his starting point[5]. So we speak of 'rounding' our sentences. Referring to the passage of Dionysius, Müller says, Hist. Gk. Lit. XXXVI. 5. note, "what is meant by the στρογγύλον appears clearly from the example given by Hermogenes from Demosthenes (Hermog. π. εὑρεσ. περὶ περιόδου. II. 240. Speng.); such a sentence is like a circle which returns necessarily into itself." But the circle of the period is not only complete and independent, but also comprehensive. This character appears especially in the Latin equivalents, circumscriptio, comprehensio verborum[6]. It is likewise called ambitus verborum, circuitus, continuatio[7], Cic. Orat. § 204. comp. §§ 38, 208: the two former exactly

---

[1] So Dion. de comp. verb. c. 2 calls it ἁρμονία λόγου.

[2] Demetr. on this defin. εὐθὺς γὰρ ὁ τὴν περίοδον λέγων ἐμφαίνει ὅτι ἦρκταί ποθεν καὶ ἀποτελευτήσει ποι καὶ ἐπείγεται εἰς τὸ τέλος, ὥσπερ οἱ δρομεῖς ἀφεθέντες.

[3] Similarly, Dion. Ars Rhet. 5 § 6. contrasts ἀπαγγελία συνεστραμμένη with διῃρημένη.

[4] αὐτοτελές. Hermog. π. περιόδου. π. εὑρεσ. τομ. δ'. II. 240. Speng. Rhet. Gr.

[5] ἔνθεν καὶ περίοδος ὠνομάσθη, ἀπεικασθεῖσα ταῖς ὁδοῖς ταῖς κυκλοειδέσι καὶ περιωδευμέναις· Demetr. u.s.

[6] Cic. de Orat. III. 51. 198. circuitum et quasi orbem verborum.

[7] Compare Quint. IX. 4. 22 who adds conclusio, and IX. 4. 124.

render the Greek περίοδος. Demetrius π. ἑρμ. l. c. has a very happy comparison of the period to a vaulted roof or dome, περιφερὴς στέγη, in which the several clauses or κῶλα are represented by the stones which by their mutual resistance and pressure upon the centre join in supporting and keeping the whole together: the διαλελυμένη ἑρμηνεία, 'loose, incoherent, style' is compared to stones lying near one another scattered and uncombined. ὥσπερ γὰρ σεσωρευμένοις ἐπ' ἀλλήλοις τὰ κῶλα ἔοικε, καὶ οὐκ ἔχουσι σύνδεσιν οὐδ' ἀντέρεισιν, οὐδὲ βοηθοῦντα ἀλλήλοις, ὥσπερ ἐν ταῖς περιόδοις[1]. Hermogenes π. εὑρεσ. τομ. δ'. has a chapter on the structure of the Period and its κῶλα. Harris, Phil. Inquiries Pt. II. ch. 4 thus illustrates the difference of the two styles. No sentences, he says, are so pleasing as the period. The reason is, that while others are indefinite, and like a geometrical right line may be produced indefinitely, the Period like a circular line is always circumscribed, returns and terminates at a given point, &c. See the excellent observations on the period in Campbell's Phil. of Rhet. Bk. III. c. 3. § 3'. See also Whately, Rhet. ch. III. p. 286. a. (Encycl. Metr.), who shows how the periodic construction was better adapted to the ancient than to the modern languages.

This εἰρομένη λέξις, to return to Aristotle, § 2, is the style of all the old writers of the age of Herodotus[2] and earlier, but is no longer employed by many. It may be defined 'that which has no end in itself but runs on until the sense comes

---

[1] Of the 'soluta oratio', Quintilian says, that its membra...insistere invicem (this is Demetrius' ἀντέρεισις.) nequeunt. VIII. 5. 17.

[2] Campbell admirably illustrates the construction of a period by the following example. "At last, after much fatigue, through deep roads and bad weather, we came with no small difficulty to our journey's end."

[3] Ἡροδότου Θουρίου. Wesseling's note, to which Gaisf. refers, merely says, after quoting Aristotle, that some had on his authority altered the text in Plut. de Exil. p. 604 and de Malig. Herod. p. 868 to Θουρίου. That Herodotus might properly be called a Thurian from his having joined the colony sent there, and there finished his history, as Strabo tells us XIV. p. 970.

Demetr. π. ἑρμ. III. pp. 264, 272. Ed. Speng. in quoting the same words has Ἀλικαρνασσῆος, as in our texts. It is doubtless one of Aristotle's ordinary slips of memory in quotation.

to an end.' It is therefore disagreeable by reason of this indefiniteness; for every one is anxious to see the end: and this is why runners in a race do not pant and gasp and become exhausted till they are close upon the goal; for up to that time, having the goal constantly in view they are insensible of the fatigue[1]. §§ 1, 2. In the κατεστραμμένη or periodic style the definition of the period is, a sentence that has a beginning and end in itself, independent, and a magnitude that can be taken in at one view[2]. This style is pleasing, because it is definite or finite; the other being indefinite or infinite, perpetua, running on for ever: and also for the reason that the listener is always fancying he is grasping or getting hold of something, because he finds something constantly concluded; whereas in the infinite continuity and incoherence of the other style there is nothing to lay hold of, nothing to get a previous conception of—as in a period you look forward to the end of

---

[1] Victorius I think altogether misunderstands this passage. The καμπτήρ in his view is not the goal, but the *turning point* of the δίαυλος, from which the goal cannot be seen. Consequently, *tunc* omnes vires contendunt, they put out all their strength, et ita spiritum effundunt et anhelant, ut prope dissolvantur (so he interprets ἐκπνέουσι καὶ ἐκλύονται). As I am not quite sure that I understand his meaning I will give the explanation in full in his own Latin. "et ita spiritum effundunt et anhelant, ut prope dissolvantur, quod ab ipsis antea non fit, quia ipsum (finem) cernant." That is, that the loss of the sight of the goal, makes them pant and almost melt away, which did not happen as long as they had it in view. But in the first place, if the race was over the double course, as V. supposes, they would *not* see the goal until they had passed the καμπτήρ; and secondly, it may be questioned whether this be true as a matter of fact. And thirdly it does not give the right interpretation of ἐκπνέουσι and ἐκλύονται; nor, I think, (here) of καμπτήρ, and the entire illustration. The general conception suggested by reading over the passage is plainly this: that the runners have the goal in sight from the very beginning of the race; consequently, having the goal or end always before them, they keep up their spirits and their efforts till they reach it; and it is not till then that they flag and grow faint. The καμπτήρ is the turning point of the δίαυλος, but the *goal* of the στάδιον or *single* race: it may therefore stand for *either;* and this is the explanation of the familiar tragic phrases, κάμπτειν βίον, and καμπτήρ βίου (where it stands for τέρμα), 'to reach the goal, i. e. the end of life'.

[2] On the length admissible in a period, see Hermog. and Demetr. ll. cc.

the sentence, and seize it by anticipation before it is concluded —nothing to accomplish or finish, get done, (ἀνύειν). It is also easy to learn, because as its symmetrical structure can be measured by number, (in § 6 he calls this its μέτρον, 'measure',) which is the easiest of all things to keep in memory, so also is the period: and this is why verse or metre is so much more easily recollected than prose. The period must contain a complete and entire sense; and that and the period must be brought to a close together. The sense must be left incomplete till the close of the period—the period must not be broken off before the sense *is* complete, which would lead to all sorts of blunders and misapprehensions—as for example in the opening lines of Euripides' Meleager (Sophocles is a slip of the author's; 'a name, not being a number', as Aristotle himself would have said, 'is less easily recollected'), if we were to put the full stop, break off the ' period', at the end of the first line, we should suppose the author to mean that Calydon is in the Peloponnesus. §§ 3, 4. The period may be either simple, consisting of only one member, μονόκωλος; or complex, of several. Quint. IX. 4. 124, 5. The limit assigned to the length of the period by the Greek Rhetoricians is four κῶλα; Quintilian allows a greater number. The period which consists of more than one 'member' must be complete in itself (as above described); its parts must be distinct and definite; and such as not to embarrass the author in the delivery by undue length or complication, εὐανάπνευστος; this latter quality must not depend upon a mere arbitrary division, like that of the lines of Euripides above-mentioned, but must have reference to the entire period, and must be effected by a proper arrangement of its several subordinate parts. The κῶλον is a part or member of this[1]. These and

---

[1] On the κῶλα in the construction of the period see Hermog. l. c. and Demetrius l. c. κῶλον is briefly defined by the former, ἀπηρτισμένη διάνοια, 'a completed sense'; and their arrangement in the construction of the period well illustrated. No period should have more than four. (Quint. IX. 4. 124 admits more). This is implied by Hermogenes, and expressed

the periods must be neither too long, nor truncated or stunted, docked or maimed, i. e. coming abruptly to a conclusion. An undue brevity gives an unpleasant check to the listener, pulls him up too short—he feels balked—and almost brings him on his knees, as it were: because he has involuntarily formed in his mind a notion of the proper measure; and when he is suddenly pulled back as he is hurrying on to his foregone conclusion, like a horse or man suddenly checked in mid career, by the sudden cessation of the sentence, is, as it were, nearly brought on his knees to the ground. Those which are too long, on the other hand, leave the hearer

---

by Demetrius αἱ μέγισται δὲ ἐκ τεττάρων. Aristotle's ἀφελής is expressed in Dem. by ἁπλοῦς: he gives as an example, the first sentence of Herodotus' history, 'Ηροδότου......ἀπόδεξις ἥδε; and adds ἡ γὰρ σαφὴς φράσις πολὺ φῶς παρέχεται ταῖς τῶν ἀκουόντων διανοίαις.

The distinction of κόμμα and κῶλον is given by Hermogenes in his next chapter περὶ πνεύματος. It rests according to him merely upon the comparative length of the two; each of them being an ἀπηρτισμένη διάνοια. The difference is illustrated by a passage of Demosthenes, q. v. This subject is much better treated by Quintilian, IX. 4. 122. 123. His division is, membrum, incisum, periodus, or circuitus. The incisum, which most define merely as a part of the membrum, is according to him, a complete sense in which however the numbers or rhythm are not yet complete: the membrum is a complete sense, and a complete rhythm; but although absolutely and per se it has a complete sense, in relation to the entire period and the entire meaning which the author has in view it is incomplete. It is like a limb severed from the body: it is perfect in itself *as a limb;* but as it is intended to form part of a given whole, the body, relatively to this it is incomplete and meaningless. One need hardly observe that our names for the 'stops' in punctuation, comma, colon, period, are borrowed from these Greek names of sentences and their subdivisions, of which they *mark* the conclusion. The Latin equivalents are membra and incisa. Cic. Orat. § 211. Quint. IX. 4. 22 and 122. The auct. ad Heren. IV. 19. 26, seems, like Aristotle, to include both under membrum; which is defined, res breviter absoluta sine totius sententiæ demonstratione; and illustrated by short clauses which Hermogenes would have called κόμματα; et inimico proderas; et amicum lædebas: the sentence, 'et inimico proderas, et amicum lædebas, et tibi ipsi non consulebas,' consists of three membra. Longinus, ars rhet. π. λέξεως. I. 309. Speng., introduces a third subdivision, περικοπή. The κόμμα consists of two or three words only; the κῶλον is double of this in length; and the περικοπή includes two or three κῶλα.

behind, in the lurch; as when people are walking (as the Greeks took their exercise) in the porticoes of a gymnasium, backwards and forwards; if one of the party goes beyond the ordinary bounds, the rest are left behind; so the hearer having the proper measure of the period in his head—this is the 'limit' of the exercising ground—if the orator exceeds that, stops short, as it were, and is left behind. These overlong periods become entire speeches (orationes Vict.), and as rambling and incoherent as the ἀναβολαί. And so, as the old joke of Democritus against Melanippides has it, when he exchanged the old antistrophic dithyramb for the modern ἀναβολαί, they become like all evil counsels and inventions, most mischievous to their author. The 'joke' consists in the substitution, in a line of Hesiod, of μακρὰ ἀναβολή for κακὴ βουλή, and cannot be represented in English. Those of which the members are excessively short make no period at all; and so, accordingly (οὖν) they hurry on the audience at a headlong break-neck pace; the audience as we say is carried away by them[1]. §§ 5, 6.

Of periods consisting of more than one member there are two kinds; one in which the parts are balanced contrasted set over against one another; opposed, ἀντικειμένη; the other in which there is no such opposition or connexion by way of contrast, but the members are merely divided, and unconnected in this sense. The latter is passed over in silence as requiring no further notice. The antithesis of the former may be conveyed in two ways: either by balancing opposite by opposite in the two contrasted members; or by uniting two opposites as it were under the vinculum of a single word, as two opposite substantives or participles by a verb. Both

---

[1] The quotation from Cicero, in Quint. IX. 4. 122, may serve as a specimen. Domus tibi deerat? at habebas. Pecunia superabat? at egebas. This illustrates the general principle, though it is not strictly speaking a period. Of course the rapidity of style is in proportion to the shortness of the members of which it is composed. Abiit, excessit, erupit, evasit, is another example. A colon, in its wider sense, may consist of a single word, as diximus.

of these varieties are illustrated by an example taken from Isocr. Paneg. 47. D. Antithesis is further exemplified by a string of instances taken with one exception from Isocrates' Panegyricus, § 7. The source of the pleasure which we derive from this figure is to be sought in that principle of our nature which leads us to desire above all things the acquisition of knowledge. (See the reff. on c. 10 § 2). For opposites when brought into contrast and placed alongside of one another are more easily recognised, and their nature better understood. Further we like it, because it bears a resemblance to one form of syllogism, the ἔλεγχος (see the analysis of II. 25), which also places opposites (opposite conclusions) side by side for the purpose of comparison; and so it wears to us the appearance of a sort of proof. παρίσωσις, another figure introduced into rhetoric by Gorgias, and adopted by his pupils and followers, consists in the equality, in point of length, of two contrasted members of a period. This is commonly called ἰσόκωλον; and is made by Demetrius (III. 267. Rhet. Gr. Spengel) a branch of παρόμοιον. It is illustrated by an example from Thucydides, in which the number of syllables in the contrasted members is precisely equal. παρομοίωσις, also introduced by Gorgias and his school, is defined by Aristotle, 'a figure which makes the extremities of two members resemble one another in sound'; when it occurs at the beginning the similarity is found in the entire words. The figure is usually called ὁμοιοκάταρκτον when the beginning is similar, ὁμοιοτέλευτον when the similar sound is at the end. This latter may be effected either by syllables, one or more, of the same sound; or by a πτῶσις, inflection, of the same word ; or by repeating the same word. All these are exemplified. These three figures, antithesis &c. may all occur in the same sentence, of which Demetrius u. s. p. 266 supplies a very complete example from Isocrates' Helen. § 17[1]. Lastly antithesis may be false ; as in the line

[1] Theophrastus, ap. Dion. de Lys. Jud. c. 12, has a more complete classification of the varieties of antithesis. ἀντίθεσις δ' ἔστι τριττῶς, ὅταν τῷ αὐτῷ

of Epicharmus, written in ridicule of the Sicilian rhetoricians his countrymen: so Demetrius, u. s. p. 266., who quotes the same line.

Ch. 10. The two following chapters treat of the means by which the liveliness and point and vividness which give an interest to composition and secure general applause may be imparted to style. These are, τὰ ἀστεῖα[1] and τὰ εὐδοκιμοῦντα. The sources of these are found to be three; metaphor[2], antithesis, and ἐνέργεια[3]. The last consists in placing

τὰ ἐναντία, ἢ τῷ ἐναντίῳ τὰ αὐτά, ἢ τοῖς ἐναντίοις τὰ ἐναντία προσκατηγορηθῇ. Victor. in his note on the passage of Aristotle thinks, that the two divisions may be identified. Theophrastus (in the same passage) has also some remarks on the use and abuse of the two figures παρίσωσις and παρομοίωσις; and Demetrius, περὶ ὁμοιοτελεύτων. (Rhet. Gr. III. 267. Speng.)

The author of the Rhet. ad Alex. treats of these three figures in cc. 27, 28, 29. The names and definitions that he gives them are nearly identical with those of Aristotle: the difference, which is but slight, is in the name and definition of the 3rd.

Quintilian, IX. 3. 75—80, treats of παρίσωσις and παρομοίωσις. 81—86 of ἀντίθετα, which he calls contraposita, distinguishing several species. The two first he refers to the general head of similia, and divides them into four species: 1. which he calls πάρισον quotiens verbum verbo simile, aut non dissimile valde, quaeritur. This may occur (apparently) in any part of the sentence. Others however refer πάρισον to *members* not dissimilar. 2. ὁμοιοτέλευτον. 3. ὁμοιόπτωτον similar (grammatical) cases in corresponding clauses. 4. ἰσόκωλον, membra aequalia, clauses of equal length.

For further illustrations, and references to various authors on this subject, see Camb. Journ. of Phil. No. VII. pp. 69—72, where these figures are classified.

[1] ἀστεῖα, 'graces of style,' 'clever things,' in general, is rendered by Vict. voces urbanae, sermo lepidus, voces acutae et elegantes. faceta oratio, Spengel on Rhet. ad Alex. c. 22. (23). In these two chapters of this author and Aristotle it seems to signify not 'wit' merely, nor 'grace' nor 'ornament,' but rather 'pungency, point, liveliness, sprightliness of style,' which keeps up the interest of an audience and relieves the weariness of long sustained attention. The directions for attaining to it are widely different in the two authors.

[2] With ἀντίθεσις παρίσωσις is afterwards included as an instrument for imparting vivacity to style, c. 11. § 10.

[3] ἐνέργεια has here its proper sense, as usually employed in Aristotle's philosophical terminology. It is actus, actuality of existence or actualisation of action, as opposed to dormant latent potential existence or capacity of action which is expressed by δύναμις. This actuality is exhibited in style by placing objects before the listener as living and moving, growing (as plants),

objects before the mind's eye πρὸ ὀμμάτων (the two are identified in c. 11 § 2. and c. 10. § 6.), as though they were living and moving; in representing things as actually going on instead of about to take place; which appears from the examples in the next chapter, § 3. This quality appears especially in endowing inanimate objects with life and motion. The source of the pleasure which we derive from style is, as usual, the gratification of the desire of knowledge instinctive in the human mind. § 2. All words therefore and figures or combinations of them which seem to convey some knowledge easily are the most agreeable and the most highly approved. Now γλῶτται have no significance at all to us, and the common terms by which objects are designated, κύρια, we know already. Of single words therefore there remain only metaphors; as when old age is compared to a dry stalk or stubble, 'the sere and yellow leaf,' we learn by means of the genus that both are withered, have lost their bloom and are fallen into decay. Poets' similes have the same effect: only not in the same degree, since they are longer and therefore less pointed: and besides they do not assert directly that one thing *is* another, and so the mind makes no inquiry into the matter. In the same way rhetorical arguments are pointed lively or interesting which convey information rapidly. §§ 2, 3. And for this reason, he adds by way of a note, neither superficial enthymemes are popular, because they are already obvious to every body; nor those which when stated are not understood; but those in which the new information comes simultaneously with, or only a little after, the statement of them. This last remark has reference to the sense or meaning of words, with which we are not here concerned. § 4. Returning now to the proper subject of the chapter, § 5, he observes that of figures of

and fulfilling the functions of animated beings, c. 11. § 2: or again, events and occurrences as in the course of actual transaction, πραττόμενα, instead of describing them in their undeveloped δύναμις as future, c. 10. § 6. This latter is well illustrated by c. 16, 7. Πραττόμενα admit of vivid description, so as to produce ἔλεος or other emotions.

speech, belonging to structure or composition, antithesis has most of the quality in question; of single words metaphor; and thirdly ἐνέργεια or vivid representation. § 6. The rest of the chapter is devoted to the exemplification of this quality in metaphor, and a number of famous examples are cited, which like Pericles' sayings had "left their sting behind them" in men's memory. It appears that the fourth kind of metaphor, the proportional, is most applauded. Aristotle is here treading on much the same ground as in c. 2., where he gave directions for the use of metaphors, pointing out what is to be sought after and avoided in the invention of them, and the sources generally from which they may be most advantageously derived. He is no doubt in the present chapter rather giving examples of notable metaphors, than rules for forming them; and his excuse for dwelling so much upon this particular subject throughout the first division of this book, is that the metaphor is, as all writers on Rhetoric acknowledge, by far the most striking and important of the ornaments of style,—that in which the ability and taste of the writer most display themselves. § 7.

Ch. 11. In pursuance of the same subject, we have now to explain more fully what we mean by the expression πρὸ ὀμμάτων ποιεῖν, and how it is to be effected. The phrase is in fact equivalent to ἐνεργοῦντα ποιεῖν, and implies a representation of things as living, moving, growing in *actual* existence: thus to call a man τετράγωνος is a metaphor, since it implies completeness, but this carries with it no ἐνέργεια: but to say that he has his vigour, all his powers "in full bloom" does so, because the metaphor is derived from the *growth* and *flourishing* of a plant. This is further illustrated by several examples from Homer, in all of which animation and active powers are ascribed to inanimate objects. §§ 1—4. The similitudes of metaphor are to be sought in things proper and appropriate to the object which is to be represented by the metaphor (c. 2. §§ 9, 12. c. 10, 4, 6. c. 11, 10.); and yet the point of similarity must not be so plain and evident that no one can help seeing it. It is in this choice of metaphor that the sagacity or cleverness and natural ability, εὐστοχία, εὐφυΐα, of the speaker are principally shown; just as the philosopher shows *his* ability in tracing resemblances in the most dissimilar things when engaged in collecting facts subservient to an induction, or to the formation of a general conception or idea. (The latter process is well illustrated by Plato, Symp. 211.) Examples of this are given, § 5.

Most of the point and vivacity of style is imparted by metaphor, which often includes a sort of temporary deception practised upon the listener; who is imposed upon for a time, as it were, by the similitude in which he does not at once trace the resemblance; and is therefore all the more struck with it, it becomes more unmistakeably evident to him that he has learnt something which he did not know before, when he discovers the meaning[1]. He seems to say to himself—"*So* it is; and I missed it! and I never thought of it!" It is to this source that Aristotle with the greatest acuteness traces the pleasure that we derive from riddles; whether they are expressed in the form of Stesichorus' apophthegm[2], or as regular enigmas; from jokes παρὰ προσδοκίαν, or παρ' ὑπόνοιαν[3] (so numerous in Aristophanes), which take you by

---

[1] παρὰ τὸ ἐναντίως ἔχειν, "from *its* being contrary to what he expected," i.e. *when he missed the point*. The phrase is interpreted by Victor of the hearer himself, who finds himself now, after he has recovered from his first suspicion, "in the opposite state" to that in which he was before.

[2] ἀπόφθεγμα, 'a terse pointed saying,' Vict. acutæ voces, specially characteristic of the Lacedæmonians, τὰ Λακωνικὰ ἀποφθέγματα, Rhet. II. 21. 8. see Xenoph. Hellen. II. 3. 56., and Plutarch's collection. ἀπόφθεγμα is a γνώμη, minus the universality and the moral purpose.

[3] παράδοξον is illustrated by Quint. VIII. 5. 15, by a couple of examples. He calls the figure ex inopinato. Demetr. π. ἑρμ. III. 296. gives specimens from Homer, Od. 369. Οὕτιν ἐγὼ πύματον ἔδομαι, and Arist. Nub. 179, ἱμάτιον ὑφείλετο, Cic. de Orat. II. 63. 255. 70. 284. jocus præter expectationem; which *he* also illustrates. The source of the amusement derived from jokes παρ' ὑπόνοιαν or παρὰ προσδοκίαν, is the surprise they cause by an 'unexpected (ἀπροσδόκητον) turn given to the sentence or sentiment. As a modern example of it may be quoted Erskine's formula of reply to all applications for subscriptions for charitable purposes. Sir, I beg to ac-

surprise; and from all verbal jests, puns, and plays upon words. These plays upon words, verbal witticisms, are included under the general name of παραπεποιημένα[1], in which the παρά implies 'perversion,' or simple 'change,' turning or twisting aside from the proper and apparent sense. Of παραπεποιημένα, τὰ παρὰ γράμμα σκώμματα[1], or jokes that depend upon a change of letter, [or upon an ambiguity occasioned by using the same word in two different senses],

knowledge the honour of the receipt of your letter, and to subscribe (here the reader had to turn over the page) myself your obedient servant &c. Rogers' Table Talk.

Another is Rogers' own memorable epigram on Lord Dudley,
They say he has no heart, but I deny it;
He *has* a heart—and gets his speeches by it.

When the Rev. Sydney Smith during his last illness was recommended by his medical attendant to "walk upon an empty stomach", he gave an 'unexpected', but not unpleasant, 'turn' to the prescription by whispering, "whose?"

[1] From the analogy of παράσημος, παρακεκομμένος, Aristoph. &c. and παραποιεῖν itself, which is to 'counterfeit, forge, falsify,' in Thuc. I. 132. and Athen., 513. A., παρὰ γράμμα is interpreted by Vict. cavillationes quæ mutatis litteris fiunt; and similarly παραπεποιημένα are, nomina ad risum excitandum leviter immutata; and so Ern. Lex. Techn. It might mean also 'jokes that depend upon the letter': παρὰ 'in accordance with'; where the jest lies in the letter, rather than in the spirit, or meaning, διάνοια. παρονομασία is called by Auct. ad Heren. IV. 2. 29. adnominatio (so Quint. IX.

3. 66) quum ad idem verbum et ad idem nomen acceditur commutatione unius litteræ aut litterarum, aut ad res dissimiles similia verba accommodantur. All the examples involve merely a similarity of sound, which is effected in various ways by change or addition &c. of letters, just as in the Greek. It is to be observed that the writer is not here defining the meaning of παρά in the original word—in fact παρονομασία is not mentioned at all—but simply describing or illustrating its acquired sense. Quintilian seems to understand the word in two different senses. In IX. 3. 80 he identifies it with ὁμοιοτέλευτον, and illustrates it by the jingle of patrimonium and matrimonium; in IX. 3. 66, when he calls it adnominatio, the application seems quite different; though it *may* possibly be included under similarity of sound. See also Hermog. π. ἰδεῶν. II. 367. Speng. Rhet. Gr. Alterum genus est (ridiculi) quod habet parvam verbi immutationem, quod in littera positum Græci vocant παρονομασίαν, ut nobiliorem mobiliorem Cato, &c. Cic. de Or. II. 63. 256. παρώνυμος, in Categ. 1. a. 11, 13. signifies change of the form or termination of the word. παράγειν τῷ ὀνόματι. Gorg. 493. A. and Cratylus, 407. C. Diog. Laert. Vit. Plat. § 26.

'literal,' verbal jests, are a variety. These are said μεταστρέφειν ὄνομα, to change or twist a word out of its proper and natural sense, or give a different 'turn' to it. As in the example, the word θράττει naturally seems to mean, and is intended so to be taken, 'you are confounded;' but it is changed or perverted in the pronunciation or application so as to imply a double taunt, Θρᾷττ' εἶ (effeminacy, and foreign extraction). Jokes or plays upon words when the same word is used in two different senses, as ἀρχή in the following example, seem not to be included under τὰ παρὰ γράμμα. They are called simply ἀστεῖα, § 7, innocent lively pleasantries, distinguishable from σκώμματα, bitter, mordant, gibes, or taunts; and if they have any distinct name given to them it is ὁμωνυμία. Ambiguum, Cic. de Or. II. 62. 253. 254. 255. § 8. In these kinds of ἀστεῖα that we are now considering, the metaphor or double entendre[1] or whatever else it may be, must always be suitable, applicable to the person or occasion, (from the connexion of προσηκόντως *in the example*, this seems to be the sense here); in this its principal merit consists. To all of them alike the same rules apply, the more briefly and antithetically they are expressed the more popular they are: the reason is as before, that the contrast of the two seems to teach more, and the brevity more quickly. § 9. In these witticisms there must always appear either a special individual application, or else they must be expressed with peculiar elegance or point; if the 'mot' is to be at once 'true' (ἀληθές, either simply 'true' in its ordinary sense; or 'apposite, well applied;' or 'sound, genuine,' and so 'carrying weight,' 'telling,' as Vict. sententiam gravem et honestam) and not on the surface, trivial, such as anybody could say, or might occur to any one. These do not always go together:

---

[1] Victorius reads ὁμωνυμίᾳ and μεταφορᾷ. He understands the words to mean, that the merit of these ἀστεῖα consists in the elegance or propriety of them, and that these are to be sought in, or conveyed by, double entendre or metaphor. I think from what follows the version in the text is right.

a phrase for example may be 'true' or 'weighty,' 'sound sense,' and yet very trite and common-place. But if it have both these qualities, if it be as before, and also pointed or well expressed, it will then be popular. In fact the more of these particular graces of style, which go to make ἀστειότης, any phrase possesses, the more vivid and striking it will be;— as metaphor, and metaphor of a particular kind, antithesis, parisosis, and ἐνέργεια. § 10. We have seen that the most important of all the aids to vivacity of style is metaphor: now similes may always be considered as in some sense (τρόπον τινά) metaphors, and those too of the best sort; and therefore they must be included in the consideration of ἀστεῖα. That these are metaphors, and of the best sort, viz. the proportional, appears from the fact that two objects are always compared in them, as when a shield is called Ares' goblet, or a bow a chordless lyre. On the ἀνάλογον in the first example see above, III. 4. 4.; and (more clearly) Poet. 21. 12. By the same analogy, I suppose, the second example is a proportional metaphor; because, the bow being the attribute of Apollo in one of his characters and the lyre in the other,—bow : Apollo (as archer) :: lyre : Apollo (as musician)[1],—to qualify the harshness of such a metaphor the word ἄχορδος is added, which shows that it is not an appendage of the god in his character of musician. (On this phrase see Demetrius π. ἑρμ. III. 282, Rh. Gr. Speng.) However, he adds as a note, the two expressions I have quoted are not simple and ordinary metaphors; to each of them a word was added: a simple naked metaphor is when one thing is said to be another, as a shield a goblet, or a bow a lyre, without any addition as a reference (πρὸς ὅ ἐστιν, Poet.[2]). § 11. Comparisons may be made without the proportional metaphor;

---

[1] In the same way, c. 6. ult., he says it is a proportional metaphor to call the sound of a trumpet ἄλυρον μέλος. See on c. 6, n. 1. Introd. p. 297. And on φιάλη Ἄρεος, c. 4. § 4. p. 290.

[2] Vict. illustrates by this ἁπλῆ μεταφορά the phrase in Poet. XXI. 12, καὶ ἐνίοτε προστιθέασιν ἀνθ' οὗ λέγει, πρὸς ὅ ἐστιν.

(see § 14) § 12, but the best contain such. In similes the poets meet with the most signal failure and success § 13. All *proverbs* also are metaphors 'from species to species;' an example is given, § 14. All *approved* hyperboles[1] are likewise metaphors. This implies that there *are* other sorts of hyperbole, but those which are expressed by metaphor are the best. As when it was said of the man with the black eye, 'you'd have taken him for a basket of mulberries'— the metaphor lies in the common quality of redness or purple; for both the mulberry and the black eye are purple: but the distinctive character of the figure lies in the excessive amount, which makes it a hyperbole. [ἀλλὰ τὸ πολὺ σφόδρα; the ellipse to be supplied seems to be ἔστιν ἐρυθρόν. The great quantity makes an excess of redness, which constitutes hyperbole.] Again the similes quoted above may be construed as hyperboles, by merely dropping the particle of comparison. Thus — you'd have taken him for Philammon in close and deadly encounter with the sack. You'd have taken his legs for parsley, so crooked are they. When expressed thus they become hyperboles. § 15. This is Quintilian's superjectio per similitudinem; illustrated by Virg. Æn. VIII. 691. Credas innare revulsas Cycladas. (This example is given by Vict. and Maj.). The hyperbole is a figure which expresses vehemence, as violent passion; it is therefore μειρακιώδης, characterised by those qualities which distinguish young men; implies fire, spirit, exuberance, exaggeration. It is therefore unbecoming in the mouth of old age. The figure is an especial favourite with the Attic orators. § 16.

Ch. 12. He now returns to the subject of propriety, in

---

[1] Hyperbole, Quint. VIII. 3. 67—76 discusses and illustrates very fully. He calls it decens veri superjectio 'a becoming exaggeration of the truth'. (The word is borrowed from Livy, Spald. ad loc.). Three of its species are expressed by similitude, comparison, metaphor, §§ 68, 69, 70. In IX. 1. 29. it is called augendi minuendive causa veritatis superlatio. According to the Auct. ad Heren. IV. 33. 44, *superlatio* est oratio superans veritatem, alicujus augendi minuendive causa. He also distinguishes one kind, cum comparatione aut a similitudine. See also Cic. Topica. x. 45.

respect of its application to the three kinds of rhetoric[1]. The same style is not suitable to written compositions, (such that is as are *intended* to be read,) and to debate[2]; nor again to the two kinds which are included under the latter, deliberative and forensic speeches. Every one who wishes to succeed and make himself a name in public life, or in fact do his duty as a citizen, in which writing as well as speaking is often required, must of necessity be acquainted with both[3]: for the one involves at any rate purity and correctness of language and grammar, a solecism or barbarism calls forth a smile or a hiss from the audience; and the other is absolutely necessary for the purpose of imparting any thing you have occasion to say to the rest of the world. § 1. Still the written style is distinguished by a nicer accuracy and a higher degree of polish and finish[4]; the style of debate is that which is best adapted to declamation or delivery. Now there are two things in particular which render a speech suitable for declamation, ἦθος and πάθος; the accommodation of the language to the delineation of (1) character, the ranks, ages, fortunes, morals, manners, habits of men; and (2) of emotions and passions[5]. These are most suitable to the ἀγωνιστικοὶ λόγοι, because in them it is most important to assume the appearance of reality. And this is why actors (whose busi-

---

[1] Compare Quint. VIII. 3. 11. seq. which seems partly taken from Aristotle.

[2] Some of the points of difference between the 'graphic' and 'agonistic' styles are pointed out by Whately, Rhet. ch. IV. p. 301. a. and 299. b. and foll. (Encycl. Metrop.).

[3] Thuc. II. 60. 5, 6. as a commentary on this.

[4] On ἀκρίβεια, high artistic finish, see above p. 11.; Grant, note on Eth. Nic. I. 7. 18. On some of its various meanings, see further in note on c. 12. § 5. Introd. p. 328. This kind of ἀκρίβεια, in style, is developed by Quintilian in the passage above referred to. VIII. 3. ἀκριβής and ἀπηκριβωμένος are applied to style by Isocrates, Paneg. § 11. and opposed to ἁπλῶς, in the sense of 'highly finished, elaborated, and adorned with all the graces of rhetoric.' The same Isocrates, περὶ ἀντιδ. § 46, seq., says that the style of the Panegyric is near akin to poetry.

[5] Compare Quint. III. 8. 12. (in concionibus deliberatio) affectus, ut quæ maxime, postulat. Nam et concitanda et lenienda frequenter est ira &c.

ness is declamation) look out for plays, and poets for *actors*[1], which express and are capable of expressing these qualities. Not but that the poets also who write to be read have their share of applause [βαστάζειν = δοκιμάζειν ap. Gramm. Vict. This interpretation seems to suit the connexion better than 'in manibus versantur,' unless that also can mean 'are popular.'] as (Chæremon[2] whose style is as finished as that of a professional speech writer (like Isocrates), and Licymnius the dithyrambic poet. When brought into comparison many of the 'composers', (as Isocrates, according to Hieronymus of Rhodes, in Dionysius, de Isocr. Jud. c. 18.) in the actual contests of the assembly or the forum appear poor and meagre, wanting in body and vigour; whilst some of the 'orators'' speeches which have enjoyed a fair reputation [which have passed muster very well by the aid of a good delivery[3] (εὖ λεχθέντες; so Vict. and Maj.)] when taken in the hand, submitted to the test of perusal, lose all their effect, and look like the work of mean and unskilful (unartistic, unprofessional, ἰδιωτικοί) composers[4]. The reason of this is because they are intended for the arena of actual debate, and to that they are adapted; they were never meant to be read, and want the nice finish which written compositions require. And so the qualities and artifices of style which tell in declamation, for which they were intended[5], when divested of this

---

[1] So Vict. and Maj. It may also be, personages for their dramas who offer marked features of character and violent passions.

[2] Chæremon's writings abounded in minute, and doubtless highly wrought, descriptions, as of flowers. Athenæus. This of course would give the opportunity for introducing the minor graces, and elaborate finish, and niceties of composition; whether shown in careful construction, or in the use of ornament and rhetorical figures.

[3] The interpretation in the text would require λόγοι. It can mean nothing but 'well spoken of', ῥήτορες being understood.

[4] On 'spoken' and 'written' speeches, as to the difference of the effect upon the audience &c., and the prejudices against the latter see Isocrates, Philip. § 25 seq. p. 87.

[5] On the illusion produced by the *delivery* of a speech, and the advantages which an orator derives from it and all the attendant circumstances of an actual contest in affecting the minds of an audience—such as the

326

aid do not 'fulfil their proper function,'—as for instance asyndeta, and the reiteration of the same word—and though the orators employ them in their debates as adapted to delivery, in the written style, 'they appear silly, and are justly reprobated.' § 2. To this is appended by way of note the following injunction; to be careful in such reiterations [to vary the voice, tone, gesture; so Vict.[1] Or rather,] to vary the form of the recurring phrases in such a way as to avoid stiffness and monotony; such variety in the construction in fact seems to pave or prepare the way to the delivery, to suggest the same variety in the declamation[2]. After illustrating this by an example from some unknown rhetorician—Aristotle seldom or never coins examples of his own[3]—and a most obscure reference to two plays of Anaxandrides, [on which Meineke, Fragm. Comm. Gr. III. 166, throws no light,] he adds; in fact if such a construction of the sentence is not helped off by the delivery it becomes intolerably stiff and awkward, like the porter in the proverb who carries the beam, (or as we say, like a

δόξα τοῦ λέγοντος, the φωνή, the μεταβολαί αἱ ἐν ταῖς ῥητορείαις γιγνόμεναι, the καιροί, and so on—as compared with a written composition, read and criticised in cold blood, see Isocr. Philip. p. 87. c. D. quoted above.

[1] τὸ μεταβάλλειν. Victor's interpretation here though apparently natural is incorrect. Major., Schrader., Ernest. Lex. Techn., Spald. on Quint. IX. 3. 38., Meineke, Fragm. Comm. Græc. III. 166., (and the passages of Anaxandrides), all understand it of the figure μεταβολή; which is described by Quint. l. c. hanc rerum conjunctam diversitatem Cæcilius μεταβολὴν vocat; and illustrated by an example from Cicero pro Cluentio, exactly corresponding with that in Aristotle's text. Major. ad loc. cites three more of the same kind from Cicero in Pisonem; and Spalding ad loc. Quint. another

from Demosth. de Cor. p. 328., given by Alexander περὶ μεταβολῆς III. 35. Sp. Rhet. Gr. It consists, as appears from the example, in expressing, for the sake of variety and animation and amplification in several distinct clauses, all sometimes introduced by the same word, a set of phrases which might all have been gathered into one sentence and connected by copulatives. It may thus be regarded as a sort of asyndeton, with which Aristotle seems to class it.

[2] ὅπερ ὡς προοδοποιεῖ τῷ ὑποκρ. seems to have much the same sense as what Dionysius says of Demosthenes, de adm. vi dic. c. 22. p. 1023. (Reiske) that his speeches, αὐτοὶ διδάσκουσιν ὡς αὐτοὺς ὑποκρίνεσθαι δεῖ, νῦν μὲν εἰρωνευόμενον...προφορᾶς.

[3] There is one exception in a subsequent chapter.

man who has swallowed a poker.) § 3. Similarly asyndeta, with which the preceding may be classed, must be varied in the delivery, and never pronounced with the same character[1] and tone, as if they all meant only one thing. While we are on the subject of asyndeta, he continues, again by way of note, it may be remarked that they have this peculiarity; that they make it appear as if several things were said in the same time, when in reality there is only one. For as it is the property of the connective particle to give a unity to several things, so the removal of this has the opposite effect of converting one into many, and accordingly serves the purpose of amplification[2]. And this is the meaning of Homer's repetition of the word $Νιρεύς$ in the Iliad, B. 671; the reiteration gives an importance to the name which fixes it in the memory for ever, though this is the only place in which he is mentioned by the poet. It is in fact the same fallacy[3] which was noticed before (III. 7. 4); the supposition viz., that if one thing is the necessary consequent of another the converse likewise is true: a person or thing of which many things are said must necessarily be frequently mentioned, but it by no means follows from this that when one is frequently mentioned many things must be said of him. § 4. Returning now to the main subject of the Chapter, he proceeds; the Deliberative style is exactly like $σκιαγραφία$—painting in light and dark shades, chiaroscuro, without colour; we may render it for the purposes of the illustration 'scene painting' —it is meant to produce its effect at a distance, and will not bear close inspection or nice criticism. But the greater the number of hearers the more distant so to speak is the point of sight[4]: the style should therefore be broad rough and tell-

---

[1] $ἤθει$, habitu animi, Vict. Maj.
[2] See Harris, Hermes, II. p. 240.
[3] It consists in assuming that antecedent and consequent are reciprocally convertible, when they are not. See Top. IX. 167. b. 1. sq. and Rhet. I. 7. 5.
[4] So in acting, the larger the theatre the more likely are any delicate shades of expression in feature, tone, action, and character, to escape the notice of the audience.

ing massive and grand; all niceties of style and language, minute touches, delicate finish, are superfluous and thrown away in both, the painting and the speeches; whereas forensic speaking, where the number of hearers is smaller, admits of this ἀκρίβεια[1] in a greater degree. Theophrastus herein follows his master. Quint. III. 8. 62. The difference between the three kinds of audience, in respect of the degree of ἀκρίβεια which each of them allows, seems to turn mainly upon the numbers of each. In a great crowd like the assembly the orator can only be imperfectly heard by reason of the actual distance, the correspondence between σκιαγραφία and a deliberative speech is therefore to be taken literally, the spectators and audience are both at a distance, and the style in each of them has to be accommodated to that distance, and the imperfect perception consequent thereupon: besides this, there are the distractions of the contest, party feeling, hope and fear, passion and excitement, which also divert the attention from minute and delicate points; these obstacles to the exercise of critical judgment upon style prevail less in a court of law; and least of all with a single judge,—as an arbiter, or, it may be, a 'critic,' (κριτής as a judge in the games, musical and theatrical contests, &c.). Forensic speaking therefore admits of a greater degree of finish of style, and

---

[1] ἀκρίβεια seems to include likewise closeness and exactness of reasoning, and keeping to the point; from what follows, ἡ δὲ δίκη ἀκριβέστερον· ἔτι δὲ μᾶλλον...ἐλάχιστον γάρ ἐστιν ἐν ῥητορικοῖς, which plainly refers to 'reasoning processes.' Compare also, c. 17. § 12. And so Victor. note on ἐπιδεικτικὴ λέξις γραφικωτάτη. The larger the assembly, the more latitude in reasoning and assertion may the speaker allow himself. And this seems to be true. Still it must refer *principally* to all the artificial graces of a *finished* composition, such as appear for instance in the writings of Isocrates: of course such an ornament as a bold and happy metaphor tells as much upon a popular audience as upon a more refined one. On the points of difference between compositions intended for speaking and for reading, and more particularly, between the latter and the forensic kind of speeches, see Isocrates π. ἀντιδ. § 46. seq. and especially, Phil. § 25, 6. It would almost seem as if Aristotle had borrowed some of his hints for this chapter from this and similar passages.

careful and minute exactness of reasoning; (for this seems to be included from what follows;) and most of all an argument conducted before a single judge or arbitrator, who is close at hand, undisturbed by noise and tumult, his judgment clear and unclouded by the passions excited by a contest[1], and who can therefore take in the case at one view, and distinguish between that which properly belongs to the subject before him and that which is not to the point. Accordingly there is here more room for 'finish,' and 'exactness' in style and reasoning. Such I think is the general meaning of this passage. Major. however makes the difference between the three audiences turn upon the degree of their refinement, and capability of judging, which requires a different mode of handling the subject specially adapted to each[2]. But there seems to be no reason why the members of a court of law, constituted as these were at Athens, should be more refined or better educated than those of the assembly; and besides Aristotle himself in the Politics, III. 10, gives a (somewhat paradoxical) opinion, that the collective judgment of the πολλοί is upon the whole superior to that of any individual, however highly cultivated, even upon questions of taste, or works of art; because the sum of the several items of taste and judgment possessed by each man in a mob must exceed the amount that any single person can possess.

And therefore, he continues, the same orators do not succeed in all these styles, and before all audiences. Where there is most opportunity for declamation, there exact finish is least in place; and this is where the qualities of voice, as power, flexibility, sweetness, and especially loud voice, find most room for their display. And as this opportunity of course varies in proportion to the size of the audience, it follows by implication, that an orator who shows his power in declamation and action is most fitted to address the assem-

---

[1] This is equally true of the 'critic' of a written composition; and is pointed out by Isocrates in the passage of the 'Philip', already quoted.

[2] This is in some degree countenanced by Top. IX. 164. b. 27.

bly: those who succeed better in close reasoning and accuracy and finish of style are more in their element at the bar.

Now of all the three kinds of rhetoric, the demonstrativum genus is most adapted for writing; for as its τέλος, and intention, is to be read, so its ἔργον or appropriate function lies in reading[1]: it appeals therefore more to exact and minute criticism; the reader has time and leisure for reflexion; and calmness and quiet and freedom from excitement and passion: and in the second degree, for the reason before mentioned, the forensic kind. § 5.

Some writers[2] on Rhetoric have introduced a further and unnecessary distinction, that style should be sweet and 'magnificent': for, why these rather than any other of the moral virtues (of which according to the philosopher, magnificence, μεγαλοπρέπεια is one)? and besides, we *have already* shown how such a style is to be attained; nothing additional is required, as if this were something distinct from the qualities already inculcated. A pleasing style will be formed by the proper mixture of the elements of style already enumerated; the familiar, and the strange or foreign, (i. e. ornamental as described. c. 2), and rhythm, and persuasiveness arising from the observance of propriety. I say a pleasing style will follow from the observance of the rules and injunctions above given; for why else have we said that style must be clear or perspicuous, and not mean and commonplace, μὴ ταπεινὴν ἀλλὰ κεκοσμημένην, σεμνοτέραν, ξενικήν, Ch. 2. § 2., but appropriate to the subject? The virtues of style like all others lie in 'the mean'. σαφήνεια for example, perspicuity, lies between the two extremes of loquacity, garrulity, tautology and such like 'in excess', and too great brevity and con-

---

[1] The relation of the ἔργον, 'the proper and natural function of anything' to its ἀρετή and τέλος—the former is determined by it, the latter determines it—is examined in Eth. Nic. I. 6. The doctrine is borrowed from Plato, Rep. I. 352. D. seq.

[2] These writers are probably Isocrates and his school. A very similar superfluous distinction is criticised, c. 16. 4.

ciseness, which tends to obscurity, (brevis esse laboro obscurus fio) 'in defect'. And so end the observations on style.

Ch. 13. We now come to the second of the two main divisions of the contents of this book, viz. τάξις, the ordering of the topics which are to be handled in the speech. By Isocrates and Aristotle's immediate predecessors the speech was made to consist of four parts, under which all the arguments and several topics of persuasion were arranged. These were προοίμιον, διήγησις, πίστεις, and ἐπίλογος[1]. The contents of these several parts, as they were usually employed, are briefly described in an extract from the Art of Theodectes, preserved by the Schol. on Aphthon.[2] (in Gaisf. nott. varr. p. 31); προοιμιάσασθαι πρὸς εὔνοιαν, διηγήσασθαι πρὸς πίστιν, ἀγωνίσασθαι πρὸς ἀπόδειξιν, ἀνακεφαλαιώσασθαι πρὸς ἀνάμνησιν: and more fully by Cicero de Or. II. 19. 80. Jubent (i.e. the current rhetorical treatises,) enim exordiri ita ut eum qui audiat benevolum nobis faciamus et docilem et attentum; deinde rem narrare ita ut veri similis narratio sit, ut aperta, ut brevis; post autem dividere causam aut pro-

---

[1] The multifarious divisions and subdivisions of the speech which were adopted by the earlier rhetoricians may be seen in Plato, Phædr. 266. E, 267. E. They are however all reducible to these four heads. The divisions of the speech are treated by Dionysius, Ars Rhet. c. X. § 12. foll., with reference to the various modes of handling them prevailing in practice. Subsequently, the usual division was into 5 parts; πίστεις being divided into confirmatio and refutatio, τὰ πρὸς ἀντίδικον. This appears regularly in Cicero; and, in reference to the judiciale genus, in Quint. III. 9. 1.

[2] This passage is cited by Schmidt (on the date of the Rhet. p. 7.) as a quotation from Doxopater, in proleg. rhet. (Waltz. rhet. gr. VI. p. 19,) and an uncertain writer in the same VII. 33.; and again, with the words slightly altered in another uncertain author VII. 33: in the second of these the words occur, τέλος δὲ τῆς ῥητορικῆς οὐ τὸ ἁπλῶς πεῖσαι ἀλλὰ τὸ πιθαναῖς χρήσασθαι μεθόδοις, as from Theodectes. This is *Aristotle's* modification of the original definition of rhetoric, "the art of persuasion." See also Spengel, Art. Script. p. 156. It does not seem *certain* however that these words are cited by the author from Theodectes. Schmidt, p. 9. takes no notice of them in arguing the question of the non-identity of the Theodectea and Aristotle's extant Rhetoric; and seems tacitly to attribute them to the author who *quotes* Theodectes.

ponere, (this as distinguished from διήγησις, narratio, does not appear in the Greek division); nostra confirmare argumentis ac rationibus; deinde contraria refutare (these are confirmatio et refutatio; but both may be included under πίστεις); tum autem alii conclusionem orationis et quasi perorationem collocant; alii jubent antequam peroretur ornandi aut augendi causa degredi, deinde concludere et perorare. See also Orat. 35. 122, where it is very briefly and clearly put. The same fourfold division appears in the Rhet. ad Alex., proceeding from the school of Isocrates. The technical names there given to them are προοίμιον, ἀπαγγελία, βεβαίωσις, ἐπίλογος[1]: and in Dion. de arte Rhet. x. § 12. προοίμιον, διήγησις, πίστεις, ἐπίλογοι; and these are described in detail in the following sections.

See further on this subject in Camb. Phil. Journ. No. VII. p. 40. and the reff. there given. Add Cic. de Inv. I. 14. 19. and Auct. ad Heren. I. 3. 4., who both make 6 divisions. These agree with the classification in Cic. de Or. II. 19. 80. In them the third, partitio or divisio, is distinguished from narratio, and is the controversiæ constitutio, the statement of the points at issue, which show under what legal head the causa falls; and also includes Aristotle's πρόθεσις, the statement of the points that you are about to prove: narratio being a narrative of the circumstances which are required to be known about the case. Lastly Quintilian IV. Procem. § 6, adopts the same division.

This current distribution of the parts of the speech, which as I have said, was first made by Isocrates, is reviewed and criticised by Aristotle, together with some of the schemes of the earlier sophistical school of rhetoricians, such as Theodorus, Licymnius, and others.

First he observes that there are in reality only two parts

---

[1] In the Rhet. ad Alex. there is a *substantial* agreement with Aristotle in the description of the ordinary and proper contents of these four divisions. ἐπίλογος is there also called παλιλλογία, as a re-enumeration or recapitulation of the preceding arguments.

of the speech, both of which as well as their distinction from one another, are natural and necessary. The object of a speech is to prove something; now you can't prove without stating what you mean to prove, nor state without proving your statements—at least the latter would be so idle and absurd that it may be called impossible[1]: therefore the two indispensable parts of every speech are πρόθεσις, propositio, setting forth a statement of what you are going to prove, and πίστεις arguments in its support; just as in dialectics you have problem[2] or statement of the question, and demonstration. The substitution of the term πρόθεσις, propositio, for the ordinary technical term διήγησις, narratio, is well explained by Quintilian, III. 9. 5. διήγησις according to the usual definition and conception of its meaning is, in the words of Cic. de Inv. x. 19. 27, (comp. auct. ad Heren. I. 3. 4), gestarum rerum aut ut gestarum expositio: that is to say, a statement in detail or narrative recital of all the preceding circumstances which are necessary to the full understanding of the case, including sometimes the statement of the case itself; and is distinct from the other parts of the speech, occupying a definite place in it. Now πρόθεσις, the setting forth of what you are about to prove, which may occur any where, and state any thing, stands to διήγησις as above defined in the relation of genus to species, and is therefore to be preferred; and again, διήγησις in the narrower sense is not universally applicable to all kinds of speeches, hâc (narratione) non semper, illâ (πρόθεσις) semper et ubique credit opus esse (Aristoteles). Accordingly Aristotle criticises the received division of the parts of the speech as absurd.

---

[1] ἀδύνατον, the 'impossibility' does not arise from the nature of things, but is only true in respect of the standard of Rhetoric. In a speech which is in any sense what it ought to be, to state a case without arguing it, or to argue without stating it, may be called impossible.

[2] πρόβλημα is properly an alternative statement of a thesis or question to be argued. διαλεκτικὸν θεώρημα (Top. A. 11. 104. b. 1.), quod in disputando quæstione bipartita efferri solebat, ex. gr. voluptas estne expetenda annon? mundus estne æternus annon? Trendel. El. Log. § 42. p. 118.

The forensic kind of rhetoric is the only one which necessarily requires a regular διήγησις in the sense usually given to it; strictly speaking, for this general assertion is afterwards qualified, (c. 16;) in the two other kinds it has no place[1]. The sort of διήγησις that is admissible in the ἐπιδεικτικὸν γένος is described c. 16. § 1; and again with regard to the third, it is true that a regular διήγησις may sometimes be found in a deliberative speech—as in the great public speeches of Demosthenes and Æschines—but this is only an accident, not of the essence of this kind of rhetoric. The time of the δημηγορικὸν γένος is the future (I. 3. 2); and a 'narrative' refers not to the future, but to the past. If it *is* introduced at all, it is as a review of past transactions, to call the facts to the memory of the assembly, and enable them to judge better of the *future* course of policy which the orator is enforcing. III. 16. 11. The same argument—of want of universality of application—will apply to two other divisions commonly assigned to the speech by writers on rhetoric[2]. How can τὰ πρὸς ἀντίδικον, refutatio adversarii, belong to an epideictic or deliberative speech, when in these two branches there *is* no adversary, properly speaking, except perhaps in the latter by accident (as for example in Demosth. de Falsâ Legatione)? The object of an epideixis is to praise or blame some one; and of a deliberative speech to persuade to or dissuade from some course of action, and nothing more. And again, if the ἐπίλογος be understood, as it usually is, to mean 'a summary review,' ἀνακεφαλαίωσις, 'of the proofs' previously brought forward, this cannot apply at any rate to all speeches; for some may not even attempt demonstration, ἀπόδειξις[3].

[1] All that Aristotle can be understood to mean here is, that narratio, as defined by the Rhetoricians of his day, and the other divisions subsequently mentioned, are *necessary* only in the δικαστικὸν γένος. They *may* occur in the others in one form or other, but are not indispensable, or of the essence of them; only accidents.

[2] Quint. III. 9. 5. disapproves of the rejection of refutatio as a division of the speech.

[3] ἢ ἐπίλογον τῶν ἀποδεικτικῶν, may also mean; an ἐπίλογος, as it is usually

This long explanation of a very few words in the original, which is so briefly expressed as to be unintelligible without it, has only brought us to the middle of § 3. The section proceeds——Again other divisions of the speech which have been assigned, as προοίμιον; ἀντιπαραβολή, comparison of opposing views and arguments; and ἐπάνοδος, review, ἀνακεφαλαίωσις (a subdivision of ἐπίλογος, sometimes identified with it, because it is its prominent feature,) are equally open to criticism. These can only appear in a deliberative speech when there is a dispute and an opponent. The object of the prooemium is to conciliate the audience and invite their attention, and briefly describe the subject of the speech. In recommending this or that measure to the assembly, unless there is an adversary who has poisoned the hearers' minds against it and its author, or some special reason, there is no occasion for this: and also, the audience is usually well acquainted with the subject. See further on this, c. 14 § 11.

defined, and with its usual contents—which are detailed in c. 19. § 1.—cannot be used in argumentative, or demonstrative, speeches. Supposing a speech to be occupied with proof *alone*, the ordinary definition and the ordinary character of the ἐπίλογος would not represent it: τῶν ἀποδεικτικῶν, neut., or with λόγων und., may very well stand for 'arguments' or 'proofs' in general. I doubt if Aristotle would use ἀποδεικνύναι and its derivatives in any other sense. Victorius however, followed by Majoragius and Schrader, understand it of the ἐπιδεικτικὸν γένος. The former cites very appositely to his view, Isocr. Panath. p. 288. D., where Isocrates in concluding his oration says, "I think now I have said enough: for the review or recapitulation in detail of all the topics that have been touched upon is unsuitable to speeches of this kind." But I don't see, in spite of Isocrates, why a summary of topics previously treated should not conclude a panegyric as well as any other kind of speech: nor do I think it possible that Aristotle would have employed the one word for the other, especially as a technical term—unless indeed it were a technicality adopted from some preceding writers, of which there is no evidence whatever. Vict. says that Isocrates uses ἀποδεικνύναι in the sense of ἐπιδεικνύναι more than once in the Panath. speech. I can't find it except in its ordinary signification, either there or in the Lexicons. Probably in the ed. he used ἀποδεικνύναι was interchanged by mistake with ἐπιδεικνύναι, the distinction not being recognised. In Paneg. § 18, ἐπιδεικνύναι is used in very much the same signification as the other. § 65.

Comparison of argument, and review, can only be required when there is an opposition. In fact by the same rule, accusation and defence (which are the matter of the forensic branch,) may be said to form a necessary part of the deliberation: for they are equally necessary when there is an adversary: they do not belong to this kind of speech, quâ deliberative[1]; but only, if ever, as an accident. The argument is a reductio ad absurdum. If the former then this; but this is manifestly absurd. Further, the ἐπίλογος[2] is not *essential* even to the forensic speech—where however it is most required—[and a fortiori, not to the two other kinds;] as when the case and the speech are short, and the facts easily remembered. For the very object and essence of the ἐπίλογος being to enumerate in brief the preceding topics and arguments, for the purpose of assisting the memory, (which is expressed by ἀφαιρεῖσθαι τοῦ μήκους) it is plain that when the arguments are already briefly expressed, and the whole case easily remembered, there can be no occasion for it[3]. The only necessary parts of the speech therefore are πρόθεσις and πίστις. § 3. These are proper to and characteristic of all. If we are to add any, let there be at the utmost the four above named. Refutatio is not a true division for it belongs to πίστεις; and so does ἀντιπαραβολή, the contrast of your own views and arguments with those of the adversary, by way of reply. You first give your own arguments in support of your case, confirmatio; then answer those of the adversary, refutatio; and then contrast the two ἀντιπαραβολή; which is, as Aristotle says, nothing more than an amplification, a setting in the most favourable light, of our own, and belongs therefore to πίστεις. For either of these proves something: not so however προοίμιον (which we allow): nor ἐπίλογος, which merely recalls them to memory. § 4. If such as these,

---

[1] Reading ᾗ, for ἡ, συμβουλή.
[2] Read with Vict. Maj. Schrader, ἀλλ᾽ ὁ ἐπίλογος ἔτι κ.τ.λ.
[3] This is Vict. Major. and I believe right.

Schrader's (whose words are by no means clear) interpretation of these obscure words, and I think must be right.

refutatio and ἀντιπαραβολή, be admitted as distinct parts, the divisions may be multiplied ad infinitum; and we might as well adopt such as those which were introduced by Theodorus and his school, ἐπιδιήγησις and προδιήγησις, ἔλεγχος and ἐπεξέλεγχος[1]. The fact is, that names of things (generic names) ought to denote a distinct kind, marked by a precise and definite difference[2] from all other things, and new words should not be introduced unless they do so: (and this, he implies, Theodorus' terms fail to do). Otherwise you have empty and meaningless and mere poetical terms, like those which Licymnius introduced into his Rhetoric; ἐπούρωσις, ἀποπλάνησις, and ὄζοι. On the import of these terms see Camb. Journ. of Phil. No. IX. p. 256.

Ch. 14. Having discussed generally in the preceding chapter the divisions of the speech, and shown that the true number of them does not exceed four, he now proceeds to describe and illustrate these, and to suggest rules for their practical application. All four are treated with reference to the three kinds of rhetoric, the deliberative, judicial, and demonstrative or panegyrical. This occupies the remainder of the book. And first of the προοίμιον. The proœmium[3] may be stated in general terms to be the beginning of the speech, to which it bears the same relation as the prologue to a tragedy, or the prelude to a piece of music: for all these are openings, and pave the way as it were for what is to follow. But here we must point out a difference between the opening as applied to epideictic speeches and to the other two kinds of rhetoric. In the former namely the connexion between the opening and the body of the speech is allowed to be much less close than in the other two[4]. For here, as there is

---

[1] See Plato, Phædr. 267. A. Plato gives instead of the two first, πίστωσις and ἐπιπίστωσις. Were they all four in Theodorus' treatise? or is this one of the not unusual slips of memory on Aristotle's part in quoting?

[2] On διαφορά, Vict. quotes Eth. N. III. 2. ὁ μὲν...ἄκων δοκεῖ, ὁ δὲ...οὐχ ἑκών. ἐπεὶ γὰρ διαφέρει (since there *is* a real difference), βέλτιον ὄνομα ἔχειν ἴδιον.

[3] On the ordinary contents of the προοίμιον, see Isocr. Paneg. § 13.

[4] On the Epideictic proœmium, (after Aristotle,) Quint. III. 8. 8, 9.

no real interest at stake, the author is allowed a much greater liberty in his choice of topics for amusing an audience; a licence which would be intolerable in a case for instance of life and death, or in the suggestion of a course of action which may involve the safety or ruin of a state. Here the audience are too eager to come to the point to admit of any trifling with their anxiety. The exordium accordingly of the epideictic branch of rhetoric is rather to be compared to the προαύλιον in the two analogous cases suggested. For a flute player in contending for the prize opens his performance with a flourish, by which he thinks he can display his powers and his instrument to their best advantage, and secure the favourable attention of the judges, which has usually no connexion whatsoever with that which is to follow, but gradually works round until it connects itself with the ἐνδόσιμον, the real commencement of his theme. The ἐνδόσιμον[1] thus seems to stand between the προαύλιον and the piece itself, to the latter of which it serves as an introduction (inter prolusionem et verum cantum. Vict.). It appears to be one or more notes struck, or a bar played, to mark the character of the piece, as the time or the key or perhaps the mode, or νόμος, 'tune, air,'—one or all; and corresponds in its use and application pretty nearly to the key note. An example of this common practice of the λογογράφοι is cited from the opening of Isocrates' Helen. There is the further advantage in this, even if the orator pass into quite a different region or climate, (the metaphor, ἐκτοπίσῃ, is from migratory birds,) that it gives variety to a kind of speaking which is apt to fall into monotony. § 1. The introductions in this branch of rhetoric are derived from praise and blame; illustrated from Isocrates and Gorgias § 2. Another topic for epideictic exordia is advice. § 3. A third may be derived from topics which properly belong to forensic

---

[1] ἐνδόσιμον, κροῦσμα, or ᾆσμα. Bos. Ellips. s. v. It is used by Aristotle, Pol. VIII. 5. 1, apparently in the sense either of an 'introduction' as here; or 'a guide,' to be followed, metaphorically. By Plutarch in two passages, quoted by Schäfer ap. Bos, for 'a signal,' or 'incentive.'

introductions; to entreat, namely, the indulgence of the audience if the subject of the speech happen to be incredible or difficult, (or harsh, unpleasant, Vict. and Maj. ardua,) or trite and stale; as Chœrilus does in his poem. Hence it appears that the προοίμια in this branch are to be derived from ἔπαινος and ψόγος, προτροπή and ἀποτροπή, and appeals to the feelings of the audience; and may be either closely connected with, or foreign to, the main subject of the speech. § 4.

The prooemium in forensic speeches is analogous to the prologue of a tragedy or the introduction of an epic poem: the epideictic bear more resemblance to the ἀναβολαί of the dithyramb. (c. 9 § 1.) § 5. In plays and epic poems it gives as it were a specimen, sample, or indication, of the subject; and so relieves the minds of the audience from the suspense and uncertainty which attend everything undefined, and keep the mind wandering in doubt and anxiety: whereas the poet by putting the opening into the hand, as it were, of the listener, gives him a 'clue' to the subject, and enables him to follow it with ease and interest. He then quotes the opening lines of the Iliad, Odyssey, and Chœrilus' 'Persian Wars,' (according to Wolf's conj. approved by Vater, Buhle, Näke, Gaisford). Similarly the tragic poets explain the subjects of their plays; if not immediately at the opening, as Euripides, at any rate in a subsequent 'introduction[1]', as Sophocles in the "Œdipus on the throne:" and so with Comedy. This then is the most necessary, and the peculiar and proper function of the prooemium, to explain the object and intention of the work; and therefore if the subject is short and plain none is required. § 6. All the other appli-

---

[1] The comm. object to προλόγῳ here because the verse quoted is in the middle of the play. But it seems that Aristotle has here used πρόλογος, in a more comprehensive sense than that which it ordinarily bears, for 'an introduction' in general, by which something that follows is better understood: and that it bears much the same relation to the ordinary signification of πρόλογος as πρόθεσις does to διήγησις in c. 13.

The same term is applied by implication to speeches in the middle of a play, in § 10.

cations of this prologue of the speech are so many remedies for the various defects of the audience; as inattention, unfavourable disposition &c.; and are common to all the three branches. They are derived from the speaker himself, from the audience, the subject, and the adversary. From the first and fourth arise the topics of raising and allaying prejudice and ill-feeling; only with this difference. The defendant must *begin* with the charges brought against him or the insinuations of his enemies, and clear them away, do away with all unfavourable impressions against him, before he proceeds to introduce himself to the audience's favourable consideration; (so Vict. Maj.); and so in his case these topics belong to the prooemium: but the accuser must reserve all that tends to raise a prejudice against the accused for the ἐπίλογος, in order that his insinuations may dwell in the minds of the audience, and leave their sting. To the second head, τὰ πρὸς τὸν ἀκροατήν[1], are referred all the topics and artifices which serve to conciliate the audience to yourself, and provoke their indignation against the adversary; or again when it is required—for this is not always the case—to make them attentive, or the reverse when our case is a bad one; or if we wish to slur over any important point which is not in our favour; and this is why orators when they feel themselves upon unsafe ground often try to raise a laugh, under cover of which they glide over the dangerous topic[2]. In fact anything or everything, meaning all that has been

[1] The three requisites in the disposition of the audience according to the later writers on the subject are that they should be, benevoli, dociles, attenti. Cic. de Inv. I. 15. 20; and frequently elsewhere. Aristotle includes the two latter under the one head of προσεκτικοί: and in fact if a man is inclined to attend, he shows already that he is desirous of learning. The two are closely connected, Cic. de Inv. I. 16. 23.

[2] This is the object of the former half of Gorgias' maxim, c. 18. 7. The propriety of Aristotle's qualification, ἐνίοτε, is contested by Quintilian, who has some very sound remarks upon it, IV. 1. 37, 38. Gaisf. quotes very appositely, Arist. Vesp. 564.
Οἱ δὲ λέγουσιν μύθους ἡμῖν, οἱ δ'
  Αἰσώπου τι γελοῖον·
οἱ δὲ σκώπτουσ', ἵν' ἐγὼ γελάσω, καὶ
  τὸν θυμὸν καταθῶμαι.

described as appropriate to the προοίμιον, (so Vict. Maj.) may be applied at the orator's pleasure, if he only treats his topics with that view, to make the audience 'dociles,' i.e. ready to receive the information which he is prepared to communicate; which is much the same as being inclined to listen to him, προσεκτικοί; and there is another thing which is of great importance for securing this object, viz. that the speaker should infuse ἦθος into his speech, i.e. set his own character and intentions in the most favourable light, make himself appear a worthy and respectable person; because people are always more inclined to attend to those whose characters they esteem. The subjects which most attract the attention of an audience are things of magnitude, momentous and important; things in which they are themselves concerned, where their own interests are involved[1]; things surprising and incredible; and things agreeable: and therefore the speaker should try to make it appear that the subject of his speech is one or other of the foregoing. If you want to make them inattentive, the opposites, trifling, painful, matters in which they have no personal interest are appropriate. § 7. However we ought to be aware that all this is beside the real point, does not belong to the *art* of rhetoric when properly defined and understood; and the necessity of it proceeds merely from the defects of the audience; for if they were what they ought to be, there would be no need of an introduction, except just to state in a summary way what the speech is to be about, that it may be as it were a body with a head[2]. § 8. At the same time it

[1] These ἴδια of Aristotle are expressed by Cic. Orat. Part. c. 8. Conjuncta cum ipsis apud quos agetur. The two others which attract attention are there given as 'magna et necessaria.' The same author, de Inv. I. 16. 23, classes them under four heads; magna, nova, incredibilia, and things relating to illustrious men, the immortal gods, and important state interests. The author of the Rhet. ad Al. c. 30. 3. enumerates many more.

[2] ὥσπερ σῶμα κεφαλήν. M. Edmond About somewhere says, in apologising for a preface, which he considers himself obliged to prefix to one of his works, that a book without a preface is like a man going out into

may be remarked that this topic is common to all the parts of the speech, and in fact more necessary everywhere than in the opening; for people's attention is much more likely to flag in the middle or at the end of the speech. Therefore orators have recourse to various artifices for giving a fillip to the drowsy audience; which Prodicus called, 'slipping in a taste of the "fifty-drachm";' i. e. his principal and most interesting lecture. § 9. All these topics for making prooemia, with the exception of the brief summary, which are beside the real subject, are plainly addressed to the hearer not merely *as a hearer*[1], as one who merely wants to be put in possession of the real facts of the case and nothing more, but as a man subject to the prejudices and defects above mentioned. This is clear from the fact that all speakers, involuntarily as it were, invariably employ the introduction in instilling prejudices into the minds of the audience against their adversary, or endeavouring to remove unfavourable suspicions which exist against themselves: showing thereby what their opinion of the character of the audience really is; that is, that they are not unbiased and what they ought to be. This is exemplified by reference to Soph. Ant. 223, and Iph. T. 1162. And so the prooemia are most useful to those who have, or fancy they have, a bad case; for it is to their advantage to dwell upon anything rather than the case itself. Similarly and for the same reason slaves when charged with a fault and excusing themselves to their masters never answer his ques-

---

the street without his hat. The opening of Gorgias' speech quoted at the end of the chapter produces exactly that effect. A man in the street is just as much a man without, as with, his hat: but custom and convention have made a hat to be regarded as part of a man, or at any rate of a gentleman, under those circumstances; and the absence of it gives him an air of incompleteness, and want of finish, like a body without a head. See the definition of σοφία, Eth. Nic. VI. 7. 3. and Stallbaum's note on Plat. Gorg. 505. D.

[1] So the jurymen in our Courts are instructed by the Judge to dismiss from their minds all that they may have heard out of Court and to attend only to the evidence of the witnesses which is then and there given. This is to make them ἀκροατὰς ἢ ἀκροατάς.

tions directly, and to the point, but always dwell upon incidental or concomitant circumstances (circumstantia, τὰ κύκλῳ), and in effect employ what is equivalent to a προοίμιον. § 10. The topics for securing εὔνοια, benevolentia, have been already treated; in Bk. II. c. 4, on φιλία; and c. 8, on ἔλεος; and the other πάθη with them in the second book. φιλία and ἔλεος are both referred to in the well-known line of Homer, Od. η'. 327; and these are the two that should be aimed at.

In the epideictic prooemia[1], the listener must be led to suppose that he is a participator in the eulogy, either personally, or by his family, and race, or his habits and pursuits, or some how or other. This is implied in the saying of Socrates (Plato) in the funeral oration, (Menexenus 235. D. quoted already I. 9. 30;) that it is easy enough to panegyrise Athenians in Athens; where every one feels himself included in the panegyric: the difficulty is to do so with effect at Sparta, amongst rivals or enemies. The topics of the deliberative prooemium are to be drawn from the same sources as the dicastic; but they are naturally most rare in this kind: for the subject is in these cases one with which the audience is acquainted; i.e. sufficiently acquainted to dispense with the preparatory summary of it; and the only necessity for using one arises from those defects of the audience above described, or from some other accident, as the opposition of an adversary. It is introduced either on account of the speaker himself, or of his opponents, or of the subject itself, if the audience make either too much or too little of it. Its topics accordingly fall under διαβάλλειν and ἀπολύεσθαι, the exciting or allaying of prejudice; and αὔξησις and μείωσις, amplification and detraction, diminution, disparagement. Or lastly it may be used merely as an ornament; for without it the speech has an off-hand, careless,

---

[1] Vater defends the introduction of this observation here, as consistent with the order of the topics of the chapter, on the ground that all that has been said about keeping up the attention of the audience refers equally to the three kinds of rhetoric.

slovenly air, ('hatless', see note 2, on p. 341) like Gorgias' abrupt opening, Ἦλις πόλις εὐδαίμων.

Ch. 15. We have seen that the ordinary contents of the προοίμιον may be reduced to two heads, each including two opposites[1]. The two last αὔξειν and μειοῦν are not peculiar to this and have been before examined (see the analysis of II. 19). It remains in continuation of the subject of the preceding chapter to analyse the remaining pair, and to classify the sources from which they may be derived. διαβάλλειν is 'to set at variance', 'to make hostile'; and so to inspire ill-will, insinuate suspicions, or prejudice a person against another. It applies as a technical term to all insinuations and accusations by which one of the parties in a case endeavours to raise a prejudice against the other, which are to be reflected upon, but do not include, the main charge or point at issue. See III. 15. 9. and compare the example, § 3. ἀπολύεσθαι is to clear oneself of such insinuated charges, to remove evil suspicions. Aristotle begins with this, because, as he told us before, it is *more* appropriate to the exordium, as the opposite is to the peroration (so Vict. Maj.). The first topic for effecting this is general; any of the methods[2] by which we encounter and do away with *suspicions* or prejudices conceived against us may be employed in rebutting the charges and insinuations of an adversary; whether they are spoken or not makes no difference, § 1. Another is to plead the 'issues' or points in controversy, either by denying the fact; or admitting that, and asserting that the alleged act was not injurious (ab utili. V.), or at any rate not to the complainant [τούτῳ; this is Victorius' reading for v. l. τοῦτο, contested by Spald. on Quint. III. 6. 60. as I think without sufficient reason.] or that the injury was not so great as stated; or that it was no wrong, or a slight one (ab aequo); or not dishonourable, or of no importance at all (ab honesto). Or to strike a balance, 'to compensate' one quality of an action by another

---

[1] With this chapter, compare the treatment of the same subject in Rhet. A. c. 30.

[2] Schrader mentions some of them.

as a set off (so Vict. and Maj. and Schrader, ἀντικαταλλάττεσθαι[1], compensare); in estimating an unjust act or wrong inflicted to 'compensate', it may be, the injury done by the honourable nature, the nobility or splendour of it; or the pain inflicted by the profit ensuing, and so on, § 2. A third, to show that the crime imputed was a mistake, or a piece of ill luck which could not be avoided[2], or done by compulsion (which relieves the agent from all responsibility); or again to substitute a different cause or motive to that alleged by the accuser; the injury that ensued was not intentional but accidental. § 3. A fourth line of argument may be adopted when the accuser is himself involved in the charge either now or formerly, or any of his near relatives or intimates: this includes recrimination, § 4. Again if others are involved who are universally acknowledged not to be liable to such a charge. [In the example some change of the received text seems necessary. Vict.'s, Maj.'s, and Schrader's, translations seem to be none of them appropriate[3]. Riccoboni and Bekker suggest εἰ ὅτι καθάριος μοιχός; which, comparing, II. 4. 15. and 24. 7, seems very probable.] You

---

[1] ἀντικαταλλάττεσθαι is interpreted by L. and Sc. Lex. "to exchange or substitute one thing for another"; as here a different name. This explanation seems unsuitable here; because the other name is not substituted, but only added; it applies better to the same word in § 3.

[2] ἀδικία, ἀδίκημα, ἁμάρτημα, ἀτύχημα, distinguished, Eth. N. V. 10. comp. Rhet. Al. 5. 9.

[3] οἷον εἰ καθαρός κ.τ.λ. neither Victor.'s nor Major.'s interpretation of this can be right. In the former the example does not agree with the τόπος; and the second does not express the Greek, nor hang together in its several parts. Schrader also translates ὁμολογοῦσι, adversarii fatentur, (it would be singular, if this were the meaning; the opponent is always spoken of as 'one') and καθ. 'sceleris purus.' Neither, I think, can Vater's explanation stand. His interpretation is, (read καθάριος) ' If because the adulterer is a neat dresser,' meaning, 'if a charge of adultery against a certain individual is made to rest upon his care of his personal appearance, then so and so and so and so, against whom there is no suspicion, must be equally open to it, or included in it. But the latter are certainly not guilty: and therefore you may argue that the charge against the former is false'. But the Greek words as they stand will not bear this sense.

have been charged with profligacy because you are a smart dresser, and take care of your person: you appeal to other well-known characters: if a man must be a rake because he is a dandy then so and so must be, for they dress as well as I do: but every body knows that their characters are above suspicion. [Either reject the article, or read εἰ ὅτι ὁ καθάριος μοιχός], § 5. Again, if your accuser or any one else has ever charged others with the same crimes that he is now alleging against you; or if without a direct accusation the same persons were ever suspected of such crimes, who have been shown to be entirely innocent; you may derive from this an argument in your favour: you infer by analogy that a mistake in the present case is equally possible; § 6. Or again you may have recourse to recrimination, and retort upon the adversary in order to shake his credit with the audience. If the accuser himself is entitled to no credit, neither are his allegations; § 7. Again, the case may have been already decided elsewhere: as Euripides in the 'exchange' case[1] replied to Hygiænon[2]—when he charged him with impiety on the ground of the famous line of the Hippolytus, v. 612; asserting that it was a downright recommendation of perjury—that he had no right to bring that forward in a court of law; the point had been already decided by the judges in the Dionysiac contest; where if any where the case ought to be tried; § 8. Again, you may inveigh against calumny and malicious insinuations in general, and show how mischievous they are, and how they raise extraneous points, and divert the attention from the facts of the case, the real point at issue[3]. This is well illustrated by Isocrates, περὶ ἀντιδ. § 18. Comp. Rhet. A. 30. 12. The topic from signs and tokens

---

[1] Sauppe, Or. Att. Fragm. III. 216.

[2] Valck. on Hippol. v. 612. p. 232, suggests the correction 'Τγιαίνετον, as more agreeable to the analogy of Greek proper names. The name is right; see Harpocration, 72. 22. 96. 3. Bekk.

[3] The words ὅτι οὐ πιστεύει τοῖς πράγμασιν are omitted by Vict. Maj. and Schrader. No notice of the omission is taken in Bekk.'s ed. and it seems to be accidental. Maj. and Schr. having probably followed Vict.'s text.

is common to both accuser and apologist. It is illustrated by an obscure reference to Sophocles' Teucer. According to what we gather from Aristotle's text, Ulysses seems to have brought a charge against Teucer of practising with the enemy, (of being on too good terms with them, or playing into their hands): in support of which he uses as a 'sign', which gives probability to the allegation, that Teucer is a near connexion of Priam, for Hesione his mother was Priam's sister: Teucer replies by a similar argument, that even his father Telamon, the husband of Hesione, was Priam's enemy, and that he was at least as likely to be so too; the one 'sign' was worth just as much in the way of evidence as the other; and also produces this further indication of his disposition towards the enemy, that when the spies were sent into the city he did not betray them to Priam[1], §9. Another, to be employed by the accuser, is to disguise your evil intention by dwelling at great length upon some trifling and unimportant topic of commendation, and then, under cover of this, to introduce in concise and pregnant terms a censure of something in the adversary's conduct which is of real importance[2]; or after a preliminary enumeration of a number of virtues and advantages in the opponent which have nothing to do with the matter in hand, to insinuate a fault which has a direct bearing on the question at issue[3]. Such tricks as these are

---

[1] Wagner, Fragm. Soph. p. 388., gives a different turn to the story and the argument; but allows that we are ignorant of the plot of the drama. His version does *not* agree so well with Aristotle's words.

[2] Victor reads τῷ and connects ἐπαιν. μικρὸν μακρῶς ψέξαι, ita vituperare ut pusillam rem magno verborum ambitu, magnam paucis, laudes. But this is not to insinuate censure, but merely to withhold or obscure praise.

Maj. interprets, si paullum laudet ut gravius vituperet, et si quod magnum atque egregium est breviter attingat: to which the same objection applies.

[3] An excellent example of the use of this topic is supplied by Victorius from Cicero, pro Flacco. Verum tamen hoc dico de toto genere Graecorum: tribuo illis litteras; do multarum artium disciplinam; non adimo sermonis leporem, ingeniosum acumen, dicendi copiam; denique etiam siqua

at the same time most artful and most unfair: for they convert what is good into an instrument of mischief by mixing them with what is bad. Another topic common to accuser and excuser is, since the same act may always be attributed to different motives, for the former always to put the worse construction upon the intention which prompted the act, the latter to interpret it in the most favourable sense. This is illustrated by the different motives which may be assigned for Diomede's choice of Ulysses to accompany him in his nocturnal exploring expedition. Il. K. 242. sq. and Theodectes, Ajax.

Ch. 16. We next come to διήγησις narratio, the second division of the speech. In the epideictic branch of Rhet. the facts of the narrative should not, as a rule, be given altogether, and in a regular string or series one after another. The διήγησις is a relation or description of the facts and actions upon which the panegyric—to take a single instance —is founded. From these the encomium is to be drawn by argument and inference; we have to show that the fact is as we state it, if it appear incredible; or that it has the character, or magnitude and importance, that we assign to it. (Hence the facts which are already provided for us without any trouble or skill of our own are, like the ἄτεχνοι πίστεις, (I. 15,) ἄτεχνα, out of the province of art; the proofs and inferences, which we supply ourselves, are ἔντεχνοι, ἐκ τῆς τέχνης, belong to the art of Rhetoric). Now if we recite all the facts together in a string, and then proceed to draw our inferences from them, this would lead to great confusion in the mind of the hearer, and render the topics very difficult to remember. We must therefore distribute them over the speech, introducing the actions severally by way of πρόθεσις, (see above, c. 13) and then put upon each of them as it occurs the required construction: as, such and such actions show that our hero

sibi alia sumunt non repugno: testimoniorum relligionem et fidem nunquam ista natio coluit; totiusque hujus rei quæ sit vis, quæ auctoritas, quod pondus, ignorant.

was just; such and such that he was wise or brave and so on. The other method is puzzling and wants plainness and simplicity. §§ 1. 2. Actions that are well known we have merely to allude to, so as to remind the audience of them; in such cases most people do not require a regular διήγησις, description in detail, [not, 'most men's actions', which is false]. For instance every body is already acquainted with the actions of Achilles; and therefore if he be the object of the panegyric, all that is required is to enlarge upon them. If it be Critias on the contrary, who is not so well known, the description is necessary. § 3. Here something has been lost, and its place supplied in many of the MSS. and early editions by a long paragraph from I. 9. 33—38; which, to say nothing of the repetition, is entirely unsuitable here. That something has fallen out appears from the sudden change, without a word of explanation, from the epideictic to the dicastic branch which is treated in the following sections; and also from the abrupt conclusion of the former, and equally abrupt commencement of the latter, subject. The words νῦν δέ which have no reference to any thing preceding suggest the same conclusion.

In the current rhetorical treatises[1]—this is aimed at Isocrates[2]—there is an absurd rule that the narrative must be rapid. In the first place there is no more reason why the narrative should be rapid than any other part of the speech: and secondly the principle is false; the narrative must be not necessarily rapid and brief, but accommodated to the subject and occasion: the true rule is that it should be of mean or moderate length, (μετρίως,) neither too long nor too short for the occasion: that is, enough to put the judges clearly in possession of the case; or to establish either the fact, or the injury, or the wrong, according to what the issue or 'status' may be; or to produce the impression of the magnitude and

---

[1] See Rhet. A. 7. 3 and 31. 4. and the notes on the latter passage.
[2] See the 3rd fragment of Isocrates' τέχνη, in Benseler's Isocrates (Teubner), II. 276.

importance of the facts which you desire to convey¹: or the opposites of these, if the other party is pleading. § 4. You may slip into the narrative any thing that tells favourably upon your own character, or unfavourably upon your adversary's, or any thing that is agreeable to the audience². § 5. The accused or defendant will not require so long a διήγησις as the other party, because the case has been already stated by the plaintiff; and all that the other has to do is to supply omissions, designed or undesigned, and correct errors and false statements. The issues he has to raise, the status, constitutiones causæ, are, first the fact; secondly if he admits that, he may plead that it did no harm; thirdly allowing that likewise, that it was not wrong or illegal; or fourthly that it was not so bad as the accuser tried to make out. It follows therefore that he should not dwell and waste time upon any thing admitted, unless it happen to make for the point which he wishes to establish; because, to take an example, if the issue is made to turn upon the justice or injustice of the act, the fact being admitted, it may be necessary to go into the details of the latter in order to throw light upon the former. § 6. Similarly in relating events, he should refer to them, for the sake of brevity, as past and gone; unless they should be of such a nature that the vivid presentation of them as actually occurring (πρὸ ὀμμάτων ποιεῖν, see note on c. 11,) admits of their being applied to awakening the compassion or arousing the indignation of the hearers. As a specimen of this mode of narration may be cited the 'story of Alcinous', in the Odyssey, IX—XII. This was one of the divisions of the work, and known under the above name; probably recited

---

¹ ἢ τηλικαῦτα ἡλίκα βούλει. I have rendered it in the text as if it were, ἢ ὅσα ποιήσει τὰ πράγματα τηλ. ἡλ. β. Victorius connects it closely with the preceding, and renders it, (perhaps better, for with this interpretation there is no change of *number* from πρᾶγμα to πράγματα,) "or in fact as much as you please, and think requisite."

² The former part of the example, ἐγὼ δ' ἐνουθέτουν, κ.τ.λ. seems to have been suggested to Aristotle by the latter half which he takes from the story in Herod. II. 30. Vict. says he has been unable to find it.

separately by the Rhapsodists. Poet. XVI. 8. Plat. Rep. x. 614. B. What Ulysses relates with all the details as actually occurring at the moment, he condenses into a summary of 60 lines[1] in repeating them to Penelope as πεπραγμένα; dry and dead, past and gone, without the life and vigour of *passing* events. Two other instances are Phayllus' treatment of the Epic Cycle (or the Cyclops, according to a var. lect.); and the prologue of Euripides' Œneus; (from the 5 lines preserved this seems to deserve the character here given of it, as a model of compact neatness.) § 7. Further the narrative should have an 'ethical' cast; to effect this we must know what imparts this ethical tone and colour to the speech. One out of many ways of producing it is to exhibit clearly the moral purpose; it is this that gives quality to action and character—it is only the moral purpose that makes an action good, wise, brave, or wicked, foolish, cowardly and so on—and the purpose itself is determined by the end aimed at, the motive which prompted the action. It follows from this definition that mathematical treatises can display no 'character', since as there is no moral object aimed at in them they do not admit of the exhibition of προαίρεσις: but the Socratic dialogues[2] (either the actual conversations of Socrates, or the dialogues in imitation of them by Plato, Xenophon, Æschines, Antisthenes, Phædo, &c.; or as Victor and Schrader think possible, all discourses on moral and social philosophy,) do this; for they treat of subjects which involve this moral purpose, the actions and moral habits of men. Secondly this ethical colour may be imparted by the introduction of any traits that accompany character, and mark a man's principles, habits or temper. As, if you say of a man, 'he talked as he was walking', [this seems to be said of a man who addresses some one or carries on a conversation in a street or public road without stopping] this shows a recklessness and

---

[1] 53 is the exact number, Vater, q. v.

[2] It seems from the context that it is not the *dramatic*, but the *moral*, character of the Socratic dialogues that is here in question.

contemptuous indifference to the opinions and feelings of others ($\theta\rho\alpha\sigma\acute{\nu}\tau\eta\varsigma$), and ill breeding ($\dot{\alpha}\gamma\rho\sigma\iota\kappa\acute{\iota}a$). Thirdly, to speak not as it were from the intellect, but from the heart; let your style bear upon it the impress, not so much of intellectual subtlety and vigour, as of good feeling and sound moral purpose: the one may be the mark of a wise man, but the other indicates a good one. The example which in this case, contrary to Aristotle's usual practice, seems to be made by himself, means, "I wished this to take place; in fact such was my purpose and intention. It is true that I have gained nothing by it; but even so it is better." Here there is no wisdom perhaps, if that consists in always pursuing one's own interest; but there is a noble spirit and goodness shown in the pursuit of honour. If any trait of character that you introduce appear incredible, (so Vict.[1] Maj. takes it for a return to the general subject, 'if any point in your narrative...') in that case add the reason and explanation; as Antigone does in Sophocles' play, (v. 911). If you happen to be unprovided with one, say that 'you know that what you are stating appears strange and incredible; but such is your nature, you can't help it: if the occasion were to arise you'd do the same again': for people never believe in disinterested motives. §§ 8, 9. Besides $\mathring{\eta}\theta o\varsigma$, the narrative should display $\pi\acute{a}\theta o\varsigma$, feeling, emotion, passion; and the usual external accompaniments and indications of such, which are well known to your audience; and any individual marks of passion or traits which are peculiar to and characteristic of yourself or your adversary: as ' he went away scowling at me from under his eyebrows': or 'hissing and shaking his fists furiously', as Æschines said of Cratylus. Such traits as these give a reality and faithfulness to the narrative which secures it credit: for the audience infers from the truth of these individual peculiarities and tokens of character and passion with which they are acquainted, to the truth of the facts

---

[1] Victorius is plainly right, we proceed from $\mathring{\eta}\theta o\varsigma$ immediately to $\pi\acute{a}\theta o\varsigma$.

stated about them which they do not know. A great number of these are to be found in Homer; as in Odyss. T. 361. Present yourself from the very outset in the character which you wish to bear in the eyes of the judges, that they may regard you in that light all through your speech; only take care not to betray your design. That it is no difficult task to convey such impressions to an audience—how quickly they seize and draw their inferences from any of these indications of emotion—appears from the rapidity with which we gather intelligence of things of which we know nothing—as for example the favourable or unfavourable complexion of news from the face and demeanour of messengers. The narrative should be distributed over the speech (as in the epideictic branch it should perhaps be prefixed to the several proofs,) and not confined to one place: sometimes it should not occupy its proper and natural place (he is speaking here of his πρόθεσις, c. 13,) at the beginning of the speech. § 10.

In the deliberative branch of rhetoric there is very little need of narrative[1], because, its time being the future, the exhortation and dissuasion which are its subject matter always have reference to the future; and there can be no narrative of things future; narrative is of the past alone. If one ever is introduced, it is of past events by way of recalling them to the memory, in order to enable the audience to form a better judgment as to their future course. Or in the way of censure or praise [Vict. and Maj. connect this with the preceding; censure or praise of those past transactions. Spengel puts them in brackets, as an interpolation]; but in these cases the narrative is an accident: the deliberative orator is not fulfilling his *proper* function, which is to exhort or dissuade. The last sentence of this chapter ἂν δ' ᾖ ἄπιστον κ.τ.λ. is very obscure, and probably corrupt; and no light

---

[1] Gaisford quotes in illustration, Dion. Halic. Ars Rhet. x. 14. ὅλη μὲν ἰδέα συμβουλευτικὴ διηγήσεως οὐ δεῖται. ἴσασι γὰρ οἱ βουλευόμενοι περὶ ὧν σκοποῦνται, καὶ δέονται μαθεῖν ὃ πρακτέον ἐστίν, οὐχ ὅπερ βουλευτέον.

whatsoever is thrown upon it by the Commentators. First of all it seems that τε after ὑπισχνεῖσθαι cannot stand; and Victorius, though he does not notice this, translates the passage as if the τε were absent. Next, Victorius who is followed by Majoragius and Schrader, renders διατάττειν by 'commissurum'; understanding δ. οἷς βούλονται, '(promise) to leave or refer the matter to the judgment of any one whom your hearers approve.' But διατάττειν has only one possible sense, 'to set out in order, duly dispose or arrange, marshal in order'; and hence it must mean here 'to set forth all your reasons in full detail, οἷς βούλονται, in the terms your hearers desire'; that is, that 'you promise to offer a full and detailed explanation, such as your hearers would like or require, of the apparent paradox or incredible statement.' But the principal difficulty lies in the application of this to the two examples, and particularly to the second. Of the contents of Carcinus' Œdipus we know nothing that will enable us to explain this, further than what the text of Aristotle itself supplies. All that we gather from it is, that in Carcinus' Œdipus Jocasta is constantly promising, in answer to the inquiries of the man who was looking after her son, that she would do something or other; probably, satisfy him. Αἵμων in the second must, I think, be corrupt. Hæmon in the Antigone appears in only one short scene, 635—765. The ῥῆσις which must be referred to, if the reading is sound, is v. 683—723.; in which Hæmon endeavours to persuade his father Creon to give way, and remit his sentence of death against Antigone. There is nothing that can be called διήγησις, 'narrative', at all; nor, as far as I can see, any 'explanation of a paradox or obscurity', in the sense intended by Aristotle. Victorius explains it thus: Hæmon, cum salutem uxoris Antigonæ contra patrem enixe tueretur, tamen ostendebat se in ejus potestate fore, ac quidquid ei visum esset facturum, cum tamen animo aliter sentiret; quod exitus postea declaravit: postquam enim eum a tam sæva sententia revocare non potuit, mori et ipse statuit. I have nothing better to offer, though this seems to me in the highest degree unsatisfactory; in fact, no illustration of the topic at all. It assumes too that διατάττειν is 'committere'.

Ch. 17. The next division of the speech, is the proof; which includes the establishment of your own case, and the refutation of your adversary's, c. 13. 4. c. 17. 14. Now there are various kinds of proof in its widest and most comprehensive sense: for instance appeals to the feelings, indications of your own or the adversary's character, evidence, and other external aids, (the latter, the ἄτεχνοι πίστεις which are used in confirmation of the statements made,) may all be included in the term πίστεις; but the proofs with which we are here concerned are argumentative or demonstrative. [ἀπόδειξις is here used loosely, including probable arguments.] The principal points to which these proofs may be applied are the several 'issues', the στάσεις, status, constitutiones causæ, as they were afterwards called; the point where the case 'comes to a stand', where 'issue is joined', between the conflicting views statements and interests of the two parties. These are according to Aristotle four, [see above 15. 2. and 16. 6. and Append. D. to this book.] which may be reduced to two general heads, the status conjecturalis, στοχαστική, the fact; and qualitas, ποιότης, where the fact is admitted, and the case turns upon the justice or injustice, harmlessness or mischief, or the amount or degree of either of these: the στάσις ὁρική, finitio, nomen, being either omitted or included under 'degree'. To establish your plea upon these the main issues and turning points of the case is of course the most important application of proof by way of argument. This relates only to the δικανικὸν γένος. [on the interpretation of the words, ὡσαύτως καὶ...τοῦτο...see Spald. on Quint. III. 6. 60. whose transl. si quæritur an *hoc* maxime factum fuerit, looks as if he meant to apply them to *a distinct* issue, the ὁρικὴ στάσις. But if this had been Aristotle's meaning he would surely have written ὡσαύτως δὲ καί. The words mean merely that the question of justice or degree is to be proved just as much, or in the same way, as that of fact]. We must remember however that the status of fact is the only one in which it may happen that one of the two parties is necessarily a rogue[1]. For in certain cases which come under this head ignorance cannot be pleaded—except in the shape of forgetfulness; see Eth. N. v. 10.—as it may when the injustice or mischievous character, or the degree of either, in a certain act, is the point contested: and therefore in cases where the issue rests upon the question of fact this topic may be safely dwelt upon, (or 'employed', $\chi\rho\eta\sigma\tau\acute{\epsilon}o\nu$, as the Scholiast reads,) in the others, not. §§ 1. 2.

In the epideictic branch most of the argument, which is only indirect, is employed upon amplification (or detraction), the facts must be taken upon trust: the orator very seldom tries to establish them by proof; or only when they are incredible, or for some other special reason. § 3.

In the public or deliberative branch of rhetoric, the four issues, that properly belong to the forensic, may be raised in the shape of a denial (1) of the future facts, i.e. of the consequences which the speaker attributes to the course of policy which he recommends; or, admitting them, (2) of the justice, (3) expediency, or (4) importance, of the line of action suggested. But though the principal attention is to be directed

[1] I think none of the Commentators has seen that this is the true meaning of the passage. Vict. apparently, and Major. expressly,'(Schrader as far as his note goes leaves the point open, but his translation seems to follow the other two,) interpret it as implying, that in this status one or the other of the two parties is always and of necessity a rascal. That this is not true is seen at once by taking the simplest example that occurs. A accuses B of murder; B denies it, and the issue arises upon the fact. But B may be innocent, and yet the circumstantial evidence so strong as fully to justify A in bringing the charge. Aristotle is referring to a particular class of cases, which he calls $\dot{\epsilon}\nu\ \sigma\upsilon\nu\alpha\lambda\lambda\acute{\alpha}\gamma\mu\alpha\sigma\iota\nu$, Eth. N. v. 10 (near the end) where there is a passage precisely parallel to this; but more explicit, and throwing light on Aristotle's meaning here: such a case as that which Victor himself supplies, and Schrader borrows; the case viz. of a disputed loan or deposit, where unless either of them can justify himself by pleading lack of memory, (Eth. Nic. l. c.) one of the parties must intend to defraud the other.

to the arguments which have reference to these main points, yet the speaker must always be on the look out for any false statement or false reasoning in the subsidiary and extraneous matter: for a direct inference may be drawn from falsehood or fallacy in the one to the existence of them in the other. § 4. Of the two instruments of all reasoning, example, the rhetorical induction, is most suitable to the deliberative; enthymeme, the rhet. syllogism, to the forensic branch: because, the former being engaged mainly with the future, examples must be drawn from past events, which by analogy may help to enable us to foresee what is likely to happen under similar circumstances; whereas no future events admit of direct proof. In a law court on the other hand, the questions, turning upon the truth or falsity of alleged facts, and fact carrying with it necessity, admit *to a greater extent*, $μᾶλλον$, of a nearer approach to, the rigorous demonstration of syllogism, the conclusions of which are necessary. This is a mere question of *comparative* exactness in reasoning: no proof in Rhetoric is really syllogistic, Rhetoric excludes all rigorous scientific proof: none of its conclusions are more than probable. § 5. As with the several facts in the epideictic $διήγησις$, (16. §§ 1, 2.,) so likewise here in the use of argumentative proofs, he recommends that they be not all brought forward in a string, but interspersed with other topics, so as to relieve the weariness and assist the intelligence of the uncultivated audience. For a long and connected chain of arguments not only puzzles and confounds a listener unaccustomed to continuous reasoning, but also wearies and overwhelms him; so that one argument coming upon another before he has fully perceived the force of the preceding, they clash together, come into conflict, as it were, and so the force and effect of the whole is weakened and destroyed ($καταβλάπτει\ ἄλληλα$)[1]. In such things there is a limit of quantity which is soon reached; as Homer says,

---

[1] Compare I. 2. 12, 13. II. 22. 2.

Od. Δ. 204.; where it appears that Homer had the same meaning, from his saying, not τοιαῦτα, but τόσα. § 6. Enthymemes are not to be employed to prove things which are plain enough without them; otherwise the same fault is committed as by those philosophers who apply their demonstrations to things more certain and better known than the premisses from which they draw their syllogisms[1]. To argue thus, to prove what is sufficiently clear already, is compared by Quint. v. 12. 8. to the absurdity of bringing out a candle into the light of the noonday sun, § 7. In painting emotion, or in working upon the feelings of the audience, use no argument: the effect of the argument and the feeling cannot coexist in their minds, one will expel the other: all 'motions' mutually exclude each other, they are either obliterated or extinguished altogether, either they are mutually destructive, or else the stronger overpowers the weaker. Nor when you are trying to give an ethical character to your speech; for argument is independent of character and moral purpose. § 8. But employ general maxims in narrative and proof, for they have an ethical colour. See II. 21. 16. This is illustrated by an example of this use of a γνώμη. If your object is to *move* the minds of your hearers, the same sentiment may be thrown into a different shape. § 9.

In this particular, as generally, public speaking is more difficult than forensic. This is in conformity with what was said at the commencement of the work upon the neglect of this the nobler and higher branch by the sophistical Rhetoricians his predecessors, but differs from the opinion of Cicero and others who consider the judicial variety the more arduous. And the reason is plain; because it deals with the future (which no one can prove), whereas the other is concerned only with the past; which, as Epimenides said, may be known even to diviners and soothsayers[2]—he accordingly

---

[1] Compare again the same two passages, p. 357, note.

[2] The καὶ τοῖς μάντεσιν, was doubtless meant by Epimenides as a sarcasm upon his prophetic brethren, who pretended to see into futurity.

never meddled with the future, but contented himself with interpreting the obscurities of the past. Besides this, pleaders in a court of justice have the law for their theme, and being furnished with this as a basis and starting-point they can easily supply themselves with arguments. Again in *public* speeches, there are few landing places, as it were, pauses in the main argument, where episodical and extraneous matter may be introduced; they admit, that is to say, of very few digressions, for which forensic speeches afford abundant opportunity; such as attacks upon the opponent, exculpatory or panegyrical remarks upon oneself, or appeals to the feelings. For these there is less room in the deliberative than in any of the three branches, unless, that is, the speaker quit his proper subject. The public speaker accordingly when at a loss for topics must do as the orators do at Athens, and Isocrates who only *writes* public speeches; they must introduce alien matter; as Isocrates in his Panegyric accuses the Lacedæmonians in the middle of his advice, and Chares in his συμμαχικός; i.e. the περὶ εἰρήνης. § 10. In epideictic speeches matter may be supplied by laudatory episodes or digression; as was Isocrates' practice who is always bringing in some one or other in this way. And this was what Gorgias meant when he remarked, that he was never at a loss for something to say. The praises of Achilles introduce those of Peleus, this brings in Æacus, then the God, next valour, and τὸ καὶ τό "so and so", any thing else that may happen to be connected however remotely with the principal subject. And this is just what I have been describing. § 11. If you have argumentative proofs to bring forward you can employ the 'ethical style[1]', to conciliate the good opinion of the audience as well—the two however are not to be mixed, or used at the same time, ἅμα. § 8.—if not, you must supply the place of direct argument with the latter. In fact it better befits a man of worth to

"Even diviners," said he, impostors as they are, "can prophesy what is *past*."

Vict and Maj. take no notice of it.
[1] The argument from character.

represent himself in his true character, than that his speech should be closely and accurately reasoned. § 12. Of enthymemes, the refutative are more popular than the demonstrative; the truth of the conclusion being much more apparent in the former, because they bring the two opposites into juxtaposition; so that the inconsistency is immediately detected, and the fallacy of that which is refuted seen at once. § 13. On the ἔλεγχος see above, on II. 22. pp. 262, 264. συναγωγὴ τῶν ἐναντίων. II. 23. 30. where the same remark is made about the comparative popularity of the two kinds of enthymemes. Introd. p. 265.

The refutatio adversarii is no distinct kind of proof, or division of the speech. The adversary's arguments may be refuted by ἔνστασις, contrary proposition, instance of the opposite, objection; or by counter syllogism. See on these in the chapter on λύσις. II. 25. supr. p. 267, seq.

In the assembly and the law courts the ordinary and natural arrangement of proofs is for the first speaker, the opener of the debate, to prove his own case first, and then reply to what may be urged on the other side, either by direct refutation, or indirectly, by pulling to pieces, cutting up, (δ ι α σύρειν) his antagonist's opinions, arguments, or character, by anticipation. This order however is not always to be observed. If the anticipated opposition is very strong, and turns on a great variety of different points, it may be advisable to attack and expose these *first*, and then support your own case by direct arguments. The reason of this, which is not given by Aristotle, seems to be, that when the arguments that may be advanced on the other side are very numerous, some of them are likely to have occurred already to your hearers, and so may have instilled a prejudice against your side of the question, which may prevent the direct and positive arguments by which you seek to prove your own case having their due weight. (so Vict.) § 14. And for the same reason, the speaker who has to reply should adopt the latter order, and more especially if the counter arguments are popular and plausible. § 14. He has as it were to make *room* for the reception of his own views in the minds of the audience, which is as it were *preoccupied* by those of the adversary; the effect of insinuations or prejudices against a speech and its proofs, being exactly similar to that which they produce upon the estimate of the character of a man: they must be removed in both cases alike before the mind is ready to receive favourably (δέχεσθαι) the one or the other. The speaker in reply must therefore *first* contend against all, or the most important, or the most popular and approved, or the most easily refuted, of the adverse arguments, and then proceed to confirm his own positions by direct proof as well as he can. This is illustrated by an example from Euripides' Troad. 969. (The first line quoted is the opening of Hecuba's reply, the second the commencement of the argument.) The poet has here shown his usual rhetorical skill by making Hecuba in her reply to Helen single out the weakest argument, τοῦ εὐηθεστάτου, of those advanced by her adversary against her, and place it in the forefront of her defence; in order that Menelaus before whom the altercation is conducted, may carry on to the rest the unfavourable impression derived from the exposure of the first. So much on the subject of proof argumentative. § 15. As regards 'ethical' proof, seeing that there are some things which are invidious to say of ourselves, or tedious, or apt to provoke contradiction, or again which when said of others reflect upon ourselves, and convey the impression that we are abusive or illbred, we may in such case adopt the artifice of Isocrates in his 'Philip', 96. D., and ἀντίδοσις, § 8., and put them into the mouth of another[1]. The same is employed by Archilochus in lampooning the daughter of Lycambes, the scurrilous insinuations against her character being represented as proceeding from the father himself: and again in another

---

[1] On the ἀντίδοσις, in connexion with this device, see Victorius. Isocrates states it all himself, § 8. There is a still more artful application of it, to which perhaps Aristotle may more directly refer, §§ 142—149.

satire the same use is made of the carpenter Charon. The verses quoted merely mark the commencement of the passages referred to, just as in the preceding reference to Euripides' Troades. And similarly Sophocles in the Antigone 683. seq. makes Hæmon in his altercation with his father convey against him through the medium of others those accusations which a son and a subject dares not bring directly against a father and a king. 692. seq. § 16. Lastly, enthymemes may be expressed as general maxims γνῶμαι, and vice versa. See the same topic treated in II. 21. 1, 2.

Ch. 18. A favourite instrument of debate with speakers in the public assembly and law courts is the interrogation of the adversary. The object of this is to enforce an argument; or to take the adversary by surprise and extract from him an unguarded admission; or to place him in an awkward dilemma, by shaping your question in such a way, that he must either by avowing it admit something which his antagonist wishes to establish, or by refusing seem to give consent by his silence to that which the questioner wishes to insinuate; or to gain some similar advantage[1]. It may be made therefore in this way subservient to proof, and so may properly be treated as an appendix to the chapter on πίστεις. In this way we may vindicate, against Vater, (quoted in the note) the insertion of this subject here. Since question and answer play such an important part in the practice of Rhetoric, it will be advisable here to describe and classify their principal τόποι, or the occasions of using them. The first of these is called by the Greek Commentator τὸ εἰς ἄτοπον ἀπάγειν,

---

[1] There is a fragment περὶ ἐρωτήσεως καὶ ἀποκρίσεως by an unknown Rhetorician, printed by Spengel as an appendix to Aristotle's work in his edition of the Rhet. Græci. It is a paraphrase of the six first sections of the 18th chapter of Aristotle's third book, which it follows exactly, and to which it serves as a commentary; once or twice supplying an illustration which is wanting in the original. The author is a stupid fellow and misunderstands Aristotle as often as he can.

Interrogatio, says Vater, quæ non nisi ex formis pronuntiatorum una est, huc non pertinet: ejus tractandæ in prima hujus libri parte locus fuisset.

the reductio ad absurdum of the adversary. The opportunity for this kind of question occurs, when by the addition of a single interrogation to something previously said by the opponent the latter can be involved in a manifest absurdity. This is illustrated by Pericles' answer to Lampon[1] the soothsayer. § 1. The second is τὸ τὰ ὁμολογούμενα ἐρωτᾶν: and the object of this also is to entrap the opponent into an unforeseen admission fatal to his own argument. When in your syllogism the second premiss is so clear and simple that no one can fail to see it, and the conclusion also so clearly follows that the adversary must needs admit it, after stating one of the premisses, you may suppress the premiss which is unmistakeable, and then express the conclusion by way of a question. This will take your adversary by surprise and throw him into confusion, and is a pointed and lively way of putting an argument. The example is from Plato's Apology 27. B, C, but somewhat differently expressed. Socrates is accused by Meletus of denying the existence of the Gods. He asks, Don't I believe the existence of τὸ δαιμόνιον? this is acknowledged. The next question is, are not the δαίμονες either the children of the Gods or some divine nature? the respondent assents. From this arises the first premiss of the syllogism. All that believe in δαίμονες believe in children of the Gods. The second or minor is omitted[2]; whoever believes in a son must needs believe in a father; as too obvious to escape any one: and thus the conclusion is drawn in the shape of a question. All that believe in δαίμονες or τὸ δαιμόνιον, of whom I Socrates am one, must needs believe in the father of them, the Gods. The Greek author (of the tract π. ἐρωτ. καὶ ἀποκρ.) absurdly says that the omitted ὁμολογούμενον is ὁ δαιμόνια νομίζων θεοὺς νομίζει; which is the conclusion. § 2. The third method is to put a question (in order to make a man contradict himself out of his own mouth,) the answer to which must involve

---

[1] Lampon, Plut. vit. Pericl. 154. F.   [2] So Vict. and Maj.
Arist. Av. 521.

a self-contradiction or paradox, which will shake the opponent's credit. An example of this is given by the Greek Rhetorician from Lysias[1] contra Eratosth. §§ 25, 26—§ 3. The fourth method is to put a question which only admits of a 'sophistical' answer, an apparent quibble, in reply; as 'it is and it is not,' or 'partly so and partly not,' or 'in one way yes and in another no': for an audience is sure to show signs of disapprobation (to clamour or hoot) at an answer like one of these, as not straightforward, and evasive of the question. Beyond these four methods, which if properly employed are all certain of effecting their object, it is not advisable to proceed in putting questions to an adversary: for if he should give you a check by interposing an 'instance' or 'objection', he will be thought to have gained a victory[2]: for you cannot carry on your questions so long as to meet and refute his objection, on account of the 'weakness' of a popular audience, who are unable to follow a long continuous chain of reasoning[3]; and for the same reason you should pack your enthymemes into as small a compass as possible. § 4. In answering, one thing to be attended to is carefully to distinguish the senses of ambiguous words and expressions by a regular explanation or definition, (διαιροῦντα λόγῳ; Vict. and Maj., 'longa oratione', opposed to συντόμως,) and not too concisely, which leads to obscurity: in replying to questions which tend to involve

---

[1] ἀπήγαγες Πολέμαρχον, ἢ οὔ; τὰ ὑπὸ τῶν ἀρχόντων προσταχθέντα δεδιὼς ἐποίουν. ἦσθα δ' ἐν τῷ βουλευτηρίῳ ὅτε οἱ λόγοι ἐγίνοντο περὶ ἡμῶν; ἦν. πότερον συνηγόρευες τοῖς κελεύουσιν ἀποκτεῖναι ἢ ἀντέλεγες; ἀντέλεγον. ἵνα μὴ ἀποθάνωμεν; ἵνα μὴ ἀποθάνητε. ἡγούμενος ἡμᾶς ἄδικα πάσχειν ἢ δίκαια; ἄδικα. εἶτα, ὦ σχετλιώτατε πάντων, ἀντέλεγες μὲν ἵνα σώσειας, συνελάμβανες δὲ ἵνα ἀποκτείναις; Lysias contra Eratosth. p. 122. § 25, 26.

[2] Thus L. Crassus put down Philippus. Quid latras? asked the latter. Furem video, was the reply. Cic. de Orat. Quint. VI. 3. 82. This is not perhaps exactly an ἔνστασις, but it is at all events a very effectual 'check'.

[3] Here again the anonymous Greek author has missed the connexion. He makes this an independent precept, overlooking the γάρ. Vict. gives it right.

you in a contradiction, give your explanation or solution at once in answering the first question, without waiting for the succeeding ones, or allowing the opponent to draw his conclusion; for the point or drift of it is always easy enough to foresee. But all this may be better learnt from the Topics. (that is, the 8th book, where Aristotle shows how captious questions are to be avoided. Maj.) § 5. If the question itself forms the conclusion of the implied syllogism, the respondent should annex the cause or explanation of his conduct, or whatever else it may be, to his reply; as Sophocles'[1] did in his answer to Pisander; and the Lacedæmonian, when called to account for his conduct in his Ephory. To avoid the risk of being thus foiled, it is expedient at all events not to continue your questions beyond the conclusion that you design to draw from your adversary's admissions; and in fact not to put the conclusion in the form of a question at all, unless it is so superabundantly clear and certain that it is impossible for the adversary to deny or evade it; for, as he says in the Topics, Θ. 2. 158. a. 7, an unscrupulous or determined opponent may spoil your argument by simply saying 'no' to your question. In fact it often happens, he continues, that an opponent will go so far as to deny a conclusion regularly drawn from the premisses, trusting to the ignorance and want of acuteness of the assistants at the debate; and therefore a fortiori is an opponent likely to deny a conclusion deduced from premisses which are *not* fully and distinctly stated. § 6. For the full treatment of the subject of τὸ γελοῖον, ridiculum, (Cicero de Or. II. 58. 236.) we are referred to some lost chapters of the Poetics. It is mentioned here because it is found extremely serviceable in debate. By well-timed ridicule, or a well-applied joke, you may often

---

[1] This is not the poet, but an orator and politician of the later period of the Peloponnesian war. He was, as we learn from this passage, one of the πρόβουλοι, appointed after the disastrous termination of the Sicilian expedition in 413. B.C., who established the oligarchical government of the four hundred. He is mentioned also in I. 14. 3.

On the second example, see Grote, Hist. Gr. II. 480. note.

silence an adversary whom you cannot convince: one of its uses being that which Gorgias mentioned in his 'Art', to spoil, namely, or destroy the effect of your adversaries' earnest by a jest, or their jest by earnest[1]. One thing however must not be passed over. Of the several kinds of jokes enumerated in the work above mentioned not all are becoming to a gentleman. You must be careful therefore, as all kinds of jokes do not suit the same people, to select those which are suitable to yourself and your own character. For example, irony is more appropriate to a well-bred and cultivated man than buffoonery; for the one is used for its own sake, with no ulterior and sordid object[2]; buffoonery looks to the reward of the applause of the vulgar. On εἰρωνεία and βωμολοχία, see Eth. N. IV. 13. sub fin. and 14. Comp. II. 7. In the former of these places there is a passage which explains the distinction here made. οἱ δ᾽ εἴρωνες ἐπὶ τὸ ἔλαττον λέγοντες (using self-disparagement) χαριέστεροι μὲν τὰ ἤθη φαίνονται· οὐ γὰρ κέρδους ἕνεκα δοκοῦσι λέγειν, ἀλλὰ φεύγοντες τὸ ὀγκηρόν· μάλιστα δὲ καὶ οὗτοι τὰ ἔνδοξα ἀπαρνοῦνται, οἷον καὶ Σωκράτης ἐποίει. And see further on propriety in jesting, Cic. de Off. XXVIII. 10—12; and de Orat. II. c. 59, seq. The distinction between the ingenuus and liberalis jocus is made to turn upon a different point to that of Aristotle. § 12.

Ch. 19. The last division of the speech is the ἐπίλογος; otherwise called ἀνακεφαλαίωσις "recapitulation" by the Greek rhetoricians; enumeratio, repetitio; (in hâc quæ repetemus... quod Græco verbo patet, decurrendum *per capita*. Quint. VI. 1. 2.) the most important and indispensable part of its contents being put for the whole. It is in Latin peroratio, conclusio,

---

[1] From Gorgias' τέχνη. The words are quoted by the Schol. on Plat. Gorg. 473. E. (Ed. Tur. p. 910). τοῦτο παράγγελμα Γοργίου, τὸ τὰς σπουδὰς τῶν ἀντιδίκων γέλωτι ἐκλύειν, τὰ δὲ γελοῖα ταῖς σπουδαῖς ἐκκρούειν. See Sauppe, Fragm. Orat. Græc. Γοργίας, τέχνη, Fr. 4. Vol. III. p. 131.

[2] αὐτοῦ perhaps masculine. The εἴρων employs his εἰρωνεία 'for his own sake', for mere amusement, with no ulterior object.

or cumulus. Quint. VI. 1. 1. This author, who treats of peroratio in the first chapter of his sixth book, describes its contents under two heads, enumeratio and affectus; the first and third of Aristotle's division being included under affectus (l. c. § 10, 11), and the second, which is *not* expressly noticed, perhaps tacitly referred to the same. See likewise on this subject, Cic. de Inv. I. 52. 98.—the division of the contents agrees with Quintilian's—hæc habet tres partes, enumerationem, indignationem (δείνωσιν), conquestionem (ἔλεον) : these are then described in detail, cc. 52—55[1]. Auct. ad Heren. II. 30. seq. Rhet. ad Al. cc. 34, 35. Apsin. Ars Rhet. ap. Speng. Rhet. Græc., I. p. 384.

The contents of the ἐπίλογος according to Aristotle may be referred to four general heads : 1. to inspire the audience with a good feeling or favourable opinion towards yourself, and a bad and unfavourable one towards the adversary ; 2. amplification and extenuation; 3. affectus, exciting emotion in the audience; and 4. ἀνάμνησις, the recalling to the minds of the hearers by a summary recapitulation the main facts and arguments already brought forward in detail. The first and third of these are common to the exordium and the conclusion. Quintilian well observes, VI. 1. 10, and 51, that there is this difference in the mode of dealing with them in the two divisions. At the beginning you have the whole speech before you in which the required impression may be produced. They may therefore be handled more sparingly, parcius ; but in the peroration in which the final impression has to be made they are to be worked up more fully and in detail; "here if any where we may let loose the full stream of our eloquence"—this point is omitted by Aristotle. That the topic of recommendation of oneself and disparagement of the adversary is properly made to succeed the third general division of the speech, πίστεις, and to occupy the first place in the peroration, is shown by this, that it is

---

[1] Cicero elsewhere (ap. Vict.) divides the peroratio into only two parts, amplificatio and enumeratio, doubtless referring the affectus to the former.

plainly the natural order, after having proved the truth of your own case and the unsoundness of your adversary's, to proceed next to praise yourself and vituperate the other party, and to dwell on, enforce, and elaborate[1] these topics. Two things may be aimed at in this; to make yourself out to be either absolutely, or relatively, good; and the adversary bad in the same way. The virtue assumed may be either virtue per se, and independent of all other considerations, as times, places, and persons—or in default of this, at any rate good to the judges or audience; as it may be, useful, or well-disposed. The topics which may be drawn upon to supply materials for this, have been already enumerated, in Bk. I. c. 9. § 1. Secondly, the facts having been already established, the next thing to be done in the natural order is to amplify the preceding topics: for it is clear that the facts must be admitted before you can venture to enlarge upon them; just as the enlargement or growth of the body arises, proceeds, from something preexisting. The topics of amplification and detraction may likewise be gathered from the analyses of foregoing chapters, as I. cc. 7. 9, 14. II. 7[2]. § 2. Where this has been done, the quality, i.e. character, and magnitude or importance, of the facts being well understood, the next thing is to awaken any of the various emotions in the minds of the audience which the case and occasion may require; such as commiseration, indignation[3], anger,

---

[1] Such seems to be the sense of ἐπιχαλκεύειν, 'to reforge,' incudi reddere, 'retouch, recast, return again and again to the work in order to complete it and bring it to perfection. So Vict. It has reference solely to the first topic, as appears from μετὰ τοῦτο at the beginning of § 2.

[2] These manifest references to the two preceding books, are quite sufficient to prove—if any proof were needed—against the impugners of the genuineness of this third book, the integrity of the entire work, and the connexion of its three parts.

[3] ἔλεος and δείνωσις are both well explained in Cic. de Inv. I. 53. 100. and 55. 106.; and noticed by Quint. VI. 1. 9. comp. VI. 2. 27. In Aristotle however, from the company in which it is found, it seems to be the emotion itself, what is usually called νέμεσις, 'righteous indignation;' and not here the 'exaggeration' of style and manner by which it may be excited. Indignatio est *oratio* per quam conficitur ut

hatred, jealousy, emulation, strife. (the last seems to be a pugnacious antagonistic feeling against the adversary or any one else, or a quarrelsome mood.) The analyses of these have also been already given in Bk. II. cc. 2—11. § 3. It remains therefore to recapitulate the principal topics of the speech. Here we may do with propriety, what some writers of rhetoric absurdly recommend us to do in the exordium— he had said before, and repeats here, that all that we want on this subject in the prooemium is a brief statement of the object of the speech—that is, repeat again and again any point that is difficult, or requires special attention, until it is fixed in the hearers' memory. § 4. The recapitulation should begin with the remark that you have performed all that you have promised, and this will naturally introduce a restatement of what you have said and why. One way of doing this is by setting your facts and arguments in comparison with those of the adverse party, which admits of two varieties: for you may either go through those only of your adversary's statements and arguments of which the subjects are common to both of you, setting your own in opposition to them individually each to each; or you may enumerate *all* those of your adversary together in one series, and then contrast your own with them, with all your own views and arguments, at the end. (This is Vict.'s expl.) The former method is κατ' ἀντικρύ, e regione collocare, to set them in direct and individual opposition one to another. Another mode of enumeration is 'ironically'—you may put for instance your own statements and arguments into the adversary's mouth, and adopt his yourself[1]. "You know, he said so and so; and I so and so"—which they very well know you and he did *not* say: or thus; "I wonder what he would have done, what airs he

in aliquem hominem magnum odium, aut in rem gravis offensio concitetur. Cic. u. s. It is employed in heightening the *atrocity* of an action or event. Præcipue δείνωσις in exaggeranda indignitate. Quint. VIII. 3. 88. See Ernesti, Lex. Techn. s. v. Demosthenes excelled all orators in δείνωσις Quint. VI. 2. 24. comp. X. 1. 108. ἔλεος deprecatio, miseratio, (Quint.) appeals to the tender and sympathetic feelings.

[1] So Major.

would have given himself, how he would have borne himself, if he had only happened to prove what is right;—so and so, and so and so—as I did; instead of what is entirely false—so and so, and so and so—as he actually did. Or thirdly by interrogation, "What have I omitted? have I not established this and that and the other?" or, "what has *he* shown? has he shown this and that?" Lastly, you may simply enumerate, without attempting to contrast them, all the foregoing topics of the speech; first what you have said yourself, and then if you please separately, what has been said by the adversary. § 6. 'An asyndeton forms an appropriate conclusion to the whole, to make it a real ἐπίλογος, and not a mere λόγος'. Perhaps the meaning of this may be what is expressed by Quint. VI. 1. 2, nam si morabimur, non jam enumeratio, sed quasi altera fiet ratio. The asyndeton by its pithy brevity well marks the close. Victor. thinks that the intention is to distinguish the ἐπίλογος, something added as an appendage, a tail-piece, from the rest of the speech by the absence of the conjunctions; (but asyndeton is admissible in the body of the speech also;) to mark by this difference that it is a true ἐπίλογος. Major. takes much the same view of the meaning.

The speeches of Lysias, against Eratosthenes, and Andocides, both conclude with an asyndeton of this kind. The first ends thus: παύσομαι κατηγορῶν. ἀκηκόατε, ἑωράκατε, πεπόνθατε, ἔχετε. δικάζετε.—which leaves no doubt as to Aristotle's real intention.

APPENDIX A. TO BOOK III. CH. II.

ὀνόματα καὶ ῥήματα. This is the primary and fundamental division of language, and even Plato carried it no farther. See Cratylus, 425 A, 431 B. λόγος—ἡ τῶν ῥημάτων καὶ ὀνομάτων ξύνθεσίς ἐστι. Theodectes and Aristotle (Dion. de Comp. Verb. c. 2. de adm. vi dic. in Demosth. c. 48. Quintil. I. 4. 17.) added a third, σύνδεσμος; and subsequent philosophers, especially the Stoics, (Dion., Quint., ll. cc.) completed the division. The third division, σύνδεσμος, is here left out of the account. This primary division is sometimes expressed in a grammatical form, as noun and verb, sometimes logically, as subject and predicate, the two ultimate elements of language. As Logic and Grammar seem to spring up simultaneously, and always go hand in hand, and grammar may be considered a branch of logic—it is hard to decide whether the logical or the grammatical conception of this distinction is the primary one. *Is* thought really antecedent to speech? probably not; but it is a grave question, not to be lightly pronounced upon[1]. At all events, with our constitutions and habits, it seems that reasoning is impossible *to us* without language; no connected continuous train of reasoning can at any rate be carried on in the mind without it. And this seems to have been Plato's opinion, as may be inferred from his constant descriptions of the conclusion of a

---

[1] *Perception*, in children, is doubtless anterior to the use of speech; whether these have the power of connecting thoughts and forming judgments at this early stage of growth, I may have my doubts, but would rather leave the decision of the question to those who are better acquainted with the habits and faculties of very young children than myself. But with regard to grown men and women, whose habits are already formed and faculties developed, I am persuaded that *they* cannot, or at all events *do* not, carry on a train of thought or of argument mentally without the suggestion of actual words.

process of reasoning, or an act of judgment, as the result of a *mental conversation*. Aristotle's ordinary conception of the distinction of ὄνομα and ῥῆμα is plainly the grammatical. This is unmistakably evident from the definitions in the Poetics, c. 20, §§ 8, 9, and the *illustrations* of the former in c. 21. ὄνομα is φωνὴ συνθετή, σημαντικὴ ἄνευ χρόνου, and includes substantives and adjectives; ῥῆμα is φ. σ. σημαντικὴ μετὰ χρόνου. And to precisely the same effect are the definitions of the de Interpr. cc. 2 and 3; and these terms are there applied to *nouns* and *verbs*. Nevertheless, to show how difficult it is to disengage the two modes of looking at them, in the same treatise c. 10. 20. b. 1, they are regarded logically, as subject and predicate; μετατιθέμενα δὲ τὰ ὀνόματα καὶ τὰ ῥήματα ταὐτὸν σημαίνει, οἷον ἔστι λευκὸς ἄνθρωπος, ἔστιν ἄνθρωπος λευκός. Here it is 'man' and 'white,' and not the *verb* ἔστι, which are transferred, or made to change their place: ἔστι is not in question at all, and ὄνομα and ῥῆμα must be distributed amongst the other two, and denote severally the *subject* and *predicate*.

Under the *grammatical* classification of the Poetics, the 'adjective' belongs to ὄνομα; so that the same word may be grammatically an ὄνομα, and logically a ῥῆμα. I think this will help to clear up the confusion which is noticeable in Aristotle's expressions on this subject; and which likewise prevails in Dr Donaldson's account of this matter, New Cratylus, § 125.

In Aristotle's *three-fold* classification, ὄνομα, ῥῆμα, and σύνδεσμος, the distribution would probably be this : ὀνόματα includes nouns, adjectives, and probably adverbs, (as a mere πτῶσις of the noun,) articles, and pronouns; ῥήματα are verbs; and σύνδεσμοι prepositions and conjunctions, connecting particles; interjections being omitted; and thus all the parts of speech are accounted for. In the Poetics, 20, 6, we are told that σύνδεσμος is a φωνὴ ἄσημος, ἢ οὔτε κωλύει οὔτε ποιεῖ φωνὴν μίαν σημαντικήν; and afterwards, which explains the other, that it is, an utterance which has no distinct sense or meaning of its own, is not 'significant,' *except in connexion with other words*, which make up *together* 'a single significant utterance,' μίαν σημαντικὴν φωνήν : *now* we get a meaning. This is equally true of prepositions (which express a mere relation) as of 'conjunctions' proper.

In the Poetics, 20. 7, ἄρθρον is added to the three other divisions. This also is an 'insignificant' utterance, and only has a meaning in connexion with other words; if it precedes, it indicates a notion following; if it follows, one that has preceded; or else it defines, as τὸ φημί, τὸ περί ("*the* words, φημί and περί"). Gräfenhan, not. ad loc.'.

---

[1] This classification of the 'parts of speech' Poet. c. 20—so called by Aristotle, τῆς λέξεως ἁπάσης τάδ' ἐστὶ τὰ μέρη—is no true grammatical classification, the members of it being heterogeneous. It consists of eight divisions, of which only four, ἄρθρον, ὄνομα, ῥῆμα, σύνδεσμος, are in reality 'parts of speech.' The remaining four are, στοιχεῖον (elementum, letter), συλλαβή, πτῶσις (inflexion, change of termination), and λόγος (the elementary proposition, combination of noun and verb, Gräfenhan, ad loc.). Aristotle in defining λόγος, § 12, says that a proposition to be intelligible need not have a verb—as the definition of man, rational animal. Expressed no doubt it need not; but understood it must. 'Rational animal' has no meaning without the addition of 'man is.' Of the four true parts of speech, two are φωναὶ σημαντικαί, and two (ἄρθρον and σύνδεσμος) ἄσημοι, 'words which *signify* nothing except in combination.'

The distribution of the parts of speech under this fourfold classification is as follows: article; ὄνομα, noun, adjective (in the definition of ῥῆμα c. 20 § 9, λευκός stands for an ὄνομα), pronoun, (unless that should be rather classed with the article, the two being originally identical), participle and adverb may either come under πτῶσις, or both belong to the class ὄνομα— as regards the latter of the two, the adverb, this is the opinion of Gräfenhan, Gesch. der Phil. I. 469, who refers to Rhet. III. 9. 9. Ταὐτὸ δὲ ὄνομα· σὺ δ' αὐτὸν καὶ ζῶντα ἔλεγες κακῶς καὶ νῦν γράφεις κακῶς. This however is also quoted as a case of πτῶσις, to which in fact it is usually referred: the passage seems not to be conclusive on the point. That the participle is an ὄνομα, appears from Top. VI. 10, where this name is given to ὠφελμκός and πεποιηκός; and de Interpr. c. 3, where ὁ λέγων and ὁ ἀκούσας are similarly designated. And so the parts of speech are all enumerated, except prepositions and conjunctions, which are both included in σύνδεσμος, and interjections, which are not recognised as one of the parts of speech. Gräfenhan thinks that the demonstrative pronoun is classed by Aristotle with the articles; both of them being called προδιόρισμοι, 'additional definitions.'

On the primary double division, Donaldson remarks, New Cratylus, § 124, looking at it from the logical side, that the Greek *verb* usually *includes* the copula; which is therefore likely to escape notice at an early stage of inquiry. ἀνὴρ βαδίζει means the same as, and almost always stands for, ἀνὴρ βαδίζων ἐστί. This is constantly implied by Aristotle: and similarly, ὁ ἵππος λευκός is fully equivalent to ὁ ἵππος ἐστὶ λευκός. See Sir W. Hamilton, Lect. on Logic, Vol. III. p. 228, and Mansel's note on the copula and predicate: and on Aristotle's classification of words, in Poet. c. XX. and elsewhere, see Grüfenhan, Gesch. der Philologie, I. 459—462. They may be classed, he says, under three heads, according to (1) the form, (2) the signification, (3) the ordinary use of language (sprachgebrauch).

APPENDIX B. TO BOOK III. CH. II.

On Metaphor.

Aristotle's definition of metaphor is given in the Poetics, c. 21. § 7. It runs thus: "Metaphor is the imposition (the assigning to any object, designating by a word, ἐπιφορά) of a foreign name, (ἀλλοτρίου, a name that does not properly belong to the thing, opposed to κύριον and οἰκεῖον) a transfer either from genus to species, or from species to genus, or from species to species, or proportionally (ἀνάλογον, i.e. by analogy or resemblance)." This definition gives a wider extension to the application of the term than would be admitted in our modern languages. The test of a metaphor in modern usage is that it must convey a direct comparison: and the merit of a metaphor consists in the ingenuity of the comparison, when remote resemblances are brought together; or in the suggestion of pleasing associations, as when a beautiful object, or one that has interesting associations, is substituted for something else of an ordinary character which wants these qualities, by reason of the resemblance which it bears to the other in one or more points. Campbell, Phil.

of Rhet., Bk. III. ch. 1. § 2, calls it "a *comparison* in epitome:" and Whately, Rhet. ch. III. § 2, defines it, "a word substituted for another *on account of the resemblance* or analogy between their significations." It might seem from this that the three first species of metaphor distinguished by Aristotle would be excluded from our conception and use of it. His two first classes might be considered mere cases of synecdoche, which either (1) puts the part for the whole, as sail for ship, or (2) genus for species, as vessel for ship, or (3) species for genus, as 'lilies of the field' for flowers in general. These examples of synecdoche are supplied by Campbell, op. cit. Vol. II. pp. 154, 159—the definition is given p. 153—and by Whately, Rhetoric, ch. III. § 2; who also remarks that Aristotle includes synecdoche under metaphor[1]. And the metaphor from εἶδος to εἶδος might be regarded as a mere case of what is commonly called μετωνυμία or ὑπαλλαγή (on the latter, Cic. Orat. c. 27), the substitution of one word for another; though of course this is never done unless there be some kind of resemblance, immediate or remote. Interpreted in this way the resemblance is insufficient to constitute a regular metaphor. At the same time Aristotle admits in Poet. c. XXII. 17, that resemblance is essential to a good metaphor, τὸ εὖ μεταφέρειν τὸ τὸ ὅμοιον θεωρεῖν; and Topic. Z. 2. 140. a. 9. πάντες γὰρ οἱ μεταφέροντες κατά τινα ὁμοιότητα μεταφέρουσιν. And in the de Gen. Anim. V. 4. 5—8, there are two exemplifications given of the metaphor, which show that the third at least of the four classes may really be brought under the meaning of the term in its proper and modern acceptation. Aristotle is speaking of σῆψις, corruption or putrefaction; a notion which he says may be applied to water, earth, and all material substances of that kind. One of the species (εἴδη) of corruption is the corruption of earthy vapour (γεωδοῦς ἀτμίδος), which is

---

[1] Twining also observes in his notes on the Poetics that the two first of Aristotle's divisions of metaphor 'belong to the trope called since Aristotle's time synecdoche.'

called 'mould'. This particular form of corruption, mould, has therefore 'vapour', ἀτμίς, for its genus. πάχνη, 'hoar frost', is another subordinate 'kind', εἶδος, of vapour: the latter in the one case taking the form of, (differenced by, *so as to make a species or kind,*) freezing, ἐὰν παγῇ; the other, differenced by corruption, becomes the species 'mould'. Now the comic poets are in the habit of comparing an old man's white hair both to mould and hoar frost (whence 'hoar hairs', 'a hoary head'), and the 'metaphor' is a good one (εὖ μεταφέρουσι). In the one case the resemblance is in 'genus': both hoar frost and whiteness of hair are kinds of vapour— whiteness of hair is a corruption of vapour § 6; in the other, mould and the white hair are both cases of corruption, σῆψις; in the latter instance the resemblance lies in the εἶδος. What the difference really is between the two cases it is not easy to see: each of them appears to be an example of resemblance in 'kind', εἶδος πρὸς εἶδος. The words are, ἡ μὲν πάχνη (ταὐτόν ἐστι) τῷ γένει· ἀτμὶς γὰρ ἄμφω· ὁ δ' εὐρὼς τῷ εἴδει· σῆψις γὰρ ἄμφω. It is possible that he calls the one γένος and the other εἶδος, because, for *the purposes* of *the present* classification, ἀτμίς is the higher genus, and σῆψις is subordinate: still in relation to ἀτμίς, πάχνη and πολιαί are certainly species. I can make nothing of it, and believe it to be a piece of carelessness, such as is extremely common in Aristotle's writings: but at all events it furnishes a good example of a *real* resemblance, sufficient to justify the application of the term metaphor ἀπὸ τοῦ εἴδους ἐπὶ εἶδος.

The same fourfold division is recognised, Rhet. III. 10. 7; where it is added, that the metaphor κατ' ἀναλογίαν is the most popular and approved. Quintilian, VIII. 6. 9, 10, likewise gives a fourfold classification of metaphors, but resting upon an entirely different basis.

The primary notion of metaphor (μεταφορά, μεταφέρειν, tralatio, transferre) is a mere 'transfer' of a word from one sense to another: it therefore includes in this original sense all cases of μετωνυμία, and ὑπαλλαγή, and συνεκδοχή, as well as metaphor proper. Isocrates, for example, ἀντιδ. §§ 284, 285, employs the word to express the misapplication of names to the softening and disguising of defects, which are *misre*-presented by indifferent or flattering, or honourable terms. This is commonly called ὑποκορισμός, and is exemplified by εὐήθης for a 'simpleton', χρηστός, ἡδύς, and γλυκύς in Plato in a similar application; by the use of diminutives, Rhet. III. 2. 15; comp. I. 9. 28, 29 for other examples, and Thuc. III. 89. Isocrates applies μεταφέρειν to the abuse of the words εὐφυεῖς, and φιλοσοφεῖν which were employed by the sophists of his time to designate something very different from their proper acceptation; μεταφέρουσιν ἀπὸ τῶν καλλίστων πραγμάτων ἐπὶ τὰ φαυλότατα τῶν ἐπιτηδευμάτων. And in a similarly general sense Cicero, de Orat. III. 37. 149, quoted above on c. 2. note 2. The subject of metaphor receives no separate treatment in the Rhet. ad Alex. It is merely mentioned, together with ἁπλοῦς and σύνθετος, as one of the three τρόποι ὀνομάτων. c. 24. 1.

Quintilian, IX. 1. 4, classifies metaphor as one of seven kinds of 'tropes': Est igitur tropus, sermo a naturali et principali significatione translatus ad aliam, ornandæ orationis gratia: vel, ut plerique grammatici finiunt, dictio ab eo loco, in quo propria est, translata in eum, in quo propria non est. ...Quare in tropis ponuntur verba alia pro aliis, ut in μεταφορᾷ, μετωνυμίᾳ, ἀντονομασίᾳ, μεταλήψει, συνεκδοχῇ, καταχρήσει, ἀλληγορίᾳ: and describes and illustrates it at length, VIII. 6. 4—18; *transfertur* nomen aut verbum ex eo loco in quo proprium est, in eum in quo aut proprium deest, aut translatum proprio melius est. The former of these two cases in which the metaphorical word is used *by necessity* to supply a defect in language, is spoken of by Cicero, de Orat. III. 38. 155, as the *only* source of metaphor: tertius ille modus transferendi verba late patet, quem necessitas genuit inopia coacta et angustiis, *post* autem jucunditas delectatioque celebravit...Verbi translatio instituta est inopiæ causa, frequentata delectationis. The origin of metaphor is the imperfection of language; where there is no term directly expressing a notion, the nearest analogy, the term which expresses that which most nearly resembles it, must be employed as a substitute. Aristotle on the other hand, Rhet. III. 10. 2, traces the frequent use of metaphor, like so many other things, to the pleasure derived from learning something; 'this is produced in the highest degree by metaphors, which bring remote members of the same genus into comparison with one another', and so suggest unexpected resemblances. With this may be compared the account given by Cicero in another place, Orat. XXXIX. 134, of the pleasure derived from metaphors; ex omnique genere frequentissimae tralationes erunt, quod ea propter similitudinem transferunt animos et referunt et movent huc et illuc; qui *motus cogitationis* celeriter agitatus per se ipse delectat. Again de Orat. III. 40. 159, 160., he attributes the frequent employment of metaphor and the pleasure it gives to *both* of those which are separately assigned in the two passages already quoted, and by Quintilian in conjunction: nam si res suum nomen at vocabulum proprium non habet...necessitas cogit, quod non habeas aliunde sumere; sed in suorum verborum maxima copia tamen homines aliena multo magis, si sunt ratione translata, delectant. And then this pleasure in metaphor is traced to four causes; we are delighted either by the ingenuity shown in passing over what lies before us at our feet (under our noses) and substituting something else that is far out of the way; or because the thought of the listener is transported to another region, yet without going astray, which is a principal source of delight; or because a resemblance is briefly suggested and illustrated by a single word; or because a well chosen metaphor realises the thing which it represents, and brings it vividly before our eyes. ($\pi\rho\grave{o}$ $\dot{o}\mu\mu\acute{a}\tau\omega\nu$ $\pi o\iota\epsilon\hat{\iota}$, Arist. Rhet. III. 10. 6.) compare Orat. § 92. In de Orat. III. 39. 137, metaphor is said to be, a contracted, concentrated, simile: and Campbell, Phil. of Rhet. Vol. II. p. 152, has the same thought.

See likewise on metaphor, Auct. ad Heren. IV. 34; Demetr. π. ἑρμην. Rhet. Gr. III. 280. (Spengel Ed.), with special reference to Aristotle; Harris, Philological Inquiries, p. 188, seq. and Campbell and Whately ll. cc. Bk. III. ch. 1. and ch. III. § 2.

APPENDIX C. TO BOOK III.

Ἀρμονία, ῥυθμός, μέτρον, μέλος, μέγεθος (τῆς φωνῆς): *and especially on rhythm, in reference to* iii. 8.

There are three properties of sounds: (1) the pitch, that is, sharpness and flatness, depending on the number of vibrations (as of a string) in a given time; the more rapid vibrations producing the higher or acuter tone, the slower vibration the lower or graver: (2), the intensity or volume, which varies in proportion as the string is more or less removed from its state of equilibrium, or the force exerted greater; and the same applies to the voice: and (3), quality or 'timbre', which is a sound of the same pitch and intensity as produced by different instruments; such as stringed instruments, wind instruments, the human voice. From Lamé, Cours de Physique: on Harmonics, Vol. II.; where also is explained the cause of sound, and the mode of its propagation.

That something of this was already known to Aristotle and the early Greek musicians, appears from the following passages of the de Gen. Anim. and Topics. ἐπεὶ δὲ βαρὺ μέν ἐστιν ἐν τῷ βραδεῖαν εἶναι τὴν κίνησιν, ὀξὺ δὲ ἐν τῷ ταχεῖαν... de Gen. An. V. 5. 4. ἀλλ' ἐπειδὴ ἕτερόν ἐστι τὸ βαρὺ καὶ ὀξὺ ἐν φωνῇ μεγαλοφωνίας καὶ μικροφωνίας (ἔστι γὰρ καὶ ὀξύφωνα μεγαλόφωνα, καὶ μικρόφωνα βαρύφωνα ὡσαύτως), ὁμοίως δὲ καὶ κατὰ τὸν μέσον τόνον τούτων· περὶ ὧν τίνι ἄν τις ἄλλῳ διορίσειεν, λέγω δὲ μεγαλοφωνίαν καὶ μικροφωνίαν, ἢ πλήθει καὶ ὀλιγότητι τοῦ κινουμένου; Ib. § 7. See also § 12. φωνὴ μὲν γὰρ ὀξεῖα ἡ ταχεῖα, καθάπερ φασὶν οἱ κατὰ τοὺς ἀριθμοὺς ἁρμονικοί. Topic. A. 107. a. 15.

Ἁρμονία and ῥυθμός are both of them general terms, from which they are transferred by metaphor and applied in a special sense to music, and composition either in poetry or prose.

ἁρμονία is 'adaptation', from ἁρμόζειν, or 'fitting'; a suitable, appropriate, combination or arrangement—apta compositio, Cic. de Offic.—of parts, serving a given purpose, or constituting a unity, or organized whole. In a fragment of Heraclitus, for instance, quoted by Plato, Sympos. 187. A. we have, ἁρμονία τόξου καὶ λύρας, to denote the stringing, or adaptation to use, of the bow and lyre. In music it denotes the orderly succession of certain sounds, determined by definite *intervals*, which appeals to an instinctive sense or taste in the human mind—some sounds, as some tastes and smells, and combinations or successions of sounds, are *naturally* agreeable, others disagreeable to the ear—and constitutes 'tune' or 'melody'[1]. Its elements are the ὀξύ and βαρύ, sharp and flat, acute and grave, produced by the 'pitch' of the voice or instrument; the indefinite matter, of which the musical intervals[2], represented by numbers and ratios, are the definite, determined 'forms'. See Lamé, u. s. In writing or composition, prose and poetry, that is, when they are delivered or recited aloud by the poet, rhapsode, or orator, the elements are the same; but the forms which they assume less numerous. Nam voces, (in singing and reading or reciting,) says Cicero, de Orat. III. 57. 216., ut chordæ sunt intentæ, quæ ad quemque tactum respondeant, acuta gravis, cita tarda, magna parva. These are the three 'tones' or 'accents', τόνοι, προσῳδίαι, Arist. Rhet. III. 1. 4. Τόνος itself means 'pitch': it is the degree of tension; the raising or

---

[1] In Dionysius, de Comp. Verb. 3. sub fin. et 13, it stands merely for 'compositio orationis, et juncturæ verborum'. Ernest. Lex. Techn. In Plato, Rep. III. 397. 398. and Arist. Pol. VIII. 7, the name of ἁρμονία is given to the various musical 'modes,' Δωριστί, Λυδιστί, Φρυγιστί, and the rest.

[2] Cic. Tusc. Q. I. 18. 41. harmoniam ex intervallis sonorum nosse possumus; quorum varia compositio etiam harmonias efficit plures.

lowering of the 'tension' of the strings of an instrument, and metaphorically, of the human voice, to a given degree, in order to produce certain definite sounds, sharp or acute, flat or grave, and middle or circumflex, notes. The 'middle' (Aristotle) or 'circumflex' accent is produced by the combination of the acute and grave. Böckh, de Metr. Pind. p. 16. On τόνος, see Mr Donkin's article on Greek Music, in Smith's Dict. of Antiq. at the beginning, and note.

'Ρυθμός[1] likewise, which signifies in general any regular measured movement; (as the strokes of the hammer in forging, the tread of horses' feet, the tramp of an army on its march, the beat of oars, or of birds' wings, the motion of the fingers, and the like;) which can be reduced to number,— ὁ δὲ τοῦ σχήματος τῆς λέξεως ἀριθμὸς ῥυθμός ἐστιν. Rhet. III. 8. 2.—or measured by number, (hence Lat. numerus,) is a genus, including several species. It may be applied to marching or walking in measured step, to dancing or gesticulation, to music, and to writing or recitation. Its element or 'matter' is time; determined by fast and slow, ταχὺ καὶ βραδύ, which in composition takes the form of 'quantity', in long and short syllables. Numeri lex est unitas plurium temporis articulorum. Böckh, u. s. p. 9. Quid igitur est numerus, nisi pulcra in temporis particularum successione forma? Ibid.

In the following passages the above description of ἁρμονία and ῥυθμός, as applied to music and writing, prose and poetry, is illustrated. Both of them belong to 'style', λέξις, in literary composition, and to music. Plat. Rep. III. 397. B. 398. D. Further on the different species of ῥυθμός, and

[1] Fragm. Longin. π. μέτρων, ap. Ernest. Lex. Techn. Gr. s.v. Quidquid est quod sub aurium mensuram aliquam cadit (ἀριθμῷ περαίνεται, Arist.) etiamsi abest a versu, nam id quidem orationis est vitium, numerus vocatur, qui Græce ῥυθμὸς dicitur. Cic. Orat. xx. 67. It belongs to prose as well as poetry; Longin. u.s. ὁ δὲ (ῥυθμὸς) ἐπὶ τοῦ προφορικοῦ λόγου (intended for delivery or declamation), κατὰ τὸ μακρὸν καὶ βραχύ, ὅσπερ μόνος καὶ μέτρον λέγεται· οὐκ ἐπὶ τῶν ποιητικῶν τε λόγων ταῦτα μόνον θεωρεῖται, ἀλλὰ καὶ ἐπὶ τῶν ῥητορικῶν.

their elements βραχὺ καὶ μακρόν, 399. E—400. B. μέτρον, ῥυθμός, and ἁρμονία, are all included in poetry, x. 601. A. Comparing Legg. II. 655. A. περὶ ῥυθμὸν καὶ ἁρμονίαν οὔσης τῆς μουσικῆς[1], with Phileb. 26. A. (see the entire passage, from 24. A.), we gather that the limiting principle, τὸ πέρας, (or the 'form', as it appears in Aristotle,) which gives a definite shape and substantial reality to the infinite or indefinite, formless, chaotic, 'potential', matter, entering into this as yet undetermined matter, the ὀξύ and βαρύ, the ταχύ and βραδύ, produces in the one ἁρμονία, in the other ῥυθμός. This will apply to the *words* of written compositions as well as to music. In the Laws, II. 664. E., we are told, that whereas all animals alike have a natural tendency to motion and utterance, man alone has the conception of order, τάξις: of this order, that which is expressed in motion is called ῥυθμός; that which is expressed by the voice in sound, arising from the mixture of the ὀξύ and βαρύ, has the name of ἁρμονία. In Sympos. 187, B. C., we find, ὅτι (ἁρμονία) ἐκ διαφερομένων πρότερον τοῦ ὀξέος καὶ βαρέος ἔπειτα ὕστερον ὁμολογησάντων γέγονεν ὑπὸ τῆς μουσικῆς τέχνης...ὥσπερ γε καὶ ὁ ῥυθμὸς ἐκ τοῦ ταχέος καὶ βραδέος διενηνεγμένων πρότερον ὕστερον δὲ ὁμολογησάντων γέγονε. See also on the same subject Phileb. 17. C. D. E. and Legg. VII. 812. D. E. Ib. II. 665. A. τῇ τῆς κινήσεως τάξει ῥυθμὸς ὄνομα εἴη, τῇ δὲ αὖ τῆς φωνῆς, τοῦ τε ὀξέος ἅμα καὶ βαρέος συγκεραννυμένων, ἁρμονία ὄνομα προσαγορεύοιτο.

Every kind of poetry and music, says Aristotle, Poet. I. §§ 4—6, carries out its imitation by means of ῥυθμός, ἁρμονία, and λόγος; only music wants the last. Dancers again represent character, passion, and action, by the aid of ῥυθμός alone. And again, Poet. VI. 3., the ἡδυσμένος λόγος of tragedy is said to possess ῥυθμός, ἁρμονία, and μέλος—the last being

---

[1] In Arist. Polit. VIII. 7. sub init. μελοποιία or μέλος is substituted for ἁρμονία, (as also in Poet. I. § 4. compared with § 13,) the element of melody or tune, as one of the component parts of music; ἐπειδὴ τὴν μὲν μουσικὴν ὁρῶμεν διὰ μελοποιίας καὶ ῥυθμῶν οὖσαν. Compare also Plat. Legg. II. 699.

the musical accompaniment. Rhet. III. 1. 4. has been already referred to. Aristotle there tells us, that those who studied the art of declamation or delivery directed their attention to three things in the regulation and management of the voice or enunciation; the intensity or volume, μέγεθος, loud or low; the pitch, in the distribution of the accents, ὀξεία, βαρεία, and μέση, ἁρμονίᾳ; and the measure or rhythm, which regulates the time or quantity, ῥυθμός[1]. See further in Rhet. III. 8., already referred to.

The source of the pleasure derived from ῥυθμός is said to be the natural love of order, regularity, symmetry. Probl. XIX. 38. ῥυθμῷ δὲ χαίρομεν διὰ τὸ γνώριμον καὶ τεταγμένον ἀριθμὸν ἔχειν, καὶ κινεῖν ἡμᾶς τεταγμένως· οἰκειοτέρα γὰρ ἡ τεταγμένη κίνησις φύσει τῆς ἀτάκτου, ὥστε καὶ κατὰ φύσιν μᾶλλον.

There is a chapter on ῥυθμός in Dionysius, de Comp. Verb., the seventeenth. He identifies πούς and ῥυθμός; τὸ δ' αὐτὸ καλῶ πόδα καὶ ῥυθμόν; apparently neglecting the important distinction between βάσις, the unit of rhythm, and πούς, the unit of metre. It contains an enumeration and description of the several metres in use. In c. 19, (p. 130. Reiske) he ascribes ῥυθμός as well as μέτρον to the Epic poets, in the sense of 'feet'; and again c. 25. p. 186, 7.

Burney, Hist. of Music, I. p. 62, defines ῥυθμός simply as 'time'. Aristides Quintil. I. 31. (p. 64.) σύστημα ἐκ χρόνων κατά τινα τάξιν συγκειμένων, "the assemblage of many parts of time which preserve a certain proportion to one another." (Burn.) Ib. (a system composed of times put together in a certain order.)

Cicero's definition of numerus is, distinctio et æqualium et sæpe variorum intervallorum percussio numerum conficit. de Orat. III. 48. 186. And to the same effect, Orat. 57. 194.

---

[1] These three qualities are assigned to sound in general and to the human voice also by Cicero, de Orat. III. 57. 216. Aristotle, and the ancient writers on Harmonics, did not recognise the third property of sound, quality or 'timbre', defined above p. 379.

(Ephorus is in error) syllabis enim metiendos pedes, non intervallis existimat. This seems to be a mistake. Rhythm in prose is determined, not by equal or varied intervals, but by the ratio of times in long and short syllables. Cicero seems to have had in his mind the recurring repeated strokes of a hammer, the measured tread of a company of soldiers, and such like. Or he may mean to *express* this ratio by intervallum; or spatium, which occurs in Orat. § 193. Compare §§ 194, 215, 217. But by these same 'intervals' in Tusc. Quæst. I. 18. 41. he characterises 'harmony'.

On rhythm in prose, see the same author, Orat. cc. 54—60. de Orat. III. 47—50.

By Hermogenes, περὶ ἰδεῶν, α', (II. p. 269. Rhet. Gr. Ed. Spengel,) it is thus described; ἡ ποία σύνθεσις τῶν τοῦ λόγου μερῶν, καὶ τὸ ὡδί πως ἀναπεπαῦσθαι τὸν λόγον ἀλλὰ μὴ ὡδί, ποιεῖ τὸ τοιόνδε ἀλλὰ μὴ τοιόνδε εἶναι τὸν ῥυθμόν.

Μέλος has two distinct significations: it denotes music or melody with and without words. In the former sense it may stand for any kind of poetical composition, which has a musical accompaniment, in general; and amongst these especially for choral odes; and again more particularly for the choral odes of the Greek Tragedy and Comedy. στάσιμον, μέλος χοροῦ. Poet. XII. 7.; and the Scholiast on Eur. Phœn. 210, (quoted by Hermann, Elem. Metr. Gr. Lib. III. c. 22. § 1.) τοῦτο τὸ μέλος στάσιμον λέγεται. ὅταν γὰρ ὁ χορὸς μετὰ τὴν πάροδον λέγῃ τί μέλος...στάσιμον καλεῖται. The πάροδος is afterwards called ᾠδή. In the latter of the two senses it is identifiable with ἁρμονία, tune or melody, or ψιλὴ ἁρμονία, music proper, without the verbal accompaniment.

I will now proceed to illustrate these two senses by passages from Plato and Aristotle, from which it will appear that the term is certainly susceptible of both these interpretations.

In Republic, III. 398. D. μέλος is first said to be composed of three elements, ἐκ τριῶν ἐστὶ συγκείμενον, λόγου τε, καὶ ἁρμονίας καὶ ῥυθμοῦ, time tune and *words:* but a little farther on, 400. A., μέλος is distinctly *opposed* to λόγος; οὓς ἰδόντα τὸν πόδα τῷ τοιούτου λόγῳ ἀναγκάζειν ἕπεσθαι καὶ τὸ μέλος, ἀλλὰ μὴ λόγον ποδί τε καὶ μέλει. Here μέλος together with πούς, which stands for ῥυθμὸς or μέτρον in general, the metrical 'foot', ('a part of rhythm',) are expressly distinguished from the 'words' of the song or ode, and employed either in the general sense of ἁρμονία, tune or harmony, or of the 'music' of the accompanying 'instruments'. And still more distinctly in a passage of the Laws, II. 669. D. E. οἱ ποιηταὶ ῥυθμὸν μὲν καὶ ῥήματα μέλους χωρὶς λόγους ψιλοὺς εἰς μέτρα τιθέντες· μέλος δ' αὖ καὶ ῥυθμοὺς ἄνευ ῥημάτων, ψιλῇ κιθαρίσει καὶ αὐλήσει προσχρώμενοι.

From Aristotle I have already quoted on the one side Poet. XII. 7., στάσιμον, μέλος χοροῦ; where the term must necessarily include the words, the musical accompaniment (which was *essential* to the performance), and rhythm or measure in its widest sense, the dances and gesticulations of the choreutæ, as well as the metre of the verses. In Poet. I. § 13, it is plainly used in the sense of melody or tune, as equivalent to ἁρμονία, for which it is actually substituted; compare § 4, where the same division is stated in different words. In this first Chapter the author, after stating his theory, that the whole art of poetry and music, to which are afterwards added dancing and painting, and the various species of poetry, are all imitative, and derived from the natural love of imitation inherent in the human race, proceeds to point out how this imitation expresses itself in several of the different kinds of poetry: and concludes the chapter, § 13, with the following remark. "Some (poets) there are that employ all the above mentioned modes, I mean measure, melody, and metre, ῥυθμῷ καὶ μέλει καὶ μέτρῳ—these had previously been designated, § 4, ῥυθμῷ καὶ λόγῳ καὶ ἁρμονίᾳ; so that μέτρον stands in § 13. for the 'words in their metrical form', whilst μέλει represents ἁρμονία—as the composers of dithyrambs, of hymns (νόμοι), of tragedy and comedy: they differ however in this respect, that some employ them all together, others only partially." The last words are explained by a passage of c. VI, which we shall also refer to as throwing some light on our subject. In § 2, is given the famous definition of tragedy. Two of its qualities are, that it must be ἡδυσμένῳ λόγῳ, and χωρὶς ἑκάστου τῶν εἰδῶν ἐν τοῖς μορίοις: the 'imitation' of tragedy is to be effected by means of language 'duly sweetened', i. e. embellished and rendered pleasurable (Twining); but this embellishment is made up of several elements, the different kinds of which must be carefully kept separate (χωρίς), and confined each to its proper sphere. The explanation of this is given in §§ 3, 4. "By ἡδυσμένον λόγον I mean, ῥυθμὸν καὶ ἁρμονίαν καὶ μέλος; and by separation of the several kinds, that the composition is to be effected in some parts by the aid of metre alone, in others again it must be aided by melody or a musical accompaniment. This is my interpretation of the passage, which enables us to retain μέλος in the text of § 3. In this case there will be a distinction drawn between ἁρμονία and μέλος. The former is the harmony of language, which is characteristic of 'metre'; whilst μέλος is the melody or music, Plato's ψιλὴ καθάρισις καὶ αὔλησις. Several of the most eminent commentators however, Victorius, Tyrwhitt, Hermann, agree in rejecting μέλος in § 3, on the ground that it is a mere repetition of ἁρμονία: Victorius substitutes μέτρον, which Tyrwhitt objects to as a tautological repetition of ῥυθμός in a different form; and Tyrwhitt himself regards it as a gloss, and, with Hermann, would exclude it altogether from the text. This I believe I have shown to be unnecessary. On the musical senses of μέλος see Twining's note 46. p. 246. (1st Ed.). He distinguishes three; which seems to me to be further than they need be carried.

In the last Chapter of the Politics Bk. VIII. (or v. according to the revised order), on Music as applied to Education, μέλος is several times joined with, and at the same time distinguished from, ἁρμονία. We have already seen that in some sense of both they are so nearly related that the one can be substituted for the other. Ἁρμονίαι throughout this Chapter is used, as by Plato in Rep. III. to denote the musical 'modes', Δωριστί, Φρυγιστί, Λυδιστί, and the rest, which were characteristic of various races and countries, and, when employed by Greek composers, appropriated to distinct kinds of poetical composition. The style of the Dorian harmony or mode was grave measured and solemn; the Phrygian had a wild excited enthusiastic character, adapted to stimulate the emotions and arouse the enthusiasm of the participants in 'orgiastic' rites, such as those of Bacchus, and the Phrygian Cybele, from whose worship it seems to have been borrowed; the Lydian[1] on the other hand was soft sweet and voluptuous. These 'modes' therefore were rather varieties of musical style and character, than distinct tunes or melodies, and therefore ἁρμονία in the more general sense may be very well distinguished in the chapter referred to from μέλη; whilst in the narrower and more special signification they are capable of being identified.

Finally μέτρα are defined by Aristotle, Poet. IV. 7, μόρια τῶν ῥυθμῶν; that is they are 'measures', or 'verses'; 'parts of rhythm', which is indefinite and never comes to an end: μέτρον is rhythm, cut, as it were, into definite lengths. But this will be described more fully in the second part of our subject, on which we are now entering, the distinction viz. and definitions of ῥυθμός and μέτρον.

ῥυθμός, μέτρον, βάσις, ἄρσις, θέσις.

The elements of rhythm are times; in writing, expressed in syllables short and long. This is the indefinite matter, ἄπειρον, ἀπέραντον, into which rhythm introduces a law, or 'form' (Ar.), or 'unity' (Plat.); (περαίνεται ἀριθμῷ, Rhet. III.

[1] Softly sweet in Lydian measures
Soon he soothed his soul to pleasures.
Dryden, Alexander's Feast.

8. 2. conf. Probl. XIX. 38. 2;) a definite regularity which constitutes its harmonious effect. The unit of time is the short syllable, which occupies the shortest time in enunciation: the long syllable, the other element, is in value equal to two short. Rhythm then resides in the ratio of these times to one another in an indefinite succession of syllables. The early writers on Music—Plato ascribes the division to Damon the Musician, Rep. III. 400. B.—distinguished three kinds of rhythm[1] and no more. (1) the heroic or dactylic, including the spondaic and anapæstic, which expresses the ratio of equality, or 1 : 1; (2) the iambic and trochaic, with the tribrach, which has the ratio of 2 : 1; and (3) the pæonic[2], including the cretic (-◡-) and bacchius (◡--), which has that of $\frac{3}{2}$: 1. This is called by Plato, after Damon, the ἐνόπλιος ῥυθμός[2], as Schneider thinks, (not. ad loc.). This last is preferred by Aristotle for prose composition because it cannot be used alone in versification, is less marked than the other two, and therefore obtrudes itself less upon the attention of the audience, μᾶλλον λανθάνει, Rhet. III. 8. This ratio or proportion is marked by the ἄρσις and θέσις[3], sublatio and positio; the ictus or stress of the voice usually (as a matter of fact) falling upon the long syllable, or the resolution of the long syllable, in each of the rhythmical βάσεις[4]. Plat. Rep. l. c. Arist. Rhet. III. 8. Quint. IX. 4. 46, 47.

[1] On these compare Cic. Orat. 56. 188.
[2] On the Pæonic rhythm (rather than metre) see Herm. Elem. D. Metr. Lib. II. c. XIX. de versibus Creticis. On the ἐνόπλιος ῥυθμός see likewise Herm. l. c. II. XXVI. 27. and on the Schol. p. 371. of Arist. Nub. 647. It was as the Scholiast on Aristoph. says, and Hermann thinks, an anapæstic measure, at all events in its ordinary application. The Scholiast however adds that others—perhaps Damon among them—gave this name to τὸν ἀμφίμακρον (-◡-), or the Cretic, which is identical in rhythm with the Pæonic. Stallbaum's note on the passage of Plato not edifying.
[3] On ἄρσις and θέσις see Böckh, de Metr. Pind. c. 4.
[4] βάσις in rhythm corresponds to πούς in metre. It takes its name from the 'step' in marching or dancing. Stallb. ad Remp. u. s. Each of the three rhythmical ratios is a βάσις. Plat. Rep. III. 400. A. ὅτι μὲν γὰρ

We now proceed to the consideration of the distinction of ῥυθμός and μέτρον. This is very clearly and well stated by Quintilian, Inst. Orat. IX. 4. 45. "rhythmi, id est numeri, spatio temporum constant: metra etiam ordine: ideoque alterum esse quantitatis videtur, alterum qualitatis." [The first consists in a mere ratio of times or quantities; the second has the 'quality' in addition, that the syllables in which the ratio resides must occur in a certain order. Böckh quarrels with this, as against his theory.] Then follows a description of the rhythmical bases and their ratios. "Sunt hi," he continues, "et metrici pedes (dactyl, pæon, iambus); sed hoc interest, quod rhythmo indifferens est dactylusne ille priores habeat breves an sequentes, (whether it be dactyl or anapæst, or indeed spondee). *Tempus enim solum metitur*, ut a sublatione ad positionem (from ἄρσις to θέσις) idem spatii sit. Proinde alia dimensio est versuum: pro dactylo poni non poterit anapæstus aut spondeus: nec pæon eadem ratione brevibus incipiet ac desinet. Sunt et illa discrimina (§ 50.), quod rhythmis libera spatia, metris finita sint; et his certæ clausulæ, illi quomodo cœperant currunt usque ad μεταβολήν, id est transitum in aliud genus rhythmi: et quod metrum in verbis modo, rhythmus etiam in corporis motu est." From this we gather; first, that rhythm, in composition at all events, is a measurement of *time alone;* secondly, that the distinction between it and metre lies in three particulars; (1) rhythm has respect only to the ratio of the times or quantities of the syllables: in rhythm, dactyl, spondee, and anapæst, are exactly equivalent: in metre, the long and short syllables must occur in a fixed order; the dactylic, anapæstic, and spondaic, are *different metres*. (2) rhythm is

τρία ἄττα ἐστὶν εἴδη ἐξ ὧν αἱ βάσεις πλέκονται ... τεθεάμενος ἂν εἴποιμι. Legg. II. 670 D. αἱ βάσεις τῶν ῥυθμῶν. Arist. Pol. II. 5. ὥσπερ κἂν εἴ τις... ποιήσειε...τὸν ῥυθμὸν βάσιν μίαν. Metaph. N. 1. 1087. b. 34. κἂν εἰ παντί...

συλλάβῃ: where βάσις is described as the measuring unit of ῥυθμός. Hermog. π. ἰδεῶν, α'. (Rhet. Gr. II. p. 269. Ed. Speng.), κατὰ δὲ τὰς βάσεις ὅση δακτυλική τε καὶ ἀναπαιστική, (is suitable to the 'sweet' style).

indefinite, metre definite; in this sense, that the former has no natural termination in the sentence, it runs on till a change occurs, whenever that may happen: metre is finite: it is rhythm cut into lengths, as it were, forming 'certas clausulas', systems or verses, which are usually repeated, in some form or other, either as single verses or stanzas, till the poem ends. (3) ῥυθμός is a genus, μέτρον a species; as we have already noticed[1].

Now in all this there is not a word of anything but 'time' or 'quantity'; rhythm is a ratio of times or quantities of syllables. Böckh however, de Metr. Pind. c. 5., would introduce a further distinction between rhythm and metre, of this nature. 'Metre,' he says, 'is a system of syllables long or short disposed in a certain order, *independent* of arsis and thesis; and it is in the ratio of arsis and thesis alone that rhythm consists.' This is derived from ancient authorities, and is no novelty of his own. The only ancient authority that he produces for it is Aristides Quintilianus, I. p. 49., where this is mentioned as a second, and apparently independent, theory. It seems to me, whether true or false in itself, to disagree at all events with all that has been above cited from Plato, Aristotle, Quintilian, &c., as to the conception of rhythm as it was understood in their times. These authors, as far as can be gathered from their expressions, make it to consist solely in the measurement of time; and make no reference whatever to the varying intensities of sound in the voice, which constitute ictus, as belonging to it. Moreover Aristotle, in another passage of the Rhetoric, III. 1. 4., expressly distinguishes μέγεθος τῆς φωνῆς from ῥυθμός; and ἄρσις and θέσις are nothing but different degrees of intensity of the

---

[1] See Suidas, quoted by Böckh, de Metr. Pind. Bk. I. ch. 4. p. 19. note 3. Also Mallius Theodorus, p. 5, quoted by Herm. Elem. Metr. Gr. Bk. II. c. 19. § 2. Si qua autem apud poetas lyricos aut tragicos quispiam repererit, in quibus certa pedum collatione neglecta, sola temporum ratio considerata sit, meminerit ea, sicut apud doctissimos quosque scriptum invenimus, non metra sed rhythmos appellari oportere.

voice; and from this I think it may be inferred that rhythm, in his opinion at least, did not reside "solely in ἄρσις and θέσις and their relation".

Specimens of these rhythms in prose composition are to be found in Dionys. de Comp. Verb. c. 25. The Cretic—"or if you prefer to call it so, the Pæonic"—rhythm is illustrated from the opening sentence of Demosthenes' speech pro Coronâ, τοῖς θεοῖς εὔχομαι πᾶσι καὶ πάσαις: the iambic from the words that follow, ὅσην εὔνοιαν ἔχων ἐγὼ διατελῶ: in the next Demosthenes reverts to the Pæonic or Cretic, τῇ πόλει καὶ πᾶσιν ὑμῖν τοσαύτην ὑπάρξαι μοι παρ' ὑμῶν εἰς τουτονὶ τὸν ἀγῶνα.

Demetrius, in his chapter, περὶ μεγαλοπρεποῦς, π. ἑρμ. (III. 270. Rhet. Gr. Speng.), referring to Aristotle, Rhet. III. 8., exemplifies the Pæonic rhythm—which he follows Aristotle in recommending for use, and also in confining the use of it to the two kinds which begin and end with a long syllable, as ἤρξατο δέ and 'Αραβία—by some words taken from Theophrastus, τῶν μὲν περὶ τὰ μηδενὸς ἄξια φιλοσοφούντων. This does not "in strictness consist of Pæons, but still is Pæonic." The heroic rhythm is illustrated by a spondaic system, ἥκειν ἡμῶν εἰς τὴν χώραν; which is disapproved on the same grounds as those that are alleged by Aristotle. And similarly the iambic.

Hermogenes, π. ἰδεῶν, α΄, II. 279 (Rh. Gr. Sp.), has some useful remarks upon rhythm in prose, and especially upon the amount of rhythmical feet that is required to give a particular rhythm to a prose sentence. The iambic rhythm, he says,—herein agreeing with Aristotle and Demetrius—being that into which the Greek language naturally falls, and therefore most usual in ordinary conversation, is only suitable for a plain and simple style, and to be avoided by those who aim at an ornamental and dignified kind of composition. Of this he gives as a specimen, ἐγὼ γάρ, ὦ ἄνδρες 'Αθηναῖοι, προσέκρουσα ἀνθρώπῳ πονηρῷ; at the same time remarking[1],

[1] See Cicero, Orat. 58—198, and 195. to the same effect.

that in order to constitute an iambic rhythm it is sufficient that such feet be introduced to a certain extent, and particularly at the beginnings of the clauses; and that the number of iambuses and trochees in the entire composition should exceed that of the anapæsts and dactyls (for instance). For it is absolutely necessary that there should be a mixture of some other feet; otherwise the speech would be in metre, and not merely rhythmical. Cic. Orat. 57. 194. Itaque ut versum fugimus in oratione, sic hi sunt evitandi *continuati* pedes, (viz. dactyl and iambus).

Cicero also, in the Orator, 65, 219, gives a specimen of Pæonic rhythm—though it is only accidentally so—from a speech of Crassus; which he says falls naturally into rhythm without any effort or intention on the part of the orator. It is an example not of numerus, but of numerosa oratio. In § 196, he gives his final opinion about the use of rhythm in prose composition. Prose should be interspersed and tempered with it, neither wholly rhythmical nor altogether loose and measureless: the pæon, in deference to Aristotle's opinion, should be most frequently employed, but blended with the other rhythms which he has passed over. Subsequently, §§ 214, 215, he expresses disagreement with one of Aristotle's rules, that the period should end with the fourth pæon, ◡◡◡–; Cicero prefers the Cretic in this position, § 218. The remarks on this subject in the de Oratore are scanty and limited; it is treated much more fully in the Orator.

APPENDIX D. TO BOOK III. CH. V.

On σύνδεσμος.

The word σύνδεσμος, as a grammatical or rhetorical—for rhetoric includes the art of composition—term, has in Aristotle a very wide and general application; it seems that at least three different senses in which it is employed are distinguishable. Its general character is defined in Rhet. III. 12. 4, ὁ γὰρ σύνδεσμος ἓν ποιεῖ τὰ πολλά; by which it seems to be meant that it unites a variety of single terms or notions or parts into one general conception; either words or sentences, as a connecting particle; or *correlative* clauses, as μέν and δέ; or a whole volume, consisting of a multitude of parts, into one great whole, as the Iliad is said to be λόγος συνδέσμῳ εἷς. In all these senses we shall find Aristotle employing it.

In a previous Appendix, A, it has been already stated upon the authority of Dionysius, that the distinction of σύνδεσμοι from ὀνόματα and ῥήματα was the second step in the grammatical analysis of language, and due to Theodectes and Aristotle. It seems however that Isocrates also recognised it;—he perhaps borrowed it from Theodectes;—for in a fragment of his τέχνη preserved by Max. Planudes, ad Hermog. v. p. 469, 8., and Joannes Sicel. vi. p. 156, 19 (in Benseler, Isocrates, Vol. ii. p. 276.), we find amongst his precepts for the regulation of style the following rule; καὶ τοὺς συνδέσμους τοὺς αὐτοὺς μὴ σύνεγγυς τιθέναι, καὶ τὸν ἑπόμενον τῷ ἡγουμένῳ εὐθὺς ἀνταποδιδόναι. The former of these clauses appears to mean, that the same conjunction or preposition or particle is not to be repeated in too close proximity to the other, that the phraseology or construction should be varied; the latter, that in correlative clauses the second member should immediately follow the first, and not after a long interval which leads to confusion. But in both cases σύνδεσμος may be interpreted 'connective particle'; in the latter of the two, the particle carries with and includes the correlative sentence to which it is attached, and of which it *expresses* the correlation.

In the Poetics, xx. §§ 1, 6., the σύνδεσμος is reckoned as one of the eight μόρια τῆς λέξεως, partes orationis. In § 6, two definitions are given, the first of which is very corrupt and obscure. The term is however illustrated by the examples μέν, ἤτοι, δή, which leaves no doubt that it includes at all events conjunctions and particles. It embraces likewise prepositions, Dion. de Comp. Verb. c. 22. p. 157, Reiske, where ἐπί is called a σύνδεσμος or πρόθεσις. In c. 25, ἄρα is an instance of σύνδεσμος. Demetrius, π. ἑρμην., περὶ συνθ. λόγου, (Rhet. Gr. III. p. 274, 5. Ed. Speng.) gives examples which include interjections, φεῦ, αἲ αἲ, together with particles, as μέν, δέ, δή, νύ: πρότερον is a σύνδεσμος, (it is regarded as a preposition) and again, p. 324, καί.

In Aristotle, σύνδεσμος, Rhet. III. 6. 6, and 12. 4, plainly stands for a 'connective', or connective particle, as a single word: and also in Probl. XIX. 20. where it is exemplified by τε—καί. And the definition of Poet. XX. 6, again describes a conjunction, preposition, or particle, by defining σύνδεσμος, φωνὴ ἄσημος (an unsignificant utterance, of course a *single word*) ἣ οὔτε κωλύει οὔτε ποιεῖ φωνὴν μίαν σημαντικήν: and secondly, φωνὴ ἄσημος ἐκ πλειόνων μὲν φωνῶν μιᾶς, (these are the words 'more than one' that it connects) σημαντικῶν δέ, ποιεῖν πεφυκυῖα μίαν σημαντικὴν φωνήν. [This last φωνή is equivalent to λόγος, a sentence *with a meaning*. An 'utterance' may be applied to one, or to several words in conjunction.] From the former definition we learn likewise, that it may be placed either at the extremities (beginning and end) or in the middle of a sentence[1]; and it is illustrated by the *single words*, μέν, ἤτοι, δέ. In this same sense it is employed by the author of the Rhet. ad Alex. c. 23. § 5. (Oxf. Ed.) χρὴ δὲ καὶ συνδέσμους ὀλίγους ποιεῖν (meaning here καί, as the connective par excellence) τὰ πλεῖστα δὲ ζευγνύναι: which is fully illustrated by Rhet. III. 6. 6, where we are told to say πορευθεὶς διελέχθην, rather than πορευθεὶς καὶ διαλεχθείς.

Harris, Hermes, Bk. II. ch. 2, thus defines a conjunction. "A part of speech devoid of signification itself, but so formed

---

[1] ἐπεί or ὥστε, for instance, may stand at the beginning of a sentence, and δέ or γάρ at the end of it—δέ so placed is extremely rare; one may conceive however such a sentence as this, οὐ πολλοὶ μὲν τοῦτο ποιοῦσι, ὀλίγοι δέ: but γάρ at the end of an interrogative sentence is by no means uncommon, as πῶς γάρ;

as to help signification, by making two or more significant sentences to be one significant sentence"—a definition which manifestly comes from Aristotle. As, 'Rome was enslaved', 'Cæsar was ambitious' become one by being connected by the particle 'because'. So in Rhet. III. 12. 4, the many significant terms ἀσύνδετα, ἦλθον, διελέχθην, ἱκέτευσα, become one by the introduction of the copula, καί. Similarly in III. 9. 1, the εἰρομένη λέξις, the loose style, which is not rounded into organized periods, in which the clauses merely 'hang together', or 'are strung together' like a rope of onions, is συνδέσμῳ μία; that is, derives the only unity and connexion that it has from conjunctions and particles.

Aristotle's definition will apply equally well to prepositions, as to conjunctions and particles, and no doubt is intended to include them. Prepositions also merely express a relation, as of time, place, cause, of one thing to another, and have no independent signification apart from the terms between which the relation lies. They also give a 'unity' to the several particulars which they connect.

These are the only parts of speech which come under the head of σύνδεσμος in Aristotle's classification.

Interjections, as mere exclamations, he seems not to have considered as parts of speech at all: at all events the definition of σύνδεσμος does not include them: all the other parts of speech are included in the classification. By some later writers, as Demetrius, interjections are classed with 'connecting particles'; a description which is certainly quite inappropriate to them.

This however is not the only sense in which this word is employed by Aristotle and other writers: it sometimes carries with it the clause to which the connecting particle, as μέν—δέ, τε—καί, is attached, and signifies a connected clause with, and sometimes even without, its connecting particle; or correlative clauses, such as those coupled by μέν and δέ. Clear examples of this usage are found in Rhet. III. 5. 2, 3, where the ἀναγκαῖος σύνδεσμος, the connexion which is de rigueur, obbligato, is the *apodosis*, ἐπορευόμην παραλαβὼν αὐτούς, the corresponding clause (to the protasis), τὸ ἀνταποδιδόμενον: here the connecting particle is wanting, but the πρότασις has its ἐπεί expressed; as also has the parenthetical clause, which is likewise called σύνδεσμος, its γάρ. Similarly of the two examples given of a σύνδεσμος in Rhet. ad Alex. c. 26. § 2., the first *may* it is true be interpreted of the conjunctions μέν and δέ alone; but in the second, σὺ γὰρ κἀκείνων αἴτιος ἐγένου καὶ τούτων αἴτιος σύ, it would seem from the introductory words, πάλιν ὅταν ὁ αὐτὸς (σύνδεσμος) συνακόλουθος ᾖ, that the repetition is meant to apply to the *three* words, καί, σύ, and αἴτιος; so that here we should understand it of the connected clause *with* its connective, καί, or of the connected clauses alone. Another certain example of its employment in this signification is Rhet. III. 5, 6., where the question is of *sentences*.

There is also a third sense of the word which seems to be distinguishable from the two preceding in Aristotle's writings. In Poet. XX. 13, περὶ Ἑρμ. 17. a. 9 and 16, Anal. Post. II. 93. b. 36, we have the phrase λόγος συνδέσμῳ εἷς; to which in the first and third passages ὥσπερ ἡ Ἰλίας is added. The author is here distinguishing two kinds of unity of phrase or description, the one where the unity is conveyed by the meaning, ὁ ἓν δηλῶν, as the definition of a man; the other which is effected by σύνδεσμος. This latter would seem to be most naturally interpreted of connexion in general. It is true that in the passage of the de Interpr. it is opposed to πολλοὶ δέ, οἱ πολλὰ καὶ μὴ ἓν (δηλοῦντες) ἢ οἱ ἀσύνδετοι: but with the last word λόγοι is to be supplied, and not σύνδεσμοι, —indeed ἀσίνδετοι σύνδεσμοι would be a contradiction in terms. And besides this, if Aristotle had meant conjunctions, &c. in the phrase which we are endeavouring to explain, he would surely have said συνδέσμοις and not συνδέσμῳ.

Ammonius, on Arist. de Interpr. p. 54. 6, (quoted by Harris, Hermes, u. s.) evidently referring to this distinction of the two kinds of unity in the λόγος, compares the first, ὁ κυρίως εἷς, to a block of wood in its natural state, which is properly and naturally one; the second, that which denotes the combination of several existences, and appears to be made one by one (or more) conjunctive particles (σύνδεσμος), to a ship made up of various pieces of timber, and deriving its unity from the nails, pegs, screws, and other fastenings; a very good illustration of the nature and use of connective particles.

Demetrius, π. ἑρμ. l. c. properly distinguishes two kinds of σύνδεσμοι. The one, which may be called κύριοι, are connectives properly so called, because they actually do 'connect' words and sentences: such are μέν, δέ, ἤτοι, ἤ, ἐπεί, γάρ, &c. The other which he calls παραπληρωματικοί, complementary, are such as γε, δή, οὖν, ἄρα, when not used as inferential, but merely continuative, restrictive, corrective or emphatic, (of which the emphatic καί is a good example). It is to these last that Demetrius refers interjections; which however strictly speaking are so far from being 'connective', that they break and interrupt the continuity of the sentence. Dionysius has the substantive παραπληρώματα in two passages; de Isocr. Jud. c. 3., p. 540, Reiske, παραπληρώμασι λέξεων οὐδὲν ὠφελουσῶν; and again, de Adm. vi dic. in Demosth. c. 39, p. 1072. παραπληρώμασι τῶν ὀνομάτων οὐκ ἀναγκαίοις.

APPENDIX E. TO BOOK III. CH. XV. XVI. XVII.

ἀμφισβητήσεις, στάσεις, status.

The legal 'issues,' afterwards called στάσεις and status, appear in Aristotle in the embryo stage of ἀμφισβητήσεις, often referred to, never exactly defined, or employed as a well determined and recognised technical and legal classification. References to these issues, on which may be made to turn the trial and decision of legal cases—more especially of criminal cases, to which Aristotle at least usually applies them—are scattered up and down the topics of his Rhetoric.

See for instance, I. 3. 6, I. 13. 9, 10. III. 15. 2; 16. 1, and 6; 17. 1. The four degrees of criminality, ἀτύχημα, ἁμάρτημα, ἀδίκημα, ἀδικία—or three, omitting (as is usually done) ἀδίκημα as distinguished from ἀδικία—may likewise be construed as so many ἀμφισβητήσεις, or issues that may be raised in determining the nature of an alleged crime. They are most explicitly enumerated in III. 16. 6. and 17. 1. They here appear as four; the question of fact, τὸ ὅτι, τὸ γεγονέναι ἢ μή; of harm or damage, τοῦ βλαβερὸν εἶναι, εἰ ἔβλαψεν; of criminality, τοῦ ἄδικον εἶναι ἢ μή, εἰ δικαίως; and of quantity or degree, εἰ τοσοῦτον, ἢ τηλικοῦτον, ὅτι οὐ τοσόνδε. In c. 16. § 1, these are otherwise classified, and reduced to three, ὅτι ἔστι δεῖξαι ἐὰν ᾖ ἄπιστον; ὅτι ποιόν; ἢ ὅτι ποσόν; fact, quality, quantity. This last coincides with one of the later and ordinary divisions. The first or fourfold division may however easily be reduced under the terms of the second, thus. The issue of fact is the same in both; we *must* know first of all whether the alleged fact is true or not. The second and third class of the former list may both be referred to the class 'quality' of the second; the damage or injury and the criminality, the justice or injustice, may both be regarded as 'qualities' of actions. And the amount or degree of criminality of an alleged offence τοσοῦτον, τηλικοῦτον, τοσόνδε, is plainly identifiable with the 'quantity' of the second division. This last is in fact what was afterwards called the ὁρικὴ στάσις, and by Cicero and the Latin Rhetoricians 'nomen' or 'finitio'. This issue is the 'definition' of the offence, the name or title which is to be given to it; and this may clearly be regarded as a question of 'degree' or 'amount' of criminality, which gives its designation to the offence; determines what it is to be called, and consequently the court by which it is to be tried, and the legal process to which it is to be subjected. For instance, the same act may be construed as αἰκία or ὕβρις, and the issue may be raised on this point. αἰκία 'assault' is a mere personal offence, and is the object of a private action or δίκη; but an act of ὕβρις is an offence against the state, and subjects the offender to a γραφή or public prosecution. The ἀμφισβητήσεις or στάσεις are likewise, as by Aristotle, *indicated*, not defined and classified, in the Rhet. ad Alex. c. 5. § 8.

The usual division of the στάσεις, when they came to be systematically classified and defined by succeeding legists and rhetoricians, was threefold; (1) στάσις στοχαστική, status conjecturalis, conjectura, the question of fact; (2) ὁρική, the definition or 'name' that was to be given to the offence charged, nomen or finitio; and (3) στ. ποιότητος, qualitas, or 'generis,' the question of the justice or injustice of the act; of right and wrong; but including also that of τὸ συμφέρον ἢ ἀσύμφορον, utile an inutile, Aristotle's βλαβερόν, the question of damage and loss. This appears from Hermogenes, c. 2. π. στασ. διαιρ. Rhet. Gr. II. 139. Ed. Speng., a chapter in which the divisions and definitions of the στάσεις are clearly and well stated; the third class has many subdivisions.

Cicero has more than one division of the status. In the de Invent. I. 8. 10, 11, 12, and 16, he gives a fourfold classification, which is also very clearly explained. The classes are, facti, nominis, generis, actionis: ut in facto conjectura, in nomine finitio, in genere qualitas, in actione jus intelligeretur. § 50. The actio, or translativa constitutio, is when the question or issue to be determined has reference to the bringing of the action (which is here separated from the nomen or finitio); quem, quicum, quomodo, apud quos, quo jure, quo tempore, agere oporteat. This fourth division is abandoned, as unnecessary, in his later works.

His ordinary division is threefold: Orat. XXXIV. 121. res (controversiam facit) aut de vero aut de recto aut de nomine. Sitne? quid sit? quale sit? de Orat. II. 30. 132. factum, quale, nomen. See also Topic. XXIV. 92—94. where the meaning of the word *status* is explained; in quo primum insistit (takes up a position to sustain an attack) quasi ad repugnandum congressa defensio. And Orat. Part. XXIX. 101, factum, facti appellatio, qualitas (rectum, concedendumve).

In the Auct. ad Heren. I. 11—15., the divisions are also three but not identical with the preceding. They are, conjecturalis, legitima, (when the issue is raised upon some *legal* point, as the interpretation of a law, the conflict of two antagonistic laws, and such like questions), and juridicalis, which corresponds to qualitas.

Lastly Quintilian has devoted a long chapter, III. 6., to the discussion of the status, and gives more suo a multitude of different divisions. His own is to be found in § 66., compare § 86. There are three status rationales, conjectura, finitio, and qualitas; and one legalis, which he formerly subdivided into five species, scripti et voluntatis, legum contrariarum, collectivum, ambiguitatis, translationis. The fourth, legalis, he now is of opinion, (§ 67.), may be withdrawn from the 'general' status, and the rationales alone remain as a *general* division. These are all examined in detail in the remainder of the chapter. In § 3 we are told that the first use of this technical term was attributed either to Hermagoras, or to Naucrates a pupil of Isocrates, or to Zopyrus of Clazomenæ: he is himself inclined to refer the earliest use of it to Æschines; who in the speech, c. Ctesiph. (§ 206. Bait. and Sauppe; p. 83. 22. H. Steph.) borrows from wrestling the term στάσις, the position or attitude which the wrestler was obliged to assume, and applies it to the 'real question at issue', from which he charges Demosthenes with straying. The name he explains either, like Cicero, and Æschines, as 'primus causæ congressus', the position or posture for resisting an attack, or 'quod in hac causa consistat'. The latter explanation seems to represent the 'real gist,' and 'essence' of the case, that which it really turns upon. In the next and following sections the *meaning* of the term is discussed. In § 49, there is a notice (apparently corrupt) of a supposed division of Aristotle's in the Rhetoric, either of the entire work, or of these στάσεις; on which Spalding's note may be consulted. See on the whole subject, Ernesti, Lex. Techn. Græc. et Lat. s. vv.

ON THE

ῬΗΤΟΡΙΚΗ ΠΡΟΣ ἈΛΕΧΑΝΔΡΟΝ.

THIS treatise on the art of Rhetoric, long attributed to Aristotle and incorporated in the collection of his works[1], derives its title from the letter prefixed, which purports to be addressed by Aristotle to his pupil Alexander during the period of his Eastern Campaign, with a present of one (or two) works on rhetoric; who is therein lectured like a school-boy upon the value and importance of the study of the art. The forger of the Epistle, whoever it may have been, or whatever may have been the motive of the forgery—Victorius opines that the object was to give an additional pecuniary value to the work by fathering it upon the distinguished philosopher—forgets, in the endeavour to observe, as he thinks, the proprieties of the situation, and to give an air of reality to his letter, by making Aristotle assume the style of a tutor in writing to his former pupil, how totally the relations between them had changed during the interval that had elapsed since he gave his lessons to the little Alexander at the Court of Philip, and that the time of instruction and education was long past. Never did a spurious document more manifestly betray itself by want of skill and inappropriateness in the composition.

As to the treatise itself, though there is *some* general correspondence, in the treatment and topics selected and

[1] In the time of Athenæus, that is early in the third century of the Christian era, not only the treatise itself, but the letter prefixed, was already ascribed to Aristotle. Athenæus, Deipn. 11. 508. A, quotes from this letter, § 4, a definition of 'law,' νόμοι, as Aristotle's.

illustrated, between this author and Aristotle, yet the numerous and important differences in detail, as well as the marked inferiority in subtlety and spirit, power and interest, the entire absence of the logical element in this work, the striking contrast of *style* between them—here, often obscure from its vagueness and indefiniteness though otherwise clear and simple, but feeble and inexpressive; there, also often obscure and elliptical, but characterised by a terse and pregnant brevity—the more scientific exactness, and the much higher moral tone that appear in Aristotle's work, all unite to prove beyond the possibility of doubt that the two arts of Rhetoric could not have proceeded from the same intellect, taste, judgment, and moral standard. The Rhet. ad Alex. is a work proceeding from an entirely different and inferior order of mind and character.

"It occupies," says Westermann, Gesch. der Beredtsamkeit, § 69, "an intermediate position between the earlier writers on the art and Aristotle; for in spite of the numerous interpolations with which the original text is here and there corrupted and disfigured, we can at any rate distinguish so much as this, that the domain of Rhetoric embraced by him was much wider than that of his predecessors." Allowing this, we must add that it presents a much nearer resemblance to the preceding Arts, and the sophistical school of rhetoricians in general, than it does to Aristotle's great work. The logical part is entirely omitted; it is totally devoid of all scientific character; and assumes altogether a practical aspect, as a series of rules and precepts for the guidance of the orator in the assembly and the law court, quite opposed, as Spengel remarks (Art. Script. p. 188.), to the 'theoretical' treatment of Aristotle. If the author followed any one of his predecessors in particular, it was Isocrates[1]; several of whose rules are borrowed, without his name, from his τέχνη. In three or four cases, to be afterwards pointed out, this is certified by extant fragments; and most probably the same

[1] We shall see hereafter that this may be considered nearly certain.

guide is followed in many other cases in which we have not the same means of ascertaining the original authority. The treatise is the best representative which we have remaining of the actual nature of the teaching of the sophistical school of rhetoric; and of this indeed it seems in many points to be quite characteristic. All this, and the fact that it is in some degree a *representative* work, representative, that is, of the mode of treatment of rhetoric characteristic of the school of the Sophistical Rhetoricians, to which Aristotle's school and system were in direct opposition and antagonism, may give it an interest and a value to us, which it would not otherwise possess, when it is examined and contrasted with Aristotle's great work. Some glaring instances of its highly immoral character I shall have occasion to notice more than once in the course of the following analysis.

It may of course be said that Aristotle's own Rhetoric, or any other system which teaches, as the *art* of Rhetoric must, to argue indifferently upon both sides of a question, is dangerous to put into the hands of novices, as all sharp and two-edged weapons proverbially are; and that it may most readily be perverted to an immoral purpose. Aristotle is perfectly aware of this, and apologises in his Introduction for the necessity he is under of treating it in this way; he suggests care and caution in the use of it, shows how it may be applied in the cause of truth and justice, and emphatically warns the students of his treatise against the *misuse* of it. We may *know how* to argue on both sides of a question without taking the wrong side; but in a world full of fraud and trickery, and in assemblies and courts of law where the object is often to deceive, we must be prepared to meet bad logic and delusive arguments, in order that truth and justice may be made to prevail over falsehood and wrong. But we must not argue from the use to the abuse of an art: in dialectics we may study and analyse and illustrate sophistries and fallacies, as an exercise for our own minds, and that we may be able to detect them when employed by others; and in rhetoric we may be able to state what is to be said on both sides of the question, and show how an argument may be turned against an opponent; not to *misuse* our skill and knowledge, to throw dust in the eyes of a jury, to promote injustice or screen the wrong doer, but to *use* it in the interest of justice and of truth, for the benefit of society and for a moral end. The true distinction between the artist and the sophist lies in the animus or προαίρεσις: it is the bad intention, the vicious moral purpose of the latter which marks the character: the accomplished dialectician and trained rhetorician can see through and unmask sophistry, without himself abusing his art to the purposes of fraud and injustice. Rhet. I. 1. 12, 13, 14. Again Aristotle's work is a Theory, with rules for practical application in the shape of Topics: it must therefore be as complete as possible in all its parts. Moreover it was never designed by its author to supersede the ordinary general education of a young man: for he expressly ascribes it to his predecessors as an imposture and a vice, that they *did* attempt to substitute it for the science of Politics, of which it is in fact only a subordinate, and comparatively unimportant branch; and so made it take the place of that complete and comprehensive science or system, which would, if duly taught, instruct the student in the 'whole duty' of a citizen[1].

But all this was entirely wanting in the systems and practice of his predecessors; and from this moral point of

[1] Spengel, Proleg. ad Anaxim. Art. Rhet. p. x., says on this subject; Hæc enim ars in oratorum usum, ut in utramque sententiam probabiliter dicas, composita est; quo fit, ut verum non curet, verisimile ubique sectetur. Id Aristotele prorsus indignum est; non enim artem docet, ut quocunque modo adversarium vincas, sed ut in omnibus causis *verum invenias et perspicias*, qui si *semel iterumque* ad illud persuadendi genus dolabi videatur, id artis levitate, non autoris consilio, factum esse credas. Nam longissime abest, qui hanc docendi rationem profiteatur. It seems to me that Spengel in this has very much understated the case against Aristotle's Rhetoric: the grounds, that is, on which it may be chargeable with an immoral tendency. The method of arguing on both sides of a question belongs to the Art of Rhetoric, *as such;* it is *essential* to it, as we have already fully shown. It there-

view we must include in our censure the treatise under consideration. They defined rhetoric as 'the art of persuasion', and made this the sole object of their teaching: persuasion, or the making of a favourable impression, by any means, and at any price. This will be substantiated by the passages we shall meet with in our review of the 'Ρητ. πρὸς Ἀλέξανδρον; and all that we know from Aristotle Plato and others of the actual contents of their writings upon the art leads us to the same conclusion with respect to the rest of them; of course with the *possible* exception of Prodicus, or this or that other individual. Besides this abuse of logic—of which Corax's τόπος of 'the probable,' exemplified by Aristotle amongst the 'fallacies', Rhet. II. 24. 11, is a striking instance—these earlier 'arts' treated of style, of the divisions of the speech and the contents of each, and especially of appeals to the feelings; all of them according to Aristotle extra artem[1]. The students who passed under their hands had entrusted to

fore pervades the whole treatise, and is by no means confined to 'one or two places', semel iterumque. The qualification of the object originally proposed by the art, which is implied in Aristotle's own definition of Rhetoric, referred to by Spengel in the first words printed in Italics, no doubt deserves to be taken into account. But so far as Aristotle's system *can* be defended against the charge of a tendency to pervert, or at all events to invalidate, or encourage a disregard of, the natural distinctions of right and wrong, truth and falsehood, it must be, as it seems to me, by the considerations I have suggested in the text. Whether in this point he is altogether free from reproach, I will not take upon me to decide: but it is certain that Plato's indignant rejection of the Art as one that prefers probability to truth, aims only at persuasion, and thereby admits of imposture and deceit, belongs to a higher and a purer Morality.

[1] Such were the contents of their written treatises. For the practical training of their pupils, by the cultivation of habits of readiness and dexterity in speaking and argument, collections of 'topics' were provided, of two kinds: 'probable,' (or plausible, such as would be likely to persuade, or impose upon, an uncultivated jury or assembly) arguments, on *both* sides of certain questions and cases legal and political, known by experience to be of constant recurrence; which again may be illustrated by Corax's τόπος: and secondly, 'Elegant extracts,' or choice specimens of rhetorical composition, either selected from actual speeches of repute, or composed for the occasion by the teachers themselves. These last are what are called 'communes loci' by the Latin Rhetoricians.

them without check or warning this powerful instrument of mischief, with which they were at once let loose upon society, uncontrolled and unguarded by any moral or religious training whatsoever; all other education being superseded—so we are given to understand—by this new art of rhetoric.

As to the authorship of the treatise, it has been held by most writers of authority from the time of Victorius, who in his preface to the Rhetoric first gave this opinion, founded on the well-known passage of Quintilian, III. 4. 9,—Buhle, (Aristotle,) who had been at first in favour of the older view which ascribed it to Aristotle, Pref. to Rhet. vol. IV. pp. 5—7, offers in the subsequent volume, Pref. pp. IV. seq., a most candid and complete retractation, convinced by the arguments and authority of Spalding in his note on the passage of Quintilian—to be the work of Anaximenes, the historian and rhetorician, contemporary of Aristotle, whose own Art of Rhetoric was preceded by this of Anaximenes at the interval of a few years. This fact is considered to be so completely established, that Spengel, who has done more than any one else to establish it; first in his Art. Script. pp. 182—191; secondly in a paper published in the Zeitschrift für Alterthumswissenschaft (in answer to Lersch), 1840. pp. 1258—67; and thirdly in the note to his Edition of this work, on Ch. I. p. 99; has gone so far as to print the name of Anaximenes as the author of the treatise on the title page of his edition. The evidence, which is not quite all that could be desired, is best given, and the whole case most convincingly argued, in his Artium Scriptores above referred to. It amounts to this. Quintilian, Inst. Orat. III. 4. 9, has the following sentence. Anaximenes judicialem et concionalem generales partes esse voluit; septem autem species, hortandi, dehortandi, laudandi, vituperandi, accusandi, defendendi, exquirendi quod ἐξεταστικὸν dicit; quarum duæ primæ deliberativi, duæ sequentes demonstrativi, tres ultimæ judicialis generis sunt partes. On which Spengel triumphantly remarks, Art. Scr. p. 190, that *he* knows no one else (besides Anaximenes) who has ascribed two genera and seven species to rhetoric. And therein in fact lies the strength of the case; most of the remaining evidence adduced in its support is even contradictory. But first of all, does the author (of the Rhet. ad Alex.) recognise two or three genera or branches of Rhetoric? At the opening of his treatise he seems to tell us that rhetoric has, not two, but three divisions or γένη; 'libri omnes τρία γένη' Speng. not. ad loc.: Oh but, says Spengel, l. c., *Aristotle* was the first that distinguished three classes or genera of rhetoric, and the alteration of δύο into τρία, and the interpolation of τὸ δ' ἐπιδεικτικόν, (which is remorselessly expunged) were introduced by some later copyist or Editor who believed the work to be Aristotle's, and naturally missed two of the characteristics of *his* system of rhetoric; and *therefore* we must alter the text, and read δύο γένη τῶν πολ. εἰσι λόγων; which he accordingly proceeds to do[1]. Victorius on the other hand for the same reason preferred altering and supplementing the text of *Quintilian* in conformity with that of the Rhet. ad Alex. Doctors *will* disagree.

The next piece of evidence is a passage of Syrianus ad Hermogenem, quoted in Art. Script., and the note of the Edition. Here we are told that *Aristotle*, (Ἀριστοτέλης δὲ δύο γένη κ.τ.λ.), not Anaximenes at all, recognised two kinds of πολιτικοὶ λόγοι, and seven species; just as Quintilian gives them. But of course this presents no difficulty to the undaunted critic, who without hesitation pronounces that as the first and last syllables (is that so?) of the two names, Ἀριστοτέλης and Ἀναξιμένης, are the same, the one might very easily be substituted for the other; and further argues that 'some sciolist,' knowing that Aristotle's distinction of the classes of rhetoric was three-, and not, two-fold, and finding Aristotle's name prefixed to the Rhet. ad Alex., altered

---

[1] There is another passage further on, c. 18. (Oxf. Ed.) § 6. Spengel Ed. c. 17. ult., where τρία εἴδη seems again to be applied to denote the three branches of rhetoric, and, as here, there is no various reading. I have commented upon this in my analysis of that Chapter. (c. 17.)

δύο into τρία, and added de suo τὸ δ' ἐπιδεικτικόν. If ''Αριστοτέλης' in Syrianus *is* a mistake, as I suppose it must be, I should rather prefer accounting for it by supposing that Syrianus himself attributed the Rhet. ad Alex. to Aristotle. If Athenæus in the 3d. century of the Christian era believed this to be the work of Aristotle, there is every reason for concluding that Syrianus, nearly two centuries later, should have held the same opinion.

Another bit of evidence, No. 3, in the note from which we are quoting, is more convincing.

The letter prefixed to the treatise concludes with the words, περὶ τῶν πολιτικῶν καὶ τῶν δικανικῶν παραγγελμάτων, ὅθεν πρὸς ἑκάτερον αὐτῶν εὐπορήσεις κ.τ.λ.; whence it seems to follow that the author of the letter, found two, and not three, kinds or classes of rhetoric mentioned at the opening of the work.

The fourth argument in the same note is to this effect. From the contents of the Art itself no one can prove that the author distinguished three kinds of rhetoric; the inferences are all in favour of two. Had his division really been by three genera, like Aristotle's, he could not have failed to state and enumerate them, like Aristotle also. But in fact he treats the topics of rhetoric under the heads of the seven *species;* not of two or three *genera;* and whereas we do find λόγοι δικανικοί, προοίμια δικανικά, δικανικὴ πραγματεία, and the same with δημογορικός, δημηγορεῖν, δημηγορία, whereby two genera are really indicated; similar phraseology with ἐπιδεικτικός never appears, from which we should infer that this is not recognised as a distinct branch. We do however find τρία εἴδη, meaning apparently three genera or branches, at the end of c. 18. (Oxf. Ed.). Spengel of course condemns this as corrupt, and substitutes πάντων. (comp. p. 407. not. 1.)

The evidence of style, upon which, as far as I am aware, no writer on this subject has entered, seems to me upon the whole as far as it goes to be rather against the Anaximenian authorship. Anaximenes was a professed rhetorician, and had therefore studied Greek composition; and although Dionysius, de Isæo Jud. c. 19, who nevertheless *compares* him as a writer with Isocrates and Gorgias and Alcidamas and Theodorus of Byzantium, gives an unfavourable account of his powers of making an impression, styling him *in this respect* ἀσθενῆ καὶ ἀπίθανον; yet he finds no fault with the purity of his style; and in fact one can see no reason why Anaximenes educated as he was should have been guilty of barbarisms in language any more than Isocrates himself.

I have however noted a few objectionable or suspicious words and phrases, some of them apparently indicative of a later stage of the Greek language, of which I will give a list, with one or two observations.

In c. 2. § 19 (Oxf. Ed.) c. 1. p. 8, 28. (Speng.) we find the Homeric and Ionic form εἵνεκα which Gaisford and Spengel retain, though three MSS. give the common form ἕνεκα. Why Anaximenes, if he was the author, should have chosen to adopt this antiquated and poetical form instead of the one commonly in use I have no explanation to offer.

ἰδέα, for εἶδος or γένος, occurs in c. 4. § 6. (Oxf.) p. 20, 19 (Speng.); and again, c. 7. § 5. This in the general sense of a fashion, guise, manner, or even 'kind', may perhaps be defensible; Dionysius, for example, Ars Rhet. x. 14, has ὅλη μὲν ἰδέα συμβουλευτικὴ διηγήσεως οὐ δεῖται: but it seems to belong in this definite sense rather to the later Greek. [After all, it may imply nothing more in the author than ignorance of logic and its terminology.]

In the next chapter, § 1, p. 22, 7, (Speng.) we have the extraordinary word καθυποπτευθέντων, offences or crimes "that have been suspected against us," or, of which we have been suspected. No other authority is cited by the Lexicons except this passage.

In c. 21 (Oxf.), c. 20 (Speng.), at the beginning, we have παλιλλογία, for ἀνακεφαλαίωσις or ἐπάνοδος, and παλιλλογεῖν, in the sense of a 'repetition' or 'recapitulation;' and both of these frequently recur throughout the remainder of the treatise. This word again, occurs both in Homer and Herodotus. In the former, the adjective παλιλλόγος, Il. A. 126, παλίλλογα ταῦτ' ἐπαγείρειν, but with a totally different signification, "re-collected." In Herodotus παλιλλογεῖν is, as here, iterum dicere, repetere. Besides these two, neither of them a very good authority for the use of it by a writer of Attic Greek Prose, the word is found, so far as can be learnt from the Lexicons, only in a doubtful passage of Theophrastus, at the end of his first 'character'; where, even if the passage be genuine, it is employed in an entirely different sense. See Ast's note[1]. It does however occur also in Plut. Vit. Hom. § 32. as a 'figure of rhetoric'; and with the same signification in two late and obscure Rhetoricians, Zonæus, and an Anonymous, in Spengel's collection of Rhet. Græc. III. pp. 165, 182., where it is defined (alike in both), λέξις ἡ φράσις τοῦ μὲν προηγουμένου κώλου κατάληξις, τοῦ δὲ ἀρχομένου ἀρχή, "a figure or expression, where the same word ends one clause of a sentence and begins the next." [These three last do *not* appear in the Lexicons.]

In c. 29, 4 (Oxf.), c. 28 (Speng.), the word προγυμνάσματα, "preparatory exercises," very common in the later Rhetoricians, appears long before its due time. Spengel notices it merely 'as the earliest use of the term'; not. ad loc.

The use of μήτε, apparently for οὔτε—I can find no other explanation—twice in c. 30, 5. (Oxf.), c. 29. p. 55, 10. (Speng.), seems to savour of a later period of Greek composition, when the distinction between the two forms of the negative had become partially obliterated : a trained rhetorician of the middle of the 4th century B.C. had no business to be guilty of such a solecism.

The short chapter, 32. (Oxf.), 31 (Speng.), is in its entire structure and expression, a very indifferent specimen of Greek prose. Of single words, we have first, in *most* of the MSS.—*no*

---

[1] Photius gives, s. v. παλιλλογία, ταυτολογία. Hesychius has παλίλλογα, παλινσύλλεκτα, referring to the word as used by Homer; and παλιλλογία, ταυτολογία: and Suidas the same.

various reading is given by Bekker in the quarto Ed.— δράματα in the *most unusual*, (indeed almost a solecism in prose,) application, for πράγματα[1], 'acts'; for which afterwards πράξεις is substituted. Spengel however finds πράγματα in three MSS., and introduces this into the text. Next comes the monstrum verbi, πραγματολογοῦντες, for which there is no authority earlier than Diogenes Laertius. Then we have πρόρρησις, a ἅπαξ λεγόμενον in the sense in which it is here employed, 'a previous, or preparatory statement': and lastly another poetical form, φροίμιον; though this is partially defended by Aristotle's employment of the verb (φροιμιάζεσθαι) twice in Polit. Bk. VII.; which is likewise found in three places of this treatise.

Near the end of c. 33 (Oxf.), 32 (Speng.), we find the extraordinary phrase, τὴν προτροπὴν πέρατι ὁρίσαι, (or ὁρίσαι); which Buhle translates, propositio (did he mistake προτροπὴν for πρότασιν?) conclusione terminanda est. But to express that, if it really be the meaning, by 'determining or limiting by an end or termination,' is hardly worthy of a Greek Rhetorician of the 4th century.

In c. 35. 7. (Oxf.), 36. p. 69. 14 (Speng.) the preposition πρός is employed in what seems to me a very unusual application, which I do not remember to have noticed in any good Greek author. οἱ πρὸς αὐτόν is opposed to οἱ παλαιοὶ πρόγονοι, apparently in the sense of "near relations,"— proximi, Buhle,—πρός standing for, 'in close relation to.'

The last word but two of c. 36, (35), is εἰδήσομεν; which may indeed be partly defended by similar grammatical monstrosities in Aristotle, who in fact uses this very form himself, Top. A. 18. 108. a. 28. as well as εἰδῆσαι, and other enormities. Plato, (Laches,) and the same Aristotle, have σκέπτεσθαι; and Demosthenes in one place σκεψάσθωσαν[2].

---

[1] It is true that Plato employs δρᾶμα *in a certain sense* for πρᾶγμα 'a deed': see Heind. on Theæt. 150.A.; but never, I think, as a mere synonym; always with some additional connotation; either to convey some special emphasis, or intentionally as a poetical word.

[2] I have a small collection of these irregularities of the best writers,

No shadow of authority for ἀναλογητέον, which is used in c. 37, 26 (Oxf.), c. 36. p. 78. (Speng.), in the sense of 'recapitulating' or 'counting (λόγος) over again'—the ἀνά having the same force as in ἀνακεφαλαιοῦσθαι[1]—is found till we come to Plutarch, who in the Symposiaca, Probl. E, has, χειμῶνι τῆς νυκτὸς ἀναλογεῖν δοκούσης: but in the totally different signification of "to be proportional (ἀνάλογον), or, correspond, answer to."

In the same chapter, §§ 5, 6, 7, ὑπεναντίος is wantonly, and without any difference of meaning, substituted three several times for ἐναντίος, 'contrary'.

These are the most prominent and glaring deviations from the standard of pure classical Greek that I have noticed in this work: whether they are sufficient when taken together to support a case of later authorship than Anaximenes' time, I must leave to others to judge. I have already observed that Aristotle often employs forms of words for which there is no earlier authority, and which grammarians pronounce to be solecisms; but no one would think of condemning on this ground alone any particular work of his as spurious. Plato and Demosthenes and the very best writers, as I have noted above, are occasionally guilty of such abnormal eccentricities, proceeding most likely from a momentary inattention or carelessness, and by sound judging critics are easily forgiven, and thought little the worse of on that account.

Spengel, Art. Script. pp. 188, 9., has endeavoured to fix the probable limits of time within which the Rhet. ad Alex. was composed or published. The conclusion at which he arrives is the probable one, that it was between 340 and 330

which this is not the proper place for enumerating. I hope to find a more favourable opportunity for doing so in the notes of the Edition that is to follow.

[1] Spengel, who seems not to have observed this, proposes in his note to read τὴν ἀντιλογίαν παλιλλογητέον, for τὴν αἰτίαν ἀναλογητέον of the MSS.; a violent and unnecessary alteration. The MSS. give as various readings, ἀναλογιστέον, and the vox nihili, ἀναλογιτέον.

B.C.; that is, a little earlier than the publication of Aristotle's Rhetoric; a conclusion founded upon two or three chronological references in the work itself. On the other point, the date of Aristotle's Rhetoric, I have already given Spengel's opinion (Introd. p. 38.), with his reasons for it, that it was not published till at least 330 B.C. From the essential difference in the conception and general treatment of the subject, as well as in numerous points of detail, we may certainly infer that the author of this work was not acquainted with Aristotle's treatise, to which he makes no allusion whatsoever, direct or indirect. We also know that he *was* acquainted with Isocrates' τέχνη, from which he borrows in several places. This is no doubt, as far as it goes, in favour of the authorship of Anaximenes, though not absolutely conclusive: and still more so, the twofold division of rhetoric, supposing that we accept Spengel's alteration of δύο for τρία, and the rest, at the opening of the treatise. For although it is quite possible, though perhaps unlikely, that a comparatively modern writer of the Christian era may not have had access to Aristotle's Rhetoric, or not have chosen to follow it, it does *not* seem probable that, after Aristotle's threefold division of the Art had been established and universally recognised, any subsequent writer on the same subject would have abandoned it, and adopted one which is so manifestly inferior and insufficient.

Upon the whole I am inclined to think that the weight of evidence preponderates in favour of attributing this work to Anaximenes. The internal evidence derived from style and manner, being mere matter of inference, opinion, and taste, can never be absolutely relied on, as we rely upon any positive statement or external and independent matter of fact; though these too are by no means free from uncertainties of their own. Thus in the case before us, it is certainly *possible* that Anaximenes may in spite of his rhetorical education and practice have been really chargeable with the solecisms which the text of the Rhet. ad Alex. presents: or on the other hand these may be corruptions or interpolations of incompetent transcribers or critics: but as we have not attained to complete certainty upon the question I think it would be as well if the name of Anaximenes on the title page of Spengel's next Edition were replaced by the more modest 'Anonymus'.

I now proceed to give some account of the contents of this Art of Rhetoric, chiefly for the purpose of comparing it with that of Aristotle, by bringing into view the numerous points of difference between them; and also of illustrating and confirming what I have elsewhere said of the mischievous and immoral character of these early rhetorical systems, and the sentiments and practice they inculcate, when used, as they were intended, as the sole instruments of education; and substituted for a genuine moral and intellectual discipline, tending to the formation of virtuous habits and the due performance of the duties of a man and a citizen, such as is recommended by the philosophers.

Before we proceed to examine the details of the work, we will first enumerate one or two of the *general* differences which mark the divergence of the two works, and prove to demonstration that they cannot be ascribed to the same author.

On the essential difference of style, tone, and character of *composition* I have already spoken. Another marked and characteristic difference between the two authors lies in the manner of *illustration* employed by each. Aristotle, with a single exception[1] in III. 16., invariably quotes the speeches or writings or remarkable sayings, of *others:* the author of the Rhet. ad Alex. with precisely the same degree of consistency, that is, with one exception corresponding to that of

---

[1] This is unnoticed by Spengel, who in his Prolegomena, u. s., has the remark, Ar. *nullum* de suo dat exemplum: an omission which is balanced by one corresponding on the other side, autor noster (Anaximenes) *omnia exempla ipse fingit;* which in like manner leaves out of the account an exceptional quotation from Euripides' Philoctetes, in chapter 18.

Aristotle, always manufactures *his own* illustrations to order, as the occasion requires. This says Spengel, Proleg. u. s., is characteristic. The one habit marks the 'rhetorician', who makes speeches himself; the other the philosopher, who seeks to give weight by the authority of *others* to his own precepts and observations. Spengel, Proleg. p. x, would include amongst these general and characteristic differences the method pursued by each of them severally in respect of its moral tendencies and influences; see above, p. 404. not. 1. I have endeavoured, pp. 403—5. to estimate the amount of difference which exists between them in this respect. *Some* difference no doubt there is. Another, which Spengel notes, u. s. p. xi., lies in the use of the personal pronoun when the author is speaking of himself: Aristotle always employs the plural (this I believe is the fact; I remember no instance to the contrary in any of his writings): 'our author', sometimes says, διειλόμην, διωρισάμην, διεξῆλθον, εἶπον, and so on.

Ch. 1[1]. The treatise, if we adopt Spengel's emendations, founded upon the passage of Quintilian, III. 4. 9, and the hypothesis thence deduced that Anaximenes is the author of it, opens with the statement, that there are *two* branches or classes (γένη) of 'political or public speeches', πολιτικοὶ λόγοι, the δημηγορικόν, concionale, public or political oratory, addressed to the general assembly, and commonly called συμβουλευτικόν, deliberativum, deliberative, or hortatory; and δικανικόν, forense, judicial or forensic, addressed to the judge or judges of a court of law: each of them being determined by its *audience*. This is a marked and very essential distinction, in which the difference between this system and Aristotle's first shows itself. Aristotle, as we learn from Quintilian, III. 4, 1. and 7, 1., was the first writer on rhetoric who

---

[1] In numbering the chapters of this work I have followed Spengel, who very properly excludes 'the letter' from the enumeration, and begins it with the treatise itself. Bekker and the Oxford text include the letter; so that Spengel's *first* chapter becomes with them the *second*, and so on throughout.

adopted the threefold classification, distinguishing the ἐπιδεκτικὸν γένος from the two others. This goes to prove that the Rhet. ad Alex. was antecedent to the publication of Aristotle's Rhetoric: all the subsequent arts recognise the tripartite division: the inference therefore is that the Rhet. ad Alex. was published before Aristotle's, and *so far* is in favour of the authorship of Anaximenes.

These two genera are subdivided into seven species, the hortative and dissuasive, the panegyrical and reprehensory or censorious, the accusatory and defensive, and lastly, one which appears nowhere else as a distinct kind of speaking, the inquisitory or critical, ἐξεταστικόν[1]: the whole division in this form being peculiar to Anaximenes: though the six first are found, under a different name and in a different classification, in the Aristotelian system, as the constituent elements or materials of the three genera of rhetoric. These seven species or kinds may be employed in public speaking, and especially in addresses to the general assembly, in forensic pleading, and in private conversations. § 1. The analysis of the first two species follows, and occupies cc. 1, 2. In § 3, definitions of προτροπή and ἀποτροπή are given: these two fall under the head of deliberative rhetoric. In § 6. the τέλη (ὧν δεῖ ὀρέγεσθαι, the author does not use Aristotle's *technical term*,) of exhortation and dissuasion are introduced: and here again we have a division entirely different to that of Aristotle. They are six; the just, the legal, (the 'just' is the ἄγραφος and κοινὸς νόμος, the 'legal' the γεγραμμένος, the written and conventional laws of any given state,) the expedient, the fair and noble, the pleasant, and the easy: and in the last resort two others, the possible and the neces-

---

[1] τὸ ἐξεταστικὸν εἶδος, is a kind seldom employed separately, but usually in combination with the other species. It denotes 'critical inquiry', either into a man's life, character and actions; or into the administration of an office or of the government; or the criticism of a speech. See c. 37. It is exemplified in Æschines' speech against Timarchus, which is entirely occupied with the examination and criticism of his conduct and character. Spengel, note on c. 37. init.

sary. These are the τέλη of one who has to exhort or recommend: one who dissuades has to show, that the course to which he is opposed is one or more of the opposites of these: all actions are capable of either construction. This is the substance of §§ 3—11. Materials for applying these, for showing that actions, &c. are just, and so forth, and the reverse, may be derived from the following τόποι. First, from the actions and things themselves; secondly, from cases analogous and similar, ἐκ τῶν ὁμοίων τούτοις; thirdly, from things opposite; fourthly, from 'authority' of various kinds, ἐκ τῶν ἤδη κεκριμένων ὑπὸ θεῶν ἢ ὑπ' ἀνθρώπων ἐνδόξων ἢ ὑπὸ κριτῶν ἢ ὑπὸ τῶν ἀνταγωνιστῶν ἡμῖν. Then follows the illustration of the application of these τόποι to the three first τέλη of deliberative rhetoric. §§ 12—24.

Ch. 2 treats of the subjects on which advice is given in councils and popular deliberative assemblies. These are seven, § 2: religion, laws, the constitution of the state, alliances, treaties, commercial and other, with foreign states, war, peace, and revenue. This differs, rather perhaps in form than in substance, from the list of subjects for a similar purpose given by Aristotle in Rhet. I. 4. Aristotle's list is, revenue or ways and means, war and peace, the defence of the country, fortification &c., exports and imports, and legislation. These topics are treated in detail in the remainder of the chapter. The unscientific, if not immoral and unscrupulous, character of the system which this treatise represents is well illustrated by some of the arguments suggested in § 25. When your object is to dissuade from an alliance, you may argue, either that there is no necessity for it, or that the proposed allies are unjust, or that they have done your country wrong at some former time; or, if none of these can be maintained, that their situation is remote, and consequently that they would have no power to render assistance on an emergency: or in other words, that the proposed allies do not deserve such a favour or honour, or that they had forfeited their claim by previous injuries: as if a *statesman* would take any thing else into account but the advantage or disadvantage accruing to his country by the alliance in question. Now it may fairly be asked, what would be the use of suggesting such arguments as Nos. 2 and 3, for example, to a statesman or orator, whose sole object should be the true interest of his country, except for the purpose of aiding him in his endeavours, right or wrong, to carry his point or 'persuade,' and gain a temporary advantage over an opponent? Is it consistent either with the science of Politics, or the duty of a citizen, to employ such like trifling, plausible and ad captandum arguments in matters of serious importance, and with such a purpose? And does it not savour of immorality and recklessness to suggest any considerations to a speaker in a case where his country's interests are at stake but such as have a real tendency to promote her welfare? and will not the familiarity arising from the constant association with bad principles and bad reasoning necessarily engender and foster sophistry and vice in a man's mind! If the facts on which these arguments are supposed to be based are true, they suggest themselves, and need not have a place in an Art of Rhetoric; if they are not, the only possible motives for employing them are such as I have stated.

Ch. 3. This chapter treats of the analysis of the third and fourth species of rhetoric, the laudatory and disparaging or censorious. In § 1, the terms, $\dot{\epsilon}\gamma\kappa\omega\mu\iota\alpha\sigma\tau\iota\kappa\acute{o}\nu$ and $\psi\epsilon\kappa\tau\iota\kappa\acute{o}\nu$ are defined: and their $\tau\acute{\epsilon}\lambda\eta$ stated. These are precisely the same as those of the preceding species:—Aristotle on the contrary, Rhet. I. 3., as we have seen assigns a single $\tau\acute{\epsilon}\lambda$ος to each of his genera; though it is true that in each case he elsewhere admits one of the others, as subordinate and supplementary to the principal and most prominent end which is distinctive and characteristic of the genus. For the analysis and description of them we are accordingly referred to the preceding Chapter. Then follows, § 2, a brief general account of the mode of applying them to individual cases; and, § 3, an illustration of three of these $\tau\acute{o}\pi$οι, $\tau\grave{o}$ $\dot{\epsilon}\kappa$ $\tauο\acute{\upsilon}\tauου$

ἐπισυμβαῖνον, the result; τὸ ἕνεκα τούτου, the motive; and τὸ μὴ ἄνευ τούτου, the necessary condition. Next we have a series of topics of amplification αὔξησις, §§ 4—10; disparagement, ταπείνωσις, is effected by the employment of their opposites. § 11. αὔξησις and ταπείνωσις may no doubt be employed advantageously in all the species alike, but their principal use and highest value appear in panegyric and censure. § 12. *Not a word is said of these two being subordinate to any genus.* There is no ἐπιδεικτικὸν γένος here.

Ch. 4 treats of the two species, accusation and defence, included in the forensic genus, "which deals with the business of the law court." These are defined, § 1. The aims or objects of the pleader in these two branches seem to be much the same as in the four preceding, § 2, comp. § 8: and in fact in c. 6. § 1. we are told that the just, the legal, the expedient, &c. are common to all the εἴδη, though most especially applicable to the first, τὸ προτρεπτικόν. The modes of enforcing an accusation are given in §§ 3—7; and three methods of defence in § 8. The two first of these include the three general status, στάσεις, constitutiones causarum; viz. the issue of fact, status conjecturalis; and the status or constitutio juridicialis, subdivided into (1) absoluta which admits the fact but altogether denies the wrong; and (2) assumptiva, or ποιότης, which admits the fact and the wrong, but denies the alleged amount, magnitude, or degree, of the offence charged. Speng. note, p. 147. Ernest. Lex. Techn. Lat.

In §§ 9—11, ἀδικία, ἁμάρτημα, ἀτυχία, are distinguished, and the modes of handling them described; and in § 12, the course of proceeding required in τιμητοὶ and ἀτίμητοι ἀγῶνες. And this concludes the special treatment of the dicastic branch.

Ch. 5. Ἐξέτασις, τὸ ἐξεταστικὸν εἶδος, the subject of the fifth chapter, is in general the "criticism" of purposes or intentions, actions, and language, by a comparison of these either with one another or with the rest of a man's life and conduct, in order to detect any inconsistency that may exist between them, past or present. § 1. This is of course to be applied especially to the character and conduct either of the adversary in a process at law, or of a political opponent. §§ 1—4.

All these species (Buhle) may be either blended together in one speech, or may form the subject of a separate treatment: for with great differences, there is still a considerable similarity between them, and therefore they are capable of 'inter-communion' (ἐπικοινωνοῦσι) in their application. In this respect they resemble the human race; who with many individual differences bodily and mental yet bear a general resemblance to one another.

Ch. 6. After the particular examination of the special εἴδη, the writer proceeds to give an account of the topics, arguments, modes of treatment, and divisions, common to all. Of these the 'objects aimed at' (Aristotle's τέλη) have been already examined (in c. 1). Αὔξησις and ταπείνωσις, 'amplification' and 'disparagement,' are also common to all kinds of speeches, though especially appropriate to the laudatory and censorious. These also have been already treated, (in c. 3.). The third of these 'common' elements of rhetoric is πίστεις, probable arguments, calculated to induce 'persuasion' or 'belief' (whence the name), rhetorical proofs. For these again there is most room for employment in forensic pleadings, because accusation and defence admit of, or 'require', more than all the other discussion pro and con. Aristotle has a similar observation in his Rhetoric. The enthymeme, or direct rhetorical proof, he says, is most readily employed in the dicastic branch, because this is always referred to *fact past;* which admits more of argument or proof than the fact future or prospective to which the deliberative or hortative speaker has to look. Besides these the following τόποι are common to all the species of rhetoric. Προκατάληψις, 'anticipation' of the opponent's charges or arguments (c 18): αἰτήματα, solicitations, prayers, petitions, to the audience or judges (c. 19): παλιλλογίαι, recapitulation (c. 20): μῆκος λόγου, μετριότης μήκους, βραχυλογία, amplification, propriety, abbreviation, in *composition*, (c. 22): and lastly, ἑρμηνεία, style or 'expression', choice of language, arrangement, or composition *in general* (cc. 23—28).

Ch. 7 is on πίστεις. Of these there are two kinds; one arising immediately out of the speech itself, the circumstances of the case, and the persons engaged—as the ἐξέτασις, for instance, or criticism of character and conduct—and constructed by the speaker in accordance with the rules of art; the other ἐπίθετοι, 'added' (from without), adventitious, corresponding to Aristotle's ἄτεχνοι πίστεις, (on which and ἔντεχνοι π. see Rhet. I. 2. 2. and I. 15). Of the former there are seven subordinate species; εἰκός, παράδειγμα, τεκμήριον, ἐνθύμημα, γνώμη, σημεῖον, ἔλεγχος: of the latter only three are found in the text, μαρτυρίαι, ὅρκοι, βάσανοι; but in c. 14 another is mentioned, δόξα τοῦ λέγοντος, which Spengel inserts here. § 3. Follows, the analysis of εἰκός. In all these matters especially, which are connected with logic, the differences between this author and Aristotle are most prominent and glaring: and this again may serve as an argument for the priority of publication of this treatise, and its Anaximenian authorship. If Aristotle's logic and rhetoric had been accessible to the writer, it seems hardly possible that he could have thus passed them over without notice. If the author was Anaximenes, and not a later rhetorician, though contemporary with Aristotle he was altogether alienus a philosophiæ studiis, and might therefore very likely be unacquainted with the Organon, as he certainly must have been with the Rhetoric. To resume. εἰκός is defined, § 4. The definition is as follows; "That is probable which, when mentioned, immediately suggests similar or analogous cases to the minds of the hearers;" that is, what is in accordance with a man's ordinary experience: and this is illustrated by one or two familiar examples. When a man hears another give utterance to a popular sentiment, or maxim of the current and prevailing morality; if for example he hears another say that he desires the greatness of his country, the welfare of his relations and friends, and misfortune to his enemies, or anything else of the same kind, he thinks this probable, because he is conscious of the existence in himself of the same or similar sentiments and wishes. We must therefore in addressing an audience always be on the look out for this, whether we are likely to find them sympathetic, or conscious themselves of having the same sentiments and principles as we are about to enunciate: for to such they are most likely to lend a willing ear. § 5. The probable has three species, determined by the πάθη, ἔθος, and κέρδος, which all belong to human nature. Probability—so far at least as human actions are concerned, which are the principal objects with which rhetoric has to deal—rests upon the common human nature in all individuals; and probable arguments are appeals to this common nature, and derive their validity from these three classes of feelings motives and incentives to action; these are universally recognised, and everything done, or suggested as being done, in accordance with them seems 'probable': we must therefore employ them in our speeches as the origin and source of actions which we wish to account for. The πάθη, or feelings, are scorn, fear, pleasure, pain, desire, and its opposite, either satiety or apathy, and such like. These we must (take along with, συμπαραλαμβάνειν,) associate with, express in, the speech in accusation and defence; because, being common to human nature in general, they are known to and recognised by the hearers, and a sympathy is thus established between the speaker and those whom he is addressing—they are brought in this way to *understand* one another. (This I presume to be the meaning of a rather obscure passage: the sense seems clear enough at a distance on first inspection, but melts away into a haze as we approach nearer to examine it closely.) The second motive which prompts to action is habit: the appeal to which in our speech again establishes an understanding between ourselves and the audience, which makes what we say appear probable. And the third of these common elements is profit, one's own interest. This is so prevailing an incentive to action[1], that men are often induced by it to act in violation of their own nature and character; and is as common to the whole human race as the feelings and acquired habits which are also the ordinary springs of human action. §§ 6, 7. I have thought it worth while to give the substance of the last four sections at some length, because they seemed to me to be somewhat more ingenious than usual, and to throw some real light upon the subject of εἰκός and its treatment. This is followed by the application of τὸ εἰκός to speaking in its various branches, in illustration of the modes of rendering probable either things, facts, or human actions; §§ 8—11. In § 8, however, we return to a former topic, which belongs to the *deliberative* branch of rhetoric; the use viz. that may be made of 'analogous cases' in making *facts* appear probable: in the two latter, §§ 9, 10, we pass to the illustration of the modes of applying the incentives and motives to action; only two of which are here exemplified, the πάθη being noticed in § 16.

In the remaining sections, 12—16, the defensive side (τὸ ἀπολογεῖσθαι) of forensic pleading is illustrated, and various feeble and shuffling excuses are suggested, for the purpose of 'persuading' the judges that the pleader is innocent of the charge brought against him, or of transferring it to some one else. The πάθη are introduced in § 16; in the rest the arguments are derived from ἔθος and κέρδος.

Here again we may note that the epideictic is *not* recognised as a distinct genus; the only two that are illustrated are the deliberative and forensic.

Ch. 8, treats of παράδειγμα. Here also an important difference between this author and Aristotle shows itself in the total omission of the logical bearing and application of the 'example', which in Aristotle's system is predominant. See Rhet. I. 2. 8, 19. II. 20; also above, Introd. p. 105—107.

---

[1] Inde nascitur, says Spengel in his note, Cassianum illud, *cui bono*.

The example is here defined; "Facts that have occurred similar, or opposite, to those which we are now stating." They are to be employed when the topic of 'probability' fails us, as evidence of the truth of an incredible or improbable statement, by the allegation of analogous acts or events that have actually occurred, § 1. They are of two kinds, the antecedently probable, those which occur κατὰ λόγον, in accordance with ordinary reckoning and calculation, which are used to support our own case, and confirm our own arguments; and the improbable or unexpected, τὰ μὴ κατὰ λόγον, which are employed to refute or invalidate the statements of the opponent, § 2. These are illustrated in §§ 3—6. If for instance it is our object to show that the rich are less disposed to dishonesty and wrong-doing than the poor, in this case the general rule or probability is on our side; and we can easily find examples in support of our assertion: but we may also want to prove the opposite, in the *accusation* of some rich man who has been bribed perhaps to betray his country's interests; and then we must find instances of (*improbable*) *exceptions* to the general rule, which will make the commission of the act of treachery in question unexpectedly or against probability probable (εἰκὸς παρὰ τὸ εἰκός or παρὰ λόγον), and invalidate the assertion of the adversary. In §§ 8—11 we have directions when and how to employ them; and in § 12, the sources from which they may be derived: these are actions and events past and present: all such are pervaded by a general principle of similarity which furnishes a ground for the proof of one *by* another[1]. If the same sort of thing which you are trying to establish has been frequently done or happened, especially if it be in accordance with a general rule, it is a proof of the probability that what you assert is also true.

Ch. 9. τεκμήριον differs in toto from Aristotle's τεκμήριον; see Rhet. I. 2. 16, 17. Introd. pp. 160—163. It is

---

[1] The man has conceived an indistinct notion of the argument from analogy.

defined here as an argument that may be derived from an inconsistency or incompatibility between facts and the opponent's speech, or contradictions in the speech itself. For from such inconsistencies and contradictions most hearers at once draw a conclusion (τεκμαίρονται) of the utter unsoundness (μηδὲν ὑγιές) both of his words and actions; that the one must be false, the other wrong.

Ch. 10 is on the enthymeme. The meaning here assigned to the term, as a *special* kind of argument, and the sense in which Aristotle employs it, have been already fully explained in this Introduction, pp. 100—105. I will here only add Spengel's note on the passage. Aristoteli ἐνθύμημα genus est probationis, ῥητορικὸς συλλογισμός, quaevis sententia cui ratio addita est. Anaximeni, ut Isocrati, aliisque oratoribus, *species;* sententia cui *qualiscunque ἐναντίωσις* inest. I may observe in passing that we have here an indication, by the correspondence in this point with Isocrates, of the rhetorical school from which the treatise proceeds.

This ἐναντίωσις, or opposition, is explained in its various applications in § 1. The argument is derived like the preceding from the detection of any inconsistency or contradiction, either in the opponent's speech itself, or in his actions, to what is just and right, or legal, or expedient, or fair and noble, or possible, or easy, or probable, or to the character of the speaker, or to facts and events in general. The difference therefore between this and the preceding 'species' of argument, is that this is derived from 'opposition' in general, the former from two particular cases of it. § 2 informs us how this kind of argument may be inverted, and applied to the establishment of our own case; and § 3 recommends that it should be brief, reduced to the narrowest compass, and treated with the smallest possible expenditure of words.

Γνώμη, c. 11, is καθ' ὅλων, (or perhaps better with Spengel, καθόλου) τῶν πραγμάτων δόγματος ἰδίου δήλωσις, an expression of private opinion on 'things in general': with καθόλου the meaning is, "a general expression of opinion", which is the usual definition. In *this* sense it is equivalent to the δόξα τοῦ λέγοντος of ch. 14. It has two varieties, like the example, ἔνδοξος and παράδοξος. When it is of the former kind, a current and generally accepted maxim or opinion, there is no occasion to assign any reason for it, or adduce arguments in its support; but when it runs counter to popular opinion, these must be brought forward, but concisely, in order to avoid long-windedness and incredibility: the reasons, if short and pointed, are more likely to carry conviction. The ordinary signification, 'a general sentiment or maxim', is, if not included in the definition, at all events conveyed in the examples; § 1. They must be appropriate, οἰκεῖαι τῶν πραγμάτων. They may be derived from τῆς ἰδίας φύσεως, § 2; from ὑπερβολή, § 3; and from παρομοίωσις, §§ 4, 5. All these are illustrated. The points of agreement and disagreement between this author's γνώμη and Aristotle's, have been already noticed in this Introduction, p. 258, on Bk. II. c. 21; to which the patient and tractable reader is referred.

Ch. 12. In treating of σημεῖον, the subject of this chapter, the author omits as usual all notice of its logical import and value.—This is supplied by Aristotle, as we have seen, in *his* introduction, Rhet. I. 2. 16 and 18, and Anal. Pr. II. 27; and may also be found in mine, supr. pp. 160—163.—His definition is, 'one thing is a sign of another—not any one chance thing of any other, nor everything of everything else, but that which is the ordinary concomitant of something else either before, or after, or simultaneously.' Not only may a thing that has happened be a sign of something else that *has* happened, but also of something that has *not* happened; and in like manner that which has not happened may be a sign of what does *not* exist, as well as of that which *does*. § 1. One kind of sign produces mere opinion, the other knowledge: the best is of course that which conveys actual knowledge, the next best that which carries with it the most plausible opinion. The first of these two seems to be identical with Aristotle's τεκμήριον, who himself tells us in the Rhet. u. s. §§ 16, 17, that σημεῖον is a general term including τεκμήρια and σημεῖα proper: and if so this will be another point of correspondence in this chapter between the two treatises; which, as they are so rare, should not be overlooked. The chapter concludes with an account of the sources from which 'signs' may be derived.

Ch. 13. On ἔλεγχος. This seems to be according to this author, not, as Aristotle defines it, a contradiction of the opponent's conclusion, or refutation, by counter syllogism or enthymeme; but any conclusive argument, or, apparently, positive assertion, or statement that can't be contradicted, either in support of something which we want to prove ourselves, or in refutation of an argument of the adversary. Spengel, following Ernesti, Lex. Techn., who supposes, s. v., that these ἔλεγχοι are always founded upon some kind of evidence, as witnesses, torture, documents, contracts, common rumour, says of them in his note, de testibus et quæstionibus dicitur ἔλεγχος, unde hoc genus ad ἀτέχνους pertinere πίστεις plures censent. One however at least of the kinds of it, τὰ φύσει ἀναγκαῖα, has nothing to do with evidence of any sort; as appears from the example, κατὰ φύσιν ἀναγκαῖόν ἐστιν οἷον τοὺς ζῶντας σιτίων δεῖσθαι; which is so absolutely certain as to be unanswerable. We may argue in this way not only from what is naturally necessary, but from what we, or the adversary, assert to be necessary, [this is according to Spengel's emendation, ἢ ἀναγκαίων ὡς ἡμεῖς λέγομεν, κ.τ.λ.]; and similarly from what is naturally impossible, and from what we or the adversary assert to be so. The two last are thus illustrated; it is naturally impossible for a little child to steal more money than he can carry, and make off with it: and the refutation of an impossibility affirmed by the opponent, or the proof of impossibility in one of his statements, is exemplified by this; it will be impossible, if he asserts that we signed the contract at a particular time at Athens, supposing that we can prove an alibi, that we were at that time absent abroad. Surely all this is rather trifling with an important subject.

In Ch. 14, the author points out the differences between the various arguments above enumerated; some of which I have already noticed, and the rest, being evident on the face of them, hardly deserve a detailed description. They do however in some sort serve as a commentary upon the preceding definitions. §§ 1—5. Having thus dispatched the direct logical πίστεις, or πίστεις proper, we may now proceed to describe the ἐπίθετοι (or ἄτεχνοι) πίστεις, the additional or adventitious proofs that may be employed in support of a case.

The first of these is the δόξα τοῦ λέγοντος. § 6. 'The speaker's own opinion' or 'authority', may be given with advantage in arguing his case; provided he shows the hearers that he is thoroughly conversant with his subject, and that it is his interest to speak the truth : [of course he would not do so if it were not.] the adversary's opinion must be shown at the same time to be as worthless as himself. If this cannot be done, you must point out that even men of skill and experience (such as the adversary has been shown, or is known, to be,) are often liable to error : or if this again prove impossible—if you can't show that he is likely to be mistaken—say that it is against your opponent's interest to speak the truth. §§ 6, 7. I think I may venture to affirm that such a direct suggestion, if not recommendation, of slander and falsehood is not to be found in Aristotle's Rhetoric.

Ch. 15 is on evidence, μαρτυρία; and the subject is very differently treated by Aristotle, Rhet. I. 15. 13—19. Evidence is defined, the voluntary (read ἑκοντός with Spengel,) testimony, or admission, of one who was privy to the fact. This excludes all evidence but that of the *living and present witness*, who, as Aristotle has it, shares in a criminal case the defendant's risk. There are three kinds of evidence, distinguished by the degree of credibility and value of each, the πιθανόν, ἀπίθανον, and ἀμφίβολον or 'ambiguous'. We have then a series of topics of argument, on both sides, pro and con, similar, but very inferior to those of Aristotle, that may be applied to evidence, to confirm or invalidate it, according as it is favourable or unfavourable to our cause in attack and defence. In support of what I have said of the flimsy and feeble and unscientific character of some parts of this treatise, I will here quote one of the suggestions in § 1. "When the evidence is credible, and the witness to be relied on, the evidence needs no concluding summary, unless you might like to finish off with a concise 'sentiment' (γνώμη), or enthymeme, for the purpose of giving point and smartness to it." (τοῦ ἀστείου ἕνεκεν). This is harmless, but unnecessary, and rather ἔξω τοῦ πράγματος: but what shall we say to the following? One of the topics suggested (in §§ 5, 6) for the invalidation of the testimony of an adverse witness is κλέπτειν τὴν μαρτυρίαν, to pass off evidence in disguise or surreptitiously, to swear falsely in such a way that it shall not be detected, or at any rate not render you liable to a prosecution for perjury. The illustration is this. "Bear witness for me, Lysicles. No by heaven! not I; (replies L.) for I tried to prevent him when he did this": thus *seeming* to refuse, οὔκουν ἐγώ, and then admitting the fact, which is assumed (from what follows) to be false; καὶ διὰ τούτου ἐν ἀποφάσει ψευδομαρτυρῆσαι ψευδομάρτυρος δίκην οὐχ ὑφέξει. If the *adversary* has recourse to a like expedient, we shall expose his villany—so that it is acknowledged to be villanous—and bid him give his evidence in writing. Such a barefaced and audacious recommendation of fraud and perjury is most certainly not to be found in *Aristotle's* work: and further the immorality of the suggestion is only equalled by its absurdity: but how *could* it be right to put into the hands of young men, as an instrument of education, and a guide to their practice, a book that contains such a precept as this?

The analysis of βάσανος, 'the question', in c. 16, bears a general resemblance to that of Aristotle in the fifteenth chapter of his first book, but the latter has much more brevity and point. The arguments that may be employed for and against the use of it are similarly given; but there is here no unmistakeable indication of opinion, as in Aristotle, of its cruelty, and uselessness for the ascertaining of the truth. The definition of it is 'an *involuntary* admission by a party to the transaction, or an accomplice, or one privy to it; the 'compulsory' character of the evidence distinguishes it from the preceding, μαρτυρία, or *voluntary* evidence, which is, ὁμολογία συνειδότος ἑκοντός.

In c. 17, the 'oath' is very briefly treated in the same way as the two preceding 'adventitious' proofs; similarly, but again in very inferior style to Aristotle's subtle analysis. According as it appears to be favourable or the reverse to our side, we must magnify, extol, enlarge upon its advantages (αὔξειν), or if we decline to take it ourselves or offer it to the adversary, we take the opposite course of disparaging, depreciating, vilifying it (ταπεινοῦν). The definition is, "a statement or assertion, unsupported by proof (ἀναπόδεικτος), with an adjuration or appeal to heaven in attestation of it," (μετὰ θείας παραλήψεως). The explanation of this last phrase has been already given above; Introd. p. 207, n. 1.

In the last clause of this chapter occurs another instance according to all the MSS. of the mention of τρία εἴδη, which can mean, if it is allowed to stand, nothing else but the 'three kinds of rhetoric', the deliberative, dicastic, and epideictic. There is no various reading. We may no doubt have recourse to the supposition that the same transcriber or commentator who ascribed the work to Aristotle, and consequently altered δύο into τρία at the beginning, made a similar change here and substituted τρία for the true reading, which, according to Spengel, who tacitly adopts this supposition, is πάντων τῶν εἰδῶν; which is as much as to say ἑπτά. This conjecture is founded upon the hypothesis of the authorship of Anaximenes, and upon that alone. His note is merely this; ἃ τῶν τριῶν εἰδῶν ἐστι, hæc corrupta sunt; [there is no evidence of this but his own conjecture] non enim tres sed septem sunt species, ἑπτὰ εἴδη, neque genera intelliguntur, duo enim genera probat autor, ut initio vidimus. This is again assuming the correctness of his other emendation at the commencement of the book, for which there is just as little MSS authority as there is for this. It is possible that Spengel may mean to found another argument upon the use of εἶδος for a 'branch' of Rhetoric, which Aristotle always calls γένος: if so, I think it is worth nothing; for I have already pointed out that the author of this treatise is completely ignorant of logic and its terms; and even if he were not, εἶδος and γένος being actually interchangeable according to their position in a logical classification, an εἶδος becoming a γένος in relation to its subordinate kinds, and a γένος an εἶδος in relation to that which is superior to it, any writer who was not bound at the moment to extreme accuracy and precision might easily be pardoned for substituting the one for the other; and the error, if it be one, is no proof of anything but carelessness. I really think that with so much negative evidence against Anaximenes' claims to the authorship of this work we should pause at any rate before we venture to print his name in the front of it[1].

It had been observed in c. 6, that of the various kinds of topics of arguments that may be employed in rhetoric, three, viz. the τέλη, τὸ δίκαιον, τὸ συμφέρον, and the rest, αὔξησις and ταπείνωσις, and the πίστεις, though in some sense common to all the species, are especially appropriate each of them to one pair of these, the τέλη to the hortative and dissuasive, the second to the laudatory and censorious, and the third to the forensic branch, accusation and defence. These have been all considered in detail, and it now remains to

---

[1] There seems to be an unconscious argument against his own view in Spengel's note: I will quote it, and leave my readers to judge. Tria sunt quæ docuit (autor), vid. cap. 6: τὰ τελικὰ κεφάλαια quorum usus imprimis in deliberativo genere est, tum αὔξησιν καὶ ταπείνωσιν quæ in *demonstrativo* (i.e. *genere*) frequentautur, denique τὰς πίστεις quibus judiciale genus carere non potest. Is not this a distinct recognition, ascribed to Anaximenes, of the three genera of rhetoric?

examine the κοινοὶ τόποι, the classes of arguments 'common' to the three branches of rhetoric (as he seems to say), and to all speeches alike. These are reviewed in the following chapters, from 18 to 28.

Ch. 18, accordingly treats of προκατάληψις; which is, a forestalling of, or reply by anticipation to, the adversary's arguments or charges against us, and the removal of objections or suspicions or bad impressions which may chance to be entertained by the audience against ourselves, our case, or our statements. The topics that furnish materials for this are then stated and exemplified. (a) The methods of removing prejudices from ourselves and our case are first illustrated in the deliberative branch, §§ 1—3, and then in the forensic, §§ 4—9; some of these suggestions are cunning enough: and next, (β) the modes of anticipating the adversary's arguments or charges are exemplified in the forensic branch alone. §§ 10—14. None of them are applied to the epideictic branch: probably however, because, as there *are* no adversaries with arguments, they are of no use there; though to be sure a speaker in this branch may have to remove prejudices in his audience. In the last section of this chapter occurs the only direct quotation that is to be found in this treatise: it is taken from Euripides' Philoctetes. The two last lines are corrupt, and have not been satisfactorily emended.

Αἰτήματα, c. 19, are prayers, petitions, or requests, addressed to the audience, and are divided into two classes, the fair or just, and the unfair or illegal: it is somewhat doubtful whether it is intended that we should employ this latter sort ourselves; but it is at all events necessary that we should be acquainted with them, for the purpose—not, observe, of avoiding them, or discountenancing an illegal or immoral practice, but—of exposing and discomfiting, or checking an adversary if he makes use of them. These petitions are illustrated by Spengel, in his note, from the orators, in whose speeches they are very numerous.

παλιλλογία, c. 20, σύντομος ἀνάμνησις, is a concise repetition of the facts and heads of arguments previously brought forward, for the purpose of recalling them to the minds of the audience, who may have forgotten them altogether, or become insensible to their force and cogency. It may be introduced in any part of the speech; but its most appropriate place is at the end, περὶ τὰς τελευτάς. It is this generality of application that constitutes the difference between it and the *special* and *detailed* ἀνακεφαλαίωσις, or 'recapitulation', of the ἐπίλογος. It differs in two points, universality and brevity. It has five species, διαλογίζεσθαι, 'division'; (a good example of this is supplied by Spengel in his note from Isocrates, Evag. § 69.); ἀπολογίζεσθαι, 'a reckoning up, enumeration', (see the example in § 3, and one from Demosth. de F. L. in Spengel); προαιρεῖσθαι, 'a summary to show the *purpose* or general *intention* of our statements or arguments'. Spengel's illustration from Isocr. Phil. § 154, is much more *illustrative* of this topic than that which the author supplies de suo in § 4; προσερωτᾶν, 'to put a question' [πρός, 'to' the adversary or audience; expresses 'direction to', as προσεντείνειν Dem. Mid. προσομιλεῖν 'to associate *with*'.] such as, "and I should be glad to know...", "and will the honourable member, or my learned friend, allow me to ask him, so and so, and so and so, and so and so?"

The fifth species, εἰρωνεία, forms the subject of the next Chapter, 21.

Ch. 21. εἰρωνεία. This topic properly belongs to the preceding, παλιλλογία, of which it is one of the five divisions. This appears not only from the conclusion of this chapter, which, after the description of εἰρωνεία, ends with the words, διὰ τούτων μὲν οὖν συντόμως ἀναμιμνήσκοντες ταῖς παλιλλογίαις χρησόμεθα κ.τ.λ. plainly including it with the other branches of 'repetition;' but also at the end of c. 33, it is enumerated again, with the remaining four species.

The definition—"to say something whilst you are pretending not to say it, or to call things by their opposite names"—is in conformity with the ordinary application of the term 'irony'. But the first example that is given of its application to παλιλλογία, in illustration of the first division of the definition, by which 'whilst we are pretending all the while to omit it, we give a succinct recapitulation of all the foregoing statements and arguments,' (it is to be introduced by some such phrase as this, "and I suppose there is no occasion for me to remind you that &c."; in which the 'irony' lies¹), is by no means in accordance with the ordinary employment of the figure. Aristotle in the Nic. Ethics defines it "mock humility," referring the origin of it to Socrates' practice: and in the passing notice of it in Rhet. III. 18. 7, says not a word of any 'pretended omission of a recapitulation.'

The second example, which illustrates the latter half of the definition, the application to things of names opposite to those that you really mean, is a genuine exemplification of the figure in its ordinary acceptation. The adversary is styled χρηστός, and you call yourself φαῦλος; in both cases the exact opposite being intended.

Ch. 22 treats of τὸ ἀστεῖον, the means of imparting spirit, point, grace, liveliness, a tone of pleasantry and sprightliness to the speech; and with it, of the modes of lengthening and shortening the speech at pleasure. Spengel remarks on the contents of this Chapter, multo accuratius hoc Aristot. Rhet. III. 10—11 enarrat, ut indignus sit noster autor qui cum illo conferatur. In fact Aristotle's directions for giving point to style are altogether different. The former of these two branches is treated by the author in the most scanty and insufficient manner, in §§ 1, 2; the rest of the chapter, §§ 3—8, is devoted to the various modes of spinning out and abbreviating the handling of a topic. One remark is made in the concluding section which deserves to be quoted, that 'the characters of the speech should be made as far as possible to coincide with the characters of the men,' (I presume, who deliver them). If this is what is really meant, it will represent Aristotle's ἦθος ἐν τῷ λέγοντι.

¹ The 'irony' is in fact the 'pretence'.

Ch. 23 seems to belong to ἑρμηνεία, the last of the 'common subjects' of c. 7. There are three kinds of ὀνόματα, (substantives, and adjectives), simple, compound, and metaphorical— a most vicious division; the first two and the third belonging to two entirely different classes. And three kinds of composition of words, determined by the position of the vowels and consonants at the junction[1]: that is, (1) when the first word ends, and the second begins, with a vowel; (2) when two consonants are similarly brought into combination; and (3) when vowel meets consonant. § 1. And four modes of arranging them (τάξεις) in the speech; (1) by placing similar words side by side or dispersing them over the sentence, or speech; (2) by employing the same words or exchanging them with others; (3) by applying one word or several to designate a thing. ['to designate a thing by several words,' is to give a description or definition of it, in place of its ὄνομα κύριον or οἰκεῖον, proper name.] (4) to state the facts in their natural order, or transpose them by hyperbaton. [ὑπερβιβάζειν, which Buhle translates 'præterire'! as if it were ὑπερβαίνειν, or *that* had any meaning here.] § 2. None of these four are illustrated, and the application of the two first is by no means clear. The second, as he is speaking of

---

[1] The reading of all or most of the MSS. appears to be συμβολαῖς, which is retained by Bekker, who gives *no* var. lect. Buhle and Spengel have συλλαβαῖς, which applies the same rule to the *syllables*, as the other reading does to *entire words in sentences*. It is hard to say which of the two is more appropriate to the sense and connexion in which the sentence stands. This stands between two sentences, the former of which treats of *single words*, to which 'syllables' would be more appropriate: but that which immediately follows, to the end of the chapter deals with the combinations of *words*, with which συμβολαῖς would be better connected. It seems to me too that a division of *words* founded upon the concluding and initial letters of their syllables is too trivial and valueless even for the author of the Rhet. ad Alex. A similar classification of words with a view to their mutual position in composition, is not *quite* so unimportant, as it involves hiatus (the meeting of two vowels), and has a direct bearing upon rhythm. One of these 'conjunctions' or 'clashings', the hiatus namely, is mentioned in c. 25 § 1, as a succession or sequence to be avoided.

τάξεις, cannot mean metaphor; and the literal acceptation of it seems almost too trifling to find a place in a grave treatise on Rhetoric, and also not properly to be included under the general head of composition or combination of words.

We have next in the following chapters, 24—28, the treatment of ἑρμηνεία, interpretatio, style, or expression of thought, or composition in general.

Ch. 24. The first thing to be done in ἑρμηνεία is ἑρμηνεύειν εἰς δύο; of the six modes of which this chapter proceeds to give an account with exemplifications. The author's intention seems to be, to give an elementary division or classification of language, or perhaps rather of topics of argument; exemplified by the analysis of a single topic, δύναμις, 'faculty, ability,' or τὸ δυνατόν, 'the possible,' selected for the purpose, and analysed into six alternative divisions, which are supposed to exhaust it. This I think may be gathered both from the analysis itself in § 1, and the examples that follow to the end of the Chapter. The analysis of this topic is proposed as a model scheme or exemplar which may be applied similarly to all other topics alike. σχήματα μὲν οὖν τοῦ εἰς δύο ἑρμηνεύειν ὧδε ποιήσεις ἐπὶ τῶν πραγμάτων ἁπάντων τὸν αὐτὸν τρόπον μετιών.

Spengel's views of the meaning of the classification are stated in his note on the passage, and, if I rightly understand them, do not quite agree with my own. He says, p. 189, In his facile grammaticæ et rhetoricæ aspicias primordia; variis quæ fieri possunt sententiis certas imponere formas voluerunt, non inepte, ut ex uno quasi fonte qua ratione diversa exirent, docerent; id autem fit imprimis subjecti et objecti quod dicitur mutatione. The last observation I confess I do not fully understand; nor can I see that any distinction of subject and object is implied in the classification. What follows I fully agree with; that we miss here the 'subtilem perscrutationem, qualem *philosophus* v. c. in libro περὶ ἑρμηνείας explicat: indeed we have here a most striking indication of the difference between the two authors.

The chapter concludes with the notice that the next consideration as regards style and expression is perspicuity, to which we now at once pass on.

Ch. 23. Σαφήνεια, 'perspicuity,' in style may be attained by the observance of the following rules. First we are to call things by their proper or appropriate names, the names which properly belong to them, τοῖς οἰκείοις ὀνόμασιν; [called also τὰ ἴδια ὀνόματα by Aristotle, Rhet. III. 5, 3, who there gives a similar precept, 'nostro accuratius,' says Spengel. Isocrates also in his τέχνη had previously laid down the same rule: ὀνόματι δὲ χρῆσθαι ἢ μεταφορᾷ μὴ σκληρᾷ ἢ τῷ καλλίστῳ καὶ τῷ ἥκιστα πεποιημένῳ (ὡς τὸ σίζειν καὶ δοῦπος· ταῦτα γὰρ πεποιημένα) ἢ τῷ γνωριμωτάτῳ. Spengel, Art. Script. p. 162. et not. ad h. l. Benseler, Isocr. Fragm. τέχνης, II. 276:] and to avoid ambiguity. Secondly, the collision, or 'sequence,' of two vowels is to be guarded against. This also comes from Isocrates' Art. δεῖ τῇ μὲν λέξει τὰ φωνήεντα μὴ συμπίπτειν· χωλὸν γὰρ τὸ τοιόνδε. Art. Scr. p. 161. Thirdly, the use of the 'articles' is to be carefully attended to; 'in order to avoid obscurity,' as is added in § 4. Fourthly, confusion in the order of the words, and hyperbaton, are vices of style, and tend likewise to obscurity[1]. Lastly, in respect of 'connectives,' σύνδεσμοι, we must be careful to supply the proper correlative particle in the apodosis to that with which the protasis is introduced. This also is derived from Isocrates' τέχνη, quoted by Benseler, Isocr. II. 276. and Spengel, Art. Scr. p. 161. The passage is more fully given by Joh. Sicellotes, VI. 156, from whom Spengel (not. p. 191) cites the following words. καὶ τοὺς συνδέσμους τοὺς σαφεῖς μὴ σύνεγγυς τιθέναι,

---

[1] This fourth precept appears likewise to be borrowed from Isocrates' τέχνη. The series of extracts from this work preserved by Maximus Planudes in his commentary on Hermogenes, and by Johannes Sicellotes, and cited by Benseler amongst the fragments of Isocrates, II. p. 276—already referred to in the text—concludes with these words: διηγητέον δὲ τὸ πρῶτον καὶ τὸ δεύτερον καὶ τὰ λοιπὰ ἑπομένως· καὶ μὴ πρὶν ἀποτελέσαι τὸ πρῶτον ἐπ' ἄλλο ἰέναι, εἶτα ἐπὶ τὸ πρῶτον ἐπανιέναι ἀπὸ τοῦ τέλους· καὶ αἱ ἐπὶ μέρος δὲ διάνοιαι τελειούσθωσαν ἐφ' ἑαυτὰς περιγραφόμεναι.

καὶ τὸν ἑπόμενον τῷ ἡγουμένῳ εὐθὺς ἀνταπυδιδόναι, τοὺς μὲν ὡς τὸ ταῦτα μὲν τοιαῦτα, ἐκεῖνα μέντοι ἑτέρως, τοὺς δὲ ὡς τὸν μὲν καὶ τὸν δὲ καὶ τὸ ὡς καὶ τὸ οὕτως. The same observation is made by Aristotle, Rhet. III. 5. 2, probably also after Isocrates. §§ 1, 2. These precepts are then illustrated, but in the reverse order, in the remaining sections of the Chapter. The use of connectives is exemplified by μὲν —δέ, and καὶ—καί. Confusion of language, by δεινόν ἐστι τοῦτον τοῦτον τύπτειν: which may be amended thus, δεινόν ἐστι τοῦτον ὑπὸ τούτου τύπτεσθαι. The proper use of the article is illustrated by οὗτος ἄνθρωπος τοῦτον τὸν ἄνθρωπον ἀδικεῖ. On this it is observed, that in the present instance the introduction of the article makes the sentence perspicuous, the withdrawal of it would cause obscurity: but that sometimes the reverse of this is the case: which I suppose can mean no more than this, that the (definite) article is used to define some particular object; when this is not required, the use of the article would only lead to obscurity. The caution against bringing two vowels into collision is next repeated: this can only be allowed "when the sense cannot be otherwise clearly expressed, or when there is a pause[1], or a division of any other kind (in sense or sound)." The ambiguity which is to be avoided is illustrated by the incautious use of a word which has more than one meaning. The example given is, in spite of the aspirate, ὁδός or ὀδός: οἷον ὁδὸς τῶν θυρῶν καὶ ὀδὸς ἦν βαδίζουσιν. Spengel remarks upon this, vetustissimus locus qui jam antiquis spiritum neglectum esse in pronuntiando docet. Might it not rather be construed as an indication of a later date of composition of

---

[1] I have adopted Knebel's emendation ἀνάπαυσις for the MSS. reading ἀνάπτυξις, which seems to be devoid of meaning here. The Lexicographers explain the latter as equivalent to ἀνάπλωσις, an unfolding, revelation, or 'explanation'; a sense in which it is found in Plutarch and Athenæus. But I do not see how this meaning can be applied here. Spengel has this note on the word, p. 192. clausulam quandam sententiæ intelligere videtur, neque tamen alibi hoc vocabulum id significat; and then quotes Knebel's suggestion.

the work in which it is found than the third quarter of the 4th century B.C.? When you have occasion to employ such an ambiguous word, the proper and special term, τὸ ἴδιον, that expresses it should always be added (συμπαραλαμβάνειν).

Cc. 26—28 treat of ἀντίθεσις, παρίσωσις, and παρομοίωσις, on which see Introd. pp. 314—316 and p. 315 n. 1. (on Rhet. III. 9.) 'Ἀντίθετον is defined, that which conveys an opposition in word or sense between two contrasted members of a sentence; or in either one of these. These three cases of antithesis in word, in sense or the thing, and in both at once, are illustrated; and c. 26 concludes with the observation that the opposition in both is the best, though the two others are also genuine antitheses. This threefold division of antithesis is adopted by Demetrius, π. ἑρμ. § 22. Speng. Rhet. Gr. III. 265. With the definition of παρίσωσις in c. 27, ὅταν δύο ἴσα λέγηται κῶλα, that of Aristotle, Rhet. III. 9. 9. exactly coincides. A few long clauses may be made equivalent (in length) to several short ones; and the size of one be compensated by the number of the other. (This appears to be the meaning of the rather obscure, καὶ ἴσα τὸ μέγεθος ἴσοις τὸν ἀριθμόν.) The 'equality' in this figure lies merely in the length of the balanced clauses; it includes no other kind of resemblance, nor opposition. The definition of παρομοίωσις differs from that given by Aristotle, Rhet. III. 9. 9. The latter limits it to similarity, i.e. of sound, between the 'extremities of the clauses'; that is, between the beginnings and ends of them, each to each. Here it is made to include equality of the clauses, as well as the similarity produced by the employment of 'similar' (sounding) words. This is illustrated by ὅσον δεῖ σε λόγου μίμημα, φέρε πόθου τέχνασμα. [One can't help noticing the want of skill shown throughout this work in the manufacture of these illustrative examples, which stands in striking contrast to the point and pungency and interest of those with which Aristotle's wonderful memory supplied him. This author's examples are for the most part stupid and pointless: the one here given does not even illustrate the 'equal length' of the two members of the clause.] The author seems to extend the 'resemblance' to all parts of the clause, with the remark however, that the most perfect similarity is produced by ὁμοιοτέλευτον, §§ 1, 2.

The remainder of this chapter (29) is occupied with a recapitulation of the foregoing contents of the work, §§ 3, 4; and we now pass on to the consideration of the last subject of the treatise, the parts of the speech[1], their order and arrangement, the topics appropriate to each, and the mode of handling them. These subjects, the order and arrangement of the parts of the speech, and the divisions that they severally belong to, are examined and analysed under four heads: of which the first includes the two kinds exhortation or recommendation, and dissuasion, which together make up the deliberative branch, and occupies cc. 29—34; the second, deals with the two kinds of epideictic speaking, the laudatory and reprehensory, in c. 35; a corresponding treatment of the forensic branch under the two heads of accusation and defence, is contained in the long chapter 36; and the critical kind, τὸ ἐξεταστικόν, similarly, but much more briefly dealt with in c. 37. The third of these branches, the forensic, is the only one of the four in which the fourfold division of the speech, προοίμιον, διήγησις, πίστεις (βεβαίωσις), ἐπίλογος is *expressly* recognised: but in the first, the deliberative, it seems to be implied, by the order in which the topics which, as we learn from c. 36, are appropriate to the ἐπίλογος are taken for examination; the appeals to the feelings, the proper subject of the peroration, being introduced after the treatment of βεβαίωσις—the third division. And though it is true that the separation between the two

---

[1] The fourfold division of the speech, adopted by this author, agrees with that of Isocrates. (See above, Introd. p. 331.) It consists of προοίμιον; ἀπαγγελία or διήγησις, c. 31. ult. c. 38. 5.; πίστεις, including βεβαίωσις confirmatio, and τὰ πρὸς τοὺς ἀντιδίκους the answer to the adversary, refutatio; and ἐπίλογος, (c. 36. 48,) usually styled in this work παλιλλογία.

is not in this instance distinctly marked, still we may perhaps assume from the topics illustrated that the ἐπίλογος is tacitly recognised. In the epideictic branch, c. 35, the narratio and confirmatio *may* be included together in the topics of §§ 3—14, and the latter represented by the αὔξησις, which may be regarded as a sort of confirmation or aid to proof; and the summary repetition of § 14, with its concluding γνώμη or enthymeme, may possibly be meant to serve for a peroration: however this supposition is not necessary, for the two topics of the ἐπίλογος are distinctly ascribed to the encomiastic branch, with the two others, in c. 36. 42. The omission of it in the chapter specially devoted to this branch, c. 35, shows the carelessness of the writer. It certainly seems that the fourfold division of topics was not considered by this author essential to all kinds of speeches. The summary ἀνάμνησις is expressly mentioned in c. 38. 9. as included in the ἐπίλογος.

And first, common to the seven εἴδη, and suitable to all occasions—herein differing from Aristotle, Rhet. III. 13— is the,

Προοίμιον, c. 30, which is described in general terms in § 1. "The prooemium, speaking generally, is a preparation, παρασκευή, of the audience (i. e. the putting them in a certain frame of mind by way of 'preparation' for what is to follow), and a summary setting forth or explanation of the subject of the speech, or the matter in hand, to an audience not as yet acquainted with it, that they may know what the speech is to be about, and be able to follow the argument, and to invite them to attention, and, so far as can be effected by the speech, give them a favourable disposition towards us." The employment of it in its application to the deliberative branch of rhetoric is then illustrated throughout the remainder of the chapter in a detailed and comprehensive analysis. The ordering of its four principal topics, the anticipation of charges and removal of unfavourable impressions, the preliminary summary of the contents of the speech, the invitation of the attention, and conciliation of the feelings, of the audience, and the occasions on which the first of these may be omitted, are briefly handled in the two last sections, 21 and 22. The treatment of the προοίμιον is to be directed towards securing the goodwill and attention of the audience, and meeting and anticipating any hostile suspicions that may have been insinuated, or charges that may have been made, (both included under the general head of διαβολή,) either directly by the adversary, or such as we know that we are rendered liable to by our character, circumstances, or past conduct; and this hostile feeling may be directed either against the person, or the thing, (the case, for instance any course of policy that we may be recommending,) or the (tone or line of argument of) the speech itself, § 8.

And here the unscientific and immoral—or if not immoral, at any rate *unmoral*, regardless of all moral considerations—character, which not only pervades this treatise, but is distinctive also, as appears from all that is recorded of it, of the entire rhetorical school to which it belongs, is brought out into strong relief. Truth of fact and exactness of reasoning are the very last things at which the speaker has to aim: to persuade, or to gain one's point, is the sole object to be kept in view; to gain this end any argument may be advanced, any fallacy maintained, any consideration urged, expedient or the reverse on public grounds, any falsehood asserted: political science and the true interests of our country may be disregarded, and all our efforts are to be concentrated upon the promotion of our own. The refutation of an adversary, real or supposed, is the first consideration, to which all others must give way; and to attain this end any means may be employed, any sophistry or fallacy, any art trick or device, any shift, subterfuge or evasion, that ingenuity can suggest and recklessness venture to recommend. This I believe is no exaggerated description of the tendencies of such a system of Rhetoric as we are now engaged in analysing.

We learn from the comparison of some of the sections of this Chapter with passages of Isocrates' speeches, quoted by Spengel in his notes, that the precepts and recommendations of §§ 11, 12, 15, 16, are probably borrowed from that author —see Speng. Comm. pp. 203, 4, 7, 8, 9.—which together with the coincidences already pointed out and others to be noticed hereafter, seem sufficient to establish a close connexion between this writer and the school of Isocrates, of whose 'arts of rhetoric' and mode of dealing with the subject in general this treatise is the sole surviving representative.

Ch. 30 treats of what was commonly called διήγησις, narratio, 'the statement of the case to be discussed or the policy to be pursued', but by this author ἀπαγγελία,—the ordinary designation is applied to it in c. 31. § 3. It is described, § 1, as 'a narration or recalling to the memory of the audience of past facts, or explanation of facts present, or statement of a future course of action'. And this also is applied in the rest of the Chapter to deliberative oratory. The first topic illustrated is the mode of delivering the report of an embassy, and excuses are suggested by which we may shift from ourselves the blame of failure. §§ 2, 3. When we are speaking in the character of counsellors, whether we are relating past facts and occurrences, or explaining present, or anticipating future, our 'narrative' must be brief, clear, and plausible: "clear, that the hearers may thoroughly understand what is stated; concise, that they may remember what has been said; and plausible (looking as if they could be relied on), in order that our statements may not be condemned and rejected by the audience at first sight, before they have been substantiated and confirmed by evidence and arguments. The various modes in which these three objects may be attained are then described down to the end of the Chapter, § 9.

On this subject our author is in two points in disagreement with Aristotle. The latter in Rhet. III. 13. 3, expressly disallows the διήγησις except in the forensic branch of rhetoric: if it be found in either of the two others, it is an accident, like the reply to an adversary, which does however sometimes occur in a public oration. But in narrating, as well as in accusing or panegyrising, the deliberative orator is not discharging his proper function, which is to give advice. III. 16. 11. The precept that the narrative must be brief is in direct opposition to what is said in Rhet. III. 16. 4. νῦν δὲ γελοίως τὴν διήγησίν φασι δεῖν εἶναι ταχεῖαν. It comes from Isocrates, whose followers, as Quintilian tells us, Inst. Orat. IV. 2. 32, volunt esse (narrandi rationem) lucidam, brevem, verisimilem. This rule, that the narrative should be brief or rapid, was no invention of Isocrates, but already existed in the 'Arts' of Tisias and Gorgias, as we learn from Plato, Phædr. 267, A.B.; but the exact correspondence of the two rules for the composition of a διήγησις here and in the passage of Quintilian is another clear proof of the close connexion of this treatise with the Sophistico-rhetorical school of Isocrates. Subsequent writers on rhetoric, Cicero, Quintilian, the Auct. ad Heren. and others of still later date abandoned on this point the guidance of Aristotle and followed Isocrates. Spengel, in his note p. 215, has illustrated the observance of it from Isocrates' own writings, and other orators. They often call attention themselves to their own endeavours to be concise, and thus to save the hearers as much trouble as possible.

Ch. 31. In respect of the 'ordering' or arrangement of the διήγησις, it may be either attached as an appendix to the προοίμιον, if the facts we have to state are few and well-known: or if not, they must be treated individually in a series (συναπτάς), and in detail, and the facts made to assume the appearance of fairness, expediency, honour, as the case requires; not for the purpose merely of making the speech simple and perspicuous, but also of gaining over the judgment of the listeners. If the facts that we have to state are of moderate length and not already known, we must arrange them, whether it be narrative, or report, or explanation, or anticipation, separately and distinctly (σωματοειδῆ, each with its own substantial, definite, bodily shape,) after the prooemium. This will be done by recounting the facts nakedly, each by itself, from beginning to end, without including or mixing up anything else in the treatment of them. I have already noticed the accumulation of odd Greek words, and the general deficiencies in point of style, that distinguish this short Chapter.

Ch. 32. Next to this comes βεβαίωσις, confirmatio, the confirmation by argument or evidence of our previous suggestions or the statements which we undertook to prove, and of their justice and expediency. When they are presented in a connected series, the most appropriate to public speaking are, the evidence of custom in confirmation of the truth of a fact (that such things are usual), example, enthymeme (so Spengel conj.: ἐπενθυμήματα, MSS., seems from what follows, § 3, to mean nothing more than 'supplementary enthymemes.') and the speaker's own opinion, § 1. Any other kind of rhetorical proof may be inserted parenthetically in the series. The order of succession should be, first the speaker's opinion; or in default of that, custom; to show that what we state, or something like it, is usual. Next example, "and if there *is* any resemblance, [what would be the use of employing it if there were not?] we must apply it (so as to show its analogy) to our own statements." "We must select examples that are most appropriate, or intimately connected, with our facts, and the nearest to the hearers in time or place; if there are none such at hand, we must supply their place with the most striking and remarkable and the best known that can be found. Next we must adduce a γνώμη or general sentiment in point; and also the parts which contain the arguments from probability (i.e. custom,) and examples may be ended with enthymemes and γνῶμαι. §§ 2, 3. Proof of facts, when they are notorious, may be omitted; and its place supplied by showing that they are just, legal, expedient, and the rest, § 4. The topic of 'just', if our case admits of its application, must be placed in the forefront of the arguments, and we must then go through all the topics immediately connected with it, as that which resembles what is just, and that which is contrary to it, and that which has been pronounced just by authority, or decided to be just: all of which may be similarly applied. The examples must also have this same character. Topics will be supplied by men's private and individual notions of justice, (these I presume are the universal notions of right and wrong, implanted in us by nature,) or the special enactments of the city in which you are speaking, or in other cities. § 5. When all this has been gone through, and we have concluded the topic with our $\gamma\nu\hat{\omega}\mu\alpha\iota$ and enthymemes, if this part of the speech be long, we may give a concise recapitulation of its heads; if it be of moderate length and easily remembered, we may first sum it up in a definition, and then immediately (in the same sentence) proceed to the next topic, as expediency." This valuable suggestion is illustrated by an example. Similar rules are applied to $\tau\grave{o}\ \sigma\nu\mu\phi\acute{e}\rho o\nu$. And so one part is to be connected with another, and the entire speech woven together into one web. §§ 6, 7. "When you have gone through all your proofs in support of your recommendations, then in a summary way, and with $\gamma\nu\hat{\omega}\mu\alpha\iota$ and enthymemes or 'figures', show that not to do as you propose would be unjust, and inexpedient, and disgraceful, and unpleasant; and contrast with this, likewise in a summary way, the justice and expediency and honour and pleasure that will follow from complying with your counsels. And after you have enunciated sufficient general maxims, give a definition of what you have recommended by way of conclusion. And in this way we shall confirm our previous statements—and now we will pass on to $\pi\rho o\kappa\alpha\tau\acute{a}\lambda\eta\psi\iota\varsigma$." § 8.

Ch. 33. $\pi\rho o\kappa\alpha\tau\acute{a}\lambda\eta\psi\iota\varsigma$ is the anticipation of the adversary's arguments or charges for the purpose of 'pulling them in pieces', exposing and refuting them. In doing this, you must make your opponent's arguments appear as trifling and insignificant as possible, and at the same time 'magnify', and give importance to your own. When your own argument is superior, more convincing, than that of the opponent, you may bring them into contrast singly, one to one; otherwise they may be compared collectively, several to several; or one to many, or many to one; through all the various modes of contrast and comparison; your own magnified, your adversary's depreciated. When this has been gone through, you may recapitulate, employing any of the above mentioned (in c. 20.) figures, διαλογισμός (division), ἀπολογισμός (enumeration), προαίρεσις, ἐπερώτησις, εἰρωνεία.

The 'anticipation' of this chapter, and the final summary, complete the third division of the speech, βεβαίωσις. In the next chapter,

Ch. 34, we pass to the last of the four, ἐπίλογος, conclusio, peroration; which though not actually named here, may be seen by comparison with c. 36, §§ 41, 2, to be the division to which the topics herein discussed belong. The technical term ἐπίλογος, occurs in c. 36, 48, and 38, 9. The σύντομος ἀνάμνησις, which is represented both by this author, c. 36, 41, and by Aristotle, Rhet. III. 9. 1, as one of the essential elements of the ἐπίλογος, is here omitted. It is recognized as specially belonging to it, c. 38. 9; but we had been told before that it is everywhere appropriate.

In recommending for example, the policy of aiding or defending any one, individual or state, it is most important to inspire those whom you are endeavouring to persuade to this course with the three feelings of love, gratitude, and pity: the motives and incentives of these three are then briefly (and very insufficiently) analysed, in order to show what circumstances and what representations must be put forward in order to produce these emotions in the hearers, which will give them favourable inclinations towards the applicants for assistance, and probably a desire to comply with their request. They are to be employed in the following order; love first;

if there be not ground for that, then gratitude may be appealed to; and, as a last resource, compassion. §§ 1—4. In dissuading a similar policy the reverse processes must be used; the order remains the same. § 5. But dissuasion may be employed by us either independently, (on our own bottom as it were, without regard to any one else, καθ' αὑτούς;) or in answer to the opposite recommendation of an adversary. The latter will require a slight alteration in the topics and their arrangement. We shall have now to state in the prooemium what we are going to reply to, and then show that our adversary's proposal and reasons are all unjust, disgraceful, inexpedient and everything else that is mean and wrong. But if this cannot be done, the next best way of proceeding is, in case he has established the justice of what he advises, to draw your arguments from the topics that he has omitted, and try to prove that it is disgraceful, or inexpedient, or laborious, or impossible; or if he have expediency on his side, *you* endeavour to show that it is unjust; and so on for the rest. Then, as in the hortative kind, exalt and magnify the course you yourself advise, and depreciate that which is recommended by the adversary; and, again as in the other kind, introduce general sentiments and enthymemes, meet and refute the opponent's 'anticipations,' and conclude with a recapitulation: §§ 6—9. And lastly, as in a hortatory speech you have to show in conclusion that those on whose behalf you are seeking aid are friendly and well disposed to the audience you are addressing, and have earned their gratitude by former services; so on the dissuasive side you must endeavour to make them out to be deserving of anger or envy or hatred. § 10. Animosity may be engendered in them by showing that they have been illtreated against right and nature by the present applicants or their friends, either themselves or those that they care for: anger, in the like cases, by suggesting to them that they have suffered from them either 'slight' or injustice. Envy is directed against those who can be shown either to have already met with, or to be in the present enjoyment of, or likely to enjoy hereafter, undeserved prosperity; or have never been, or are never likely to be, deprived of any good, past present or future; or who have had no experience past or present, nor have any future prospect of misfortune. This brings us to the end of the analysis of the προτρεπτικὸν (including ἀποτρεπτικὸν) εἶδος, its divisions, topics, and materials.

I have given the contents of this chapter almost in extenso for the purpose of contrasting it with Aristotle's most acute and interesting analysis of these same πάθη or emotions, and the characters and dispositions of their subjects and objects, and the motives and causes that excite them; Rhet. II. cc. 2. 4. 7. 8. 10. On this contrast Spengel truly enough remarks (note p. 224.) ut ibi (apud Aristotelem) subtile et uberrimum dialectici, [why not philosopher, or man of science?] ita hic sterile et vulgare rhetoris ingenium agnosces. Amidst all this striking dissimilarity however there is in one point a very curious coincidence; each of them assigns as the sting or exciting cause of anger ὀλιγωρία, 'slight', the contempt and wantonness that aggravates the insult, nay may even take the place of the injury in stirring the emotion. Aristotle's definition of anger is, "an impulse, (or impulsive longing,) accompanied with pain, after an *evident* (one that the aggrieved person actually *witnesses;* otherwise there is no compensation,) vengeance, arising from an *evident* slight, offered to oneself or to any of one's friends, when the slight has no justification." [τοῦ ὀλιγωρεῖν μὴ προσήκοντος, if the slight be not *due* to us, where we don't *deserve* it, either by reason of the inferiority of our rank and condition, which might justify it as proceeding from a superior, or perhaps of some meanness of which we are conscious

---

[1] As I wrote this I happened to look at Aristotle's chapter on anger, and the difference is really amazing. There one feels oneself to be in the hands of a master, here of a—Rhetorician, as Spengel says.

in our character or conduct: no mere injury would justify 'slight'.]

The recipe for the manufacture of a laudatory and censorious speech is supplied in the following chapter, 35. The order of the parts of the speech is first described in its application to these two kinds. The προοίμιον is to be similarly constructed to that of the preceding species; only to the topics there given for attracting attention are to be added τὸ θαυμαστὸν καὶ περιφανές, the marvellous and striking. §§ 1, 2. For these are topics which are not appropriate to ἀγῶνες, where the issue is a serious one, but rather belong to ἐπίδειξις. In the place of the διήγησις, and next to the προοίμιον, should be introduced a division of 'goods', into those which reside in virtue, and those 'outside of it': our hero must of course be endowed with all of the former class. These are wisdom, justice, courage, and reputable pursuits and habits: the others are such as birth, wealth, strength, beauty. The former are the proper objects of panegyric (ἐγκωμιάζεται), the latter must be smuggled in (κλέπτεται) indirectly: for the strong, the handsome, the well-born, and the wealthy, ought not to be 'praised' but congratulated[1]. The first topic of this detail of virtues internal and external is γενεαλογία, placed here because this is the first indication that any *animal* can give of a disposition or probable tendency to virtue (fortes creantur fortibus, &c.). So that when a man or any other *animal* is the object of our panegyric, we must begin with his genealogy; if it be a πάθος, [meaning probably a disposition or character, an 'affection' in a wide

---

[1] Here the author agrees partially with Aristotle in making ἔπαινος, or moral approbation, the test and mark of virtue, which is therefore distinguished from μακαρίζειν. He however deprives himself of any credit that he might have obtained from this distinction, by confounding it on the other hand with ἐγκώμιον, for which it is repeated as a substitute: ἐγκωμιάζειν is in the next clause rendered by ἐπαινεῖν. I have already given an account of Aristotle's distinctions of these three terms, with the opinions of others on the same point, in Append. B. to Rhet. I. 9. Introd. p. 212. foll. Compare especially with what is said here, Aristotle on ἐγκώμιον, Ib. p. 215.

but peculiar sense: not, I think, here "emotion". Buhle, indolem. It may be merely 'a quality, property, or accident'.] or an act, or a speech, or any property ($κτῆμα$)[1], we may omit the genealogy, and start at once with any estimable quality that they may be supposed to possess. §§ 3—5. The topics of 'genealogy' are then illustrated. §§ 5—7. If your hero should be unfortunate enough to have no claims to admiration on the score of birth, you must depreciate all such advantages (nam genus et proavos, &c.), and argue that true nobility depends, not upon birth, but upon virtue; or criticise those that commend a man for his ancestors by saying that many a descendant of a noble line has turned out utterly unworthy of his distinguished forefathers; or point out that it is the man himself, and not his ancestors, that you are now employed in panegyrising. § 8. In a vituperative speech all this must be reversed, and the object of your censure charged with the vices of those that went before him. § 9. The next topic of encomium is $τύχη$[2], any natural gifts and advantages due to good fortune; especially, as appears from what follows, those accomplishments and excellences bodily and mental, which are natural gifts, comprised in $εὐφυΐα$, and not acquired habits. The virtues, so far as they are natural and spontaneous, are included: for we are told to be upon our guard in applying this topic to children against dwelling long upon it, because it is generally believed that these qualities in children are due rather to their tutors and governors than to themselves. § 10. And next, after the never-failing $γνώμη$ and enthymeme, first enumerate all the admirable points in character, pursuits, actions, of your hero, especially admirable considering his youth, and then apply to these the

---

[1] On the varieties of these $ἐπιδείξεις$ see above, Introd. pp. 121—3.

[2] Spengel has arbitrarily, and 'audacter' as he himself says, without any MS. authority, printed διὰ τὴν ψυχήν in the text as a substitute for τύχην: which seems to me to be quite unnecessary, and withal no improvement.

various topics of amplification, some of which are specified. § 11. Then compare them advantageously with the acts and characters of others, "selecting for contrast the best parts of your own subject with the worst of the others;" and so on for other topics. §§ 12. 13. Then more γνῶμαι and enthymemes, and a brief summary; and then proceed to the moral virtues, justice first, then wisdom, and last courage—'if there be any', ἐὰν ᾖ. § 14. All these sections, 3—14, seem, as I have already indicated, to represent the διήγησις and βεβαίωσις of a deliberative or dicastic speech: the confirmatio is replaced here by the αὔξησις, γνῶμαι, and enthymemes; the statements of acts and virtues constitute the narrative.

The three remaining sections convey a few hints of a practical nature for the treatment of the style, in panegyrical and vituperative speeches. In the former 'magnificence' of language should be aimed at[1], which may be effected by multiplying our words, πολλοῖς ὀνόμασιν,—that is, it is to be presumed, dwelling and enlarging upon a topic, and accumulating high sounding words in the individual sentences— and the same kind of amplification is to be applied to the vituperative topics of a censorious speech. In these latter no sneering or scoffing, σκώπτειν, is to be admitted, but the man's own life and conduct examined; because arguments (λόγοι; narrationes, Buhle.) are more effective than taunts or jeers in convincing the listeners, and wounding the object of censure. The reason of this is that such taunts may be aimed at a man's personal appearance (ἰδέας) or 'belongings'; 'estate', (things comparatively trifling—Buhle, ingenium, vel hominem omnino!) but serious arguments are directed to his character and manners. Carefully avoid foul or indecent terms in describing foul actions for fear of bringing an imputation upon, setting in an unfavourable light, your *own*

---

[1] This rule may help to confirm my conjecture, (Introd. p. 330, n. 2.) that Isocrates and his school are intended by the "some writers" of Rhet. III. 12. 6.

character (or, the character of the speech)—ἵνα μὴ διαβάλῃς τὸ ἦθος—such things are to be merely hinted, or the meaning obscurely and enigmatically intimated, and the facts are to be expressed by words denoting other things. In vituperative oratory again there is room for the employment of irony and derision of the adversary, especially in the things that he prides himself upon: in a private conversation, and with few listeners the object should be to discredit him or bring him into contempt—of course by serious argument—in great crowds, any common, popular, vulgar (κοινάς), accusation will serve for a topic of abuse. αὔξειν and ταπεινοῦν may be applied in precisely the same way as in panegyric. §§ 15. 18. Such are the contents of the chapter on the two varieties of epideictic speaking.

Ch. 36 opens with the announcement that there only now remains to be treated the application of the preceding method, the analysis of the speech by its four divisions and their contents, to the forensic branch of rhetoric. The words however are these, λοιπὸν ἡμῖν εἶδος τό τε κατηγορικὸν καὶ τὸ ἐξεταστικόν. Here τὸ ἀπολογητικόν seems to be omitted and ἐξεταστικόν to be out of place: for the latter is *not* treated with the two forensic εἴδη in this chapter, nor is it exclusively confined to it. Spengel supplies the former, as usual against MS. authority, and explains the insertion of τὸ ἐξεταστικόν as a piece of careless writing, which means no more than this; that it might be treated under this head because it can be introduced in the forensic branch; the insertion of it was simply due to the fact that the author was come to the end of his enumeration of the seven εἴδη, and thought it as well to make it complete; note, p. 240. It is neither true in itself, nor in place here; but let it stand, it does no harm.

Having first briefly described the topics of this chapter in the order of their arrangement I will proceed to offer a few general remarks upon its contents. The arrangement is the same as that which is expressed in the analysis of the hortative and dissuasive kinds, and apparently implied in that of the laudatory and vituperative; that is, the topics fall under the four general heads of the speech, προοίμιον; ἀπαγγελία; βεβαίωσις or πίστεις, here subdivided into the two subsequently recognised divisions, direct proofs in support or confirmation of our own case, and the indirect 'confirmation' derived from τὰ πρὸς ἀντίδικον, or the refutation of the adversary; and ἐπίλογος, otherwise παλιλλογία, ἀνακεφαλαίωσις, or recapitulation, so called from its characteristic feature. The fourth division receives this *name* in § 48. In the first part of the chapter, to § 26, the accusatory kind is illustrated: the defensive kind occupies the rest. For the illustration of several of the topics mentioned we are referred to the previous analysis of the deliberative kinds, cc. 29—34.

The προοίμιον of the accusatory kind, as in the preceding, has three principal topics; a brief preparatory statement of the subject of the speech, an invitation of the audience to attention, and the endeavour to secure their good will. This last topic admits of several variations in the mode of treatment, according as the speaker is already regarded by the judges, either favourably, or with indifference, or with suspicion and dislike; and the last of these again may take a threefold direction, either against the speaker himself and his private character, or against what he is doing (as when a man is prosecuting a relation or friend), or the speech he is making. These prepossessions have to be met and removed, λύειν διαβολήν; and as the sooner this is done the better—because until it has been done they will listen to nothing with favour—the proper place for it is the proœmium. The analysis of this carries us down to § 13. The ἀπαγγελία, or διήγησις, is to be treated in precisely the same way as in the 'public' branch of rhetoric. § 14. In fortifying our statement or case by arguments, βεβαίωσις, the third division, when our *facts* are denied by the opponent, (constitutio conjecturalis, στάσις στοχαστική) πίστεις are to be used in reply; when the facts are admitted but the injury or wrong (injustice) in general denied, (constitutio juridicialis absoluta, Cic. de Inv. II. 24. 69.) the arguments are to be borrowed from the topics of justice and expediency. § 14. The πίστεις, ἄτεχνοι or ἐπίθετοι and ἔντεχνοι, are then enumerated in their order—these are the πίστεις of c. 8. The ἐπίθετοι π. witnesses, torture, oaths, must be put first. The remaining πίστεις, of the logical sort, must then be employed in 'confirmation' of our case. The use of πίστεις is confined to the proof of fact; if that is admitted, we must have recourse to δικαιολογία, the plea of justice. Then follows, τὰ πρὸς ἀντιδίκους, the 'refutation' of the adversary's arguments; and under this head is treated the application of 'laws', according as they are favourable or unfavourable to our case, or ambiguous. §§ 15—22. If the facts are admitted by the defendant, and he is going to argue his case on the ground of the justice and legality of what he has done, the arguments that you expect him to use must be anticipated: if he admit both the fact and the wrong, and throw himself upon the compassion of the judges, you may anticipate him here by describing his proceedings as indicative of a bad ἦθος, or declaring that a man when his crime is discovered is always ready enough to attribute it to mere mistake, and therefore if the judges show indulgence to such a fellow as this there is no knowing where it will stop. And other arguments by which his appeals to the feelings of the judges may be counteracted are suggested, §§ 23—25. Next the ἐπίλογος, which is not here so called, but expressed by the word ἀναλογητέον (see above, p. 411.), or 'recapitulation' which is characteristic of it, must contain first, a summary of the topics of the whole speech; and secondly, an attempt, as concise as possible, to excite in the judges feelings of hatred, anger, jealousy, against the opponent, (!) [merely because he is the opponent, observe, and we want to gain a victory over him, and for no other reason whatever.] and towards ourselves love, gratitude, compassion. The modes of effecting this may be looked for in the chapters on hortative and dissuasive rhetoric: we now proceed to the second kind of dicastic speeches, the defensive. § 26. The topics of this branch are very much the same as those of the preceding, with the difference, that we have not now a case to establish, but arguments to answer, and charges to defend ourselves against. We have rules given for dealing with the accuser's μάρτυρες and βάσανοι, § 27, and for answering or evading his εἰκότα, § 28, παραδείγματα, τεκμήρια, γνῶμαι, ἐνθυμήματα § 29, and σημεῖα § 30. So in direct answer to arguments on questions of fact: in the constitutio juridicialis we have recourse to arguments from justice and the laws; or plead error, ignorance, accident, (three degrees of criminality). §§ 30—32. Then we have to meet the προκαταλήψεις, anticipations, arguments already advanced by the accuser in anticipation of, to meet beforehand, what we are likely to urge in our defence: and amongst these anticipated imputations, that we are using *prepared written* speeches, or pleading *for hire as a paid advocate*, or *teaching rhetoric*, or *writing speeches for others* (acting as a λογογράφος)—all of them represented as very grave charges, which we must do our utmost to defend ourselves against—are particularly dwelt upon. §§ 33—37. Next the use of questions and answers in defence is illustrated. The *answer* to the adversary's interrogation may either *admit* the fact, but with some reservation or qualification which justifies the act or shifts the blame upon some one else; or, as in a case where two laws happen to be in conflict, you may *deny* (in a sense) the act of which you are notoriously guilty, affirming that it was the law, and not yourself, which was the real prompter of the deed. The only example given is, "Did you kill my son?" "No, not I, but the law." §§ 38—40. So far of the τὰ πρὸς ἀντιδίκους. This brings us to the last division, here called as usual in this author παλιλλογία, the recapitulation: which, it is added, may be introduced also in any other part of the speech, παρὰ μέρος "partially", as well as παρὰ εἶδος "specially" here at the end of it. The other essential element of the ἐπίλογος, viz. the appeal to the feelings of the judges is included here in παλιλλογία, because it has already been employed as one of the topics of the προοίμιον. The ἐπίλογος or παλιλλογία is especially serviceable in the accusatory and defensive kinds of rhetoric, though it is also of use in public speaking. For here we have not only to review the preceding statements of facts and proofs, and to refresh the memory of the audience, but also to secure the goodwill of the audience to ourselves, and render them hostile to the adversary; whereas in the two kinds of epideictic oratory this is not required. §§ 41, 42. The modes in which this summary review may be made are described in § 43. and, finally, the topics for conciliating the goodwill of the audience to ourselves and diverting it from the opponent are given in detail to the end of the chapter, §§ 44—48. The easy indifference with which these suggestions for calumniating the opponent, if necessary, if not, for provoking against him hatred, envy, ill will, are, not merely brought forward in illustration of a theory, but actually recommended for *use*, is —— highly characteristic of this system of rhetoric.

In fact, in this analysis of the defensive art in forensic rhetoric the vices of this system are revealed in all their naked deformity. It is a system of tricks, shifts, and evasions, showing an utter indifference to right and wrong, truth and falsehood. The truth of any statement has no value, except in so far as it carries with it an air of greater probability, and is more likely therefore to 'persuade' an audience; and the only limit to the employment of any kind of trick, fraud, or chicanery, is the 'possibility' of its producing any effect upon the audience. ἐὰν δὲ μὴ ἐνδέχηται τοῦτο, if this can't be effected, you must *then* have recourse, καταφεύγειν—to some other mode of imposition. In §§ 9, 10, 11, of this chapter the true character of some of these suggestions is conveyed with unconscious irony by the terms προφάσεις and προφασίζεσθαι which are there applied to them; they are indeed mere pretexts, excuses, shifts, evasions.

For the illustration of some of these arts and devices alike unscientific and unfair, I will now refer to one or two particular passages in which this vicious character by which the whole system is pervaded is more prominently exhibited; some others I have already noticed in passing in the course of the preceding review. In § 4 for instance, the accuser is recommended to flatter the judges by telling them that they are just and clever; that is, according to Aristotle's metaphor, to warp and distort the very rule that he is about to use to determine what is *right*. Again, in the two common or universal topics of § 9; the accuser, who is himself exposed to antecedent suspicions and prejudices in the minds of the judges, if he thinks that there is anything in his person or character that they are likely to find fault with, is told to anticipate them, to take the words out of their mouth as it were, and find fault with it himself: and secondly, if he is obliged to do anything in the prosecution of his case which may lay his motives or conduct open to suspicion or censure, he is to try if possible to turn the blame upon the adversary, or if this can't be done, upon somebody else, alleging that he did not take up the case voluntarily, but was forced to it by the other party. And this is repeated in § 12. "We must remove any prejudices that may have been conceived against us in consequence of anything that we have done (τὸ πρᾶγμα) in the prosecution of our case, by shifting the blame upon the adverse party, or by charging him with abusive language or injustice, or a grasping and greedy, or quarrelsome and contentious temper—the truth or falsehood of the charge being apparently a matter of pure indifference—and, assuming an air of indignation, imply that it was impossible to obtain justice in any other way."

In § 27 another practice is prescribed, which, though likely enough to be adopted by a pleader in a desperate extremity, one would hardly have thought a fit subject to be noticed, and still less recommended, in a professedly scientific and educational treatise; and this is spoken of as a regular τόπος, ὁ τοῦ παραλειπομένου τόπος. This consists in evading any fact or argument which can't be disputed or answered by 'passing it over' or 'omitting' it, and going on to something else where you are on safer ground. The language in which part of this is expressed is so characteristic that I will give it in the author's own words. τῶν δὲ κατηγορουμένων (we are answering charges, in the 'defensive kind') ἃ μὲν εἰδέναι τοὺς ἀκούοντας ἐποίησε, (meaning apparently, what had been so fully substantiated by evidence and argument that the judges were quite *sure* of it) παραλείψομεν, ἃ δὲ δοξάζειν, ταῦτα προθέμενοι...διαλύσομεν. Any thing that has been fully proved against him the apologist is to pass over without notice; and go on to meet the other allegations, in which the facts and arguments of the accuser have not been so strong as to produce absolute conviction in the minds of the judges, but only probable opinion (δοξάζειν)[1].

Such are only a few specimens of the tricks and sophistries suggested and recommended for practice in this treatise —the appeals to the feelings have been already noticed—and it is precisely in this, the dicastic, branch, in which justice and truth of fact should be the sole considerations, that the utter unscrupulousness and disregard of truth and justice which characterise the system show themselves in their most monstrous proportions. The general tone of morality at Athens was certainly low, and there is no doubt that most if not all of these unfair artifices will be found exemplified in the speeches of the most approved orators, Demosthenes not excepted. This however does not mend the matter; but rather shows what a pernicious effect these rhetorical systems, under which the orators were trained, must have had upon the public education and morality. The character which has exhibited itself

[1] In further illustration of the immoral character of this work see particularly the passage quoted above from c. 15, p. 429.

in the review of this treatise, the sole surviving representative of the Arts of the sophistical school of rhetoric, agrees perfectly with the notices of the earlier systems given by Plato in the Phædrus and elsewhere, illustrates his language, and, as it seems to me, fully justifies his reprobation. It shows to what consequences an art and practice of 'persuasion', pure and simple and unqualified, may be made to lead. This treatise at least may fairly be called an Art of Cheating, and illustrates nothing but the principles and practice of a pettifogging attorney.

Ch. 38 contains a brief examination of the ἐξεταστικὸν εἶδος, 'the critical kind' of rhetoric. It is first acknowledged that this kind of rhetoric is seldom found alone—Spengel mentions Æschines' speech against Timarchus as a case in point—but generally mixed up with the other species; and it is most useful in controversy, that is, in the τὰ πρὸς ἀντιδίκους. However for the sake of completeness an analysis is given of this as of the rest, under the four divisions of the speech. The 'criticism' may be applied to the speeches, actions, life and conduct of a man, or the administration and policy of a city. § 1. The topics of the προοίμιον are given in §§ 2, 3. and consist of various 'excuses' προφάσεις for venturing to undertake such an office; the διήγησις and πίστεις are represented by a statement of the sayings, doings, thoughts, motives, and intentions of the person whose character is examined, and by proving that they are all contrary to justice, law, and public and private expediency: and nothing is to be left undone which will bring upon the person subjected to criticism the utmost possible discredit. §§ 4, 5. The character and tone of the speech however must not be harsh and bitter, but mild; because such a tone has a more persuasive effect, and is less likely to subject the critic himself to unpleasant imputations. The whole is to conclude with a παλιλλογία or summary repetition of the principal contents, § 6.

Ch. 38, to § 10, where the work really ends, is a sort of moral upon the preceding exposition. It has all the air of gravity and seriousness, though its contents are so ludicrous that it rather suggests the notion of a quiz, or burlesque application of the preceding system. No one as far as I know has expressed any suspicion of its genuineness; but it seems to me so unusually foolish that rather than believe that it could proceed from a man of Anaximenes' reputation, I would suppose that it was tacked on with the remaining sections, 11—21, as an appendage to the treatise, to supply the moral, which had been inadvertently omitted by the author. The absence of all but one of the author's technical terms for the divisions of the speech, $\dot{a}\pi a\gamma\gamma\epsilon\lambda\acute{\iota}a$, $\beta\epsilon\beta a\acute{\iota}\omega\sigma\iota\varsigma$, $\pi a\lambda\iota\lambda\lambda o\gamma\acute{\iota}a$, which in this chapter are replaced by the three which afterwards became the received names, $\delta\iota\acute{\eta}\gamma\eta\sigma\iota\varsigma$, $\pi\acute{\iota}\sigma\tau\epsilon\iota\varsigma$ and $\tau\grave{a}\ \pi\rho\grave{o}\varsigma\ \dot{a}\nu\tau\acute{\iota}\delta\iota\kappa o\nu$, and $\dot{\epsilon}\pi\acute{\iota}\lambda o\gamma o\varsigma$, is very suspicious. It is true that all these terms do occur in the treatise, but not as the technical and only proper designations of the three divisions. Spengel only remarks, note p. 273, quis risum teneat, aut sophistam non miretur [he has apparently a low opinion of Anaximenes,] arti tam deditum, ut ex hujus præceptis vitæ rationem nobis gerendæ explicet?

The object of these first ten sections of the chapter is to show how life may be made to conform to the model of a speech, and a rule of life deduced from its topics and divisions. "In speaking and writing (he begins) we must endeavour to make our words correspond as nearly as possible with our actions, and habituate ourself to facility in the use of them all. (viz. the words.)" For artistic *speaking* we shall derive our rules and precepts from the preceding work, "but our attention must not be confined merely to our words, but extended to our whole life, which is to be ordered and regulated according to those ideas: *for* (note the reason) the right conduct of our life *contributes much to the power of persuading*, and the attainment of a reputation for virtue and respectability". The 'reputation of virtue' is required for the $\mathring{\eta}\theta o\varsigma\ \dot{\epsilon}\nu\ \tau\hat{\omega}\ \lambda\acute{\epsilon}\gamma o\nu\tau\iota$, to give the weight of 'character' to our statements, opinions, and arguments; so that after all the object and end of a virtuous life is to contribute to success in speaking. This goes a step beyond even Quintilian in the exaltation of the rhetorical art, who merely says that no bad man can ever be a perfect orator. §§ 1, 2. Then for the details. Our conduct is to be arranged according to the divisions of the speech, which will show us what should come first, second, third, and fourth. The prooemium accordingly takes the lead in the direction of our conduct. Two of the ordinary topics of this are the conciliation of the good will, and of the attention, of the audience. These may be transferred to ourselves; good will may be conciliated by the observance of good faith, and steady consistency in friendship, habits and pursuits; the 'attention' of others may be attracted by great and noble and useful actions [I don't think this is by any means a fair application of the system. The methods of conciliation recommended in that are certainly very different.] §§ 3, 4. The actions that have these characters are described in § 5. From the rules for the composition of the διήγησις we may learn to make our actions "rapid" and "clear," (σαφῆ means, as it is afterwards interpreted, 'intelligible to ourselves and others'; definite, precise, without overhaste or confusion in acting) and to be relied upon. These are qualities of the 'narrative' (which here, by the way, receives the *name* of διήγησις instead of ἀπαγγελία) in the system. How they are to acquire these characters is explained in § 6. The rules for the manufacture of πίστεις may be applied to conduct in this, that they teach us when we have full knowledge, to act in accordance with it; when we have not, in accordance with the ordinary experience of the probable, or what usually happens. § 7. The next section, 8, purports to give the application of τὰ πρὸς ἀντίδικον to the rule of life. As the text stands it seems to say this: that as in these arguments against the adversary's statements we confirm our own by refuting his (ἐκ τῶν λελεγμένων), so in our ordinary dealings with others we shall secure our own safety and happiness ($\beta\epsilon\beta\alpha\iota\delta\tau\eta\tau\alpha$ $\pi\epsilon\rho\grave{\iota}$ $\dot{\eta}\mu\hat{\omega}\nu$ $\pi o\iota\acute{\eta}\sigma o\mu\epsilon\nu$, in a double sense) by conforming our actions to the laws, written and unwritten, with the best witnesses of our conduct in definite times—Of the meaning of the 'definite times' I must confess my ignorance. Now it is true, as Spengel notes, that there is no true parallel here between the two cases: but the correspondence is very nearly as close as it is in the prooemium, and the amount of sense contained in the above interpretation is quite as much as one has a right to expect in such a chapter as this[1]. Spengel's emendation at all events is violent and improbable. From the Epilogus, § 9, in which we recall what has been already said to the hearers' recollection by a verbal repetition, we may learn to apply the same rule of repetition to our actions, and recall them to men's minds by the repeated performance of the same or similar ones. Good will (another topic of the Epilogue) may be conciliated by doing what will be considered good services past present or future: and lastly we may apply the topic of 'amplification', (another of the ordinary topics of the peroration) $a\check{v}\xi\epsilon\iota\nu$, here rendered by $\mu\epsilon\gamma\acute{a}\lambda a$ $\pi\rho\acute{a}\tau\tau\epsilon\iota\nu$ 'to magnify', to the conduct of our lives by a multitude of noble actions[2].

On the remaining sections appended to this chapter I will content myself with quoting Spengel's note; quæ sequuntur ex primo libelli capite excerpta et paucis mutata, lector ut præ cæteris quæ attenderentur digna repetiisse videtur. And this brings us to the end of the Rhetorica ad Alexandrum.

I will add here to the examples of doubtful Greek cited from this work, above pp. 409—12, a passage in which

[1] A certain amount of sense and parallelism is obtained by giving a double meaning to $\beta\epsilon\beta\alpha\iota o\hat{v}\nu$, to confirm, and to secure, i.e. to ensure and render permanent, as I have done in the text.

[2] The above is a literal abstract, without the least exaggeration or embellishment, of the contents of this very remarkable chapter.

two departures from the ordinary grammar occur for which I can see no reason or justification. They are found close together εἰ μὲν τὰ πράγματα πιστὰ ᾖ, and immediately afterwards, and in precisely the same sense as far as the particles and verbs are concerned, εἰ δ' εἶεν οἱ μάρτυρες.... to which an indicative, if it were expressed, would follow as the apodosis. Now I am well aware that εἰ with the subjunctive is found in several places of good authors, and that Hermann in particular has laboured hard (with but limited success) to make out a distinction between that and other similar combinations; and also that εἰ εἶεν, if indefiniteness were meant to be conveyed, or if an optative followed in the apodosis, or in other possible cases, might be undeniable Greek; but here in both instances there is no more than a simple hypothesis, and the indicative ought in both to have been employed. It looks to me like the careless inaccuracy of the composition of a later age, when grammatical distinctions were lost, when the rules which once had regulated the usages of the language in its prime had fallen into abeyance, when μή and οὐ could be interchanged without sensible loss of meaning.

www.ingramcontent.com/pod-product-compliance
Lightning Source LLC
Chambersburg PA
CBHW051848300426
44117CB00006B/314